Using dBASE™ IV 1.1

Using dBASE™ IV 1.1

Edward Jones

Osborne **McGraw-Hill**
Berkeley New York St. Louis San Francisco
Auckland Bogotá Hamburg London Madrid
Mexico City Milan Montreal New Delhi Panama City
Paris São Paulo Singapore Sydney
Tokyo Toronto

Osborne **McGraw-Hill**
2600 Tenth Street
Berkeley, California 94710
U.S.A.

For information on translations and book distributors outside of the U.S.A., please write to Osborne **McGraw-Hill** at the above address.

Using dBASE IV™ 1.1

1234567890 DOC 99876543210

ISBN 0-07-881676-9

Acquisitions Editor: Liz Fisher
Technical Reviewers: Bob Hoch, Lisa Biow
Copy Editors: Kay Luthin, Jeff Green
Proofreaders: Barbara Conway, Julie Anjos
Cover Design: Bay Graphics Design, Inc.
Production Supervisor: Kevin Shafer

Contents at a Glance

Table of Contents

Acknowledgments

The fun of writing acknowledgments comes from the awareness that, as an author, you're finally done with the book! It's also an opportunity to thank others whose help was invaluable in quickly turning out a comprehensive book. I would like to thank Lee The' for invaluable help. I could not have written the book without it. No small amount of thanks go to Bob Hoch and Lisa Biow, whose outstanding technical editing helped provide a first-rate product. Thanks to my editor Liz Fisher for tying together what seemed like thousands of details in production, and to Kevin Shafer, whose finesse with balky screen dumps is becoming legendary. Wendy Goss deserves a note of thanks for dealing with incoming chapters under a tight schedule. Copy editors Kay

Luthin and Jeff Green, as well as proofreaders Barbara Conway and Julie Anjos, also deserve special thanks. And again, thanks to Ashton-Tate, for keeping this member of the army of dBASE consultants gainfully employed.

Introduction

Many changes have taken place in the few years between the introduction of dBASE II and the introduction of dBASE IV 1.1. When dBASE II was introduced, microcomputers were largely the province of dedicated hobbyists who were challenged by the task of learning in-depth programming skills. By the time dBASE IV came along, however, millions of business professionals were using microcomputers in their day-to-day working environment.

These professionals do not all wish to become programmers, but they do have one thing in common: they want to put the power of the personal computer and of software packages like dBASE IV to use. This book is for them.

Using dBASE IV 1.1 covers the topics that you'll need to know to put dBASE IV to work in your business. Chapters 1 and 2 introduce dBASE IV and the concepts of database design. Creating, changing, and rearranging your database and using entry forms are the topics of Chapters 3, 4, 5, and 6. Chapter 7 details the use of query by example to refine your searches for data. Chapter 8 provides an introduction to reporting, outlining the various ways you can produce reports with dBASE IV.

In Chapter 9, you'll learn how you can use macros to automate often-used tasks. Chapter 10 shows how you can manage files and perform DOS operations without leaving dBASE IV. In Chapter 11, more advanced topics regarding reports are covered. Chapter 12 shows how you can put dBASE IV's relational capabilities to effective use.

In Chapters 13 through 16, you learn how to use command files to automate many operations that are time-consuming when performed manually. In Chapter 17, you learn to bridge the gap between dBASE IV and other popular software, including Lotus 1-2-3 and WordPerfect. Chapter 18 details the use of the applications generator, a powerful feature of dBASE IV that helps you write programs to manage a complete task (or "application").

Chapter 19 describes the use of dBASE IV on a local area network (LAN). Sample applications that you can create are provided in Chapter 20. Appendix A provides a glossary of dBASE IV commands, while Appendix B provides a glossary of functions.

The best way to learn dBASE IV is to use it. This book presents a series of exercises that explain the various dBASE IV menu options and commands, and then has you use those options and commands in a practical application. Using your copy of dBASE IV, you should follow along with the examples.

The database and program files used in this book, including the sample applications in Chapter 20 and additional sample applications, are available on diskette. The complete cost of the diskette package is $20.00, which covers the costs

Why This Book Is for You

Because you want to utilize the full capabilities of dBASE IV as quickly as possible, this book is for you. With this book as your guide, you will be managing and retrieving data by the end of the third chapter. Also, since the later chapters delve into the more advanced features of dBASE IV, this book gives you all the information you need to put dBASE IV to effective use.

If you are an experienced user of dBASE III or dBASE III PLUS and are upgrading to dBASE IV, you will find this book to be a great help in discovering the features of dBASE IV which are not available in earlier versions of dBASE, including how to use windows effectively, and how to fully utilize the significantly enhanced Applications Generator. If you have relied on the menus or the dot prompt and stayed away from programming, this book will help you become familiar with programming concepts needed to build sophisticated applications. And once you have become familiar with dBASE IV, the Command Reference and Function Reference included in the Appendixes will provide a helpful dictionary-style listing which you can refer to when needed.

Because dBASE IV version 1.1 includes many enhancements over earlier versions of dBASE, if you have purchased dBASE IV or are considering the use of dBASE IV, you'll need an effective guide that specifically covers this product, including the revisions in version 1.1. This book is that guide.

CHAPTER

1

Introduction to dBASE IV

Welcome to dBASE IV, a high-powered relational database manager for the IBM PC and compatibles. If you are feeling somewhat tense about learning a program of this magnitude, this book should put you more at ease. Learning to use database managers can appear to be a daunting task, but the hands-on approach you are starting will have you managing your data with dBASE IV in short order.

You can use dBASE IV to create files that contain the necessary data. And you can display information in a format that best meets your needs with the various capabilities built into dBASE IV. Figure 1-1 shows an example; in it, dBASE IV is used to examine a listing of employee social security numbers, names, and addresses.

You'll perform many tasks within dBASE IV through the *Control Center,* which can be thought of as dBASE IV's "main menu." The Control Center provides a series of menus that let you use most dBASE IV features. From the Control Center, you can perform a variety of data management tasks, such as creating files to store your data, viewing and editing the data, selecting specific information, and producing reports.

Figure 1-1.

Records Organize Fields Go To Exit

SOCIALSEC	LASTNAME	FIRSTNAME	ADDRESS	CITY
123-44-8976	Morse	Marcia	4260 Park Avenue	Chevy Ch
121-33-9876	Westman	Andrea	4807 East Avenue	Silver S
232-55-1234	Jackson	David	4102 Valley Lane	Falls Ch
901-77-3456	Mitchell	Mary Jo	617 North Oakland Street	Arlingto
121-90-5432	Robinson	Shirley	270 Browning Ave #2A	Takoma P
495-00-3456	Jackson	Cheryl	1617 Arlington Blvd	Falls Ch
343-55-9821	Robinson	Wanda	1607 21st Street, NW	Washingt
876-54-3210	Hart	Edward	6200 Germantown Road	Fairfax

Browse | E:\...dbdata\ABCSTAFF | Rec 1/8 | File

dBASE IV in use

Creating a database to store your data is a straightforward process. After choosing the Create option from the Data panel of the Control Center, you define the names and types of fields you will use. You can store a variety of different kinds of data with dBASE IV, such as text, numeric values, dates, and logical (true or false) information. Figure 1-2 shows the process of creating a database in dBASE IV.

Once your database exists, you can enter data in Browse mode, as illustrated in Figure 1-1, or through on-screen forms, which can resemble the paper forms used in an office. You can also design custom forms to contain categories of data at locations you desire, along with borders or descriptive text.

To extract subsets of data from your database, you can use dBASE IV's query-by-example facility, accessible from the Queries panel of the Control Center. Figure 1-3 shows the Query Design screen being used to create queries.

To get more detailed information from your dBASE IV databases, you will want to build detailed reports. dBASE IV provides a report *hot key* that lets you create a quick columnar-style report with no more than one function-key combination. If you need additional flexibility, you can use the powerful report generator built into dBASE IV to design custom reports in a format of your choosing.

If you are an advanced user, you will find that dBASE IV has the power to match your complex database management needs. Using the relational capabilities of dBASE IV, you can draw complex relationships between multiple database files. You can make use of *macros,* which are automated series of actions that dBASE IV carries out as if individual commands had been entered at the keyboard. You can also use the command language that is an integral part of dBASE IV to write programs that perform complex tasks. If you have no desire to learn to write programs, you can use the applications generator provided by dBASE IV, an

Figure 1-2.

Layout Organize Append Go To Exit 10:55:18 am

Bytes remaining: 3837

Num	Field Name	Field Type	Width	Dec	Index
1	SOCIALSEC	Character	11		Y
2	LASTNAME	Character	15		N
3	FIRSTNAME	Character	15		N
4	ADDRESS	Character	25		N
5	CITY	Character	15		N
6	STATE	Character	2		N
7	ZIPCODE	Character	10		N
8	PHONE	Character	12		N
9	BIRTHDAY	Date	8		N
10	DATEHIRED	Date	8		N
11	DEPENDENTS	Numeric	2	0	N
12	SALARY	Numeric	5	2	N
13	ASSIGNMENT	Character	20		N
14	HOURLYRATE	Numeric	5	2	N
15	EVALUATE	Memo	10		N

Database E:\...dbdata\ABCSTAFF Field 1/15
Enter the field name. Insert/Delete field:Ctrl-N/Ctrl-U
Field names begin with a letter and may contain letters, digits and underscores

Creating a dBASE IV database

Figure 1-3.

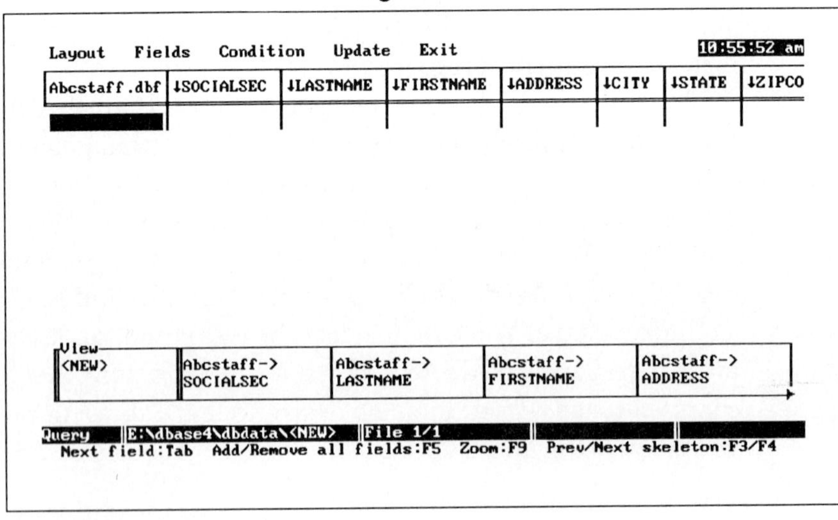

Example of a query

automated system that writes dBASE IV programs for you by providing a series of menus that contain questions about the program you want to create.

What Is a Database?

Although *database management* is a computer term, it can also apply to the ways in which information is catalogued, stored, and used manually. At the center of any information management system is a *database,* which is any collection of related information grouped together as a single item. Figure 1-4 is an example of a database. Metal filing cabinets with customer records, a card file of names and phone numbers, and a notebook with a penciled listing of a store inventory are all databases. However, a file cabinet or a notebook does not by itself constitute a database; the way information is organized makes it a database. Objects like

Figure 1-4.

Name	Address	City	State	ZIP	Phone No.	Cust. No.
J. Billings	2323 State St.	Bertram	CA	91113	234-8980	0005
R. Foster	Rt. 1 Box 52	Frink	CA	93336	245-4312	0001
L. Miller	P.O. Box 345	Dagget	CA	94567	484-9966	0002
B. O'Neill	21 Way St. #C	Hotlum	CA	92346	555-1032	0004
C. Roberts	1914 19th St.	Bodie	CA	97665	525-4494	0006
A. Wilson	27 Haven Way	Weed	CA	90004	566-7823	0003

A simple database

cabinets and notebooks only aid in organizing information, and dBASE IV is one such aid to organizing information.

Information in a database is organized and stored in tables, with rows and columns. In the mailing list shown in Figure 1-4, for example, each row contains a name, an address, a phone number, and a customer number. Each row is related to the others because they all contain the same types of information. And because the mailing list is a collection of information arranged in a specific order—a column of names, a column of addresses, a column of customer numbers—it is a table. One or more tables containing information arranged in an organized manner is a database, as you saw in Figure 1-4. The multiple tables used to manage your data within dBASE IV are referred to as *database files.*

Rows in a database file are called *records,* and columns are called *fields.* Figure 1-5 illustrates this with a comparison of a

Figure 1-5.

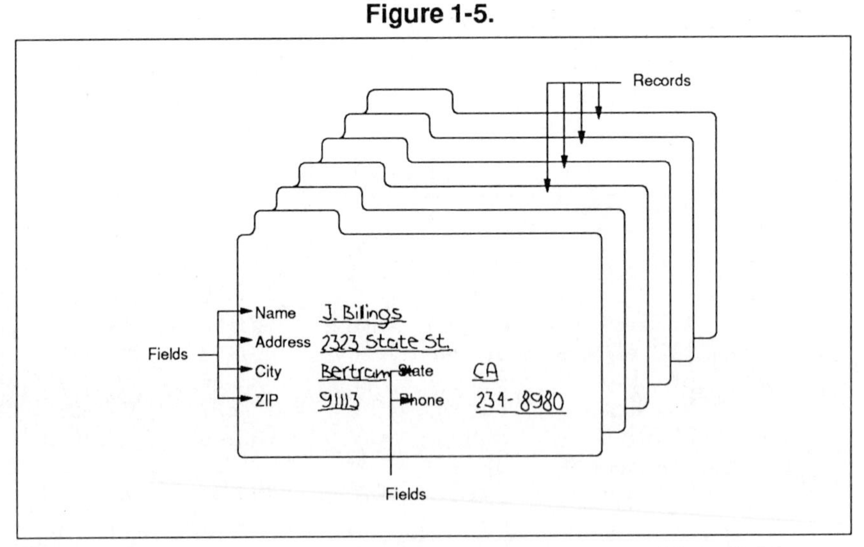

Each card represents a record; information is separated into fields

Figure 1-6.

Name	Address	City	State	ZIP	Phone No.	Cust. No.
J. Billings	2323 State St.	Bertram	CA	91113	234-8980	0005
R. Foster	Rt. 1 Box 52	Frink	CA	93336	245-4312	0001
L. Miller	P.O. Box 345	Dagget	CA	94567	484-9966	0002
B. O'Neill	21 Way St. #C	Hotlum	CA	92346	555-1032	0004
C. Roberts	1914 19th St.	Bodie	CA	97665	525-4494	0006
A. Wilson	27 Haven Way	Weed	CA	90004	566-7823	0003

A record and a field in a database

simple database to an address filing system kept on three-by-five file cards.

Since every card in the box has the same type of information, the card box is a database. Each card in the box is a single record, and each category of information on a card is a field. Fields can contain any type of information that can be categorized. In the card box, each record contains six fields: a name, address, city, state, ZIP code, and phone number.

Figure 1-6 identifies a record and a field in the mailing-list database.

Using a Database

In theory, any database is arranged in such a way that information is easy to find. In Figure 1-6, for example, names are arranged alphabetically. If you want to find the phone number of a customer, you simply locate the name and read across to the corresponding phone number.

You are already interested in how a computerized filing (database) system can make information storage and retrieval more efficient than a traditional filing system can, and you will find that dBASE IV offers many advantages. A telephone book, for example, is fine for finding telephone numbers, but if all you have is the address of a person and not the person's name, the telephone book is useless for finding that person's telephone number. A similar problem will plague conventional office filing systems: if the information is organized by name and you want to find all of the clients located in a particular area, you could be in for a tedious search. In addition, organizing massive amounts of information into written directories and filing cabinets can consume a great deal of space.

A manual database can also be difficult to modify. For example, adding a new phone number to the listing may mean rearranging the list. If the phone company were to assign a new area code, someone would have to search for all phone numbers having the old area code and replace that code with the new one.

When a database is teamed with a computer, many of these problems are eliminated. A computerized database provides speed: finding a phone number from among a thousand entries, or putting the file in alphabetical order, takes just seconds with dBASE IV. A computerized database is compact: a database with thousands of records can be stored on a single floppy disk. A computerized database is also flexible: it has the ability to examine information from a number of angles, so you could, for example, search for a phone number by name or by address.

Tasks that are time-consuming to accomplish manually are more practical with a computer. In principle, a database in a computer is no different from a database recorded on paper and filed in cabinets. In reality, however, the computer does the tedious work of maintaining and accessing a database, and it does it fast. A computerized database that can do all of this is known as a *database management system,* or *DBMS* for short.

Relational Databases

There are a number of ways to store information in a computer, but not all of these ways are *relational.* A word-processing program can be used to organize data in the form of a list. However, it will offer only limited flexibility; you still must sort, rearrange, and access the information. At a level above word processors are simple file managers and spreadsheets with simple database management capabilities. Most file managers (and those spreadsheets that have data management capabilities) can also perform sorting and other data management tasks.

Relational database managers can also store information in database files. However, in addition to being more sophisticated than file managers, they can access two or more database files simultaneously. By comparison, file managers can access only one database file at a time. This type of constraint can be severely limiting. If a file manager is accessing information from one database file and needs three pieces of information from a second file, it must finish reading the current file first. But what good is this when the file manager needs information from both files simultaneously? The only solution is to instead use a single file that contains all the needed fields. Fortunately, this is easy for a relational database manager such as dBASE IV.

Suppose a mailing list stores customer information for a warehouse that distributes kitchen appliances. The warehouse would also have a separate database file within the database for customer orders, which would include fields for customer number, merchandise number, price per unit, quantity ordered, and total cost. The mailing-list and customer-order database files comprise a relational database because they have the customer number field in common, as shown in Figure 1-7. By searching for the customer number in the mailing list and matching it to the customer number in the order form, the database manager can determine who the purchaser is and where the purchaser is located from one database file, and what the purchaser ordered and the total cost of the purchase from the other database file. A database manager that draws information from different database files linked by one or more common fields is known as a *relational database manager.*

Figure 1-7.

Mailing List

Name	Address	City	State	ZIP	Phone No.	Cust. No.
J. Billings	2323 State St.	Bertram	CA	91113	234-8980	0005
R. Foster	Rt. 1 Box 52	Frink	CA	93336	245-4312	0001
L. Miller	P.O. Box 345	Dagget	CA	94567	484-9966	0002
B. O'Neill	21 Way St. #C	Hotlum	CA	92346	555-1032	0004
C. Roberts	1914 19th St.	Bodie	CA	97665	525-4494	0006
A. Wilson	27 Haven Way	Weed	CA	90004	566-7823	0003

Customer Order

Cust. No.	Merchandise No.	Price per Unit	Quantity	Total Price
0001	15A	1500.00	5	7500.00
0001	15B	1750.00	10	17500.00
0002	311	500.00	3	1500.00
0003	555	1000.00	4	4000.00
0004	69	650.00	7	4550.00
0005	1111	300.00	2	600.00

Relationship between database files

To handle the same task with a file manager would be very difficult, since the file manager cannot access the mailing list when it comes time to find out where the merchandise should be shipped. The only solution would be to combine the two database files, but this would result in a clumsy and inefficient database. For example, to represent both of R. Foster's purchases, you would have to duplicate his name, address, and phone number as shown in Figure 1-8. If R. Foster had purchased 100 items instead of 10, the extra typing would take far longer and use up valuable memory space.

Figure 1-8.

Name	Address	Phone No.	Merch-andise No.	Price per Unit	Quan-tity	Total Price
J. Billings	2323 State St. Bertram CA 91113	234-8980	1111	300.00	2	600.00
R. Foster	Rt. 1 Box 52 Frink CA 93336	245-4312	15A	1500.00	5	7500.00
R. Foster	Rt. 1 Box 52 Frink CA 93336	245-4312	15B	1750.00	10	17500.00
L. Miller	P.O. Box 345 Dagget CA 94567	484-9966	311	500.00	3	1500.00
B. O'Neill	21 Way St. #C Hotlum CA 92346	555-1032	69	650.00	7	4550.00
C. Roberts	1914 19th St. Bodie CA 97665	525-4494	15A	1500.00	1	1500.00
A. Wilson	27 Haven Way Weed CA 90004	566-7823	555	1000.00	4	4000.00

Combined customer-order invoice and mailing-list database; unnecessary customer number field was eliminated

How You Will Use dBASE IV

Figure 1-9 shows the relationship between the database, the user, and the database software. At the core is the database from which you will retrieve, add, and delete information. The database is made accessible to the user by means of the available menu options and commands provided within dBASE IV.

Figure 1-9.

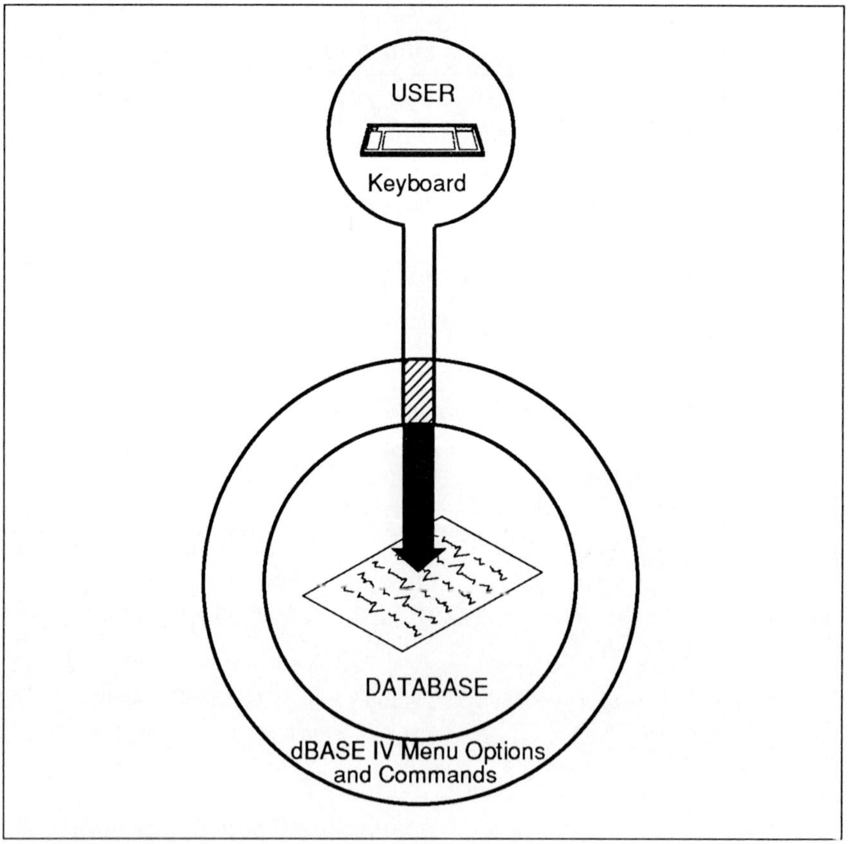

Simplified layout of database manager

dBASE IV lets you carry out operations in one of two ways: by choosing the options from a detailed series of menus starting at a screen called the Control Center, or by typing in a series of commands at a screen prompt known as the *dot prompt.* Whatever you want done to the database has to be communicated to the computer by using the correct dot-prompt command or menu option.

The various commands and menu options in dBASE IV offer you a host of ways to manage information. Among all these commands and menu options, however, you won't find a single command that creates a database, inputs the information into it, and prints the database on the printer. In any application, you probably will not be able to use only one command or make one menu choice that will perform the entire task. Instead, you will have to divide the task into smaller chores that dBASE IV will handle. For example, to create a mailing list, you will need to perform the following steps:

1. Create the database structure.

2. Input information into the database.

3. Print the contents of the database.

Even after breaking down the problem this far, you will need to segment the process further, since, for example, there is no single command that inputs information into the database.

How will you know when the task is divided into sufficient steps for dBASE IV to cope with it? The answer is experience. You have to know the program, and you have to know what you can and cannot get away with. This book is designed to provide you with that knowledge.

History of dBASE IV

No introduction to dBASE IV would be complete without a brief look at the program's colorful history. dBASE IV is the latest in a line of database managers bearing the name "dBASE." The first product in this line, dBASE II, was the first popular database manager for microcomputers. The program had its beginnings long before the personal computer became popular. Scientists at the Jet Propulsion Laboratory (JPL) in Pasadena, California, were using a database management system on mainframe computers to track information received from JPL's deep-space probes. Wayne Ratliff, a software systems designer for JPL, was impressed by the capabilities and features of the JPL database manager and set to work writing a database system for his own microcomputer, using the JPL system as a model. After its completion, Ratliff decided to market his database manager under the name "Vulcan" (in honor of Mr. Spock's home planet in *Star Trek*). Vulcan was a far cry from dBASE IV, or for that matter, dBASE II. It lacked many of the powerful sorting and indexing commands present in dBASE IV. Despite its limitations, Vulcan was a powerful program for the time, and it picked up a very small but dedicated cult following.

One of those followers was George Tate, a software distributor who heard of Vulcan's capabilities. Tate gave Vulcan a try and was sufficiently impressed to contact Ratliff in hopes of distributing the program. Ratliff, who felt far more comfortable as a programmer than as a salesman, turned over Vulcan's marketing to Tate. Tate, in turn, signed a contract providing Ratliff with royalties for sales of the program.

Tate used a number of marketing ploys to increase the sales of Vulcan. First, the name was dropped in favor of "dBASE II" (there was no dBASE I, but the II implied a newer version). At a computer show, Tate floated a gas-filled blimp with the name "dBASE II" emblazoned on its sides over the exhibit booth. Also, a famous advertisement compared competitors' similar products to a bilge pump in a rather unflattering way. The ads drew sharp criticism from the competitors (as well as from the bilge-pump maker), but the public noticed the ads and the product.

Tate teamed up with Hal Lashlee and formed a company, Ashton-Tate, to distribute dBASE II (the only individual named Ashton was Tate's parakeet, but Tate felt that "Ashton-Tate" had a nice ring to it). After years of success and advancements in the form of dBASE III followed by dBASE III PLUS, the popular database manager has grown into dBASE IV. It offers a significant number of improvements over earlier versions of dBASE.

With dBASE IV, Ashton-Tate seems to have corrected every noticeable complaint about earlier versions of dBASE, particularly dBASE III and III PLUS. dBASE IV can handle one billion records and up to 255 fields per record. Up to 4000 characters can be placed in a single character field. Up to 64,000 characters can be placed in a *memo field,* which is a field designed to store large and varying amounts of text. Memo fields can now be searched, which solves a problem experienced by dBASE III users. dBASE IV can sort multiple fields and work with up to 99 files at the same time.

This kind of power is in some ways more impressive than realistic. A few quick calculations indicate that if you created a database with one billion records of 255 fields each, it would take your PC more than a month to read through the database one time, and the database would occupy about 30 million floppy disks. Suffice to say that if your database application outgrows the capabilities of dBASE IV, you should be talking to a mainframe computer salesperson.

Changes, Enhancements in dBASE IV, Version 1.1

Version 1.1 of dBASE IV provides major enhancements and some added commands to dBASE IV.

Reduced Memory Requirements Version 1.1 needs significantly less available memory to operate, and version 1.1 makes use of extra extended or expanded memory to enhance performance. Whereas version 1.0 required 512K of free RAM to operate, version 1.1 requires just 450K of free RAM to operate. The new memory manager present in version 1.1 also speeds performance in windowing and menu operations.

Multiple Browse, Edit Sessions Simultaneous sessions of BROWSE and EDIT are now possible. You use ON commands to halt a current Browse or Edit session, change work areas, and execute another BROWSE or EDIT command.

Simplified Installation, Increased Configuration Flexibility The installation process has been simplified, and configuration parameters can now be changed using the DBSETUP program from the DOS prompt. With DBSETUP, printer drivers and other configuration settings can be changed without reinstalling dBASE IV.

Expanded Printer Support Additional drivers for HP LaserJet printers have been added. PostScript printers, including the Apple LaserWriter, are now supported.

Disk Cache Software To increase performance, a disk cache program is supplied with version 1.1. The disk cache is automatically installed during the installation process, unless you turn off the Disk Cache option. The disk cache software loads automatically when dBASE IV is loaded, and it unloads from memory when you quit dBASE IV. Note that Borland's SideKick does interfere with the disk cache software and may cause your system to hang. If you plan on using SideKick along with dBASE IV version 1.1, do not turn on the Disk Cache option when you are installing dBASE IV. If you do install the disk cache and later want to load dBASE IV without it, enter **DBASE1** at the DOS prompt.

Indexing Enhancements The INDEX command now supports a FOR clause, which can be used to build conditional indexes. Such indexes will contain only those records meeting the conditions specified by the FOR clause. (See "Indexing" in Chapter 6 for complete details.) Menu options for indexing, provided within the Organize menu, can be accessed from the Append, Browse, and Edit menus.

Variable-Width Columns in QBE Screens File skeletons in query-by-example (QBE) screens now default to the width of the field, instead of being fixed at 21 characters each as in version 1.0. You can resize any column in a QBE screen with the Size (SHIFT-F7) key. (See Chapter 7 for more details on QBE screens.)

SQL Enhancements Use of the Control Center while in SQL mode is now supported. Also, a number of operations that were prohibited in SQL mode of version 1.0 are supported in the SQL mode of version 1.1.

New Commands The SAVE SCREEN, RESTORE SCREEN, REPLACE FROM ARRAY, SET CURSOR, SET DIRECTORY, and KEYBOARD commands have been added to version 1.1. For complete details on any of these commands, see the command by name in Appendix A.

System Requirements

To use dBASE IV, you will need an IBM PC, XT, AT, PS/2, or a compatible of any of these; a Compaq Portable, Plus, Deskpro, Portable II, Portable III, or 386; a Tandy 1000, 3000, or 4000; an Epson I, II, or III; or some other 100% IBM- compatible computer. Any personal computer that is software- compatible with the IBM PC should be able to use dBASE IV. Your computer must have a minimum of 512K of free memory after DOS loads (450K for version 1.1), and it must be equipped with one floppy-disk drive and one hard-disk drive. You must be using DOS version 2.1 or later or OS/2 version 1.0 or later. dBASE IV can be used with either a monochrome or a color monitor, and with any printer. dBASE IV version 1.1 is designed to take advantage of extra memory and can use the AST RAMpage, Intel Above Board, or any memory board meeting the LIM (Lotus-Intel-Microsoft) specifications.

To use dBASE IV on a local area network, you will need workstations with a minimum of 640K of memory (on Novell networks) or a minimum of 640K base memory plus 360K extended memory (or 64K additional DOS-contiguous memory on non-Novell networks). The server or one workstation on the network must have one 5 1/4-inch 360K or 1.2Mb floppy-disk drive, or one 3 1/2-inch 720K floppy-disk drive. The server must have a hard-disk drive. The network operating system can be any of the following:

- Novell SFT Netware/286 TTS version 2.10 or later
- IBM Token Ring Network with IBM PC Local Area Network Program version 1.2 or later
- 3Com 3Plus Share version 1.3.1
- Ungermann-Bass Net/One PC version 16.0
- Any other network configuration that is completely NETBIOS compatible with DOS 3.1 or later and with the networks just listed

Specifications

Specifications for dBASE IV include the following:

Maximum number of records:	1 billion
Maximum number of fields:	255
Maximum number of characters per field:	254
Maximum number of characters per memo field:	64,000
Maximum number of numeric digits per field:	20
Maximum number of databases open simultaneously:	10
Maximum number of files open simultaneously:	99

CHAPTER

2

Database Design

You may be anxious at this point to load dBASE IV into your computer and begin using the program. Resist the temptation to use dBASE IV for a new task you've never done by computer before; there are excellent reasons for approaching the job of designing a database with patience.

Planning is vital to effective database management. Many a purchaser of database management software has gotten started with the software, created a database, and stored data within that database, only to discover with disappointment that the database does not provide all of the needed information. Although powerful databases like dBASE IV let you make up for mistakes committed during the design process, correcting such errors can become a tedious job. This chapter will focus on database design to help you avoid such time-consuming mistakes.

HINT Creating a database without proper planning often results in a database with too few or too many fields.

Database design means thinking about how the data should be stored and how you and others will ask for data from the database file. As you design your database, you will outline on paper the problem that you want dBASE IV to help you solve. Just as you should not toss a bunch of files haphazardly into a filing cabinet without designing some type of filing system, you should not place information into a database file without first designing the database. As you design it, you must define the kinds of information that should be stored in the database.

About Data and Fields

Data and *fields* are two important terms in database design. Data is the information that goes into your database; for example, the last names for a group of individuals are data. Fields are the types of data that make up the database. A field is another name for a category, so an entire category of data, such as a group of names, is considered to be a field. Names, phone numbers, customer numbers, descriptions, locations, and stock numbers are common fields that your database might contain.

In addition to thinking about what kinds of information will go into the database, you must give careful consideration to the ways in which information will come out of the database. Information comes from a database in the form of *reports*. When you ask the computer for a list of all homes in a certain area priced between $100,000 and $150,000 or for a list of employees earning less than $15.00 an hour, you are asking for a report. When you ask for John Smith's address, you are also asking for a report. A report is a summary of information. Whether the computer displays a few lines on the screen or hundreds of lines on a stack of paper, it is providing a report based on the data contained within the database file. When designing a database, you must keep in mind that every item appearing on a report must either be included in your database or be calculable from data in your database.

To practice the techniques of database design, you should follow the hands-on practice sessions in this book. They demonstrate how you can design and utilize a database with a hypothetical example. The tasks and problems of an imaginary company named ABC Temporaries is used throughout this book to illustrate the effective use of dBASE IV for database management. ABC Temporaries is a temporary services firm that must not only keep track of the number of employees working for the firm, but must also track the client companies to which those temporary employees are currently assigned.

ABC Temporaries had always handled this task with ordinary three-by-five file cards, but the paperwork load finally grew too large to be handled efficiently in this manner. A major task at ABC Temporaries is to track just how much time each temporary employee spends at a particular client's, so that accurate bills can be generated. The relational capabilities of dBASE IV will make such tracking a relatively simple matter.

Successive chapters of this text will show how the staff at ABC Temporaries used dBASE IV to manage information successfully. By following along with these examples, you will learn how to put dBASE IV to work within your particular application.

Three Phases of Database Design

Designing a database file—whether for ABC Temporaries or for your own purposes—involves three major steps:

1. Data definition (an analysis of existing data)
2. Data refinement (refining necessary data)
3. Establishing relationships between the fields

Data Definition

During the first phase of database design, data definition, you must make a list, on a piece of paper, of all the important attributes (fields) involved in your application. To do this, you must examine your application in detail to determine exactly what kinds of information must be stored in the database.

In discussing the design for the database, the staff at ABC Temporaries determined that certain items must be known about each temporary worker: the employee's name, address, date of birth, date of hiring, salary, and the name of the client firm the employee is assigned to. The resulting list of fields is shown here:

Fields
1. Employee name
2. Employee address
3. Employee salary
4. Assigned to (firm)
5. Date of birth
6. Date hired

An important point to remember is that during this design phase, you should list all of the fields your database might possibly require. Listing more fields than are actually needed by your particular application is not a problem, because unnecessary fields will be eliminated during the data refinement stage.

Data Refinement

During this phase, you will refine your initial list of fields so that the fields form an accurate description of the types of data that will be needed in the database. At this stage, it is vital to include suggestions from as many other users of the database as possible. The people who use the database are the ones who know best the kinds of information they will need to have from the database.

When the staff of ABC Temporaries took a close look at their initial list of fields, they realized that most of the refinements were obvious. The address field, for example, should be divided into street address, city, state, and ZIP code, because the staff might want to arrange (index) the data by ZIP code or select a group of records by city. In most cases, any item that might be used to determine the order of the records or to select subsets of data should be assigned a field of its own.

HINT Get suggestions from those who will use a database before starting its design.

In your own case, some refinements may become evident quickly, and others may not. Going over your written list of fields will help make any necessary refinements more obvious. For example, when the staff of ABC Temporaries further examined the initial field list, they realized that the index-card system they had previously used contained multiple occurrences of employees with the same last name. To allow the staff to uniquely identify each employee, the name field was further divided into last name and first name fields. Suggestions were also made to add the salary, the number of dependents, and the hourly billing rate charged to the client. In addition, the managers wanted a comments field for employee evaluations. The following shows the refined list of fields:

Fields

1. Employee last name
2. Employee first name
3. Street address
4. City
5. State
6. ZIP code
7. Salary
8. No. of dependents
9. Assigned to (firm)
10. Rate charged to firm
11. Date of birth
12. Date hired
13. Evaluation comments

Considering the Relationships

During the third phase of database design, you will think about future relationships between the fields. This can help you determine whether you will need to use multiple databases, keeping in mind that dBASE IV is a relational database. Relational capability means that the data within one database can be related to the data in another; when you are designing a database, it is important not to lose sight of that fact. Too many users take relational database management software and proceed to create bulky, nonrelational databases, an approach that drastically increases the amount of work involved.

Relationships can be complex. The company president might want to know how many employees who are data entry operators worked for Mammoth Telephone between July and October. The database management system must compare fields that indicate who the client worked for with fields for the type of job and the time the job was performed. These types of questions can help reveal the types of data that are redundant, which helps you eliminate such data from the database.

As an example, the proposed staff database to be used by ABC Temporaries has fields that will be used to describe each employee. A major goal of computerizing the personnel records at the firm is to provide automated billing; by creating another database that shows which employees worked at a given assignment during a certain week, the firm can prepare bills for the services it provides to its clients. If ABC Temporaries took the nonrelational approach of adding fields for a "week ending" date and for the number of hours worked, the staff could store all of the information needed in each record. However, they would also have to fill in the name, address, and other information for each employee week after week. A better solution would be to create two databases, one containing the name, address, and other pertinent fields for each employee, and the other containing the number of hours worked, the "week ending" date, the client the work was done for, and a way of identifying the employee.

When establishing the relationships, you may determine that an additional field is necessary. In the case of ABC Temporaries, the method of employee identification is by social security number, so this field was added to the proposed list of fields, resulting in the finalized list of fields shown here. The database created in the next chapter is based on this list.

Fields

1. Employee social security number
2. Employee last name
3. Employee first name
4. Street address
5. City
6. State
7. ZIP code
8. Salary
9. No. of dependents
10. Assigned to (firm)
11. Rate charged to firm
12. Date of birth
13. Date hired
14. Evaluation comments

During all three design phases, potential users should be consulted to determine what kinds of information they will expect the database to supply. Just what kinds of reports are wanted from the database? What kinds of queries will employees make of the database? By continually asking these types of questions, you will think in terms of your database, and this should help you determine what is important and what is unimportant.

It often helps to consider examples of the data you will store while you are designing the database. For example, if your database contains many names that include salutations like "Dr." or "Honorable," you may need to create a separate title field to allow indexing or selections based on such information.

HINT Look at examples of your data before finalizing your list of fields.

Keep in mind that even after the database design phases, the design of your database file is not set in stone. Changes to its design can be made later if necessary. If you follow the systematic approach of database design for your specific application, however, you have a better chance of creating a database that provides much of the information you need and does not need to be extensively redesigned.

dBASE IV lets you change the design of a database at any time, although such changes are often inconvenient to make once the database is designed. Here is an example. If you used dBASE IV to create a database file that handled a customer mailing list, you might have included fields for names, addresses, cities, states, and ZIP codes. At first glance this might seem sufficient. You might then begin entering customer information into the database and gradually build a sizeable mailing list. But if your company later decided to begin telemarketing using the same mailing list, you might suddenly realize that you have not included a field for telephone numbers. With dBASE IV, you could easily change the design to include a field for telephone numbers, but you would still face the mammoth task of going back and adding a telephone number for every name currently in the mailing list.

If this information had been added as you developed the mailing list, you would not face the inconvenience of having to enter the phone numbers as a separate operation. Careful planning and the time spent during the database design process can help you avoid such problems.

CHAPTER

3

Creating and Displaying A Database

dBASE IV comes in the form of assorted manuals and quick reference guides, one installation disk, nine system disks, three disks of samples, and a tutorial disk. (If you purchased the Developer's Edition of dBASE IV, there may be additional disks present; these contain programmer's utilities that are beyond the scope of this book but are detailed in the documentation that accompanies the Developer's Edition.) If you are not sure if all of your disks are present, refer to your dBASE IV documentation to be sure that you have the correct number of disks.

Hard-Disk Installation

Installing dBASE IV on a hard disk is a simple matter, thanks to the installation program contained on the Installation disk and the detailed instructions contained in the "Getting Started" booklet packaged with your software. If you do not have the "Getting Started" booklet, you should locate it now. Because versions of dBASE IV change and the instructions may change along with software updates, this book will provide only general tips regarding installation. You should refer to your latest dBASE IV documentation for detailed specifics on installing the program.

The installation program supplied as a part of dBASE IV will create the necessary subdirectory on your hard disk and copy the needed files into that subdirectory. Before installing dBASE IV, you should make sure that you have at least three megabytes of free disk space remaining on your hard disk. (You can tell the amount of free space by using the DIR command; the description "*xxxxx* bytes free" that appears at the bottom of the directory listing indicates the amount of free space remaining.) The program itself requires almost three megabytes of disk space for installation; however, you will certainly need adequate space for storing your databases and for sorting files.

NOTE If you are using dBASE IV for the first time, you should also be aware of the memory requirements of the program. dBASE IV requires 640K of installed memory for version 1.0, or 576K of installed memory for version 1.1. While your machine may be equipped with 640K, some memory is consumed by DOS, and memory-resident programs (such as SideKick or Superkey) will also consume available memory. Also, while dBASE IV may operate with some small memory-resident programs loaded, it will need to access the disk much more often when working with large files than it will when it has more memory to work with. For best performance you should have 640K of memory in your machine, and you should not have memory-resident programs loaded while you are using dBASE IV (unless those programs are designed to use other extended or expanded memory, which you may also have installed above 640K).

To install the program, turn on your computer and get to the DOS prompt in the usual manner. Then perform the following steps:

1. Insert the Installation disk into drive A.

2. Change the default drive to A by typing **A:** and then pressing the ENTER key.

3. Enter the following command to start the installation process:

```
INSTALL
```

Refer to the "Getting Started" booklet supplied with your dBASE IV documentation, and follow the instructions in that booklet to complete the installation process.

Creating a Batch File To Start the Program

You can create a batch file that makes starting dBASE and changing to the desired subdirectory an easier task. If you have installed dBASE in a subdirectory named DBASE on drive C of your hard disk, the commands that follow can be used to accomplish this task. If your hard disk is not in drive C, substitute your hard-disk letter and a colon for the "C:" in the following commands. If you installed dBASE IV in a subdirectory named something other than DBASE, refer to your DOS manual for specifics on creating batch files.

HINT Batch files make starting dBASE an easier process.

To create the batch file, first enter the following commands from the DOS prompt, pressing ENTER at the end of each line:

```
CD\
MD\DBASE\DBDATA
COPY CON DBASE.BAT
```

When you complete the third command, the cursor will move down a line and wait for additional entries. Type the following lines, pressing ENTER after each line:

```
PATH=C:\DBASE
CD\DBASE\DBDATA
DBASE
```

Then press the F6 key, followed by the ENTER key. You should see the message "1 file(s) copied."

From this point on, you will always be able to start dBASE and switch to the DBASE\DBDATA subdirectory simply by entering **DBASE** at the DOS prompt. Creating a subdirectory to contain your data files (in this case, C:\DBASE\DBDATA) is a wise idea, because it will help you keep your data files separate from the other program files used by dBASE IV.

HINT Keeping your data files separate from your program files will reduce the amount of clutter in your disk directories. Use separate directories for data and program files.

Starting dBASE IV

Start your computer in the usual manner. If you created a batch file by following the directions in the previous paragraphs, you can enter **DBASE** and press ENTER to switch to the proper directory and load the program. Otherwise, you must first set a path to the DBASE directory with the DOS PATH command, then switch to the subdirectory that will contain your data files, and then enter **DBASE** from the DOS prompt. As an example, let's assume that your hard disk is in drive C, that the program is stored in a subdirectory named DBASE, and that all your data files are residing in a subdirectory named C:\DBASE\DBDATA (which must already exist on your hard disk). You could start the program by entering the following commands from the DOS prompt:

```
PATH=C:\DBASE
CD\DBASE\DBDATA
DBASE
```

Once the program starts, you will briefly see an introductory screen and a copyright message. You will see this at the bottom of the screen:

```
Press ↵ to assent to the license agreement and begin dBASE IV
```

Figure 3-1.

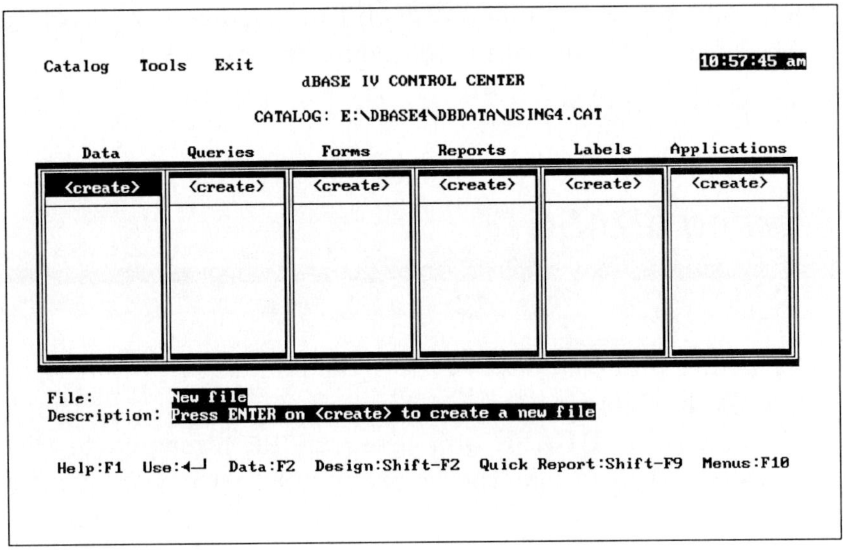

```
Catalog   Tools   Exit                                              10:57:45 am
                          dBASE IV CONTROL CENTER

                      CATALOG: E:\DBASE4\DBDATA\USING4.CAT

   Data       Queries      Forms      Reports      Labels    Applications
 <create>    <create>    <create>    <create>    <create>    <create>

File:         New file
Description:  Press ENTER on <create> to create a new file

Help:F1  Use:◄┘  Data:F2  Design:Shift-F2  Quick Report:Shift-F9  Menus:F10
```

dBASE IV Control Center

Press ENTER. Within a moment, the dBASE IV Control Center will appear, as shown in Figure 3-1.

The Control Center is a system of menus provided by dBASE IV. Using the Control Center, you can select various options for creating databases, adding and changing information, printing reports and labels, creating data entry forms, and performing most functions that can be performed within dBASE IV. The Control Center is just one of three ways in which you can use dBASE IV. The other ways—from the dot prompt, and from within a command file or program—will be discussed in more detail later.

About the Screen

The top line of your screen shows the time and the menu bar, which currently consists of three menu choices. Pressing the ALT key plus the first letter of the menu name opens the desired menu. Press ALT-C now, and the Catalog menu will be opened. An alternative method of opening a menu is pressing F10 and then using the left and right arrow keys to move to the desired menu. Whenever a menu is open, the appropriate menu options appear in a rectangular box called a *pull-down menu.*

The large area underneath the menu bar is referred to as the *work surface.* The work surface begins directly underneath the menu bar and extends to the status bar. When you are at the Control Center (as you are now), the work surface contains six panels that are used for various operations. As you create different types of files within dBASE, the names of these files will appear in the panels.

The status bar is not presently visible on your screen, but it will often appear at the bottom of the screen, depending on where you are in the program. An example of a status bar is shown in Figure 3-2. It is divided into portions, each of which contains useful information. The far-left portion of the status bar displays information that indicates what portion of the program you are using at the time. To the right of this information is the disk drive, path, and filename of any file that is currently in use. The example in the illustration shows "<NEW>" as the filename because, in this illustration, a new database file is being created.

The third portion of the status bar shows the cursor location, and the fourth and fifth portions show different types of related

Figure 3-2.

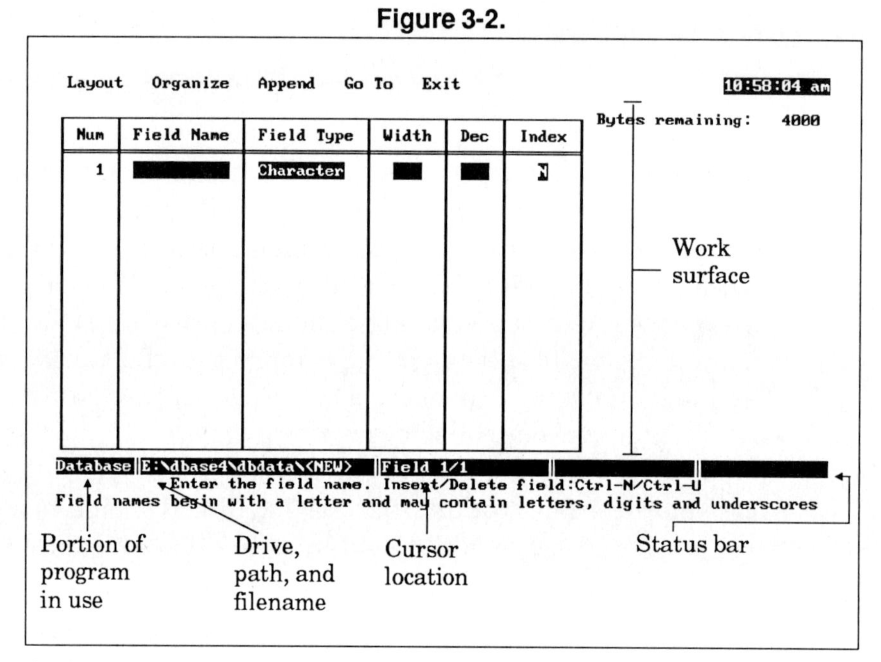

Screen with status bar

information, again depending on where you are within the program. The right edge of the status bar contains indicators that show the status of the NUM LOCK and CAPS LOCK keys.

Directly below the status bar is the navigation line. (The navigation line is currently visible on your screen; it is the line at the bottom that begins with "position selection bar.") This line provides helpful messages that tell you how to move within the various dBASE IV menus. Below the navigation line is the message line, which contains various messages as you use the program. It generally provides information about the currently highlighted option or displays error messages.

Press the right arrow key once. You'll see the Catalog menu close, and a pull-down menu for Tools will be opened. The choices displayed within the pull-down menu apply to using various tools within the program; they will be covered in more detail later. If you continue pressing the right or left arrow key, you will see the various menu choices for the Exit menu, which is used to exit to a dot prompt or to exit from the program.

Selecting Options from a Menu

Once a menu has been opened, any option on that menu can be chosen by pressing the up or down arrow key to highlight the option and then pressing ENTER. (An alternative is to press the first letter of the desired menu option.) As an example, use the left and right arrow keys to open the Tools menu; then press the down arrow key until the DOS Utilities choice on the Tools menu is highlighted. Press ENTER to choose this option.

In a moment, another set of menu choices will appear, along with a window showing the available files under DOS. Press F10 to display the menus, and use the left and right arrow keys to examine the available menu options. (These will be covered in more detail in a later chapter.)

Press ESC until dBASE asks if you wish to abandon the operation, and then type **Y** for yes. You will be returned to the Control Center.

Canceling a Selection

You can use the ESC key from any point in the Control Center to cancel an operation or a menu selection. However, you should be aware that some operations (like copying files) cannot be canceled once the process has actually begun.

HINT ESC is your most useful key wherever you are somewhere you don't want to be. In most cases, repeatedly pressing ESC will get you out of an operation.

About the Keyboard

If you are already familiar with the PC keyboard, you should skip this section and begin reading at the next section.

dBASE IV uses a number of special-purpose keys for various functions. In addition to the ordinary letter and number keys, you will often use the *function keys.* On most IBM PC and PC-compatible computers, these keys are the double row of gray keys at the left side of the PC keyboard, as shown in Figure 3-3. On newer IBM PCs and some PC-compatibles, the function keys are placed in a horizontal row at the top of the keyboard, as illustrated in Figure 3-4.

The function keys on the older PCs are labeled F1 through F10, for Function 1 through Function 10. The newer machines have twelve function keys. Usually grouped on the left side of the keyboard are three often-used keys: the Escape key (ESC), the Tab key (it may have TAB or double arrows on it), and the Alternate

Figure 3-3.

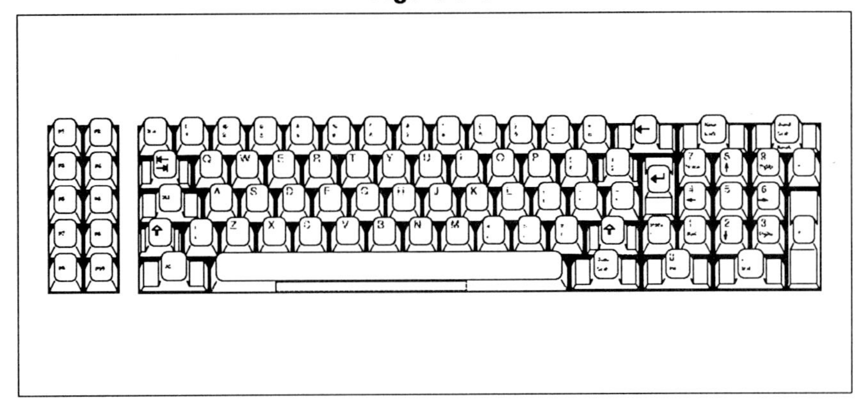

The IBM PC keyboard

(ALT) key. Some keyboards have the ESC key in a different location, and some keyboards have two ALT keys, one on each side of the keyboard. Find these keys before going further; they will prove helpful for various operations.

You should locate the template supplied with your package of dBASE IV and place it where you can refer to it when you use the

Figure 3-4.

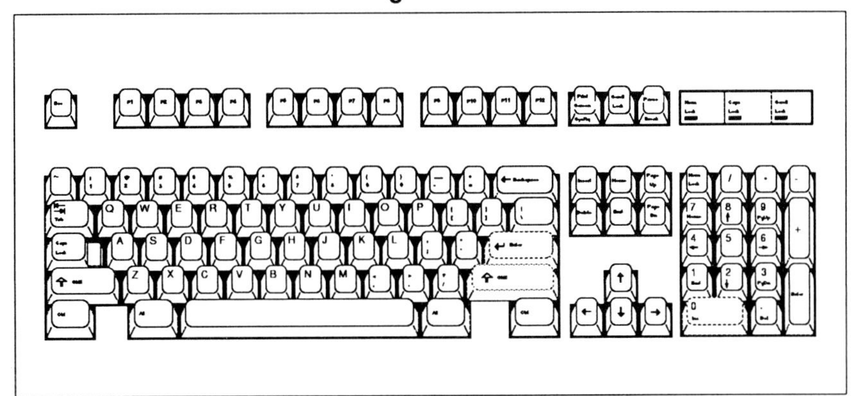

The enhanced IBM PC keyboard

function keys. The uses for these keys will be detailed in later chapters as those operations are discussed.

Toward the right side of the keyboard is one of the SHIFT keys. Usually located below the right SHIFT key is a key labeled CAPS LOCK; it is used to change all typed letters to uppercase. Newer IBM PCs and many compatible keyboards have the CAPS LOCK key located above the left SHIFT key. (The CAPS LOCK key does not change the format of the numbers in the top row of the keyboard.) Just above the right SHIFT key is the ENTER or RETURN key; it performs a function that is similar to the return key of a typewriter. In dBASE IV, the ENTER key is often used to let dBASE know that you are finished entering information. Above the ENTER key is the BACKSPACE key.

On the right side of the keyboard, in the numeric key area, is a key labeled DEL. The Delete key can be used to delete characters when you are in dBASE IV. You can also delete files with this key when you are at the Control Center by highlighting the filename and pressing DEL.

Finally, the far-right side of the keyboard has two gray keys with plus (+) and minus (-) labels. These keys will produce the plus and minus symbols when pressed. You can use these keys interchangeably with the plus and hyphen keys on the top row of the keyboard.

The far-right side of the keyboard also contains a numeric keypad. On some computers, this area can serve a dual purpose. The keys containing up, down, left, and right arrows in this area can be used to move around in a worksheet. By pressing the NUM LOCK key, you can use the same keys to enter numbers. Some keyboards have a separate area with arrow keys and a seperate area with a numeric keypad.

☞ ***REMEMBER*** When NUM LOCK is pressed, the arrow keys on many keyboards create numbers instead of moving the cursor. If you press on an arrow key and get an unwanted number, check the status of the NUM LOCK key.

The dBASE IV Dot Prompt

The Control Center is just one way in which you can use dBASE IV. Another method is the direct entry of commands from the dot prompt. The options that you can choose from a menu within the Control Center have equivalent commands that can be entered directly from the dot prompt. You will get acceptable results from dBASE IV regardless of which method you choose, but it does help to know a little about both methods.

Press the ESC key now to exit the Control Center. A message will appear on the screen, asking if you want to abandon the operation. Respond by typing **Y** for yes. At the bottom of the screen you will now see a period and the message "Command" within the status bar. The period, commonly known as the dot prompt, indicates that dBASE IV is in its interactive mode and is ready to accept a command.

dBASE IV's basic command structure becomes obvious after you try a few commands. To print information on the screen, you use the question mark. As an example, type

```
? "Using dBASE"
```

```
Using dBASE
```

As you can see, the ? command prints everything between the quotation marks except for the quotation marks themselves. The reason these characters require quotation marks will be explained later. You need not type quotation marks to print numbers on the screen:

```
? 23

23
```

dBASE IV performs addition, subtraction, multiplication, division, and square-root calculations when you use the mathematical operators listed in the following table:

Operation	Symbol
Addition	+
Subtraction	-
Multiplication	*
Division	/
Exponentiation	**

To use dBASE IV as a quick calculator, you enter the question mark after the dot prompt, followed by the numbers and appropriate operators:

```
? 5*45

225


? 5/15

0.33
```

To clear the entire screen of information, enter

```
CLEAR
```

You can go from dot-prompt mode back to the menus of the Command Center at any time simply by entering **ASSIST** at the dot prompt.

dBASE IV also accepts commands in abbreviated form. Only the first four letters of any command are necessary, so you could enter **CLEA** instead of CLEAR to clear the screen. However, all commands in this book will be used in their complete form.

REMEMBER Any time you find yourself at the dot prompt, you can get back to the Control Center by entering **ASSIST**.

Conventions

Before you start working with dBASE IV, you need to know about the conventions that will be used throughout the book. All commands are printed in UPPERCASE, but you can type them in either uppercase or lowercase. Any part of a command surrounded by left ([) and right (]) brackets is optional, and any command followed by an ellipsis (...) can be repeated. Parameters in the command are in *italics*. Every command that you enter will be terminated by pressing ENTER (or RETURN). Pressing ENTER indicates to dBASE IV that you are finished typing the command and that you want it to execute. Whenever you are asked to "enter" a command in this book, finish it by pressing ENTER unless otherwise noted. Characters to be typed in at the keyboard are shown in **boldface**.

In this book new terms are printed in *italics*. Messages that the computer displays are printed in this book within quotes, as in "Variable not found."

Getting Help

Should you need help, dBASE IV provides information on subjects ranging from basic database concepts to the use of programming commands and functions, all of which is stored in a HELP file and is accessible to dBASE IV. From either the dot prompt or the Control Center menus, you can get help by pressing F1. With either approach, a series of menus will assist you in finding the information you are searching for.

! ***HINT*** At any point in dBASE, pressing F1 reveals a help screen.

As an example, let's suppose you are working with dBASE IV from the dot prompt and need information on the CLEAR command. Press F1 now, and a main menu of five topics will appear. Pick the topic that best describes your problem; since the first choice looks as good as any, press ENTER. Next, three choices appear on a new menu, with the first choice, Alphabetical List of Commands, highlighted. Since you want to know about the CLEAR command, press ENTER. A list containing the commands for which you can obtain help appears. Use the arrow keys to highlight the CLEAR command, and then press ENTER. A description of the CLEAR command, along with the command's syntax usage and its variations, is displayed on the screen (see the example in Figure 3-5).

If you already know the name of the command, you can circumvent the menus and go directly to the explanation by entering **HELP** followed by the command name at the dot prompt, as in **HELP CLEAR**.

dBASE IV will offer you help even if you don't ask for it. If dBASE IV cannot understand how you are trying to use a command, it will display a message asking if you want to cancel the

Figure 3-5.

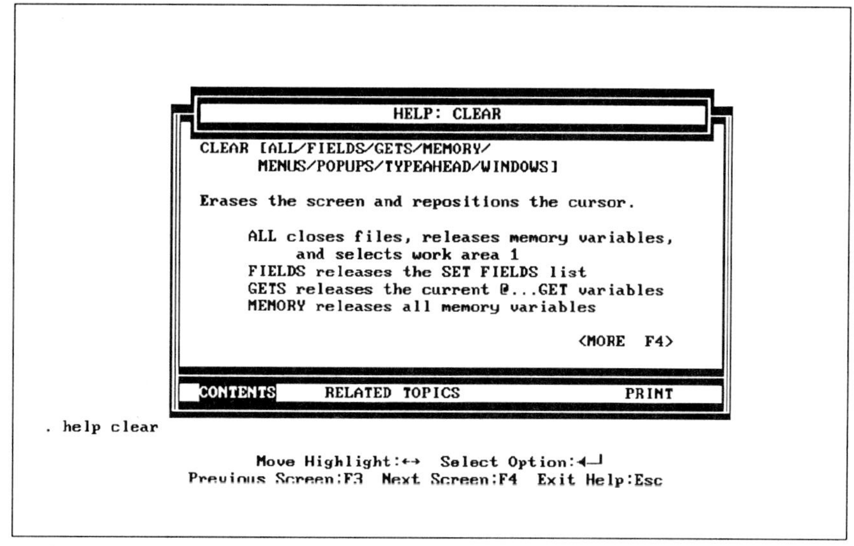

Help screen for the CLEAR command

command, correct (edit) it, or get help. To see an example, press ESC to exit the help screen and get back to the dot prompt, and then enter **CLOSE**. dBASE IV responds with an error message, as shown in Figure 3-6.

Use the right arrow key to highlight the Help option, and then press ENTER. A help screen dealing with the use of dBASE appears. In this case, you see a general help-system table of contents. If you had used a command that dBASE recognized, the help screen would have been more specific. Again, you can use the up and down arrow keys to select a desired topic and then press ENTER to see more information about that particular topic.

Pressing F1 when you are at the Control Center menus reveals similar help screens that provide information specific to the Control Center menus. The help system is *context-sensitive,* which means that the particular help screens that appear will depend on where you are in the program. The HELP file is quite

Figure 3-6.

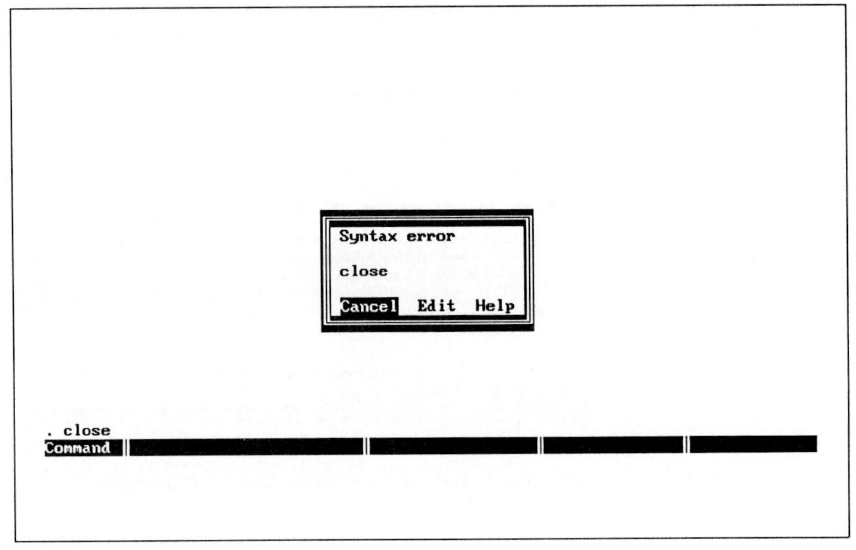

Error message

extensive, so by all means take some time to rummage through it, view the different options, and understand how the file is set up. Knowing where to locate information about a particular operation or command can be a great aid when you work with some of the more difficult operations in the book. When you are done, press ESC to exit the help screens.

Creating a Database

The Create option of the Data menu prepares a database file for use. (The CREATE command from the dot prompt performs the same task.) You normally prepare a file once, when you are beginning to create a database. When it is used to create rather than redesign a database, the Create option of the Data menu accomplishes three tasks: it creates a database file, defines the structure (design) of the database, and opens the file in preparation for entering information into the database (if desired).

Let's create the database needed by ABC Temporaries from the final list of fields. First, return to the Control Center menus if you are not already there. To do this, enter **ASSIST** at the dot prompt. The dot prompt will disappear, and the Control Center will return.

To create a database, you must highlight the Create option under the Data panel. Since you just entered the Control Center, the Create option should be currently highlighted. Press ENTER to accept the option. Within a few seconds, dBASE IV will display a screen with highlighted blocks for the entry of field names, types

Figure 3-7.

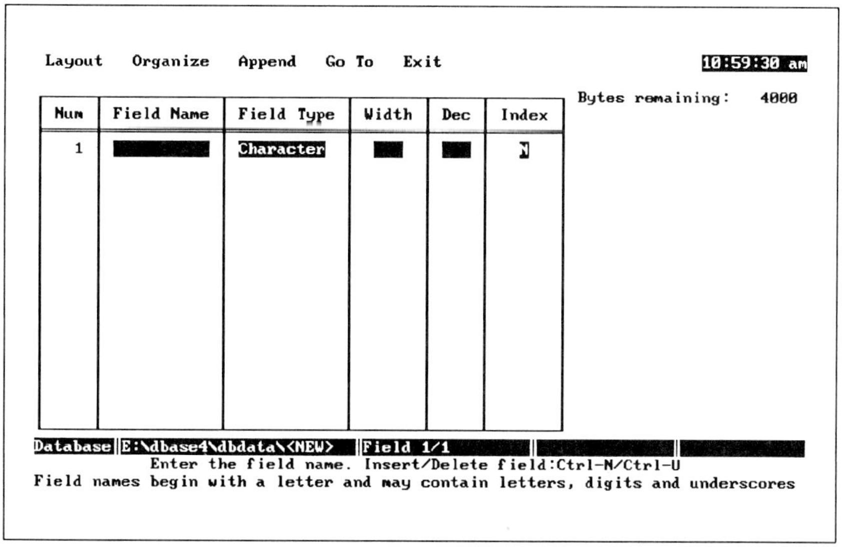

Layout Organize Append Go To Exit 10:59:30 am

Bytes remaining: 4000

Num	Field Name	Field Type	Width	Dec	Index
1		Character			N

Database E:\dbase4\dbdata\<NEW> Field 1/1
Enter the field name. Insert/Delete field:Ctrl-N/Ctrl-U
Field names begin with a letter and may contain letters, digits and underscores

Database Design screen

of fields, field widths, the number of decimal places, and whether or not an index should be created on the basis of this field (more on this topic later). This screen, known as the Database Design screen, is shown in Figure 3-7.

When you are naming a field, use a name that best describes the contents of the field. Field names can be made of letters, numbers, and underscores, but they must start with a letter. Field names can contain up to ten characters. dBASE IV will not allow the entry of field names that are too long or that contain illegal characters.

The first field on the list is the employee's social security number, so enter **SOCIALSEC** for the field name. Once you press the ENTER key, the cursor will automatically move to the Field Type block. dBASE IV allows for the entry of six types of fields:

- *Character fields* These are used to store any characters, including letters, numbers, any special symbols, or blank spaces. A character field has a maximum size of 254 characters. You usually store words, numbers that do not need to be calculated, and combinations of words and numbers in character fields.
- *Date fields* You use the date field to store dates. The default format for entering dates is *MM/DD/YY*, but this format can be changed from the dot prompt with the SET command. dBASE IV automatically inserts the slashes as you enter a date into a date field. Although you could store a date in a character field, the use of date fields allows dBASE to perform calculations based on dates.
- *Numeric fields* These fields are for numbers, with or without decimal places. Only numbers and the minus sign (the hyphen) can be entered; dBASE does *not* use commas in numbers larger than 1000, although you can format reports so that the commas appear. You can enter numbers up to 20 digits in length; dBASE IV is accurate to 15 digits, so unless you are performing scientific calculations, you shouldn't have a problem with nu-

meric accuracy. You usually use numeric fields to store any numbers that you must use in calculations, such as salary amounts, quantities of items, and so forth.

HINT Use numeric fields for numbers that must be calculated. Numbers that you never need to perform calculations on (like phone numbers) should be stored in character fields.

- *Float fields* These are numeric fields with a floating decimal point. As with numeric fields, you can enter numbers or the minus sign, and accuracy extends to 15 digits.
- *Logical fields* These fields consist of a single letter representing a true or false value. The letter T or Y represents true, and F or N represents false. Use logical fields when you want to store the response to a true-or-false question, such as whether an employee belongs to a union or not. An advantage of using a logical field (rather than a character field with a width of one character) is that dBASE will only accept T, F, Y, or N in a logical field. This kind of validation can help reduce the possiblility of your making data entry errors.
- *Memo fields* dBASE IV can store large blocks of text for each record in the form of memo fields. Up to 64,000 characters can be stored in a memo field. Use this type of field when you want to store very large amounts of text. If the text will consist of an average paragraph or less, you can usually get by with a character field instead.

Most fields in a database are character or numeric fields, although there may be times when you need all of the different field types that dBASE IV offers.

dBASE IV is still waiting for you to define the field type. Try pressing the spacebar. Each time you press it, dBASE IV displays one of the six choices for field types, and an accompanying description is shown at the bottom of the screen. You can choose a field type in one of two ways: you can continue to press the spacebar until the appropriate choice appears and then press ENTER, or you can type the first letter of the field type—C for character, D for date, N for numeric, F for float, L for logical, or M for memo.

Before you proceed, think about the field type for social security numbers. Such entries consist of numbers, so at first it might seem you should use a numeric field. However, this is not really practical. If you include the hyphens that normally appear as part of a social security number, dBASE IV will attempt to subtract the two parts of the social security number that are separated by the hyphen (which happens to be the numerical subtraction symbol), and the result will be an incorrect entry. You will never use a social security number in a numerical calculation, so it makes sense to store the entry as a character field rather than as a numeric field. A number stored in a character field cannot be used directly in a numerical calculation, although you could convert the value to a number with a dBASE IV function.

Since the social security field will contain characters in the form of hyphens, enter **C** (for character). Note that when you do so, dBASE IV asks for the field width. Remember, character fields can be up to 254 characters in length, while numeric and float fields are limited to 20 digits. Logical fields are fixed at one character, while date fields are fixed at eight characters. Earlier, in Chapter 2, ABC Temporaries calculated that the social security field would require 11 characters, so enter **11** as the field width. Once you have pressed ENTER, the cursor moves to the Index field, where dBASE IV expects you to enter **Y** for yes or **N** for no.

dBASE IV lets you define any field to be used within an *index*. When you tell dBASE IV that any particular field is to be indexed, dBASE IV treats that field differently. Designating a field as an indexed field causes dBASE IV to keep an internal index that will allow you to quickly locate or group records based on the contents of that field. The index data is stored in a master index file that shares the same name as the database but has the extension

.MDX. Since social security numbers are a useful and unique way to locate employees, enter **Y** in the Index block for the SOCIAL-SEC field. The cursor will move to the next field description.

HINT Indexes will help you keep records in order and will aid in quickly finding information.

Enter **LASTNAME** for the second field name. When the cursor moves to the Field Type area, enter **C** (for character) for the field type, and then enter **15** for the field width. This time, enter **N** for no at the Index block (or just press ENTER), and the cursor will move to the third field definition.

For the third item in the list of specified fields, the employee's first name, enter **FIRSTNAME**. Again, when the cursor moves to the Field Type area, enter **C** (or just press ENTER to accept the existing entry). Then enter **15** for the field width and **N** in the Index block. Providing different fields for the last and first names will allow you to order or locate records based on a last name.

Moving down the list, enter **ADDRESS** for the fourth field definition, **C** for the field type, and **25** for the field width. Answer **N** to the Index prompt. For the fifth field, enter **CITY**, and enter **C** for the field type, **15** for the width, and **N** for the Index prompt. For the next field enter **STATE**, enter **C** for the field type, **2** for the field width, and **N** for the Index prompt.

The next field will be ZIP code. Although ZIP codes contain numbers, the same reasoning used with the social security field applies, so enter **ZIPCODE** as the field name, **C** as the field type, **10** as the width, and **N** in response to the Index prompt.

You may recall from Chapter 2 that two of the field attributes take the form of dates: the date of birth and the date the employee was hired. dBASE IV lets you use date fields to enter dates.

Enter **BIRTHDAY** for the name of the next field, and when in the Field Type column, type **D** to indicate a date field. Note that dBASE automatically supplies a width of 8 for this type of field. Again, enter **N** in response to the Index prompt.

Enter **DATEHIRED** for the name of the next field, and when in the Field Type column, type **D** to indicate a date field. Enter **N** in response to the Index prompt. For the next field name, enter **DEPENDENTS**. (dBASE will beep as you fill up the column with the name for this field.) For the field type, enter **N** (for numeric). For the field width, enter **2**. This will create a numeric field with a maximum width of two digits. You will be able to store numbers from 0 to 99 in this field. (ABC Temporaries assumes it will never have employees with more than 99 dependents.)

Since you specified a numeric field, the cursor now moves to the Dec (decimal) column. You could, if desired, specify a number of decimal places for the numeric field. Since you are using whole numbers to describe the number of dependents, simply press ENTER to bypass the decimal entry. Finally, enter **N** in the Index block.

Enter **SALARY** for the name of the next field, and enter **N** in response to the Field Type prompt. Next, enter **5** for the field width and then enter **2** for the number of decimal places. (One digit is used for the decimal place, two digits for the dollar amount, and two for cents.) The field will be used to track the hourly salaries of the employees, in dollar amounts. Whenever you include decimal amounts, allow one digit for the decimal; also, if you are working exclusively with decimal numbers, include one digit so the decimal point can be preceded by a zero (for example, 0.1). Thus, the minimum field width for a decimal number is 3. Again, enter **N** in response to the Index prompt.

Finally, enter the remaining information for the next two fields:

Field Name	**Type**	**Width**	**Dec.**	**Index?**
ASSIGNMENT	CHARACTER	20		N
HOURLYRATE	NUMERIC	5	2	N

Depending on the individual, the EVALUATE field may need to store a lengthy series of comments. The most economical way of storing very large amounts of text is to use a memo field, so EVALUATE should be designated as a memo field. (If you were to enter comments of 100 characters or less in most records, a character field would be better; however, since some ABC managers will want to enter entire paragraphs of text, a memo field will work best for this database.) Enter **EVALUATE** as the next field name, and then enter **M** (for memo) as the field type. dBASE IV will automatically supply 10 as a field width. You may also notice that dBASE automatically places the letter N in the Index prompt here. It is not possible to index on a memo field, and in virtually all cases, there is no need to do so.

At this point, your screen should resemble Figure 3-8. While you are creating the database, notice the statistic listed at the top

Figure 3-8.

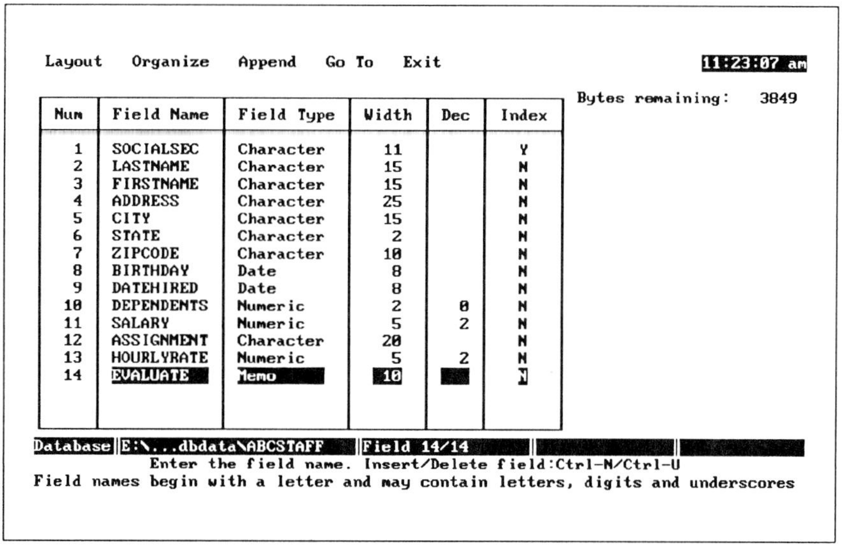

Layout Organize Append Go To Exit 11:23:07 am

Bytes remaining: 3849

Num	Field Name	Field Type	Width	Dec	Index
1	SOCIALSEC	Character	11		Y
2	LASTNAME	Character	15		N
3	FIRSTNAME	Character	15		N
4	ADDRESS	Character	25		N
5	CITY	Character	15		N
6	STATE	Character	2		N
7	ZIPCODE	Character	10		N
8	BIRTHDAY	Date	8		N
9	DATEHIRED	Date	8		N
10	DEPENDENTS	Numeric	2	0	N
11	SALARY	Numeric	5	2	N
12	ASSIGNMENT	Character	20		N
13	HOURLYRATE	Numeric	5	2	N
14	EVALUATE	Memo	10		N

Database E:\...dbdata\ABCSTAFF Field 14/14
Enter the field name. Insert/Delete field:Ctrl-N/Ctrl-U
Field names begin with a letter and may contain letters, digits and underscores

Completed sample database

of the screen. In the right corner beneath the clock is the number of available bytes remaining in the current record. This number is calculated by adding the numbers in the Width column and subtracting the total from the alloted 4000 bytes (characters) per record. The status bar at the bottom of the screen indicates the number of fields created so far. Both figures—the number of bytes remaining and the number of fields—will change as you add fields to the database. At the left side of the status bar appears the path and the subdirectory, along with the filename (in this case <NEW>, because you have not yet named the file).

Correcting Mistakes

If you make any mistakes while defining the structure of the database file, you can correct them before completing the definition process. To correct mistakes, use the cursor keys to move to the field name or field type containing the offending characters, and use the BACKSPACE key along with the character keys to make any desired corrections. You can use the arrow keys to move left, right, up, or down in the form. To insert new characters between existing characters, press the INS key and then type the correction. Pressing INS again takes you out of Insert mode. When you are not in Insert mode, any characters that you type will write over existing characters.

A more complete list of dBASE IV editing keys is shown in Table 3-1. These editing keys also work with the word processor when you are editing memo fields.

Table 3-1.

Key	Action
← or CTRL-S	Cursor back one character
→ or CTRL-D	Cursor forward one character
↑ or CTRL-E	Cursor up one field
↓ or CTRL-X	Cursor down one field
INS or CTRL-V	Insert mode on/off
DEL or CTRL-G	Delete character
BACKSPACE	Delete character to left of cursor
CTRL-Y	For appending clear field with blanks
CTRL-Q	Abort screen operation; don't add record to database
ESC or CTRL-O	Abort screen operation; add record to database
CTRL-T	Delete word or all characters until next blank
CTRL-← or CTRL-A	Move to start of field in Create; move left by word in Edit or Browse
CTRL-→ or CTRL-F	Move to end of field in Create; move right by word in Edit or Browse
TAB	Move right one column or field
SHIFT-TAB	Move left one column or field
CTRL-END or CTRL-W	Save changes and return to Control Center or dot prompt

dBASE IV Editing Keys

Saving the Database

To tell dBASE IV that you have finished defining the database structure, position the cursor on an empty field and press the ENTER key. (An alternative method is to press CTRL-END.) The screen will display the message

```
Save as:
```

prompting you for a name for the file. Each database file must have a name, and the name must not contain more than eight characters. dBASE IV automatically assigns an extension of .DBF to the name. Database files that include memo fields will also have a corresponding file with a .DBT extension created automatically by dBASE IV.

HINT In many operations (including saving a database), CTRL-END tells dBASE you are ready to save.

Enter **ABCSTAFF** as the name of the file. Within a few moments, you will see this at the bottom of the screen:

```
Input data records now? (Y/N)
```

You could begin entering records for the staff of ABC Temporaries. However, let's first display a list of database files on the disk. To do this, type **N**, and dBASE IV will return to the Control Center. Press ALT-T to open the Tools menu; then select the DOS Utilities option. When you press ENTER to select the option, a window of available files will appear.

Within the window, you should notice three new files that were not present previously: ABCSTAFF.DBF, ABCSTAFF.DBT, and ABCSTAFF.MDX. The files with .DBF and .DBT extensions comprise the database you just defined. The .DBF extension stands for "database file," and the file contains all of the data you entered (except for the text in the memo fields). The .DBT extension stands for "database text," and this file contains the text entered in the memo fields. The file with the .MDX extension contains the index information.

REMEMBER Databases with memo fields are stored in two files, with .DBF and .DBT extensions. Keep this in mind if you use DOS commands to copy or erase files.

Press ALT-E to open the Exit menu, and choose Exit to return to the Control Center. (As an alternative, you could press the ESC key and type **Y**.)

Adding Information to a File

To add information to a file, you simply highlight the desired file in the Data menu of the Control Center, and then press F2 (Data) to use that file. To add data to the ABCSTAFF file now, first highlight the filename ABCSTAFF in the Data menu (it should be currently highlighted), and then press F2 (Data) to move to the Database menu. The screen will change to reveal the simple

Figure 3-9.

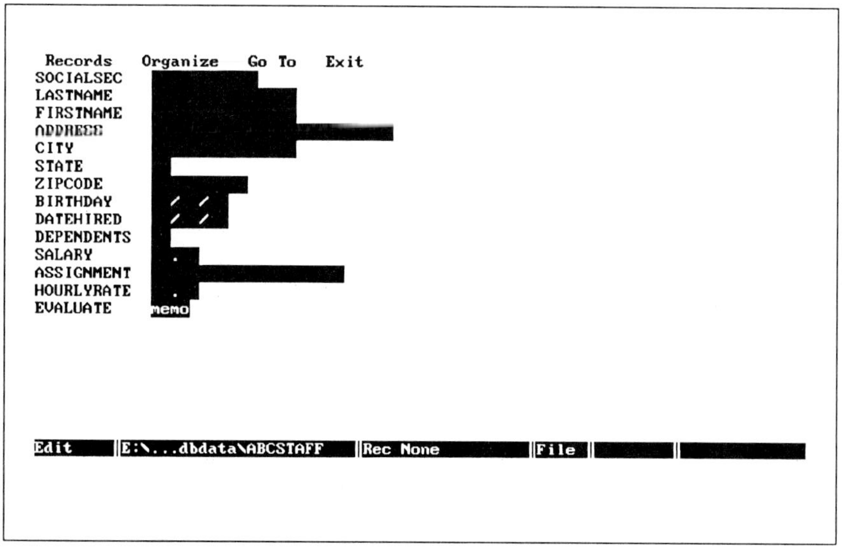

```
Records   Organize   Go To   Exit
SOCIALSEC
LASTNAME
FIRSTNAME
ADDRESS
CITY
STATE
ZIPCODE
BIRTHDAY     / /
DATEHIRED    / /
DEPENDENTS
SALARY        .
ASSIGNMENT
HOURLYRATE    .
EVALUATE    memo

Edit  ||E:\...dbdata\ABCSTAFF  ||Rec None  ||File ||  ||
```

Screen form

on-screen form shown in Figure 3-9, with blank spaces beside each corresponding field name. You will use this screen for adding and editing records.

The cursor is flashing in the SOCIALSEC field. For each field in the record, enter the following information, pressing ENTER after each entry is completed.

SOCIALSEC:	123-44-8976
LASTNAME:	Morse
FIRSTNAME:	Marcia
ADDRESS:	4260 Park Avenue
CITY:	Chevy Chase
STATE:	MD
ZIPCODE:	20815-0988
BIRTHDAY:	03/01/54
DATEHIRED:	07/25/85
DEPENDENTS:	2
SALARY:	8.50
ASSIGNMENT:	National Oil Co.
HOURLYRATE:	15.00

If you make a mistake during the data entry process, you can reach the offending data with the cursor keys and use the BACKSPACE key to correct and retype the entry. As you fill in the fields, dBASE IV will occasionally cause the computer to beep. This occurs whenever you enter data that fills the field. This is normal, but you can turn off the beep if it annoys you (how to do so will be discussed later in this book). Once you have entered all of the information shown, the cursor should be at the start of the memo field.

Entering Data in a Memo Field

Entering data in a memo field is quite different from entering data in other fields. You'll notice that the word "memo," which was supplied by dBASE when you indicated the memo field type, already appears in the field. Whenever the cursor is in a memo field (as it is now), you are at the entry point for a *memo slip* that can hold as many as 64,000 characters.

NOTE Use CTRL-HOME to get into a memo field.

To get to the memo slip, hold down the CTRL key and press HOME. The data entry form will vanish, and in its place will appear the dBASE editor. This editor lets you type text as you would with any word processing software. It isn't necessary to press the ENTER key at the end of every line; the editor will automatically move the cursor to the next line. The BACKSPACE key will erase any mistakes, and you can use the arrow keys to move the cursor around the screen for editing.

The various menu options available while you are in the editor deserve more detailed treatment in a later chapter. For now, you'll use only the text entry capabilities, and the simple editing offered by the BACKSPACE and DEL keys, to add a few comments in the memo fields. As an example, type the following:

```
Experienced in accounting, tax preparation, has MBA in business management.
```

When you have finished typing this text, you will need to get back to the data entry form. You can do so either by pressing CTRL-END or by pressing ALT-E for the Exit menu and choosing Save Changes and Exit from the menu. (As another alternative, the CTRL-W key combination can also be used to save the data.) Use either of these methods now to get back to the data entry form.

Now that you're back at the Edit screen, note that the word "memo" in the field now appears in uppercase letters. When a memo field of a record contains data, "memo" appears as uppercase. If the memo field is empty, "memo" appears as lowercase.

You can continue adding records in either of two ways: you can press the PGDN key to display another blank record, or you can press ALT-R to display the Records menu and then choose Add New Records from the menu.

Proceed to fill in the following additional records for the ABC Temporaries database. You can press ENTER or the down arrow key to move to the next field as you complete the entry in a field. Be sure to press CTRL-END after completing each entry in the final (memo) field.

```
SOCIALSEC:      121-33-9876
LASTNAME:       Westman
FIRSTNAME:      Andrea
ADDRESS:        4807 East Avenue
CITY:           Silver Spring
STATE:          MD
ZIPCODE:        20910-0124
BIRTHDAY:       05/29/61
DATEHIRED:      07/04/86
DEPENDENTS:     2
SALARY:         15.00
ASSIGNMENT:     National Oil Co.
HOURLYRATE:     24.00
EVALUATE:       Did well on last two assignments.
```

```
SOCIALSEC:      232-55-1234
LASTNAME:       Jackson
FIRSTNAME:      David
ADDRESS:        4102 Valley Lane
CITY:           Falls Church
STATE:          VA
ZIPCODE:        22044
BIRTHDAY:       12/22/55
DATEHIRED:      09/05/85
DEPENDENTS:     1
SALARY:         7.50
ASSIGNMENT:     City Revenue Dept.
HOURLYRATE:     12.00
EVALUATE:       Absentee rate high.
```

SOCIAL SEC:	901-77-3456
LASTNAME:	Mitchell
FIRSTNAME:	Mary Jo
ADDRESS:	617 North Oakland Street
CITY:	Arlington
STATE:	VA
ZIPCODE:	22203
BIRTHDAY:	08/17/58
DATEHIRED:	12/01/87
DEPENDENTS:	1
SALARY:	7.50
ASSIGNMENT:	Smith Builders
HOURLYRATE:	12.00
EVALUATE:	Too new to evaluate, but has excellent references from temporary agency in Chicago, IL where she lived previously.

Edit Mode Versus Browse Mode

Viewing and entering records in this manner gets the job done, but as you can see, it does not allow you to view more than one record on the screen at a time. dBASE IV can also display information in table form, an important feature because most users find it easier to grasp the concept of a database when it is shown in a tabular manner. It is easy to see a number of records, and the records and fields are clearly distinguished.

There will probably be times when you prefer to see the information in the form of a table, and there will be other times when you find a form like the one you have been using until now to be the best approach. dBASE IV provides the flexibility of using either method. You can move quickly between the two with the Data (F2) key. Press F2 now, and dBASE IV will display the record in the database in a tabular view. Press the PGUP key once to view all of the records you have entered so far, as shown in Figure 3-10.

Figure 3-10.

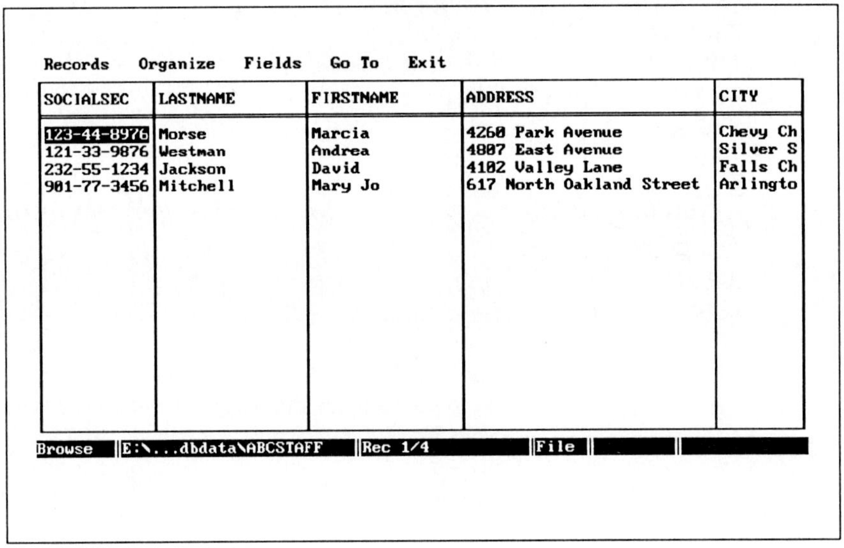

```
Records   Organize   Fields   Go To   Exit

SOCIALSEC    LASTNAME    FIRSTNAME   ADDRESS                    CITY

123-44-8976  Morse       Marcia      4260 Park Avenue           Chevy Ch
121-33-9876  Westman     Andrea      4807 East Avenue           Silver S
232-55-1234  Jackson     David       4102 Valley Lane           Falls Ch
901-77-3456  Mitchell    Mary Jo     617 North Oakland Street   Arlingto

Browse  E:\...dbdata\ABCSTAFF   Rec 1/4          File
```

Tabular view of record

This style of display is known as Browse mode; in fact, an alternative way to display data in this format is to enter the BROWSE command at the dot prompt. Moving around in the database is different when you are in Browse mode than when you are in Append or Edit mode in a data entry form. Try PGUP and PGDN, and then try using the up and down arrow keys. Whereas in Edit mode, PGUP and PGDN would have moved you up and down by a record at a time, they now move you up and down by a screenful of records. And the up and down arrow keys now move the cursor between records, instead of between fields.

HINT Once you are in Edit or Browse mode, pressing F2 repeatedly switches you between modes.

You can use the TAB key and the SHIFT-TAB key combination to move the cursor between fields. While viewing the records in either mode, you can use the F2 key to switch back and forth between Browse and Edit modes. Try pressing F2 repeatedly now, and note the effect as dBASE changes between Browse and Edit modes of operation.

You can add or edit records in Browse as well as in Edit mode. To add records, press ALT-R for the Records menu, and then choose Add New Record from the menu to continue adding records to the database. Use the mode of your choice (Browse or Edit) to continue adding the remaining records to the table now:

```
SOCIALSEC:      121-90-5432
LASTNAME:       Robinson
FIRSTNAME:      Shirley
ADDRESS:        270 Browning Ave #3C
CITY:           Takoma Park
STATE:          MD
ZIPCODE:        20912
BIRTHDAY:       11/02/64
DATEHIRED:      11/17/87
DEPENDENTS:     1
SALARY:         7.50
ASSIGNMENT:     National Oil Co.
HOURLYRATE:     12.00
EVALUATE:       Too new to evaluate.

SOCIALSEC:      495-00-3456
LASTNAME:       Jackson
FIRSTNAME:      Cheryl
ADDRESS:        1617 Arlington Blvd
CITY:           Falls Church
STATE:          VA
ZIPCODE:        22044
BIRTHDAY:       09/17/51
DATEHIRED:      09/19/87
DEPENDENTS:     1
SALARY:         12.00
ASSIGNMENT:     City Revenue Dept.
```

HOURLYRATE:	18.00
EVALUATE:	Consistently high client satisfaction with employee's work.

SOCIALSEC:	343-55-9821
LASTNAME:	Robinson
FIRSTNAME:	Wanda
ADDRESS:	1607 21st Street, NW
CITY:	Washington
STATE:	DC
ZIPCODE:	20009
BIRTHDAY:	06/22/66
DATEHIRED:	09/17/87
DEPENDENTS:	0
SALARY:	7.50
ASSIGNMENT:	City Revenue Dept.
HOURLYRATE:	12.00
EVALUATE:	Excellent PC skills, has conducted classes in dBASE, Paradox, Excel, and 1-2-3.

SOCIALSEC:	876-54-3210
LASTNAME:	Hart
FIRSTNAME:	Edward
ADDRESS:	6200 Germantown Road
CITY:	Fairfax
STATE:	VA
ZIPCODE:	22025
BIRTHDAY:	12/20/55
DATEHIRED:	10/19/86
DEPENDENTS:	3
SALARY:	8.50
ASSIGNMENT:	Smith Builders
HOURLYRATE:	14.00
EVALUATE:	Absence rate has been very excessive.

SOCIALSEC:	909-88-7654
LASTNAME:	Jones
FIRSTNAME:	Judi
ADDRESS:	5203 North Shore Drive
CITY:	Reston

STATE:	VA
ZIPCODE:	22090
BIRTHDAY:	09/18/61
DATEHIRED:	08/12/86
DEPENDENTS:	1
SALARY:	12.00
ASSIGNMENT:	National Oil Co.
HOURLYRATE:	17.50
EVALUATE:	Performed well on four assignments over the past year.

After the last record has been entered and you are in Browse or Edit mode, press CTRL-END to save the records to disk and get back to the Control Center.

An Introduction to Queries

Your data is now stored in dBASE IV, ready for use. Successive chapters will detail how you can make use of data once it has been entered into a file, but a quick introduction to how you will ask dBASE IV for information and produce simple reports is appropriate at this time.

One regular task for any database user takes the form of inquiries; you will often need to obtain a particular set of facts, such as a list of all employees living in Maryland. dBASE IV makes such a query simple with its Query menu. To quickly try an example, press the right arrow key once and then press ENTER to select the Create option on the Queries panel. In a moment, the Control Center will vanish, and a query form will appear (Figure 3-11). If you are using dBASE IV version 1.0, your query form will have wider columns than those in the figure.

Figure 3-11.

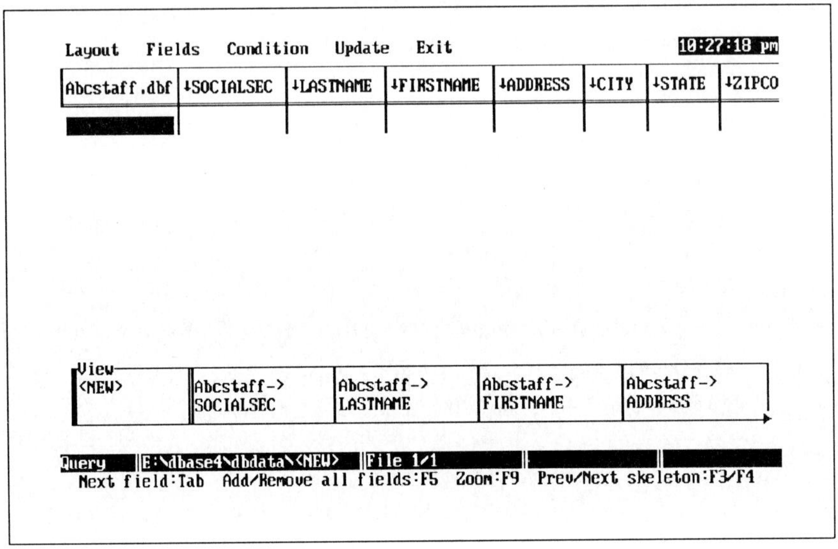

```
Layout   Fields   Condition   Update   Exit                          10:27:18 pm
Abcstaff.dbf │↓SOCIALSEC │↓LASTNAME │↓FIRSTNAME │↓ADDRESS │↓CITY │↓STATE │↓ZIPCO

View
<NEW>        │Abcstaff->  │Abcstaff-> │Abcstaff->  │Abcstaff->
             │SOCIALSEC   │LASTNAME   │FIRSTNAME   │ADDRESS

Query     │E:\dbase4\dbdata\<NEW>  │File 1/1
 Next field:Tab  Add/Remove all fields:F5  Zoom:F9  Prev/Next skeleton:F3/F4
```

Query form

The use of the query form is covered in detail in Chapter 7, but let's try it briefly here. First, remove any fields that you do not want included in the answer that dBASE IV will provide by moving the cursor to any unwanted field and pressing F5. Type matching criteria in any field to select the desired records of your choice.

As an example, press the TAB key four times to place the cursor in the ADDRESS field, and then press F5. When you do this, the ADDRESS field will be removed from the view at the bottom of the screen. Use TAB to move the DEPENDENTS field, and press F5 again; then do the same for the ASSIGNMENT and EVALUATE fields. This action tells dBASE IV that you will want the ADDRESS, DEPENDENTS, ASSIGNMENT, and EVALUATE fields excluded from the list dBASE IV provides in response to your query.

Next, use SHIFT-TAB to move the cursor back to the STATE field, and then enter

```
="MD"
```

to tell dBASE IV that you want the query to select only the records containing the letters "MD" in the STATE field.

What you have just done is basically all that you need to do to provide dBASE IV with a simple query, using its query-by-example system. There are no arcane commands or strange syntax to try to decipher; you simply omit any fields you don't want to see and fill in an example of the data you want in any desired field. Once you've done this, you can then save the query for further use when editing or creating reports. The query will tell dBASE IV to include only those fields you left in the view, and to include only those records that meet the matching criteria you specified.

Press ALT-E to open the Exit menu. Choose Save Changes and Exit from this menu. dBASE IV will ask for a name for this query; enter **QFIRST** as a filename.

To see the results of the query, once you are back at the Control Center, note that the cursor appears on the name of the new query (QFIRST) under the Queries panel. Whenever you place the cursor on the query filename and then use one of the function keys outlined at the bottom of the screen, you are telling dBASE IV to apply the criteria stored in the chosen query to the respective option. Press F2 (Data) to view the data. You will note that only those fields you included in the query are now visible. If you use the PGUP and PGDN keys to view other records, you will see that only the records for employees who live in the state of Maryland are now available. (Remember, you can repeatedly press F2 to switch in and out of Browse mode.) For future reference, note that you can also see the results of a query while you are designing the query by pressing F2 (Data) while still at the Create Query screen.

NOTE Chapter 7 provides more details on how you can design queries to retrieve specific information.

Getting an Instant Report

If you need a quick printed report of the results of a query (or of any database file), you can easily get it with a single key combination. The dBASE IV program uses the SHIFT-F9 key combination as the Instant Report key.

If you have a printer, make sure it is turned on, and paper is loaded. Press ESC (if necessary) to get back to the Control Center.

Figure 3-12.

Page No. 1
08/25/88

SOCIALSEC	LASTNAME	FIRSTNAME	CITY	STATE	ZIPCODE	BIRTHDAY
DATEHIRED	SALARY	HOURLYRATE				
123-44-8976	Morse	Marcia	Chevy Chase	MD	20815-0988	03/01/54
07/25/85	8.50	15.00				
121-33-9876	Westman	Andrea	Silver Spring	MD	20910-0124	05/29/61
07/04/86	15.00	24.00				
121-90-5432	Robinson	Shirley	Takoma Park	MD	20912	11/02/64
11/17/87	7.50	12.00				

31.00 51.00

Results of instant report using a query

Next, make sure the query filename (QFIRST) is highlighted by the cursor. This will tell dBASE IV to use the query when it prints the report. Finally, press SHIFT-F9. In a moment, a Print menu will appear. The choices on this menu will be covered in more detail shortly, but for now, the Begin Printing option can be used to tell dBASE IV to route the data to the printer.

With the Begin Printing option highlighted, press ENTER. You should get a printed report based on the temporary file created by the query; the report will resemble the example shown in Figure 3-12.

You can use the same SHIFT-F9 key combination to produce a report of your entire database. When the Control Center is again visible, and with the QFIRST query file highlighted, press ENTER. From the next menu that appears, select Close View to stop using the view. Then use the arrow keys to highlight the ABCSTAFF database. Next, press SHIFT-F9. From the Print menu that appears next, choose Begin Printing. This time, you should get a printed report based on the entire ABCSTAFF file. The report will resemble the example shown in Figure 3-13.

You can produce far more detailed reports in dBASE IV; such reports can include customized headers and footers, customized placement of fields, word-wrapping of large amounts of text, and numeric results based on calculations of fields. Such reports are covered in detail from Chapter 8 onward.

The Concept of Catalogs

As you work with dBASE IV, the files that you work with are added to a *catalog*. Since dBASE does this automatically, it may not seem of major importance. However, as you start to work with

Figure 3-13.

```
Page No.  1
08/25/88

SOCIALSEC  LASTNAME     FIRSTNAME    ADDRESS              CITY          STATE ZIPCODE
BIRTHDAY DATEHIRED DEPENDENTS SALARY ASSIGNMENT       HOURLYRATE EVALUATE

123-44-8976 Morse        Marcia       4260 Park Avenue       Chevy Chase    MD    20815-0988
03/01/54 07/25/85  2      8.50  National Oil Co.    15.00     Experienced in accounting, tax preparation,
has MBA in business management.

121-33-9876 Westman      Andrea       4807 East Avenue       Silver Spring  MD    20910-0124
05/29/61 07/04/86  2     15.00  National Oil Co.    24.00     Did well on last two assignments.

232-55-1234 Jackson      David        4102 Valley Lane       Falls Church   VA    22044      12/22/55
09/05/85  1        7.50  City Revenue Dept.   12.00     Absentee rate high.

901-77-3456 Mitchell     Mary Jo      617 North Oakland Street  Arlington   VA    22203
08/17/58 12/01/87  1      7.50  Smith Builders      12.00     Too new to evaluate, but has excellent
references from temporary agency in Chicago, IL where she lived previously.

121-90-5432 Robinson     Shirley      270 Browning Ave #3C   Takoma Park    MD    20912
11/02/64 11/17/87  1      7.50  National Oil Co.    12.00     Too new to evaluate.

232-55-1234 Jackson      Cheryl       1617 Arlington Blvd    Falls Church   VA    22044      09/17/51
09/19/87  1       12.00  City Revenue Dept.   18.00     Consistently high client satisfaction with
employee's work.

343-55-9821 Robinson     Wanda        1607 21st Street, NW   Washington     DC    20009
06/22/66 09/17/87  0      7.50  City Revenue Dept.  12.00     Excellent PC skills, has conducted classes
in dBASE, Paradox, Excel, and 1-2-3.

876-54-3210 Hart         Edward       6200 Germantown Road   Fairfax        VA    22025      12/20/55
10/19/86  3        8.50  Smith Builders       14.00     Absence rate has been very excessive.

909-88-7654 Jones        Judi         5203 North Shore Drive  Reston        VA    22090      09/18/61
08/12/86  1       12.00  National Oil Co.     17.50     Performed well at four assignments over past year.
```

Results of instant report using ABCSTAFF file

many different files for different tasks, you will use catalogs to better organize your work. You will learn more about catalogs in a later chapter, but there are a few points you should be aware of before proceeding.

When you start dBASE, it opens the last catalog that was in use. If no catalog has yet been chosen or named with the options of the Catalog menu, dBASE uses a catalog called UNTITLED.CAT. The name of the catalog in use appears on your screen just above the panels of the Control Center.

Catalogs contain the names and locations of files, along with optional descriptions of those files. The files that you see in the various panels of the Control Center are contained in the catalog that is currently in use. This is important to know, because dBASE opens whatever catalog was last opened when the program is started. If someone else used dBASE on your computer and selected the Use a Different Catalog option of the Catalog menu to change to another catalog, you would not see the contents of your catalog when you next started dBASE, and you might assume incorrectly that the files had been erased.

☞ ***REMEMBER*** If you start dBASE and you can't see files you know are present, you're probably using the wrong catalog.

If, when you start dBASE, you do not see the files you have been working with, you are probably in a different catalog. You can get back to the catalog you were last using by opening the Catalog menu, selecting the Use a Different Catalog option, and choosing the desired catalog from the list that appears. Before going on, you may want to note the name of your current catalog so you will remember it if your catalog is ever changed by you or anyone else.

Dot-Prompt Options for Displaying a Database

A few shortcuts for displaying your data from the dot prompt may prove useful. Although using commands from the dot prompt requires a precise recall of how the commands should be entered, many users find that using dot-prompt commands is faster than using Control Center menus.

When you first start dBASE IV, you must choose a database file for use. From the dot prompt, this action can be performed with the USE command. The syntax for this command is

USE *filename*

Press ESC and then type **Y** to leave the Command Center and get to the dot prompt. Then enter the following:

```
USE ABCSTAFF
```

dBASE IV will open the ABCSTAFF database file. Since the file was previously open, this step was unnecessary; however, if you were just starting dBASE IV, you would need the USE command or its Control Center menu equivalent to open a file before working with that file. When you are working from the dot prompt, you can tell whether a file is currently open by looking for the name of the file within the status bar.

Viewing a Database

You can use the LIST and DISPLAY commands to examine the contents of a database. Typing **LIST** by itself will show the entire contents of a database unless you specify otherwise, but you can limit the display to certain fields by including the field name after you enter **LIST**.

If you specify more than one field, separate them by a comma. For example, at the dot prompt, enter the following:

```
LIST LASTNAME, SALARY
```

dBASE IV shows only the last names and salary amounts contained in the database:

```
Record#     LASTNAME  SALARY
      1     Morse       8.50
      2     Westman    15.00
      3     Jackson     7.50
      4     Mitchell    7.50
      5     Robinson    7.50
      6     Jackson    12.00
      7     Robinson    7.50
      8     Hart        8.50
      9     Jones      12.00
```

If you had entered **LIST** without any field names, you would have seen a list of all of the fields.

The DISPLAY command lets you view selected information. With the DISPLAY command, you must tell dBASE IV exactly what you would like to see displayed. Enter the following:

```
GO 3
DISPLAY
```

You will now see the third record in the database. This happens to be the location in the file that dBASE IV is currently viewing. Enter the following:

```
GO 2
DISPLAY NEXT 3
```

You should now see three records, beginning with record number 2. To see the entire database, enter

```
DISPLAY ALL
```

There is one significant difference between DISPLAY and LIST. If the database is large, the LIST command will cause the contents to scroll nonstop up the screen; you must use CTRL-S to start and stop the scroll. If you use the DISPLAY command, the screen will pause after displaying every 20 lines, and you can press any key to resume the scrolling.

If it is followed by a specific condition, the DISPLAY command can also be used to search for specific information. If you understand the logic, this use of the DISPLAY command lets you get an effect similar to that of a simple use of the Control Center's Queries panel, but with less work. As an example, you could display only the name, city, state, and salary fields for all employees earning more than $10.00 per hour by entering

```
DISPLAY ALL FIELDS LASTNAME, FIRSTNAME, CITY, STATE, SALARY FOR
SALARY > 10.00
```

Because of printing limitations, this command appears on two lines in this book, but you must enter it all on one line at the dot prompt.

You can add TO PRINT after any DISPLAY or LIST command, and the data will be printed (turn on your printer first). For example, entering

```
LIST LASTNAME, FIRSTNAME TO PRINT
```

will cause the names in the database to be printed.

HINT The TO PRINT option of the DISPLAY or LIST command is a useful way to get a fast report.

Searching Within a Field

There may be occasions when you want to search for information that is contained within a field, but you know only a portion of that information. This can cause problems, because dBASE IV does not search "full text," or within a field, unless you give it specific instructions to do so. To demonstrate the problem, if an ABC Temporaries' manager calls and asks for the name of an employee who lives on North Oakland Street, how do you find that record? The manager can't recall the employee's name.

You could try searching for an employee who lives on North Oakland Street by entering the following:

```
DISPLAY FOR ADDRESS = "North Oakland"
```

Don't feel that you've done something wrong when the record does not appear. dBASE normally begins a search by attempting to match your characters with the first characters of the chosen field. In this database, there is no record that begins with the characters "North Oakland" in the ADDRESS field. As a result, dBASE IV failed to find the data.

To get around this problem, you can search within a field. The normal layout, or *syntax,* for the necessary command is

DISPLAY FOR "*search-text*" $ *fieldname*

where *search-text* is the actual characters that you want to look for and *fieldname* is the name of the specific field that you wish to search. To try an example, enter the following command:

```
DISPLAY FOR "North Oakland" $ ADDRESS
```

This time, dBASE IV will find the desired information.

HINT Use the dollar sign when searching for partial text within a field.

You can use this technique to search for data within the text of a memo field. The ability to search memo fields is a major improvement over earlier versions of dBASE.

Keeping Track of Records

Whenever dBASE IV looks at a database, it examines one record at a time. Even when you list all of the records in the database, dBASE IV starts with the first record in the file and then examines each additional record, one by one. The program keeps up with where it is by means of a *pointer*. The dBASE IV pointer is always pointing to a particular record, whenever you are using a database. You can move the pointer to a specific record with the GO command.

Enter **GO TOP** and then enter **DISPLAY**. The pointer will be at the first record in the file:

```
1  123-44-8976  Morse  Marcia...
```

To move the pointer to the fourth record, enter **GO 4** and then enter **DISPLAY**, and you will see the fourth record:

```
4  901-77-3456  Mitchell  Mary Jo...
```

You can go to the first record by entering **GO TOP**, or you can go to the end of a database by entering **GO BOTTOM**. If you don't know the record number but need to find a particular record, you can use the LOCATE command to find it. For example, enter this:

```
LOCATE FOR LASTNAME = "Morse"
```

dBASE IV responds with "Record = 1." If you now enter **DISPLAY**, you will see that the pointer has been repositioned to record 1.

At first glance, the LOCATE command may not seem any different from a selective use of the DISPLAY command. The major difference is that LOCATE does not cause the record to be displayed on the screen; it only finds a record based on the criteria supplied with the LOCATE command.

If this is a good time for a break, enter **QUIT** from the dot prompt. The QUIT command saves any work in progress and exits the program. The Command Center alternative to leave dBASE IV is to open the Exit menu and choose Quit to DOS.

REMEMBER Always exit dBASE with a QUIT command, or by choosing Quit from the Exit menu. Never quit by turning off your computer.

Now that you have a file containing data, you will want to know how you can manipulate that data better to obtain the results you want. The next chapter covers this area in more detail.

Quick Reference

To start dBASE Switch to the directory containing your data files, and set a path to the directory containing the dBASE IV program files. Then enter **DBASE** at the DOS prompt. (Remember, you can create a batch file to do all of this automatically.)

To get to the Control Center At the dot prompt, you enter **ASSIST**.

To leave the Control Center and then get to the dot prompt Press ESC, and then answer Y for yes when dBASE asks if you want to abandon this operation.

To get help From anywhere in dBASE, press F1.

To create a database Choose the Create option from the Data panel, or enter **CREATE** at the dot prompt. When the Database Design screen appears, enter the desired field names, field types, widths, and number of decimal places. Place a Y in the Index field if you want an index on that field of the database. When done, press CTRL-END. dBASE will ask for a name for the database; enter any name of eight characters or less, with no spaces.

To add data to a database From the Control Center, highlight the database by name in the Data panel and press F2. Then open the Records menu with ALT-R and choose Add New Record. Or, from the dot prompt, enter **USE *filename*** (where *filename* is the name of your database file) and then enter **APPEND**.

To enter or edit data in a memo field Place the cursor in the memo field and press CTRL-HOME. Make the desired entries or edits, and press CTRL-END.

To get an instant report From the Control Center, place the cursor on the name of a database file (or on a query) and press SHIFT-F9. Choose Begin Printing from the menu that appears next.

CHAPTER

Changing Your Database

dBASE IV has a number of menu options and commands that you can use to change records and fields. You can edit information in a record, such as a person's name or phone number on a mailing list, and you can change the structure of a database, adding fields for items that you did not plan for or deleting fields that you no longer use. You can also expand or shorten the width of a field. Let's begin by editing records in the ABC Temporaries database.

Editing a Database

First get into the database. With the Command Center visible on the screen, highlight the data file name, ABCSTAFF. Then press F2 (Data) to access the data. The ABCSTAFF database will appear, with the records displayed in Browse mode. Press F2 (Data) once, and dBASE will switch to Edit mode, with a single record visible on the screen (Figure 4-1).

At this point you are in Edit mode, which means you can make changes to the data contained within the chosen record. The cursor is flashing underneath the first character of the first field in the record. Try pressing the up, down, left, and right arrow keys a few times, and notice that each keypress moves the cursor either one character or row at a time. If you keep pressing the

Figure 4-1.

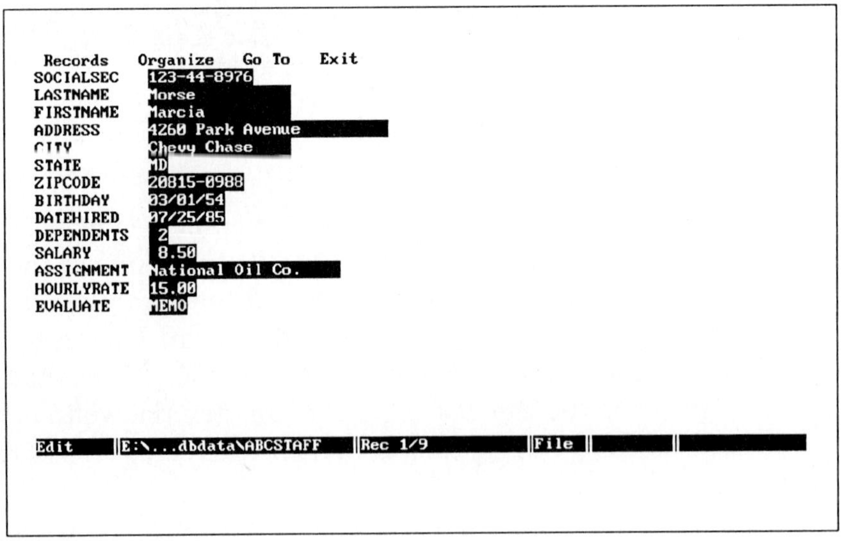

```
Records    Organize   Go To    Exit
SOCIALSEC   123-44-8976
LASTNAME    Morse
FIRSTNAME   Marcia
ADDRESS     4260 Park Avenue
CITY        Chevy Chase
STATE       MD
ZIPCODE     20815-0988
BIRTHDAY    03/01/54
DATEHIRED   07/25/85
DEPENDENTS   2
SALARY       8.50
ASSIGNMENT  National Oil Co.
HOURLYRATE  15.00
EVALUATE    MEMO

Edit    E:\...dbdata\ABCSTAFF    Rec 1/9    File
```

Record visible in Edit mode

down arrow key, you'll see that dBASE IV takes you to the next record in the file. Pressing the up arrow key repeatedly will take you to the previous record in the file, unless you are already at the first record. You can use the arrow keys to move the cursor to any location in the record.

Try pressing F1 and then the ESC key. Doing so will show and hide the help screen that provides information about editing.

While you are in Edit mode, you can also use the PGUP and PGDN keys to move around in the database. The PGDN key takes you one record forward, while the PGUP key moves you one record back. If you are at the last record in the file, pressing the PGDN key will display the "Add new records?" prompt at the bottom of the screen. If you are at the first record in the file, pressing PGUP will have no effect.

Suppose that while you are in the mode, you learn that Ms. Shirley Robinson has moved to a different apartment on the same street, and you wish to correct the address without retyping the entire line. Use the PGUP or PGDN key to find the record for Ms. Shirley Robinson. Place the cursor in the ADDRESS field, use the right arrow key to move the cursor to the apartment number, and use the BACKSPACE or DEL key to delete the old apartment number. Enter **#2A** as the new apartment number.

At this point, you could save the change by using the CTRL-END key combination, by moving to another record with PGUP or PGDN, or by pressing the arrow keys repeatedly. Instead, let's first examine the menus available to you when you are editing records.

Press F10 now, and the Records menu will open (Figure 4-2). This menu is one of three menus (four if you are using version 1.1 or later) available at the menu bar when you are in Edit mode. It contains options that directly affect the records you are editing. When the menu bar is not visible, pressing F10 will display it.

REMEMBER You can also use ALT-R to open the Records menu.

Figure 4-2.

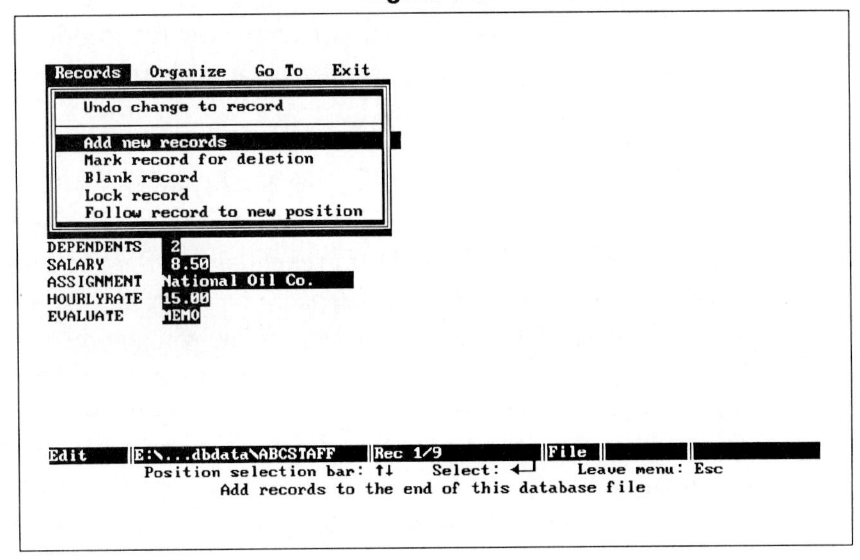

Records menu

The Undo Change to Record option is used to "undo," or reverse, any changes that you have just made to a record. Once you leave the record and go to a different record, you can no longer undo any changes to the record you just left.

The Add New Records option displays a blank record, ready for the addition of new data. Note that from the dot prompt, the APPEND command accomplishes the same task. You can also add new records by pressing the PGDN key until the "Add new records?" prompt appears at the bottom of the screen, and then responding with the letter Y to begin adding records.

The Mark Record for Deletion option lets you mark a particular record for deletion. (Deleting records is a topic that is covered in detail shortly.) The Blank Record option tells dBASE IV to erase the contents of every field in the record currently on the screen. This can be useful if you have filled in the fields of a record and then decide that you want to put different data into those fields.

The Lock Record option applies only to network users of dBASE IV. It allows you to "lock" records so that other network users cannot modify the records at the same time. Finally, the Follow Record to New Position option applies to records that have an index that is in active use. If this option is set to On and the field on which the index is based changes, the dBASE pointer will follow the record to the new position based on the index. (More details on the topic of indexing will be covered in Chapter 5.)

In dBASE IV version 1.1, the next press of the right arrow key causes the Organize menu to open. (In version 1.0, this menu is available only when changing the design of a database.) The Organize menu contains options for sorting or indexing a database. These options will be covered in detail in Chapter 6.

Press the right arrow key once more, and the Go To menu shown in Figure 4-3 will open. This menu provides ways to move around within the database. The Top Record and Last Record options, when chosen, will move you to the start or the end of the database,

Figure 4-3.

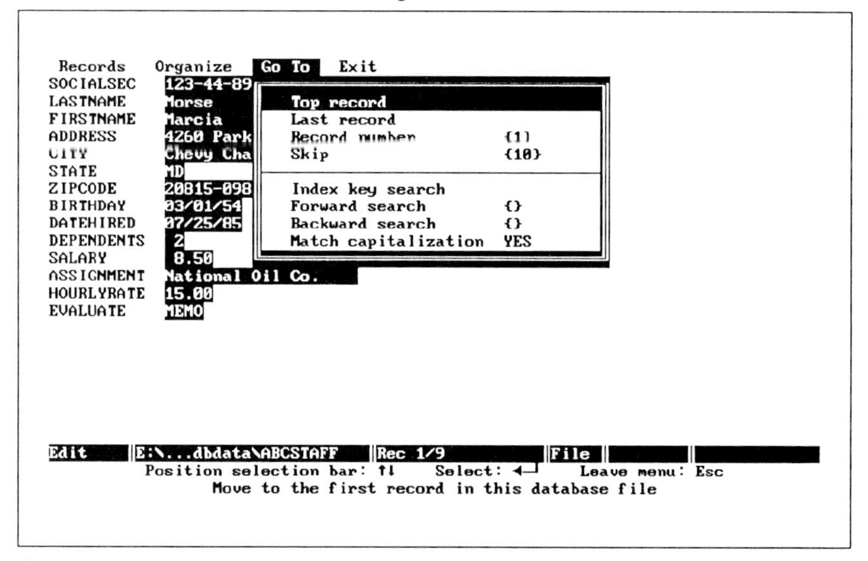

Go To menu

respectively. If you choose the Record Number option, you can enter a specific record number and dBASE will move to that record. Choosing the Skip option and entering a number tells dBASE to move by the specified number of records. A positive number moves you forward in the file, and a negative number moves you in reverse.

If the file is indexed on a particular field, choosing the Index Key Search option lets you search for a particular record based on that field. The Forward Search and Backward Search options let you search forward or backward for a specific record. To use a search option, place the cursor in the field you want to search, choose the desired option (Forward Search or Backward Search) from the menu, and enter the search string when prompted. The Match Capitalization option determines whether uppercase and lowercase letters are significant in searches.

Pressing the right arrow key once more reveals the contents of the Exit menu (Figure 4-4). Here, there are just two choices; Exit and Transfer to Query Design. Use the Transfer to Query Design option if you want to build a query that selects specific records (as you did briefly in the prior chapter) or use the Exit option to save any current changes and exit back to the Control Center.

If the purpose behind each of these options is not clear at this time, don't be too concerned. Throughout the chapter, you'll have the chance to use these options.

The menu options can provide a handy way of locating a specific record. For example, suppose you quickly want to find the record for Mr. Hart. First press ESC to leave the menus, and then place the cursor in the LASTNAME field, since this is the field you want to search. Press ALT-G to open the Go To menu, and then choose Forward Search. In response to the prompt that asks you for a search string, enter

```
Hart
```

and you will see the desired record appear.

Figure 4-4.

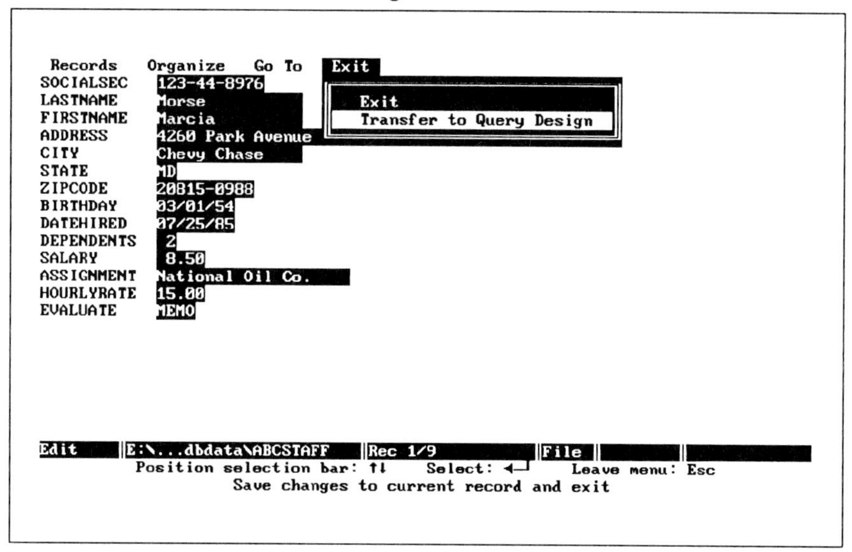

Exit menu

REMEMBER Place the cursor in the field you want to search before choosing the Forward Search option.

If you know the record number of the desired record, you can use the menu options of the Go To menu to find the record. For example, if you want to edit record 5, press ALT-G to open the Go To menu. Select the Record Number option, and enter **5** in response to the prompt. You will see that dBASE jumps to record 5, which happens to be the record for Ms. Shirley Robinson. You can also note that you have moved to a desired record number by viewing the record number as shown in the status bar. (If your status bar does not appear, someone has turned off the option. You can display it by getting to the dot prompt with ESC and entering a SET STATUS ON command.)

As with all Control Center menu options, the editing operations can also be performed with dot-prompt commands. From the dot prompt, once you have opened a file for use with the USE command, you can edit records by using the command EDIT *n,* where *n* is the record number of the record you wish to edit. Or you can use the command GO *n,* where *n* is the record number of the record you wish to edit, and then enter the EDIT command without any record number after the command. As an example, from the dot prompt, you could enter

```
GO 3
EDIT
```

to edit the contents of record number 3. Once in Edit mode, you can save your changes either by using CTRL-END or by choosing the Exit option of the Exit menu.

From the dot prompt, you can also use the LOCATE command as described in the previous chapter to perform a search in a manner similar to the search options on the menus. By default, LOCATE starts its search from the top of the file rather than from the current record. However, you can conduct a forward search by using the CONTINUE command after the LOCATE command. For example, if you use the command

```
LOCATE FOR LASTNAME = "Robinson"
```

and the name you find is not the Robinson you want, you can then enter

```
CONTINUE
```

to find additional occurrences of that same name. If dBASE responds with an "End of LOCATE scope" message, it means no additional records by that name exist.

More About Browse Mode

Another useful way of editing data is from Browse mode, which was introduced in the previous chapter. Browse mode displays more than one record at a time on the screen, so you can conveniently access a number of records for editing. If you are at the dot prompt now, enter **ASSIST** to get back to the Control Center. To use Browse Mode, press the F2 (Data) key now. If you are viewing a record, simply press F2 (Data) to switch from Edit mode to Browse mode. When the display of records appears, press PGUP to see all of your records (Figure 4-5).

Browse mode displays as many fields as will fit on the screen and can display 20 records in a horizontal format. If there are

Figure 4-5.

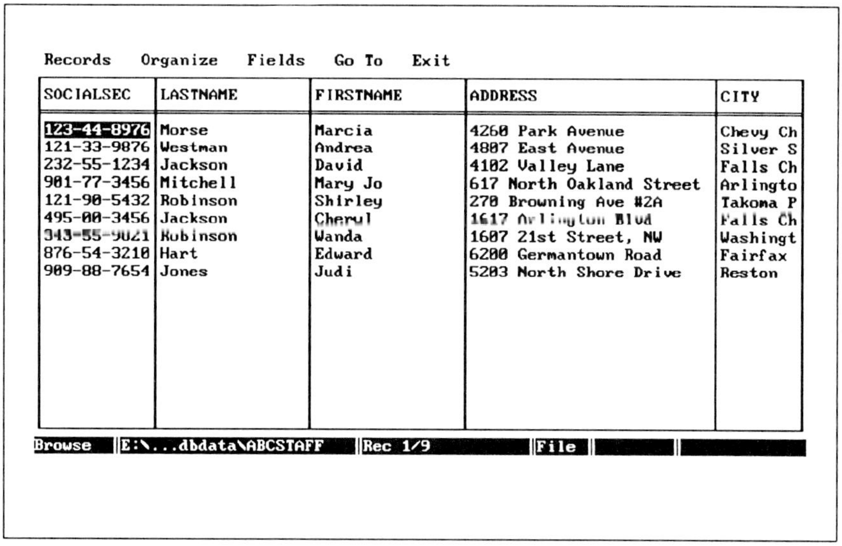

Records Organize Fields Go To Exit

SOCIALSEC	LASTNAME	FIRSTNAME	ADDRESS	CITY
123-44-8976	Morse	Marcia	4260 Park Avenue	Chevy Ch
121-33-9876	Westman	Andrea	4807 East Avenue	Silver S
232-55-1234	Jackson	David	4102 Valley Lane	Falls Ch
901-77-3456	Mitchell	Mary Jo	617 North Oakland Street	Arlingto
121-90-5432	Robinson	Shirley	270 Browning Ave #2A	Takoma P
495-00-3456	Jackson	Cheryl	1617 Arlington Blvd	Falls Ch
343-55-9021	Robinson	Wanda	1607 21st Street, NW	Washingt
876-54-3210	Hart	Edward	6200 Germantown Road	Fairfax
909-88-7654	Jones	Judi	5203 North Shore Drive	Reston

Browse ‖E:\...dbdata\ABCSTAFF ‖Rec 1/9 ‖File ‖

Browse mode

more fields in a record than will fit on a screen, only the first fields will appear, as the ABC Temporaries database demonstrates; fields after the CITY field are not visible. All that Browse mode can show you in this case are the SOCIALSEC, LASTNAME, FIRSTNAME, and ADDRESS fields, and part of the CITY field. The other fields are to the right of the display. Pressing F10 makes the menus available; pressing ESC removes the menus from the Browse screen.

When in Browse mode, you can scan across the database to bring the other fields into view by using the TAB and the SHIFT-TAB key combination. Press the TAB key four times. The fields shift from right to left, with the SOCIALSEC field disappearing off the left side of the screen and the STATE field coming into view on the right side of the screen. If you continue to press the TAB key, fields on the screen will disappear as remaining fields come into view. Pressing ENTER will also move you one field to the right, just as the TAB key does.

Press SHIFT-TAB repeatedly, and you'll notice the opposite effect. The fields that disappeared at the left of the screen reappear, and the fields on the right side disappear. Continue pressing SHIFT-TAB until the SOCIALSEC field returns to the screen.

To quickly move the cursor from the first field in the database to the last, use the HOME and END keys. HOME moves the cursor to the first field, and END moves the cursor to the last field.

Try using the PGUP and PGDN keys. These two keys move the cursor through the database one screenful at a time. Since ABC Temporaries' list of employees is rather short, pressing PGDN will move the cursor to the end of the database. To move the cursor up or down by one record, use the up and down arrow keys.

You can also edit records while you are in Browse mode. You can type changes in a field, and they will take effect just as they did when you were using Edit mode. Because Browse mode displays a screenful of records instead of one record at a time, it is easier to access a particular field when in Browse mode.

As in Edit mode, moving to a different record in Browse mode (with the up or down arrow key or with PGUP or PGDN) saves any changes you made to the record. Pressing ESC before leaving the record cancels any changes to that record and returns you to the Control Center.

Let's try adding a record while in Browse mode. Press the PGDN key until the last record in the file is reached, and then press the down arrow key once. At the bottom of the screen, dBASE IV will display

```
Add new records? (Y/N)
```

Type **Y** to tell dBASE IV that you wish to add another record. Now add the following record to the database:

```
SOCIALSEC: 495-00-3456
LASTNAME: Abernathy
FIRSTNAME: Sandra
ADDRESS: 1512 Redskins Park Drive
CITY: Herndon
STATE: VA
ZIPCODE: 22071
BIRTHDAY: 10/02/59
DATEHIRED: 02/17/88
DEPENDENTS: 1
SALARY: 10.00
ASSIGNMENT: City Revenue Dept.
HOURLYRATE: 18.00
EVALUATE: Too new to evaluate
```

When you reach the memo field, use the same CTRL-HOME key combination to reach the dBASE editor and enter the text of the memo. Then exit the editor with the CTRL-END key combination (or with the Save Changes and Exit option of the Exit menu while you are in the editor). When you are back in Browse mode, press HOME once to ensure you are at the first field before going further.

REMEMBER The same CTRL-HOME key combination used in Edit mode can be used to enter a memo field while in Browse mode.

The Fields Menu Options

While you are in Browse mode, note the menu bar that appears at the top of the screen when you press F10. Three of the menu choices—Records, Go To, and Exit—are the same choices provided in Edit mode, and they operate in the same fashion. The Organize choice, which appears only in dBASE IV version 1.1 and later, is used to sort or index a database; it is covered in more detail in Chapter 6. The one new choice in Browse mode is the

Figure 4-6.

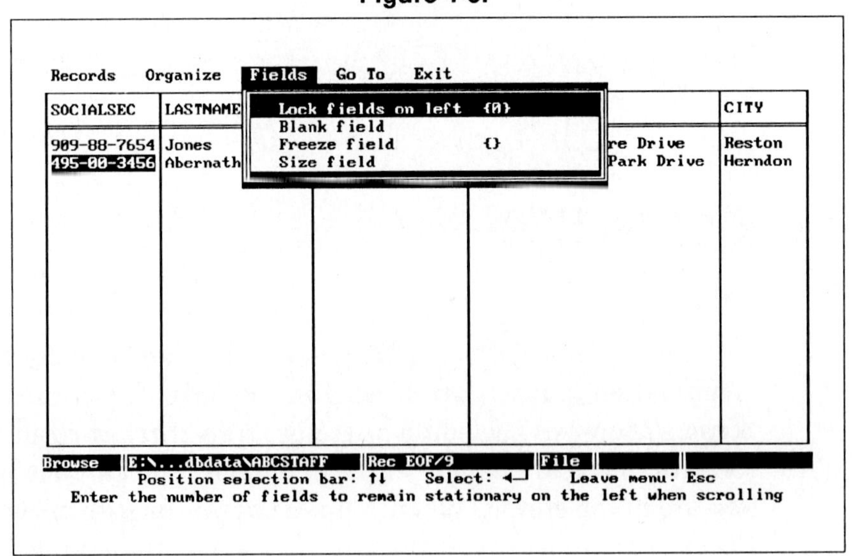

Fields menu

Fields menu, which lets you control the display of fields while in Browse mode. Press ALT-F now to open the Fields menu (Figure 4-6). The available options on the screen are Lock Fields on Left, Blank Field, Freeze Field, and Size Field. When your database contains more fields than will fit on the screen at once and you are editing fields at the right side, a common problem is that the names (or other identifying fields) have vanished off the left side. This makes it difficult to tell whose record you are editing. The Lock Fields on Left option solves this problem by letting you "lock" a selected number of fields so they will not move from the left side. Choose the Lock Fields on Left option now. A prompt asks you for the number of fields that are to remain stationary. In this example, you'll lock the first two fields, SOCIALSEC and LASTNAME, so enter **2** in response to the prompt.

NOTE Your menu options may appear different; remember, the Organize menu is not present in version 1.0 of dBASE IV.

Now try pressing the TAB key repeatedly. You'll notice that as you reach the right side of the screen, the SOCIALSEC and LASTNAME fields remain in view as the other fields change position. Continue pressing the TAB key until the SALARY field comes into view, and move the cursor to the record for Ms. Westman. Press F10 again to display the Fields menu.

REMEMBER You can also use ALT-F to get to the Fields menu.

The Blank Field option of the Fields menu lets you erase the contents of a single field while in Browse mode. Choose Blank Field now, and you will see the SALARY entry for Ms. Westman vanish. Enter **16.00** as the new salary in this field, and then press TAB to move the cursor to the HOURLYRATE field. Press F10 again to display the Fields menu.

The Freeze Field option lets you select a specific field for editing, limiting the cursor movements to that field. Choose Freeze Field now, and dBASE IV will ask you to enter a field name. Enter **HOURLYRATE** in response to the prompt. Now try the TAB or SHIFT-TAB key. You'll note that instead of moving to the other fields, the cursor remains in the HOURLYRATE field and moves from record to record. This option can prove useful for major editing of a single field, such as salary updates or price changes, because you can change the same field in each record by entering data and simply pressing TAB or ENTER to move to the next record.

You can cancel the effect by opening the Fields menu with F10, choosing the Freeze Field option again, using BACKSPACE to erase the field name from the prompt that appears, and pressing ENTER alone without specifying a field name. Do so now, and then press SHIFT-TAB until the FIRSTNAME field is again beside the LASTNAME field (remember, SOCIALSEC and LASTNAME are still locked).

HINT Freeze Field is a very useful option when you need to change a single field (like a salary field) in a large number of records.

The Size Field option of the Fields menu lets you change the width of the columns while you are in Browse mode. The change is not permanent, but will remain in effect until you stop using the database. To try this, place the cursor in the LASTNAME field and press F10 to open the Fields menu. Choose the Size Field option. A message at the bottom of the screen will read

```
Change current column width (← →) End sizing (↵)
```

Try pressing the left arrow key now, and you'll see the column width narrow. Using the right arrow key reverses the effect.

When you get the column to the size you prefer, press ENTER to leave the column at the new size.

If you are working for a prolonged time in Browse mode, resizing your columns may help you view additional columns at one time. Note that if you make the column so narrow that not all of the data fits in the new width, you can still see or change the data by moving to that field and scrolling with the arrow keys.

Using Browse from The Dot Prompt

Dot-prompt users can enter the BROWSE command at the dot prompt to get into Browse mode. Once in Browse mode, the same menu options and key combinations described earlier can be used to update records.

HINT The BROWSE options available at the dot prompt give you more flexibility than Browse from the Control Center menus.

Options can also be specified along with the BROWSE command when you enter it at the dot prompt. These options provide ways to lock certain fields in place so that they will not be lost from view when you pan with the CTRL and cursor keys, just as the Lock Fields on Left menu option of the Fields menu does. Other dot-prompt options let you show or edit selected fields when using BROWSE.

The FIELDS option of the BROWSE command lets you name the fields that you want to display with BROWSE. This option is particularly helpful when you want to edit specific information while you are using BROWSE. The syntax for this form of the command is

BROWSE FIELDS (*field1, field2, field3*)

As an example, you might wish to change the salary amounts to reflect new salaries for some ABC Temporary employees. You only wish to see the names and salary amounts. Press CTRL-END to get back to the menus. Then, use ESC to get to the dot prompt, and try this command:

```
BROWSE FIELDS LASTNAME, FIRSTNAME, SALARY
```

The resultant display (see Figure 4-7) shows only the fields that you named within the command. Since these are the only fields that are displayed, these are the only fields that can be edited at the present time.

Figure 4-7.

Records   Organize   Fields   Go To   Exit

LASTNAME	FIRSTNAME	SALARY
Morse	Marcia	8.50
Westman	Andrea	16.00
Jackson	David	7.50
Mitchell	Mary Jo	7.50
Robinson	Shirley	7.50
Jackson	Cheryl	12.00
Robinson	Wanda	7.50
Hart	Edward	8.50
Jones	Judi	12.00
Abernathy	Sandra	10.00

Browse ║E:\...dbdata\ABCSTAFF ║Rec 1/10 ║File ║

Selected fields with BROWSE

The LOCK option of the BROWSE command locks a field at the left side of the screen, which produces the same result as using the Lock Fields on Left option of the Fields menu. The locked field remains stationary when you use the CTRL and cursor keys to pan left or right. The syntax for the command with this option is

BROWSE LOCK (*x*)

where *x* is a numeric value that tells dBASE IV how many fields should be locked.

To lock the first two fields of the database, press CTRL-END to get back to the dot prompt, and then try the following command:

```
BROWSE LOCK 2
```

Use the TAB and SHIFT-TAB keys to pan across the database. Notice that the SOCIALSEC and LASTNAME fields of the database remain locked, while the other fields pan across the screen.

The FREEZE option of the BROWSE command lets you limit any editing to a specific field. This is the dot-prompt equivalent of the Freeze Field option on the Fields menu. All fields are displayed, but only the specified field can be changed. The syntax for the command is as follows:

BROWSE FREEZE (*fieldname*)

To try this option, use CTRL-END to get back to the dot prompt, and then enter

```
BROWSE FREEZE ASSIGNMENT
```

You will see that only the ASSIGNMENT field can be edited.

The WIDTH option of the BROWSE command lets you set a default width for all fields except memo fields and logical fields. For example, if you want to set the width of the fields to ten characters, you could enter this command at the dot prompt:

```
BROWSE WIDTH 10
```

You can use the dot-prompt options of the BROWSE command in combination with each other. As an example, the command

```
BROWSE FIELDS LASTNAME, FIRSTNAME, CITY, STATE, SALARY FREEZE
SALARY
```

displays the LASTNAME, FIRSTNAME, CITY, STATE, and SALARY fields, and allows you to edit just the SALARY field. (If you try this command, be sure to enter **BROWSE** alone at the dot prompt to restore the full display afterwards, or you may not be able to see all the fields you'll want to edit in the following section.)

Using Calculated Fields with BROWSE

One advantage that BROWSE from dot prompt offers is the ability to display calculated fields. Calculated fields are fields that do not acually exist in a database but instead result from a calculation based on one or more database fields. You can use the syntax

BROWSE FIELDS *field1, field2, calcfield = basis-of-calculation*

to display a calculated field along with other fields while in Browse mode. Since calculated fields are not real database fields, they cannot be edited; you can only view the data in a calculated field.

As an example, perhaps you would like to see a standard weekly rate of pay for each employee, based on a 35-hour week. The hourly salaries are stored in the database, so it would be a simple calculation of the SALARY field multiplied by 35. You can display such a calculation within a field of a Browse display by giving the calculated field a name and including the basis of the calculation as part of the BROWSE command. At the dot prompt, enter the following:

```
BROWSE FIELDS LASTNAME, FIRSTNAME, SALARY, WEEKLY=SALARY*35
```

and the result appears as shown in Figure 4-8. The calculation for each record appears in the column labeled WEEKLY. If you

Figure 4-8.

Records Organize Fields Go To Exit

LASTNAME	FIRSTNAME	SALARY	WEEKLY
Morse	Marcia	8.50	297.50
Westman	Andrea	15.00	525.00
Jackson	David	7.50	262.50
Mitchell	Mary Jo	7.50	262.50
Robinson	Shirley	7.50	262.50
Jackson	Cheryl	12.00	420.00
Robinson	Wanda	7.50	262.50
Hart	Edward	8.50	297.50
Jones	Judi	12.00	420.00
Abernathy	Sandra	10.00	350.00

Browse ‖E:\...dbdata\ABCSTAFF ‖Rec 1/10 ‖File

Calculated field with BROWSE

try to edit any of the entries in the WEEKLY field, the computer will beep, because changes can't be made to calculated fields.

Mode Differences

If Browse mode is so all-powerful, why must you bother with the Edit mode? Edit mode shows you more of the complete record on the screen at once. Browse mode, on the other hand, shows you only those fields that fit on the screen. If your database contains many fields, Browse mode will have to display it in small pieces.

After you change or add information in Browse mode, you can return to the Control Center or the dot prompt by pressing CTRL-END or by choosing Exit from the Exit menu. Use either method to save your changes and get back to the Control Center now. If you are at the dot prompt, enter **ASSIST** to get to the Control Center.

Deleting Records

dBASE IV uses a combination of two menu options, or equivalent dot-prompt commands, to delete records. From the menus, these are the Mark Record for Deletion option on the Records menu and the Erase Marked Records option on the Organize menu. From the dot prompt, the two commands are DELETE and PACK.

☞ ***REMEMBER*** Records you mark for deletion are still visible (unless you use SET DELETED ON). You must perform a PACK to permanently remove the records.

The Mark Records for Deletion option on the Records menu (or its dot-prompt equivalent, the DELETE command) prepares a record for deletion, but does not actually delete the record. This method of marking records for later deletion allows you to mark as many records as you wish at one time. By identifying records in this way, dBASE IV provides a built-in safeguard: you have the opportunity to change your mind and recall the record. (How this is done will be discussed later in this section.)

Let's say that the record that you just added for Sandra Abernathy needs to be deleted from the database. You must first move the pointer to the record. Since you just added the record to the file, you'll find it at the end of the file. You can move to the desired record in a number of ways. You could visually search the database while in Browse mode, but this method is impractical if there are hundreds of records in the file. A better method is to use the search options on the Records menu (or their dot-prompt equivalent, the LOCATE command) to find the desired record.

From the Control Center, with the ABCSTAFF file highlighted by the cursor, press F2 (Data) to access the database. Since you will search for a last name, use the TAB key to place the cursor in the LASTNAME field. Open the Go To menu with ALT-G. Choose the Forward Search option, and enter **Abernathy** in response to the prompt. dBASE IV will move the cursor to the desired record.

Open the Records menu with ALT-R. Choose the Mark Record for Deletion option. You will not see a visible change to the record itself. However, at the bottom of the screen, note that the letters

"Del" appear at the right side of the status bar. This indicates that the record presently on the screen has been marked for deletion.

While in Browse or Edit mode, you may want to keep in mind a faster shortcut for deleting records. You can place the cursor at the desired record manually or with the search options of the Go To menu. Once the cursor is anywhere in the desired record, you can press the CTRL-U key combination, which marks a record for deletion with less effort than using the menu options.

HINT With the cursor anywhere in the desired record, CTRL-U quickly deletes the record.

Dot-prompt users can use the LOCATE command to find desired records, followed by the DELETE command to mark the records for deletion. To see how this works, press CTRL-END to get back to the Command Center, press ESC, and then type **Y** to get to the dot prompt. You may recall from the previous chapter that the format for the LOCATE command is:

LOCATE FOR (*fieldname*) = "*search-term*"

If you are searching a character field, you must surround the search term with quotes. Capitalization must also match inside the quotes; you will not find the desired record if you enter **jackson** when what's really stored in the field is "Jackson." If you are searching a date field, surround the search date with the { and } curly braces. If you are searching a numeric field, just enter the number alone without any braces or quotes.

NOTE When searching for data, capitalization can be important. dBASE normally considers uppercase letters to be different from lowercase letters.

As an example, enter the following:

```
LOCATE FOR LASTNAME = "Jackson"
```

dBASE should respond with the message "Record = 3." If you instead see an error message or the message "End of locate scope," recheck your spelling of the command or the last name, and try the command again. Then, since record 3 is the one you want to mark for deletion, enter

```
DELETE
```

You will see the confirmation "1 record deleted."

If you know the record number, you can specify the command DELETE RECORD #*n,* where #*n* is the number of the record to be deleted. Suppose that Shirley Robinson, listed in record 5, also needs to be removed from the list. Enter the command

```
DELETE RECORD 5
```

Again, the "1 record deleted" message appears. Now enter the command

```
LIST LASTNAME, FIRSTNAME
```

and you will see that the marked records have not been removed from the database. When the LIST command is used, an asterisk appears besides the marked records, indicating that these records are marked for deletion.

If you decide that deleting a record is not the thing to do, you can use the RECALL command to undo the damage. For example, enter this command to recall the fifth record:

```
RECALL RECORD 5
```

The confirmation "1 record recalled" appears. Now reenter the LIST LASTNAME, FIRSTNAME command. A shortcut is available here: by pressing the up arrow key at the dot prompt, you can display the dot-prompt commands you entered earlier. When you see the desired command (in this case, LIST LASTNAME, FIRSTNAME), just press ENTER to repeat the command. Once you do so, the database will show that only records 3 and 10 are still marked for deletion. You can remove all delete marks with the command RECALL ALL. For now, recall record 3 by entering **RECALL RECORD 3** at the dot prompt.

When a record has been marked for deletion it remains in the database, and various operations, such as COUNT and SUM (which will be discussed later), can still use the record in calculations as if it had never been deleted. To avoid displaying and using records that have been marked for deletion, you can use the SET DELETED command. Enter

```
SET DELETED ON
```

Now repeat the LIST LASTNAME, FIRSTNAME command by pressing the up arrow key until the command appears and then pressing ENTER. You will see that record 10, which was marked for deletion, is no longer visible. To make the record visible again, enter

```
SET DELETED OFF
```

When you try the LIST command again, the record marked for deletion will again be visible in the database.

There is no need to delete records one by one with the DELETE command. You can mark more than one record for deletion by specifying the number of records to be deleted. For example, enter the command

```
GO 5
DELETE NEXT 2
LIST LASTNAME, FIRSTNAME
```

GO 5 moves the pointer to record 5; then DELETE NEXT 2 marks records 5 and 6 for deletion.

The RECALL command can be used in the same manner. Enter

```
GO 5
RECALL NEXT 2
LIST LASTNAME, FIRSTNAME
```

and records 5 and 6 will be unmarked.

To make the deletion process final, you must either enter the PACK command from the dot prompt or select the file at the Control Center, choose Modify Structure/Order, and then choose Erase Marked Records from the next menu that appears. Note that in dBASE IV version 1.1, you can also find the Erase Marked Records option in the Organize menus of the Browse and Edit screens.

Let's try the menu method now. Enter **ASSIST** from the dot prompt to get back to the Control Center. With the filename ABCSTAFF highlighted, press ENTER. From the next menu that appears, choose Modify Structure/Order. In a moment, the Control Center will disappear, and the Organize menu will appear.

Most choices on this menu will be covered in a later chapter. The last two options on the menu, Unmark All Records and Erase Marked Records, correspond to the RECALL ALL and PACK commands from the dot prompt. The Unmark All Records option will remove all deletion markers, and the Erase Marked Records option will remove all marked records from the database.

Like its dot-prompt equivalent, PACK, the Erase Marked Records option makes the deletion process final. This option removes the marked records, and it renumbers the remaining records to fill any empty spaces created by the deleted records. Choose the Erase Marked Records option from the menu now. dBASE IV will ask for confirmation; type **Y**, and the marked record will be deleted.

Press F10 to get to the menus, and choose Save Changes and Exit from the Exit menu to get back to the Control Center.

NOTE The Erase Marked Records option (or its dot-prompt equivalent, PACK) can be time-consuming with large files.

Deleting Files

You can also delete files from within dBASE IV. From the dot prompt, you can use the DELETE FILE command. For example, the command

```
DELETE FILE NAMES2.DBF
```

would erase a file called NAMES2.DBF from the disk. If you prefer the menu approach, you can press F10 at the Control Center to open the menus, choose the DOS Utilities option of the Tools menu, highlight the desired file in the directory that appears, and press the DEL key. dBASE will display a confirmation menu, and you must choose the Proceed option to delete the file. Then press ESC and type **Y** (or open the Exit menu and press ENTER) to get back to the Control Center.

Use either of these options for deleting files with care. Once a file has been deleted, you cannot recall it without special programs or techniques that are beyond the scope of this book.

Global Replacements From the Dot Prompt

Suppose that you wanted to replace the five-digit ZIP code with the new nine-digit ZIP codes for all employees in Washington, DC. You can change the ZIP code for every Washington, DC, entry with the CHANGE command from the dot prompt. However, you only need to use CHANGE once because it is a *global* command. A global command performs the operation of the command on the entire database, not just on a single record.

The CHANGE command consists of a two-step process: it first finds the proper field, and it then asks you to enter the correction. The format of the command is

CHANGE FIELD *fieldname* FOR *keyfield* = "*keyname*"

For *fieldname* enter the field where you want the changes to occur, and for *keyfield* enter the field where CHANGE should search for the occurrence of *keyname*. You must surround *keyname* with quotes.

In the following example you will use the CHANGE command to change the ZIPCODE field for each occurrence in the database that has the word "Robinson" within the LASTNAME field. Get to the dot prompt, and enter the following:

```
CHANGE FIELD ZIPCODE FOR LASTNAME = "Robinson"
```

Record 5 is the first record containing Robinson in the LASTNAME field. Notice that dBASE only displays the field that will be changed.

The cursor is flashing at the first character, so you can enter **20912-1234** as the new ZIP code for record 5. After you fill the field, you will see record 7. (You can tell the record number from the center of the status bar, or from the "Record No." indicator at the top of the screen when the menus are not active.) Enter **20009-1010** , and the dot prompt will reappear. To see the results, enter

```
LIST LASTNAME, CITY, ZIPCODE
```

The new ZIP codes you entered will be displayed.

Record#	LASTNAME	CITY	ZIPCODE
1	Morse	Chevy Chase	20815-0988
2	Westman	Silver Spring	20910-0124
3	Jackson	Falls Church	22044
4	Mitchell	Arlington	22203
5	Robinson	Takoma Park	20912-1234
6	Jackson	Falls Church	22044
7	Robinson	Washington	20009-1010
8	Hart	Fairfax	22025
9	Jones	Reston	22090

REPLACE operates very much like CHANGE, except that REPLACE does not ask you to type in the change after it finds the field. Instead, you specify the change within the command and it will be made automatically. The format of the command is

REPLACE [*scope*] *fieldname* WITH *field-replacement* FOR *keyfield* = "*keyword*"

The *scope* parameter is optional and is used to determine how many records REPLACE will look at. If ALL is used as the scope, REPLACE will look at all records; but if NEXT 5 is used as the scope, REPLACE will only look at the next five records from the pointer's current position. If you don't specify the scope, RE-

PLACE only looks at the current record, which may or may not be what you had in mind. NEXT is always followed by the number of records REPLACE will look at.

The field where the change will occur is *fieldname,* and *field-replacement* is what will be inserted if *keyfield,* which is the field REPLACE is searching for, matches *keyword.*

There is plenty going on with REPLACE, so it might be best described by an example. Enter the following:

```
REPLACE ALL CITY WITH "Miami" FOR CITY = "Falls Church"
```

This means, "Search for all CITY fields containing the words 'Falls Church' and then replace those fields with the word 'Miami.'" When the prompt reappears, enter

```
LIST LASTNAME, CITY
```

You'll see that the Falls Church employees have been relocated to Miami. They probably would not enjoy the commute to work, so let's move them back.

Enter the command

```
REPLACE ALL CITY WITH "Falls Church" FOR CITY = "Miami"
```

Again, enter

```
LIST LASTNAME, CITY
```

Now the CITY field is correct.

The REPLACE command is handy for updating salaries or prices on a global basis. If every employee is to receive a 50-cent per hour increase, do you really want to update each record manually? It would be much faster to use the REPLACE command to perform the task. From the dot prompt, enter the following commands:

```
LIST LASTNAME, SALARY
REPLACE ALL SALARY WITH SALARY + .50
LIST LASTNAME, SALARY
```

The results show how quickly a global update can be performed with the REPLACE command.

As you work with dBASE IV, you'll find that REPLACE is a handy command for changing area codes, dollar amounts, and other similar applications. But you should be careful: REPLACE has the potential to wreak havoc on a database if used improperly. If you doubt whether REPLACE will have the desired effect, make a copy of the database file under a different name and experiment on the copy instead of the original.

HINT The REPLACE command can be used much like a word processor's search-and-replace feature. You can change values in a group of records or in all records, depending on how you structure the REPLACE command.

There are no direct equivalents for the CHANGE and REPLACE commands in the Control Center menus. However, you can perform global updates from the menus by creating an *update query*. This will be covered in Chapter 7.

Modifying the Structure Of a Database

You'll often use a database for a while and then decide to enlarge a field, delete a field, or add a field for another category. dBASE allows you to make these changes in the structure of a database.

From the dot prompt, you use the MODIFY STRUCTURE command. From the Control Center, you highlight the desired file and select it by pressing ENTER, choose Modify Structure/Order from the next menu, and then press ESC to close the Organize menu and begin changing the structure. When you change the structure of a database, dBASE IV copies the entire database into a temporary file and then modifies the database according to your instructions.

If ABC Temporaries suddenly decides that the database should include all of the employee phone numbers, you could add a field for them. To make this change, from the dot prompt enter

```
MODIFY STRUCTURE
```

From the Control Center, highlight the ABCSTAFF file and press ENTER, choose Modify Structure/Order from the next menu, and

Figure 4-9.

Layout Organize Append Go To Exit   10:52:29 pm

Bytes remaining: 3849

Num	Field Name	Field Type	Width	Dec	Index
1	SOCIALSEC	Character	11		Y
2	LASTNAME	Character	15		N
3	FIRSTNAME	Character	15		N
4	ADDRESS	Character	25		N
5	CITY	Character	15		N
6	STATE	Character	2		N
7	ZIPCODE	Character	10		N
8	BIRTHDAY	Date	8		N
9	DATEHIRED	Date	8		N
10	DEPENDENTS	Numeric	2	0	N
11	SALARY	Numeric	5	2	N
12	ASSIGNMENT	Character	20		N
13	HOURLYRATE	Numeric	5	2	N
14	EVALUATE	Memo	10		N

Database E:\...dbdata\ABCSTAFF Field 1/14

Enter the field name. Insert/Delete field:Ctrl-N/Ctrl-U
Field names begin with a letter and may contain letters, digits and underscores

ABC Temporaries database structure

then press ESC to hide the Organize menu that appears. You will see the structure of the ABC Temporaries database as shown in Figure 4-9.

The first field in the structure is highlighted, indicating that dBASE IV is ready to modify it. Since you want to add a field, move the cursor to the BIRTHDAY field with the down arrow key. You will enter the field name, type, and width exactly as you did when you created the database in Chapter 3, but before you do, you need room to add a new field.

Notice the message in the message line at the bottom of the screen. It mentions that fields can be inserted with CTRL-N and deleted with CTRL-U. Press the CTRL-N key once, and a new field will appear above the BIRTHDAY field. Since you want to enter phone numbers, the word "phone" would be a good title for the field; enter **PHONE**. Once you press ENTER, the cursor will move to the Field Type category. You want to use C for the character types—since phone numbers are never used in calculations, they need not be numeric—so press ENTER to move on to the next category.

HINT To add a new field in the midst of an existing structure, move the cursor to the spot for the new field and press CTRL-N.

At the width category, enter **12**. This will leave room for a ten-digit phone number, plus two hyphens. You can leave the default of N in the Index block.

When you modify a database, data will be returned from the fields of the temporary file to the fields in the modified database automatically only if the field names or field types match. If you rename a field or change the type of a field, dBASE IV may or may not not restore the data in that particular field, since it doesn't always know where to find the data or how to convert the data type.

REMEMBER When you modify a database structure, be careful when changing field types. dBASE may lose data if a change in field types doesn't allow an orderly transfer of data.

You can change field types without losing data as long as the change "makes sense" to dBASE within the new data type. For example, you can change a character field filled with digits to a numeric field without data loss. You can also change a field's name without losing data, as long as you do not make any other changes in the structure at the same time.

When you press CTRL-END (or choose Save Changes and Exit from the Exit menu), you'll see a yes/no confirmation prompt, as shown in Figure 4-10. Along with the prompt, notice the message that appears at the bottom of the screen:

Database records will be APPENDED from backup fields of the same name only!!

Figure 4-10.

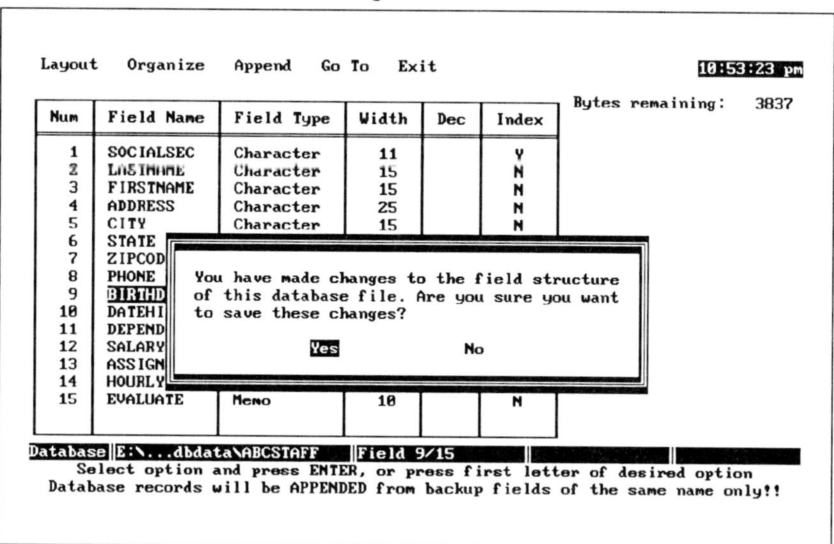

Confirmation prompt

This indicates that dBASE IV is ready to copy the data from the temporary file into the modified database. You are asked to confirm whether data should be copied from all fields. Select Yes from the prompt. After a short delay (during which dBASE IV automatically rebuilds the database), you should see the Control Center or the dot prompt.

Get to the dot prompt with ESC if you're not already there, and enter the command

```
BROWSE FIELDS LASTNAME, FIRSTNAME, PHONE FREEZE PHONE
```

If you press PGUP, you'll see that all of the PHONE fields are present but empty. To complete the database, type in the phone numbers for the employees as shown here:

LASTNAME	FIRSTNAME	PHONE
Morse	Marcia	301-555-6678
Westman	Andrea	301-555-2912
Jackson	David	703-555-8778
Mitchell	Mary Jo	703-555-6874
Robinson	Shirley	301-555-0201
Jackson	Cheryl	703-555-5432
Robinson	Wanda	202-555-4545
Hart	Edward	703-555-1201
Jones	Judi	703-555-2638

Had this field been planned in advance during the database design stage, as outlined in Chapter 2, you wouldn't have the inconvenience of returning to each record to type a phone number.

Quick Reference

To edit records in a database From the Control Center, highlight the database by name in the Data panel, and then press F2 once to edit in Browse mode or press F2 twice to edit in Edit mode. From the dot prompt, enter **USE *filename***, where *filename* is the name of the database, enter **BROWSE** to edit in Browse mode, or enter **EDIT** to edit in Edit mode.

To save changes when done with Browse or Edit Press CTRL-END or choose Save Changes and Exit from the Exit menu.

To find a record while in Browse or Edit mode Place the cursor in the field you want to search. Open the Go To menu with ALT-G, and choose Forward Search (to search forward) or Backward Search (to search in reverse). Enter a search term when prompted.

To switch between Edit and Browse modes Press F2.

To find a record from the dot prompt Use the LOCATE command. You can use the syntax LOCATE FOR *fieldname* = "*search-term*". When searching for a character string, surround the search term with quotes. Surround dates with curly braces.

To search within numeric fields, enter the numbers without any quotes.

To mark a record for deletion First, find the desired record using the menu options or the LOCATE command. Then open the Records menu with ALT-R and choose Mark Record for Deletion (or, at the dot prompt, enter the DELETE command).

To permanently remove all records marked for deletion At the Control Center, highlight the filename in the Data panel and press ENTER. From the next menu, choose Modify Structure/Order. From the Organize menu that next appears, choose Erase Marked Records. Or, from the dot prompt, enter the PACK command.

To modify the structure (or the design) of a database From the Control Center, highlight the filename in the Data panel and press ENTER. From the next menu, choose Modify Structure/Order. When the Organize menu appears, press ESC to hide the menu. Make the desired changes to the fields of the database, and press CTRL-END. Or, from the dot prompt, enter the MODIFY STRUCTURE command. Make the desired changes to the fields of the database, and press CTRL-END.

CHAPTER

5

Creating Entry Forms

When you are in Edit mode and you add data or make changes to a database, you are presented with a simple on-screen entry form that lists the various fields, along with highlighted areas that contain the actual data. For the purposes of demonstrating how to add or change data within a database, this has been sufficient. However, such a straightforward approach to adding data to a database can create problems.

One drawback is in the unfriendly screen presented to the computer user. If an ABC Temporaries employee does not know what is meant by "HOURLYRATE" on the screen, the help screens or the dBASE manual will not offer any assistance. Another drawback is the lack of control you have in Edit mode; if for any reason you wish to prevent the editing of a particular field, you cannot do so.

To overcome such limitations, dBASE IV lets you design flexible *entry forms*. An entry form is simply a form that appears on the screen, which is used for data display and data entry. Using the Form Design screen, you can build forms that resemble the printed forms commonly used in an office. You can also restrict entry by omitting certain fields and including other fields in the form. You can limit fields to accept certain types of data, such as amounts that fall within a predefined range. And you can tell dBASE IV to use a specific form when working with a database, so that the form automatically appears when you add or edit records. The forms you create can be used for the entry or the display of data in a database.

HINT If you desire, you can design screen forms that resemble paper-based forms used in an office.

dBASE IV builds three files for each form that you create. One file has an extension of .SCR, and the second has an extension of .FMO. dBASE IV uses these files to build the actual form. The third file has an extension of .FMT. This file can be used within a DBASE IV program or command file, a subject that will be discussed in a later chapter.

If you're not already in dBASE IV, load the program and get to the Control Center. Highlight ABCSTAFF and press ENTER, and then select the Use File option from the next menu that appears.

Creating a Data Entry Form

Data entry forms can be created by choosing the Create option from the Forms panel. (From the dot prompt, you can also use the CREATE SCREEN command. For the purpose of illustration, however, we will use the Control Center.) Highlight the Create option under the Forms panel, and press ENTER to select this option. The Control Center will be replaced with the Form Design screen shown in Figure 5-1.

The Form Design screen uses a menu bar and pull-down menus similar to those used in the Browse and Edit modes of dBASE IV.

Figure 5-1.

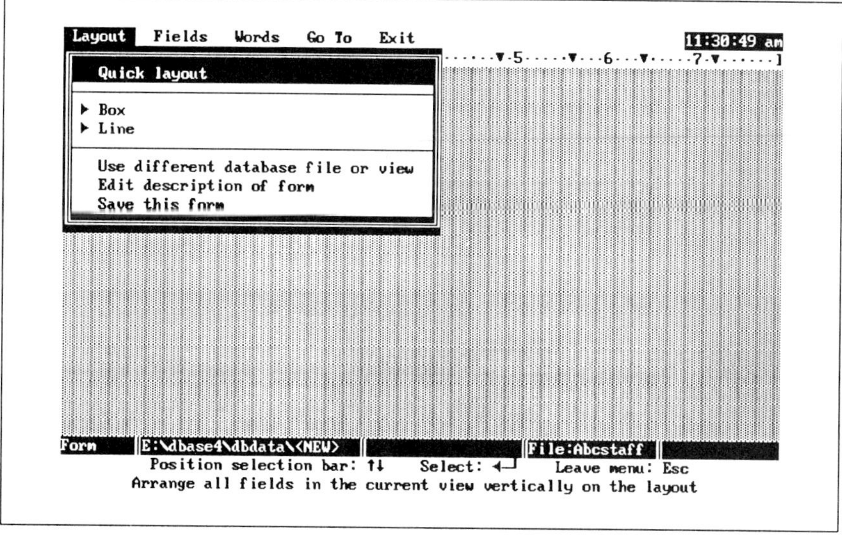

Form Design screen

The first menu is the Layout menu. It offers a number of options for designing the form, choosing different database files for use with the form, or laying out a form quickly. The Fields menu provides options for adding, changing, or deleting fields within the form, and the Words menu provides options that affect the display of text. Finally, the Go To and Exit menus perform the same tasks as they do in the Edit and Browse screens. The options in the Layout, Fields, and Words menus will be covered in more detail shortly.

The basic idea when you design a form is to place the fields for data entry and editing in the desired locations on the screen. You can add a single field with the Add Field option of the Fields menu. However, with 15 fields in the database, this would mean selecting the Add Field option 15 times. Fortunately, there is an easier way. The Quick Layout option of the Layout menu will lay out all of the fields in the ABCSTAFF database in a vertical arrangement on the screen. Choose the Quick Layout option from the Layout menu now. In a moment, all of the fields in the database will appear, as is shown in Figure 5-2. Note that cursor movement in a screen form is from top to bottom, and, within the same line, from left to right.

HINT To quickly design a screen, choose the Create option of the Forms panel. At the next screen, choose Quick Layout from the Layout menu.

When you are in the work area of the Form Design screen (as you are now), you can draw your desired data entry form. Fields can be moved around, lines and borders can be added, and more descriptive names can be entered to describe the fields. As in other parts of dBASE IV, you can display the menus at any time by pressing ALT and the first letter of the menu name, and you can leave the menus and return to the Form Design screen without picking an option with the ESC key.

Figure 5-2.

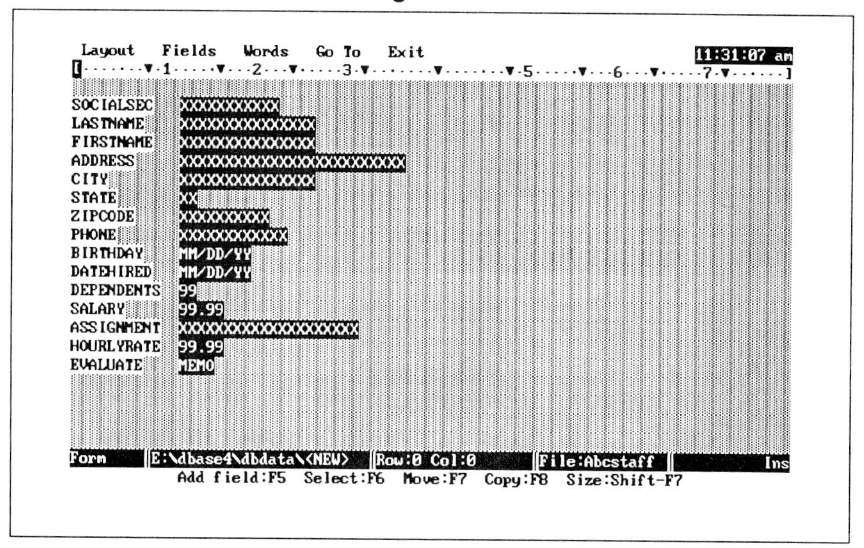

Form Design screen with all fields

When you first load fields into a form and begin using the Form Design screen, the field names appear at the left side of the screen. The highlighted areas that appear to the right of the field names represent the actual fields and are called *field templates.* It is important to recognize the difference between the actual fields, as represented by the field templates, and the field names, because the Modify Field menu offers options that apply specifically to the fields. On your screen, the word "LASTNAME" is a field name, not a field. The first highlighted "X" to the right of the LASTNAME label marks the start of the actual field, as represented by the field template.

The characters in these highlighted areas represent the types of data that will appear in those fields when you use the completed form. The letter X is used to indicate a character field. The number 9 is used to indicate numeric fields, and MM/DD/YY indicates date fields. The letter L indicates a logical field, and MEMO indicates a memo field.

The status bar at the bottom of the screen tells you the row and column position of the cursor while you are working within the screen. Cursor movement is performed with the same editing keys you use in Edit mode.

HINT The row and column indicators in the status bar are helpful for determining the cursor location when designing forms.

Try pressing the Insert key (INS) repeatedly. As you do so, note that "Ins" appears and disappears from the status bar. Pressing the INS key moves you in and out of Insert mode. When you are in Insert mode, all characters that you type are added to the existing text to the left of the cursor location. When you are out of Insert mode (and thus in Overwrite mode), all characters that you type replace any existing characters. Insert mode is normally turned on when you start creating a form.

The cursor is currently at the letter S in SOCIALSEC. The form would look less cluttered if there were open space at the top of the screen, so press the INS key until you are in Insert mode. Then press ENTER to insert a blank line at the top of the screen. Move the cursor to the letter B in the field name BIRTHDAY, and press ENTER once to insert a blank line between the PHONE and BIRTHDAY fields.

Next, let's use the Form Design screen to add a descriptive title to the form. Move the cursor to row 3, column 41 (remember, the position of the cursor is indicated by the status bar). Then enter this title:

ABC TEMPORARIES ENTRY FORM

NOTE If your database has a large number of fields, you can create multiple-page screens. Place as many fields as desired on the form, then use PGDN to get to a blank screen, and place more fields. Later, when you use the form, PGUP and PGDN will access the various screens.

Moving Fields

The form is starting to look better already, but more changes would improve its appearance. A sensible arrangement would be to place the CITY and STATE fields on the same line. You can easily move a field by placing the cursor at the beginning of the field, pressing F6 (Select) and then F7 (Move), placing the cursor in a new location, and pressing ENTER.

As an example, place the cursor at the start of the STATE field (the first letter X within the highlighted block). Once the cursor is at the first character within the field, press F6 to select the field for movement, and then press F7 to move the field. The message below the status bar now indicates that you can use the cursor keys to reposition the field. Move the cursor to row 6, column 34. This location will leave sufficient room to add the field name. Press ENTER, and the field will be moved to the new location (Figure 5-3).

When moving fields to new locations, you must be careful to measure whether there is sufficient room to fit the entire field at the screen location that you choose. If, for example, you attempt to place a field that is 20 characters long at column 62, you will cut off the display of the last two characters, because the screen ends at the character position 80.

A field name is needed for the repositioned field, so place the cursor at row 6, column 28. Press the INS key until you are in Overwrite mode ("Ins" does *not* appear in the status bar), and type **STATE**. Then move the cursor to any location within row 7. Open

Figure 5-3.

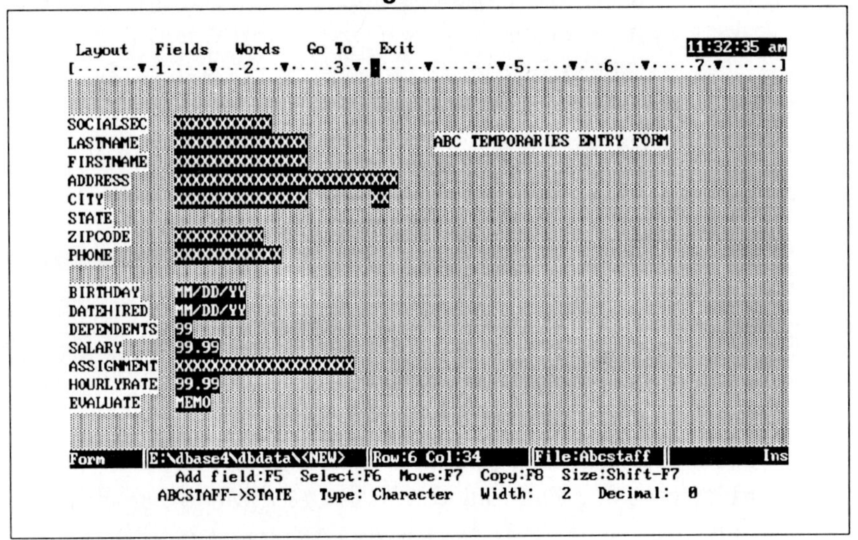

New location of STATE field

the Words menu with ALT-W, and choose Remove Line to delete the line under the CITY and STATE fields.

HINT You can also move a group of fields at once. To do this, place the cursor at the start of the first field and press F6. Move the cursor until the highlight covers all desired fields, and press ENTER. Then press F7, and use the cursor keys to move the group of fields.

To reduce the visual clutter still present in the form, let's move the memo field, EVALUATE, to the right side of the form. Place the cursor at the start of this field (the letter M in MEMO) and press F6, and then press F7. Move the cursor to row 10, column 45, and press ENTER again to reposition the field. To add a field name, move the cursor to row 9, position 36, and type **EVALU-**

ATE. Then move the cursor back to the original EVALUATE field name, and use the DEL key to remove that name.

One benefit of designing a custom form is that it allows you to add descriptive messages to a form. ABC Temporaries employees may not instinctively understand how to enter data in the memo field. To add an explanation, move the cursor to row 9, column 52, and type the following message:

```
(Control-Home edits.)
```

Finally, one of the field names could use some clarification. It may not be clear to new users what the name SOCIALSEC refers to. The Form Design screen lets you change the labels that refer to the names of the fields. Changing these labels does not change the actual names of the fields within the database. To change the labels on the form, you can type over them when you are in Overwrite mode, or you can use the DEL key to delete the labels and type in new ones when in Insert mode.

Press the INS key until you are in Insert mode. Next, move the cursor to the second S in the SOCIALSEC field name. Press the spacebar once, and then add a period after the letters SEC. Your screen should now resemble the one shown in Figure 5-4.

The entry form is now ready for use. Press ALT-E to open the Exit menu and choose the Save Changes and Exit option. dBASE will ask you for a name for the form; enter **ABCFORM** as the name. The form will be saved on the disk, and the Control Center menus will reappear.

REMEMBER CTRL-END can also be used to save changes to a form.

Once you have made the selection, there will be no noticeable immediate change; you will be returned to the Control Center menus. However, from this point on, your custom form can be

Figure 5-4.

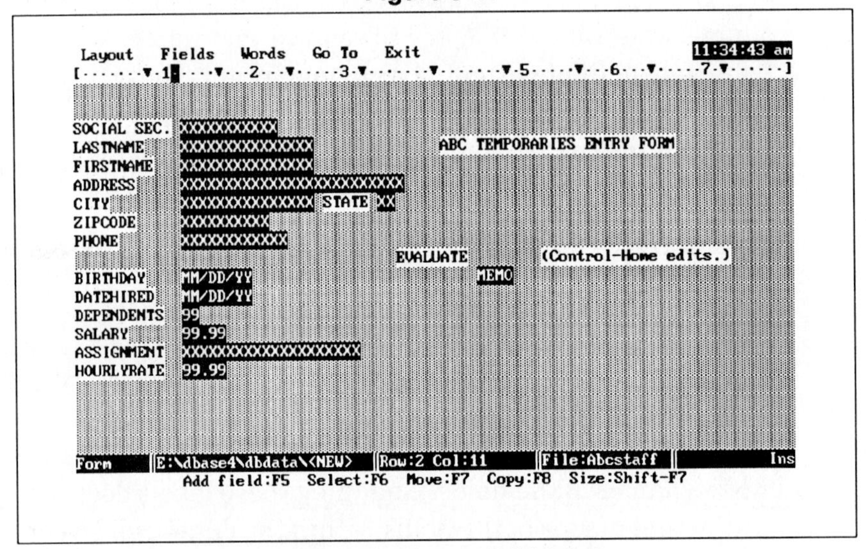

Form containing moved fields and new field label

used for adding and editing records (until you tell dBASE IV not to use that form). To use any form you create for adding or editing records, just highlight that form on the Control Center Forms panel, and press F2 (Data).

NOTE From the Control Center, you place any database and its corresponding screen form in use at the same time by placing the cursor on the form in the Forms panel and pressing F2 (Data).

To see the results of your work, with ABCFORM currently highlighted, press F2 (Data). Instead of the standard append/edit form, you will be greeted with the record displayed within the custom form that you designed with the Form Design screen. Try pressing the PGUP and PGDN keys to move around in the database. Changes can be made to any of the records with the same editing keys you use in Edit mode. When you are done examining the effects of the entry form, press ESC to leave the form and return to the Control Center menus.

About Form Design Menus

From the Control Center, highlight ABCFORM in the Forms panel, and press SHIFT-F2 (Design) to get back to the Form Design screen. You will add a new field and change some field characteristics shortly. Before doing so, however, let's consider the available menu options in more detail.

Press F10 to display the menus, and the Layout menu will open on your screen (Figure 5-5). The first option of this menu, Quick Layout, is the option used to quickly produce a default form that

Figure 5-5.

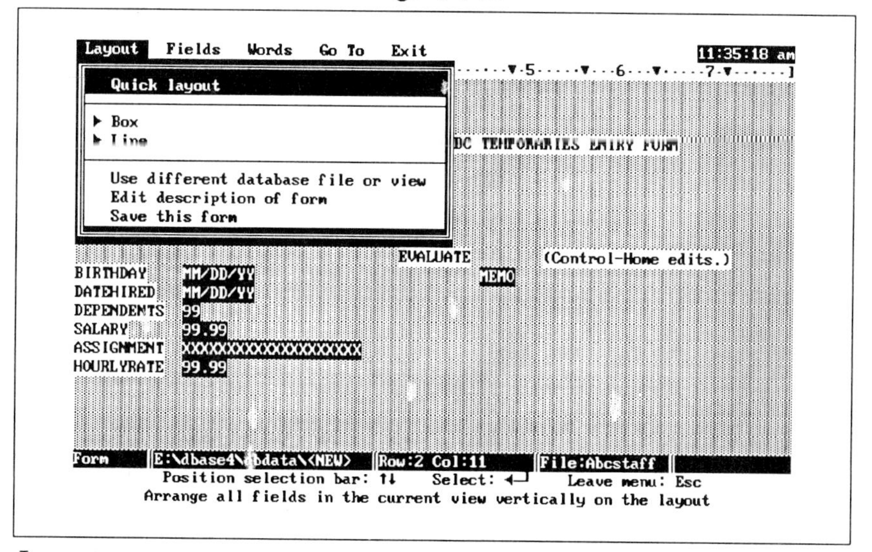

Layout menu

you can then modify, as you did in this example. Once you have chosen Quick Layout to produce the default form, you can modify that form as desired by moving fields around on the screen, adding fields, or deleting fields. Choosing Quick Layout places all of the fields in a database file (or view) onto the form. Each field appears on a separate line, with the field name appearing at the far left and the field template appearing one space to the right of the field name.

REMEMBER You can use ALT plus the first letter of the menu to open any menu.

The Box and Line options of the Layout menu are used to draw boxes or lines on a form to add visual emphasis. Boxes or lines can be made of single lines, double lines, or any special character that you specify after choosing the Box or Line menu option.

The Use Different Database File or View option lets you choose a different database file (or a view) to use when creating the form. This can be a very useful option if you intend to use a single form with more than one database file (assuming the database files have the same design, or structure). You could modify the form, switch databases with the Use Different Database File or View option, and then save the form under a different name.

The Edit Description of Form option lets you add or edit a one-line description for the form. Enter any descriptive text you desire here; the text then jogs your memory whenever you highlight the form from the Control Center. When you have numerous forms in existence, adding these descriptions helps keep track of the purpose of each form.

The Save This Form option of the Layout menu lets you save any changes to the form while you remain at the Form Design screen. (By comparison, the Save Changes and Exit option of the Exit menu saves the changes, but exits from the Form Design screen back to the Control Center.) You'll also want to use this option to save an existing form under a new name; whenever you use the Save This Form option, dBASE asks you for a filename for the form.

If you press the right arrow key once, the Layout menu closes, and the Fields menu opens (Figure 5-6). This menu lets you add or remove fields and modify the characteristics of fields. To add a field to the form, place the cursor in the desired location for the new field, and choose Add Field from this menu. From the list of fields that appears, you select the desired field to add, and then press CTRL-END. You can also add calculated fields and change the display characteristics while using the Add Field option; these topics are discussed shortly.

To remove a field, use the Remove Field option of the Fields menu. You can place the cursor on the desired field and then choose Remove Field from the menu, or you can place the cursor anywhere in the work area (but not on a field) and choose Remove Field. A list of fields then appears, and you can choose the desired field by name from the list.

Figure 5-6.

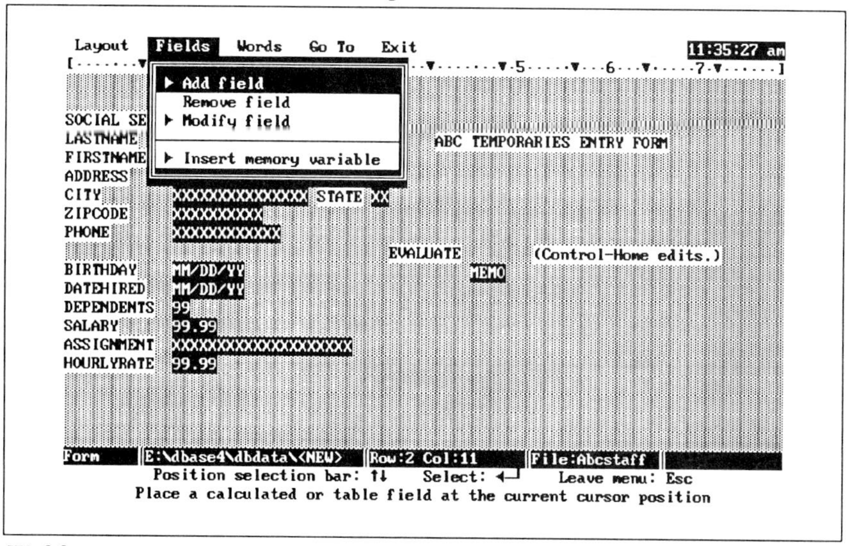

```
Layout  Fields  Words  Go To  Exit                          11:35:27 am
         ▶ Add field
           Remove field
SOCIAL SE▶ Modify field
LASTNAME                                 ABC TEMPORARIES ENTRY FORM
FIRSTNAME▶ Insert memory variable
ADDRESS
CITY       XXXXXXXXXXXXXXX STATE XX
ZIPCODE    XXXXXXXXXX
PHONE      XXXXXXXXXXXX
                               EVALUATE          (Control-Home edits.)
BIRTHDAY   MM/DD/YY                      MEMO
DATEHIRED  MM/DD/YY
DEPENDENTS 99
SALARY     99.99
ASSIGNMENT XXXXXXXXXXXXXXXXXXXX
HOURLYRATE 99.99
Form  E:\dbase4\dbdata\<NEW>  Row:2 Col:11  File:Abcstaff
      Position selection bar: ↑↓   Select: ◄┘   Leave menu: Esc
      Place a calculated or table field at the current cursor position
```

Fields menu

HINT You can also remove a field by placing the cursor on the field and pressing DEL.

The Modify Field option lets you change various display and editing options for a particular field. (While you are in the Forms Design screen, you can also use the F5 key as a shortcut to display these menu options.) As with the Remove option, you can place the cursor on the desired field and then choose Modify Field from the menu, or you can place the cursor anywhere in the work area (but not on a field) and choose Modify Field. A list of fields then appears, and you can choose the desired field by name from the list. Once you perform either step, another menu appears, similar to the example shown in Figure 5-7.

The various specifications for the field appear in the upper half of the menu box; these are taken from the database design, so you cannot change them from this menu. The lower half of the screen

Figure 5-7.

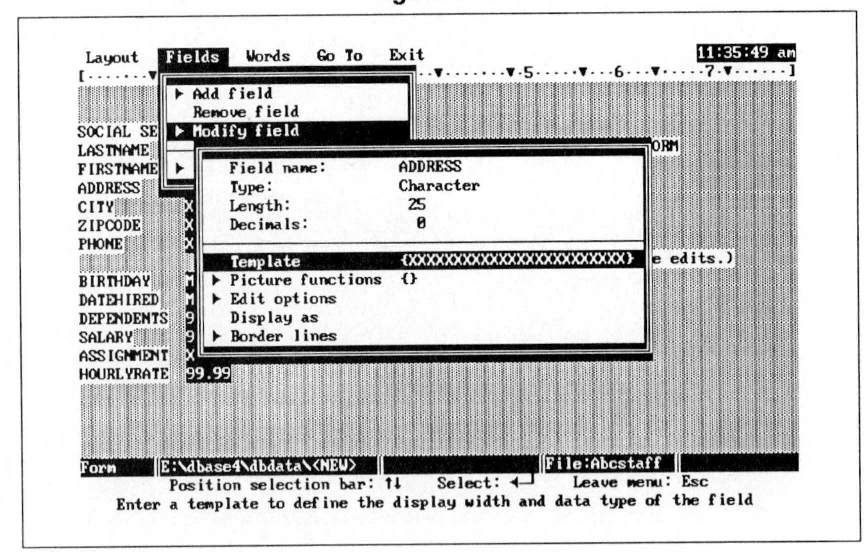

Modify Field menu options

contains display and editing options that you can change. The changes that are available will depend on the type of field you have selected. The Template and Picture Functions options apply to character, numeric, and floating fields, and they let you specify formats for the data that is entered; for example, you might want all phone numbers to have a format of (999) 999-9999. Edit Options applies to all types of fields and lets you control such features as whether editing will be allowed, the minimum and maximum values permitted, and messages that can appear at the bottom of the screen when a user is editing that field. The Display As option lets you specify whether memo fields should be displayed in a "marker" (as they are shown on your form now) or in a window. If you choose to display a memo field within a window, the Border Lines option lets you choose the type of border lines to use for the window.

The Insert Memory Variable option of the Fields menu lets you add a memory variable to the form. Memory variables are commonly used for programming in dBASE or working with SQL databases. Both subjects are more advanced topics that will be covered in later chapters; for now, you can ignore this particular option.

Press the right arrow key once to open the Words menu (Figure 5-8). The available options in this menu let you control the appearance of words and fields in the form.

The Display option lets you change the colors of selected text and fields. (On a system with a monochrome monitor, you can change display attributes such as intensity and underlining.) You can select the desired text (which can include fields) by placing the cursor at the start of the desired area, pressing F6 (Select), moving the cursor to the end of the area, and pressing ENTER. Then choose the Display option of the Words menu. Select the desired colors (or attributes on monochrome systems) from the list of choices that appears, and then press CTRL-END. When you use the form, the areas you selected will appear in the chosen colors or attributes.

Figure 5-8.

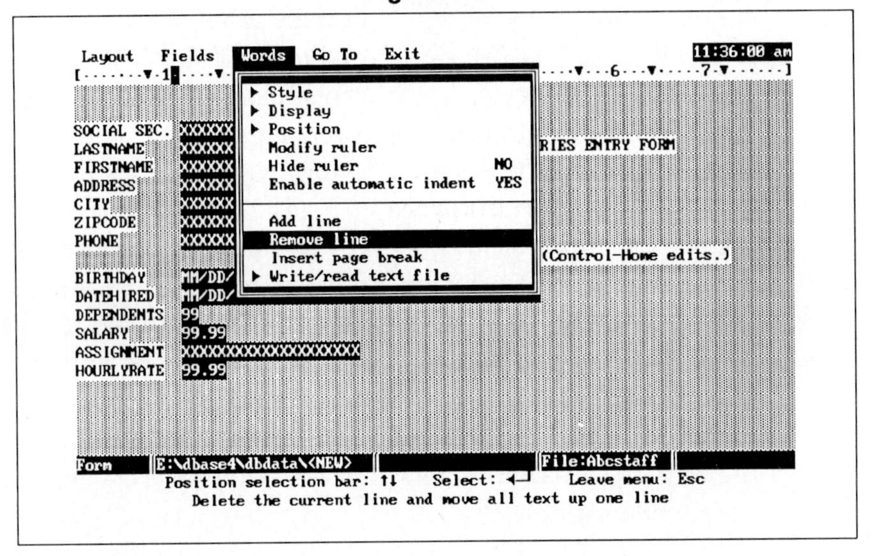

Words menu

The Position option lets you specify where objects within a selection should appear in relation to the margins of the selection. The choices provided are left, center, and right. For example, if you select an area that includes a group of field names and then choose Position and then Right, the labels will be aligned flush right in the selected area.

The Modify Ruler option is used to change the ruler line (just underneath the menu bar) for controlling margins and tab stops. After you select this option, you can move the cursor along the ruler line. Type [at any desired location to set a new left margin, and type] at any desired location to set a new right margin. Type ! at any desired location to set a new tab. To remove an existing tab, move to that tab stop (indicated by the upside-down triangle) and press the DEL key. When you have finished making any changes to the ruler line, press CTRL-END.

The Add Line and Remove Line options can be used to add or remove lines from a form. When you choose Add Line, a new blank line is added directly below the cursor. If you choose Remove Line, the line at the cursor location is removed. (Note that any fields and text on a line will be removed along with the line.) The Write/Read Text File option lets you read a text file into the current cursor location. The remaining options in the Words menu do not apply to editing forms, and are therefore dimmed on the screen and unavailable as valid choices.

HINT You can also remove a line (and any fields within the line) by placing the cursor on the line and pressing CTRL-Y. You can add a new line with CTRL-M.

The Go To and Exit menus perform the same functions as has been described in previous chapters. One option worth noting is the Go to Line Number option that appears under the Go To menu. You can quickly move the cursor to a specified line (row) of the form by choosing this option and entering the desired line number.

Adding a Calculated Field

You can add fields at any time by choosing the Add Field option of the Fields menu and selecting the desired field from the list of fields. You can also add *calculated fields* to the form. These fields are used to display the results of calculations that are usually based on the contents of other fields in the database. Calculated fields are not actual fields in a database; they do not consume space because they are not stored in any permanent location. Adding a calculated field simply tells dBASE to perform a calculation and to display the results in the calculated field of the form.

REMEMBER Because calculated fields do no exist in the database, you cannot edit them. Calculated fields are "display-only" fields.

When you create a calculated field, dBASE will ask for an expression that provides the basis of the calculation. For example, the managers at ABC Temporaries desire a "profitability" field, which will display the difference between the hourly rate charged to the customer and the employee's salary. To add a new field to the database for this information would be a waste of time, since the information can be readily obtained by subtracting the salary amount from the hourly rate amount. The result can be displayed as a calculated field.

Press ESC to close the menus, and place the cursor at row 17, column 12. This will be the position of the new calculated field. Open the Fields menu with ALT-F, and choose Add Field. A *list box* appears, showing the existing fields in the database and all calculated fields (Figure 5-9). Since no calculated fields exist, the

Figure 5-9.

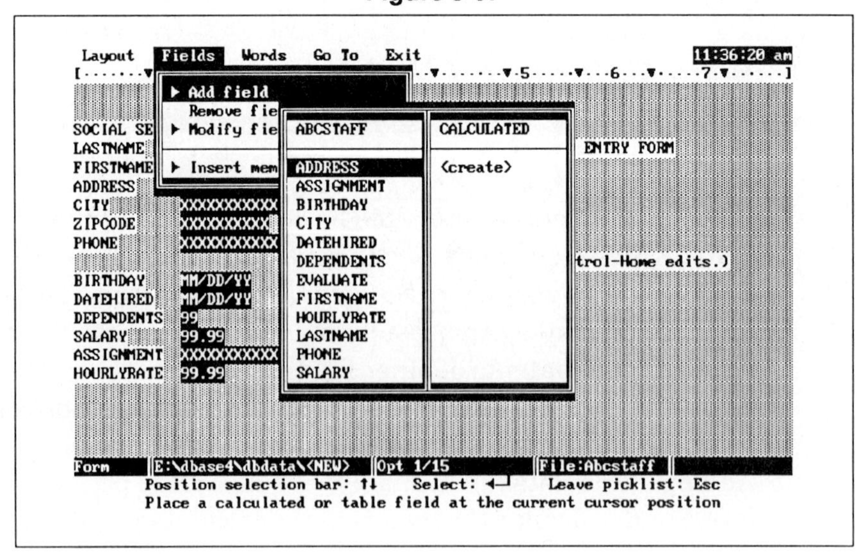

List box of fields

Figure 5-10.

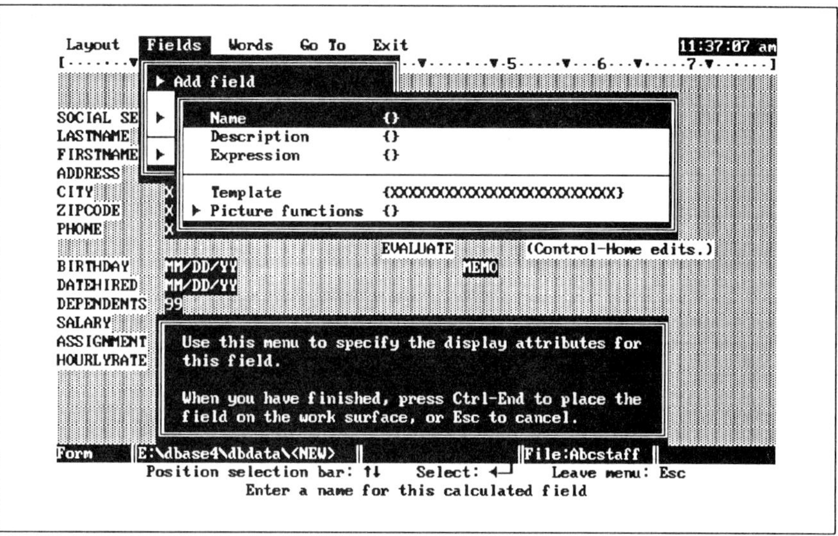

Menu options for creating a calculated field

list box is empty underneath the CALCULATED heading. Highlight the Create option in the Calculated panel and press ENTER. Another menu will appear, as shown in Figure 5-10.

In the upper half of this box, you will enter a name for the field, a description, and the expression that is used as the basis for the calculation. The lower half of the box contains options that let you change the way the data in the field is displayed; you will not use them at this time.

With the Name option highlighted, press ENTER. Enter **PROFIT** as the field name. Move down to the Description option, and press ENTER to select it. Enter **difference between hourly rate and salary** in this field.

Move down to the Expression option, and select it by pressing ENTER. In this case, what is wanted is a valid numeric expression, HOURLYRATE - SALARY. You could enter this manually, but for the sake of experience, try a feature called the *Pick List* to build the expression. You may have noticed the message "Pick operators/fields-Shift-F1" at the bottom of the screen. This message refers to the Pick List feature.

Press SHIFT-F1 now, and a list of field names, operators, and valid dBASE functions appears. Some of the operators and functions may not make much sense at this point; they are covered in more detail in the programming chapters of this text. Highlight the HOURLYRATE field name in the Field Name panel (by repeatedly pressing the down arrow key until the field appears), and then press ENTER. You'll see the field name entered automatically in the Expression option of the menu.

REMEMBER The most commonly used math symbols in expressions are + (addition), - (subtraction), * (multiplication), and / (division).

Press SHIFT-F1 to display the Pick List again, and choose the minus symbol (-) under the Operator panel. It will also be added to the expression once you select it by pressing ENTER. Finally, press SHIFT-F1 and choose SALARY from the Field Name panel of the Pick List. Once you have pressed ENTER, the expression will read as

```
HOURLYRATE-SALARY
```

in the Expression option of the menu. Press ENTER again to accept this as the desired expression. This will tell dBASE to subtract the value in the SALARY field from the value in the HOURLYRATE field and to display the result.

Press CTRL-END to accept all of the options for the calculated field. When you do so, the field will appear on the form. Press HOME to move the cursor to the left margin. Press INS until you are in Overwrite mode ("Ins" does not appear in the status bar), and then type **PROFIT RATE** as the heading.

Note that when you are using the form, if you change the data in a field that serves as the basis for the calculation, the contents of the calculated field do not immediately change. You must move to another record and then back to the changed record to see a change in the calculated field.

Changing the Display Characteristics of a Field

Using the Modify Field option of the Fields menu, you can change the manner in which data is displayed in a field. You can also limit the user's ability to edit particular fields. These changes are possible with the Template, Picture Functions, and Edit options that appear when you choose Modify Field from the Fields menu.

To get an idea of how these options can be used, consider this example. All of the personnel department's staff shouldn't be permitted to make changes to the hourly rate for an employee. Only higher-level managers are permitted to make these changes, so you want to restrict access to the HOURLYRATE field for this form, which is used by the entire personnel staff.

The Edit Options choice provides an ideal way to do this. Place the cursor anywhere that is not directly on a field, go to the Fields menu with ALT-F, and choose Modify Field. From the list of fields that appears, select HOURLYRATE as the field to modify. From the next menu that appears, choose Edit Options. You will see the menu shown in Figure 5-11.

Before going on, an explanation of the various options on this menu is in order. The first choice, Editing Allowed, lets you specify whether editing will be permitted when this form is used. The second choice, Permit Edit If, lets you specify whether editing of

Figure 5-11.

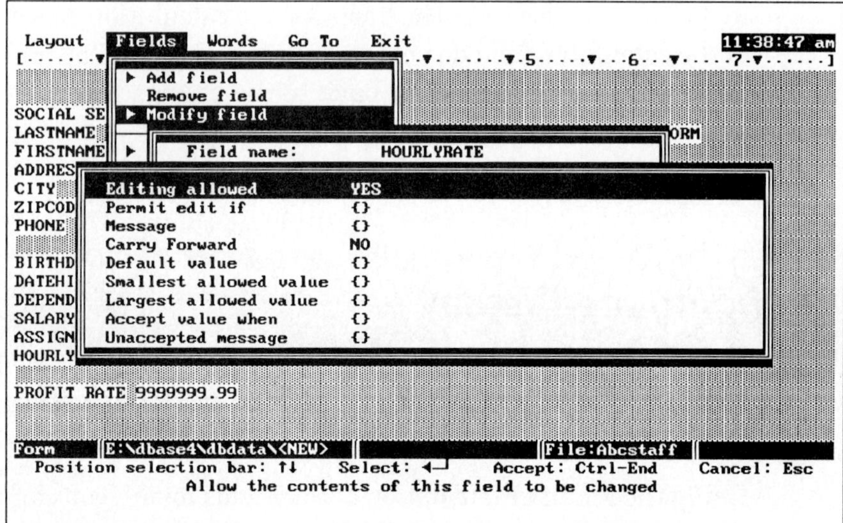

Edit Options menu

the field will be permitted if a certain condition is true. For example, you might want to allow editing of a salary field if the amount was 10.00 or less; you could select Permit Edit If and enter the expression **SALARY <= 10.00** to specify this control over the editing.

The Message option lets you enter a one-line message that will appear in the message line when the cursor reaches the field within the form. The Carry Forward option, which can be set to Yes or No, lets you tell dBASE to carry forward any value placed in the field to the next blank record when new records are being added. This is often helpful with fields like CITY or STATE, in which the same value may be repeated over dozens of records.

HINT The Message option is useful for providing customized help. You can enter a line of "help text" explaining the purpose of a field.

The Default Value option lets you enter a default value that will automatically appear in this field in new records. The Smallest Allowed Value and Largest Allowed Value options let you set minimum and maximum values for a field. You can use these options with date fields and character fields as well as numeric fields. (Character strings must be enclosed in quotes.)

The Accept Value When option lets you specify a condition that must be true before data will be accepted into the field. Along with this option, you can use the Unaccepted Message option to display a message in the message line if the condition for acceptance is not met. As an example, a valid condition for the ASSIGNMENT field might be "accept value when: SALARY > 0." This particular expression would prevent a user from entering an assignment into the ASSIGNMENT field of a new employee if the salary rate had been left blank.

In the case of ABC Temporaries, you want to specify that no editing of the HOURLYRATE field will be allowed, so highlight the Editing Allowed option and press ENTER to change the option from Yes to No. You may notice that the other options are immediately dimmed; because editing will not be allowed for the field, the options no longer apply. Press CTRL-END twice, once to accept the options and once to close the menus. To see the results, choose Save Changes and Exit from the Exit menu or press CTRL-END again. When you are back at the Control Center with the form name ABCFORM highlighted, press F2 (Data). You'll notice that you can no longer edit the contents of the HOURLYRATE field.

Using Picture Functions, Template, and Range

The Picture Functions and Template options are used to format the manner in which data is displayed on the form. With these options, you can display all characters as uppercase letters, or you can display dates in American or European date format. You can also use these options to restrict the way data can be entered into the system. You can specify that only letters or only numbers be accepted, and with numeric fields you can specify a range of acceptable numbers.

The Picture Functions option is used to restrict entry to letters, to identify any lowercase-to-uppercase conversion of data from the database, and to format an entry (when used in combination with a picture template). As an example, you might wish to convert all characters entered in the LASTNAME field to uppercase letters. Press ESC to get to the Control Center, highlight ABCFORM in the Forms panel, and press SHIFT-F2 to get to the Form Design screen.

Move the cursor to the start of the LASTNAME field (make sure the cursor is in the field template, not the field name), and open the Fields menu. Choose Modify Field, and from the next menu that appears, choose Picture Functions. Another menu appears (Figure 5-12), highlighting the available choices. These choices

Figure 5-12.

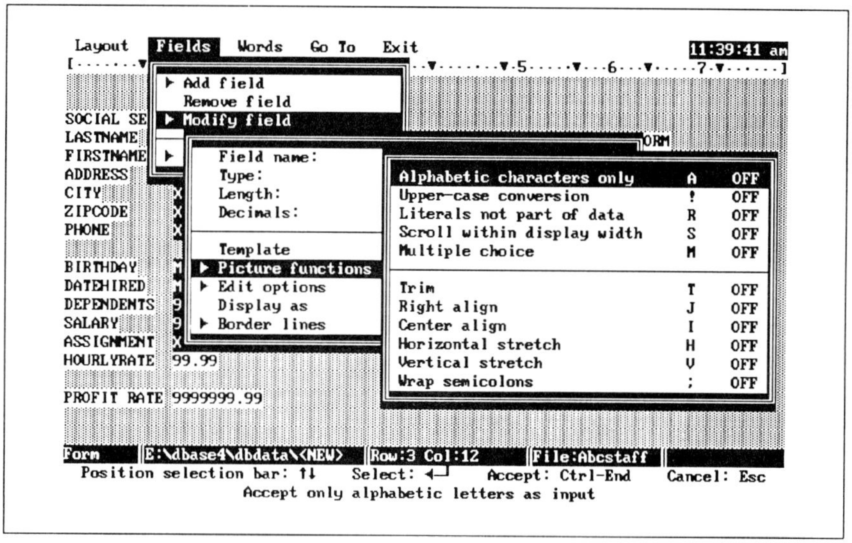

```
Layout  Fields  Words  Go To  Exit                                11:39:41 am
[·······▼          ··▼·······▼·5·····▼···6···▼·····7·▼·····]
          ▸ Add field
            Remove field
SOCIAL SE ▸ Modify field
LASTNAME
FIRSTNAME ▸  Field name:
ADDRESS      Type:            Alphabetic characters only       A    OFF
CITY         Length:          Upper-case conversion            !    OFF
ZIPCODE      Decimals:        Literals not part of data        R    OFF
PHONE                         Scroll within display width      S    OFF
             Template         Multiple choice                  M    OFF
BIRTHDAY   ▸ Picture functions
DATEHIRED  ▸ Edit options     Trim                             T    OFF
DEPENDENTS   Display as       Right align                      J    OFF
SALARY     ▸ Border lines     Center align                     I    OFF
ASSIGNMENT                    Horizontal stretch               H    OFF
HOURLYRATE 99.99              Vertical stretch                 V    OFF
                              Wrap semicolons                  ;    OFF
PROFIT RATE 9999999.99

Form  E:\dbase4\dbdata\<NEW>  Row:3 Col:12  File:Abcstaff
  Position selection bar: ↑↓   Select: ←┘   Accept: Ctrl-End   Cancel: Esc
                Accept only alphabetic letters as input
```

Picture Functions options

are described in Table 5-1. Note that the functions actually available vary with the type of field; for example, you can't use the numeric-type functions for displaying amounts as debit (DB) or credit (CR) with a character field, even if it does contain data entered as numbers.

The Uppercase Conversion option is used to tell dBASE IV that all characters entered into this field will be converted to uppercase. Highlight the Uppercase Conversion option, and press ENTER to set this Picture Functions option to On. Next, you'll choose an option for Template.

Table 5-1.

Symbol	Meaning
Picture Functions:	
!	Converts letters to uppercase
A	Displays alphabetic characters only
S	Allows horizontal scrolling of characters
M	Allows multiple choice
T	Trims trailing spaces
B	Left alignment of entry
I	Center alignment of entry
C	Positive credits followed by CR
X	Negative credits followed by DB
(	Uses () around negative numbers
L	Displays leading zeros
Z	Displays zeros as blanks
$	Displays numbers in financial format
^	Displays numbers in exponential format
R	Allows use of literals within a template without having those literals stored in the database
Templates:	
A	Allows only letters
L	Allows only logical data (true/false, yes/no)
N	Allows only letters or digits
X	Allows any character
Y	Allows Y or N
#	Allows only digits, blanks, periods, or signs
9	Allows only digits for character data, or digits and signs for numeric data
!	Converts letters to uppercase
other	Used to format the entry; for example, with hyphens and parentheses to format a phone number, as in (999) 999-9999

Picture Functions and Templates Available from Modify Field Option

The Template option lets you choose what types of data users of the form will see and be allowed to enter. It also lets you format a field by adding special characters. As an example, you could use Template to cause all phone numbers in a database to be displayed with parentheses and hyphens, as in (202)555-1212. The parentheses and hyphens would not be contained in the database, but they would appear within the form.

REMEMBER Changing data formats with the Picture Function and Template options does not change existing data in the database. New or edited data entered through the form will conform to the new formats.

To try using Template, accept your changes so far and close the Picture Functions option menu with CTRL-END, and then select the Template option. The help screen shown in Figure 5-13

Figure 5-13.

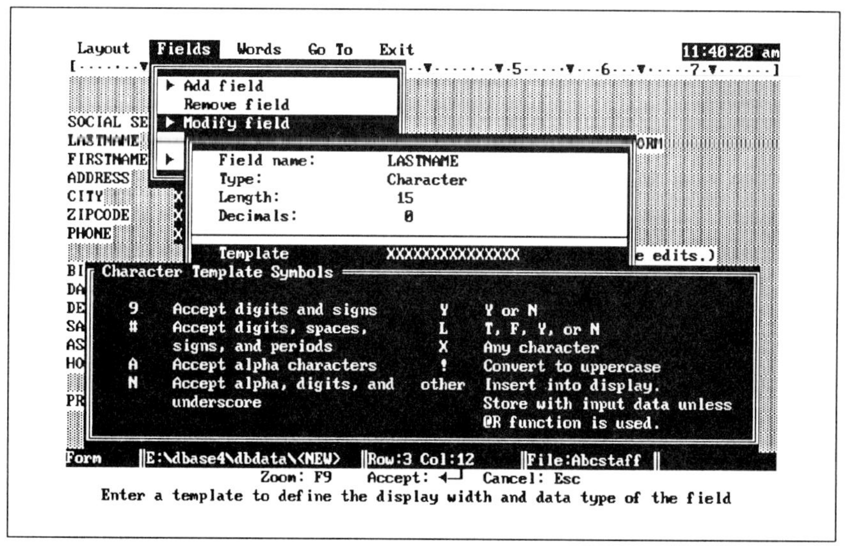

Template help screen

appears, displaying the available choices with Template. (These options are also described in Table 5-1.) Choice A allows entry of letters only. For our example, this choice will be used, although you should be aware that this could cause a problem depending on the application. By using the A option, you will prohibit a name with an embedded space, such as Van Huesen. For your own applications, you'll want to decide whether or not such an approach would create a problem.

Create a template for uppercase letters only by using the BACKSPACE key to delete all of the X's, and then enter **A** 15 times. (When creating a template, the template character must be entered once for each desired position in the field; hence, you will need the letter A in each of the 15 spaces.) Press ENTER and then CTRL-END to accept the options. Next, move the cursor to the SALARY field. You will use the allowable value options to specify the dollar amounts that will be accepted as a minimum and maximum salary level.

With the cursor in the SALARY field, open the Fields menu. Choose Modify Field, and select Edit Options from the next menu that appears. Choose the Smallest Allowed Value option and enter **6.50**. Then choose the Largest Allowed Value option and enter **20.50**.

Press CTRL-END twice, once to accept the option and once to close the menus. Then save the modified form with CTRL-END again or with the Save Changes and Exit option of the Exit menu. When the Control Center reappears, press F2 (Data). You will note that if you try to enter lowercase letters in the LASTNAME field, they will be stored as uppercase letters.

This use of Template can be a noticeable help for using dBASE IV. dBASE IV is *case-specific,* which means it considers uppercase letters to have different values than lowercase letters. Rather than risk having some users of a database enter data in all lowercase letters while others enter data in uppercase letters, you can design an entry form that forces all users to add character data in uppercase letters only.

Note that while the data previously entered in the LASTNAME field now appears as all uppercase, it is still stored in the database as uppercase and lowercase letters. New data that is entered by using the form will be stored as uppercase as well as displayed in uppercase.

Try entering an amount of $4.50 for the hourly salary. An error message showing the acceptable range will be displayed in the message bar when you try to do this. Press ESC when you're done to cancel the changes and return to the Control Center.

Using Memo Windows

By default, memo fields are displayed as markers containing the word MEMO on the screen. dBASE IV also offers the option of displaying memo fields within *windows*. You can place these windows anywhere you desire on the screen, and they can be of varying sizes. This lets you view memo field data while still viewing the other fields in the database.

To change a memo marker to a memo window, you use the Display As Marker/Window option from the Modify Field menu. To see how this can be done, highlight ABCFORM at the Control Center Forms panel and press SHIFT-F2 (Design). Place the cursor in the memo field, EVALUATE, and open the Fields menu. Choose Modify Field, highlight the Display As option, and press ENTER. When you press ENTER, you'll see that the option changes from Marker to Window.

With Window as the selected choice, move down to the Border Lines option and press ENTER. From the next menu to appear, choose Double Line to specify a double-line border for the memo window. Then press CTRL-END to accept the options. You'll see a large memo field window that covers most of your screen, as in Figure 5-14.

HINT Adding border lines helps clearly define the position of your memo windows.

You can resize the window with SHIFT-F7 followed by the cursor keys, and you can move the window with F7 followed by the cursor keys. Press SHIFT-F7 now, and then use the cursor keys to shrink the window to a size of about 40 columns by 8 rows. (This entails eliminating 10 columns and 9 rows.) Press ENTER to anchor the new size, and then press F7 and use the cursor keys to move the window to the lower-right corner of the screen, as illustrated in Figure 5-15.

Figure 5-14.

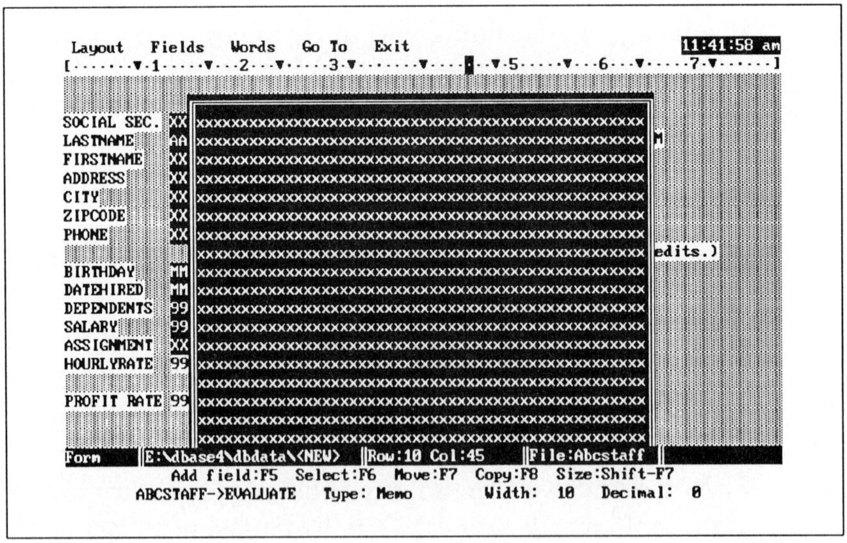

```
Layout  Fields  Words  Go To  Exit                                11:41:58 am
[·······▼·1·····▼···2···▼·····3·▼·······▼····█··▼·5·····▼···6···▼·····7·▼······]

SOCIAL SEC. XX XXXXXXXXXXXXXXXXXXXXXXXXXXXXXXXXXXXXXXXXXXXXXXXXXX
LASTNAME    AA XXXXXXXXXXXXXXXXXXXXXXXXXXXXXXXXXXXXXXXXXXXXXXXXXX M
FIRSTNAME   XX XXXXXXXXXXXXXXXXXXXXXXXXXXXXXXXXXXXXXXXXXXXXXXXXXX
ADDRESS     XX XXXXXXXXXXXXXXXXXXXXXXXXXXXXXXXXXXXXXXXXXXXXXXXXXX
CITY        XX XXXXXXXXXXXXXXXXXXXXXXXXXXXXXXXXXXXXXXXXXXXXXXXXXX
ZIPCODE     XX XXXXXXXXXXXXXXXXXXXXXXXXXXXXXXXXXXXXXXXXXXXXXXXXXX
PHONE       XX XXXXXXXXXXXXXXXXXXXXXXXXXXXXXXXXXXXXXXXXXXXXXXXXXX
               XXXXXXXXXXXXXXXXXXXXXXXXXXXXXXXXXXXXXXXXXXXXXXXXXX edits.)
BIRTHDAY    MM XXXXXXXXXXXXXXXXXXXXXXXXXXXXXXXXXXXXXXXXXXXXXXXXXX
DATEHIRED   MM XXXXXXXXXXXXXXXXXXXXXXXXXXXXXXXXXXXXXXXXXXXXXXXXXX
DEPENDENTS  99 XXXXXXXXXXXXXXXXXXXXXXXXXXXXXXXXXXXXXXXXXXXXXXXXXX
SALARY      99 XXXXXXXXXXXXXXXXXXXXXXXXXXXXXXXXXXXXXXXXXXXXXXXXXX
ASSIGNMENT  XX XXXXXXXXXXXXXXXXXXXXXXXXXXXXXXXXXXXXXXXXXXXXXXXXXX
HOURLYRATE  99 XXXXXXXXXXXXXXXXXXXXXXXXXXXXXXXXXXXXXXXXXXXXXXXXXX
               XXXXXXXXXXXXXXXXXXXXXXXXXXXXXXXXXXXXXXXXXXXXXXXXXX
PROFIT RATE 99 XXXXXXXXXXXXXXXXXXXXXXXXXXXXXXXXXXXXXXXXXXXXXXXXXX
               XXXXXXXXXXXXXXXXXXXXXXXXXXXXXXXXXXXXXXXXXXXXXXXXXX
               XXXXXXXXXXXXXXXXXXXXXXXXXXXXXXXXXXXXXXXXXXXXXXXXXX
Form    ║E:\dbase4\dbdata\<NEW>  ║Row:10 Col:45    ║File:Abcstaff  ║
        Add field:F5  Select:F6  Move:F7  Copy:F8  Size:Shift-F7
     ABCSTAFF->EVALUATE   Type: Memo      Width:  10   Decimal:  0
```

Memo field window

Figure 5-15.

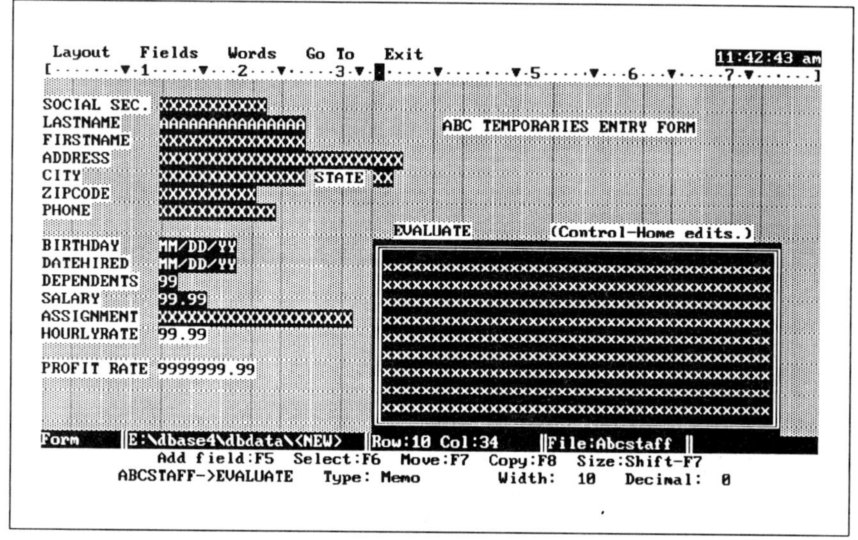

Memo window in new location

For a finishing touch, place the cursor anywhere in the memo window so that the entire window is selected. Open the Words menu with ALT-W, and choose the Display option. If you are using a color monitor, select a different set of foreground and background colors for the field by using the cursor keys to highlight the selected colors. If you are using a monochrome monitor, try a different attribute, such as high intensity. Press CTRL-END to accept the changes. Save the changes to the form by pressing CTRL-END once more. Once you are back at the Control Center, you can see the results by pressing F2 (Data).

Keep in mind that you cannot edit text inside of the memo field window without pressing CTRL-HOME first. You must use CTRL-HOME if you want to make changes to the text contained in the memo field.

Drawing Lines and Boxes on a Form

To improve a form's appearance, you can draw lines and boxes composed of lines. This is done by selecting the Box option or Line option from the Layout menu and by using the cursor keys to draw the line or box.

Add a box to the ABC Temporaries form now by performing the following steps. With ABCFORM highlighted in the Control Center Forms panel, press SHIFT-F2 (Design). Next, open the Layout menu with ALT-L, and choose the Box option. Then choose Double Line. The message in the message line now asks you to position the cursor at the box corner. Place the cursor just above and to the left of the heading "ABC Temporaries Entry Form." Press ENTER to mark this corner of the box.

The message line now asks you to stretch the box with the cursor keys. Place the cursor below and to the right of the word "FORM" in the heading, and press ENTER to mark this corner. A double-line border will surround the heading, as shown in Figure 5-16. To draw a line, you would simply place the cursor on the same line when marking the corners, and a single line instead of a box would then be drawn. Save the modified form now with CTRL-END or with the Save Changes and Exit option of the Exit menu.

! ***HINT*** Boxes drawn around groups of fields often enhance the visual appearance of a form.

Figure 5-16.

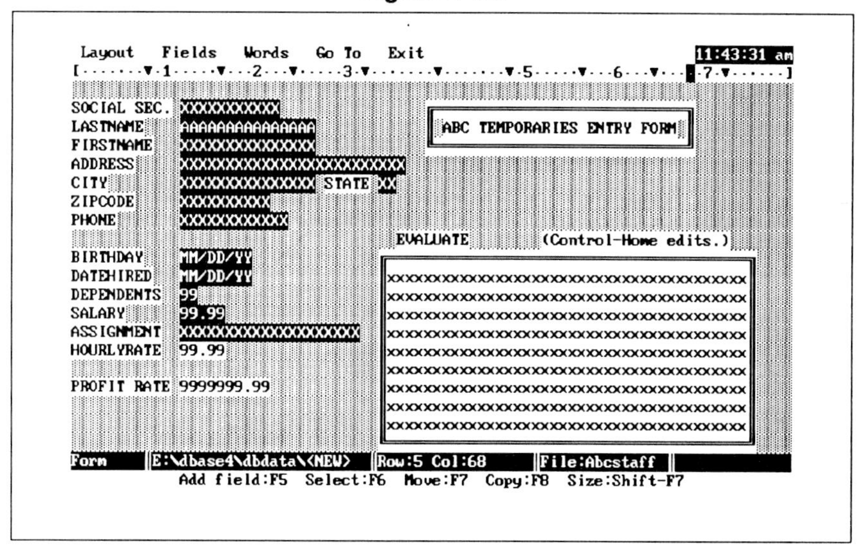

Heading with border

Boxes, Lines, and Your Printer

If you use the SHIFT-PRTSCR key to print screen images to your printer, any form containing lines or boxes created by Form Design may not print out as you might expect. In most cases, the lines on the form will print as alphabetic characters on your printer. Only printers that can print the IBM Extended Graphic Character set will print these lines as they actually appear on a form.

For Dot-Prompt Users Only

Since the process of creating a form uses the Form Design screen, dot-prompt and Control Center users perform the same steps in designing a screen form. The only difference is in getting the process started. From the dot prompt, you first open the desired database file with the USE *filename* command. You then get to the Forms Design screen by entering the command

```
CREATE SCREEN filename
```

where *filename* is the filename for the screen you are building. To make changes to an existing screen, you can enter the command MODIFY SCREEN *filename* at the dot prompt.

Quick Reference

To begin creating a data entry form From the Control Center, highlight the Create option of the Forms panel, and press ENTER. From the dot prompt, enter CREATE SCREEN.

To quickly place all fields onto a form Open the Layout menu with ALT-L, and choose Quick Layout.

To place a single field in a desired location Move the cursor to the location for the field. Open the Fields menu with ALT-F, and choose Add Field. Select the desired field from the list that appears, and press CTRL-END.

To move a field to a different location Place the cursor at the start of the field, and press F6 (Select) and then F7 (Move). Move the cursor to the new location for the field, and press ENTER.

To modify characteristics for a field Place the cursor anywhere in the field, open the Fields menu with ALT-F, and choose Modify Field. Use the Template, Picture Functions, and Edit Options choices that appear in the next menu to modify the desired characteristics.

To change a memo field marker to a memo window Put the cursor anywhere in the field, open the Fields menu with ALT-F, and choose Modify Field. Highlight the Display As option, and press ENTER until it changes to WINDOW. Press CTRL-END. Resize the window as desired with SHIFT-F7 followed by the cursor keys, and move the window to the desired location with F7 followed by the cursor keys.

To draw boxes or lines Open the Layout menu with ALT-L, choose Box or Line, and then choose Single Line or Double Line. Place the cursor at one corner of the box (or one end of the line) and press ENTER. Move the cursor to the diagonal opposite corner of the box (or the other end of the line) and press ENTER.

To save the completed form Press CTRL-END or choose Save Changes and Exit from the Exit menu. Supply a name for the file when prompted. dBASE IV will take a few moments to compile the necessary instructions and save the form.

CHAPTER

6

Sorting and Indexing Your Database

After a database is built, you may need to arrange it in different ways. With the ABCSTAFF database, for example, managers might want to refer to the listing of employees by salary amount, the accounting department might want a list in alphabetical order by last name, and the payroll department might want the list in order by ZIP code, because the Post Office offers discounts for mail presorted in this way. You can arrange a database in a number of different ways by using the SORT and INDEX commands from the dot prompt or their equivalent options in the Control Center menus.

In this chapter, an increasing number of commands will be executed from the dot prompt, rather than through Control Center menus. Although you can perform your sorting and indexing tasks with either method, many of the more complex sorting and indexing operations can be performed more quickly from the dot prompt. Since it is good to have an understanding of both methods, the chapter will include coverage of both methods; use whichever method you are more comfortable with for your own use.

Sorting

When dBASE IV sorts a database, it creates a new file with a different filename. If you were to sort a database of names in alphabetical order, the new file would contain all of the records that were in the old file, but they would be arranged in alphabetical order, as shown in Figure 6-1.

From the dot prompt, the basic format for the SORT command is as follows:

SORT ON *fieldname* [/A/C/D] TO *new-filename*

As a brief example, the command

```
SORT ON LASTNAME TO NEWFILE
```

from the dot prompt creates another database called NEWFILE that has the same records as the original database but is sorted in alphabetical order by the LASTNAME field.

Figure 6-1.

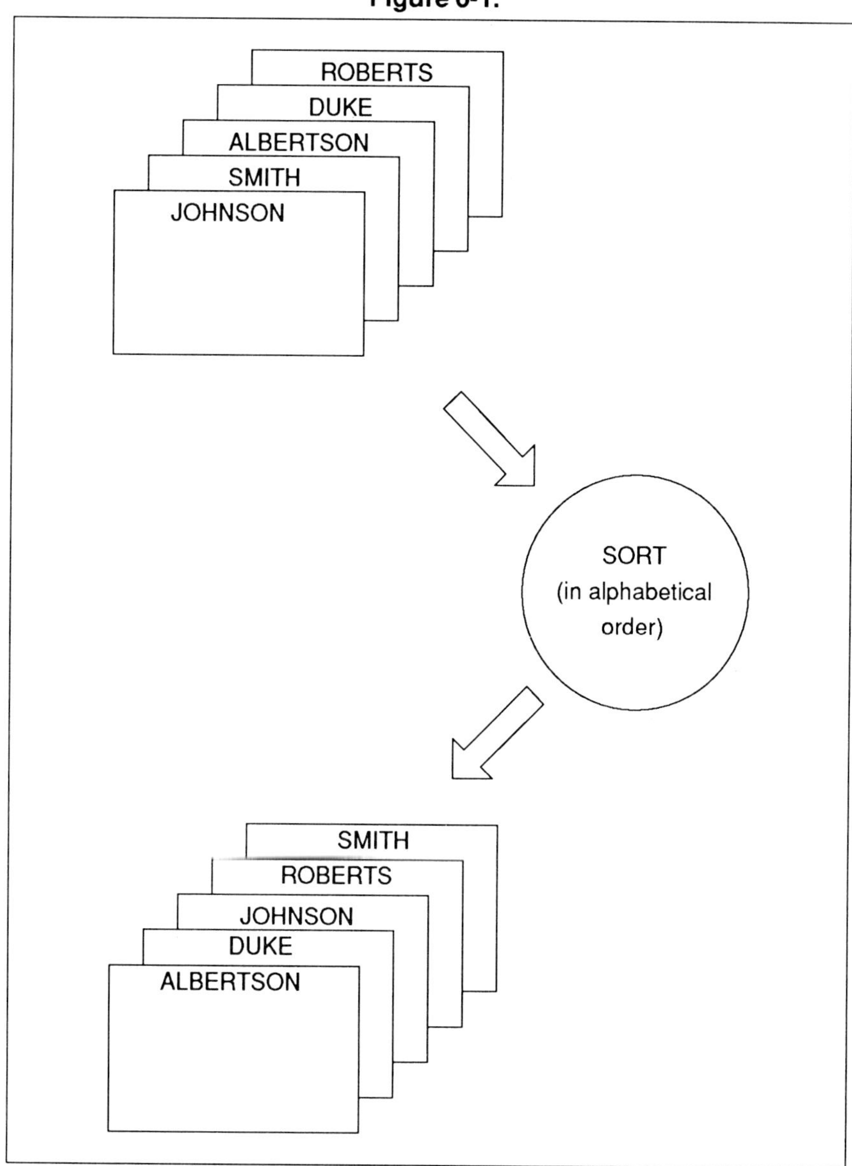

Sorting records in a database

From the Control Center, you highlight the database file to be sorted, press ENTER, and choose Modify Structure/Order. You then choose Sort Database on Field List from the Organize menu that appears, fill in the desired fields for the sort order, and enter a name for the sorted file. A new file is created, sorted by the field that you specify.

Users of dBASE IV versions 1.1 and later should note that you can also get to the Organize menu, used for sorting or indexing files, from the Browse and Edit screens. While in Browse or Edit mode, press ALT-O to open the Organize menu. The menu choices are then the same as described here.

If you specify the A option, the file will be sorted in alphabetical order, or numeric fields will be sorted in numerical order. If you use the D option, character fields are sorted in descending order—Z to A—or numeric fields are sorted from highest to lowest. If you do not use A or D, dBASE IV assumes that ascending order is your preference. If you sort on date fields, they will appear in chronological order. You cannot sort on logical fields or on memo fields.

Sorts are also normally in ASCII order, with uppercase letters treated differently than lowercase letters. Ascending ASCII order is A through Z and then a through z. Descending ASCII order is Z through A and then z through a. If you want uppercase and lowercase letters treated equally in the sorting order, include the C option.

Try sorting the file to alphabetize the employees in the ABCSTAFF file. From the Control Center, highlight ABCSTAFF and press ENTER. From the next menu to appear, choose Modify Structure/Order. When the Organize menu appears, select Sort Database on Field List. You will now see an entry screen similar to the one shown in Figure 6-2.

In the Field Order column, you can enter the name of the field that will control the sort order. In the Type of Sort column, you can press the spacebar to change the order from ascending to descending and from ASCII order (capitals before small letters) to dictionary order (capitals and lowercase letters treated alike).

Figure 6-2.

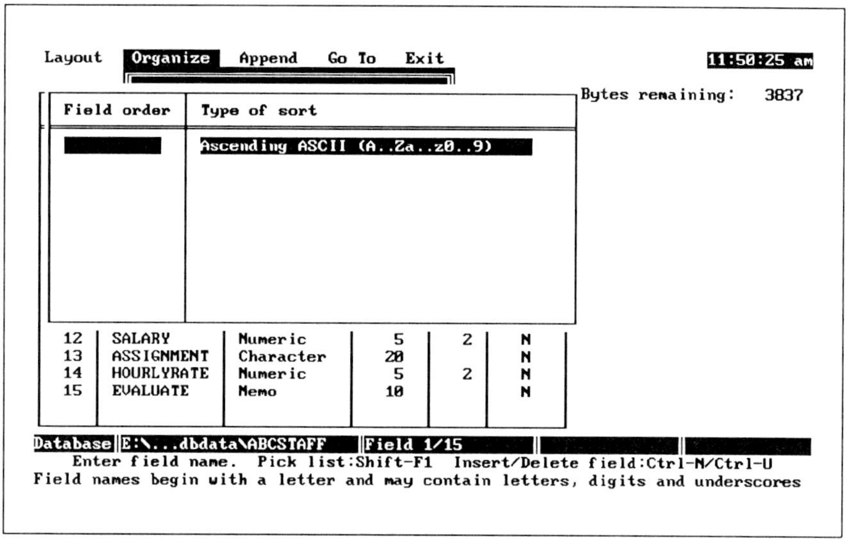

```
Layout  Organize  Append  Go To  Exit                         11:50:25 am
                                          Bytes remaining:   3837
  Field order | Type of sort
              | Ascending ASCII (A..Za..z0..9)

 12 | SALARY      | Numeric    |  5 | 2 | N
 13 | ASSIGNMENT  | Character  | 20 |   | N
 14 | HOURLYRATE  | Numeric    |  5 | 2 | N
 15 | EVALUATE    | Memo       | 10 |   | N
Database E:\...dbdata\ABCSTAFF   Field 1/15
  Enter field name.  Pick list:Shift-F1  Insert/Delete field:Ctrl-N/Ctrl-U
Field names begin with a letter and may contain letters, digits and underscores
```

Entry screen for sort fields

Enter **LASTNAME** as the desired field, and the cursor will move to the box for the type of sort. Try pressing the spacebar repeatedly, and notice the various choices. Continue pressing the spacebar until the Ascending Dictionary choice is displayed, and then press CTRL-END to accept it. You will be prompted for a name for the sorted file; enter **STAFF2** as the filename. Once you enter the filename, the sorting process will begin. If you are using version 1.1 from the menus, you will be prompted for a description of the new file; you can simply press CTRL-END to bypass this. When the sorting process is complete, press CTRL-END again to leave the Modify Structure/Order screen and return to the Control Center.

REMEMBER Sorting always creates a duplicate of the original file. You must put the new file in use to view or print the sorted records.

The file has been sorted, but you are still using the original ABCSTAFF file at this point. To see the results, you must use the new file. Highlight STAFF2 and press ENTER, select Use File from the menu that appears, and then press F2 to see the data. In Browse mode it is apparent that the new file is in alphabetical order by last name, as shown in Figure 6-3.

The old file, ABCSTAFF, still exists in its unchanged form. The sorting operation has added a new file called STAFF2 that is in alphabetical order. Remember, a file cannot be sorted onto itself in dBASE IV; each time a sort is performed, a new file must be created.

Now try a sort option from the dot prompt. Press ESC twice, once to get to the Control Center and once to exit from the Control Center menus. Answer **Y** to the "Abandon operation?" prompt to get to the dot prompt.

Figure 6-3.

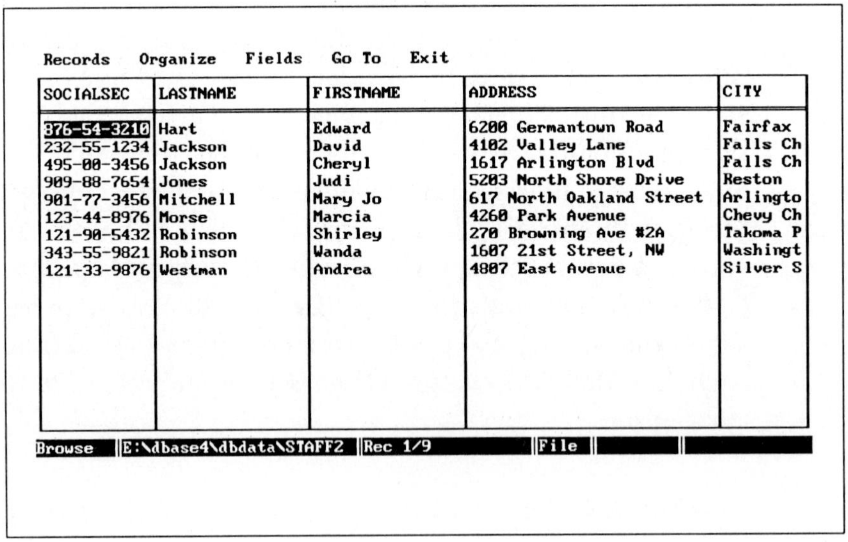

Records Organize Fields Go To Exit

SOCIALSEC	LASTNAME	FIRSTNAME	ADDRESS	CITY
376-54-3210	Hart	Edward	6200 Germantown Road	Fairfax
232-55-1234	Jackson	David	4102 Valley Lane	Falls Ch
495-00-3456	Jackson	Cheryl	1617 Arlington Blvd	Falls Ch
909-88-7654	Jones	Judi	5203 North Shore Drive	Reston
901-77-3456	Mitchell	Mary Jo	617 North Oakland Street	Arlingto
123-44-8976	Morse	Marcia	4260 Park Avenue	Chevy Ch
121-90-5432	Robinson	Shirley	270 Browning Ave #2A	Takoma P
343-55-9821	Robinson	Wanda	1607 21st Street, NW	Washingt
121-33-9876	Westman	Andrea	4807 East Avenue	Silver S

Browse E:\dbase4\dbdata\STAFF2 Rec 1/9 File

Records sorted by last name

First you must use the file you want to sort, so you need a USE *filename* command followed by the desired SORT command. Try the following commands:

```
USE ABCSTAFF
SORT ON DATEHIRED TO STAFF3
```

In a few moments, you'll see a message indicating the completion of the sorting process and the message "Copying text file." The "Copying text file" message indicates that the text of the memo field is being copied to the new file. Once the dot prompt reappears, enter

```
USE STAFF3
LIST LASTNAME, DATEHIRED
```

You will then see the following:

Record#	LASTNAME	DATEHIRED
1	Morse	07/25/85
2	Jackson	09/05/85
3	Westman	07/04/86
4	Jones	08/12/86
5	Hart	10/19/86
6	Robinson	09/17/87
7	Jackson	09/19/87
8	Robinson	11/17/87
9	Mitchell	12/01/87

This shows that the records in the new file are arranged in the order of the hire date, with the earliest dates first. Enter

```
USE ABCSTAFF
```

Now try the SORT command with the /D option (for descending order) on the LASTNAME field by entering the following.

```
SORT ON LASTNAME /D TO STAFF4
```

To see the results, you need to list the new file you created. Enter this:

```
USE STAFF4
LIST LASTNAME
```

The results should be

```
Record#          LASTNAME
      1          Westman
      2          Robinson
      3          Robinson
      4          Morse
      5          Mitchell
      6          Jones
      7          Jackson
      8          Jackson
      9          Hart
```

Return to ABCSTAFF by entering **USE ABCSTAFF** at the dot prompt. Then, for an example of numerical sorting, enter

```
SORT ON SALARY TO STAFF5
```

To see the results, enter

```
USE STAFF5
LIST LASTNAME, SALARY
```

This listing should appear:

Record#	LASTNAME	SALARY
1	Jackson	8.00
2	Mitchell	8.00
3	Robinson	8.00
4	Robinson	8.00
5	Hart	8.50
6	Morse	9.00
7	Jackson	12.00
8	Jones	12.50
9	Westman	16.50

It shows the salaries arranged in ascending order.

Before going back to the Control Center to consider the topic of sorting on multiple fields, you may want to perform some housekeeping by deleting the example files you just created. This can easily be done from the dot prompt. First enter

```
USE ABCSTAFF
```

to close the file you are currently working with, and then open the original ABCSTAFF database. (You will get an error message if you ever try to erase a file that is open.) Next, enter these commands to erase the files:

```
DELETE FILE STAFF2.DBF
DELETE FILE STAFF3.DBF
DELETE FILE STAFF4.DBF
DELETE FILE STAFF5.DBF

DELETE FILE STAFF2.DBT
DELETE FILE STAFF3.DBT
DELETE FILE STAFF4.DBT
DELETE FILE STAFF5.DBT
```

REMEMBER You can also erase files with the DOS Utilities, available through the Tools menu of the Control Center. DOS utilities are covered in Chapter 10.

Sorting on Multiple Fields

Sometimes you may need to sort on more than one field. For example, if you alphabetize a list of names that is divided into FIRSTNAME and LASTNAME fields, you would not be able to sort only on the LASTNAME field if there were three people with Williams as their last name. You would also have to sort on the FIRSTNAME field to find the correct ordering of the three Williamses.

Fortunately, dBASE IV can sort on more than one field. This can be done from the dot prompt by listing the fields as part of the SORT command, separating them with commas. From the Control Center, sorting on multiple fields is done by entering more than one field name in the entry screen for the sort fields. You can also sort on a combination of different types of fields, such as a numeric field and a character field, at the same time.

As an example, consider the recent sort you did by salary amount. Although the salary amounts were in order, there were a large number of employees with the same salaries, and employees within that salary group fell in random order. Sorting the file in order of salary, and within equal salary groups by order of the employees' last names, would provide a more logical listing. Try it first from the Control Center. Enter **ASSIST** to get back to the Control Center, highlight ABCSTAFF, and press ENTER. From the next menu to appear, choose Modify Structure/Order. When the Organize menu appears, select Sort Database on Field List. In a moment, the entry screen for the sort fields will appear.

Enter **SALARY** as the desired field order, and the cursor will move to the Type of Sort box. The choice for Ascending ASCII is fine, so press ENTER to move to the next line. Enter **LASTNAME** as the second field for the sort order. In the Type of Sort box, press the spacebar until Ascending Dictionary appears as the choice. Press CTRL-END to accept the choice, and enter **STAFF2** as the name for the sorted file.

When the sorting process is complete, press CTRL-END again to leave the Modify Structure/Order screen and return to the Control Center. Highlight the new file, STAFF2, in the Data panel and press F2 to see the data sorted by salary and last name, as shown in Figure 6-4. (In the figure, the SOCIALSEC and LASTNAME fields have been locked to allow the LASTNAME and SALARY fields to be viewed at the same time.) When you

Figure 6-4.

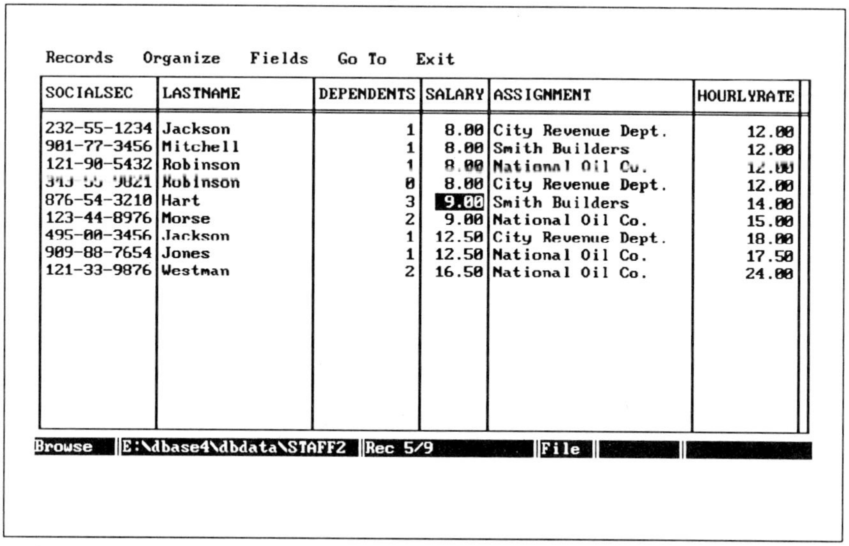

Records   Organize   Fields   Go To   Exit

SOCIALSEC	LASTNAME	DEPENDENTS	SALARY	ASSIGNMENT	HOURLYRATE
232-55-1234	Jackson	1	8.00	City Revenue Dept.	12.00
901-77-3456	Mitchell	1	8.00	Smith Builders	12.00
121-90-5432	Robinson	1	8.00	National Oil Co.	12.00
343-55-9821	Robinson	0	8.00	City Revenue Dept.	12.00
876-54-3210	Hart	3	9.00	Smith Builders	14.00
123-44-8976	Morse	2	9.00	National Oil Co.	15.00
495-00-3456	Jackson	1	12.50	City Revenue Dept.	18.00
909-88-7654	Jones	1	12.50	National Oil Co.	17.50
121-33-9876	Westman	2	16.50	National Oil Co.	24.00

Browse | E:\dbase4\dbdata\STAFF2 | Rec 5/9 | File

File sorted by SALARY and LASTNAME fields

have finished viewing the data, press ESC to get back to the Control Center.

To do this type of sort from the dot prompt, the format for the command is

SORT ON *1st-field /D , 2nd-field /D... last-field /D*
TO *new-filename*

You could perform the same sort as you just performed from the Control Center by getting to the dot prompt and entering commands like

```
USE ABCSTAFF
SORT ON SALARY, LASTNAME /AC TO STAFF2
```

The database would be sorted on both fields in ascending order because the /D option was not specified. The /C option was included, so the sort would be in dictionary order instead of ASCII order.

To see the results of a descending-order sort on multiple fields, use ESC to get back to the dot prompt and enter these commands:

```
USE ABCSTAFF
SORT ON SALARY /D, LASTNAME /D TO STAFF2
```

Because you are now trying to overwrite a file you have already created (STAFF2.DBF), you will see a message warning you that the file exists. Select Overwrite from the message box to tell dBASE that you want to overwrite the previous file, and the sort will occur. To see the results, enter

```
USE STAFF2
LIST LASTNAME, SALARY
```

and the results this time will resemble the following:

Record#	LASTNAME	SALARY
1	Westman	16.50
2	Jones	12.50
3	Jackson	12.00
4	Morse	9.00
5	Hart	8.50
6	Robinson	8.00
7	Robinson	8.00
8	Mitchell	8.00
9	Jackson	8.00

This shows the file is sorted in descending order by salary, and where the salaries are equal, in descending order by last names. In this sort, the SALARY field is the *primary field.* A primary field is the field that will be sorted first by the SORT command. After the database has been sorted by the primary field, if there is any duplicate information in the first field, SORT will sort the duplicate information by the second field listed in the command, known as the *secondary field.*

It is possible to sort further with additional secondary fields; you can, in fact, sort with all fields in the database. As an example, try these commands:

```
USE ABCSTAFF
SORT ON STATE, SALARY, LASTNAME TO MASTER
```

This creates a database called MASTER that alphabetizes records by state. Inside each group of states, records are arranged by salary and then by employees' last names. In this example, STATE is the primary sort field and SALARY and LASTNAME are secondary fields.

When the sort is complete, enter this:

```
USE MASTER
LIST STATE, SALARY, LASTNAME
```

The database with the STATE, SALARY, and LASTNAME fields will be displayed, as shown here:

Record#	STATE	SALARY	LASTNAME
1	DC	8.00	Robinson
2	MD	8.00	Robinson
3	MD	9.00	Morse
4	MD	16.50	Westman
5	VA	8.00	Jackson
6	VA	8.00	Mitchell
7	VA	8.50	Hart
8	VA	12.00	Jackson
9	VA	12.50	Jones

Sorting with Qualifiers on a Subset of a Database

Adding a *FOR statement* as a qualifier to a SORT command lets you produce a sorted file that contains only a specific subset of the records in the database. The format for this kind of SORT command is

SORT ON *fieldname* [/A/C/D] TO *new-filename* FOR *condition*

To produce a new database, sorted by salary amounts and containing only records with Virginia addresses, try the following commands:

```
SORT ON SALARY TO VAPERSON FOR STATE = "VA"
USE VAPERSON
LIST LASTNAME, STATE, SALARY
```

The results will appear as

Record#	LASTNAME	STATE	SALARY
1	Jackson	VA	8.00
2	Mitchell	VA	8.00
3	Hart	VA	8.50
4	Jackson	VA	12.00
5	Jones	VA	12.50

This shows the result of the use of the qualifying FOR condition. The new database contains only the records of employees located in Virginia.

Additional examples of the conditional use of SORT include the following:

```
SORT ON LASTNAME, SALARY TO STAFF2 FOR SALARY < 10

SORT ON ZIP TO PACIFIC FOR ZIP >= "90000"
```

You may want to note that the arrangement of the command components can differ and still have the same results. For example, the command

```
SORT TO MYFILE ON LASTNAME, SALARY FOR SALARY > 8
```

will have the same result as the command

```
SORT ON LASTNAME, SALARY TO MYFILE FOR SALARY > 8
```

Selective sorting is one area in which working at the dot prompt, once you know the syntax of the commands, can be much faster than using the Control Center menus. To do this type of selective sort from the Control Center, you would have to create a query that would limit the records to those that meet your desired condition, and you would have to include a sorting order within that query. In the time it takes to finish the query form, you could have entered the entire command from the dot prompt to do the job.

Why Sort?

Now that you've learned all about sorting with dBASE IV, you should know why you should not sort a database—at least, not very often. Sorting with dBASE IV is relatively fast, particularly when compared with earlier versions of dBASE. Still, sorting can be very time-consuming, particularly when you are sorting large files or sorting on multiple fields. Sorting also uses a lot of disk space. Each time a sort occurs, dBASE IV creates a new file that is as large as the original. For this reason, you must limit the database to no more than half the space on the disk if you are going to sort it.

Adding records to a database merely complicates matters. After you add records, chances are that the database must be sorted to maintain the desired order. If you need to view a database in several different orders, the sorting time can become prohibitive. There is a more efficient way of arranging a database alphabetically, numerically, or chronologically: by using index files.

Indexing

An *index* is a file that lets you view or list a database in a particular order without actually rearranging or copying the database records. An index file consists of at least one field from the database. The field is sorted alphabetically, numerically, or

Figure 6-5.

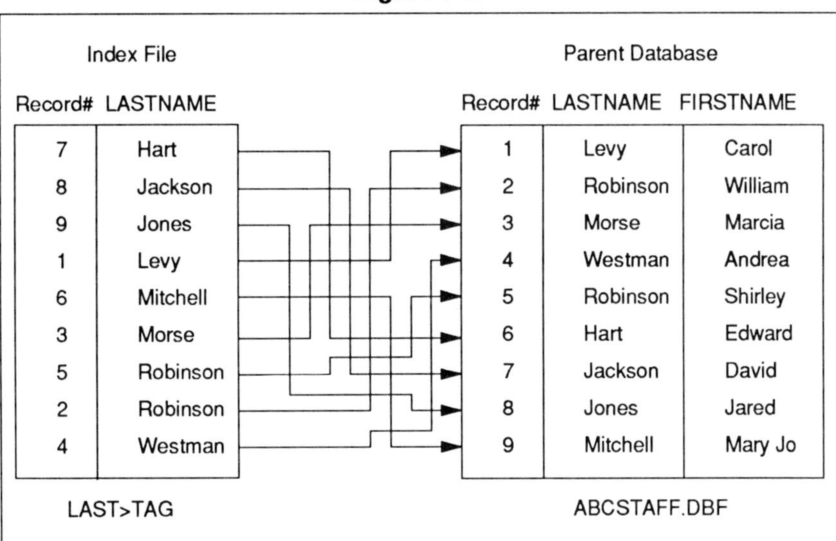

Index file alphabetized by LASTNAME and database

chronologically, and with each entry in the field is the corresponding record number from the database. The record number is used to reference the record in the parent database, as in Figure 6-5.

In effect, an index file provides an "imaginary sorting" of the database, since none of the records in the database are sorted. Just as a book index is a separate section that indicates where information is located, a dBASE IV index file is a separate file that contains information regarding the location of individual records in the database.

When the database file is opened along with the index file, the first record to be retrieved is not the first record in the database; instead, it is the first record listed in the index. The next record retrieved will be the second record listed in the index, and so on. Remember, indexing does not affect the order of the records within the database. Indexes can be updated automatically to accommodate new records or other changes to your data, and indexes also allow you to quickly find records.

Types of Indexes

dBASE IV can maintain its index information in one of two ways; either method accomplishes the same result of keeping things in order. The first method uses a *multiple index file* with an extension of .MDX. This file maintains information on the different indexes that you create within a single file. dBASE IV can have more than one multiple index file open at a time, and each multiple index (.MDX) file can contain data about more than one index. However, only one index file—the active index file—will control the order of the records you see. (You will learn more about this later in the chapter.)

When you check the Index box while designing or modifying the structure of a database, the information used to later maintain that index gets saved in an .MDX file that by default has the same name as the database. This .MDX file, known as the *production .MDX file,* is then opened and updated automatically whenever you open the database file. You can also add new indexes to the production index file at any time with the Create New Index option of the Organize menu; any index that you create with this option becomes a part of the production .MDX file.

The second method of indexing your files is to create individual .NDX index files for each index desired. With this approach, the information for every index is stored in a separate file. If you wanted to index a file on last names and also on ZIP codes, you would need two separate .NDX files to do this.

The two methods of indexing exist for an important reason: compatibility with earlier versions of dBASE (specifically dBASE III and dBASE III PLUS). The first method of indexing, using the multiple index file to hold all the index information, is faster and more efficient. However, dBASE III and dBASE III PLUS cannot use the multiple index files. dBASE IV therefore provides menu options and dot-prompt commands that let you work with .NDX index files, which are the index-file style used by dBASE III and dBASE III PLUS. If you must share data with other users of dBASE III or dBASE III PLUS, you may want to create and use the .NDX-style index files to maintain compatibility.

The .NDX-style index files can also be used for indexes that are used infrequently. As an example, you might have an index for use with a monthly report that you might not want to update every time you use the index. However, when you do want to update indexes regularly or when compatibility with earlier versions of dBASE is not required, you can stick with the newer versions of the index files and ignore the .NDX file options.

From the dot prompt, the general format of the INDEX command is similar to the format of the SORT command:

INDEX ON *fieldname* TAG *index-tag-name*

This version of the INDEX command will add an index "tag" to the production .MDX index file. If compatibility with dBASE III/III PLUS is needed, the command takes on a slightly different form:

INDEX ON *fieldname* TO *filename*

This variant of the INDEX command produces a single .NDX index file containing the index information.

When you type **Y** for yes in the Index box during the design of a database, dBASE IV automatically creates a production .MDX file to accompany the database. The index file is given the same name as the database file, but it has an extension of .MDX. Therefore, ABCSTAFF.MDX is the production index file that is currently controlling the order of your records when you use the ABCSTAFF database.

Depending on the type of index you create, dBASE IV appends the extension .MDX or .NDX to all index files. To list these files with the DIR command from the dot prompt, you must explicitly supply the .MDX or .NDX extension. For example, the command

```
DIR *.MDX
```

will generate a list of .MDX index files.

Creating an Index

Suppose that you need to arrange the employee list in alphabetical order by city for ABC Temporaries. You can create an index file by getting to the dot prompt and entering the following commands:

```
USE ABCSTAFF
INDEX ON CITY TAG TOWNS
```

Enter **LIST LASTNAME, CITY** and you will see the result of the new index file:

```
Record#     LASTNAME    CITY
      4     Mitchell    Arlington
      1     Morse       Chevy Chase
      8     Hart        Fairfax
      3     Jackson     Falls Church
      6     Jackson     Falls Church
      9     Jones       Reston
      2     Westman     Silver Spring
      5     Robinson    Takoma Park
      7     Robinson    Washington
```

Notice that the record numbers are not in order. The order of the records is now controlled by the index tag you just created, so the records appear in alphabetical order by city.

If you wanted to build the same type of index while maintaining compatibility with earlier versions of dBASE, the command would be

```
INDEX ON CITY TO TOWNS
```

It would create the TOWNS.NDX index file containing the index information. It is a good idea to give an index file a name that is related in some manner to the indexed field. This helps you and others keep track of how the file was indexed and what field was used.

From the Control Center, you can index a file by highlighting the desired file and pressing ENTER, then choosing Modify Structure/Order from the next menu to appear. When the Organize menu appears, choose Create New Index. Once you choose this option, you will be prompted for a name for the index and for an index expression. This expression is usually the name of the field on which you wish to index, but it can be a combination of fields. dBASE IV version 1.1 users should keep in mind that the Organize menu is also available from the Edit and Browse screens by pressing ALT-O.

To try indexing from the Control Center, enter **ASSIST** at the dot prompt. When the Control Center appears, with ABCSTAFF highlighted, press ENTER. Choose Modify Structure/Order from the next menu to appear. In a moment, the Organize menu will appear (see Figure 6-6).

The options in the upper half of the Organize menu all apply to index files. The first option is used to create a new index, while the next option, Modify Existing Index, lets you change the order of an index created previously. The Order Records by Index option lets you choose an index tag or an index file to control the order of the records. The Activate .NDX Index File option lets you specify a dBASE III-style index file that will be kept current as changes are made to the database. The Include .NDX Index File option lets you add a dBASE III-style index file to the catalog that is currently active. (A *catalog* is a list of the files that you are using; catalogs are covered in more detail in Chapter 12.) Finally, the Remove Unwanted Index Tag option lets you remove an index tag from the index file currently in use.

In this case, a new index is desired, so choose the first option, Create New Index. When you do so, another menu will appear, as shown in Figure 6-7. With the name of the index highlighted, press ENTER and enter **BYNAMES**. For the Index Expression entry, press ENTER to begin the entry and enter **LASTNAME** as the expression. Version 1.1 users have a FOR clause as the next option. This option lets you build selective indexes, a topic dis-

Figure 6-6.

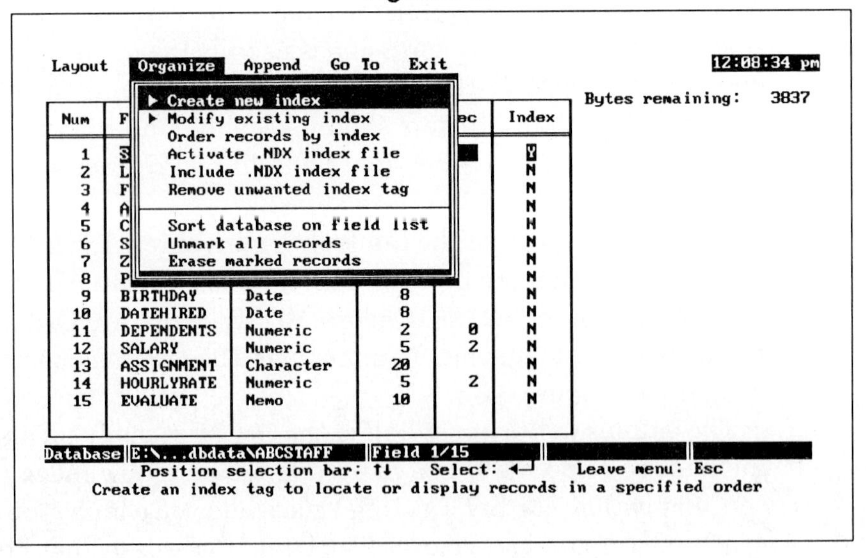

Organize menu

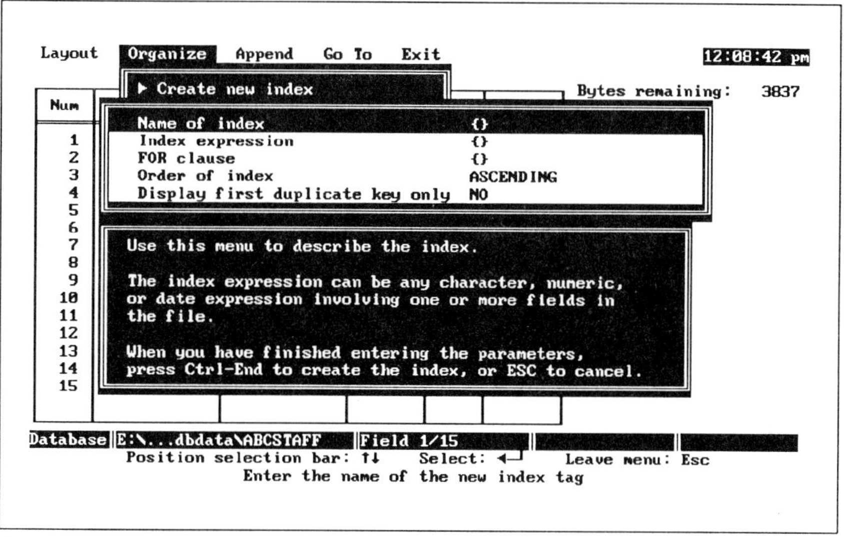

Secondary menu options

cussed in detail later in this chapter. For now, press down arrow to skip past this option if you have it. The Order Of Index option is fine with its default value of Ascending, so you needn't change it. You can also leave the last option, Display First Duplicate Key Only, set to its default of No. If this option is set to Yes, only the first record of multiple records with the same index value would be included in the index.

Press CTRL-END to accept the changes and create the index. When the indexing is completed, press CTRL-END again to get back to the Control Center. With ABCSTAFF highlighted, press F2 (Data) to view the file; it will appear in order, by last name. Before continuing, press ESC twice and then type **Y** to get back to the dot prompt.

Indexing on Multiple Fields

You can index by several fields. The process is similar to sorting on multiple fields. There is one limitation, however: you cannot directly index multiple fields that are not of the same field type. For example, you could not index by last name and salary, because SALARY is a numeric field and LASTNAME is a character field. You can, however, circumvent this problem by using special operators known as functions; this technique will be discussed later.

Examine the effect of the BYNAMES index again by entering **LIST LASTNAME, FIRSTNAME**. Now notice that Cheryl Jackson is listed after David Jackson, which is not a fully alphabetical order. Because you indexed the file on last names only, the order of the first names was ignored. To correct the situation, enter

```
INDEX ON LASTNAME + FIRSTNAME TAG ALLNAMES
```

In the index, records having the same last name are now indexed by last names and then by first names. To see the results, enter

```
LIST LASTNAME, FIRSTNAME
```

HINT Press the up arrow key to repeat the LIST command you used earlier.

The listing should be as follows:

Record#	LASTNAME	FIRSTNAME
8	Hart	Edward
6	Jackson	Cheryl
3	Jackson	David
9	Jones	Judi
4	Mitchell	Mary Jo

```
1           Morse           Marcia
5           Robinson        Shirley
7           Robinson        Wanda
2           Westman         Andrea
```

You can use this technique to create an index file on any number of fields within a record. The plus symbol (+) is always used with the INDEX command to tie the fields together. For example, the INDEX command

```
INDEX ON ZIPCODE + LASTNAME + FIRSTNAME TAG TOTAL
```

would result in a database that is indexed on three levels: by ZIP codes, by last names for records having the same ZIP code, and by first names for records having the same last name. The dBASE III- and III PLUS-compatible version of the command would be

```
INDEX ON ZIPCODE + LASTNAME + FIRSTNAME TO TOTAL
```

As you might expect, multiple-key indexes are valuable aids when you are dealing with a large database and must organize it into comprehensible subgroups.

Indexing on Multiple Fields From the Control Center

You will also need to use the plus symbol to build a list of multiple index fields if you use the Control Center menus to index your files. To see how this works, enter **ASSIST**.

With ABCSTAFF highlighted, press ENTER. Choose Modify Structure/Order from the next menu, and the Organize menu will appear. Select Create New Index, and enter **SAMPLE** as the name for the index. The next entry needed in the menu that now

Figure 6-8.

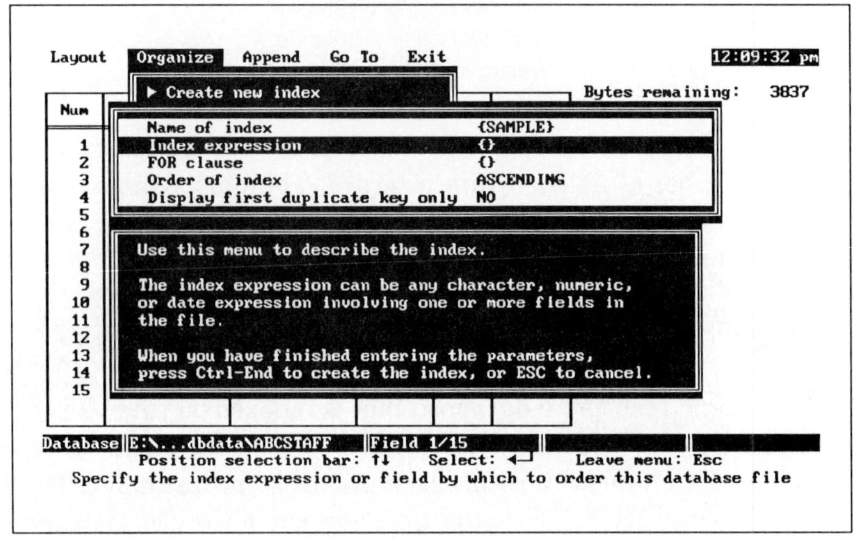

Index option from Control Center menu

appears is the Index expression (Figure 6-8). What this doesn't tell you (at least, not in a clear fashion) is that in addition to entering the name of a single field, you can enter multiple fields separated by plus signs.

As an example, enter the following:

```
ZIPCODE + LASTNAME + FIRSTNAME
```

Notice that as you enter a long string, the characters in the window scroll to make room for the complete character string. Once you have pressed ENTER, you can press CTRL-END to accept the remaining options and create the index. The new index file, arranged in order of the fields that you specified, will be created.

REMEMBER As with sorting, when you index on multiple fields, the first field named takes priority.

When the indexing is complete, you can examine the results by pressing CTRL-END to get back to the Control Center and pressing F2 (Data) to view the file. When you are done, press ESC twice and then type **Y** to get back to the dot prompt.

Indexing on Fields of Different Types

One of the INDEX command's limitations is that in its basic form, it does not allow you to directly index on combinations of fields that are of different types. For example, you cannot index on a combination of the last name and rental amount fields in the ABC Realty database. To see the problem, try either of the following commands at the dot prompt:

```
INDEX ON LASTNAME + SALARY TAG TEST

INDEX ON LASTNAME + BIRTHDAY TAG TEST
```

The resulting error message, "Data type mismatch", tells you that dBASE IV cannot index on a combination of fields that are of differing data types (such as date and character fields).

The secret to indexing on fields that are not of the same type is to use *functions* to convert fields that are not character data into character data. Functions are used to perform special operations that supplement the normal dBASE IV commands, and will be explained in greater detail in the programming portion of this text. For now, it is sufficient to know about two functions: the DTOS (Date-to-String) function, and the STR (String) function. The DTOS function will convert the contents of a date field into a string of characters. The STR function will convert the contents of a numeric field into a string of characters. You can use the

DTOS and STR functions in combination with your INDEX commands to accomplish the same result as indexing on combinations of different types of fields.

The normal format for an INDEX command, when combined with these functions, is

> INDEX ON *character field* + STR(*numeric field*) +
> DTOS(*date field*) TAG *index-tag-name*

As with all INDEX commands, you can use a combination of additional fields in whatever order you prefer to build the index. As an example of the use of these functions, to build an index file that is indexed in alphabetical order by state and in chronological order by date within each group of states, you would enter this command:

```
INDEX ON STATE + STR(SALARY) TO TEST
```

You would then enter

```
LIST LASTNAME, STATE, SALARY
```

to see the results of the index file.

NOTE For more details on functions, see the programming portion of this text. For a complete list of functions, see Appendix B.

You can also use these functions within the Control Center menus by entering the functions along with the field names when the menu prompts you for the index expression.

Selective Indexing

If you are using dBASE IV version 1.1 or later, you can use the FOR clause with the INDEX ON command (or the FOR option which appears after you choose Create New Index from the menus) to add a clause that limits the records stored in the index. From the dot prompt, the syntax for the index command becomes

INDEX ON *expression* TO *filename* FOR *condition*

where *condition* is any expression that evaluates to a logical true or false. This is a powerful indexing option that can, in effect, filter the database of unwanted records while placing records in order at the same time. Using the SET FILTER command along with the INDEX command would accomplish the same result, but assuming an updated index already exists, using FOR with INDEX ON is faster. As an example, you can easily produce a listing of those employees living in Maryland or Virginia, indexed in ZIP code order. If you are using version 1.1 or later, at the dot prompt, enter the following commands:

```
INDEX ON ZIPCODE TAG ZIPS FOR STATE = "MD" .OR. STATE = "VA"
LIST LASTNAME, STATE, ZIPCODE
```

You will see from the resultant listing that the index contains only those records with "MD" or "VA" in the STATE field. The records with "DC" in the STATE field are still in the database, but because they were not included in the index, they do not appear when you use the LIST command. If you now close the index file by closing and reopening the database and again perform a listing with the commands

```
USE ABCSTAFF
LIST LASTNAME, STATE, ZIPCODE
```

you will see that the records are still present in the database.

Note that you can only use the FOR clause with multiple index (.MDX) files. You cannot use FOR with dBASE III PLUS-style index files.

Using SET ORDER

In many cases you will create and work with more than one index for a database. However, the order in which the records appear (or are printed) is controlled by only one index. For an index to control the order of the records, it must be *active*. An index that has just been created is active; the SET ORDER command makes a dormant index active.

HINT When more than one index is open, use SET ORDER to tell dBASE which index should control the order of the records.

The SET ORDER command is the dot-prompt equivalent of choosing the Order Records by Index option from the Organize menu. Remember that you can only use SET ORDER with an open index; if the index file has not been opened, you cannot use SET ORDER.

Suppose that you need three lists from the ABCSTAFF database. The first list must be in order by salary, the second by last name, and the third by ZIP code. Create the indexes from these three fields now with the following commands:

```
INDEX ON LASTNAME TAG NAME
INDEX ON SALARY TAG PAY
```

```
INDEX ON ZIPCODE TAG ZIP
```

These commands create three indexes in your production index file: NAME, PAY, and ZIP. Each index contains the appropriate field from each record and the corresponding record numbers. NAME, for example, contains last names in alphabetical order and the matching record numbers for each last name. Since ZIP was the last index created, it is the active index.

By using the SET ORDER command you can activate any index. You can also use it to activate a dBASE III- or III PLUS-compatible .NDX file. For example, to activate and display the database organized by salary instead of by ZIP code, enter

```
SET ORDER TO TAG PAY
LIST LASTNAME, SALARY
```

The display should appear as follows:

```
Record#         LASTNAME       SALARY
      3         Jackson        8.00
      4         Mitchell       8.00
      5         Robinson       8.00
      7         Robinson       8.00
      8         Hart           8.50
      1         Morse          9.00
      6         Jackson        12.00
      9         Jones          12.50
      2         Westman        16.50
```

Now try the same method to activate and display the ZIP file:

```
SET ORDER TO TAG ZIP
LIST LASTNAME, ZIPCODE
```

The display should appear as follows:

```
Record#         LASTNAME       ZIPCODE
      7         Robinson       20009-0101
```

1	Morse	20815-0988
2	Westman	20910-0124
5	Robinson	20912-1234
8	Hart	22025
3	Jackson	22044
6	Jackson	22044
9	Jones	22090
4	Mitchell	22203

Remember, ZIP codes are stored as characters, so they will be indexed "alphabetically," which explains why the nine-digit ZIP codes are not at the bottom of the list.

Open Index Tags and Open Files

Although you can have only one index active at a time, you can have up to seven *open files*. If an index file is open, any changes you make to the parent database will automatically be updated in all the index tags contained within that index file. For example, adding a record to ABCSTAFF will place the LASTNAME field of the new record and the record number in the NAME index and alphabetize the index file again, if ABCSTAFF.MDX (the multiple index file that contains the NAME index) is open. You do not need to explicitly open the production .MDX file, because it is opened automatically when you open the database. This is one of the main advantages of the production .MDX file, because it means that all of its tags are updated automatically whenever you update the database.

You can open an index with the USE INDEX command. (You can use the SET INDEX command to accomplish the same task, but SET INDEX will only open the file; in the case of .MDX files, it will not make any specific tag within that file active.) List the index files that you want opened after the USE INDEX command. For example, the command

```
USE INDEX ABCSTAFF
```

would open the ABCSTAFF.MDX index file, and all indexes in that file would be updated as the database is changed.

You can list more than one index filename with either the USE INDEX or the SET INDEX commands. As an example, the command

```
SET INDEX TO COSTS, NAMES
```

would open the COSTS and NAMES index files if they were not already open. You do not have to supply the .NDX extension in the command.

An active index is also an open index, so using SET INDEX will open a file. If you list more than one file with SET INDEX, all files will be open but only the first will be active.

To get an idea of why it is important to keep needed index files open, get to the dot prompt now (if you are not there already) and create two dBASE III- or III PLUS-compatible index files by entering the following commands:

```
INDEX ON LASTNAME TO NAMESDB3
INDEX ON ZIPCODE TO ZIPSDB3
```

Then you use the SET INDEX command to open both the ABC-STAFF.MDX index file and the NAMESDB3.NDX index file you just created.

```
SET INDEX TO ABCSTAFF, NAMESDB3
SET ORDER TO PAY
```

The two index files (that is, ABCSTAFF.MDX, containing PAY, and NAMESDB3.NDX) are now open. Enter

```
LIST LASTNAME, SALARY
```

The resulting display shows that the PAY index you specified with the SET ORDER is the active index, but NAMESDB3.NDX is also open. This is important if you add or edit records in the database, because as long as the index files are open they will be updated automatically.

To see how this works, enter **APPEND**. When the new blank record appears, enter this data:

```
SOCIALSEC: 111-22-3333
LASTNAME: Roberts
FIRSTNAME: Charles
ADDRESS: 247 Ocean Blvd
CITY: Vienna
STATE: VA
ZIPCODE: 22085
SALARY: 13.00
```

The remaining fields in the record may be left blank for now. Press CTRL-END to store the new record and get back to the dot prompt. Now enter this command again:

```
LIST LASTNAME, SALARY
```

The index file now includes the new entry in the proper order of salary.

This brings up an important point: whenever you make changes or add records to a database, dBASE IV automatically updates all open index files, which may slow down the entire operation—particularly if more than one index file is open at once. If you wish, you can close all open index files with the CLOSE INDEX command described shortly.

Using REINDEX

If you changed a database but didn't remember to open an index file, you can update the index with the REINDEX command. If the index file in use is a multiple index file, all tags contained within the file will be updated with REINDEX. You will want to do this with the ZIP index file, for example; because you did not open the ZIP index file, it does not include the newly added record. You can verify this by using the ZIP index and looking at the names in the database. Enter the following:

```
SET INDEX TO ZIPSDB3, ABCSTAFF
LIST LASTNAME
```

As you can see, the name "Roberts" does not appear in the database—the ZIP index was not open when you added the record:

```
Record#        LASTNAME
      7        Robinson
      1        Morse
      2        Westman
      5        Robinson
      8        Hart
      3        Jackson
      6        Jackson
      9        Jones
      4        Mitchell
```

To update an index that was not open at the time you added or edited records, you can use the REINDEX command. Try it now by entering **REINDEX**. You will see from the status messages, which appear on the screen, that whenever you reindex, all open files are indexed; in this case, this means all of the tags in the production .MDX file, as well as ZIPSDB3.

To display the updated result, enter **LIST LASTNAME**. The results are as follows:

Record#	LASTNAME
7	Robinson
1	Morse
2	Westman
5	Robinson
8	Hart
3	Jackson
6	Jackson
10	Roberts
9	Jones
4	Mitchell

The Roberts entry is now in the indexed ZIP file. Mr. Roberts is no longer needed in the database. Enter **DELETE RECORD 10** and then enter **PACK** to remove him from the list. Since the ZIP index file and the ABCSTAFF.MDX production index file are open, Roberts' ZIP code will be removed from all those indexes.

REMEMBER The PACK command automatically reindexes all open index files.

NOTE A power failure or hardware malfunction may damage an index file. If this happens REINDEX may not work properly. You'll need to use the INDEX command instead to reconstruct the index from scratch.

Using CLOSE INDEX

If you decide that you do not want to use an index file that is not the production .MDX file, the CLOSE INDEX command will close the index file and leave the associated database open. (CLOSE INDEX has no effect on the production .MDX file, which is always open as long as the database is open.) To execute the command from the dot prompt, you enter

```
CLOSE INDEX
```

Note that direct equivalents of the REINDEX and CLOSE INDEX commands are not available from the Control Center menus. To rebuild an index file while you are at the menus, you could choose the Modify Existing Index option of the Organize menu and create another index file with the same name and index expression as the old index file. However, with large databases, this is slower than using REINDEX at the dot prompt.

Searching for Specifics

You can use two additional dBASE IV commands with indexed files: FIND and SEEK. These commands quickly find information in an indexed file. Both commands operate only on the active index.

The format for the FIND command is

FIND *character-string*

where *character-string* is a group of characters that do not have to be surrounded by quotation marks. The format for SEEK is

SEEK *expression*

The *expression* can be a number, a character string (which must be surrounded by single or double quotes), an operator, or a variable (operators and variables are discussed in the programming portion of this text). When you are in Browse or Edit mode, you can accomplish the equivalent of the FIND and SEEK commands by choosing the Index Key Search option of the Go To menu.

FIND and SEEK will search the active index file and find the first record that matches your specifications. The record itself will not be displayed; the FIND and SEEK commands will simply locate the record pointer at the desired record and display the record number. If no match is found, dBASE IV will respond with a "Find not successful" error message.

To try the FIND command, enter

```
SET ORDER TO NAME
FIND Mitchell
DISPLAY
```

The result is shown here:

```
SOCIALSEC      LASTNAME      FIRSTNAME      ADDRESS...
901-77-3456    Mitchell      Mary Jo        617 North Oakland...
```

To try the SEEK command, enter

```
SET ORDER TO PAY
SEEK 16.50
DISPLAY
```

The result is shown here:

```
SOCIALSEC      LASTNAME      FIRSTNAME     ADDRESS...
121-33-9876    Westman       Andrea        4807 East Avenue...
```

Keep in mind that the FIND command expects a character string, so you need not enclose the character string with quotes. The SEEK command expects an expression, so if that expression is a character string, it must be surrounded by quotes. As an example, the following two commands have the same result, assuming that the active index is the LASTNAME field:

```
FIND Westman

SEEK "Westman"
```

Since SEEK expects an expression, you can use the SEEK command with numbers and dates when your indexes are based on numeric or date fields. (Remember to enclose dates in curly braces.)

REMEMBER A menu equivalent of the SEEK command is available from the Browse and Edit screens. From Browse or Edit mode, open the Go To menu with ALT-G, choose Index Key Search, and then enter your search expression.

The FIND and SEEK commands offer the advantage of speed over the LOCATE command (as discussed in Chapter 4). LOCATE is simple to use, but slow. In a database containing thousands of records, a LOCATE command can take several minutes. A FIND or SEEK command can accomplish the same task in a matter of seconds, because these commands make use of the active index to look up the record, rather than reading through the entire database from top to bottom. Keep in mind that the FIND command searches for an exact match in terms of the character string entered. If the ABC Realty database index is set to NAME, for example, the following commands would both find the record for Westman:

```
FIND Wes

FIND Westman
```

dBASE only looks at the number of characters in the search expression—in this case, it only looks at the first three characters of the index key when you enter **FIND Wes**. Note that the command

```
FIND wes
```

would not find the record, because dBASE IV considers uppercase and lowercase letters to be different characters. As far as dBASE IV is concerned, "Westman" and "westman" are different names.

One way to prevent problems with the case-sensitivity of dBASE IV is to design entry forms that store your character data as all uppercase letters. Another method is to use a dBASE IV function known as the UPPER function, which will be discussed in a later chapter.

Housekeeping

Adding numerous tags to a production index file will slow things down, because dBASE must take the time to update each file

Figure 6-9.

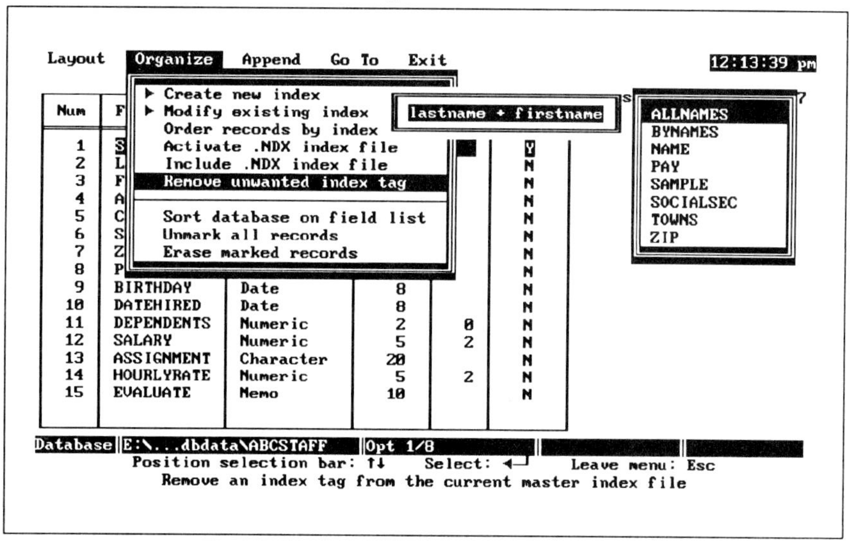

List of index tags

when you make changes. You may have already noticed that the REINDEX and PACK operations are now time-consuming, because your production index file contains numerous tags that must be updated. If you are no longer using tags you created earlier, you should remove those tags to speed up performance. You can do this by choosing the Remove Unwanted Index Tag option from the Organize menu.

To try this, enter **ASSIST** at the dot prompt to get back to the Control Center. Highlight the ABCSTAFF filename and press ENTER; then choose Modify/Organize Structure from the next menu. When the Organize menu appears, choose Remove Unwanted Index Tag. A pick list of available index tags will appear, similar to the example shown in Figure 6-9.

Select ALLNAMES from the list. Then choose the Remove Unwanted Index Tag option again; this time, choose BYNAMES from the list that appears. Repeat this process, and remove SAMPLE, TOWNS, and ZIP from the list. Finally, press CTRL-END twice, once to leave the menu and once to get back to the Control Center.

Indexing, Tips, and Unusual Cases

With all the different ways to arrange a file, you may occasionally run into some problems when indexing. The following sections cover some of the more unusual areas of indexing, along with hints for making your indexing as efficient as possible.

The Multiple Numeric Field Trap

With multiple numeric fields, things may not always turn out as you expect, due to the way dBASE IV builds an index expression. Consider a database of department store sales, with fields for customer name, high credit amounts, and balance amounts. You are preparing a mailing, and you want to target customers who have high credit lines and low account balances as likely prospects for heavy spending. You'd like to get an idea of who these customers are, so you prepare a report to show records sorted by high credit amounts. Where the high credit amounts are the same, you'd like to order the records by outstanding balance. If you use the INDEX command to do something like

```
USE SALES
INDEX ON HIGHCREDIT + BALANCE TO MAILER
LIST STORE, CUSTNAME, CUSTNUMB, HIGHCREDIT, BALANCE
```

the results will be as follows:

STORE	CUSTNAME	CUSTNUMB	HIGHCREDIT	BALANCE
Collin Creek	Artis, K.	1008	1200.00	0.00
Oak Lawn	Jones, C.	1003	900.00	350.00
Galleria	Johnson, L.	1002	1200.00	675.00
Six Flags	Keemis, M.	1007	2000.00	0.00
Collin Creek	Williams, E.	1010	2000.00	0.00
Prestonwood	Smith, A.M.	1009	2000.00	220.00
Prestonwood	Allen, L.	1005	2000.00	312.00
Downtown	Walker, B.	1006	1300.00	1167.00
Prestonwood	Smith, A.	1001	2000.00	788.00
Downtown	Jones, J.	1011	2000.00	875.00
Collin Creek	Jones, J.L.	1004	2000.00	1850.00

Rather than concatenating the two numbers, dBASE IV has added them and indexed in the order of the sum, which is not what you had in mind. The reason for this is that the plus symbol operates differently with numeric expressions than it does with string (character-based) expressions. The plus symbol adds numbers, but combines character expressions. If instead you use the SORT command, as indicated in the following commands:

```
USE SALES
SORT ON HIGHCREDIT,BALANCE TO SALES1
USE SALES1
LIST STORE, CUSTNAME, CUSTNUMB, HIGHCREDIT, BALANCE
```

The results will appear as:

STORE	CUSTNAME	CUSTNUMB	HIGHCREDIT	BALANCE
Oak Lawn	Jones, C.	1003	900.00	350.00
Collin Creek	Artis, K.	1008	1200.00	0.00
Galleria	Johnson, L.	1002	1200.00	675.00
Downtown	Walker, B.	1006	1300.00	1167.00
Six Flags	Keemis, M.	1007	2000.00	0.00
Collin Creek	Williams, E.	1010	2000.00	0.00
Prestonwood	Smith, A.M.	1009	2000.00	220.00

```
Prestonwood     Allen, L.      1005      2000.00   312.00
Prestonwood     Smith, A.      1001      2000.00   788.50
Downtown        Jones, J.      1011      2000.00   875.00
Collin Creek    Jones, J.L.    1004      2000.00  1850.00
```

What you get is what was expected: a file in numeric order by high credit, and where high credit is the same, in order of the outstanding balance. The unexpected results when using INDEX occurred because the INDEX command, when used with multiple fields, depends on a math expression. In this case, dBASE IV added the amounts, building the index on the value that was the sum of the amounts. To index on the combined numeric fields and get the desired results, you would have to first convert the numeric expressions into string values, then use the plus symbol to combine the string values. In the previous example, you could issue a command like

```
INDEX ON STR(HIGHCREDIT) + STR(BALANCE) TO CSALES
```

to accomplish the same result as the SORT command.

Using Functions to Standardize Case

The UPPER function (and less commonly, the LOWER function) is used to avoid problems arising due to the case-sensitive nature of dBASE IV. The functions can be used as part of an index expression, resulting in an index containing all uppercase characters (or all lowercase, if the LOWER function is used). The problem that can arise if you are not consistent when entering data is shown in the following example, which uses a database of names in which some of the names are entered with an initial capital letter, some are entered as all uppercase, and some are entered as all lowercase:

```
USE SAMPLE
INDEX ON NAME TO NAMES
LIST
```

Record#	NAME	AGE
1	ADDISON, E.	32
2	Addison, a.	28
3	Carlson, F.	45
4	McLean,R.	28
5	Mcdonald, s.	47
7	Smith, S.	55
8	Smith, b.	37
10	adams, j.q.	76
6	de laurentis, m.	25
9	edelstien, m.	22

Unless told otherwise, dBASE IV puts lowercase letters after uppercase letters in the index, and the results are probably not what you had in mind. If you use the UPPER function to build the index, you get acceptable results, as shown with the following commands:

```
USE SAMPLE
INDEX ON UPPER(NAME) TO NAMES
LIST
```

This results in the following listing:

Record#	NAME	AGE
10	adams, j.q.	76
2	ADDISON, A.	28
1	Addison, E.	32
3	Carlson, F.	45
6	de laurentis, m.	25
9	edelstien, m.	22
5	Mcdonald, s.	47
4	McLean,R.	28
8	Smith, b.	37
7	Smith, S.	55

To find such records in the index, simply enter all uppercase letters in the expression along with the FIND or SEEK command. As an example, with the index just created, the command

```
SEEK "ADDISON"
```

would find the record, regardless of the case of the letters in the actual record.

Indexing on a Date Field Combined with Other Fields

When you need an index based partially on a date field, dBASE IV can present a bit of a challenge. It's no problem when you want to see the database in order by just one date field. Consider an example of a small medical database, containing patient names and an "admitted" field with the date of admission to a hospital. You can use commands like

```
USE PATIENT
INDEX ON ADMITTED TO DATESIN
LIST PATIENT, ADMITTED
```

to create a listing such as the following:

```
Record#     PATIENT         ADMITTED
      1     Smith, A.       04/05/85
      2     Johnson, L.     04/15/85
      3     Jones, C.       04/15/85
      4     Jones, J.L.     04/15/85
      5     Allen, L.       05/20/86
      6     Walker, B.      05/20/86
      7     Keemis, M.      05/20/86
      8     Artis, K.       05/20/86
```

```
      9        Smith, A.M.     05/20/86
     10        Williams, E.    06/14/86
     11        Jones, J.       06/22-86
```

The database is now indexed in the order of the entries in the date field. Things get more complex when you want a database indexed on a combination of fields, and one of the fields is a date field. Since dBASE IV doesn't let you directly index on multiple fields of different types, you must use the DTOS() function to convert the date into a character string. This function converts a date value to a character value of YYYYMMDD, where YYYY is the year, MM the month, and DD the day. When an index is built using the DTOS() function, the result comes out in true chronological order. Assuming the medical database contains a date field named DIAGNOSED and a character field named PATIENT, and you want it indexed by date and then by the name of the patient, the following commands provide an index based on date and patient name, in the correct chronological order:

```
USE PATIENT
INDEX ON DTOS(DIAGNOSED) + PATIENT TO COMBO
LIST PATIENT, DIAGNOSED
```

The results will appear as follows:

```
Record#        PATIENT         DIAGNOSED
      3        Jones, C.       02/08/85
      4        Jones, J.L.     03/02/85
      2        Johnson, L.     03/06/85
      1        Smith, A.       03/17/85
      9        Smith, A.M.     02/03/86
      7        Keemis, M.      02/23/86
      8        Artis, K.       04/19/86
      5        Allen, L.       05/12/86
      6        Walker, B.      05/16/86
     10        Williams, E.    06/01/86
     11        Jones, J.       06/13/86
```

Indexing .NDX Files on Dates In Descending Order

If you need a dBASE III PLUS-style index file in reverse chronological order (latest date to earliest), you can use the little-known technique of indexing on negative values to build an index file based on negative date values. Simply subtract the dates from any date that is larger (or later) than the latest date in the database. Some arbitrary date far in the future works well for this. The technique is shown in this example:

```
USE PATIENT
INDEX ON {12/31/99} - DIAGNOSED TO REVERSE
LLIST PATIENT, DIAGNOSED
```

The results appear as follows:

Record#	PATIENT	DIAGNOSED
11	Jones, J.	06/13/86
10	Williams, E.	06/01/86
6	Walker, B.	05/16/86
5	Allen, L.	05/12/86
8	Artis, K.	04/19/86
7	Keemis, M.	02/23/86
9	Smith, A.M.	02/03/86
1	Smith, A.	03/17/85
2	Johnson, L.	03/06/85
4	Jones, J.L.	03/02/85
3	Jones, C.	02/08/85

In this example, the index is built on a number that represents the difference in number of days between 12/31/99 and the date field (DIAGNOSED) in the database. With each earlier date, this number increases, causing the position of the date to be further down in the index file. If you are using dBASE IV's multiple index (.MDX) tags, you can perform this kind of task easily by using the DESCENDING option of the INDEX command.

Power Hints When Indexing

A few tips for when you are using index files will help speed things along in dBASE IV.

Use short keys when you don't need long ones. Most indexes are directly based on a series of character fields. And in real life, most character fields get unique around the tenth character, if not sooner. If you can get by with indexing on fewer characters, do so. dBASE IV will manage the index in less time. Take a real-world example: you are building a customer file for a store in a medium-sized city (with a population of around 100,000), so you do not need to deal with the duplicity of names that exists in New York or Los Angeles. The customer base is manageable: you might see a maximum of 5000 to 10,000 records in the file over the next 10 years. The store manager despises labels with names cut off for lack of field width, so you've specified a width of 30 characters each for the LASTNAME and FIRSTNAME fields. You are going to index on a key field of customer number as the primary index, but you also want an index based on a combination of last and first names so you can quickly find a record when a customer is on the phone and does not have his or her customer number handy. In this situation, do you really need an index based on the LASTNAME and FIRSTNAME fields? Quite likely not, but this is often done out of force of habit, and dBASE IV must work harder for it. If instead you do something like

```
INDEX ON LEFT(LASTNAME,10)+LEFT(FIRSTNAME,10) TAG NAMES
```

the use of the LEFT function (explained in more detail in Appendix B) will result in an index that contains 20 characters per entry, as opposed to an index that contains 60 characters per entry. Given the small customer base, indexing on the first 10 characters of the last and first names should be more than enough to keep the records in order and find a given record. And the index file will use considerably less disk space.

Store numbers in character fields if you are never going to perform calculations on those numbers. If you use numbers as a unique identifier (such as part numbers, employee numbers, invoice numbers, and so on) and you plan to use this data as a part of the index, don't store it in a numeric field. Use a character field instead. dBASE IV does a better job of indexing on character fields than it does on numeric fields. When you try indexing with very large files, it becomes apparent that dBASE IV takes longer to index a numeric field than a character field of equivalent size. If you are not going to calculate such fields, they don't need to be numeric fields.

Perform routine maintenance often. When dBASE IV must perform sequential operations while your index files are open, it has to work harder. You can cut down on processing time by regularly putting your database files back in their natural order. To do this, open the file along with the index you use most often, and use the COPY TO *filename* command to copy the contents of the file to another file. Then delete the original database, rename the new database to the same name as the original database, and rebuild the necessary indexes. (If the database has memo fields, remember to rename the corresponding .DBT file.) In applications using large files that are regularly updated, this simple step can make a dramatic difference to the users in terms of response time when performing any reporting or processing that is based on sequential operations in dBASE IV. Part of the speedup may also be due to the fact that the creation of a new database with the COPY command results in a new file under DOS that may have its data arranged in sectors located side-by-side on the hard disk. Often when a file has been updated over months of time, it may be arranged in sectors that are scattered all over the hard disk. Depending on how much free space exists on your hard disk, you may be able to use the above technique to reduce such fragmentation of files over a hard disk, or you can use one of the many "disk optimizer" software packages available to clean up your hard disk and make all of your files more accessible to your software.

Quick Reference

To sort a database From the Control Center, highlight the file in the Data panel, and press ENTER. Choose Modify Structure/Order. Choose Sort Database on Field List from the Organize menu. Enter the fields to sort on in the Field Order column. Choose the direction of the sort by pressing the spacebar in the Type of Sort column. When done, press CTRL-END to start the sorting process.

From the dot prompt, use the SORT ON *fieldname*[/A/C/D]TO *filename* command. Use /A for ascending order (the default if no letter option is included), /C for Dictionary sort (uppercase and lowercase letters treated the same), or /D for descending order.

To sort on multiple fields From the Control Center, use the method just described. Place the *primary field* (the most important field to sort) in the first row of the Field Order column, and choose Type of Sort for that field. Place the *secondary field* (the next most important field to sort) in the next row of the Field Order column, and choose Type of Sort for that field. Continue adding more fields as needed in the same manner.

From the dot prompt, use the command SORT ON *1st fieldname* [/A/C/D], *2nd fieldname* [/A/C/D], *3rd fieldname* [/A/C/D] TO *filename*. The slash options work as previously described. You can add as many fields as necessary to sufficiently sort the database.

To perform a selective sort Add the FOR option and a condition to the SORT command, as performed from the dot prompt. The syntax for the SORT command becomes SORT ON *fieldname* [/A/C/D] TO *filename* FOR *condition*. For example, the command SORT ON LASTNAME TO MYFILE FOR STATE = "VA" would produce a sorted file containing only those records with "VA" in the STATE field.

To create an index From the Control Center, highlight the file in the Data panel, and press ENTER. Choose Modify Structure/Order. Choose Order Records by Index from the Organize menu. In the next menu box to appear, enter the name of the index file, the expression (usually a field name or a combination of field names) to index on, and select the order for the index (ascending or descending). To index on multiple fields, use the format *fieldname1* + *fieldname2* + *fieldname3* in the expression. Version 1.1 users can also specify a FOR clause here to build a selective index. Press CTRL-END when done to build the index.

From the dot prompt, use the command INDEX ON *expression* TO *filename*. (*expression* is usually the field name or field names that the index will be based on.) To index on multiple fields, use the format *fieldname1* + *fieldname2* + *fieldname3* in the expression. If the index needs to be built in descending order, add the word DESCENDING to the end of the command. Version 1.1 users can also specify a FOR clause here to build a selective index. The format of the command then becomes INDEX ON *expression* TO *filename* [DESCENDING] FOR *condition*.

To index on multiple fields of different types Use functions to convert fields to the same type. The DTOS() function converts a date to a year-month-day character string, and the STR() function converts a number to a character string.

To change the index in use, when more than one index file is open From the Organize menu, choose the Order Records By Index option. Select the desired index from the list that appears. From the dot prompt, use SET ORDER TO TAG *tagname,* where *tagname* is the name of the index tag.

CHAPTER

7

The Power of Queries

Now that you have significant sets of data stored within a dBASE IV database, it is time to examine more complex ways to get at the precise data you will need. You've already used the helpful search options of the Records menu to quickly locate a record, but this is only a simple form of query. You will often need to isolate one or more records based on a matching condition. For example, you may need to generate a list of all employees working at a particular assignment or all employees earning more than $9.00 per hour.

This chapter will describe how you can use the Query Design screen to compose queries. This powerful feature of dBASE IV uses a principle called "query-by-example" to make complex requests easy for the user. You do not have to think about the arcane logic behind a detailed set of commands; with query-by-example, you add the fields you want included in the results, and provide examples or ranges of the data you wish to extract. dBASE IV does the rest for you.

You can also use queries to add or delete records, with the additions or deletions based on the results of the query. In addition, you can update values in one database, based on a query of another database.

dBASE IV provides two types of queries: *view queries* and *update queries*. Using view queries, you can design a "view" of your data, limiting the ways in which data is displayed or printed. With a view query you can select only those records that meet certain conditions, and you can choose specific fields from those records. The specific data that results can be seen on the screen (as in Browse mode) or it can be printed by using a quick report or a custom report.

Update queries are used to perform global changes, or updates, to your database. Using an update query, you could, for example, increase the salaries of all employees earning more than $10.00 per hour by 5%, and increase the salaries of all employees earning $10.00 per hour and less by 7%.

☞ ***REMEMBER*** If you are using version 1.0 of dBASE IV, your screens may appear different than the ones shown throughout this chapter. Version 1.0 sets columns in queries to a preset width, while versions 1.1 and later vary column widths to fit the field sizes. The techniques described throughout this chapter are the same for versions 1.0 and 1.1, regardless of the appearance of the screens.

Displaying the Query Design Screen

Queries are built in the Query Design screen (Figure 7-1). You can get to this screen in various ways. If you are at the Control Center, you can highlight the Create option of the Queries panel and press ENTER. Dot-prompt users can enter the command CREATE QUERY *filename*. If you want to modify an existing query, you can highlight that query at the Queries panel and press SHIFT-F2 (Design); from the dot prompt, you can enter MODIFY QUERY *filename*. Finally, users of dBASE III PLUS can continue to use the CREATE VIEW *filename* and MODIFY VIEW *filename* commands that were used in dBASE III PLUS.

Figure 7-1.

```
Layout   Fields   Condition   Update   Exit                                9:37:06 am
Abcstaff.dbf | ↓SOCIALSEC | ↓LASTNAME | ↓FIRSTNAME | ↓ADDRESS | ↓CITY | ↓STATE | ↓ZIPCO

View
<NEW>        | Abcstaff->  | Abcstaff-> | Abcstaff->  | Abcstaff->
             | SOCIALSEC   | LASTNAME   | FIRSTNAME   | ADDRESS

Query    ||E:\dbase4\dbdata\<NEW>  ||File 1/1  ||  ||
 Next field:Tab  Add/Remove all fields:F5  Zoom:F9  Prev/Next skeleton:F3/F4
```

Query Design screen

In dBASE IV, these commands are equivalent to CREATE QUERY and MODIFY QUERY.

HINT Whenever you're in Browse or Edit mode, you can also get to the Query Design screen by choosing the Transfer To Query Design option of the Exit menu.

The Query Design screen uses a visual model of your data to design your queries. The screen is divided into two main parts. In the upper half is the *file skeleton.* This area can be thought of as a model of the databases you use to construct the query. Field names from the database in use appear in this area. Since a query can be based on more than one database file, it is possible to see

Figure 7-2.

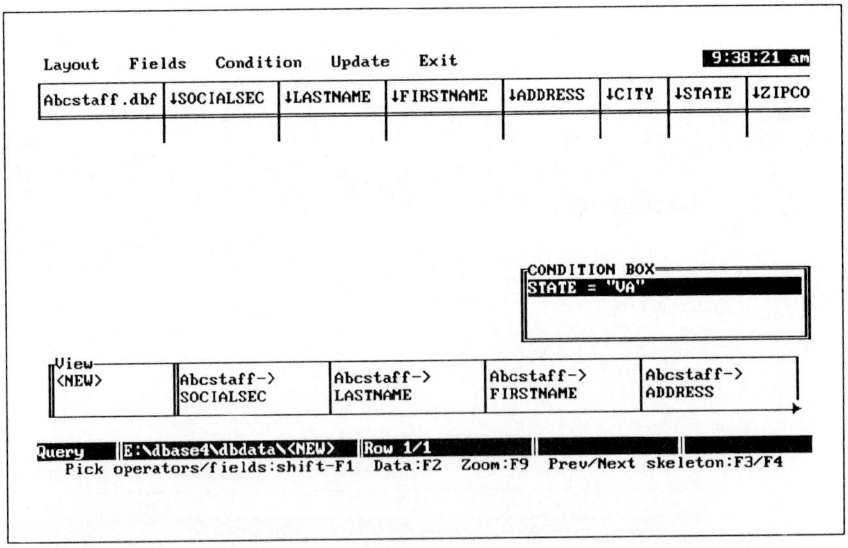

```
Layout   Fields   Condition   Update   Exit                                9:38:21 am
Abcstaff.dbf | ↓SOCIALSEC | ↓LASTNAME | ↓FIRSTNAME | ↓ADDRESS | ↓CITY | ↓STATE | ↓ZIPCO

                                              CONDITION BOX
                                              STATE = "VA"

View       | Abcstaff->  | Abcstaff-> | Abcstaff->  | Abcstaff->
<NEW>      | SOCIALSEC   | LASTNAME   | FIRSTNAME   | ADDRESS
Query  E:\dbase4\dbdata\<NEW>  Row 1/1
  Pick operators/fields:shift-F1  Data:F2  Zoom:F9  Prev/Next skeleton:F3/F4
```

Query Design screen with condition box

fields from multiple files arranged in successive rows of the file skeleton.

The lower portion of the Query Design screen contains an area called the *view skeleton*. It can be thought of as a model of the fields that will appear in the resulting view. (Note that when you are designing an update query, this area is empty; the view skeleton only appears with view queries.)

A *condition box* can also appear on the Query Design screen. You will use it when you are specifying complex conditions that involve many different fields. Figure 7-2 shows a Query Design screen containing a condition box. In this example, the Query Design screen was produced from a single table of data, the ABCSTAFF database. Queries of a relational nature will be covered in more detail in Chapter 12, but for now note that you can repeat this query process for additional databases and make use of example variables to link common fields in order to build a query that is dependent on multiple database files.

Hints on Navigation

To move around the columns (fields) within the skeletons, you can use the TAB key and SHIFT-TAB key combination. You can also move up or down between the file skeleton and the view skeleton by using the F3 (Previous) and F4 (Next) keys. Moving between the rows of a skeleton can be accomplished with the up and down arrow keys, and you can use the HOME and END keys to move to the far-left or far-right sides of the skeleton.

Users of dBASE IV version 1.1 or later can also resize the columns with SHIFT-F7. Press SHIFT-F7 and then use the left or right arrow keys to resize the column as desired. Press ENTER when done.

Building a Simple Query

To build a simple query, you usually need to perform just two basic steps. In the first step, you select the fields you want displayed in the result. You do this either by adding all fields in the file skeleton to the view skeleton and then removing unwanted fields or by starting with a blank slate (no fields) in the view and adding the fields you desire. (Note that if you create a query when a database file is already open, all fields in that file automatically appear in the view.)

To add a single field to the view, move the cursor to the desired field within the file skeleton, and then choose the Add Field to View option of the Fields menu or press F5 (Field). You can also add all fields in the file skeleton to the view skeleton at once by placing the cursor underneath the filename (at the far-left side of the skeleton) and pressing F5.

To remove a field from the view, move the cursor to the desired field (in either the file skeleton or the view skeleton). Then choose the Remove Field from View option of the Fields menu, or press F5 (Field). If all of the fields in a file skeleton are already in the view skeleton, you can remove all of them at once by moving the cursor to the far left, under the name of the file skeleton, and pressing F5 (Field).

For the second step, simply enter a matching expression in any desired field. (This is only necessary if you want to limit your query to include a specific subset of records; if you want to see all records, you can omit this step.) As an example, if you wanted to see all employees with the last name of Robinson, you would move the cursor to the LASTNAME field and type **="Robinson"**. To select records in which the employee was hired before January 1, 1987, you would enter **< {1/1/87}** in the HIREDATE field (curly braces must surround any dates you enter). And if you wanted all employees who earned between $7.50 and $9.00 per hour, you

Figure 7-3.

```
Layout   Fields   Condition   Update   Exit                                   9:39:44 am
Abcstaff.dbf |↓PHONE |↓BIRTHDAY |↓DATEHIRED |↓DEPENDENTS |↓SALARY              |↓ASSIG
                                                          >=7.50, <=9.00

View
<NEW>        Abcstaff->      Abcstaff->      Abcstaff->      Abcstaff->
             SOCIALSEC       LASTNAME        FIRSTNAME       ADDRESS

Query   E:\dbase4\dbdata\<NEW>   Field 12/15
 Prev/Next field:Shift-Tab/Tab  Data:F2  Pick:Shift-F1  Prev/Next skel:F3/F4
```

Example of filled-in Query Design screen

could enter **>=7.50, <=9.00** in the SALARY field, as shown in the example in Figure 7-3. There are many variations that can also be used, but these are the basic steps in constructing a query.

REMEMBER You need to use quotes around character expressions in queries.

Saving and Applying the Query

Once the Query Design screen has been filled in, pressing a single key, F2 (Data), will apply the query. The results will appear in Browse mode, as shown in the example in Figure 7-4. The results are not permanent, however. You can choose to save the query to a file so that it can be used to apply the chosen conditions repeatedly. While you are still at the Query Design screen, you can press ALT-E and choose Save Changes and Exit (or use the CTRL-END key combination) to save the query. If necessary, dBASE will ask you for a filename for the query.

Once the query is saved, you are returned to the dot prompt or the Control Center. To apply the query, select it at the Control Center Queries panel. From the dot prompt, you can activate a view query at any time with the SET VIEW TO *filename* command.

Remember that you do not have to save a query to a file to use the results. You can move back and forth between the Query Design screen and the data as defined by the query in Edit or Browse mode by pressing F2 (Data). In addition, you can press Quick Report (SHIFT-F9) to produce a printed report of the data. However, you must save the query to a file if you want to be able

Figure 7-4.

SOCIALSEC	LASTNAME	DEPENDENTS	SALARY	ASSIGNMENT	HOURLYRATE
232-55-1234	Jackson	1	8.00	City Revenue Dept.	12.00
901-77-3456	Mitchell	1	8.00	Smith Builders	12.00
121-90-5432	Robinson	1	8.00	National Oil Co.	12.00
343-55-9821	Robinson	0	8.00	City Revenue Dept.	12.00
123-44-8976	Morse	2	9.00	National Oil Co.	15.00
876-54-3210	Hart	3	9.00	Smith Builders	14.00

Results of example query

to use it again after closing the database.

HINT You can press SHIFT-F9 to generate a quick report while you're still in the Query Design screen.

In many cases, these steps are all that is necessary to get the kind of information that you need from your database. You can quickly produce reports of critical data by designing a query with the desired fields (you may want to limit the fields so they will fit on a single page), filling in any desired conditions to isolate the needed set of matching records. Press F2 (Data) to see the results while in Browse mode, or press SHIFT-F9 for a quick report based on your query.

Although the columns in the Query Design screen are narrow, the expressions that you enter to define selection criteria can be up to 254 characters in length. If you wish to see all of the expression as you are entering it, you can use the Zoom key (F9) to edit the entry. When you are done editing, press F9 (Zoom) again to shrink the entry back to its normal size. Version 1.1 users can also resize columns by pressing SHIFT-F7 followed by the left or right arrow keys.

Query Design Menu Options

When you are in the Query Design screen, the available menus provide you with choices that apply to constructing your queries. Figure 7-5 shows the Layout menu. Its Add File to Query option adds a database file to the file skeleton, and the Remove File from Query option removes a file from the file skeleton. The Create

Figure 7-5.

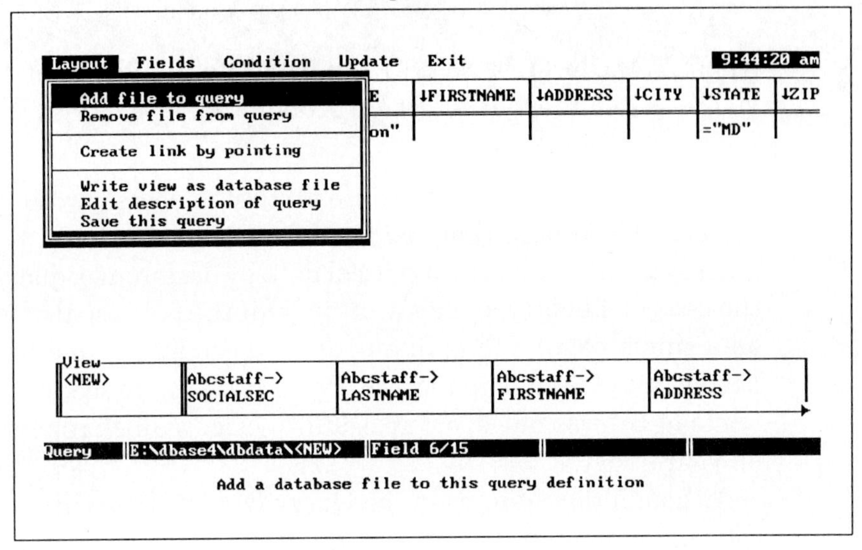

Layout menu

Link by Pointing option lets you create a relational link between multiple files; this topic is covered in detail in Chapter 12.

The Write View as Database File option lets you create another database file, using the records selected by the view. Use the Edit Description of Query option to create or edit a one-line description for the query. Finally, the Save This Query option lets you save a query to disk and continue working within the Query Design screen.

The Fields menu, shown in Figure 7-6, lets you perform operations related to the fields when you are designing a query. The Add Field to View option adds a field to the view skeleton, and the Remove Field from View option removes a field. The F5 (Field) key can also be used for these actions; if the current field is not in the view, F5 adds it, and if it is in the view, F5 removes it.

The Edit Field Name option lets you change the name of a field that is in the view without changing the field name in the database itself. This option is most often used to distinguish fields

Figure 7-6.

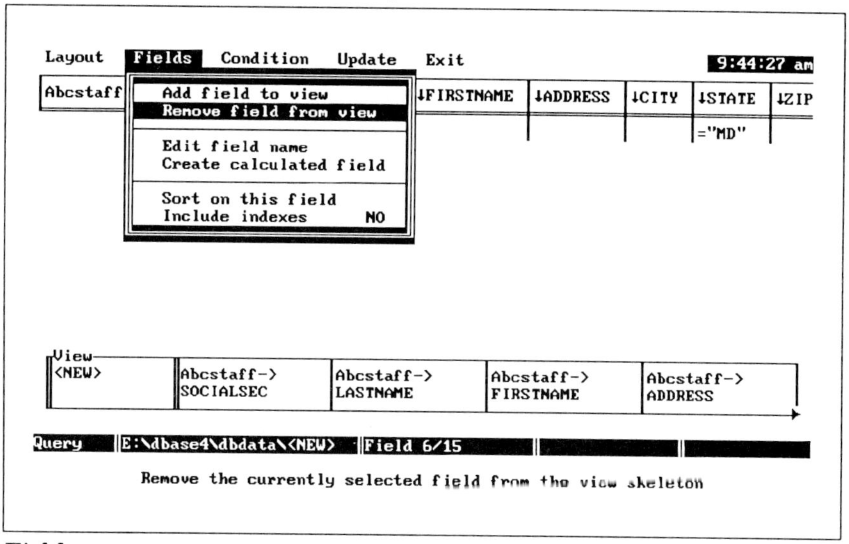

Layout Fields Condition Update Exit
9:44:27 am
Abcstaff
Add field to view
Remove field from view
Edit field name
Create calculated field
Sort on this field
Include indexes NO
↓FIRSTNAME ↓ADDRESS ↓CITY ↓STATE ↓ZIP
="MD"
View
<NEW>
Abcstaff-> SOCIALSEC
Abcstaff-> LASTNAME
Abcstaff-> FIRSTNAME
Abcstaff-> ADDRESS
Query E:\dbase4\dbdata\<NEW> Field 6/15
Remove the currently selected field from the view skeleton

Fields menu

Figure 7-7.

Layout Fields Condition Update Exit
9:44:34 am
Abcstaff.dbf ↓SOC
Add condition box
Delete condition box
Show condition box
NAME ↓ADDRESS ↓CITY ↓STATE ↓ZIP
="MD"
View
<NEW>
Abcstaff-> SOCIALSEC
Abcstaff-> LASTNAME
Abcstaff-> FIRSTNAME
Abcstaff-> ADDRESS
Query E:\dbase4\dbdata\<NEW> Field 6/15
Create an empty condition box

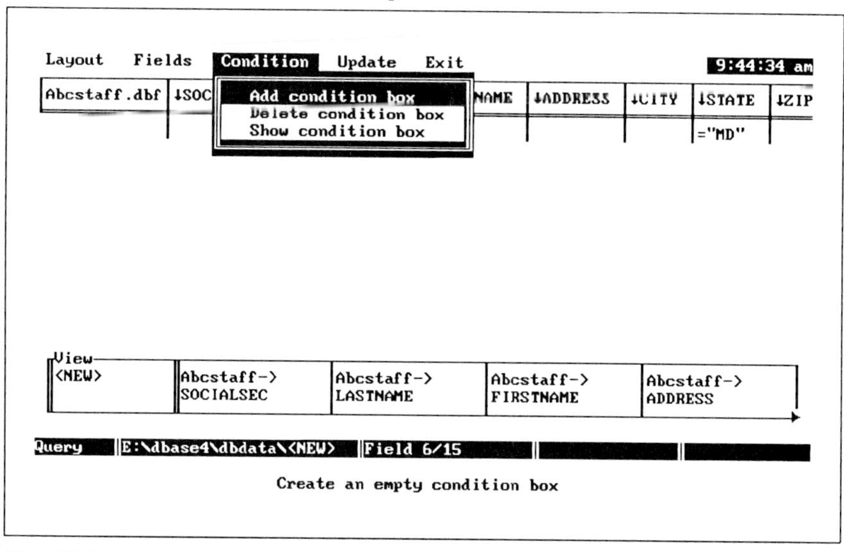

Condition menu

with the same name in different files. The Create Calculated Field option lets you create a calculated field from within the Query Design screen.

The Sort on This Field option lets you sort a database while you are performing the query. The results of your query will then be in the desired order. The Include Indexes option lets you mark key fields (or key expressions) as a column in the file skeleton, so you can group or link related files by that key field or expression.

The Condition menu, shown in Figure 7-7, has three choices, all of which apply to the use of the optional condition box. The possible options are Add Condition Box, Delete Condition Box, and Show Condition Box. Condition boxes are used to contain conditions that apply to all files in the query, and they will be discussed in detail shortly.

The Update menu (Figure 7-8) offers choices for designing and performing update queries. The Perform the Update option tells

Figure 7-8.

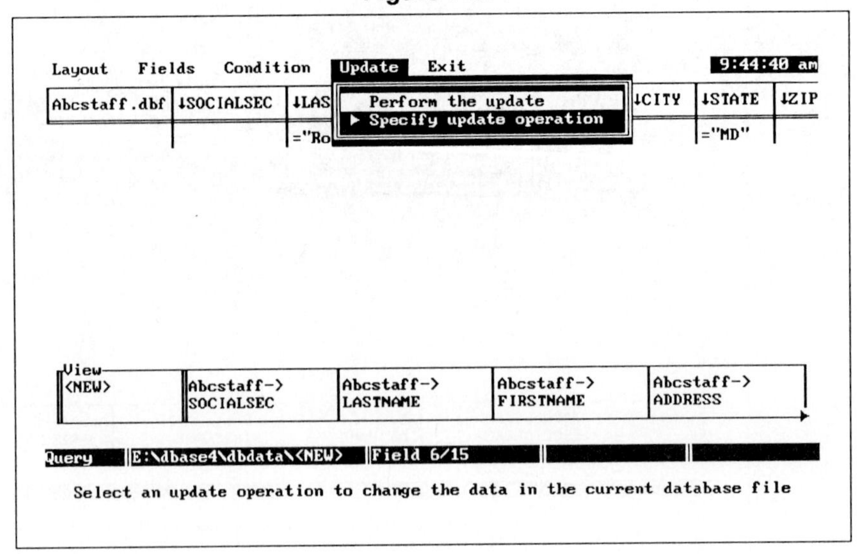

Update menu

dBASE to apply the instructions contained in the update query to the database in use. The Specify Update Operation choice is used to begin building the query that will control how the records are updated when the query is performed.

The Exit menu's options are identical to those used in other parts of dBASE IV, with choices for saving changes or for abandoning work with no changes saved.

Table 7-1.

Symbol	Meaning
+	Addition
-	Subtraction
*	Multiplication
/	Division
=	Equal to
>	Greater than
<	Less than
>=	Greater than or equal to
<=	Less than or equal to
< > or #	Does not equal
like	Pattern matching for any characters
$	Contains
sounds like	Similar to (spelling need not be exact)
date( )	Date in field matches today's date
avg	Average of values
max	Maximum of the values
min	Minimum of the values
sum	Sum of the values
cnt	Count (number) of the values

Valid Query Symbols and Operators

Valid Query Symbols

You can use any of the symbols and operators listed in Table 7-1 to assist you in building your queries. These symbols will let you select records based on a wide variety of numeric conditions, pattern matches, and ranges.

Note that the syntax of the $ operator differs from the syntax used at the dot prompt; the symbol comes *before* the operator when you are constructing a query. As an example, the expression

```
$ "North Shore Drive"
```

is valid in the ADDRESS column of a query, although it would not be valid with a LIST command at the dot prompt.

Pattern Matching

On occasion, you may need to find a group of records in which characters match a specific pattern. dBASE IV lets you use certain *wildcards,* along with the Like operator, as a part of the query expression as it applies to character fields. Valid wildcard operators are the asterisk (*), which represents any number of characters, and the question mark (?), which indicates any single character. As an example, you could use the expression

```
like "J*n"
```

to query a name field for names that might include Jackson, Jonson, and James-Albertson.

Practice Queries

Your first task as the personnel manager for ABC Temporaries is to find a person living in Maryland whose last name is Robinson. Get into dBASE IV and to the Control Center if you are not already there. If the database file ABCSTAFF.DBF is not open, open the file now by highlighting ABCSTAFF at the Data panel and pressing ENTER twice. This is done so that when you create a new query all of the fields for ABCSTAFF will be included by default in the file skeleton.

To begin the query, choose the Create option of the Queries panel. Once you choose the option, the Query Design screen will appear. In the resulting view, you want to select a record based on the last name, so press TAB twice to move the cursor to the LASTNAME field within the file skeleton and enter the following:

```
="Robinson"
```

Press TAB until the cursor moves to the STATE field, and then enter

```
="MD"
```

Then press F2 (Data). The records matching the query appear, as shown in Figure 7-9.

If your results do not match those in the figure, make sure that your criteria in the Query Design screen match the actual data in the database. For example, if you are trying to locate a record in which the last name has been entered as "Robinson," you cannot find the record if you enter "robinson" or "ROBINSON" in the Query Design screen.

Figure 7-9.

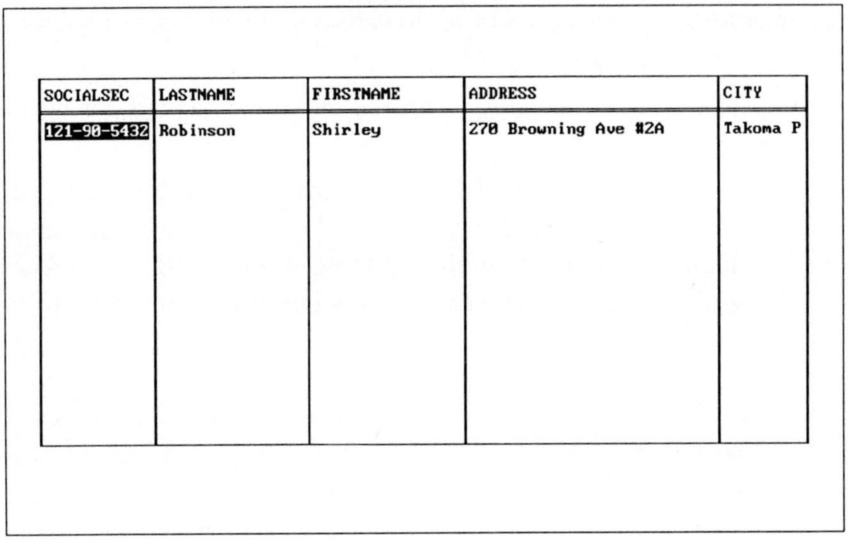

SOCIALSEC	LASTNAME	FIRSTNAME	ADDRESS	CITY
121-90-5432	Robinson	Shirley	270 Browning Ave #2A	Takoma P

Results of first practice query

Matching on Two or More Fields

To search for records that meet criteria in two or more fields, simply enter the criteria in the proper format within each field of the Query Design screen. If, for example, you need to see all employees who live in Virginia and earn more than $10.00 per hour, you will need to enter **="VA"** in the STATE field of the file skeleton and **>10.00** in the SALARY field of the file skeleton.

To try this, first press SHIFT-F2 (Design) to get back to the Query Design screen, and delete the prior entry in the LASTNAME field. A shortcut is available here: by moving to any field and pressing CTRL-Y, you can delete the contents of that field in the skeleton.

Press HOME to move the cursor under the name ABC-STAFF.DBF in the file skeleton. Open the Fields menu with ALT-F, and choose the Remove Field from View option to remove all of the fields in the view skeleton. Then use the TAB key to move to the LASTNAME field, and press F5 (Field) to add the field to the view skeleton. Use TAB to move to the FIRSTNAME field, and press F5 again. Use TAB to move to the STATE field, and press F5 to add that field.

While you are still in the STATE field, enter the following:

```
="VA"
```

Then move to the SALARY field. Press F5 to add this field to the view skeleton. While you are still in the SALARY field, enter

```
>10
```

Because a whole amount is desired, the decimal point and trailing zeros are unnecessary in this case.

Press F2 (Data) to apply the query. The results will appear in the records shown in Browse mode (Figure 7-10). Notice that

Figure 7-10.

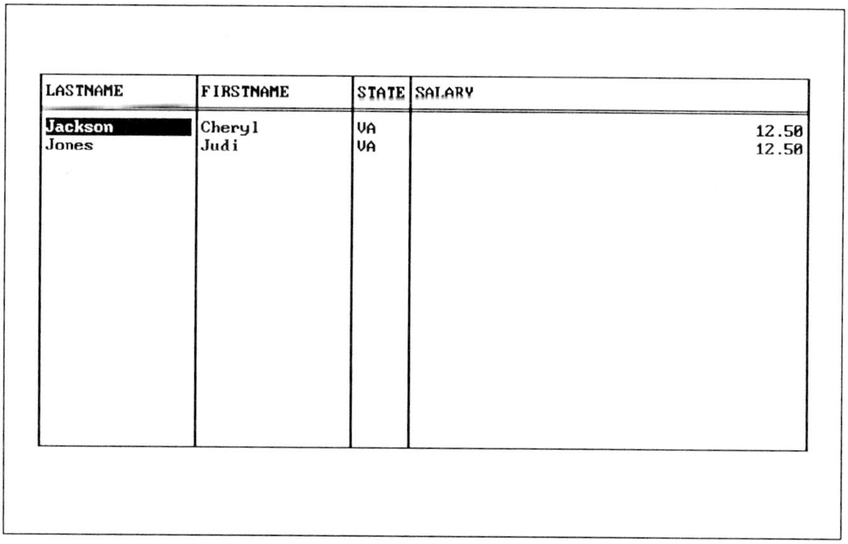

LASTNAME	FIRSTNAME	STATE	SALARY
Jackson	Cheryl	VA	12.50
Jones	Judi	VA	12.50

Results of second practice query

because you started with an empty view skeleton and added the LASTNAME, FIRSTNAME, STATE, and SALARY fields, these are the only fields that appear when you are in Browse mode.

A Note About Editing

When you switch to viewing the data by pressing F2 (Data), in most cases you can update the database—that is, make changes to the records—just as you can when using Browse or Edit mode outside of a query. Any changes made through the view query apply to the data in the database. In a few cases, however, the view will be *read-only* and "Read only" will appear at the right side of the status bar. You will be unable to make any changes to the data if this is the case. The data becomes read-only data if you sort the records within the view or use calculated fields in the view. Both sorting and the use of calculated fields in a view are covered later in this chapter.

Using Inexact Matches

One very useful feature of dBASE IV's query-by-example facility is its ability to use the Sounds Like operator as a condition for finding inexact matches. For example, the expression "sounds like Morrs," when used in the LASTNAME field of a query of the ABCSTAFF database, should find a record that sounds like the word "Morrs," or Marsha Morse. Let's try it now. Press SHIFT-F2 (Design) to get back to the Queries Design screen, and clear the previous entries in the SALARY and STATE fields. Enter the following in the LASTNAME field of the file skeleton:

```
sounds like "Morrs"
```

☞ ***REMEMBER*** Press CTRL-Y to delete an entry in a query field.

Press F2 to view the results of the query. The answer should show the record for Ms. Marcia Morse, because the last name "Morse" sounds like "Morrs."

This capability of dBASE IV can be quite useful for finding names when you aren't quite sure of the spelling. The Sounds Like operator is also helpful for maintaining mailing lists, when you are trying to weed out accidental duplicates of the same record.

Using Ranges

The range operators <, >, <=, >=, and < >, shown among the operators in Table 7-1, are very useful for ensuring that records fall within a selective range. You can use the range operators with all types of dBASE IV fields; they are by no means limited to numeric values. Consider a list of employees whose last names fall between the letters M and Z. Press SHIFT-F2 to get back to the Query Design screen, and delete the prior entries. In the LASTNAME field of the Query Design screen, enter the following expression:

```
>="M", <="Zz"
```

This represents "Greater than M, and less than or equal to Zz." The second letter z ensures that all names starting with z are included in the query. Press F2 (Data) to apply the query, and the results shown in Figure 7-11 will appear.

Note in this example that a *comma* is used to separate the two possibilities. Remember that whenever you want to enter more

Figure 7-11.

Ins

LASTNAME	FIRSTNAME	STATE	SALARY
Mitchell	Mary Jo	VA	8.00
Morse	Marcia	MD	9.00
Robinson	Shirley	MD	8.00
Robinson	Wanda	DC	8.00
Westman	Andrea	MD	16.50

Results of practice query with operators limiting names

than one selection criterion in a field, you must separate the criteria with commas. Another example, this time performed with dates, illustrates this point. Suppose you need a report of all employees who were hired during 1986. Press SHIFT-F2 to get back to the Query Design screen, and delete the prior entry in the LASTNAME field. Move the cursor to the DATEHIRED field, and enter the following expression:

```
>={1/1/86}, <={12/31/86}
```

REMEMBER Whenever you use dates, surround them with curly braces.

Press F2 to process the completed query. The result, shown in Figure 7-12, displays the employees who were hired by ABC Temporaries in 1986.

Figure 7-12.

LASTNAME	FIRSTNAME	STATE	SALARY
Westman	Andrea	MD	16.50
Hart	Edward	VA	9.00
Jones	Judi	VA	12.50

Results of query of 1986 employees

You may have noticed another point from the nature of this query. The limiting criterion for records was the date hired, and yet the DATEHIRED field was not picked for inclusion in the view skeleton. dBASE IV does not necessarily need to have the fields that are used to select the records included in the results. However, it is often a good idea to include the field on which you are selecting records in the view to make sure that you stated the criteria properly.

You can also use the accepted operators listed in Table 7-1 to build queries based on other types of ranges. Consider the common personnel problem of deciding who qualifies for vacation and who does not qualify for vacation. At ABC Temporaries, every employee with one year or more of service qualifies for vacation. If suddenly you need a list of employees eligible for vacation, a simple query will do the task.

Press SHIFT-F2 to get back to the Query Design screen, and delete the prior entry. Next, with the cursor still in the DATEHIRED field, enter the expression

```
>=DATE( )-365
```

which translates to "Greater than or equal to today's date minus 365 days." If you refer back to Table 7-1, you will note that dBASE IV uses Date( ) as a function indicating today's date, as measured by the computer's clock.

Press F2 (Data) to process the query, and you will see a list of employees who have been with the firm for one year or more. Depending on the date maintained by your PC's clock and the dates you entered for the employees, this list may or may not include every employee of the company.

Matching Records Based On OR Criteria

The types of queries you've done so far will work fine for conditions in which all of the criteria you specify need to be met before a record is included. Such cases of criteria are also referred to as *AND logic,* because you are qualifying a record where a certain condition is met *and* another certain condition is met. Sometimes, however, you need a different sort of qualification.

Suppose you want to find records that meet one criteria or another criteria, such as all employees who live in either Maryland or Virginia. This calls for a different type of logic, known as *OR logic*—you want employees in Maryland *or* in Virginia. Fashioning such queries in dBASE IV is simple. You just add as many lines to the Query Design screen as necessary; each line contains a separate condition that can be met to qualify the records.

For an example, press SHIFT-F2 (Design) to get back to the Query Design screen, and clear the last entry in the DATEHIRED field. Press HOME to get the cursor to the far left, under the filename ABCSTAFF.DBF. With the cursor under the filename, press F5 until the view skeleton at the bottom of the screen clears, and then press F5 once more. Because the cursor was in the first field, this action will tell dBASE IV to move every field from the file skeleton to the view skeleton, so that every field will be included in the result.

Next, place the cursor in the STATE field and in the first row, and enter **="MD"**. Move the cursor down one line by pressing the down arrow key once, and enter **="VA"**. Note that as you move the cursor down, the length of the file skeleton automatically extends to provide room for another condition. Finally, press F2 (Data) to process the query. The results should show all the employees who live in either Maryland or Virginia.

! ***HINT*** You can add multiple rows for multiple OR conditions by pressing the down arrow key as many times as needed.

If the Query Design screen fills with different conditions, you can press PGDN to get more viewing room on the screen. This should give you sufficient room to execute the most complex of queries by using OR logic.

☞ ***REMEMBER*** You'll need to save your queries if you want to use them later. Use the Save changes and Exit option of the Exit menu to do this.

Complex Matching

You can use the powerful query-by-example facility of dBASE IV to match criteria for various fields and thereby set up complex searches. You can also combine AND and OR logic to isolate the results to the precise records you'll need. As an example, suppose that you wish to see all the employees who live in Virginia or in Maryland, were hired in 1986, and are earning at least $9.00 per hour. If this sounds like overkill, rest assured that it isn't; management reports often require more complex conditions than these before upper management is satisfied with the results.

In this example, dBASE IV needs to know three facts as selection criteria. First, the states must be equal to MD or VA. Second, the date hired must be >={1/1/86} and <={12/31/86}. Finally, the salary value must be >=$9.00.

To begin, press SHIFT-F2 to get back to the Query Design screen, and delete the prior entries. Press HOME, and then press F5 until the view skeleton (at the bottom of the screen) clears. Using the TAB key to position the cursor, select the following fields, and enter the following matching criteria:

- In the LASTNAME, FIRSTNAME, STATE, DATEHIRED, and SALARY fields, press F5 to add the field to the view skeleton.
- In the STATE field, on the first row, enter **="VA"**. On the second row of the same field, enter **="MD"**. (Use the down arrow key to get to the second row.)
- In the DATEHIRED field, on both the first and second rows, enter this expression:

  ```
  >={1/1/86}, <={12/31/86}
  ```

- In the SALARY field, on both the first and second rows, enter **>= 9**.

Figure 7-13.

LASTNAME	FIRSTNAME	STATE	DATEHIRED	SALARY
Hart	Edward	VA	10/19/86	9.00
Jones	Judi	VA	08/12/86	12.50
Westman	Andrea	MD	07/04/86	16.50

Results of complex query

Finally, implement the query by pressing F2 (Data). The results should be similar to the example shown in Figure 7-13.

Creating the HOURS Database

Because dBASE IV is a relational database, you can use it to work extensively with multiple databases at the same time. Later chapters will explain how relationships can be drawn between multiple databases. For now, however, the ability to work with numeric amounts will come in handy, because ABC Temporaries needs an additional database that will show how many hours were worked by a given employee for a given firm while on assignment. You should create this database, called HOURS, now; it will be used (along with the ABCSTAFF database you created earlier) throughout the remainder of this text.

After some analysis of the needed attributes has been done by the management staff at ABC Temporaries, it is decided that the following attributes need to be tracked.

Field Name	Field Type	Length	Decimals
ASSIGNMENT	Character	20	
SOCIALSEC	Character	11	
WEEKENDING	Date		
HOURS	Numeric	4	1

Press ESC and then type **Y** to get back to the Control Center, and choose Create from the Data panel to create a new database. Using the attributes just shown as a guide, create the four fields that will be used in the HOURS database. Once you finish defining the fields, the structure should look like the example shown in Figure 7-14.

Figure 7-14.

```
Layout   Organize   Append   Go To   Exit                          12:15:02 pm

                                                        Bytes remaining:   3957
 Num  Field Name   Field Type  Width  Dec  Index
  1   ASSIGNMENT   Character    20           Y
  2   SOCIALSEC    Character    11           N
  3   WEEKENDING   Date          8           N
  4   HOURS        Numeric       4     1     N

Database E:\dbase4\dbdata\HOURS   Field 1/4
        Enter the field name.  Insert/Delete field:Ctrl-N/Ctrl-U
Field names begin with a letter and may contain letters, digits and underscores
```

Structure of HOURS database

Use the Save Changes and Exit option of the Exit menu to save the new file. When prompted for a name, enter **HOURS**. Once you are back at the Control Center, press F2 (Data) to begin adding records. Add the records shown in Table 7-2 to the new database. When you are finished adding the records, press CTRL-END to save the additions and return to the Control Center.

Summarizing Records in Queries

You may find the reserved words that apply to numeric calculations to be of use in your own applications. As you saw in Table 7-1, these words can be used as a part of a query, to find totals,

Table 7-2.

Assignment	Social Security	Weekend Date	Hours Worked
National Oil Co.	909-88-7654	01/16/88	35
National Oil Co.	121-33-9876	01/16/88	30
National Oil Co.	121-90-5432	01/16/88	27
National Oil Co.	123-44-8976	01/16/88	32
City Revenue Dept.	343-55-9821	01/16/88	35
City Revenue Dept.	495-00-3456	01/16/88	28
City Revenue Dept.	232-55-1234	01/16/88	30
Smith Builders	876-54-3210	01/23/88	30
Smith Builders	901-77-3456	01/23/88	28
Smith Builders	876-54-3210	01/23/88	35
City Revenue Dept.	232-55-1234	01/23/88	30
City Revenue Dept.	495-00-3456	01/23/88	32
City Revenue Dept.	343-55-9821	01/23/88	32
National Oil Co.	121-33-9876	01/23/88	35
National Oil Co.	909-88-7654	01/23/88	33

New Records for HOURS Table

minimum and maximum values, averages, or counts of occurrences. To see how they can be used, choose the Create option of the Queries panel. Since you are now working with a new database (HOURS), the file and view skeletons that appear on the screen contain the fields from the HOURS database.

For planning purposes, perhaps you need to know the average number of hours worked by the staff. Move the cursor to the HOURS field of the Query Design screen, enter **AVG**, and press F2. When the results appear, you will see what resembles a screen in Edit or Browse mode, but with no records present. (Press F2 again to switch to Browse mode if you are not already there.) The empty fields are normal; when you use one of the calculation expressions, only the calculated value appears in the appropriate field. In the HOURS column, dBASE IV displays the average hours worked per employee.

Press SHIFT-F2 to move back to the HOURS field of the Query Design screen, and press CTRL-Y to delete the entry. Then enter **MAX** and press F2. The resulting answer shows the maximum number of hours worked by any single employee. If you had entered MIN as the expression, the result would have been the minimum number of hours worked.

If you press SHIFT-F2 to move back to the HOURS field of the Query Design screen and change the expression to **SUM** and press F2, dBASE IV will sum the hours worked and display the total hours worked per week for the entire staff.

HINT If you want to perform these types of summaries from the dot prompt, you can use the CALCULATE command. See CALCULATE in Appendix A for details.

Obtaining Summaries by Group

You can also divide your numeric summaries into groups with the Group By operator. Simply enter the words "Group By" in the field you want to use for dividing the records into groups. When you perform the query, any of the summary operators you are using will provide values for each group.

As an example, consider the sum value you just obtained for the number of hours worked. Perhaps what you really wanted is a sum by group of employees at each assignment. Press SHIFT-F2 to get back to the Query Design screen. With the Sum operator still in the HOURS field, move the cursor back to the ASSIGNMENT field and enter **Group By**. Then press F2 for the results. You'll note that the sum totals of the hours worked are broken into three totals for each of the three assignments.

Sorting Within Queries

If the records chosen through a query need to be in some type of order, you can sort and perform the query at the same time. The Sort on This Field option of the Fields menu can be used to accomplish this task. Simply place the cursor in the field you want to sort, open the Fields menu with ALT-F, and choose Sort on This Field. Then choose the desired sort order (ascending or descending, and ASCII or dictionary order) from the menus that appear.

To see an example, first get back to using the ABCSTAFF file. Press ESC and then type **Y** to abandon the query. When you are at the Control Center, highlight ABCSTAFF in the Data panel and press ENTER; then choose Use File from the next menu. Next, highlight the Create option in the Queries panel, and press ENTER to get to the Query Design screen.

Perhaps you need to see a list of all employees living in Virginia, sorted in alphabetical order by last name and then first name. Move the cursor to the STATE field and enter the condition:

```
="VA"
```

Then move to the LASTNAME field. Open the Fields menu with ALT-F, and choose Sort on This Field. From the next menu to appear, choose Ascending Dictionary. When you make the selection, you will notice that the term "AscDict1" is automatically entered into the LASTNAME field of the file skeleton. You could have manually typed this entry to get the same results, but the menu makes the correct entry for you.

Move the cursor to the FIRSTNAME field. Open the Fields menu with ALT-F, choose Sort on This Field, and again choose Ascending Dictionary. This time "AscDict2" is entered into the FIRSTNAME field of the file skeleton.

Press F2 to apply the query. The sort will take place, and in a moment, you will see the selected records in alphabetical order by last name and first name (see Figure 7-15).

Using Condition Boxes

An optional feature offered to you by dBASE IV's query-by-example system is the ability to build conditions inside of a condition

Figure 7-15.

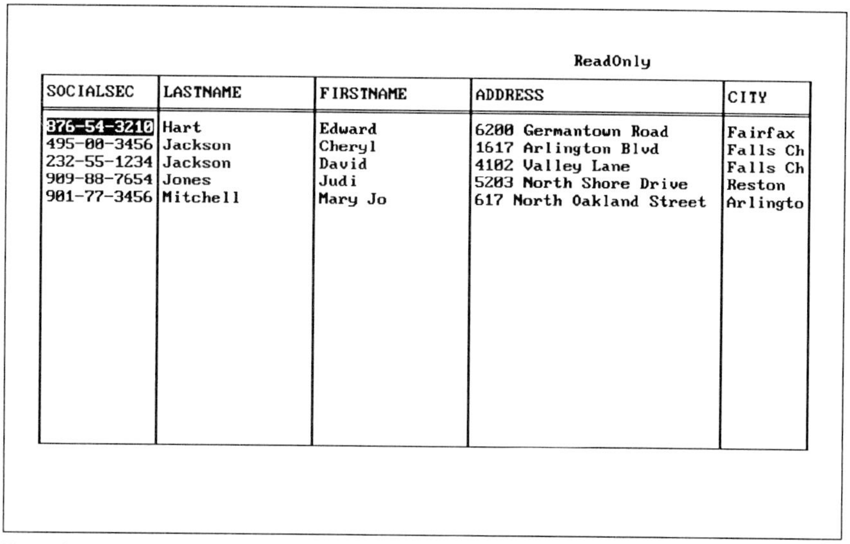

ReadOnly

SOCIALSEC	LASTNAME	FIRSTNAME	ADDRESS	CITY
876-54-3210	Hart	Edward	6200 Germantown Road	Fairfax
495-00-3456	Jackson	Cheryl	1617 Arlington Blvd	Falls Ch
232-55-1234	Jackson	David	4102 Valley Lane	Falls Ch
909-88-7654	Jones	Judi	5203 North Shore Drive	Reston
901-77-3456	Mitchell	Mary Jo	617 North Oakland Street	Arlingto

Results of sorted query

box that will apply to every record and database file on the Query Design screen. Experienced users of dBASE III and dBASE III PLUS may prefer the condition box, because it lets you enter the logic that will define the chosen records in a single visual area, much like the filter and query methods used with dBASE III and dBASE III PLUS.

To add a condition box, you select the Add Condition Box option of the Condition menu. When you do so, a condition box appears at the lower-right corner of the screen, as shown in Figure 7-16. You can enter the desired conditions manually, or you can press SHIFT-F1 to display a pick list of field names, operators, and dBASE functions with which you can build the condition.

For example, entering the expression **CITY = "Falls Church"** in the condition box would have the same effect as entering **="Falls Church"** in the CITY field of the file skeleton. Both methods would limit the records available for display or printing to those containing "Falls Church" in the CITY field.

Figure 7-16.

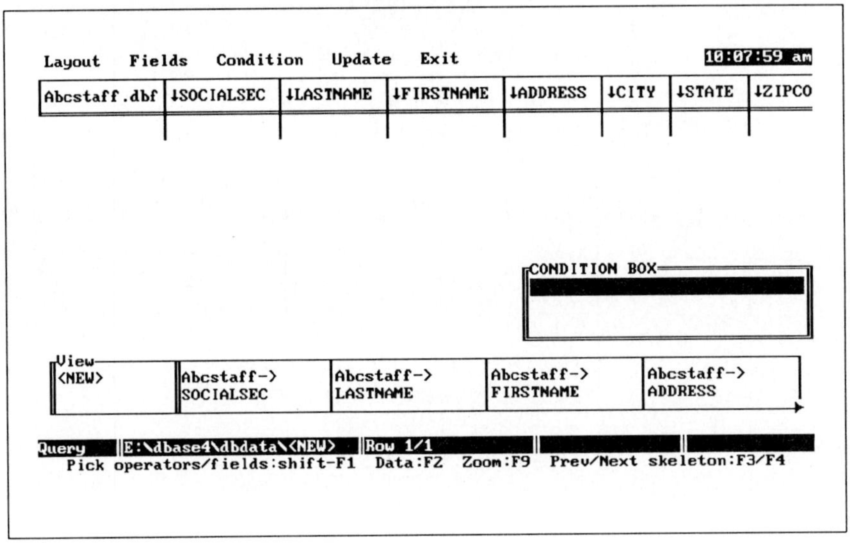

```
Layout   Fields   Condition   Update   Exit                          10:07:59 am
Abcstaff.dbf |↓SOCIALSEC |↓LASTNAME |↓FIRSTNAME |↓ADDRESS |↓CITY |↓STATE |↓ZIPCO

                                                CONDITION BOX

View          Abcstaff->      Abcstaff->      Abcstaff->      Abcstaff->
<NEW>         SOCIALSEC       LASTNAME        FIRSTNAME       ADDRESS

Query    E:\dbase4\dbdata\<NEW>    Row 1/1
  Pick operators/fields:shift-F1  Data:F2  Zoom:F9  Prev/Next skeleton:F3/F4
```

Condition box

You can view more of the entries in the condition box by pressing F9 (Zoom) to enlarge the box to a full screen. Pressing F9 again will shrink the condition box back to its original size. Once you have entered the desired conditions in the condition box, you can press F2 (Data) to see the records meeting the specified conditions, or you can save the query as a file for later use.

Using Update Queries

While view queries can be readily used for editing records and generating reports, another type of query is available for global replacements or updates of records: the update query. Update queries provide four possible operators: Replace, Append, Mark, and Unmark. These operators let you specify how the database will be changed when the update query is performed.

Use the Replace operator to replace the values in specified fields with another value. The Append operator lets you add chosen records to a file (the target) from another file (the source). The Mark and Unmark operators let you mark selected records for deletion or remove deletion markers from selected records.

Building an update query is very similar to building a view query. The major difference is that one of the four operators—Replace, Append, Mark, or Unmark—must be entered directly under the database filename in the file skeleton. If you have more than one database file displayed on the screen, the operator must be entered under the name of the file that you wish to update.

You can enter the desired operator by typing it directly under the filename, or you can place the cursor under the filename and choose Specify Update Operation from the Update menu. When you choose this option, a second menu appears, providing your choice of the four operators. Choose the desired option from the menu, and the operator will be entered automatically in the file skeleton.

Once you enter the desired operator, you then enter the necessary conditions in the same manner as you did with view queries. For example, entering **MARK** as the operator directly underneath the filename and then entering **="Robinson"** in the LASTNAME column would cause the query, when performed, to mark for deletion all employees whose last name was Robinson.

Once you have entered the desired conditions, the simplest way to perform the update is to open the Update menu while you are still at the Query Design screen, and choose the Perform the Update option. When the update is completed, you will still be at the Query Design screen. You can view the data with F2, or you can exit from the Query Design screen.

If you do not plan to perform the same update again, there is no need to save the update query once it has been performed. If you wish to perform the update later (which is sometimes preferable because updates on large databases are time-consuming), you can save the update query with the Save Changes and Exit choice of the Exit menu. You can then perform the update query later by getting to the dot prompt and entering the command

```
DO updatename.UPD
```

where *updatename* is the name you gave the update query when you saved it.

An example of an update query can be done now on the ABCSTAFF database. In a prior chapter, the salaries were increased by a set amount. However, no increase has been made to the billing rates, and profits at ABC Temporaries are growing thin. To rectify the situation, you will perform an update query that increases the hourly rate by $1.00 per hour.

Since you will be replacing the contents of the HOURLYRATE field with a new amount, you will need to use the Replace operator. Press SHIFT-F2 to get back to the Query Design screen, and delete any prior entries in the fields of the file skeleton. Move the cursor back to the far left by pressing the HOME key. Open the Update menu with ALT-U, and choose Specify Update Operation from the menu. You will see another menu containing the four possible update operators, as shown in Figure 7-17.

The Replace choice is currently highlighted, so press ENTER. A message box will warn you that you are changing the view into an update view, and in the process you will delete the existing view skeleton. You don't need to save the view skeleton, so choose Proceed from the menu. The Replace operator will appear under the filename.

Press the END key to quickly get to the end of the list of fields, and then use SHIFT-TAB to get back to the HOURLYRATE field. Enter the following:

```
WITH HOURLYRATE + 1
```

Figure 7-17.

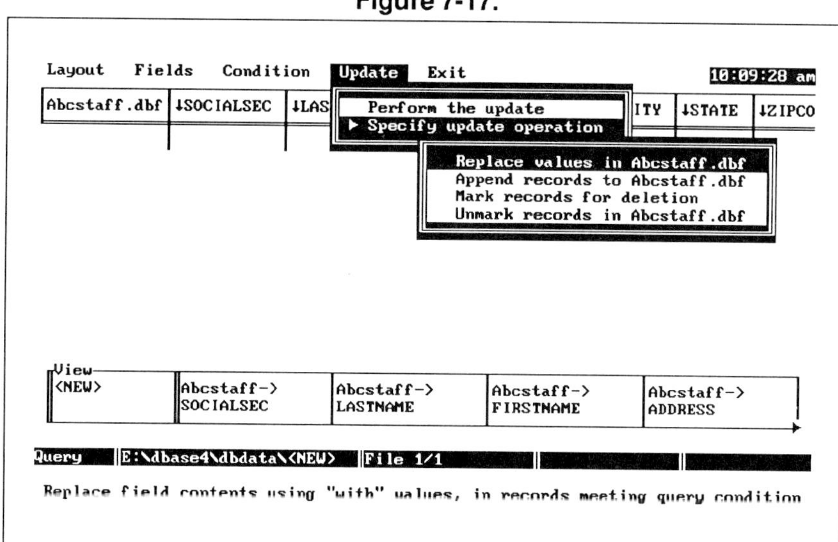

Update operators menu

This tells dBASE to replace the contents of the HOURLYRATE field with the current amount plus $1.00. If you wished, you could enter other conditions that would limit the replacements to a specific subset of records. For example, the expression, < >"National Oil Co." in the ASSIGNMENT field would cause the update to occur only for records that had clients other than the National Oil Company in the field. However, in this example, no other conditions are needed. Open the Update menu with ALT-U, and choose Perform the Update. When the update is completed, you will still be at the Query Design screen.

Press F2 (Data), and tab over to the HOURLYRATE field. Your screen should resemble the example in Figure 7-18, with the increased hourly rates in place.

One significant type of query that has not been covered in this chapter is a query of a relational nature; that is, one that works with more than one file. Relational queries are covered in detail in Chapter 12.

Figure 7-18.

SOCIALSEC	LASTNAME	DEPENDENTS	SALARY	ASSIGNMENT	HOURLYRATE
123-44-8976	Morse	2	9.00	National Oil Co.	16.00
121-33-9876	Westman	2	16.50	National Oil Co.	25.00
232-55-1234	Jackson	1	8.00	City Revenue Dept.	13.00
901-77-3456	Mitchell	1	8.00	Smith Builders	13.00
121-90-5432	Robinson	1	8.00	National Oil Co.	13.00
495-00-3456	Jackson	1	12.50	City Revenue Dept.	19.00
343-55-9821	Robinson	0	8.00	City Revenue Dept.	13.00
876-54-3210	Hart	3	9.00	Smith Builders	15.00
909-88-7654	Jones	1	12.50	National Oil Co.	18.50

View of increased hourly rates

Quick Reference

To get to the Query Design screen From the Control Center, select the Create option in the Queries panel. From the dot prompt, enter either **CREATE QUERY *filename*** or **MODIFY QUERY *filename***.

To move around the Query Design Screen Use TAB and SHIFT-TAB to move between columns. Use F3 and F4 to move between the file skeleton and the view skeleton. Use HOME and END to move to the far-left or far-right ends of a skeleton.

To design a query First choose the fields you want displayed in the view. You can press F5 repeatedly to add and remove fields from the view skeleton. After the fields you want are in the view skeleton, enter the desired conditions in the fields of the file skeleton. Remember to surround character expressions with quotes, and dates with curly braces.

To apply the query Press F2 (Data). The results will appear in a Browse or Edit screen. Press F2 again to switch between Edit and Browse modes. To get back to the Query Design screen, press SHIFT-F2.

To save a query for later use From the Query Design screen, open the Exit menu with ALT-E. Choose Save Changes and Exit. When prompted, enter a name for the query file.

To use an existing query From the Control Center, highlight the query name in the Queries panel, and press F2 (Data). From the dot prompt, enter **SET VIEW TO *filename***, where *filename* is the name you gave the query file when you saved it.

To perform summary queries based upon numeric fields
At the Query Design screen, enter the desired keyword in the numeric field of the file skeleton. Keywords you can use include AVG (for average), MAX (for maximum), MIN (for minimum), and SUM (for sum total). Press F2 (Data) to apply the query and display the summary values.

To sort a database while performing a query At the Query Design screen, open the Fields menu with ALT-F, and choose Sort On This Field. Select the desired sort order from the menu that appears. Press F2 (Data) to apply the query.

To perform an update query Design the query conditions as you normally would. Then enter one of the four update operators—MARK, UNMARK, APPEND, or REPLACE—directly under the database filename in the file skeleton. Open the Update menu with ALT-U, and choose Perform The Update.

CHAPTER

8

Introducing Reports

Creating reports is, for many users, what database management is all about. While a query is a powerful tool for gaining immediate answers to specific questions, much of your work with dBASE IV will probably involve generating reports. Detailed reports are easy to produce with dBASE IV, thanks in part to the program's Quick Report option, which can be combined with queries to obtain reports of selective data.

dBASE IV provides several ways to print reports. You can print quick reports with a single key combination. From the dot prompt, you can also use a combination of the LIST and DISPLAY commands to print information. You can use dBASE IV's sophisticated built-in report generator to create custom reports. You can also print form letters or mailing labels.

This chapter provides an introduction to the many ways you can produce reports. More advanced reporting topics, including form-oriented reports, mailing labels, and form letters, are covered in Chapter 11. Before going any further, be sure that your printer is turned on and ready; otherwise, you may lock up your system when trying to print.

Report Design

Before you start to design your custom reports, you should plan the design of the report. This may mean asking the other users of the database what information will actually be needed from the report. In the case of ABC Temporaries, you would consider what information the managers need from the report, and how you want the report to look.

In many cases, you'll find it advantageous to outline the report's contents and format on paper. Once the report has been designed on paper, your outline should resemble the actual report that is produced by dBASE IV. You may also find it helpful to print a list of fields from the database structure, particularly if you are designing a report that contains a large number of fields. This can be done by selecting the filename from the Control Center, choosing Modify Structure/Order, and choosing the Print Database Structure option from the Layout menu.

dBASE IV Reports

The two types of reports available in dBASE IV are *quick reports* and *custom reports.* Quick reports contain all of the fields in the file (or view, if the report is based on a view query). The field names that were supplied during the database design are used as column headings within the report.

Figure 8-1a.

Page No. 1
09/09/88

ASSIGNMENT	SOCIALSEC	WEEKENDING	HOURS
National Oil Co.	909-88-7654	01/16/88	35.0
National Oil Co.	121-33-9876	01/16/88	30.0
National Oil Co.	121-90-5432	01/16/88	27.0
National Oil Co.	123-44-8976	01/16/88	32.0
City Revenue Dept.	343-55-9821	01/16/88	35.0
City Revenue Dept.	495-00-3456	01/16/88	28.0
City Revenue Dept.	232-55-1234	01/16/88	30.0
Smith Builders	876-54-3210	01/23/88	30.0
Smith Builders	901-77-3456	01/23/88	28.0
Smith Builders	805-34-6789	01/23/88	35.0
City Revenue Dept.	232-55-1234	01/23/88	30.0
City Revenue Dept.	495-00-3456	01/23/88	32.0
City Revenue Dept.	343-55-9821	01/23/88	32.0
National Oil Co.	121-33-9876	01/23/88	35.0
National Oil Co.	909-88-7654	01/23/88	33.0

Example of a quick report (columnar)

Figure 8-1b.

```
Page No. 1
09/09/88

ASSIGNMENT          National Oil Co.
SOCIALSEC           909-88-7654
WEEKENDING          01/16/88   HOURS WORKED:35.0

ASSIGNMENT          National Oil Co.
SOCIALSEC           121-33-9876
WEEKENDING          01/16/88   HOURS WORKED:30.0

ASSIGNMENT          National Oil Co.
SOCIALSEC           121-90-5432
WEEKENDING          01/16/88   HOURS WORKED:27.0

ASSIGNMENT          National Oil Co.
SOCIALSEC           123-44-8976
WEEKENDING          01/16/88   HOURS WORKED:32.0

ASSIGNMENT          City Revenue Dept.
SOCIALSEC           343-55-9821
WEEKENDING          01/16/88   HOURS WORKED:35.0

ASSIGNMENT          City Revenue Dept.
SOCIALSEC           495-00-3456
WEEKENDING          01/16/88   HOURS WORKED:28.0

ASSIGNMENT          City Revenue Dept.
SOCIALSEC           232-55-1234
WEEKENDING          01/16/88   HOURS WORKED:30.0
```

Example of a custom report (form)

Figure 8-1b. (continued)

```
ASSIGNMENT        Smith Builders
SOCIALSEC         876-54-3210
WEEKENDING        01/23/88  HOURS  WORKED:30.0

ASSIGNMENT        Smith Builders
SOCIALSEC         901-77-3456
WEEKENDING        01/23/88  HOURS  WORKED:28.0
```

Example of a custom report (form)

Custom reports, by comparison, are reports that you create or modify to better fit your specific needs. A significant plus of the report generator in dBASE IV is that it doesn't force you to design custom reports from scratch, starting with a blank screen. The report generator provides a Quick Layouts option that lets you choose one of three automatic designs for reports: columnar (with printed data appearing in columns), form (with printed data arranged in rows resembling a form), and mailmerge (for use with form letters).

Custom reports that you design with the report generator can contain any data you desire from the fields of the database. They can include numeric information, such as totals or calculations based on numeric fields. Reports can also include headings that contain the specified title of the report, the date (as determined by the PC's clock), and the page number for each page. Such headings are commonly used with columnar reports. Figure 8-1a shows an example of a report in columnar layout, and Figure 8-1b shows an example of a report in form layout.

By far the fastest way to produce printed reports in dBASE IV is to use a quick report, because it needs no designing in advance. To produce a quick report, simply highlight the database file (or view query, if the report is to be based on a view) and press SHIFT-F9 (Quick Report). From the Print menu that appears next, choose Begin Printing (after making sure your printer is turned on).

The report shown in Figure 8-1a was produced from the HOURS database by means of the Quick Report key. Note that the report illustrates the design of a quick report. The page number appears at the upper-left corner of the page, and the date appears directly underneath. The field names appear as column headings, and the data appears in single-spaced rows beneath the headings.

If you generate your own quick report by highlighting the ABCSTAFF file (not the HOURS file) and pressing SHIFT-F9, you may notice one trait of a quick report that may not be very appealing to you. Depending on the number of fields in the file and how your printer handles lines that are wider than 80 columns, one or more columns of text may be cut off at the right margin. You could solve this problem by changing widths or moving the locations of columns in a custom report. If you don't want all the fields in the report, another way to obtain a quick report with the selected fields you desire is to base the report on a view query. Create a query that selects only the fields you want, and while at that query use SHIFT-F9 to generate a quick report.

Sending Reports to the Screen or to a File

When you press SHIFT-F9 to print a quick report, the default selections that appear on the Print menu cause the data to be sent to the printer. You can choose instead to direct the output of a report to the screen or to a disk file as ASCII (American Standard Committee for Information Interchange) text. To do this, highlight the desired database file or view from the Control Center and press SHIFT-F9 (Quick Report). When the Print menu appears, choose the View Report on Screen option if you want the report to go to the screen; otherwise, choose the Destination option. After you choose Destination, another menu will appear, as shown in Figure 8-2.

Pressing ENTER while the Write To option is highlighted will change the selection from Printer to DOS File. When DOS File appears, move the menu bar to the Name of DOS File option, press ENTER, and enter the desired filename (you can include a drive path if desired). If you omit this step, the file will be stored in the current directory with a default name of PRTOUT.PRT (under version 1.0), or with the same name as the database in use (under version 1.1). (The .PRT extension is the default extension, so if you name the file and omit an extension, the file will be assigned the .PRT extension.) Press ESC to close the secondary menu, and

Figure 8-2.

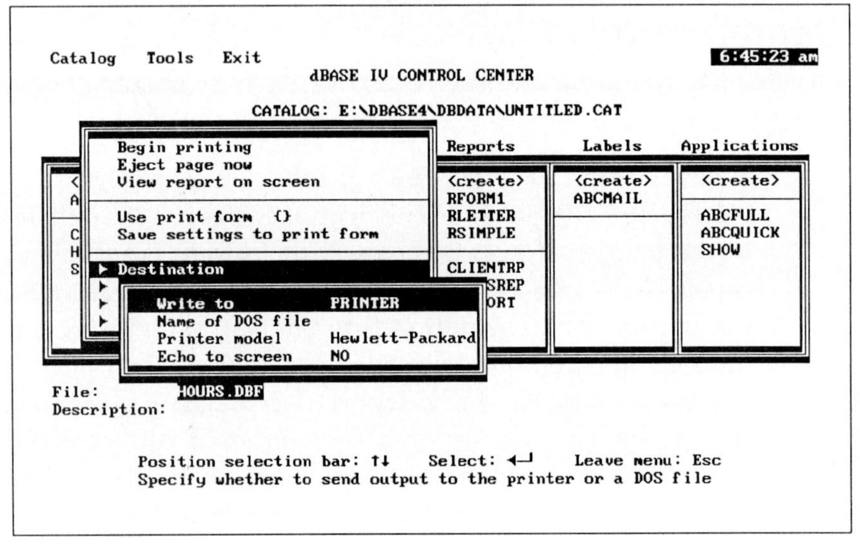

Secondary menu for Print Destination

choose Begin Printing to send the file to disk (or to the screen if you chose the View Report on Screen option).

If you choose View Report on Screen, the first page of the report appears on the screen. If there is more than one page of the report, you will see the message

Cancel viewing: ESC, continue viewing: spacebar

You can repeatedly press a key to display successive pages of a report.

REMEMBER When sending reports to a DOS file, change the Printer Model option in the submenu that appears to "ASCII" if you don't want printer control codes included in the DOS file.

If you send the report to a DOS file, note that ASCII text is stored in the file in the same format as it appears on the screen—with the headings, title and page numbers, and large amounts of white space (blank lines) between successive pages. This option of sending data to a disk file can be very useful for merging the contents of a report with a document; nearly all word processors for the IBM PC and compatibles can read an ASCII file produced in this manner. Consult your word processor's manual for details on how to do this.

The Print Menu Options

While we are on the topic of printing, further explanation of the various options in the Print menu is in order. The first option, Begin Printing, tells dBASE to send the output of the report to the printer or, if you have changed the Destination setting to DOS File as just described, to a DOS text file.

The Eject Page Now option sends a page eject, or printer form-feed escape code, to your printer. This helps you begin and end pages at the printed perforations, and with laser printers it helps you feed the last sheet of paper out of the printer (you can also use the printer's form-feed button for this task). The View Report on Screen option lets you display the report on the screen rather than send it to the printer. This is a useful option for visually checking the appearance of a report before printing it.

The Use Print Form option lets you recall printer settings that were previously saved in a print form. This option works along with the next option, Save Settings to Print Form. When you make various changes to printer settings for styles of print, page controls, and the optional use of escape codes, you may want to save these settings to avoid having to choose them again later. Use the Save Settings to Print Form option to save the settings. Then, when you print at a later time, select the Use Print Form option to recall the saved settings. How you actually make these settings is covered in succeeding paragraphs.

The Destination option lets you direct the output of the report. Note that when you choose DOS File, the text file that is generated meets the requirements of your printer. Therefore, the text file may contain escape codes or initialization strings at the start of the report if the printer you chose when installing dBASE normally uses these. You can alleviate this problem by changing the printer setting to ASCII Text, as described shortly.

When you choose Destination, a submenu offers four more choices: Write To, Name of DOS File, Printer Model, and Echo to Screen. The Write To option offers Printer or DOS File as the output device; pressing ENTER changes the setting. At the Name of DOS File option, you enter the name for the DOS text file. If you want to see all of a long path name as you enter it, press F9 (Zoom) to expand the size of the entry.

! ***HINT*** You'll need to install a printer if you want to make use of special styles such as italics and bold print. Note that most but not all printers support these styles.

The Printer Model option lets you select from as many as five of the printers you installed when you installed dBASE. (If you didn't install printers when you installed dBASE, you can add them by running DBSETUP from the subdirectory containing the dBASE program; see the end of this chapter for details.) The Printer Model option also provides a choice of ASCII Text, which is useful if you want a DOS file produced containing no control codes. Finally, the Echo to Screen option lets you display a report on the screen while it is printing. Note that you can cycle through

Figure 8-3.

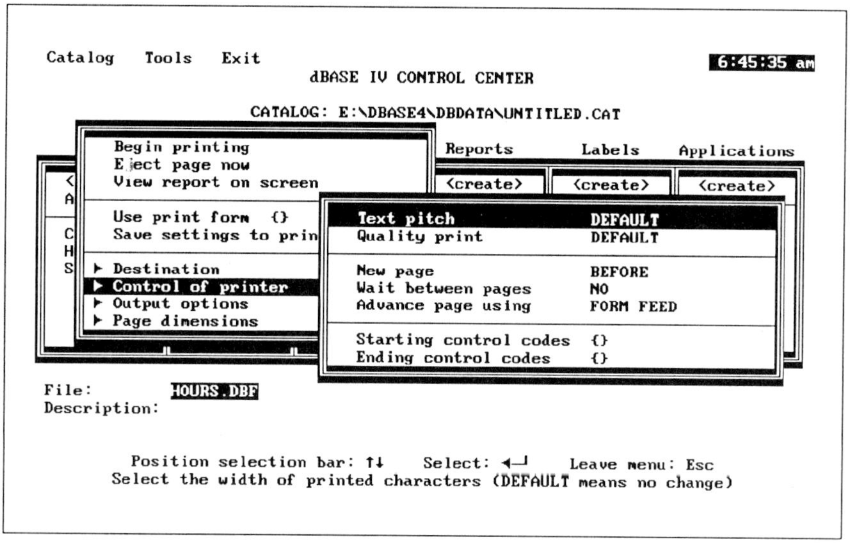

```
Catalog   Tools   Exit                                          6:45:35 am
                         dBASE IV CONTROL CENTER

               CATALOG: E:\DBASE4\DBDATA\UNTITLED.CAT

    Begin printing                    Reports      Labels      Applications
    Eject page now
    View report on screen           <create>     <create>      <create>

    Use print form  {}         Text pitch                  DEFAULT
    Save settings to prin      Quality print               DEFAULT

  ▶ Destination                New page                    BEFORE
  ▶ Control of printer         Wait between pages          NO
  ▶ Output options             Advance page using          FORM FEED
  ▶ Page dimensions
                               Starting control codes      {}
                               Ending control codes        {}
File:          HOURS.DBF
Description:

     Position selection bar: ↑↓    Select: ◄─┘     Leave menu: Esc
   Select the width of printed characters (DEFAULT means no change)
```

Control of Printer submenu

all of the available options on each of these submenus by pressing ENTER repeatedly.

The Control of Printer option, when chosen, displays the submenu of options shown in Figure 8-3. These options let you control the print quality and paper-handling aspects of printing. You can choose various text sizes with the Text Pitch option: Pica or 10 Chars per Inch, Elite or 12 Chars per Inch, Condensed, and Default (or no change). The Quality Print option selects near-letter-quality printing, if your printer supports this feature. The New Page option determines whether new pages are printed before the report starts, after the report ends, before and after, or not at all.

HINT To print an entire report in compressed print, choose Control of Printer from the Print menu, then choose Text Pitch. Press ENTER until condensed appears, then press CTRL-END.

Wait Between Pages lets you tell dBASE to pause between each page (which is useful for manually-fed printers). The Advance Page Using option lets you choose either Form Feeds (the most common method) or Line Feeds to advance to the top of each page. Finally, the Starting Control Codes option lets you send escape codes directly to your printer at the start of a report. See your printer manual for details about escape codes that can be used with your particular printer. You can enter escape codes as ASCII values by placing them inside curly { } braces. For example, an entry of **{015}** would enter an ASCII code of 15, which turns on compressed printing with most Epson-compatible printers.

The Output Options choice, when chosen, displays the submenu shown in Figure 8-4. These options let you select which pages of the report should be printed, as well as the number of copies to be printed. Use the Begin on Page and End After Page options to specify a starting and ending page for the report when you don't want the entire report printed. This can be very useful

Figure 8-4.

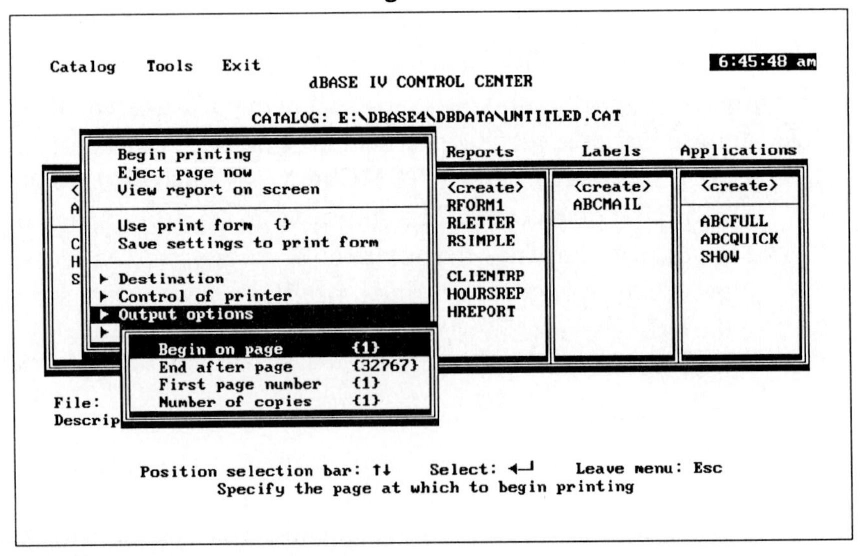

Output Options submenu

when your printer jams on page 87 of a 90-page report; after clearing the printer jam, you can use these options to restart the report without printing the first 86 pages all over again. The Begin on Page option can be set as low as 1, and the End After Page setting can be set as high as 32,767.

The First Page Number setting lets you make the first page of the report print with a page number other than page 1. Finally, the Number of Copies option lets you specify that more than one copy of the report is to be printed (although you will put less wear and tear on your computer and printer if you use a copying machine for this kind of task).

The Page Dimensions option displays the submenu shown in Figure 8-5. These options let you control the placement of text on the pages of the report. Use Length of Page to change the number of single-spaced lines that will fit on a page. The default is 66, but if you are using legal-size or European standard paper, you may

Figure 8-5.

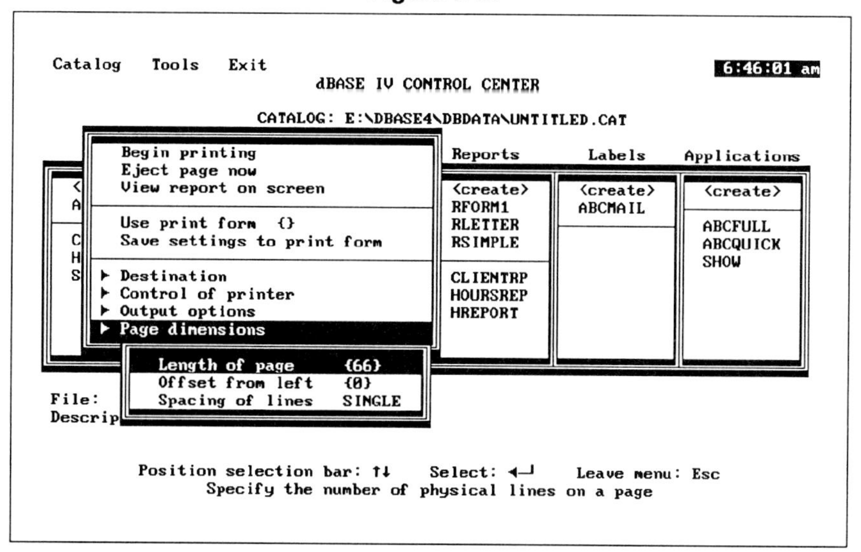

Page Dimensions submenu

want to change this setting to fit your paper (this may take some experimentation on your part). The Offset From Left option lets you establish a left offset (by default, set at 0) for the printing. This option is functionally equivalent to the SET MARGIN TO command available at the dot prompt. Finally, the Spacing of Lines option lets you select single, double, or triple line spacing in a report.

Producing Selective Reports with Ease

If you want maximum results in a minimum amount of time, keep in mind the flexibility that dBASE IV provides by letting you design queries that provide selective views of data. You can use views to generate your reports. In many cases, you can also solve formatting problems by including selected fields and omitting unwanted fields in the views.

Take the quick report produced if you highlight the ABCSTAFF database file and press SHIFT-F9 to print the report. Obviously, there are far too many fields to fit on a standard sheet of paper. Perhaps all you are really interested in are the LASTNAME, SALARY, HOURLYRATE, and ASSIGNMENT fields, and you know that these will comfortably fit on a standard sheet of paper.

Get to the Control Center if you are not there already, and select the Create option of the Queries panel. In a moment, a query form appears, with the cursor under the field name ABCSTAFF.DBF. From the prior chapter, you may recall that pressing F5 (Field) while the cursor is under the filename in the file skeleton will remove all fields from the view. Since you only want four fields in the view, it would be faster to remove all of the fields and then add the fields you desire.

Press F5 (Field) to remove all the fields of ABCSTAFF.DBF from the view skeleton. Now press TAB twice to move to the LASTNAME field and press F5 (Field) to add the LASTNAME field to the view. Use the TAB key to move to the SALARY field, and press F5 (Field) to add this field to the view. Using the same technique, add the ASSIGNMENT and HOURLYRATE fields to the view. Press F2 (Data) to apply the results of the query to the file. When the data appears, press SHIFT-F9 and choose Begin Printing to print the quick report.

The report that results should contain all of the records from the staff database, but with only the desired fields, as shown in Figure 8-6. If you wanted specific records in the report, you could use the query-by-example methods described in the prior chapter to produce a subset of records in the view. Also, if you wanted to

Figure 8-6.

Page No. 1
09/09/88

LASTNAME	SALARY	ASSIGNMENT	HOURLYRATE
Morse	9.00	National Oil Co.	16.00
Westman	16.50	National Oil Co.	25.00
Jackson	8.00	City Revenue Dept.	13.00
Mitchell	8.00	Smith Builders	13.00
Robinson	8.00	National Oil Co.	13.00
Jackson	12.00	City Revenue Dept.	19.00
Robinson	8.00	City Revenue Dept.	13.00
Hart	8.50	Smith Builders	15.00
Jones	12.50	National Oil Co.	18.50

Quick report based on query with selected fields

see the records within the quick report in some specific order, you could specify a sort selection within the Query Design screen and then apply the query and print the report. In cases where you want to include all fields and all records, but you do want the records in a specific order, you can just use the Order Records by Index option of the Organize menu before printing the report. Using these techniques, you can generate detailed reports based on complex conditions with little or no custom-report designing.

HINT If you sort or index a file before printing a report, the records in the report will appear in the order of the sort or index. Remember that in the case of sorts, you must put the sorted file in use.

Dot-Prompt Options: Using LIST with Printers

From the dot prompt, the LIST command is useful for printing data as well as examining data on the screen. The SET PRINT ON command directs all output to the printer as well as the screen for all subsequent LIST commands, and SET PRINT OFF stops output from being sent to the printer.

To use these commands, first get to the dot prompt and enter

```
USE ABCSTAFF
```

to close and reopen the database file. Doing so will cancel the effects of the query that you worked with earlier. Make sure your printer is ready, and then enter these commands:

```
SET PRINT ON
LIST LASTNAME, FIRSTNAME, SALARY, HOURLYRATE
```

Anything that you type with SET PRINT ON will be directed to the printer, including all commands that you type and any error messages. Enter

```
SET PRINT OFF
```

to turn off the output to the printer. If you are using a laser printer, you may also need to enter **EJECT** at the dot prompt. The EJECT command sends a printer form-feed code, causing the printed sheet to feed out of the printer.

A more precise method of directing output to the printer is to use the TO PRINT option with the LIST command. This prevents all your command words from printing on the page along with the desired data. The normal format of the command with this option is as follows:

LIST [*fieldname1, fieldname2...fieldnameX*] TO PRINT

To try this command, enter

```
LIST LASTNAME, CITY, STATE TO PRINT
```

to print all the name, city, and state fields for each record in the database.

You can be selective by specifying a FOR condition with the LIST command, and still send output to the printer with TO PRINT. For example,

```
LIST LASTNAME, FIRSTNAME, CITY FOR LASTNAME = "Robinson" TO PRINT
```

prints the last names, first names, and cities of Shirley Robinson and Wanda Robinson. The command

```
LIST LASTNAME, CITY, STATE, SALARY FOR SALARY > 9.00 TO PRINT
```

provides a printed listing like the following, with the last names, cities, states, and salary amounts for all employees earning more than $9.00 per hour:

Record#	LASTNAME	CITY	STATE	SALARY
2	Westman	Silver Spring	MD	16.50
6	Jackson	Falls Church	VA	12.00
9	Jones	Reston	VA	12.50

Margin Settings and Page Ejects

You can change your printer's left margin with the SET MARGIN command. dBASE IV normally defaults to a printer margin value of 0. Entering **SET MARGIN TO 12**, for example, would cause the printer to indent 12 spaces at the beginning of each line. (This command affects only the left margin; the right margin cannot be set with a command in dBASE IV.)

The equivalent of the SET MARGIN command can be reached through the Control Center menus by choosing the Settings option on the Tools Menu and selecting the Margin option. (The Offset From Left option on the Page Dimensions submenu on the Quick Report menu discussed earlier has the same effect.)

The EJECT command, as mentioned earlier, causes the printer to perform a form feed (to advance to the top of the next sheet). This command is not available from Control Center menus; it must be entered at the dot prompt. An alternative is to use the form-feed button on your printer to accomplish the same task.

REMEMBER Most laser printers will not feed the last page of a report generated with a LIST...TO PRINT statement unless you add an EJECT command after the report has completed.

Designing a Custom Columnar Report

There will be times when you prefer to place your fields as you want them, change formatting attributes, add custom headers and footers, and so on. Designing a custom report is the desired route when you need this kind of flexibility. Depending on how complex your needs are, the precise steps involved in the report's design may vary in complexity. You will learn here about the basic process in designing a custom report, following the columnar format used by the quick report.

You first choose Create at the Reports panel of the Control Center to begin the report's design process. (Dot-prompt users can enter the CREATE REPORT *filename* command to begin creating the report.) In a moment, the Report Design screen will appear and the Layout menu will be opened. If you want to use (or modify) one of the quick-layout styles of report, choose the Quick Layouts option from this menu and then select the desired layout (Column, Form, or Mailmerge). The column style is covered in detail in this chapter; the other styles, form and mailmerge, are covered in Chapter 11.

Once you make the selection, dBASE IV displays the *report specification,* as shown in Figure 8-7. If you chose the Quick Layouts option, the fields in the database will be included in the report automatically. In the process of designing a custom report,

Figure 8-7.

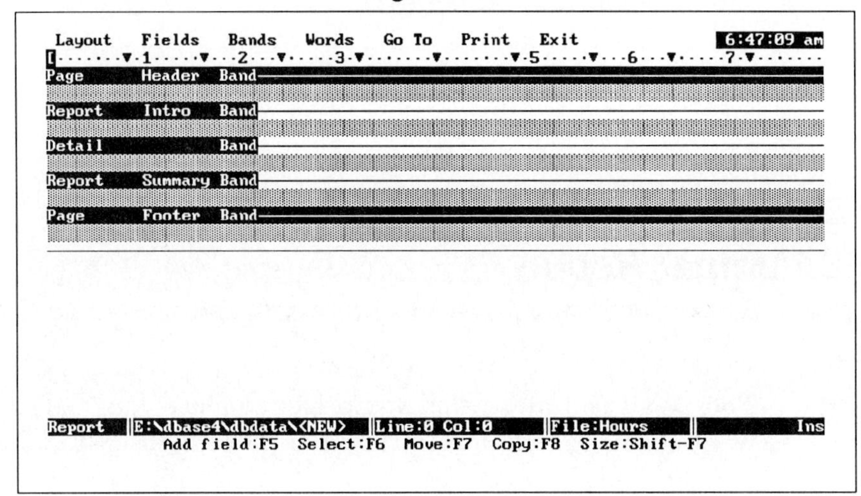

Report specification

you can move fields, add and delete headings, and make other changes to the report.

The Report Specification

The report specification is made up of several important parts, as shown in Figure 8-8. dBASE IV views each portion of the report as a horizontal area known as a *report band.* As the figure shows, there is a Page Header band, a Report Intro band, a Detail band, a Report Summary band, and a Page Footer band. There can also be optional Group bands present in the report design. These bands control what the report contains and how it will appear when printed.

The Page Header band appears once for each page of the report. In many cases, you'll place such information as the date or time of the report and a report title in this area. The Page Footer band at the bottom of the report design has the same purpose as the header but is for footers, the information that typically appears at the bottom of each page.

Report Intro bands contain any information that should appear at the beginning of the report. Such information can be simple (as in a series of headings) or more complex (as with a paragraph of explanatory text or a form letter). Report Summary bands contain summary information that will be printed at the end of the report. You usually include numeric totals in this area.

The Detail bands indicate the actual information (usually fields) that will appear in the body of the report. The values in the Detail bands are represented by symbols called *field templates;* examples are AAAAAAA for alphanumeric fields, 999999 for numeric fields, and mm/dd/yy for date fields, like those seen in the Form Design screen.

Group bands, which are optional, are printed once for every

Figure 8-8.

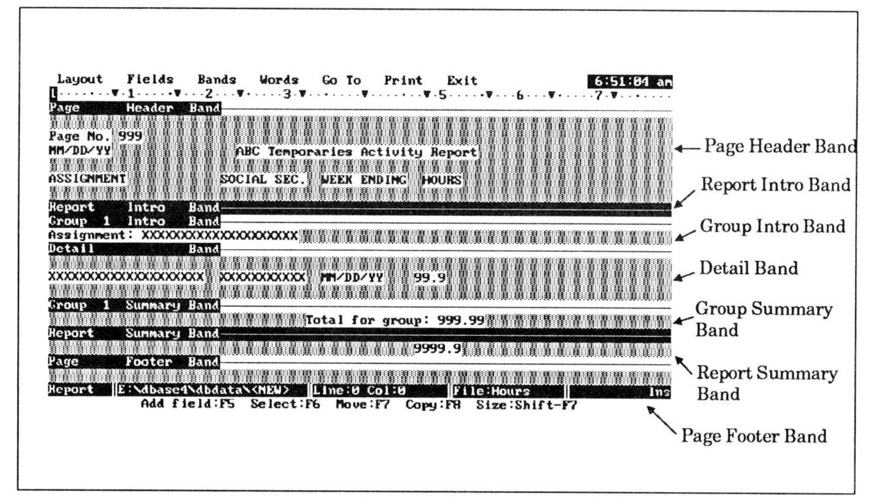

Parts of a report specification

group of records in a report. You may or may not want to group records in a report; as an example of grouping, you might decide to print a list of employees for ABC Temporaries by assignment. If you decide to include groups, dBASE IV lets you have an unlimited number of Group bands in a single report.

Making Changes to the Report's Design

Once the report design appears on the screen, you can use various options of the menus to rearrange or remove fields, set display formats, add bands for grouping, or make other desired changes. If you press F10 while the Report Design screen is visible, you will display the available menus.

The first menu is the Layout menu (Figure 8-9). It provides

Figure 8-9.

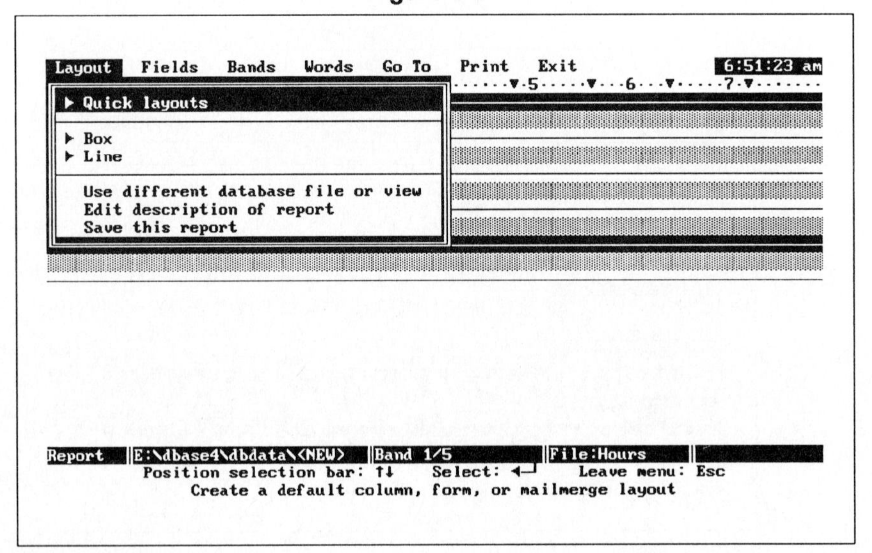

Layout menu

options for changing the overall layout of the report or the database file used by the report, for adding a description of the report, and for saving the report. The first option, Quick Layouts, provides a choice of column, form, or mailmerge layout when selected. You can choose one of these three standard types of reports as the format of your report. The Column choice creates a report with fields arranged in a columnar format. The Form choice arranges each field on a separate line, as on a printed form. The Mailmerge choice designs the report as a design for form letters.

The Box and Line options on the Layout menu let you add boxes or lines to the report in a manner similar to that with forms. (Note that your printer must have the capability of printing the IBM extended ASCII graphics character set to print the lines or boxes correctly.) The Use Different Database File or View option lets you change the database (or view) being used to produce the report. The Edit Description of Report option lets you add or edit a one-line description for the report, which is displayed when you highlight the file at the Control Center. The Save This Report option lets you save a report and continue working on it.

Pressing ALT-F opens the Fields menu (Figure 8-10). It contains the choices that are used to add, remove, and change fields. In operation, the menu options are very similar to those found in the Fields menu when you are designing forms. The Add Field option is used to add new fields to the report, and the Remove Field option will remove an existing field. Use the Modify Field option to change the field's characteristics (such as the template and picture functions described in Chapter 5). The Change Hidden Field option also changes field characteristics, but it does so for hidden fields. Calculated and summary fields can be hidden with the Hidden option that appears on a menu when you first create the field. They can later be modified by using the Change Hidden Field option. You might hide a field if you only wanted to use it as the basis for another calculation later in the report.

Pressing ALT-B reveals the Bands menu (Figure 8-11). This menu is used to change the characteristics of the report bands and to add, change, or remove the Group bands that divide the report into groups of records. Most of the options appearing within the Bands menu refer to Group bands.

Use the first three options to add, remove, or modify Group bands. The Group Intro on Each Page option tells dBASE to print the contents of the Group Intro band at the top of the page whenever the contents of the Detail band extend past the bottom of the prior page.

The Open All Bands option is used to open any temporarily closed bands in the report's design (closed bands do not print in the report). The Begin Band on New Page option can be set to Yes for any particular band, creating a new page (printer form feed) whenever the contents of the chosen band begin printing. The Word Wrap Band option can be set to Yes to tell dBASE to turn

Figure 8-10.

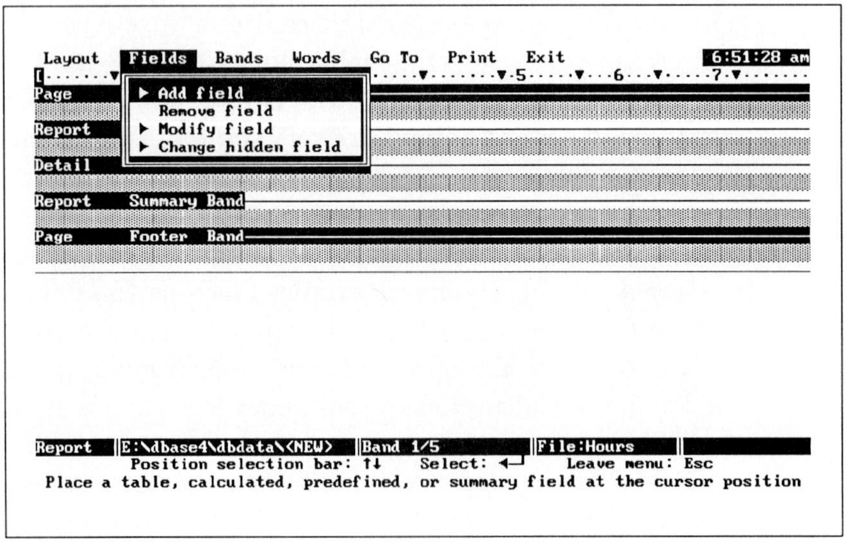

```
Layout  Fields  Bands  Words  Go To  Print  Exit                 6:51:28 am
[.......▼                     .....▼.......▼.5.....▼...6...▼.....7.▼.......
Page           ► Add field
               Remove field
Report         ► Modify field
               ► Change hidden field
Detail
Report   Summary Band
Page     Footer  Band

Report  ‖E:\dbase4\dbdata\<NEW>  ‖Band 1/5        ‖File:Hours    ‖
          Position selection bar: ↑↓    Select: ◄┘     Leave menu: Esc
 Place a table, calculated, predefined, or summary field at the cursor position
```

Fields menu

on word wrap for the chosen band. While word wrap is usually off when you are designing reports, it can be turned on with this option. Word wrap is needed when you are adding paragraphs of text (such as in a form letter) to one of your reports.

The Text Print for Band and Quality Print for Band options both affect the style of printed text. Text Print for Band can be set to Default (or no change), Pica, Elite, or Condensed. The Quality Print for Band option can be set to Default (or no change), Yes, or No. Note that in order for these options to work correctly, your printer must support the features, and you must have properly installed your choice of printer during the installation process, or by using DBSETUP, as described at the end of this chapter. Finally, the Spacing of Lines for Band option lets you change the line spacing within a particular band.

NOTE The Text Print for Band and Quality Print for Band options only affect the print style for the current band (the band

Figure 8-11.

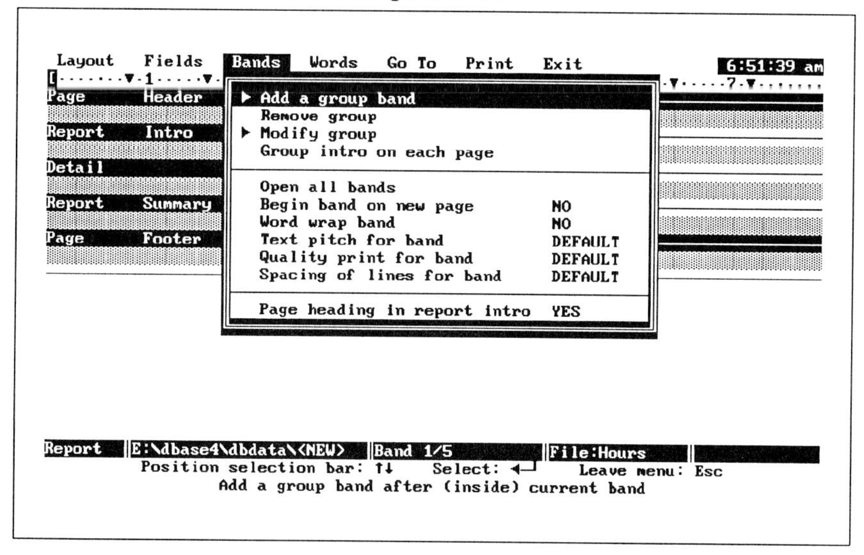

Bands menu

Figure 8-12.

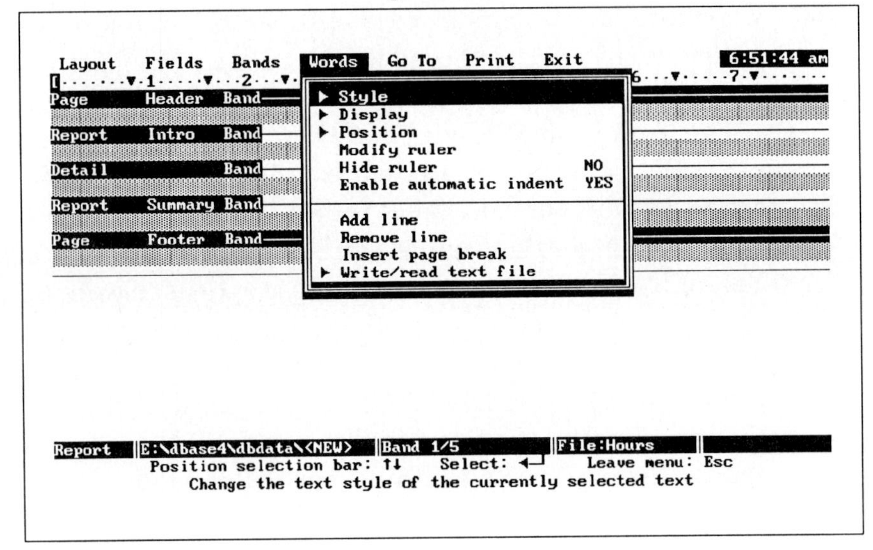

Words menu

where the cursor is when you choose the option). Use Control of Printer on the Print menu to change these styles for an entire report.

Pressing ALT-W reveals the Words menu (Figure 8-12). This menu provides options to control the appearance of text throughout the report. Also contained in the menu are options for adding and removing lines, inserting the contents of other files, and adding page breaks.

The Style option of the Words menu lets you change the style of selected text. Note that the Style option only applies to selected text, or text that has been selected with F6. (The Display option, which works for screen forms, is not used in reports and is therefore dimmed on the screen.) The Position option lets you left-align, right-align, or center selected text within the margins of the selection.

HINT You can use the Style option of the Words menu to select bold or italics print for a portion of a report.

The Modify Ruler option lets you change the ruler line's tabs, margins, or paragraph indent. (The ruler line is the line located directly beneath the menu bar.) The Hide Ruler option lets you hide the ruler line.

The Enable Automatic Indent option is used only when you are in Word Wrap mode (which is when you set Word Wrap Band in the Bands menu to On, or when you choose Mailmerge as a quick layout format). If you are in Word Wrap mode and you turn on Enable Automatic Indent, dBASE will use the spaces or tabs you enter at the beginning of a paragraph to set the indent for the remainder of that paragraph.

The Add Line option adds a new line after the current line, and the Remove Line option will remove the current line, moving all remaining text up by one line. The Insert Page Break option will insert a page break above the current line. The Write/Read Text File option lets you read the contents of a text file into the report at the cursor location or write selected text out to a text file. You are not likely to use this option with anything other than a form.

Pressing ALT G reveals the Go To menu (Figure 8-13). When designing a report, you use the Go To menu options to move the cursor to various locations or text, or to search for selected text and replace that text with other text.

The Go to Line Number option lets you specify a line number or row on the report to move the cursor to. The Forward Search and Backward Search options search for text, either from the cursor position forward (toward the bottom of the screen) or from the cursor position backward (toward the top of the screen). The Replace option lets you replace a specified text string with another string. These search and replace options may prove useful when you are working with form letters, which may contain large amounts of text. Finally, the Match Capitalization option, used

Figure 8-13.

```
Layout   Fields   Bands   Words   Go To   Print   Exit                 6:51:54 am
[·······▼·1·····▼···2···▼·····3·▼·
Page     Header  Band         Go to line number        {0}
Report   Intro   Band         Forward search           {}
Detail           Band         Backward search          {}
                              Replace                  {}
                              Match capitalization     NO
Report   Summary Band
Page     Footer  Band

Report  ║E:\dbase4\dbdata\<NEW>  ║Band 1/5        ║File:Hours      ║
          Position selection bar: ↑↓    Select: ◄┘     Leave menu: Esc
                           Move to the specified line
```

Go To menu

with the search and replace options, tells dBASE whether the difference between upper- and lowercase letters should be significant. If Match Capitalization is set to Yes, the case of the search text must match any text that is to be found.

The Print and Exit menus perform the same tasks as they do in other parts of dBASE IV.

Saving and Running the Report

Once you have made the desired changes to the report design, press CTRL-END, or choose Save Changes and Exit from the Exit menu to save the report. To run a report from the Control Center, highlight the report by name in the Reports panel and press ENTER; then choose Print Report from the next menu that appears, and when the Print menu appears, choose Begin Printing. You can also run a report from the dot prompt by entering the command

REPORT FORM *filename* TO PRINT

where *filename* is the name that you saved the report under. Omit the TO PRINT designation if you simply wish to view the report on the screen.

Practice Designing a Custom Report

ABC Temporaries needs a personnel report with more to offer than the standard format created by the Quick Report key. The report must include the LASTNAME, FIRSTNAME, PHONE, DATEHIRED, and SALARY fields arranged in a set of columns on the page. The date and time of the report should appear in the upper-right corner of the first page, and a report title should be centered at the top of the first page. Page numbers should be centered at the bottom of each page.

To begin designing the report from the Control Center, highlight the Create option of the Reports panel and press ENTER. (The dot-prompt equivalent of this action is the CREATE REPORT command.) Within a moment, the Report Design screen will appear. Press ESC once to close the Layout menu and to reveal the entire screen (see Figure 8-14).

Let's begin with the headings. The date and time are to appear at the upper-right corner of the first page, so these items must be placed in the Page Header band. Press the down arrow key once. With the cursor in the Page Header band, move the cursor to column 50. Remember, the status bar shows the cursor location; it should display "LINE:0 COL:50" when the cursor is correctly positioned. Use ALT-F to get to the Fields menu, and choose the Add Field option. A pick list of available fields will appear (Figure 8-15).

Note that there are four panels containing the four types of fields that can be added to the report. The panel on the far left contains the field names from the current database. The next panel contains any calculated fields; you can use the Create option of this panel to add a new calculated field. The Predefined panel contains predefined fields for the current date and time, the record number of the current record, and the page number of the report. Finally, the Summary panel contains fields used to obtain numeric (summary) values, such as averages, minimum or maximum values, or a sum of values.

Figure 8-14.

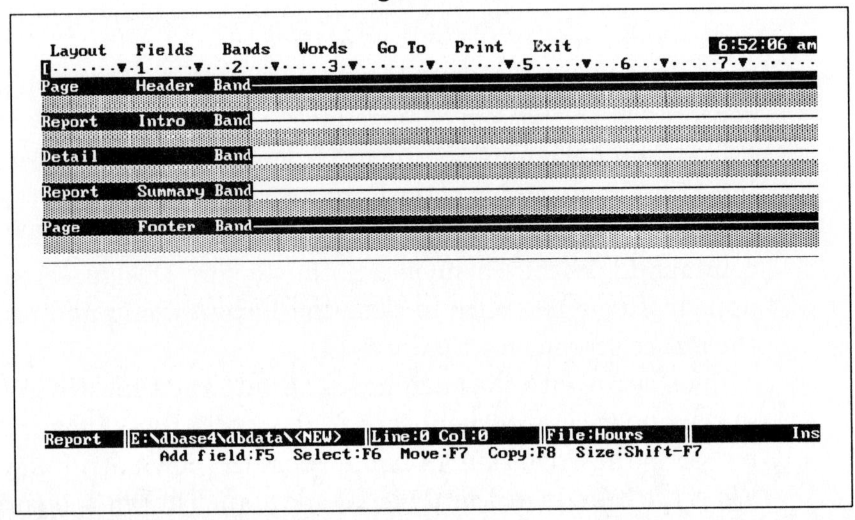

Report Design screen

Move the cursor to Date in the Predefined panel, and press ENTER. Another menu appears, with the field name DATE present in the selected option (Figure 8-16). Try pressing ENTER repeatedly, and you will see that you can change the predefined field to any of the other choices. Continue pressing ENTER until "DATE" reappears in the Name entry.

The Template and Picture Function values perform the same tasks as they did in Chapter 5. (Note that the Template and Picture Function options cannot be changed for date or time fields.) The Suppress Repeated Values option lets you tell dBASE not to print the contents of a field if its value is the same as in the prior record.

With Date selected as the type of predefined field, press CTRL-END. You'll see the date designation (MM/DD/YY) appear at the cursor location.

Press ENTER once to add a new line to the Page Header band.

Figure 8-15.

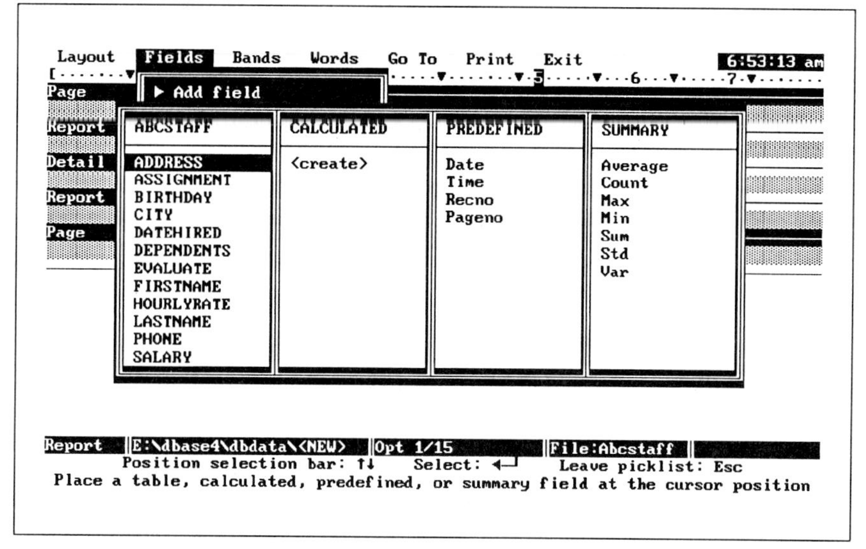

Pick list of fileds available for report

Place the cursor at line 50 directly underneath the DATE field template you just added. Open the Fields menu with ALT-F, choose Add Field, and select Time from the Predefined panel of the pick list. Then press CTRL-END to accept these values.

Move the cursor down four lines to the Detail band, and press HOME to move the cursor to the left margin. Press ALT-F to open the Fields menu, and choose Add Field. From the pick list that appears, choose LASTNAME. Press CTRL-END to accept the default options for the use of the field.

HINT Whenever you are in a pick list of field names, you can type the first few letters of a field's name to quickly move the cursor to the desired field.

Move the cursor right one space to column 16. (*Do not* use the

Figure 8-16.

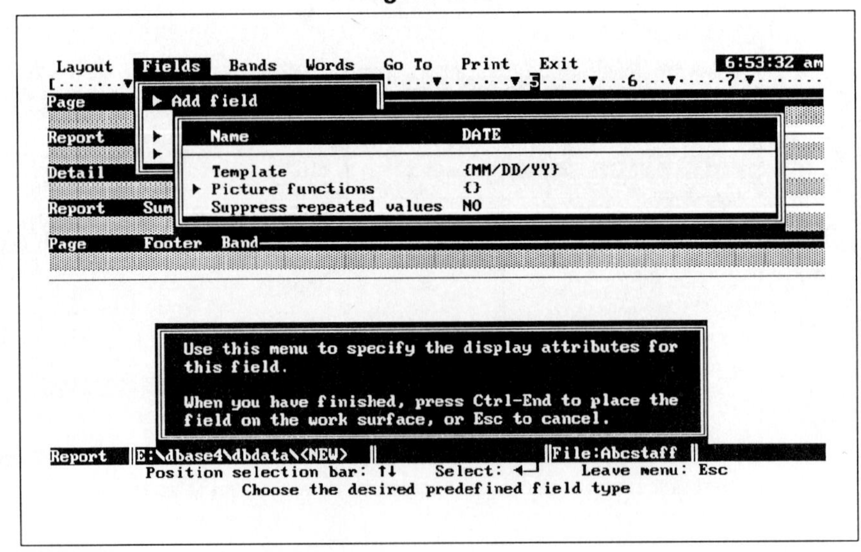

Secondary menu for Add Field

spacebar to do this; use the right arrow key instead. If you use a space to separate the fields, they will run together in the report, causing uneven columns.) Open the Fields menu with ALT-F, and choose Add Field. This time, pick FIRSTNAME from the menu, and again press CTRL-END to accept the options.

Move the cursor to column 35. Open the Fields menu with ALT-F, and select Add Field. Choose PHONE from the menu, and press the CTRL-END key.

Move the cursor to column 50. Open the Fields menu with ALT-F, and select Add Field. Choose DATEHIRED from the menu, and press CTRL-END.

Move the cursor to column 60. Open the Fields menu with ALT-F, and select Add Field. Choose SALARY from the menu, and press CTRL-END.

Next, the headings over the columns of data can be added. Move the cursor up into the Report Intro band, and press ENTER once to add a blank line. With the cursor at the far-left margin of line 1, type **Last Name**. Move the cursor to column 16, and type **First Name**. At column 35, type **Phone**. Then move the cursor to column 50, and type **Hire Date**. Finally, move the cursor to column 60, and type **Salary**.

Press ENTER once after the last heading (Salary) to add another blank line below the headings. The two blank lines now present in the Report Intro band will result in white space (blank lines) above and below the headings when the actual report is printed.

You also want page numbers centered at the bottom of the page. Move the cursor into the Page Footer band, and then press ENTER to add a blank line between the data on the actual report and the page footers. Move the cursor to column 35, open the Fields menu, and choose Add Field. From the predefined list of fields, choose Pageno., and then press CTRL-END to accept the default options. Your screen should now resemble the example shown in Figure 8-17.

The custom report, which will provide the employee name, phone number, hire date, and salary, is nearly completed. All

Figure 8-17.

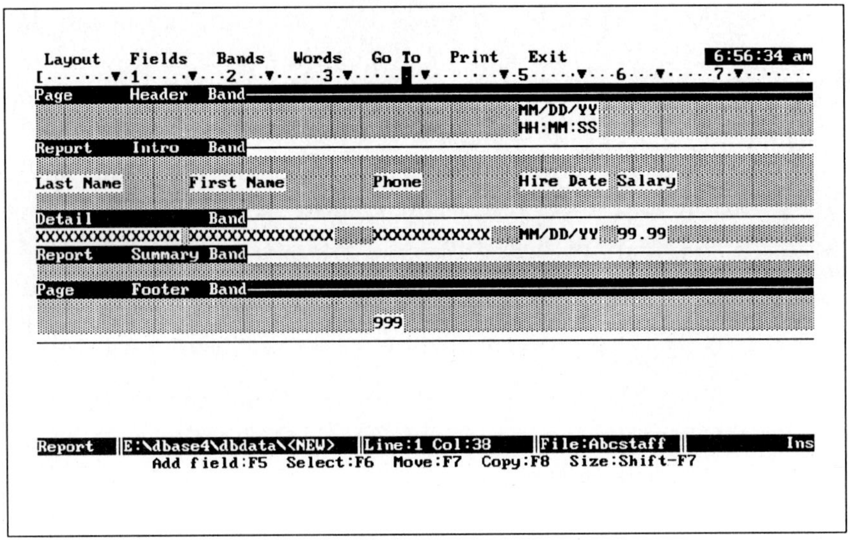

```
Layout  Fields  Bands  Words  Go To  Print  Exit                    6:56:34 am
[·······▼·1·····▼···2···▼·····3·▼·····▼·▼·······▼·5·····▼···6···▼·····7·▼·······
Page        Header  Band
                                                  MM/DD/YY
                                                  HH:MM:SS
Report      Intro   Band

Last Name         First Name          Phone        Hire Date Salary

Detail              Band
XXXXXXXXXXXXXXX XXXXXXXXXXXXXXX    XXXXXXXXXXXXX   MM/DD/YY  99.99
Report     Summary Band
Page        Footer  Band

                                   999


Report  E:\dbase4\dbdata\<NEW>  Line:1 Col:38  File:Abcstaff              Ins
          Add field:F5  Select:F6  Move:F7  Copy:F8  Size:Shift-F7
```

Completed report

that's left is to save the report for future use. Get to the Exit menu with ALT-E, and choose Save Changes and Exit (or press CTRL-END). dBASE will ask you for a name for the report. Enter **RSIMPLE** as a report filename. The report will be saved, and you will be returned to the Control Center.

With RSIMPLE still highlighted, press ENTER. From the next menu that appears, choose Print Report. In a moment, the Print menu will appear. With your printer ready, choose Begin Printing to see the results of the new report. It should resemble the form shown here:

09/02/88
09:16:41

Last Name	First Name	Phone	Hire Date	Salary
Morse	Marcia	301-555-6678	07/25/85	9.00
Westman	Andrea	301-555-2912	07/04/86	16.50
Jackson	David	703-555-8778	09/05/85	8.00
Mitchell	Mary Jo	703-555-6874	12/01/87	8.00
Robinson	Shirley	301-555-0201	11/17/87	8.00
Jackson	Cheryl	703-555-1234	09/19/87	12.00
Robinson	Wanda	202-555-4545	09/17/87	8.00
Hart	Edward	703-555-1414	10/19/86	8.50
Jones	Judi	703-555-2638	08/12/86	12.50

An Alternate Method: Using Quick Layouts

You may want to make use of the Quick Layouts option of the Layout menu to quickly design reports that are based on one of the three default reports described earlier. To see how this can be done, get to the Control Center and choose the Create option at the Reports panel to create another report. When the Report Design screen appears, with the Layout menu open, choose Quick Layouts. From the next menu to appear, choose Column Layout. dBASE will place a page number and date at the left side of the Header band, and the field names will appear as column headings. The actual fields (as represented by field templates) will be placed in the Detail band, as shown in Figure 8-18. Any numeric fields in the database will have summary fields placed in the Report Summary band.

REMEMBER You can use queries to design a report based on a quick layout, and only those fields present in the query will appear in the report.

With the quick-layout style serving as a guide to get you started, you could modify the headings as desired and remove or add fields. If you wanted to move a field from one location to another, you could use the Remove Field option of the Fields menu to remove the field from its current location; you could then use the Add Field option of the same menu to add the field to its new location. Or you could use F6 to select the field and F7 to move it, just as in moving fields in forms. Once done, you could save the

Figure 8-18.

```
Layout   Fields   Bands   Words   Go To   Print   Exit                 6:58:37 am
Page        Header  Band
Page No. 999
MM/DD/YY
SOCIALSEC    LASTNAME          FIRSTNAME         ADDRESS                     CITY
Report      Intro  Band
Detail             Band
XXXXXXXXXXX  XXXXXXXXXXXXXXX  XXXXXXXXXXXXXXX  XXXXXXXXXXXXXXXXXXXXXXXXX  XXXXXX
Report      Summary Band
Page        Footer  Band

Report  E:\dbase4\dbdata\<NEW>  Line:0 Col:0   File:Abcstaff              Ins
         Add field:F5  Select:F6  Move:F7  Copy:F8  Size:Shift-F7
```

Quick layout of columnar report

Figure 8-19.

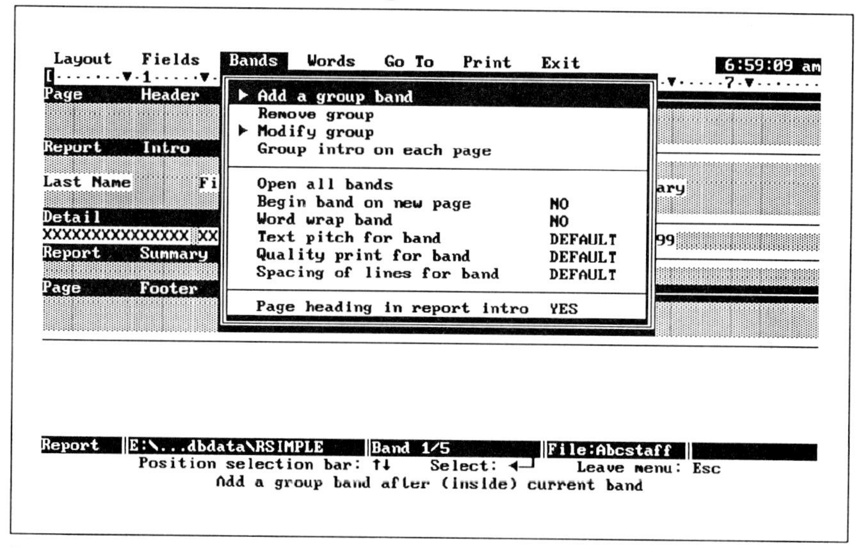

Bands menu

report by using the Save Changes and Exit option of the Exit menu. In this case, the report is not needed, so press ESC and then type **Y** to abandon the report design process and return to the Control Center.

Using the Group Menu Options

You can use the various group options of the Bands menu to work with groupings of records within a report. Most likely, you will need to arrange reports broken down by groups. As an example, you might like to see all employees divided into groups by state of residence or by the name of the assignment. By utilizing the

Add a Group Band, Remove Group, and Modify Group options of the Bands menu, you can define multiple levels of grouping.

While more than three levels of groups may seem like overkill to some, it is nice to know that dBASE IV is accomodating when you must base a complex report on a large number of subgroups. Multiple groupings can be quite common in business applications. In something as simple as a national mailing list, for example, you might need to see records by groups of states, and within each state group by city, and within each city group by ZIP code. That represents three levels of grouping alone. If you cut the data in the table even more specifically—for example, by other categories like income levels—you can quickly come to appreciate dBASE IV's ability to perform effective grouping.

When you open the Bands menu while designing a report, the menu options seen in Figure 8-19 are displayed. The Add a Group Band option lets you insert new group bands into the report, and the Remove Group option lets you delete existing groups from the report. Finally, the Modify Group option lets you change the ways existing groups are defined.

To add a new group to the report, first place the cursor at the desired location at which the band is to appear. Choose Add a Group Band from the Bands menu. The next menu to appear will display three options: Field Value, Expression Value, and Record Count. If you want to establish the group by field (such as groups of records from the same state or with the same assignment), choose Field Value. You can also group records based upon a valid dBASE expression; choose Expression Value if you desire this kind of grouping. As an example, if you were using an index tag based on a combination of LASTNAME + FIRSTNAME to control the order of the records, you could enter **LASTNAME + FIRSTNAME** to define the grouping. Finally, dBASE IV lets you establish groups by a set number of records. You could set the report's design to isolate records into groups of 10, 15, or any set number of records per group. Choose Record Count to select grouping by number of records.

After you select the desired type of grouping, dBASE IV will insert a new Intro band and a new Summary band for the group. Intro bands appear immediately below the cursor, so the cursor must be above the Detail band when you select the option. Group bands must fall outside of the Detail band. Figure 8-20 shows a sample report design for the ABCSTAFF personnel that includes a Group band for employees grouped by state.

REMEMBER You cannot add a Group band inside a Detail band.

Once you've placed the desired group, you can check to see if the results are what you desire by pressing ALT- P for the Print menu and choosing View Report on Screen from the menu. The resulting report that appears will be divided by group. Note that the file *must* be sorted or indexed on the field you are grouping by to get the records in the proper group order; you may need to

Figure 8-20.

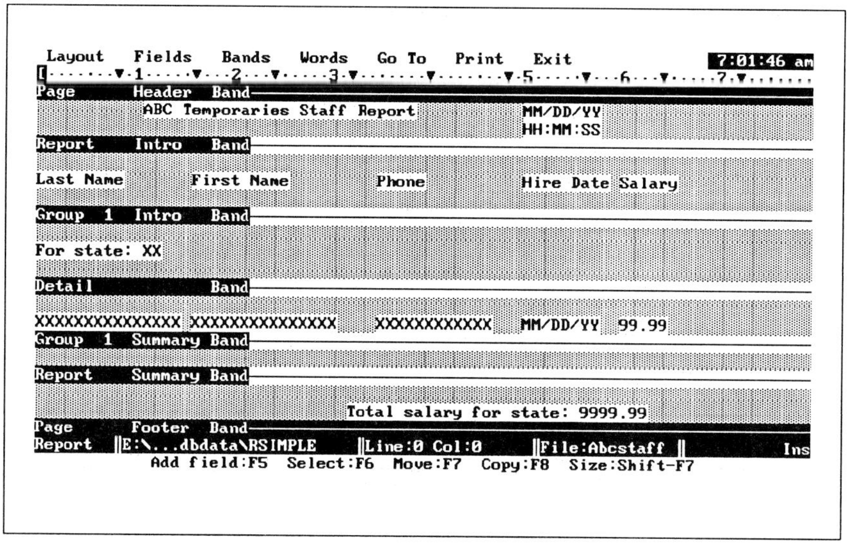

```
Layout   Fields   Bands   Words   Go To   Print   Exit                    7:01:46 am
[·······▼·1·····▼···2···▼·····3·▼·······▼·······▼·5·····▼···6···▼·····7·▼·······
Page        Header  Band
                ABC Temporaries Staff Report             MM/DD/YY
                                                         HH:MM:SS
Report       Intro    Band
Last Name       First Name          Phone              Hire Date Salary
Group   1   Intro     Band
For state: XX
Detail                Band
XXXXXXXXXXXXXXX XXXXXXXXXXXXXXX    XXXXXXXXXXXX      MM/DD/YY   99.99
Group   1   Summary Band
Report       Summary Band
                                  Total salary for state: 9999.99
Page        Footer  Band
Report    ||E:\...dbdata\RSIMPLE    ||Line:0 Col:0     ||File:Abcstaff ||        Ins
             Add field:F5  Select:F6  Move:F7  Copy:F8  Size:Shift-F7
```

Report design with single level of grouping

save the report, index or sort the file from the Control Center or dot prompt, and then run the report. When you are satisfied with the results, save the report specification with the Save Changes and Exit option of the Exit menu.

Adding a Group to the Personnel Report

Try adding a group by assignment name to the existing personnel registry report you created earlier in the chapter. From the dot prompt, you can enter **MODIFY REPORT RSIMPLE**, or at the Control Center, highlight RSIMPLE and press SHIFT-F2 (Design). The report specification for the report you designed earlier will appear. To add the group to the report, first place the cursor on the last line of the Report Intro band. Next, open the Bands menu with ALT-B, and choose Add a Group Band to insert a new group. The report is to be grouped by assignment name (which is a field), so choose Field Value from the next menu to appear. The pick list that now appears shows the fields available in the file; choose ASSIGNMENT from the list. Your screen should now resemble the example shown in Figure 8-21.

Save the report by choosing Save Changes and Exit from the Exit menu. Then, if you are at the Control Center, highlight the database file, ABCSTAFF, and press ENTER. Select Modify Struc-

Figure 8-21.

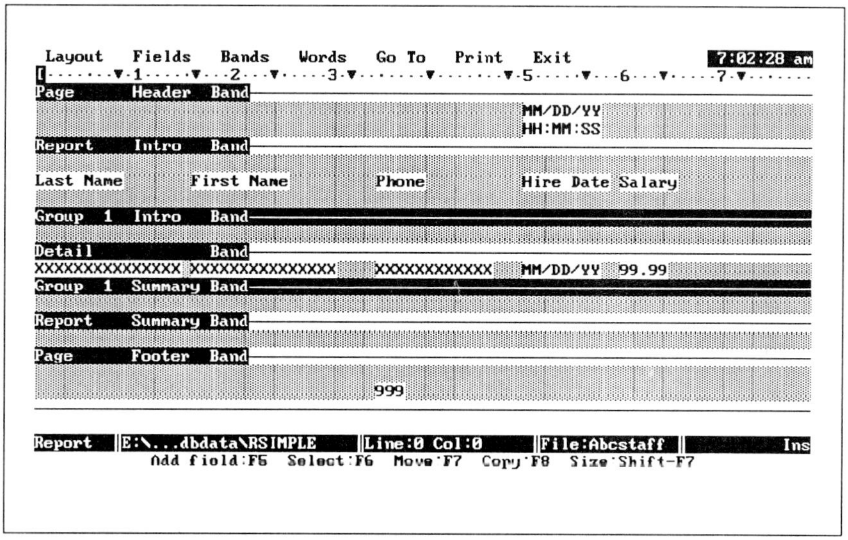

```
Layout   Fields   Bands   Words   Go To   Print   Exit                7:02:28 am
[·······▼·1·····▼···2···▼·····3·▼·······▼·······▼·5·····▼···6···▼·····7·▼·······
Page      Header  Band
                                                  MM/DD/YY
                                                  HH:MM:SS
Report    Intro   Band
Last Name        First Name         Phone         Hire Date Salary
Group  1  Intro   Band
Detail            Band
XXXXXXXXXXXXXXX XXXXXXXXXXXXXXX     XXXXXXXXXXXX  MM/DD/YY  99.99
Group  1  Summary Band
Report    Summary Band
Page      Footer  Band
                                    999
Report    E:\...dbdata\RSIMPLE   Line:0 Col:0     File:Abcstaff          Ins
          Add field:F5  Select:F6  Move:F7  Copy:F8  Size:Shift-F7
```

Report specification with group added

ture/Order, choose Create New Index from the next menu, and call the index ASSIGNED. For the index expression, enter **ASSIGNMENT**. Press CTRL-END twice, once to create the index and once to get back to the Control Center. If you are positioned at the dot prompt, you can enter the command

```
INDEX ON ASSIGNMENT TAG ASSIGNED
```

and the file will be indexed in the order needed to provide the groups within the report.

From the Control Center, highlight the report name, RSIMPLE, press ENTER, and choose Print Report followed by Begin Printing. Or from the dot prompt, enter

```
REPORT FORM RSIMPLE TO PRINT
```

The report will be printed, and should resemble the following:

```
                                                          09/02/88
                                                          10:40:51

Last Name     First Name     Phone          Hire Date   Salary


Jackson       David          703-555-8778   09/05/85      8.00
Jackson       Cheryl         703-555-1234   09/19/87     12.00
Robinson      Wanda          202-555-4545   09/17/87      8.00


Morse         Marcia         301-555-6678   07/25/85      9.00
Westman       Andrea         301-555-2912   07/04/86     16.50
Robinson      Shirley        301-555-0201   11/17/87      8.00
Jones         Judi           703-555-2638   08/12/86     12.50


Mitchell      Mary Jo        703-555-6874   12/01/87      8.00
Hart          Edward         703-555-1414   10/19/86      8.50
```

Note that the actual contents of the ASSIGNMENT field do not appear with each group; to add this, you'll need to place the field where you want it to appear. You can place the field used to control the group within the Group band, and it will then print once for each occurrence of that group. To see how this works, with RSIMPLE highlighted in the Control Center, press SHIFT-

F2 for the Report Design screen. Place the cursor inside the Group 1 Intro Band. At the far-left margin, type **Assignment:** as the heading and add a space after the colon. Then use ALT-F to get to the Fields menu, choose Add Field, and select ASSIGNMENT from the menu of fields as the field to place in the band. Finally, press CTRL-END to accept the default options for the format of the field. A field template representing the Assignment field will appear in the Group band.

To see the results, press ALT-P and choose Begin Printing from the Print menu. The report will appear or be printed, and this time the contents for the ASSIGNMENT field will appear along with each group, as shown here:

```
                                                              09/02/88
                                                              10:57:23

Last Name        First Name       Phone           Hire Date  Salary

Assignment: City Revenue Dept.
Jackson          David            703-555-8778    09/05/85     8.00
Jackson          Cheryl           703-555-1234    09/19/87    12.00
Robinson         Wanda            202-555-4545    09/17/87     8.00

Assignment: National Oil Co.
Morse            Marcia           301-555-6678    07/25/85     9.00
Westman          Andrea           301-555-2912    07/04/86    16.50
Robinson         Shirley          301-555-0201    11/17/87     8.00
Jones            Judi             703-555-2638    08/12/86    12.50

Assignment: Smith Builders
Mitchell         Mary Jo          703-555-6874    12/01/87     8.00
Hart             Edward           703-555-1414    10/19/86     8.50
```

Save the report and return to the main menu by pressing CTRL-END or by choosing Save Changes and Exit from the Exit menu.

Creating a Report with Multiple Groups

You can insert additional groups to further define your groups. As an example, consider the HOURS database, which contains records of the employee hours worked at different assignments. If what you need is a report grouped by assignment, and by "week ending" date within each assignment group, you must create a report that contains more than one group.

From the Control Center, highlight the HOURS database file and press ENTER, and choose Use File from the menu that appears. Next, choose Create from the Reports panel. When the Layout menu appears, choose Quick Layouts, and then select Column as the type of layout. In the headings that appear for the field names, you may want to add a space between "SOCIAL" and "SEC" and between "WEEK" and "ENDING." Otherwise, the standard report format will do for this example.

In this case, what is wanted is a report grouped by assignment name, and within each assignment name, by groups of week ending dates. Place the cursor at the start of the Report Intro band, just above the Detail band. Press ALT-B to get to the Bands menu, and choose Add a Group Band to insert a new group; from the next menu to appear, choose Field Value to base the new group on a field.

From the list of field names, choose ASSIGNMENT, and the new Group band will appear. Place the cursor on the blank line between the start of the Group Intro band and the Detail band. Type **Assignment:** as the heading and add a space after the colon. Then open the Fields menu, choose Add Field, and select ASSIGNMENT from the pick list that appears. Press CTRL-END to accept the default options.

Figure 8-22.

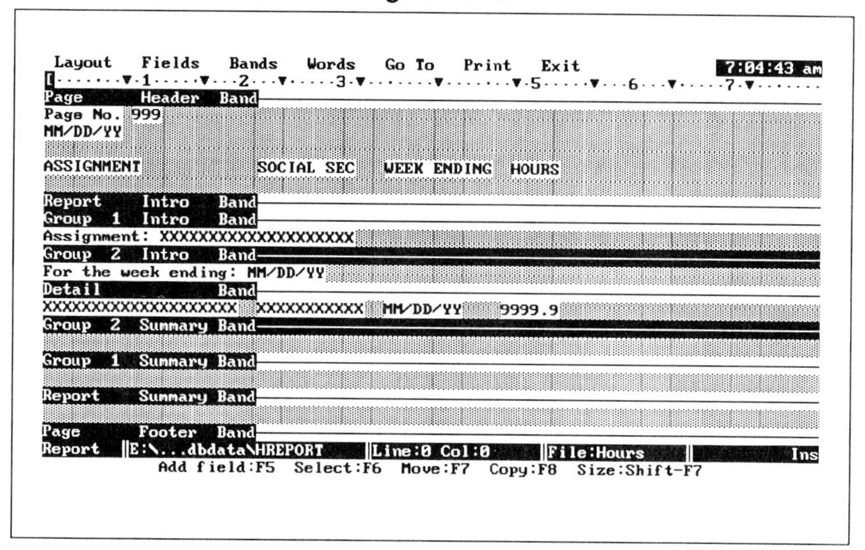

Report specification containing multiple groups

To add the second group, press ALT-B for the Bands menu, and then choose Add a Group Band from the menu. Choose Field Value from the next menu. From the list of fields, choose WEEK-ENDING.

Press the down arrow key and then press HOME to move the cursor to the start of the blank line between the Group 2 Intro band and the Detail band. Type the heading

For the week ending:

Then open the Fields menu, choose Add Field, and select WEEKENDING from the pick list that appears. Press CTRL-END to accept the default options. Your screen should resemble the one shown in Figure 8-22.

REMEMBER You must create or activate an index, or sort the file, before a report containing groups will print properly.

Because the report will be grouped by assignment and then by "week ending" date, the database must be sorted or indexed on a combination of the ASSIGNMENT and WEEKEND fields for the groupings to appear in the correct order. Save the report by choosing Save Changes and Exit from the Exit menu; type **HREPORT** as a report name. Then, if you are at the Control Center, highlight the database file, HOURS, and press ENTER. Select Modify Structure/Order, choose Create New Index from the next menu, and call the index ASSIGN2. For the index expression, enter

```
ASSIGNMENT + DTOS(WEEKENDING)
```

The DTOS() function is used to allow indexing on a combination of a date field and a character field. This function will convert the date to a character string but will preserve the proper date order (which is important for working with dates that span different years). Press CTRL-END twice, once to create the index and once to get back to the Control Center. If you were at the dot prompt, you can enter the command

```
INDEX ON ASSIGNMENT + DTOS(WEEKENDING) TAG ASSIGN2
```

and the file will be indexed in the order needed to provide the groups within the report.

From the Control Center, highlight the report name, HREPORT, press ENTER, and choose Print Report followed by Begin Printing. Or from the dot prompt, enter

```
REPORT FORM HREPORT TO PRINT
```

The report will be printed, and should resemble the following:

Page No. 1
09/02/88

ASSIGNMENT	SOCIAL SEC	WEEK ENDING	HOURS
Assignment: City Revenue Dept.			
For the week ending: 01/16/88			
City Revenue Dept.	343-55-9821	01/16/88	35.0
City Revenue Dept.	495-00-3456	01/16/88	28.0
City Revenue Dept.	232-55-1234	01/16/88	30.0
For the week ending: 01/23/88			
City Revenue Dept.	232-55-1234	01/23/88	30.0
City Revenue Dept.	495-00-3456	01/23/88	32.0
City Revenue Dept.	343-55-9821	01/23/88	32.0
Assignment: National Oil Co.			
For the week ending: 01/16/88			
National Oil Co.	909-88-7654	01/16/88	35.0
National Oil Co.	121-33-9876	01/16/88	30.0
National Oil Co.	121-90-5432	01/16/88	27.0
National Oil Co.	123-44-8976	01/16/88	32.0
For the week ending: 01/23/88			
National Oil Co.	121-33-9876	01/23/88	35.0
National Oil Co.	909-88-7654	01/23/88	33.0
Assignment: Smith Builders			
For the week ending: 01/23/88			
Smith Builders	876-54-3210	01/23/88	30.0
Smith Builders	901-77-3456	01/23/88	28.0
Smith Builders	805-34-6789	01/23/88	35.0

Using Summary Fields

You can also use summary fields to show numeric totals of data within the report. To try this, highlight HREPORT in the Reports panel, and press SHIFT-F2 to get back to the Report Design screen. You can place your desired fields in the Summary bands for the groups or for the entire report. For example, by placing a summary field for the HOURS field in the Group 2 Summary band, you would get a total of hours printed each time the "week ending" date changed. If you placed a summary field for the HOURS field in the Group 1 Summary band, you would get a total of hours printed each time the assignment changed. If you placed a summary field for the HOURS field in the Report Summary band, you would get a total of hours printed at the end of the report. You can place these fields in more than one band, if desired.

Place the cursor in the Group 1 Summary band at column 48 (just below the HOURS field that's already in the Detail band). Open the Fields menu with ALT-F, and choose Add Field. From the Summary panel of the pick list that appears, choose SUM.

When the next menu for the field's specifications appears, enter **SUMHRS** as the name for the new field. You can skip the description, and leave the default (SUM) in the Operations entry. At the Field to Summarize On entry, enter **HOURS**. In the Template entry, enter **999.99**. Finally, press CTRL-END twice, once to accept the values for the summary field and once to save the report. Press CTRL-END again to save the report.

From the Control Center, highlight the report name, HREPORT, press ENTER, and choose Print Report followed by Begin Printing. The report will be printed and will include the totals for the HOURS field each time the contents of the ASSIGNMENT field changes.

More Dot-Prompt Options: Using Conditionals with Report Commands

As mentioned earlier, dot-prompt users can print custom reports with the REPORT FORM *filename* command; adding the TO PRINT designation at the end of the command routes the report to the printer. You can also use additional statements along with the REPORT FORM command to get specific information from the report.

Get to the dot prompt, and try the following commands:

```
USE ABCSTAFF
REPORT FORM RSIMPLE FOR STATE = "MD" TO PRINT
```

In response, a report with only those employees who live in Maryland will be printed. Now enter

```
REPORT FORM RSIMPLE FOR SALARY > 9.00 TO PRINT
```

A report showing the employees earning more than $9.00 per hour will be printed.

You can use curly braces surrounding a date to convert a date field into a string of characters. That string of characters can then be used to form a conditional command for printing a report. This is a very handy tool for printing reports that indicate activity within a certain time period. As an example, the command

```
REPORT FORM RSIMPLE FOR DATEHIRED <= {10/01/87} TO PRINT
```

will produce a report of all records with hire dates earlier than October 2, 1987. A report of all employees with hire dates within a particular month could be produced with a command like this one:

```
REPORT FORM RSIMPLE FOR DATEHIRED > {09/30/87} .AND. DATEHIRED
< {11/01/87} TO PRINT
```

A Word About Files

The dBASE IV report generator creates three files for each report you design and save. The filename for all three files is the same as the name you assigned the report, while the extensions are .FRO, .FRM, and .FRG. The .FRM file is used by dBASE in the design of the report, while the .FRO file is used to run the report. The .FRG file contains a dBASE IV program that, when run inside of dBASE, will also produce the report.

You should keep these files together as long as you are using the report. If the report is no longer needed and you erase files from DOS or from the DOS Utilities option of the Tools menu, be sure to erase all three files.

A Word About Other Reports

This chapter serves as a detailed introduction to creating and producing reports, whether you use the Report Design screen to design detailed reports, or whether you use SHIFT-F9 to produce quick reports for most of your needs. There are numerous reporting topics not covered in this chapter, such as designing and printing mailing labels and form letters, and producing reports that are of a form-oriented nature. These topics are covered in detail in Chapter 11.

Adding Printer Drivers to dBASE IV

If you have not already installed printer drivers that match your particular printer, you should do so. Installing the correct printer driver lets you take advantage of additional type styles and other features your printer may offer. dBASE IV supports a number of popular printers, including the HP LaserJet and compatible printers, and most Epson, NEC, and Okidata printers. Version 1.1 of dBASE IV adds support for PostScript printers (including the Apple LaserWriter). The various menu options discussed in this chapter for changing the style of characters printed in reports depend on dBASE being able to fully support your printer, and it can only do this if it knows what kind of printer you are using.

Installing printer drivers is a simple task, thanks to the DBSETUP program. To use DBSETUP, exit dBASE IV and get back to DOS. Use the DOS CD command to switch to the directory containing the dBASE IV program (not the data files). Unless you specified otherwise when you installed the program, this directory should be named DBASE. You can enter CD\DBASE at the DOS prompt to get to this directory.

Once in the directory with the dBASE IV program, enter **DBSETUP** at the DOS prompt to load the DBSETUP program. In a moment, a copyright screen will appear. Press ENTER, and the DBSETUP menus will appear. The CONFIG.DB menu opens as soon as you start using DBSETUP. From this menu, choose Modify Existing CONFIG.DB. (CONFIG.DB is the name of a special file that is used to store all your configuration settings.)

Another prompt appears, asking where the CONFIG.DB file should be loaded from. The current drive and directory name appear by default. Press ENTER to accept this default. Once you do this, eight configuration menus will appear, as illustrated in Figure 8-23.

The various menu options can be used to modify numerous settings of dBASE IV, including available printers. The Printer menu should already be open; if not, press ALT-P to open it. Choose Drivers from the Printer menu. When you do this, another menu box appears, with room for up to four printers (Figure 8-24).

With the cursor in the printer name entry, press SHIFT-F1. A list of available printers will appear. Choose your printer brand by name. In most cases, another list box showing specific printer models will appear after you have chosen the brand of printer. Select the desired model from this list (if it appears).

Once you have chosen a printer brand and model, the cursor moves to the device column. Press SHIFT-F1 again, and a list of printer ports appears. In most cases, you will want the first choice, LPT1. (This corresponds to the default parallel port on most IBM-compatible computers.) Check your computer's documentation if you think you should be using a different printer port.

After you have chosen the desired device (printer port), you can move the cursor down and repeat these steps for up to three more printers. When you are done choosing printers, press CTRL-END to get back to the DBSETUP menus.

Open the Exit menu with ALT-E, and choose Save and Exit. Another prompt appears, asking where the CONFIG.DB file should be saved to. The current drive and directory name appear by default. Press ENTER to accept this default, then choose OK from the next menu box to overwrite the old CONFIG.DB file. Finally, choose Exit to DOS from the Exit menu.

When you next start dBASE IV, the specified printer drivers

Figure 8-23.

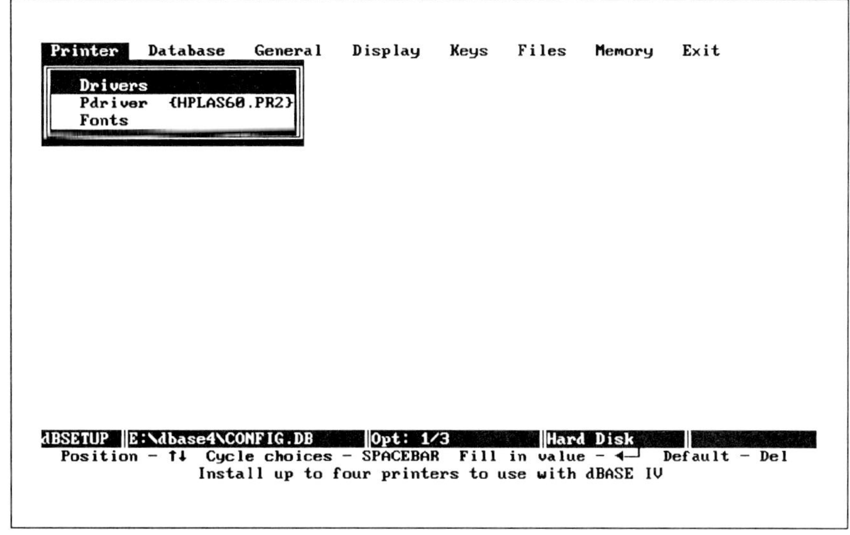

Configuration menus

Figure 8-24.

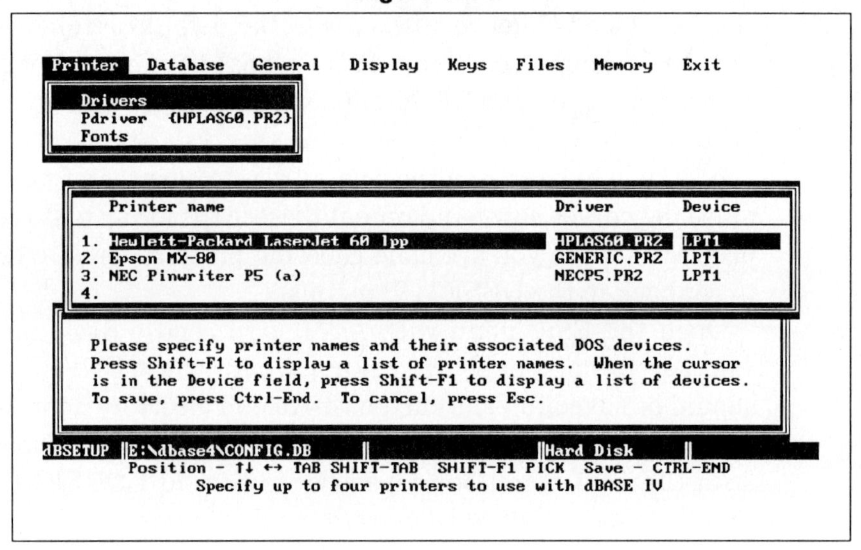

Menu Box with available printers

will be loaded automatically. You can select any of the drivers from the Print menu, which appears when you print a report, by choosing Destination, and then choosing Printer Model from the next menu that appears. Note that the first printer driver you installed will be the default printer driver; if you do not make a selection before printing a report, the default printer driver will automatically be selected by dBASE IV.

Quick Reference

To produce a quick report If you want all records in the report, highlight the database file in the Data panel of the Control

Center. If you want selected records in the report, design and save a query that selects the desired records, then highlight the query in the Queries panel. Press SHIFT-F9. From the next menu that appears, choose Begin Printing to print the report, or choose View Report on Screen to see the report on the screen.

To select a different printer If you have multiple printer drivers installed, you can select a desired printer by pressing SHIFT-F9 to reveal the Print menu, choosing Destination from the next menu, and choosing Printer Model from the next menu. Press ENTER repeatedly until the desired printer appears, then use CTRL-END to store the new setting.

To produce reports based on selected fields or records Base the report on a query, rather than on a database file. Use the Query Design screen, outlined in Chapter 7, to design a query that includes the selected records and/or fields. Save the query by choosing Save Changes and Exit from the Exit menu of the Query Design screen. Highlight the query in the Queries panel of the Control Center, press SHIFT-F9, and choose Begin Printing from the next menu to print the report.

To print records using the LIST command Add the words TO PRINT to the end of the LIST command. For example, entering **LIST LASTNAME, FIRSTNAME, SALARY TO PRINT** would cause the contents of the fields named to be printed. With some printers, you may need to enter an EJECT command to force the paper to feed out of the printer.

To design a custom report Place the database or query on which the report will be based into use. Then, choose the Create option of the Reports panel (or from the dot prompt, enter **CREATE REPORT**). Add fields at the desired locations by moving the cursor there, opening the Fields menu with ALT-F, choosing

Add Field, and selecting the desired field from the list. Note also that you can quickly add all fields in the file or the query to the report by choosing the Quick Layouts option of the Layout menu. If Group Bands are needed, add them by using the Add a Group Band option of the Bands menu. When you are done designing the report, save it by choosing Save Changes and Exit from the Exit menu (or by pressing CTRL-END).

To display or print a custom report From the Control Center, highlight the report in the Reports panel, press ENTER, and choose Print Report from the next menu to appear. When the Print Menu appears, choose Begin Printing. From the dot prompt, enter the command **REPORT FORM *filename* TO PRINT**, where *filename* is the name that you saved the report under.

CHAPTER

9

Automating Your Work with Macros

dBASE IV provides macros, which are combinations of keystrokes that can automate many of the tasks you normally perform while within dBASE. Macros let you record a sequence of characters in a single key combination. You can save the macro and later use it to play back those key sequences by pressing the assigned key combination. When the macro is played back, dBASE IV acts as if you had manually performed the actions contained within the macro.

You can use a macro to store a complex series of menu choices or commands, frequently used phrases, names, or complete paragraphs of text. You are not limited to one key combination; you can use various combinations of letter keys and function keys for macros. If you must print daily reports or perform similar repetitive tasks, you can save many keystrokes by using macros.

HINT Macros are ideal for automating repetitive tasks performed through the Control Center menus.

If you use commercially available keyboard enhancers like Superkey and ProKey, you are familiar with the advantages of automating your work with macros. Users of other keyboard enhancers may wonder whether they should simply continue to use such products instead of using dBASE IV's macro capability. The advantage of using the macro capability within dBASE IV is twofold. First, you will not consume additional memory that could be used by the program because you have loaded a memory-resident keyboard enhancer. dBASE IV requires a full 640K of RAM; unless your memory-resident keyboard enhancer can use extended or expanded memory, you are sure to run into "Insufficient memory" messages when you try to use it with dBASE. Second, you will avoid any possible conflicts between the operation of dBASE IV and the memory-resident keyboard enhancer. Memory-resident programs have, in the past, been known to conflict with various Ashton-Tate software packages. As of this writing, Ashton-Tate does not recommend the use of memory-resident packages when Ashton-Tate products are used. During the writing of this book, Borland's Sidekick was used with dBASE, with no ill effects; however, that experience is no guarantee that you will not encounter problems if you are using memory-resident packages with dBASE IV.

Creating a Macro

REMEMBER ALT-F10 cannot be assigned as a macro key.

To create a macro, follow these four steps:

1. Press SHIFT-F10, and then select Begin Recording from the next menu that appears. (An alternate method for this step is to choose the Macros option of the Tools menu, choose Record Macro, and then choose Begin Recording.)

2. Press the letter key or function key that is to be assigned to the macro. You can use any of the 26 letter keys or 9 function keys from F1 to F9.

3. Enter the keystrokes that will make up the macro. If you make an error, press SHIFT-F10 and then type **E** to end the recording, and start again.

4. Once all the keystrokes have been entered, press SHIFT-F10, and then select End Recording to stop the macro recording. (Or you can choose the Macros option of the Tools menu, choose Record Macro, and then choose End Recording.)

! ***HINT*** Macros assigned to function keys can easily be played by pressing ALT plus the assigned function key.

After the macro has been recorded, you can at any time press ALT-F10 followed by the assigned macro key to play back the macro. If you assigned the macro to a function key, you can press ALT plus that function key to play back the macro. As an alternate method of playing a macro, you can choose the Macros option of the Tools menu, choose Play Macro, and enter the key assigned to the macro.

For a quick example of what macros can do for you, get to the Control Center (if you are not there already) and open the ABCSTAFF file by highlighting the file and pressing F2 (Data). At this point, you should be in Browse mode, viewing the records in the ABCSTAFF file. Perhaps you regularly update records by locking the three leftmost fields and performing a forward search of the LASTNAME field for a desired last name. A macro would automate much of this process.

Press SHIFT-F10 and choose Begin Recording from the menu that appears. dBASE will ask you to press the key that will be used to call the macro. Type **S**. In the message line at the bottom of the screen, you will now see the message

```
Recording Macro; Press Shift-F10 E to end.
```

This indicates that dBASE is now recording each of your keystrokes in the form of a macro. Press the HOME key once. (This is done as a precaution to ensure that the cursor is at the leftmost field, since a user could start the macro from any location in the file.) Press ALT-F to open the Fields menu, and then type **L** to choose the Lock Fields on Left option. Enter **3** as the number of fields to remain stationary.

Press the TAB key once to move the cursor to the LASTNAME field. Next, press ALT-G to open the Go To menu and type **F** to choose the Forward Search option. When the prompt for a search value appears, press SHIFT- F10 and then choose End Recording to stop the recording of the macro.

To try the macro, first press ESC twice to close the menus and get back to a normal browsing mode. Assuming you now wanted to lock the first three fields and search for a particular name, you could use the macro to carry out all steps except the final one of entering the name to search for. Press ALT-F10 (Play Macro) now. dBASE will ask you to press the key assigned to the macro. Type **S**. All of the keystrokes are entered from the macro, and you are presented with the prompt for a last name to search for. Go ahead and enter any last name in the database. When the search is complete, press ESC until you are back at the Control Center.

Saving Macros

Macros that you create are saved in temporary memory and are not saved permanently on the disk. If you want to keep a permanent record of your macros, you must use the Save Library option, which appears on the Macros menu when you choose Macros from the Tools menu.

☞ ***REMEMBER*** The macros you create must be saved to a macro file if you want to use them during a later session.

Open the Tools menu, and choose Macros. From the next menu to appear, choose Save Library. dBASE will ask you for a name for the macro library; enter **MYMACROS** as the filename. (Note that macro libraries are saved with a .KEY extension.) The Save Library option saves all macros currently in memory to the designated macro file. This includes all macros created during the current work session, plus any that were loaded from a macro file during this work session.

Once the library has been saved, you can exit dBASE. When you return to the program, you can reload the macros you saved by choosing Macros from the Tools menu and then selecting Load Library from the next menu that appears.

One important point to note: while recording this macro, the ALT-key shortcuts to menu choices were purposely used. You could have used the cursor keys and the ENTER key to choose menu options, but when you build macros, it is a good idea to get into the habit of avoiding the cursor keys whenever possible. Not only does it mean less overall keystrokes in the macro, but also there is less chance during playback of an error caused by a list of available options being different than it was during recording. This can be a particular problem when you are choosing filenames from a pick list, because the list changes as files are added to or deleted from your directory.

For Dot-Prompt Users Only

Macros can also be used to repeat a series of dot-prompt commands, but this is not the speediest way to carry out a series of dot-prompt commands. You could start a macro with SHIFT-F10, assign a key to the macro, and enter a series of commands at the dot prompt, and then stop the recording and save the macro. When you play back the macro, all of those dot-prompt commands would be repeated, just as if you had typed them. However, dBASE will execute a series of dot-prompt commands much faster if they are stored in a command file (or program). Details on creating programs begin with Chapter 13.

Macros Menu Options

When you choose the Macros option of the Tools menu, another menu appears, called the Macros menu (Figure 9-1). The Begin Recording option of this menu is used to start the recording of the macro. (The alternate method to do this is to use SHIFT-F10, and then type **B** to select Begin Recording.) When you choose this option from the menu, the Macro Display table appears (Figure 9-2), showing all of the macros currently in memory and the keys assigned to those macros. The top half of the list displays the macros that are assigned to the function keys, and the bottom half

Figure 9-1.

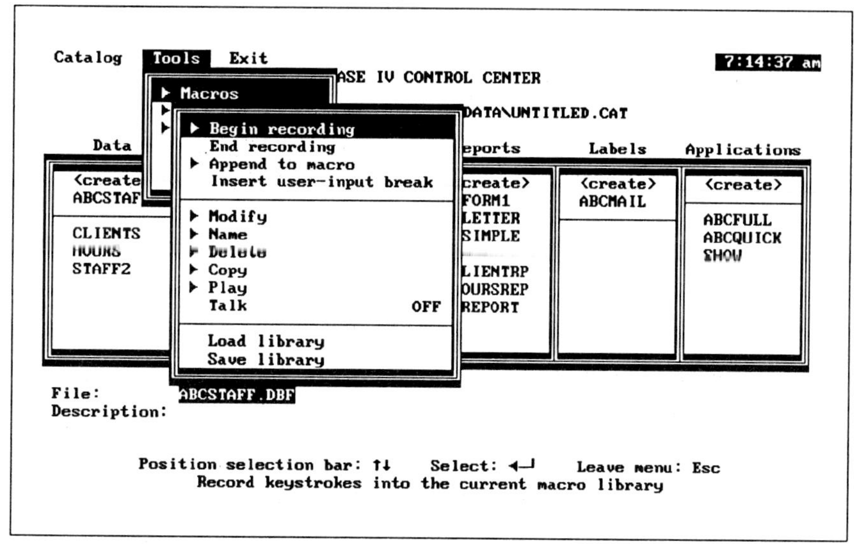

Macros menu

Figure 9-2.

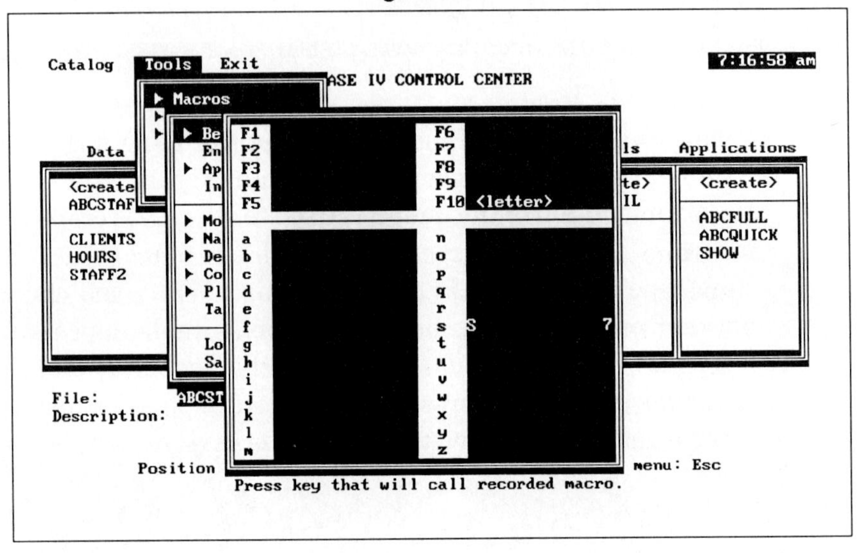

Macro Display table

of the list shows the macros that are assigned to the letter keys. (Note that if you assign a function key to a macro, you can start the macro playback from elsewhere within dBASE by pressing the ALT key and the assigned function key.) To record the macro, press the function or letter key you want to assign to the macro. If that key was used earlier, dBASE will ask for confirmation before overwriting the old macro in memory. After pressing the desired key, you can proceed to perform the actions you wish to store in the macro. When you are done, press SHIFT-F10 and then type **E** to stop the recording. The End Recording option of the Macros menu can also be used to stop the recording of the macro.

The Append to Macro option is used to append actions to the end of an existing macro. Choose this option, and the Macro Display table will appear. Press the key assigned to the macro, and you can then begin recording. Your actions will be added to the end of the existing macro.

The Input User Break option is used to let you enter a break in the macro. When the break occurs during playback, the macro will stop, allowing the user to make a choice or enter data. Pressing SHIFT-F10 then restarts the macro at the next action after the break.

Note that neither the End Recording nor the Input User Break option would actually be selected from this menu. These options would be selected from the macro window that is displayed with SHIFT-F10 while you are recording the macro.

The Modify option lets you edit a macro with the editor, and the Name option lets you change the name assigned to a macro. The Delete option is used to delete a macro from the current macro library. The Copy option of the menu lets you copy a macro into a different slot in the Macro Display table, while the Play option displays that table and lets you pick by name a macro to be played. Dot-prompt users should note that the Play option of the menu has a dot-prompt equivalent, the PLAY MACRO *macroname* command.

The Talk option of the Macros menu lets you show the macro steps in the message line as the macro is being played. Finally, the Load Library and Save Library options let you load a macro library into memory or save the current macros in memory to a library. The dot-prompt equivalents for these commands are RESTORE MACROS FROM *macro library filename*, which loads the macro library, and SAVE MACROS TO *macro library filename*, which saves the current macros to the named file.

Because you can save different libraries under different filenames, you can have an unlimited number of macros. One helpful hint in keeping track of your macro libraries is to give them the same name as the associated database file. Macro libraries are saved to a file with an extension of .KEY.

Macro Rules and Limitations

One macro cannot be made a part of itself. (For example, if a macro can be called with the Macro menu's Play option followed by the letter J, you cannot call up the Macros menu, choose Play, and enter the letter J within the macro.) Such a technique would set up an anomaly known in programming as a *recursive loop,* where the program chases its own tail. dBASE IV will not let you get away with this; an error beep will sound if you try it.

Allowable key combinations for assigning macros are the function keys F1 to F9 and the alphabetic keys. An attempt to use any other keys to assign a macro will produce an error beep. You cannot assign ALT-F10 to a macro, since ALT-F10 is the key combination for playing back macros.

Editing Macros

You may want to make changes to macros without being forced to recreate the entire macro. You can edit macros from the Edit Macro screen. To edit a macro, open the Tools menu and choose Macros. Next, choose Modify and press the key assigned to the macro. In a moment the editor will appear, containing the text of the macro (Figure 9-3).

The Edit Macro screen displays the characters and keystrokes contained within the macro. To edit a macro, use the same cursor

Figure 9-3.

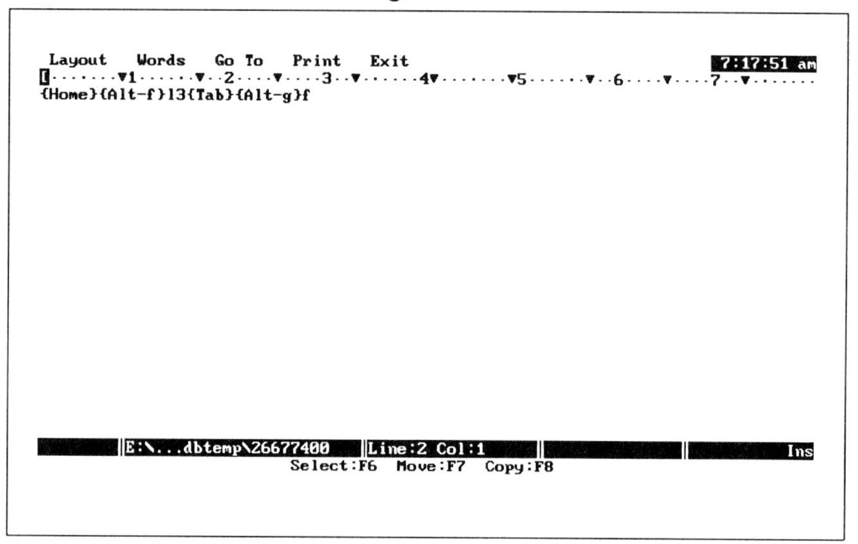

Edit Macro screen

movement and keyboard keys (DEL, INS, BACKSPACE) that you normally use during editing. You can manually construct a macro (or parts of one) within the editor by typing the desired symbols and keystrokes. Any of the alphabetic, numeric, or symbol keys are stored in macros as the exact character. Nonalphabetic keys are stored in the form of abbreviations inside of curly braces; the common ones are listed for your reference in Table 9-1.

Once you have finished editing the macro, press CTRL-END or choose Save Changes and Exit from the Exit menu. Remember, this saves the macro to memory, but you must save all macros in memory to a macro library if you want a permanent record of the macro on disk.

Table 9-1.

Abbreviation	Key Name
{Backspace}	BACKSPACE key
{Ins}	INS key
{Del}	DEL key
{uparrow}	Cursor Up key
{downarrow}	Cursor Down key
{leftarrow}	Cursor Left key
{rightarrow}	Cursor Right key
{PgUp}	PGUP key
{PgDn}	PGDN key
{Home}	HOME key
{End}	END key
{Esc}	ESC key
{Tab}	TAB key
{Enter}	ENTER or RETURN key
{F1}	Function keys
{F2}	
{F3}	
{F4}	
{F5}	
{F6}	
{F7}	
{F8}	
{F9}	

Common Nonalphabetic Macro Keys

Quick Reference

To create a macro Press SHIFT-F10, select Begin Recording, and press the letter or function key that is to be assigned to the macro. (You cannot use the F10 key.) Then, perform the actions that will be stored in the macro. When done, press SHIFT-F10 and type **E** to halt recording of the macro.

To play back a macro Press ALT-F10, followed by the key assigned to the macro. If you have assigned a function key to the macro, you can play the macro by pressing ALT plus the assigned function key.

To save all macros in memory to a macro file Open the Tools menu with ALT-T, choose Macros, and choose Save Library from the next menu to appear. Enter a filename for the macro library when prompted.

To load all of the macros in a macro file back into memory Open the Tools menu with ALT-T, choose Macros, and choose Load Library from the next menu to appear.

To edit the contents of a macro Open the Tools menu with ALT-T, choose Macros, and then choose Modify from the next menu to appear. Press the key assigned to the macro, and the contents of the macro will appear inside the Editor. Make the desired changes, and press CTRL-END (or choose Save Changes and Exit from the Exit menu) to save the macro.

CHAPTER

10

Managing Your Files

This chapter's topic is file operations—copying files, renaming and erasing files, and using more than one database file at a time. Although some file operations are normally performed from your operating system (DOS or OS/2), these operations can also be performed without leaving dBASE IV.

In addition to performing file operations without returning to the operating system, you can also transfer information between database files—all the data in a file, or selected data. dBASE IV lets you set various conditions for transferring files. You can also open and work with more than one file at once. The use of multiple files is common in a relational database manager like dBASE IV, and you will find it a virtual necessity for performing some types of tasks, such as inventory and complex accounting functions. You will be using multiple files shortly.

Using the DOS Tools

Various options for managing files are available through the Control Center by choosing the DOS Utilities option of the Tools menu. Get to the Control Center if you are not already there, and open the Tools menu with ALT-T. From the menu, select DOS Utilities. The Control Center will be replaced by the DOS Utilities screen, as shown in Figure 10-1. This screen is made up of a menu

Figure 10-1.

```
DOS   Files   Sort   Mark   Operations   Exit                              7:18:38 am
                              E:\DBASE4\DBDATA
 Name/Extension      Size     Date & Time         Attrs    Space Used

 <parent>            <DIR>    Feb 17,1989  8:50a  ****
 CHAP18              <DIR>    Feb 17,1989  9:02a  ****
 DATA                <DIR>    Feb 17,1989  9:06a  ****
 DBTEMP              <DIR>    Mar  6,1990  1:29a  ****
 EMPLOYEE            <DIR>    Feb 17,1989  9:10a  ****
 INVOICE             <DIR>    Feb 17,1989  9:14a  ****
 MAILING             <DIR>    Feb 17,1989  9:04a  ****
 PAYROLL             <DIR>    Feb 17,1989  9:05a  ****
 PROGRAMS            <DIR>    Feb 17,1989  9:08a  ****
 SQLFILES            <DIR>    Feb 17,1989  9:09a  ****
 TESTSQL             <DIR>    Apr  7,1990 12:49a  ****

Total  <marked>                0  (   0 files)                        0
Total  <displayed>       586,294  ( 194 files)                  970,752

  Files:*.*                                              Sorted by: Name

DOS util  E:\dbase4\DBDATA                                               Ins
     Position selection bar:↑↓   Mark file:←┘   Directories:F9
```

DOS Utilities screen

bar that contains menu options for various file operations, and a *files list,* which appears in a large rectangular box in the work surface. The files list displays all of the files in your current directory, and it is divided into five columns. The first column shows the name and extension (if any) of the file. Directories and subdirectories are displayed inside of angle brackets; in the figure, the filename *<parent>* at the top of the files list denotes the parent directory, E:\DBASE4 in this example.

The Size column shows the size of each file, in bytes, and the Date and Time column shows when the file was created, according to the time stamp put on the file by your operating system. The Attrs column shows the attributes of the file, as determined by your operating system. Up to four letters can appear in this column: A for archive, H for hidden, R for read only, and S for system. More information about file attributes can be found in your DOS manual.

The Space Used column shows the actual space used by the file. This figure is usually larger than that of the file size because of the way the operating system arranges files on a disk. With most versions of DOS, the minimum file size is either 1024 or 2048 bytes, and the space used will be the nearest multiple of these values necessary to store the file.

Notice the two lines that appear at the bottom of the files list. These lines show the total number of marked files (you can mark a group of files to perform a single operation on them) and the total number of files in the directory.

Moving Around the Files List

You can use the up and down arrow keys and the PGUP and PGDN keys to move the cursor within the files list. Try PGDN and your down arrow key now to see the effects. You can also use the HOME and END keys to quickly move to the beginning and end of a directory.

As you highlight a particular file, you can press ENTER to place a marker beside that file. Pressing ENTER again removes the marker from the file. In this way, you can mark a group of files for a selected operation you wish to perform later (such as deleting all marked files or copying them to another location). How to perform such operations on marked files will be covered shortly.

You are not limited to a single directory. By highlighting a parent or a subdirectory name and pressing ENTER, you can switch to that directory. You may want to try moving around your hard disk now by highlighting the <parent> directory name at the top of your list and pressing ENTER. When you do so, the directory containing all of your dBASE IV files appears (unless you have set up your hard disk differently).

After experimenting with moving around, be sure to get back to the subdirectory that contains your working files (it will probably be DBASE\DBDATA, unless you set up your hard disk differently at the start of this book). If you somehow get lost and can't find your way back, just press ESC and answer Yes at the "Abandon operation?" prompt, and then choose DOS Utilities from the Tools menu again. dBASE IV will automatically put you back in the working directory.

Deleting a File

You can use menu options (covered shortly) to delete a single file or a group of files, but there is a faster way to delete a single file.

Figure 10-2.

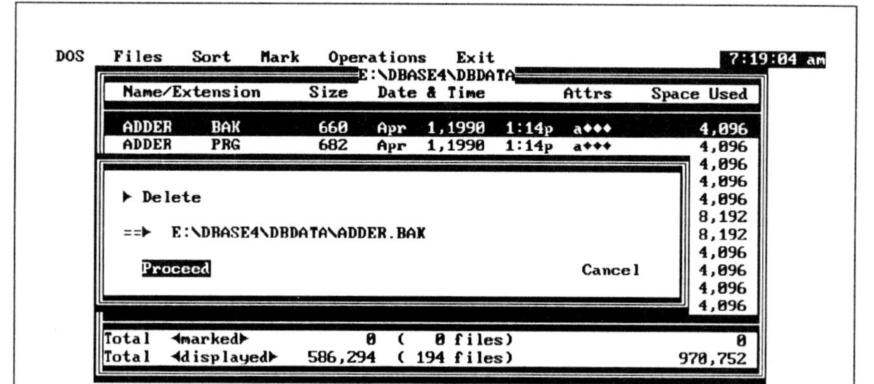

Prompt for deleting files

You can delete any file by highlighting that file in the files list and pressing the DEL key. A prompt similar to the example shown in Figure 10-2 will appear.

You must select Proceed from the menu to delete the chosen file. If you do not want to delete the file, choose Cancel.

REMEMBER Exercise care when deleting files. dBASE does not prevent you from deleting its own program files.

Using the Directory Tree

dBASE IV also lets you see your various directories by means of a *directory tree.* You may have noticed the message in the message bar which reads "Directories: F9." When you are in the files list, pressing F9 (Zoom) displays the directories in the form of a directory tree. Press F9 now, and the directory tree will be created. In a moment, your display should resemble the one shown in Figure 10-3. (Your directory names will certainly be different than the ones shown in this example, since they will reflect the directories that your hard disk contains.) At the top of the directory tree appears the root directory. Subdirectories appear as branches off of the line that runs down from the root directory.

Figure 10-3.

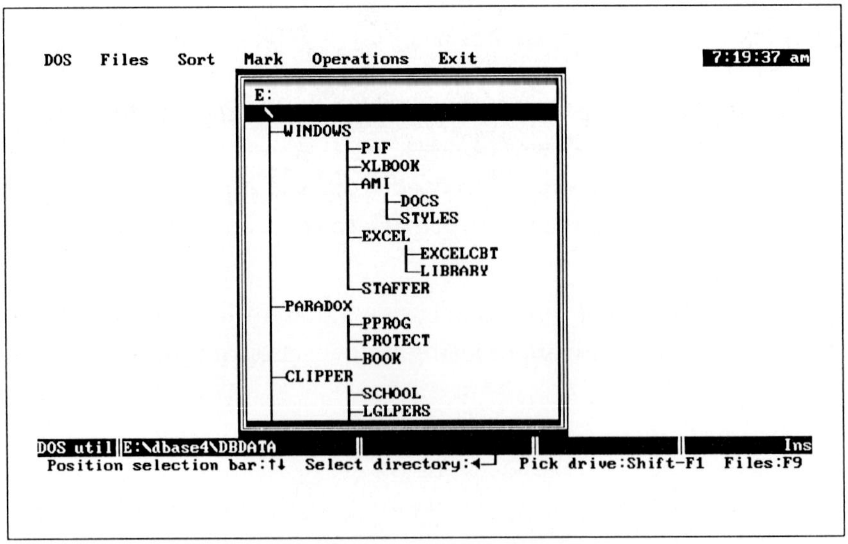

```
DOS   Files   Sort   Mark   Operations   Exit                    7:19:37 am
                            E:
                            \
                             ├WINDOWS
                             │       ├PIF
                             │       ├XLBOOK
                             │       ├AMI
                             │       │   ├DOCS
                             │       │   └STYLES
                             │       ├EXCEL
                             │       │     ├EXCELCBT
                             │       │     └LIBRARY
                             │       └STAFFER
                             ├PARADOX
                             │       ├PPROG
                             │       ├PROTECT
                             │       └BOOK
                             ├CLIPPER
                             │       ├SCHOOL
                             │       ├LGLPERS
DOS util E:\dbase4\DBDATA                                                 Ins
Position selection bar:↑↓  Select directory:◄─┘  Pick drive:Shift-F1  Files:F9
```

Directory tree

HINT To quickly move from one directory to another, press F9 to show the directory tree. Highlight the desired directory, and press ENTER.

You can switch the files list to display any directory by highlighting the desired directory in the directory tree and pressing ENTER. The files list will then reappear, and you will be in that directory. You can also change disk drives by moving to the top of the directory tree (the HOME key can be used for this purpose) and pressing ENTER. A list of available drives on your system will then appear; you can highlight the desired drive and press ENTER to switch the files list to that drive.

Before going on, get back to the subdirectory containing your dBASE IV data files, if you're not still there. If you're still at the directory tree, highlight the subdirectory with your data files and press ENTER to get back to the files list with your data files displayed.

Using the Menu Options

The DOS Utilities screen provides six menus: DOS, Files, Sort, Mark, Operations, and Exit. The Exit menu works just as it does elsewhere in dBASE IV, so we will not discuss it here.

Pressing ALT-D reveals the DOS menu (Figure 10-4). This menu is used to perform DOS file operations without returning to the operating system. The first option, Perform DOS Command, lets you enter a DOS command from within dBASE. When you choose this option, dBASE prompts you for the name of the DOS command. When you enter the command, it will be carried out. When it has completed, the message, "Press any key to return to dBASE

Figure 10-4.

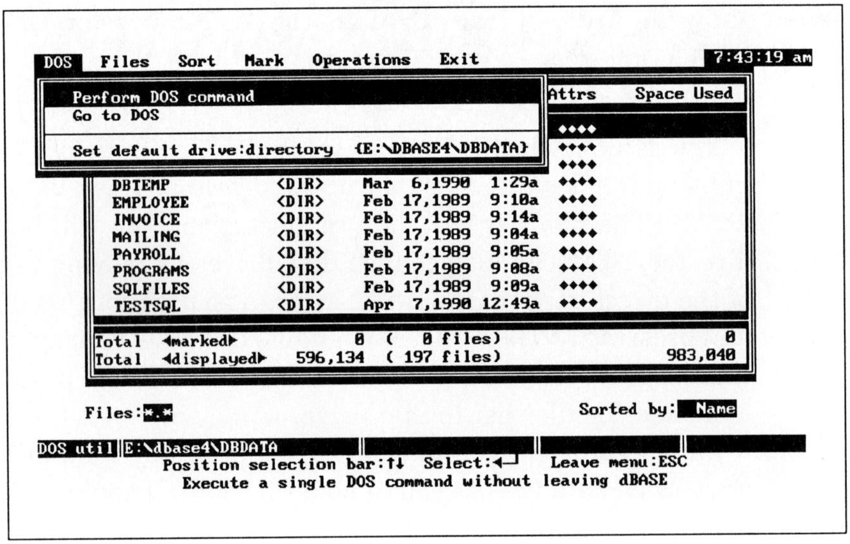

```
DOS  Files  Sort  Mark  Operations  Exit                          7:43:19 am
 Perform DOS command                              Attrs    Space Used
 Go to DOS
                                                  ****
 Set default drive:directory  {E:\DBASE4\DBDATA}  ****
                                                  ****
   DBTEMP        <DIR>   Mar  6,1990   1:29a      ****
   EMPLOYEE      <DIR>   Feb 17,1989   9:10a      ****
   INVOICE       <DIR>   Feb 17,1989   9:14a      ****
   MAILING       <DIR>   Feb 17,1989   9:04a      ****
   PAYROLL       <DIR>   Feb 17,1989   9:05a      ****
   PROGRAMS      <DIR>   Feb 17,1989   9:08a      ****
   SQLFILES      <DIR>   Feb 17,1989   9:09a      ****
   TESTSQL       <DIR>   Apr  7,1990  12:49a      ****

 Total ◄marked►              0  (   0 files)                   0
 Total ◄displayed►     596,134  ( 197 files)             983,040

   Files:*.*                                      Sorted by: Name

DOS util  E:\dbase4\DBDATA
      Position selection bar:↑↓   Select:◄┘    Leave menu:ESC
         Execute a single DOS command without leaving dBASE
```

DOS menu

IV" appears in the message line. Press a key, and you will be returned to the files list.

The Go to DOS option lets you jump to DOS through a "DOS shell." You can then proceed to enter assorted DOS commands, if you prefer to perform your file management tasks from DOS. When you are done, enter **EXIT** at the DOS prompt to return to dBASE. The EXIT command is a DOS command that returns you from a DOS shell back to the program you were running (in this case, dBASE IV). If you forget to use EXIT and try to enter **DBASE** to load dBASE IV instead, you will see the error message "Program too big to fit in memory."

The Set Default Drive:Directory option lets you change the default drive and/or directory being used by dBASE to store your data. When you choose this option and enter the desired drive and directory path, dBASE IV will store all your data in the new directory.

Figure 10-5.

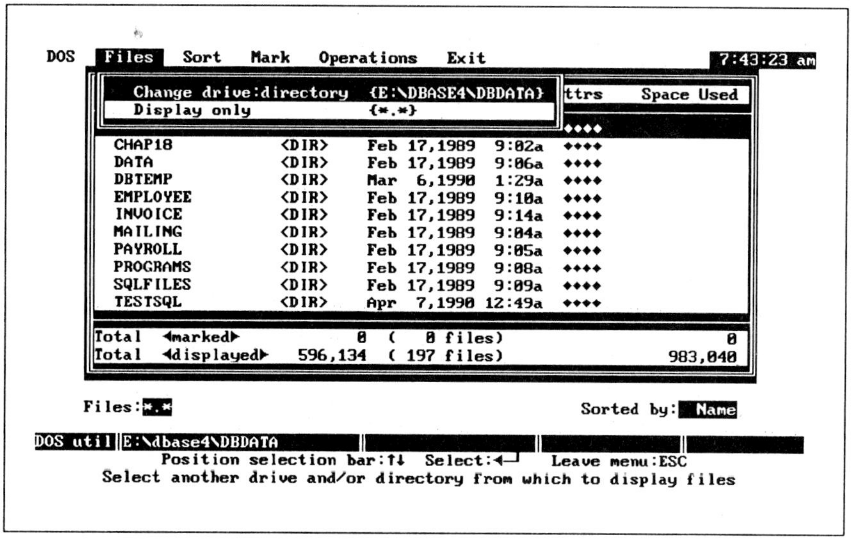

```
DOS  Files  Sort  Mark  Operations  Exit                              7:43:23 am
       Change drive:directory   {E:\DBASE4\DBDATA}  ttrs    Space Used
       Display only             {*.*}
                                                    ****
     CHAP18          <DIR>     Feb 17,1989   9:02a  ****
     DATA            <DIR>     Feb 17,1989   9:06a  ****
     DBTEMP          <DIR>     Mar  6,1990   1:29a  ****
     EMPLOYEE        <DIR>     Feb 17,1989   9:10a  ****
     INVOICE         <DIR>     Feb 17,1989   9:14a  ****
     MAILING         <DIR>     Feb 17,1989   9:04a  ****
     PAYROLL         <DIR>     Feb 17,1989   9:05a  ****
     PROGRAMS        <DIR>     Feb 17,1989   9:08a  ****
     SQLFILES        <DIR>     Feb 17,1989   9:09a  ****
     TESTSQL         <DIR>     Apr  7,1990  12:49a  ****
    Total  ◄marked►            0  (   0 files)                        0
    Total  ◄displayed►   596,134  ( 197 files)                  983,040

    Files:*.*                                        Sorted by: Name
DOS util ║E:\dbase4\DBDATA
         Position selection bar:↑↓   Select:◄┘   Leave menu:ESC
      Select another drive and/or directory from which to display files
```

Files menu

Pressing ALT-F will reveal the Files menu (Figure 10-5). It provides two choices that affect the display of files in the files list. The first option, Change Drive:Directory, lets you change the drive and directory displayed in the files list. (As you've seen, you can accomplish the same task by highlighting the directory or drive name in the files list and pressing ENTER.) The second choice, Display Only, lets you filter the display of files to show a particular type of file.

To see how this works, select the Display Only option now, and enter

```
*.DBF
```

You will see the files list change so that it displays only database files. To go back to the normal display of all files, open the Files menu again with ALT-F, choose Display Only, and then enter

* *

to restore the display to all files. DOS wildcards (such as the asterisk, which means all files) can be entered here; see your DOS manual for details on the use of wildcards.

Pressing ALT-S displays the Sort menu (Figure 10-6). The Sort menu lets you change the sorting order for the display of files in the files list. The Name option (which is the default) causes the files to be arranged in alphabetical order by name. The Extension option reorders the list by extension. The Date and Time option sorts the list by date, and where dates are the same, by time. The Size option sorts the list by the size of the file. Try these Sort menu options now, and note the effect on the display in the files list. Regardless of how you sort the directory, the <parent> directory will always appear at the top of the list.

Pressing ALT-M opens the Mark menu (Figure 10-7). Use the first option, Mark All, to mark all files in a directory. The second

Figure 10-6.

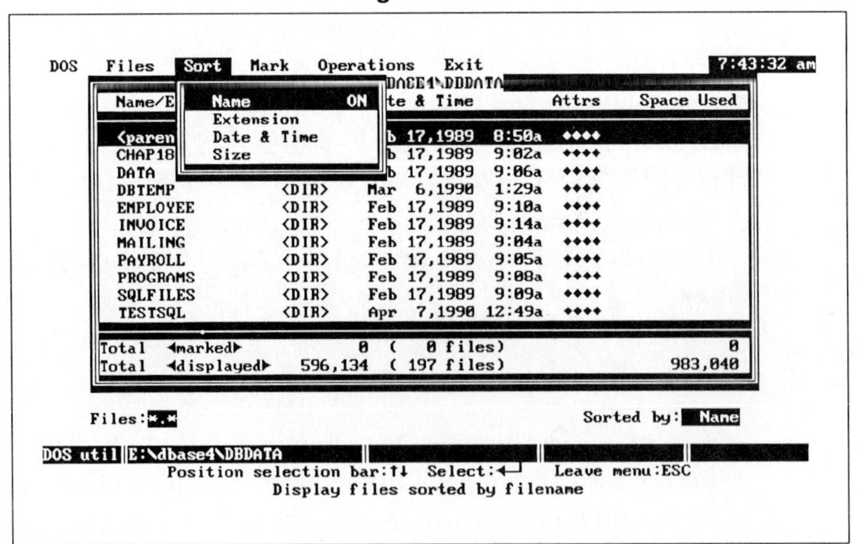

Sort menu

Figure 10-7.

```
DOS   Files   Sort   Mark   Operations   Exit                          7:43:36 am
                                         \DBDATA
 Name/Extensio | Mark all         | Time          Attrs    Space Used
               | Unmark all       |
 <parent>      | Reverse marks    | 1989  8:50a   ****
 CHAP10                             1989  9:02a   ****
 DATA             <DIR>    Feb 17,1989  9:06a   ****
 DBTEMP           <DIR>    Mar  6,1990  1:29a   ****
 EMPLOYEE         <DIR>    Feb 17,1989  9:10a   ****
 INVOICE          <DIR>    Feb 17,1989  9:14a   ****
 MAILING          <DIR>    Feb 17,1989  9:04a   ****
 PAYROLL          <DIR>    Feb 17,1989  9:05a   ****
 PROGRAMS         <DIR>    Feb 17,1989  9:08a   ****
 SQLFILES         <DIR>    Feb 17,1989  9:09a   ****
 TESTSQL          <DIR>    Apr  7,1990 12:49a   ****

Total  ◄marked►              0  (   0 files)                    0
Total  ◄displayed►     596,134  ( 197 files)              983,040

Files: *.*                                       Sorted by: Name

DOS util ||E:\dbase4\DBDATA
        Position selection bar:↑↓  Select:◄┘   Leave menu:ESC
Mark all files in current display window, including those scrolled out of view
```

Mark menu

option, Unmark All, has the opposite effect—it removes the markers from all marked files. The Reverse Marks option marks all files that are unmarked and unmarks all files that are marked. As mentioned earlier, you can mark a single file by highlighting that file in the files list and pressing ENTER.

Pressing ALT-O opens the Operations menu (Figure 10-8). The choices on this menu let you perform the common file operations of deleting, copying, moving, or renaming files. You can also view files and edit files with the dBASE editor (these options should only be used with text files or files that have no control codes in them.)

The first option, Delete, lets you delete a single file, a marked group of files, or all files displayed in the directory. When you choose this option, another menu appears, offering the three choices described. If you choose Single File, the file that is highlighted in the files list is deleted (you are asked for confirmation first). If you choose Marked Files, all files that are marked will be

Figure 10-8.

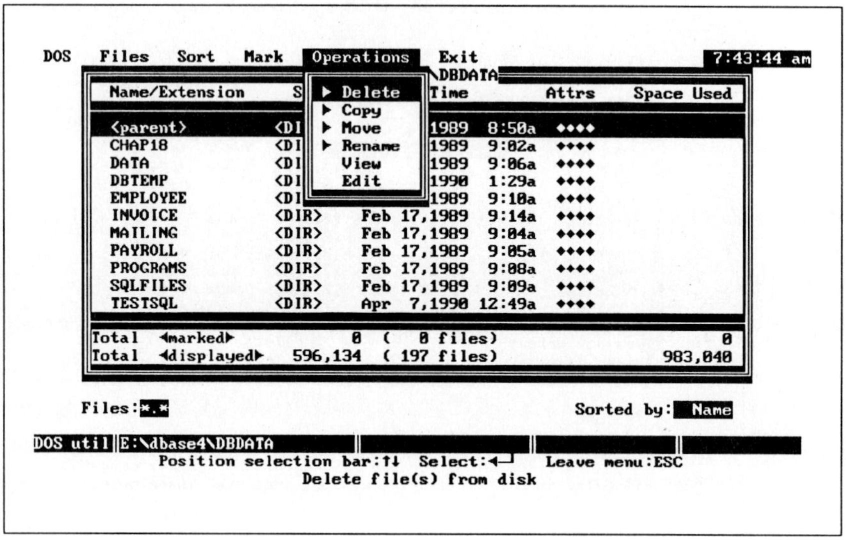

```
DOS   Files   Sort   Mark   Operations   Exit                          7:43:44 am
                                         \DBDATA
  Name/Extension         S  ▶ Delete   Time          Attrs    Space Used
                            ▶ Copy
  <parent>             <DI  ▶ Move     1989  8:50a   ****
  CHAP18               <DI  ▶ Rename   1989  9:02a   ****
  DATA                 <DI    View     1989  9:06a   ****
  DBTEMP               <DI    Edit     1990  1:29a   ****
  EMPLOYEE             <DI             1989  9:10a   ****
  INVOICE              <DIR>    Feb 17,1989  9:14a   ****
  MAILING              <DIR>    Feb 17,1989  9:04a   ****
  PAYROLL              <DIR>    Feb 17,1989  9:05a   ****
  PROGRAMS             <DIR>    Feb 17,1989  9:08a   ****
  SQLFILES             <DIR>    Feb 17,1989  9:09a   ****
  TESTSQL              <DIR>    Apr  7,1990 12:49a   ****

Total  ◄marked►             0  (   0 files)                          0
Total  ◄displayed►    596,134  ( 197 files)                    983,040

  Files:*.*                                          Sorted by: Name

DOS util ║E:\dbase4\DBDATA      ║                  ║                ║
        Position selection bar:↑↓   Select:◄┘    Leave menu:ESC
                        Delete file(s) from disk
```

Operations menu

deleted after you confirm the operation. If you choose Displayed Files, all files shown in the directory will be deleted after your confirmation.

Since deleting files is usually done to keep a hard disk manageable, you may want to try this option now to see how it works. Close the menu (if it is open) with ESC, and then use PGDN and the arrow keys to highlight VAPERSON.DBF. Press ENTER to mark the file. Then highlight VAPERSON.DBT, and press ENTER to mark that file. Use the same technique to mark QFIRST.QBE and QFIRST.QBO. These four files were created in the exercises in earlier chapters. They will not be needed later in the book, so it is safe to delete them from your disk.

With the files marked, open the Operations menu with ALT-O and choose Delete. Select Marked Files from the next menu. You will be asked to confirm the operation by choosing Proceed from a menu box. With Proceed highlighted, press ENTER, and the files will be deleted.

The Copy option of the Operations menu lets you copy files to another disk or directory. As with the Delete option, selecting Copy presents another menu with the choices of Single File, Marked Files, or Displayed Files. You may find the Marked Files option useful for performing an incremental backup of selected files. After selecting one of the three options, enter the drive and path (if any) of the destination to which the files are to be copied. If you are copying marked files or all displayed files, you will need to press CTRL-END to perform the file copy.

The Move option of the Operations menu lets you move files to another directory. As with the Copy option, choosing this option presents another menu with choices of Single File, Marked Files, or Displayed Files. Select the desired choice, and then enter the drive and directory path to which the file or files are to be moved. Once you press CTRL-END to complete the process, the files will be moved (copied to the destination directory and then deleted from the source directory). Note that when you are copying or moving database (.DBF) files with memo fields, you should also copy or move the associated .DBT files.

The Rename option of the Operations menu lets you rename files. As with the Move option, choosing this option presents another menu with choices of Single File, Marked Files, or Displayed Files. Select the desired choice, and then enter the new name for the file. You can rename more than one file at a time by using DOS wildcards; for example, if you wanted to rename MASTER.DBF and MASTER.DBT to new names FIRST.DBF and FIRST.DBT, you could mark those files and enter **FIRST.*** as the new name for the files. Once you enter the new name, the file or files will be renamed.

The View and Edit options are designed for use with text files. You can view the contents of a file or use the editor to edit the files. Highlight the desired text file and then open the Operations menu and choose View or Edit. If you choose View, the text will appear one screenful at a time. Press the spacebar to see the next screenful, or press ENTER to start or stop a file scrolling. If you choose the Edit option, the highlighted file will be loaded into the dBASE editor, and you can use all of the features of the editor to edit the file. Note that the editor is not designed to work with files containing program codes such as .EXE, .COM, or .OVL files, or with your dBASE database files (.DBF or .DBT extensions). You should not attempt to edit such files.

Dot-Prompt Options for File Management

If you prefer, you can also use a number of dot-prompt commands for performing file management. You can even run a DOS command from a dot prompt. You can also perform selective copying of records within a database file to another file.

The RUN Command

To exit dBASE temporarily and run a DOS command, use the RUN command from the dot prompt. The syntax for this command is

RUN *DOS-command-or-program-name*

It causes dBASE to temporarily suspend itself in memory and exit to DOS. Note that a substantial portion of dBASE remains in memory when you do this, so while you technically can run other programs, you will probably find very few programs that run in this manner.

The RUN command is primarily useful for executing DOS commands you may be familiar with, such as COPY, DIR, RENAME, and so on. To see how this works, get to the dot prompt and enter the following command

```
RUN DIR /P
```

You will see the directory of your disk displayed just as if you had entered **DIR /P** at the DOS prompt. When the command completes, you will be returned to the dot prompt.

Note that you should never attempt to run a program that will modify your PC's memory with the RUN command. All memory-resident programs fall into this category, as does the PRINT command in DOS.

The COPY FILE Command

You can use the COPY FILE command as an equivalent to the COPY command in DOS to make copies of entire files. The format for this command is

COPY FILE *source-filename* TO *destination-filename*

You must include any extensions when using this command. As an example, if you wanted to make a copy of a file named LETTER1.TXT and the copy was to be named MYFILE.TXT, you could do so from the dot prompt with the following command:

```
COPY FILE LETTER1.TXT TO MYFILE.TXT
```

Drive identifiers and path names are optional and can be included before the filenames. Note that if you use this method to copy a database file, be sure to also copy any .DBT (memo field) file that may accompany the database. Remember, whenever a database contains memo fields, it is made up of two files: one with a .DBF extension, and another with a .DBT extension.

NOTE With very large files, using COPY at the DOS level will be much faster than using COPY FILE within dBASE.

The COPY Command

The COPY command is used to copy all or parts of a database file. Its format is

COPY TO *filename*

where *filename* is the name of the new file that you want the records copied to. You must first use the USE command to open the file that you want to copy from. For example, if you enter

```
USE ABCSTAFF
COPY TO FILE1
USE FILE1
LIST
```

all of the records in the ABCSTAFF database will be copied to the new file, FILE1. One advantage of the COPY TO command is that you need not worry about copying the memo field (.DBT) file; it is copied automatically.

The COPY command offers significant flexibility when you choose to copy specific fields. To select the fields to be copied, use the format

COPY TO *filename* FIELDS *field-list*

By adding the word "FIELDS" after the filename and then adding a list of fields, you tell dBASE IV to copy the fields that you place in the list to the new database. Copy just the LASTNAME, FIRSTNAME, CITY, and STATE fields in FILE1 by entering

```
COPY TO FILE2 FIELDS LASTNAME, FIRSTNAME, CITY, STATE
USE FILE2
LIST
```

Only those fields you specified by name in FILE1 are copied to FILE2.

You can also use FOR to select specific data from a database. FOR is an optional phrase that indicates that the COPY command will apply to every record in the database for which the specified condition is true. The format of the COPY command with FOR is

COPY TO *filename* FIELDS *fields-list* FOR *condition*

Using the FOR phrase as part of the COPY command, you can copy the LASTNAME and SALARY fields from FILE1 for all records in which the salary is less than $10.00 per hour. To do this, enter

```
USE FILE1
COPY TO FILE3 FIELDS LASTNAME, SALARY FOR SALARY < 10
```

The FOR condition specified before the SALARY field resulted in the new file, FILE3, containing only those employees earning less than $10.00 per hour. To see the results, enter

```
USE FILE3
LIST
```

This kind of selective copying is an advantage the dot prompt offers over the Control Center. There is no direct way to make such a selective copy of a file from the Control Center menus. You could design a view query with the fields and records you wanted, and then select the Write View as Database File option of the Layout menu; however, you could not do so as quickly as you can enter commands like the ones just shown.

Organizing Your Work With Catalogs

dBASE IV lets you store an associated group of database files, index files, query files, report format files, and label format files in a special file known as a *catalog*. When you are using that catalog, only those files will be accessible from the panels of the Control Center. This feature comes in particularly handy when numerous files begin to clutter your hard disk. By placing various files in different catalogs, you do not have to search through excessively long lists of files in a directory. Any new files that you create when a particular catalog is open will be added to that catalog. dBASE IV stores the information that makes up a catalog in a special kind of database that is assigned the .CAT extension. When you choose a catalog from the Catalog menu of the Control Center, dBASE IV looks into the special database to find the files associated with that particular catalog.

To manage your catalogs, use the various options of the Catalog menu. From the Control Center, press ALT-C to open the Catalog menu (Figure 10-9). The Use a Different Catalog option lets you

Figure 10-9.

```
Catalog  Tools  Exit                                               7:44:05 am
 Use a different catalog                  CENTER
 Modify catalog name
 Edit description of catalog              TA\UNTITLED.CAT

 Add file to catalog                      orts      Labels      Applications
 Remove highlighted file from catalog     eate>     <create>    <create>
 Change description of highlighted file
                                          ENTRP     ABCMAIL     ABCFULL
 CLIENTS      RELATE3                     HOURSREP              ABCQUICK
 HOURS                                    HREPORT               SHOW
 STAFF2                                   RFORM1
                                          RLETTER
                                          RSIMPLE

File:         New file
Description:  Press ENTER on <create> to create a new file

      Position selection bar: ↑↓    Select: ←┘    Leave menu: Esc
               Select a different catalog or create a new one
```

Catalog menu

change to a different catalog or create a new catalog. When you choose this option, a list of available catalogs will appear. Choose the desired catalog from the list, or choose the Create option on the list to create a new catalog. Once you choose a new catalog, any files you create will be stored in that catalog.

The Modify Catalog Name option lets you change the filename for the existing catalog, and the Edit Description of Catalog option lets you change the description for the catalog. (The description appears on the screen as you are choosing a catalog with the Use a Different Catalog option of the Catalog menu.) The Add File to Catalog option lets you add an existing file to a catalog. When you choose this option, a list of files appears. The files you see in the list are of the same type as the panel the cursor is in. For example, if the cursor is in the Reports panel, you will see report format files when you choose the Add File to Catalog option. If the cursor is in the Data panel, you will see database files when you choose the option.

The Remove Highlighted File from Catalog option lets you remove a file highlighted on the Control Center from the current catalog. Finally, the Change Description of Highlighted File lets you change the description of the file currently highlighted.

When you are creating a new application, or set of databases and associated files to handle a particular task, it is a good idea to first create a new catalog before creating any of the database files, indexes, reports, screen formats, and so on. Choose Use a Different Catalog from the Catalog menu, and select the Create option from the pick list that appears; then enter a name for your new catalog. You'll see the catalog name appear near the top of the screen (above the Control Center panels). You can now proceed to create the databases, index files, reports, and so forth that will be used in your application. The new catalog will contain those files as long as it is open when the files are created.

Work Areas and Active Files

dBASE IV can access any database file that is open. Basically, opening a database file amounts to telling dBASE IV, "I am ready to work with a database file that is stored on disk; now go get it." You can tell this to dBASE IV ten times, because it allows you to have ten open database files at any given time.

dBASE IV can read any information in the database from an open database file, but that is all. If you want to change, add, or delete any information in a database, the database file not only must be open, but it must be active as well. Commands like EDIT, APPEND, and DELETE can only operate on active database files. dBASE IV allows only one active database file at a time, so out of a possible ten open database files, only one can be active.

Opening a database file from disk requires that it be assigned to a *work area*. No database file can be open unless it resides in a work area. As you might have guessed, there are ten work areas in dBASE IV, numbered from 1 to 10. Assigning a database file to a work area—or opening a database file—is a two-step process: you tell dBASE IV what work area you want the file to be placed in, and you load the file into that work area. The SELECT command enables you to choose the work area, and the USE command loads the file. For example, if you wanted to open ABCSTAFF in work area 2, you could first select the work area by entering

```
SELECT 2
```

To load ABCSTAFF into the current work area, you would enter

```
USE ABCSTAFF
```

As an alternative, you can also perform both steps—specifying the work area and opening the file—on a single command line by using the IN option along with the USE command. As an example, the following command tells dBASE to open ABCSTAFF in work area 2:

```
USE ABCSTAFF IN 2
```

If you had specified a different filename, for example HOURS instead of ABCSTAFF, that file (HOURS) would have been loaded into work area 2. In fact, any database file that you now load with the USE command will be directed into work area 2 until you use the SELECT command to choose a different work area.

The current work area is always the last area you chose with the SELECT command. The active database file is the last database file you loaded into the current work area. As an example, open the HOURS file in work area 1 and ABCSTAFF in work area 2 by entering the following commands:

```
SELECT 1
USE HOURS
SELECT 2
USE ABCSTAFF
```

ABCSTAFF is now the active database, because work area 2 was the last work area selected; thus, dBASE IV is pointed to ABCSTAFF. dBASE IV can now change or access any information in ABCSTAFF but can only access information from the HOURS database. If you want HOURS to be the active file, after opening both database files you would enter **SELECT 1**. The active database file will switch from ABCSTAFF to HOURS, although ABCSTAFF remains open.

When you start a session, dBASE IV selects work area 1 as the default work area. Also, when you select a file from the Control Center, it is opened in work area 1 by default. This is why in the other chapters you did not have to use the SELECT command first in order to load ABCSTAFF. Note that you could also select a file and work area by specifying the *alias* after the SELECT command. (You will learn more about aliases shortly.) For example, once ABCSTAFF is opened in work area 1, entering **SELECT ABCSTAFF** would switch to work area 1 and open the file.

Until now you've worked with only one database file at a time, so when you referenced a field you didn't need to include the filename; whatever file you were working with was the active file. If you need information from a neighboring open database file, however, it is necessary to include the filename with the field. For example, enter the following:

```
SELECT 2
LIST
```

You will see from the listing that ABCSTAFF, open in work area 2, is the active file. To inspect the WEEKENDING field in HOURS in work area 1 while ABCSTAFF is active in work area 2, enter

```
LIST HOURS->WEEKENDING
```

The hyphen and the greater-than sign are combined to form a "pointer" for the field name. If you want to list the HOURS, WEEKENDING, and SOCIALSEC fields from the HOURS database, include the filename and pointer for all three:

```
LIST HOURS->HOURS, HOURS->WEEKENDING, HOURS->SOCIALSEC
```

Listing the filename while referencing a neighboring work area can be tedious, especially if the filename is long or difficult to remember. To alleviate part of the problem, you can give a shorter or more descriptive alias to a file when you assign it to a work area. In fact, dBASE IV assigns the default alias of A to work area 1, B to work area 2, C to work area 3, and so on. Instead of entering LIST HOURS->WEEKENDING, for example, you can enter **LIST A->WEEKENDING** and the same result will appear.

If you are dissatisfied with the default names, you can name your own alias when you load a database file into a work area by including the ALIAS option with the USE command. The format for assigning an alias is

USE *filename* ALIAS *aliasname*

The same naming conventions for a filename apply to an alias name, but the .DBF extension is not included with an alias name. As an example, the following command will give the alias ABC to the ABCSTAFF database file in work area 2:

```
SELECT 2
USE ABCSTAFF ALIAS ABC
```

Using CLOSE DATABASES

Another command that you will use often is the CLOSE DATABASES command. It closes all database and index files and returns dBASE IV to work area 1. Enter

```
CLOSE DATABASES
```

to close all of the database files that you have opened earlier.

Combining Files

dBASE IV lets you transfer records from one database file to another by using a variation of the APPEND command that you have used to add records to a database. However, the format of the command is somewhat different when it is used for transferring records from another database. Instead of simply entering APPEND, you must enter the command in the format

APPEND FROM *filename*

where *filename* is the name of the file from which you wish to transfer records. The file to which you are adding the records must be the active database file. (The equivalent for this command from the Control Center is the Append Records from Database File option shown on the Append menu when you are at the File Design screen.)

For example, to transfer records from the newly created FILE3 database to the FILE2 database, you should first activate FILE2. Enter

```
USE FILE2
```

You can append the records to FILE2 with

```
APPEND FROM FILE3
```

When you list the database to see the appended records, your display should resemble the listing in Figure 10-10.

One characteristic of the APPEND FROM command becomes apparent when you examine the list: only fields having the same names in both databases are appended. Remember, you gave different structures to these files as a result of the selective use of the COPY command. FILE2 contains the LASTNAME, FIRSTNAME, CITY, and STATE fields, while FILE3 contains only the LASTNAME and SALARY fields. When you appended from FILE3 to FILE2, dBASE IV found just one field common to the two database files—LASTNAME.

Even if the field name is the same, dBASE IV may or may not append the field if the data type is different. If dBASE can make sense of the transfer, it will append the data. For example, a numeric field will transfer to a character field of another

Figure 10-10.

Record#	LASTNAME	FIRSTNAME	CITY	STATE
1	Morse	Marcia	Chevy Chase	MD
2	Westman	Andrea	Silver Spring	MD
3	Jackson	David	Falls Church	VA
4	Mitchell	Mary Jo	Arlington	VA
5	Robinson	Shirley	Takoma Park	MD
6	Jackson	Cheryl	Falls Church	VA
7	Robinson	Wanda	Washington	DC
8	Hart	Edward	Fairfax	VA
9	Jones	Judi	Reston	VA
10	Morse			
11	Jackson			
12	Mitchell			
13	Robinson			
14	Robinson			
15	Hart			

Appended records in FILE2

database, with data appearing in the character fields as numbers. A character field, if it contains only numbers, will transfer to a numeric field. A memo field will not transfer to any other type of field. In addition, if the field being copied has a field size larger than the field receiving the record, character data will be truncated and asterisks will be entered for numeric data.

The file that you append from does not have to be a dBASE IV database file. The APPEND FROM command is also commonly used when you want to transfer data from other programs, such as spreadsheets or word processors. This aspect of using dBASE IV will be detailed more thoroughly in Chapter 19.

Copying a Database Structure

Another helpful dBASE IV command, COPY STRUCTURE, lets you make an identical copy of the database structure (in effect, an empty database). You can use COPY STRUCTURE to create empty copies of a database on multiple floppy disks, which others can use at their machines (provided they have dBASE IV) to add records. Later, the records can be combined at a single site with the APPEND FROM command just discussed.

To use this command, first open the database you want to copy the structure from with the USE command; then, at the dot prompt, enter the command

COPY STRUCTURE TO *filename*

where *filename* is the desired name of the file. You can precede the filename with a path or a drive identifier if desired. For example, the commands

```
USE ABCSTAFF
COPY STRUCTURE TO A:REMOTE
```

would copy an empty database containing the structure of ABC-STAFF to a file called REMOTE.DBF on the disk in drive A. If the file contains memo fields, both a .DBF and a .DBT file will be copied under the new name.

Quick Reference

To use the DOS Tools Open the Tools menu by pressing ALT-T. Select the DOS Utilities option. When the DOS Utilities screen appears, select the desired menu by pressing ALT plus the first letter of the menu name. Use the menu options of the Operations menu to delete, copy, and rename files. To mark files for deletion, place the cursor next to the desired file, and press ENTER. To delete a single file, place the cursor next to that file and press the DEL key.

To display the disk directory tree Open the Tools menu by pressing ALT-T. Select the DOS Utilities option. When the DOS Utilities screen appears, press F9. In a moment, the directory tree will appear. To change to another directory shown on the tree, move the cursor to that directory, and press ENTER.

To access DOS from within dBASE IV From the Control Center, open the Tools menu by pressing ALT-T, select DOS Utilities, and from the DOS Utilities screen open the DOS menu with ALT-D and choose Go To DOS. When done, enter **EXIT** at the DOS prompt to return to dBASE IV.

To use a DOS command from within dBASE IV From the Control Center, open the Tools menu by pressing ALT-T, select

DOS Utilities, and from the DOS Utilities screen open the DOS menu with ALT-D and choose Perform DOS Command. Enter the name of the DOS command when prompted. Or, from the dot prompt, use the syntax RUN *command-name,* where *command-name* is the name of the DOS command you want to run.

To change catalogs At the Control Center, open the Catalog menu with ALT-C, and select Use a Different Catalog. Select the desired catalog from the list that appears (no list appears if only one catalog currently exists), or select the Create option to create a new catalog.

To access multiple work areas Use the SELECT command, followed by the number of the desired work area. For example, enter **SELECT 2** to select work area 2, and so on. You can open a different database in each work area with the USE command.

To copy the structure (design) of a database to an empty database file Get to the dot prompt, and use the command syntax COPY STRUCTURE TO *D:filename* where *D:* is the letter of the disk drive where the new file should be stored, and *filename* is the name to be assigned to the file.

Figure 11-1.

```
Page No.   1
09/11/88

SOCIALSEC      123-44-8976
LASTNAME       Morse
FIRSTNAME      Marcia
ADDRESS        4260 Park Avenue
CITY           Chevy Chase
STATE          MD
ZIPCODE        20815-0988
PHONE          301-555-6678
BIRTHDAY       03/01/54
DATEHIRED      07/25/85
DEPENDENTS     2
SALARY         9.00
ASSIGNMENT     National Oil Co.
HOURLYRATE     16.00
EVALUATE       Experienced in accounting, tax preparation, has
               MBA in business management.


SOCIALSEC      121-33-9876
LASTNAME       Westman
FIRSTNAME      Andrea
ADDRESS        4807 East Avenue
CITY           Silver Spring
STATE          MD
ZIPCODE        20910-0124
PHONE          301-555-2912
BIRTHDAY       05/29/61
DATEHIRED      07/04/86
DEPENDENTS     2
SALARY         16.50
ASSIGNMENT     National Oil Co.
HOURLYRATE     25.00
```

Example of default form-layout report

Figure 11-1 (*continued*)

EVALUATE	Did well on last two assignments.
SOCIALSEC	232-55-1234
LASTNAME	Jackson
FIRSTNAME	David
ADDRESS	4102 Valley Lane
CITY	Falls Church
STATE	VA
ZIPCODE	22044
PHONE	703-555-8778
BIRTHDAY	12/22/55
DATEHIRED	09/05/85
DEPENDENTS	1
SALARY	8.00
ASSIGNMENT	City Revenue Dept.
HOURLYRATE	13.00
EVALUATE	Absentee rate high.

Example of default form-layout report

Producing a Selective Form-Style Report

As with columnar reports, you can use view queries to generate form-layout reports that meet your precise needs. You can often save time by limiting the fields produced by the view query, and basing a report that uses the default form-layout design on that view. As an example, perhaps you need a quick mailing list. You only need the names and addresses of the employees; and for this example, you only need those employees who live in Maryland.

Get to the Control Center. Open ABCSTAFF by choosing the file and selecting Use File from the next menu to appear. Next,

Figure 11-2.

```
Page No.  1
09/11/88

LASTNAME      Morse
FIRSTNAME     Marcia
ADDRESS       4260 Park Avenue
CITY          Chevy Chase
STATE         MD
ZIPCODE       20815-0988

LASTNAME      Westman
FIRSTNAME     Andrea
ADDRESS       4807 East Avenue
CITY          Silver Spring
STATE         MD
ZIPCODE       20910-0124

LASTNAME      Robinson
FIRSTNAME     Shirley
ADDRESS       270 Browning Ave #2A
CITY          Takoma Park
STATE         MD
ZIPCODE       20912-1234
```

Form-oriented report of Maryland employees

select the Create option of the Queries panel to start a new query. Press F5 once to remove all fields in the file skeleton from the view. Then use TAB and F5 to add the LASTNAME, FIRSTNAME, ADDRESS, CITY, STATE, and ZIPCODE fields to the view. Move back to the STATE field within the file skeleton, and enter

```
="MD"
```

Then choose Save Changes and Exit from the Exit menu. For a name, call the query file MDONLY.

When the Control Center reappears, choose the Create option of the Reports panel to start a new report. When the Layout menu appears atop the Report Design screen, choose Quick Layouts and then choose Form Layout. In a moment, the fields you placed in the view appear within the report's Detail band. Open the Print menu with ALT- P and choose Begin Printing (or choose View Report on Screen).

The results, similar to the listing shown in Figure 11-2, demonstrate how quickly you can combine a view query and a report by using a form layout to produce the desired results. If you wanted to use this report along with the query in the future, you could save the report with the Save Changes and Exit option of the Exit menu. In this case, however, the report will not be needed later, so choose Abandon Changes and Exit from the Exit menu now to discard the report and return to the Control Center.

Designing a Custom Report With a Form Layout

You will probably want to change the default design of the form-layout report to meet your own needs. As with columnar reports, dBASE IV offers a great deal of flexibility for designing reports in a form-oriented layout. You can rearrange the location of fields, delete unwanted fields, or add calculated and summary fields. You can also change margins and use grouping options to generate reports with records divided into specific groups.

REMEMBER You can test a report's design before saving it by choosing View Report on Screen from the Print menu.

The reports that you design with a form layout or a mailmerge layout are quite similar to the columnar reports you've already designed in Chapter 8. The parts of the reports are the same; the Page Header bands, Group bands, Report Intro bands, Report Summary bands, and Detail bands are used for the same purposes. You also use the same menu options described in detail in Chapter 8. About the only difference is in the way you lay out the report. Instead of placing all of your fields in an even row to form columns and using a narrow Detail band, you place the fields where needed, and you often use a much wider Detail band. In the case of form letters (mailmerge), the Detail band may contain multiple paragraphs of text, with fields of a database inserted into the text.

Before proceeding, choose MDONLY from the Queries panel, and choose Close View from the next menu to appear. Then choose ABCSTAFF from the Data panel, and choose Use File from the next menu to appear.

Creating a Custom Personnel Listing

In the case of ABC Temporaries, the managers desire a custom personnel listing that will resemble the format shown in Figure 11-3. Let's create one now. At the Control Center, choose the Create option of the Reports panel. When the Report Design screen appears, press ESC to close the Layout menu.

The line containing the date, page number, and "Personnel Listing" heading in the proposed format is to be printed on each page, so it needs to be placed in the Page Header band. Move the cursor into that band, and with the cursor at the far-left margin,

Figure 11-3.

```
(date)                 Personnel Listing              (page no.)

Name: XXXXXXXXXX XXXXXXXXXX  Soc Sec.: 999-99-9999
Address: XXXXXXXXXXXXXXXXXXXXXXXXX
City: XXXXXXXXXXXXXXX  State:XX     Zip Code: 99999

Date Born: MM/DD/YY           Date Hired: MM/DD/YY
```

Format for personnel listing

open the Fields menu with ALT-F. Choose Add Field, and then select Date from the predefined list of fields that appears. Press CTRL-END to accept the default values that appear for the Date field.

HINT You can also add fields by placing the cursor at the desired location, pressing F5 (Field), and selecting the desired field from the list.

Move the cursor to column 20, and type this heading:

```
Personnel Listing
```

Then move the cursor to column 50, open the Fields menu with ALT-F, and choose Add Field. This time select Pageno from the predefined list of fields that appears. Again, press CTRL-END to accept the default values that appear for the page number field.

Move the cursor into the Detail band, and press HOME to get to the far-left margin. Make sure you are in Insert mode (press the INS key until "Ins" appears in the status bar at the right margin). Then press ENTER once to add a blank line in the Detail band. On the new blank line, enter **NAME:** followed by a blank space.

Open the Fields menu with ALT-F and choose Add Fields. Choose FIRSTNAME from the list of fields in the ABCSTAFF database. Press CTRL-END to accept the default values for the field.

Press the spacebar once to add a space after the FIRSTNAME field. You want to insert a space instead of simply moving the cursor, because inserting a space allows the TRIM function (which is a default picture function for the field) to pull the last and first names together automatically. If you don't add a space with the spacebar but instead move the cursor over by one space, a name combination like

```
Marsha Morse
```

would be printed in the report as

```
Marsha       Morse
```

using the full width of the field.

☞ ***REMEMBER*** When you use the spacebar to separate two character fields, they appear in the report separated by a space. When you use the cursor keys to separate the fields, they appear in the report separated by the full width of the fields.

Open the Fields menu with ALT-F, choose Add Field, and select LASTNAME from the list of fields. Press CTRL-END to accept the default values for the field. Press ENTER once to move to the next line. Type **ADDRESS:** and add a space at the end. Open the Fields menu with ALT-F, choose Add Field, and select ADDRESS from the list of fields. Press CTRL-END to accept the default values for the field.

Press ENTER again to move to the next line. Type **CITY:** and add a space at the end. Open the Fields menu with ALT-F, choose

Add Field, and select CITY from the list of fields. Press CTRL-END to accept the default values for the field.

Press the spacebar once, type **STATE:**, and add a space at the end. Open the Fields menu with ALT-F, choose Add Field, and select STATE from the list of fields. Press CTRL-END to accept the default values for the field.

Move the cursor right two spaces, type **ZIP CODE:**, and add a space at the end. Open the Fields menu with ALT-F, choose Add Field, and select ZIPCODE from the list of fields. Press CTRL-END to accept the default values for the field.

Press ENTER twice to move down two more lines. Type **DATE OF BIRTH:** and add a space. Open the Fields menu with ALT-F, choose Add Field, and select BIRTHDAY from the list of fields. Press CTRL-END to accept the default values for the field.

Move the cursor to column 30. Type **DATE HIRED:** and add a space. Open the Fields menu with ALT- F, choose Add Field, and select DATEHIRED from the list of fields. Press CTRL-END to accept the default values for the field.

Finally, press ENTER once more to add another blank line in the Detail band. When you have finished, your report's design should resemble the example shown in Figure 11-4.

You can test the design before saving the report. Press ALT-P to open the Print menu, and choose View Report on Screen. When you have finished viewing the report, choose Save Changes and Exit from the Exit menu. For a name, call the report RFORM1.

Using Different Styles in a Report

If you have installed a printer driver that supports your printer, you can make use of different type styles in a printed report. (See

Figure 11-4.

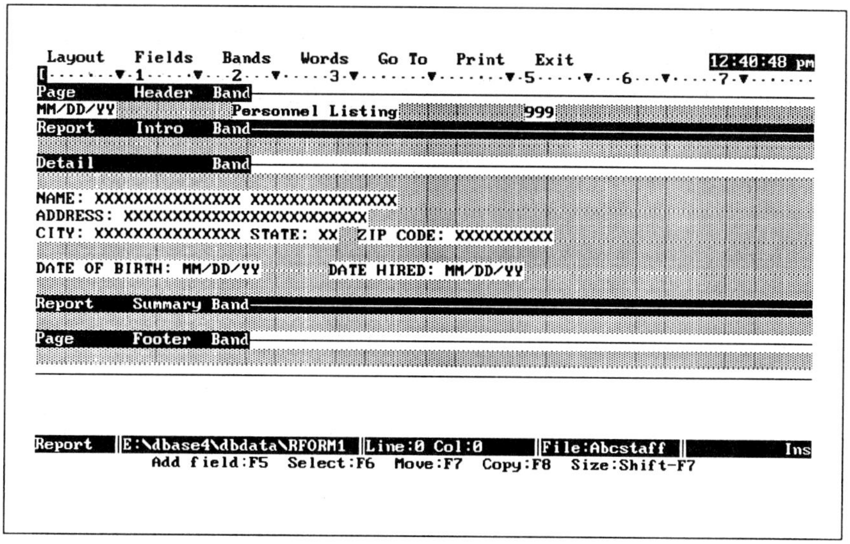

```
Layout   Fields   Bands   Words   Go To   Print   Exit                12:40:48 pm
[·······▼·1·····▼···2···▼·····3·▼·······▼·······▼·5·····▼···6···▼·····7·▼·······
Page        Header   Band
MM/DD/YY             Personnel Listing                 999
Report      Intro    Band
Detail               Band
NAME: XXXXXXXXXXXXXXX XXXXXXXXXXXXXXX
ADDRESS: XXXXXXXXXXXXXXXXXXXXXXXXX
CITY: XXXXXXXXXXXXXXX STATE: XX  ZIP CODE: XXXXXXXXXX
DATE OF BIRTH: MM/DD/YY       DATE HIRED: MM/DD/YY
Report      Summary Band
Page        Footer   Band

Report  ||E:\dbase4\dbdata\RFORM1 ||Line:0 Col:0  ||File:Abcstaff ||      Ins
            Add field:F5  Select:F6  Move:F7  Copy:F8  Size:Shift-F7
```

Sample report design for personnel listing

the end of Chapter 8 if you have not installed a printer driver.) To apply different styles to text or fields in a dBASE report, simply select the text or the fields while at the Report Design screen, and then use the Style option of the Words menu to apply the desired style.

As an example, perhaps ABC Temporaries' staff would like to see the names and addresses in italics, the date of birth underlined, and the date hired in bold print. To try this, highlight the RFORM1 report in the Reports panel and press SHIFT-F2 (Design) to modify the report.

Place the cursor at the start of the word NAME in the Detail Band. Press F6 to begin the selection, move the cursor to the end of the ZIPCODE field, and press ENTER to complete the selection. This will result in the entire address being highlighted. Open the Words menu with ALT-W, and choose Style. From the next menu to appear, choose Italic. Doing this will apply the italic typestyle to the entire name and address selection.

Move the cursor to the start of the words "Date of Birth". Press F6 to begin the selection, move the cursor to the end of the accompanying date field, and press ENTER to complete the selection. Open the Words menu with ALT-W, and choose Style. From the next menu to appear, choose Underline.

Move the cursor to the start of the words "Date Hired". Press F6 to begin the selection, move the cursor to the end of the date field, and press ENTER to complete the selection. Open the Words menu with ALT-W, and choose Style. From the next menu to appear, choose Bold.

Open the Print menu with ALT-P, and choose Begin Printing. Assuming your printer supports these features and the proper printer driver has been installed in dBASE, your report will be printed with the names and addresses in italics, the dates of birth underlined, and the dates hired in bold print. If you want to save these styles with the report, choose Save Changes and Exit from the Exit menu; otherwise, just press ESC and answer yes to the "Abandon changes" prompt that appears.

☞ ***REMEMBER*** Some printers that do not support italics will print any selections you set to italics as underlined text.

Keep in mind that you can also change some style settings for the entire report with the Control of Printer option available from the Print menu. When you choose Control of Printer from the Print menu, you can then use the Text Pitch and Quality Print options (on the next menu that appears) to change between 10 pitch (Pica) and 12 pitch (Elite) sizes, and between normal, compressed, and emphasized (quality) print. Again, your printer must support these options for the choices to take effect.

Designing Form Letters

You can also generate form letters with the dBASE report generator. The Mailmerge option on the Quick Layouts menu is specifically designed for this task. When you choose this option, you produce a report in which all bands except the Detail band are condensed automatically and the Word Wrap option is turned on. Since literal text can be entered anywhere you wish within the report's Detail band, you simply type the text of the form letter into the Detail band. Use the Add Field option on the Fields menu to insert the fields in the locations at which you wish to see those fields appear.

To see how this can be done, choose the Create option of the Reports panel to start a new report. From the Layout menu, choose Quick Layouts; then choose Mailmerge Layout from the next menu to appear. In a moment, the default layout for the mailmerge style of report will appear (Figure 11-5).

Before typing the text, you will need to set a margin for the word-wrap feature to follow. Open the Words menu with ALT-W and choose Modify Ruler. When you choose this option, the cursor will appear on the ruler line. Move the cursor to position 65 and type] (a right bracket symbol) there to indicate a new setting for the right margin. Press CTRL-END to complete the change to the ruler line.

Place the cursor on the Page Header band. Press ENTER to add a blank line. Move the cursor down to the new line, type **To:**, and add a space after the colon. Open the Fields menu with ALT-F and choose Add Field; then select FIRSTNAME from the list of fields. Press CTRL-END to accept the default options for the field.

Figure 11-5.

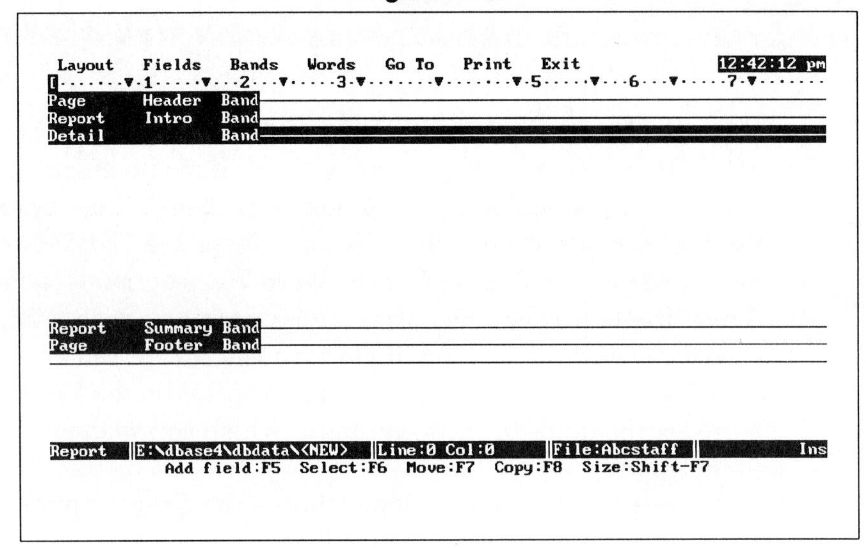

Default style of mailmerge report

Press the spacebar to add a space after the FIRSTNAME field. Then open the Fields menu again, choose Add Field, and select LASTNAME from the list of fields. Press CTRL-END again to accept the default options for the field.

Press ENTER to get back to the left margin and move down by one line. Type **Date:** followed by a space, and open the Fields menu with ALT-F. Choose Add Field, choose Date from the predefined list of fields, and press CTRL-END to accept the default options.

Press ENTER to add another blank line and get back to the left margin, and then move the cursor down to the first line in the Detail band. Type the following text:

The temporary assignments for the upcoming month have been finalized. Our records now show that your assignment for this month will be at the

Add a space after the last letter. Then open the Fields menu, choose Add Field, and choose ASSIGNMENT from the list of fields. Press CTRL-END to accept the default values for the field.

Press the END key to get to the end of the newly placed field, and add a space. Then complete the text of the letter by typing

```
offices. If you have any questions regarding this assignment, please contact
Administration as soon as possible.
```

Press HOME, move the cursor down three lines, and type the following:

```
Sincerely,

Mary Doe
ABC Temporaries
```

When you finish the text of the letter, open the Print menu with ALT-P, turn on your printer, and choose Begin Printing to see the results. When the letters have completed printing, save the report by choosing Save Changes and Exit from the Exit menu. For a name, call the report RLETTER.

Creating and Printing Mailing Labels

dBASE IV provides a Label Design screen for creating mailing labels. It also offers nine predefined label sizes that match most sizes of office mailing labels, including the popular Cheshire binder, Rolodex, and Xerox copier formats. If you don't like any of the predefined sizes, you can create your own label size by entering various dimensions. You can also print labels in the common "three-across" format, where the labels are placed on the label sheet in rows of three labels each. Label designs are stored on disk with an .LBL extension.

Creating the Label

To create a label from the Control Center, you highlight the Create option of the Labels panel. From the dot prompt, you enter **CREATE LABEL *filename***. Use either of these methods now to start creating a new label design. When you do so, the Label Design screen shown in Figure 11-6 will appear.

Figure 11-6.

```
Layout   Dimensions   Fields   Words   Go To   Print   Exit            12:42:37 pm

                    [·······▼·1·····▼···2···▼·····3·▼·]

Label   E:\dbase4\dbdata\<NEW>   Line:0 Col:0   File:Abcstaff            Ins
          Add field:F5  Select:F6  Move:F7  Copy:F8  Size:Shift-F7
```

Label Design screen

In appearance and operation, the Label Design screen is similar to the Report Design screen. There are seven menus: Layout, Dimensions, Fields, Words, Go To, Print, and Exit. The Fields, Words, Go To, Print, and Exit menus perform the same tasks as they do in the Report Design screen; because they are explained in detail in Chapter 8, they will not be covered here. The Layout menu, which can be opened with ALT-L, displays three choices: Use Different Database File or View, Edit Description of Label Design, or Save This Label Design. The Use Different Database File or View option lets you change the file or view that the label will be based upon. The Edit Description of Label Design option lets you add or edit a one-line description of the label. The Save This Label Design option lets you save and continue working on the label design.

Press ALT-D now to reveal the Dimensions menu (Figure 11-7). You use this menu to control the dimensions of your mailing labels. The Predefined Size option is currently highlighted. Press

Figure 11-7.

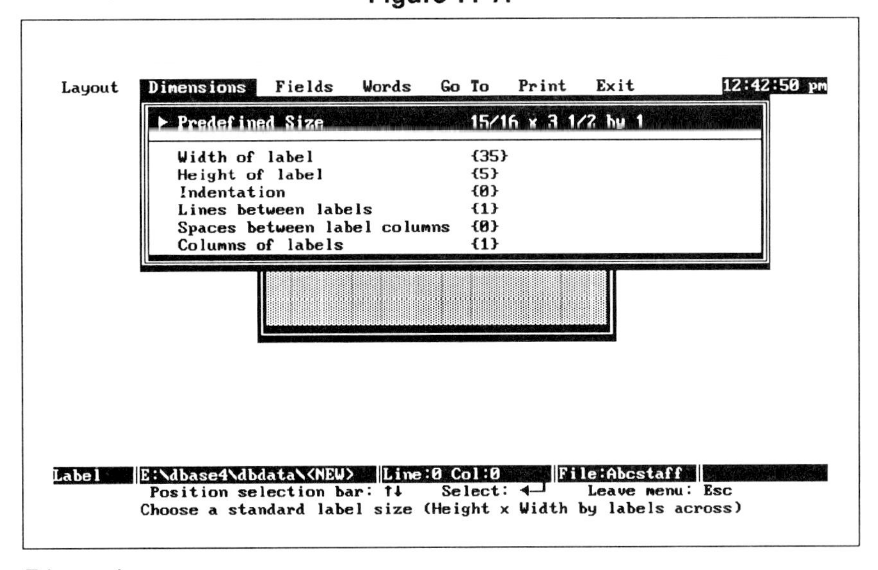

Dimensions menu

ENTER now, and you will see an additional menu showing the nine possible predefined label sizes. The measurements are in inches. The first value indicates the height of the label, and the second value indicates the label's width. The third value (when shown) indicates the number of labels across a page. Note that as you choose any of the predefined sizes, the default values for the remaining options of the Dimensions menu, such as the height and width, will automatically change to match the predefined size you have selected.

HINT If you need a custom label size that doesn't match any of the predefined sizes, pick the predefined size closest to your label. Then press ALT-D again, and change the individual settings in the lower half of the menu as needed.

Choose the second option (15/16 by 3 1/2 by 2). For our sample label you will use this option, which will produce a printout that matches mailing labels that are 15/16 by 3 1/2 inches, two across to a page. Once you press ENTER to accept the size, the menus will close. The size of the layout area that appears is directly controlled by your choice of dimensions; the bigger the label you choose, the larger the design area you get to work with. Oncc you have chosen your label dimensions, you proceed to lay out the label in much the same manner as you would lay out a report—by placing fields in the desired locations with the Add Field option of the Fields menu.

Place the cursor at line 1, column 2 of the label. (Check the status bar at the bottom of the screen to see where the cursor is located.) Open the Fields menu with ALT-F, and choose Add Field. From the list of fields, choose FIRSTNAME. Press CTRL-END to accept the default values for the field. Press the spacebar once to insert a blank space between the FIRSTNAME and LASTNAME fields. Open the Fields menu with ALT-F, choose Add Field, and select LASTNAME from the list of fields. Press CTRL-END to accept the default values for the field.

Move the cursor to line 2, column 2 of the label. Open the Fields menu with ALT-F, choose Add Field, and select ADDRESS from the list of fields. Press CTRL-END to accept the default values for the field.

Move the cursor to Line 3, column 2. Open the Fields menu with ALT-F, choose Add Field, and select CITY from the list of fields. Press CTRL-END to accept the default values for the field.

Next, enter a comma and then press the spacebar once. Open the Fields menu with ALT-F, choose Add Field, and select STATE from the list of fields. Press CTRL-END to accept the default values for the field.

Move the cursor right two spaces, open the Fields menu with ALT-F, choose Add Field, and select ZIPCODE from the list of fields. Press CTRL-END to accept the default values for the field. Your label design should resemble the one shown in Figure 11-8.

To preview the label before printing, press ALT-P to open the Print menu, and choose View Labels on Screen. Note that the labels will appear in "two-across" format on the screen (unless you are using version 1.1 or later) and they will print in the chosen format. When you have finished viewing the labels, choose Save Changes and Exit from the Exit menu. For a name, call the labels ABCMAIL.

Once you have saved the labels you design to a file, you can print them at any time. From the Control Center, highlight the desired label file by name, press ENTER, and choose Print Label from the next menu to appear. From the dot prompt, you can enter the command

LABEL FORM *filename* [FOR *condition*] [TO PRINT]

Figure 11-8.

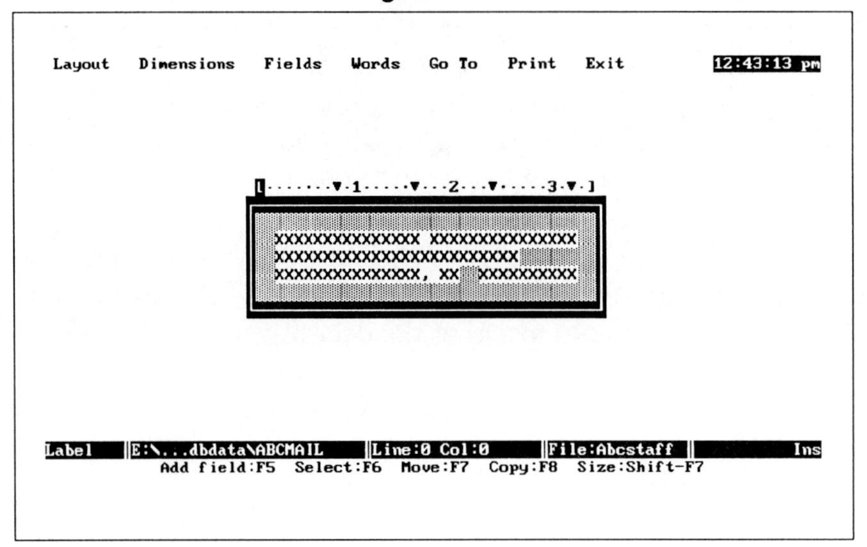

Completed label design

As in other commands, the FOR condition and TO PRINT clauses are optional. Try the LABEL FORM command now by getting to the dot prompt and entering

```
LABEL FORM ABCMAIL TO PRINT
```

The results should resemble the listing in Figure 11-9 (yours should contain more records than are shown in the figure).

REMEMBER You can also base a label on a query. Highlight the query in the Queries panel, press ENTER, and choose Use Query. Then design or print the labels.

If you want the labels printed in a certain order, simply index or sort the database first as desired. Then use the LABEL FORM command (or select the label by name from the Control Center).

Figure 11-9.

Marcia Morse 4260 Park Avenue Chevy Chase, MD 20815-0988	Andrea Westman 4807 East Avenue Silver Spring, MD 20910-0124
David Jackson 4102 Valley Lane Falls Church, VA 22044	Mary Jo Mitchell 617 North Oakland Street Arlington, VA 22203
Shirley Robinson 270 Browning Ave #2A Takoma Park, MD 20912-1234	Cheryl Jackson 1617 Arlington Blvd Falls Church, VA 22044

Results of the LABEL FORM command

It is usually wise to print a test run of labels on plain paper first and to visually align the printout with a sheet of blank labels. If the alignment looks correct, you can proceed to print on the labels themselves.

From the Control Center, you can design and apply view queries that will specify a group of records for which you want to print labels. Also, from the dot prompt, you can combine conditional FOR clauses to print labels for specific records, just as you did with reports. For example, the command

```
LABEL FORM ABCMAIL FOR STATE = "VA" TO PRINT
```

will print mailing labels for employees in Virginia. The command

Figure 11-10.

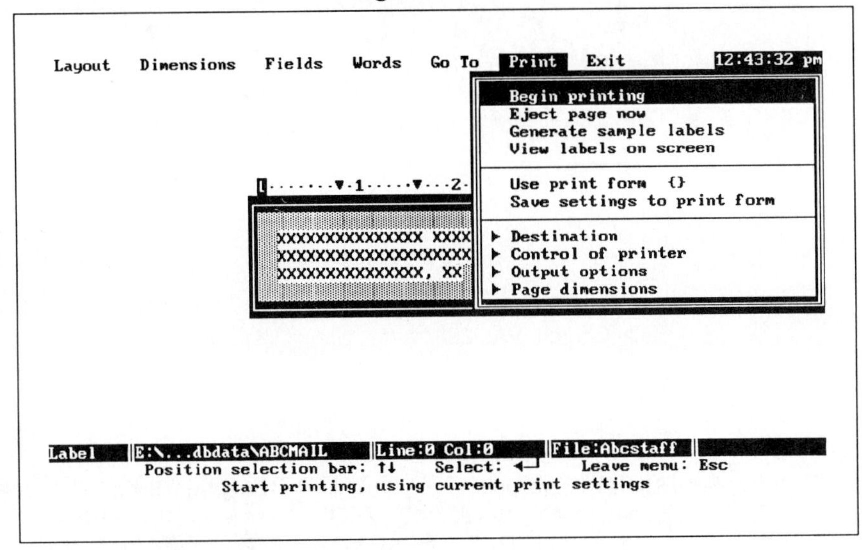

Print menu with Generate Sample Labels option

```
LABEL FORM ABCMAIL FOR HIREDATE > {07/31/87} .AND. HIREDATE
< {09/01/87} TO PRINT
```

will print labels for only those employees who were hired during the month of August in 1987.

When you select a label by name from the Control Center and then choose Print Labels from the next menu, the familiar Print menu appears (Figure 11-10). You should note, however, that there is one option in this menu that doesn't appear with reports—the Generate Sample Labels option. If you choose this option, dBASE will print the label you've designed in the chosen format but will fill the fields with X's. This lets you check the label alignment in your printer before you start to print the actual records from the database. From the dot prompt, you can accomplish the same task by adding the SAMPLE clause to the LABEL FORM command. For example, the command

```
LABEL FORM ABCMAIL TO PRINT SAMPLE
```

would tell dBASE to print sample labels one at a time and to display a "More samples? Y/N" prompt after each sample label. Once you answer with N, the actual labels will be printed.

HINT Generate sample labels to test alignment before printing a long run of labels (especially with dot-matrix printers).

A Final Bit of Advice

The majority of the operations you perform when designing reports are the same with columnar reports as with form-layout and mailmerge reports. The main differences are these:

- With columnar reports, all fields are placed on the same line of the Detail band, and Word Wrap is turned off.
- In reports designed with a form-oriented layout, fields are placed wherever they are needed, and the Detail band is often much wider than a single line.
- With mailmerge-layout reports, large amounts of text are usually placed in the Detail band, and the Word Wrap option is turned on.

Most other options are the same between the types of reports, and you can perform similar steps to design your columnar, form, and mailmerge reports. See Chapter 8, if you haven't already examined it, for additional important details on report design.

Quick Reference

To quickly produce a default report with a form-oriented layout Place the database or query in use, then choose the Create option of the Reports panel. When the Report Design screen appears, select Quick Layouts from the Layout menu. From the next menu, choose Form Layout. Press CTRL-END (or choose Save Changes and Exit from the Exit menu) to save the report.

To design a custom report with a form-oriented layout Place the database or query on which the report will be based into use. Then, choose the Create option of the Reports panel (or from the dot prompt, enter **CREATE REPORT**). Add fields at the desired locations on different lines, rather than putting all fields on the same line (as is done with columnar reports).

To add a field, place the cursor where you want the field to appear, open the Fields menu with ALT-F, choose Add Field, and select the desired field from the list. Note, also, that you can quickly add all fields in the file or the query to the report by choosing the Quick Layouts option of the Layout menu, and choosing Form from the next menu to appear. If Group Bands are needed, add them by using the Add a Group Band option of the Bands menu. When done designing the report, save it by choosing Save Changes and Exit from the Exit menu (or by pressing CTRL-END).

To display or print the custom report From the Control Center, highlight the report in the Reports panel, press ENTER, and choose Print Report from the next menu to appear. When the Print Menu appears, choose Begin Printing. From the dot prompt, enter the command **REPORT FORM *filename* TO PRINT**, where *filename* is the name that you saved the report under.

To use different type styles in a report While designing the report, place the cursor at the start of the fields, labels, or text which is to use the different style. Press F6 (Select), move the cursor to the end of the fields, labels, or text, and press ENTER to select the entire area. Open the Words menu with ALT-W, choose Style, and select the desired type style from the next menu.

To create mailing labels Place the database or query in use, and then choose the Create option of the Labels panel. When the Label Design Screen appears, press ALT-D to open the Dimensions menu, and choose your desired label size. Next, place the desired fields in the label by putting the cursor at the desired location, opening the Fields menu with ALT-F, and choosing Add Field. When done adding the desired fields, save the label by pressing CTRL-END (or by choosing Save Changes and Exit from the Exit menu).

To display or print mailing labels From the Control Center, highlight the label in the Labels panel, press ENTER, and choose Print Labels from the next menu to appear. When the Print Menu appears, choose Begin Printing. From the dot prompt, enter the command **LABEL FORM *filename* TO PRINT**, where *filename* is the name that you saved the labels under.

CHAPTER

12

Using the Relational Powers of dBASE IV

As you learned in Chapter 1, dBASE IV is a relational database manager. The relational capabilities of dBASE IV let you use more than one database file at a time and to define relationships between two or more database files. This chapter will describe a number of ways in which you can take advantage of the relational capabilities of dBASE IV. By using example variables within the Query Design screen, you can link multiple database files by means of a field that is common to each database file.

The hands-on practice examples in this chapter will make extensive use of the ABCSTAFF and HOURS databases created in Chapters 3 and 7. Therefore, if you did not create those database files as outlined earlier, do so now before proceeding.

Consider the ABCSTAFF and HOURS files. The HOURS file contains records of the hours worked by each employee and the client for whom (or assignment at which) the employee performed the work. However, the HOURS file does not contain the names of the employees. The ABCSTAFF file, on the other hand, contains the full name of each employee, but no record of the hours worked.

The payroll coordinator at ABC Temporaries needs a report in a format illustrated by Figure 12-1.

This report will be used by the payroll department to handle check requests when processing the payroll. A report with this kind of information is a relational report because it draws its

Figure 12-1.

Last name	First name	Assignment	Hours worked
Westman	Andres	National Oil Co.	37
Smith	William	Smith Builders	40
Jones	Judi	City Revenue Dept.	35
Abernathy	Frank	City Revenue Dept.	35

Desired relational report

information from more than one file. The ABCSTAFF file contains the LASTNAME and FIRSTNAME fields; the HOURS file contains the ASSIGNMENT, WEEKENDING, and HOURS fields. To produce a report based on these fields, you can design a view query that will retrieve data from both files and link them through a relational view. The data provided by the view can then be used to produce the desired report.

The key to retrieving data from a relational database is to link desired records on some sort of matching (or common) field. In this context, the term *common field* is used to indicate a field that is common to both database files. Consider an example of two files, one of which contains records of computer parts and the other containing records of purchasers who have ordered certain parts. These files (in this example, called PARTS and ORDERS) are typical examples of database files that benefit from the use of relational commands. The PARTS file, as shown by the file structure listed here, contains part numbers, descriptions, and the cost of each part:

Name of Field	**Type**
PARTNO	Numeric
DESCRIPT	Character
COST	Numeric

The ORDERS file, on the other hand, contains the names and customer numbers of the customers who order computer parts, as well as the part numbers and quantities of the parts that have been ordered.

Name of Field	**Type**
CUSTNO	Numeric
CUSTNAME	Character
PARTNO	Numeric
QUANTITY	Numeric

Using two separate database files is a better solution than using a single database file in this case, because a single database file would require unneeded duplication of the information. If you had a single database file with all of the fields present in these two files, each time a customer ordered a part that had been previously ordered by another customer, you would have to duplicate the part description and part cost. To avoid such duplication, you can use two files and link the files together based upon the contents of the common PARTNO field, as shown in Figure 12-2.

With all relational databases, this kind of link between common fields can be drawn, linking a particular record in one file with a corresponding record in another file. Take ABC Temporaries' problem of the payroll again. If you need to know how many hours Andrea Westman worked, you could find out by looking at the data from the two files, shown in Figure 12-3. To find the answer manually, you would first look at the listing from the ABCSTAFF

Figure 12-2.

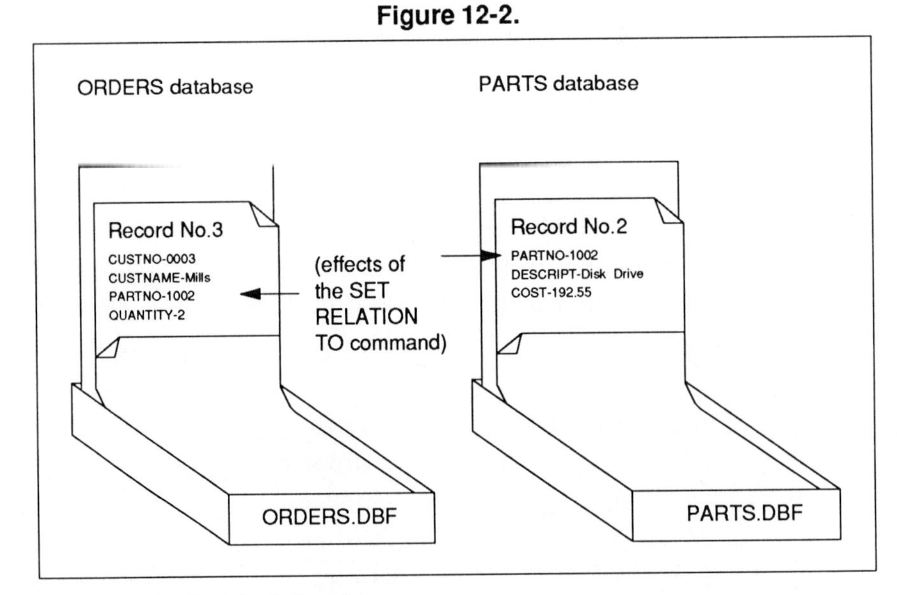

Concept of relational database

Figure 12-3.

SOCIALSEC	LASTNAME	FIRSTNAME	CITY	STATE
123-44-8976	Morse	Marcia	Chevy Chase	MD
121-33-9876	Westman	Andrea	Silver Spring	MD
232-55-1234	Jackson	David	Falls Church	VA
901-77-3456	Mitchell	Mary Jo	Arlington	VA
121-90-5432	Robinson	Shirley	Takoma Park	MD
495-00-3456	Jackson	Cheryl	Falls Church	VA
343-55-9821	Robinson	Wanda	Washington	DC
876-54-3210	Hart	Edward	Fairfax	VA
909-88-7654	Jones	Judi	Reston	VA

ASSIGNMENT	SOCIALSEC	WEEK ENDING	HOURS
National Oil Co.	909-88-7654	01/16/88	35.0
National Oil Co.	121-33-9876	01/16/88	30.0
National Oil Co.	121-90-5432	01/16/88	27.0
National Oil Co.	123-44-8976	01/16/88	32.0
City Revenue Dept.	343-55-9821	01/16/88	35.0
City Revenue Dept.	495-00-3456	01/16/88	28.0
City Revenue Dept.	232-55-1234	01/16/88	30.0
Smith Builders	876-54-3210	01/16/88	30.0
Smith Builders	901-77-3456	01/23/88	28.0
Smith Builders	876-54-3210	01/23/88	35.0
City Revenue Dept.	232-55-1234	01/23/88	30.0
City Revenue Dept.	495-00-3456	01/23/88	32.0
City Revenue Dept.	343-55-9821	01/23/88	32.0
National Oil Co.	121-33-9876	01/23/88	35.0
National Oil Co.	909-88-7654	01/23/88	33.0

HOURS, ABCSTAFF database files

file and find the social security number for Ms. Westman, which is 121-33-9876. You would then refer to the listing of the HOURS file and look for all the records with the matching social security number. The HOURS fields from these records could be used to calculate the salary for Ms. Westman. The process of matching social security numbers between the files could be repeated for every employee in the company.

Unless a field in each of the database files contains matching data, such a relational link is not possible. This is one reason that the design of complex, relational databases is not a process to be taken lightly. If an important field is not included in a database file, you may find it difficult or impossible to access multiple files in the desired manner. As Figure 12-3 shows, the SOCIALSEC field makes it possible to access data simultaneously from both files.

To link multiple files in dBASE IV, you use a query in a manner similar to the way in which you used nonrelational queries in Chapter 7. The one notable difference is that you use *example variables* in the common fields of the file skeletons. The example variables tell dBASE IV which fields are used to provide the links between files.

Querying from Two Files

Because the design of a relational query can be complex, the next few paragraphs will describe the overall process. Don't try to build a relational query yet, but read these steps for clarification. In the next part of the chapter, you'll build an actual relational query.

To query from two database files, first close any open database files. (This step isn't mandatory, but it reduces visual clutter by letting you start the query from a blank screen.) Choose the Create option from the Queries panel, and a new Query Design screen appears. From the Layout menu, choose Add File to Query. Select the first database file desired from the pick list that appears, and choose the desired fields for inclusion in the view in the normal manner by moving to those fields and pressing F5 (Field). You can also set any selection criteria that the records must meet by entering these criteria in the fields of the file skeleton, as described in Chapter 7.

When the first file skeleton contains the desired criteria, choose Add File to Query from the Layout menu, and select the name for the second database file. dBASE IV places a file skeleton for the second file below the first. You can again proceed to add the desired fields to the view and enter any desired selection criteria. Figure 12-4 shows a Query Design screen containing two file skeletons from the ABCSTAFF and HOURS files, with selected fields of LASTNAME and FIRSTNAME from the ABCSTAFF file, and fields of WEEKENDING and HOURS from the HOURS file.

Finally, enter the example variable that is used to link the database files. To enter an example variable, place the cursor in the common field of the file skeleton and enter an example variable. Next, move the cursor to the common field in the second file skeleton, and fill in the same example variable used in the

Figure 12-4.

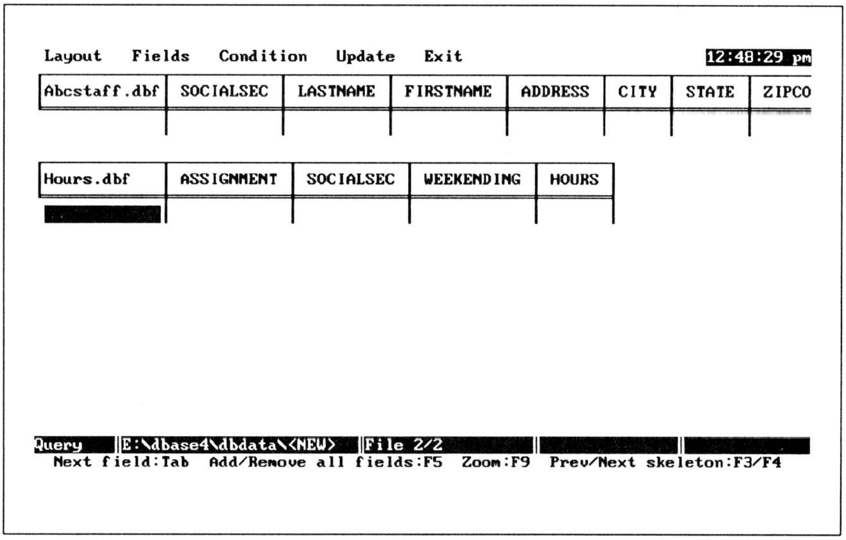

```
Layout   Fields   Condition   Update   Exit                               12:48:29 pm

Abcstaff.dbf | SOCIALSEC | LASTNAME | FIRSTNAME | ADDRESS | CITY | STATE | ZIPCO

Hours.dbf | ASSIGNMENT | SOCIALSEC | WEEKENDING | HOURS

Query  |E:\dbase4\dbdata\<NEW>  |File 2/2
 Next field:Tab  Add/Remove all fields:F5  Zoom:F9  Prev/Next skeleton:F3/F4
```

Example of partially filled-in queries for two database files

common field of the first file skeleton to provide the link between the fields.

Figure 12-5 shows the queries with the same example variable entered into the SOCIALSEC fields of both file skeletons. (Note that the Create Link by Pointing option of the Layout menu can also be used to link the common fields.) Example variables are not arbitrary values. What's important is what the examples represent—that is, the same value in two separate files. The example variable "identical" entered in both SOCIALSEC fields of Figure 12-5 could have been entered as **nonsense**. You can enter any set of letters (but no spaces, punctuation marks, or reserved dBASE command words) as an example variable, but the example variables entered into the fields of the two files must be the same.

Figure 12-5.

```
Layout  Fields  Condition  Update  Exit                                6:10:26 am

Abcstaff.dbf | SOCIALSEC | ↓LASTNAME | ↓FIRSTNAME | ADDRESS | CITY | STATE | ZIPCO
             | identical |           |            |         |      |       |

Hours.dbf | ASSIGNMENT | SOCIALSEC | ↓WEEKENDING | ↓HOURS
          |            | identical |             |

View
<NEW>  | Abcstaff->  | Abcstaff->  | Hours->     | Hours->
       | LASTNAME    | FIRSTNAME   | WEEKENDING  | HOURS

Query  |E:\dbase4\dbdata\<NEW>  |Field 3/4
  Prev/Next field:Shift-Tab/Tab  Data:F2  Pick:Shift-F1  Prev/Next skel:F3/F4
```

Queries with example variables

Performing the Query

Once you have entered the example variables, added the desired fields to the view, and supplied any record selection criteria, you are ready to perform the query. Press F2 (Data), and the results based on the query will appear in Browse mode as shown in Figure 12-6. The results are in read-only format, as indicated by the words "Read Only" in the status bar. You cannot edit records while you are in Browse mode supplied by a relational query.

Note that the order you follow in supplying the data does not matter. You could first fill in the example variables, then pick the fields to be included in the result, and then provide any record selection criteria; or you could perform all needed steps for one file, proceed to perform all the steps for the second file, and then

Figure 12-6.

Records Organize Fields Go To Exit

LASTNAME	FIRSTNAME	WEEKENDING	HOURS
Westman	Andrea	01/16/88	30.0
Westman	Andrea	01/23/88	35.0
Robinson	Shirley	01/16/88	27.0
Morse	Marcia	01/16/88	32.0
Jackson	David	01/16/88	30.0
Jackson	David	01/23/88	30.0
Robinson	Wanda	01/16/88	35.0
Robinson	Wanda	01/23/88	32.0
Jackson	Cheryl	01/16/88	28.0
Jackson	Cheryl	01/23/88	32.0
Hart	Edward	01/23/88	30.0
Hart	Edward	01/23/88	35.0
Mitchell	Mary Jo	01/23/88	28.0
Jones	Judi	01/16/88	35.0
Jones	Judi	01/23/88	33.0

Browse ‖E:\dbase4\dbdata\<NEW> ‖Rec 1/9 ‖View ‖ReadOnly‖

Answer to relational query

press F2 (Data) to process the query. Regardless of the order, once you process the query, the results appear. If you need a printed report at this point, the easiest way to get one would be to press SHIFT-F9 for a quick report. You can view or list the results in a particular order by saving the query as a new database file and sorting or indexing that file.

Practice Querying from Two Files

To get a listing containing the employee social security number, last name, assignment, "week ending" date, and the number of hours worked, with both files linked through the common social security field, follow the steps described here.

First, close any database file that is currently in use by selecting the filename directly under the Create option of the Data panel and choosing Close File from the next menu to appear.

REMEMBER If a file is in use, be sure to close it before designing a relational query. This prevents the new query from having all fields of a file in the view.

Next, choose the Create option of the Queries panel to start a new query. From the Layout menu, choose Add File to Query and select ABCSTAFF as the file. Tab over to the SOCIALSEC and LASTNAME fields, and press F5 at each of these fields to include them in the view. Move the cursor back to the SOCIALSEC field, and enter the following as the example variable:

```
ABCD
```

Press ALT-L for the Layout menu, choose Add File to Query, and this time select HOURS as the name of the file. When the file skeleton for the second file appears, use the TAB and F5 keys to add the ASSIGNMENT, WEEKENDING, and HOURS fields to the view skeleton. Then move the cursor back to the SOCIALSEC field, and enter

```
ABCD
```

again as the example variable. Finally, press F2 (Data), and the result of the relational query should appear on the screen, as shown in Figure 12-7.

REMEMBER When entering selection criteria in a query field, enclose character strings in quotes.

Figure 12-7.

Records Organize Fields Go To Exit

SOCIALSEC	LASTNAME	ASSIGNMENT	WEEKENDING	HOURS
121-33-9876	Westman	National Oil Co.	01/16/88	30.0
121-33-9876	Westman	National Oil Co.	01/23/88	35.0
121-90-5432	Robinson	National Oil Co.	01/16/88	27.0
123-44-8976	Morse	National Oil Co.	01/16/88	32.0
232-55-1234	Jackson	City Revenue Dept.	01/16/88	30.0
232-55-1234	Jackson	City Revenue Dept.	01/23/88	30.0
343-55-9821	Robinson	City Revenue Dept.	01/16/88	35.0
343-55-9821	Robinson	City Revenue Dept.	01/23/88	32.0
495-00-3456	Jackson	City Revenue Dept.	01/16/88	28.0
495-00-3456	Jackson	City Revenue Dept.	01/23/88	32.0
876-54-3210	Hart	Smith Builders	01/23/88	30.0
876-54-3210	Hart	Smith Builders	01/23/88	35.0
901-77-3456	Mitchell	Smith Builders	01/23/88	28.0
909-88-7654	Jones	National Oil Co.	01/16/88	35.0
909-88-7654	Jones	National Oil Co.	01/23/88	33.0

Browse | E:\dbase4\dbdata\<NEW> | Rec 1/9 | View | ReadOnly

Results of first practice query

Selection criteria can be used in either database file to limit the records available in a relational query. As an example, perhaps you only want to see records for the City Revenue Department so you can bill that particular client for services rendered by the staff of ABC Temporaries. Press SHIFT-F2 to get back to the Query Design screen. In the file skeleton for the HOURS file, move the cursor to the ASSIGNMENT field, and enter

```
="City Revenue Dept."
```

as the selection criteria. Press F2 (Data), and the results shown in Browse mode (Figure 12-8) display only those employees who put in time for the City Revenue Department.

dBASE IV lets you add a selection criteria in the same query field as the example variable; just use a comma to separate the

Figure 12-8.

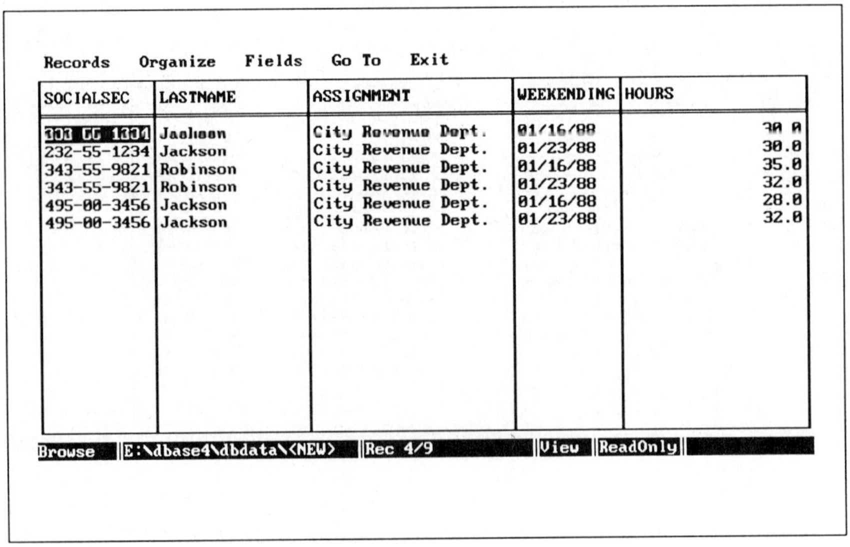

Records   Organize   Fields   Go To   Exit

SOCIALSEC	LASTNAME	ASSIGNMENT	WEEKENDING	HOURS
[illegible]	[illegible]	City Revenue Dept.	01/16/88	30.0
232-55-1234	Jackson	City Revenue Dept.	01/23/88	30.0
343-55-9821	Robinson	City Revenue Dept.	01/16/88	35.0
343-55-9821	Robinson	City Revenue Dept.	01/23/88	32.0
495-00-3456	Jackson	City Revenue Dept.	01/16/88	28.0
495-00-3456	Jackson	City Revenue Dept.	01/23/88	32.0

Browse | E:\dbase4\dbdata\<NEW> | Rec 4/9 | View | ReadOnly

Results of practice query for City Revenue Dept.

Figure 12-9.

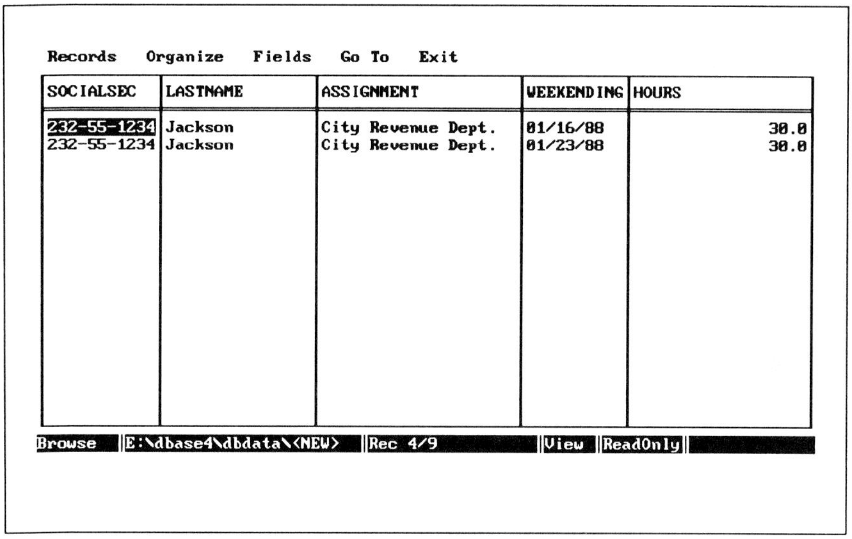

Records Organize Fields Go To Exit

SOCIALSEC	LASTNAME	ASSIGNMENT	WEEKENDING	HOURS
232-55-1234	Jackson	City Revenue Dept.	01/16/88	30.0
232-55-1234	Jackson	City Revenue Dept.	01/23/88	30.0

Browse | E:\dbase4\dbdata\<NEW> | Rec 4/9 | View | ReadOnly

Relational query for a single name

example variable and the selection criteria. As an example, perhaps you wish to retrieve records using the fields you have already chosen for inclusion in the view, but you only want to see records for Mr. David Jackson. Press SHIFT-F2 to get back to the Query Design screen, and use CTRL-Y to delete the prior selection criteria from the ASSIGNMENT field.

Move the cursor up to the ABCSTAFF file skeleton with F3 (Previous) to the SOCIALSEC field. Add a comma after the example variable, and then enter the following:

```
="232-55-1234"
```

Press F2 (Data) to process the query. The results will show the records for Mr. Jackson, as shown in Figure 12-9.

Using Linked Database Files With AND Selection Criteria

dBASE IV does not limit the way you use selection criteria; you have the same flexibility as you do in queries performed on a single file. As an example, perhaps you need a listing of employees who worked for the City Revenue Department and worked during the week ending 1/23/88.

! **HINT** You can use CTRL-Y to delete a prior entry in a query field.

Press SHIFT-F2 to move back to the Query Design screen, and delete the equal symbol, quotation marks, social security number, and the comma in the SOCIALSEC field (leave the example variable). Press F4 (Next) and move the cursor to the WEEKENDING field of the HOURS file skeleton, and then enter

```
={01/23/88}
```

Next, move the cursor to the ASSIGNMENT field, and enter

```
="City Revenue Dept"
```

Press F2 (Data) to process the query. The results, shown in Figure 12-10, provide all employees who worked for the City Revenue Department and worked during the week ending on 1/23/88.

The conditions do not need to be in the same file. You might need a listing of all employees assigned to National Oil Company who are earning more than $10.00 per hour. The fields you are using to limit the records, SALARY and ASSIGNMENT, are in two different files.

Figure 12-10.

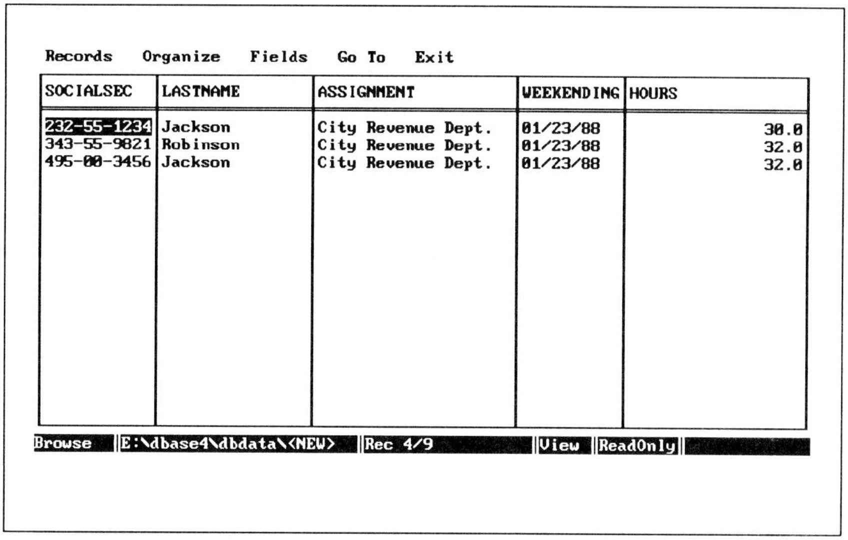

Records Organize Fields Go To Exit

SOCIALSEC	LASTNAME	ASSIGNMENT	WEEKENDING	HOURS
232-55-1234	Jackson	City Revenue Dept.	01/23/88	30.0
343-55-9821	Robinson	City Revenue Dept.	01/23/88	32.0
495-00-3456	Jackson	City Revenue Dept.	01/23/88	32.0

Browse | E:\dbase4\dbdata\<NEW> | Rec 4/9 | View | ReadOnly

Query of linked database files using AND condition

Press SHIFT-F2 (Design) to get back to the Query Design screen. Delete the prior conditions in the ASSIGNMENT and WEEK-ENDING fields of the HOURS file skeleton. Then press F3 (Previous) to move to the ABCSTAFF file skeleton. In the SALARY field, enter

```
>10
```

Then move back to the file skeleton for HOURS.DBF with F4. Move to the ASSIGNMENT field, and enter the following as the condition:

```
="National Oil Co."
```

Finally, press F2 to process the query. The results, shown in Figure 12-11, display the records meeting the two conditions.

Figure 12-11.

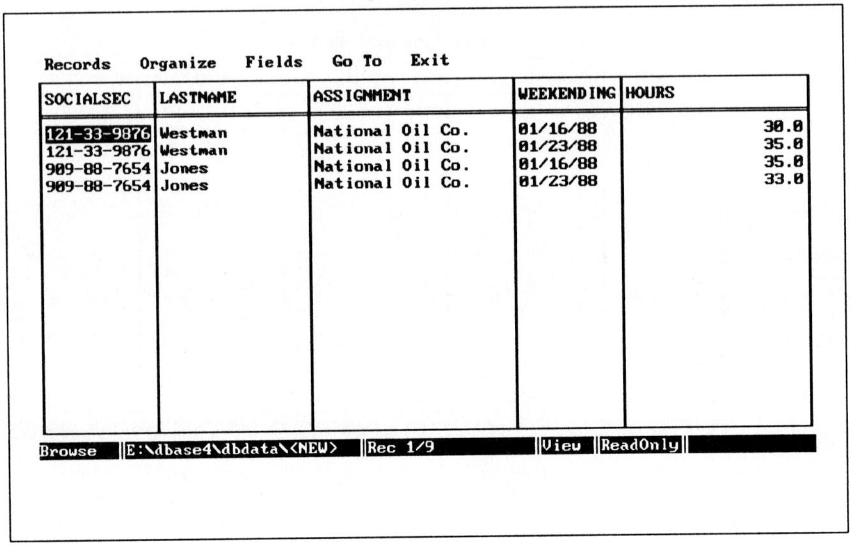

Records Organize Fields Go To Exit

SOCIALSEC	LASTNAME	ASSIGNMENT	WEEKENDING	HOURS
121-33-9876	Westman	National Oil Co.	01/16/88	30.0
121-33-9876	Westman	National Oil Co.	01/23/88	35.0
909-88-7654	Jones	National Oil Co.	01/16/88	35.0
909-88-7654	Jones	National Oil Co.	01/23/88	33.0

Browse | E:\dbase4\dbdata\<NEW> | Rec 1/9 | View | ReadOnly

Query of linked database files using conditions in separate database files

Using Linked Files with OR Selection Criteria

You can enter additional criteria in the additional rows of the file skeletons to specify OR conditions, in which records are selected when one *or* another condition is met. As an example, perhaps you want to see all employees who are assigned to National Oil Company or to the City Revenue Department. First press SHIFT-F2 to get back to the Query Design screen. Use F3 (Previous) to get to the ABCSTAFF file skeleton, and delete the prior entry in the SALARY field.

You will need to use something a little different for queries of multiple files using OR conditions. You must enter example variables that will link either of the conditions on each line of the file skeleton. Move to the SOCIALSEC field, delete the previous example variable of ABCD, and enter

ONE

as the example variable. Move the cursor down one line, and enter

TWO

as the name for the second example. Move to the HOURS file skeleton and place the cursor in the SOCIALSEC field. Delete the prior example variable; then enter

ONE

as the matching example variable for linking the database files.

Since National Oil Company is one of the desired assignments, you can leave the existing condition (="National Oil Co.") in the ASSIGNMENT field. Move the cursor down one line and back to the ASSIGNMENT field. Enter

="City Revenue Dept."

as the selection criteria for this row of the query. Move the cursor over to the SOCIALSEC field, and enter

TWO

as the matching example variable for linking the files. At this point, your query should resemble the example illustrated in Figure 12-12.

Before you process this query, take a moment to think about how it is structured. The first line of the file skeleton for HOURS, which will select records that contain "National Oil Co." in the ASSIGNMENT field, is linked to the ABCSTAFF file through the

Figure 12-12.

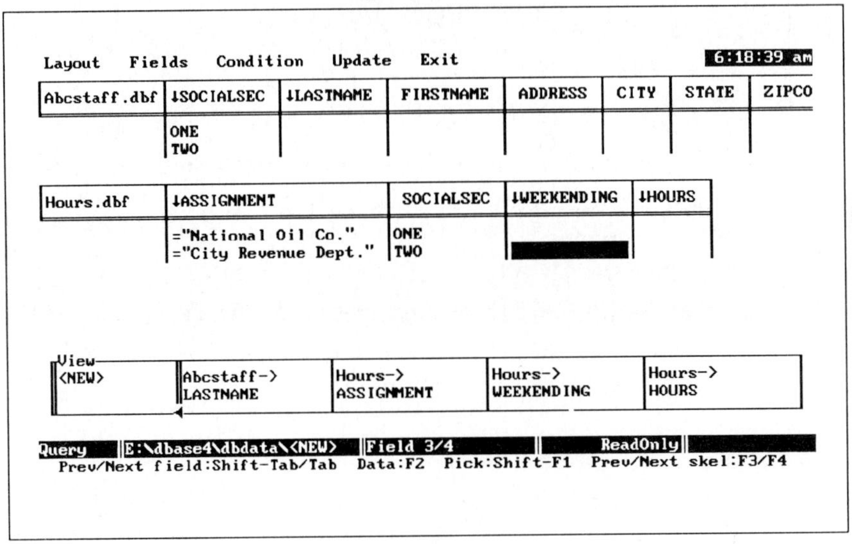

Layout Fields Condition Update Exit 6:18:39 am

Abcstaff.dbf	↓SOCIALSEC	↓LASTNAME	FIRSTNAME	ADDRESS	CITY	STATE	ZIPCO
	ONE TWO						

Hours.dbf	↓ASSIGNMENT	SOCIALSEC	↓WEEKENDING	↓HOURS
	="National Oil Co." ="City Revenue Dept."	ONE TWO		

View <NEW>	Abcstaff-> LASTNAME	Hours-> ASSIGNMENT	Hours-> WEEKENDING	Hours-> HOURS

Query E:\dbase4\dbdata\<NEW> Field 3/4 ReadOnly
Prev/Next field:Shift-Tab/Tab Data:F2 Pick:Shift-F1 Prev/Next skel:F3/F4

Filled-in file skeletons for OR conditionals

Figure 12-13.

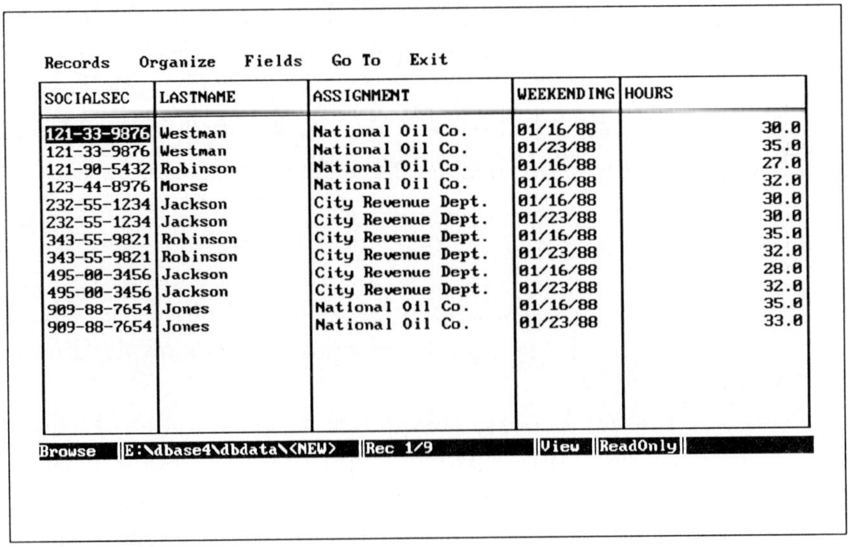

Records Organize Fields Go To Exit

SOCIALSEC	LASTNAME	ASSIGNMENT	WEEKENDING	HOURS
121-33-9876	Westman	National Oil Co.	01/16/88	30.0
121-33-9876	Westman	National Oil Co.	01/23/88	35.0
121-90-5432	Robinson	National Oil Co.	01/16/88	27.0
123-44-8976	Morse	National Oil Co.	01/16/88	32.0
232-55-1234	Jackson	City Revenue Dept.	01/16/88	30.0
232-55-1234	Jackson	City Revenue Dept.	01/23/88	30.0
343-55-9821	Robinson	City Revenue Dept.	01/16/88	35.0
343-55-9821	Robinson	City Revenue Dept.	01/23/88	32.0
495-00-3456	Jackson	City Revenue Dept.	01/16/88	28.0
495-00-3456	Jackson	City Revenue Dept.	01/23/88	32.0
909-88-7654	Jones	National Oil Co.	01/16/88	35.0
909-88-7654	Jones	National Oil Co.	01/23/88	33.0

Browse E:\dbase4\dbdata\<NEW> Rec 1/9 View ReadOnly

Results of OR query based on two database files

example variable called ONE. The second line of the file skeleton for HOURS, which will select records with "City Revenue Dept." in the ASSIGNMENT field, is linked to the ABCSTAFF file through the example variable called TWO. In the case of OR conditionals like this one, dBASE IV is actually performing two separate queries at the same time: one to link records based on having "National Oil Co." in the field, and the other to link records based on having "City Revenue Dept." in the field. To see the results (shown in Figure 12-13), press F2.

Linking More than Two Database Files

As many database files as you need (up to the limit of nine possible open databases and a catalog) can be linked to provide you with the results you need while you use dBASE IV. You can see an example of this if you create one more database file, named CLIENTS, which will contain the addresses of the clients for whom ABC Temporaries performs work.

Press ESC, and then choose Yes to save the query; call the query TEST1. When you are back at the Control Center, choose the Create option of the Data panel to create a new database file. Define the following fields:

Field Name	Field Type	Width	Index?
CLIENT	Character	20	Y
ADDRESS	Character	25	N
CITY	Character	15	N
STATE	Character	2	N
ZIP	Character	5	N

When you have defined the structure, save the file by pressing CTRL-END. Call the file CLIENTS when asked for a filename. Answer **Y** to the "Input Data Records Now?" prompt, and add the three records shown here to the new file:

Client name: National Oil Co.
Address: 1201 Germantown Road
City: Fairfax
State: VA
ZIP: 20305
Client name: City Revenue Dept.
Address: 2000 Town Hall Square
City: Alexandria
State: VA
ZIP: 22045

Client name: Smith Builders
Address: 2370 Rockville Pike
City: Rockville
State: MD
ZIP: 30504

Press CTRL-END to save the records and get back to the Control Center.

Perhaps you need a listing of the assignments, the city of each assignment, the name of employee, and "week ending" dates so that you can track the validity of expense reports for car mileage handed in by your staff. The fields you need are in three different files, so you must fill in three file skeletons to get the result you need.

From the Control Center, highlight CLIENTS in the Data panel and press ENTER. Then choose Close File from the next menu to close the file. Choose the Create option of the Queries panel to begin creating a new query. From the Layout menu, choose Add File to Query, and select ABCSTAFF as the desired file. When the file skeleton appears, move the cursor to the SOCIALSEC field and enter

ABCD

as the example. Then move the cursor to the LASTNAME field and press F5 (Field) to add it to the view.

Open the Layout menu with ALT-L, choose Add File to Query, and choose HOURS as the filename. When the file skeleton appears, move the cursor to the SOCIALSEC field and enter

ABCD

as the example. Then move the cursor to the WEEKENDING field and press F5 to add it to the view.

Move the cursor to the ASSIGNMENT field and enter

EFGH

as the example variable that will provide the link to the third database file. Then open the Layout menu with ALT-L, choose Add File to Query, and choose CLIENTS as the desired file. Move the cursor to the CLIENT field and enter

EFGH

as the example variable. Press F5 to add the CLIENT field to the view. Tab over to the CITY field, and press F5 again to add this field to the view.

Press F2 to process the query. The results, shown in Figure 12-14, include the desired fields selected from the ABCSTAFF, HOURS, and CLIENTS database files.

One additional point can be noted from this example. The example variable used to link the second and third database files was placed in two fields that had different field names. (The HOURS database file stored the name of the client in a field called ASSIGNMENT, while the CLIENTS database file stored the name of the client in a field called CLIENT.) dBASE IV does not require you to give the fields identical field names before you can

Figure 12-14.

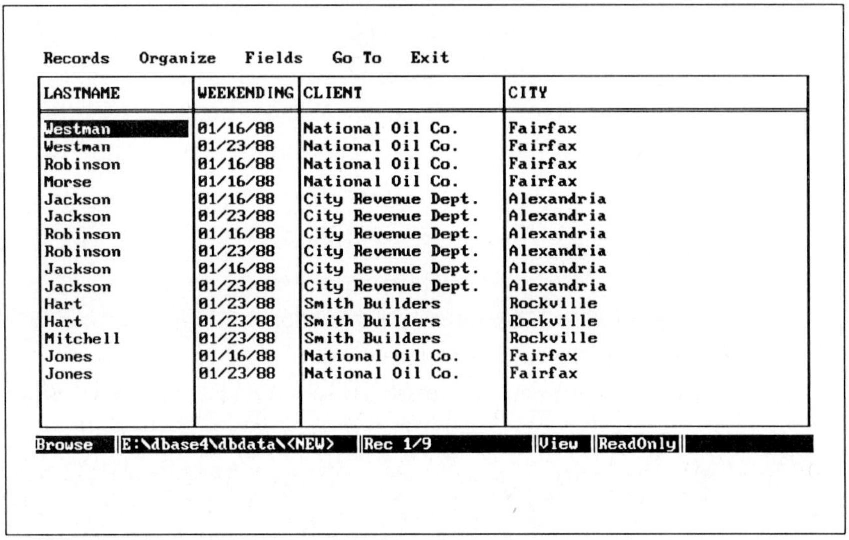

Records Organize Fields Go To Exit

LASTNAME	WEEKENDING	CLIENT	CITY
Westman	01/16/88	National Oil Co.	Fairfax
Westman	01/23/88	National Oil Co.	Fairfax
Robinson	01/16/88	National Oil Co.	Fairfax
Morse	01/16/88	National Oil Co.	Fairfax
Jackson	01/16/88	City Revenue Dept.	Alexandria
Jackson	01/23/88	City Revenue Dept.	Alexandria
Robinson	01/16/88	City Revenue Dept.	Alexandria
Robinson	01/23/88	City Revenue Dept.	Alexandria
Jackson	01/16/88	City Revenue Dept.	Alexandria
Jackson	01/23/88	City Revenue Dept.	Alexandria
Hart	01/23/88	Smith Builders	Rockville
Hart	01/23/88	Smith Builders	Rockville
Mitchell	01/23/88	Smith Builders	Rockville
Jones	01/16/88	National Oil Co.	Fairfax
Jones	01/23/88	National Oil Co.	Fairfax

Browse | E:\dbase4\dbdata\<NEW> | Rec 1/9 | View | ReadOnly

Results of query on three database files

draw links between different database files. What *is* required is that the data contained in the linked fields can be matched. It would make no sense to try to draw a link between two fields containing such dissimilar data as phone numbers and dates of birth.

Generating Relational Reports

Generating reports from a relational database is no different than generating reports from a nonrelational database. You design your reports in the same manner as with other database files, as outlined earlier (in Chapter 8). You simply base the report on the relational view query. To see how this works, press ESC, and answer Yes to the prompt that asks if you wish to save this query. When prompted for a name, call the file RELATE3. When back at the Control Center, highlight RELATE3 at the Queries panel, press ENTER, and select Use View from the next menu.

Next, select the Create option of the Reports panel to create a new report. When the Report Design screen appears, choose the Quick Layouts option of the Layout menu. From the next menu to appear, choose Form Layout. A standard layout for a form-oriented report will appear. Notice that the fields in the report are based on the fields present in the view you just created.

To see the effects of this report, open the Print menu with ALT-P, and choose Begin Printing (or choose View Report on Screen). The resulting report contains all of the fields present in the view. You could, if you wished, save the report for future use. In this case, when the report has completed, choose Abandon Changes and Exit from the Exit menu to get back to the Control Center without saving the report.

Remember that a view must be in use before you can design a relational report based on that view. To put any view into use, just highlight the desired view from the Control Center and press ENTER. From the next menu that appears, select the Use View option. To stop using a view, highlight the view at the Control Center and press ENTER; then choose Close View from the next menu that appears.

Relating Files from the Dot Prompt

The relational powers provided by dBASE IV are also available from the dot prompt. A variety of commands, including SET RELATION and SET FIELDS, will enable you to establish the same kinds of relationships from the dot prompt as you do from the view queries accessed through the Control Center.

Whenever you are working from the dot prompt, you can link databases together with the SET RELATION command. This command links the files together by means of a common field. In our example, you will draw a relation between the HOURS database and the ABCSTAFF database by linking the common SOCIALSEC field. Then, whenever you move to a record in the HOURS database, the record pointer in the ABCSTAFF database will move to the record that contains the same social security number. The format of the SET RELATION command is

SET RELATION TO *key-expression* INTO *alias*

The key expression is the common field present in both databases. The alias is usually the name of the other database to which the active database is to be linked. One important requirement of this command is that you must index the file that will be linked on the common field. In our case, the ABCSTAFF database must be indexed on the SOCIALSEC field. (Since this is already the case, you don't need to build the index again; you'll just use the ORDER clause of the USE command to make sure the index is in use.)

To work with multiple database files, you will need to open more than one database file at a time. As mentioned in Chapter 10, you do this by using different work areas that contain the database files. You choose the work area with the SELECT command; for example, entering **SELECT 2** at the dot prompt would choose work area 2. (If no SELECT command is used, work area 1 is chosen by default.)

Get to the dot prompt if you're not already there. Open the HOURS and ABCSTAFF database files by using the following commands:

```
CLOSE DATABASES
SELECT 1
```

```
USE HOURS
USE ABCSTAFF IN 2 ORDER SOCIALSEC
```

A little explanation of the last command is in order. The USE ABCSTAFF IN 2 portion of the command line tells dBASE IV to open the database file ABCSTAFF, but to open it in work area 2 without actually switching work areas (hence the "IN 2" designation). The ORDER SOCIALSEC clause tells dBASE to set the index tag to SOCIALSEC.

It is now possible to link the files by the SOCIALSEC field with the SET RELATION command. The HOURS database is the active database, so you will link the ABCSTAFF database to the HOURS database. Enter

```
SET RELATION TO SOCIALSEC INTO ABCSTAFF
```

No changes are immediately visible, but dBASE IV has linked the files. To see the effects, enter the commands

```
GO 3
DISPLAY
```

You will see the third record in the HOURS database. The record indicates that an employee having the social security number of 121-90-5432 worked 27 hours at National Oil Company. To see just who this employee is, enter these commands:

```
SELECT 2
DISPLAY
```

The ABCSTAFF database (open in work area 2) will become the active database. The record pointer will be at record 2 (the record containing the social security number 121-90-5432), showing that the employee in question is Shirley Robinson.

Get back to the HOURS database with these commands:

```
SELECT 1
GO 2
DISPLAY
```

Again, you can see that the relation has found a matching social security number in the ABCSTAFF database by entering these commands:

```
SELECT 2
DISPLAY
```

Wherever you move in the HOURS database, the record pointer will try to find a matching social security number in the ABCSTAFF database. If dBASE IV cannot find a match according to the relation that you have specified, the record pointer will be positioned at the end of the database. (At the end of a file, all fields are blank. You can use this fact to test for failures to find a match by listing key fields from both databases.)

You can retrieve data in the related file by including the alias name and pointer (*filename*->) along with the field name. For example, in the expression

```
ABCSTAFF->FIRSTNAME
```

the filename ABCSTAFF is the alias, while FIRSTNAME is the field name. The combination of the hyphen and greater-than symbol make up the pointer.

To see how this works, try the following commands:

```
SELECT 1
LIST ABCSTAFF->LASTNAME, HOURS, ASSIGNMENT, WEEKENDING
```

The results show that such use of the SET RELATION command to establish the relational link, combined with the use of the alias and pointer, can be a powerful tool for obtaining data of a relational nature.

Record#	ABCSTAFF-> LASTNAME	HOURS	ASSIGNMENT	WEEKENDING
1	Jones	35.0	National Oil Co.	01/16/88
2	Westman	30.0	National Oil Co.	01/16/88
3	Robinson	27.0	National Oil Co.	01/16/88
4	Morse	32.0	National Oil Co.	01/16/88
5	Robinson	35.0	City Revenue Dept.	01/16/88
6	Jackson	28.0	City Revenue Dept.	01/16/88
7	Jackson	30.0	City Revenue Dept.	01/16/88
8	Hart	30.0	Smith Builders	01/16/88
9	Mitchell	28.0	Smith Builders	01/23/88
10	Hart	35.0	Smith Builders	01/23/88
11	Jackson	30.0	City Revenue Dept.	01/23/88
12	Jackson	32.0	City Revenue Dept.	01/23/88
13	Robinson	32.0	City Revenue Dept.	01/23/88
14	Westman	35.0	National Oil Co.	01/23/88
15	Jones	33.0	National Oil Co.	01/23/88

You could add the TO PRINT clause at the end of the LIST command to generate a printed list like the one just shown.

When you are working with related files from the dot prompt in this manner, keep in mind that you can test for mismatched records (such as an entry in the HOURS file with no matching social security number) by listing the key fields from the related files. For example, once the relationship has been established, the command

```
LIST HOURS->SOCIALSEC, ABCSTAFF->SOCIALSEC,
ABCSTAFF->LASTNAME
```

should produce a listing with a matching employee for each entry in the HOURS file. If an employee name and social security number turns up blank next to an entry in the HOURS listing, it is clear that a mismatch exists. Such a mismatch could be caused by a social security number entered incorrectly into the HOURS file.

Another command that is useful when you are working with related files from the dot prompt is the SET FIELDS command. Use this command to establish a pool of fields for further use. Also include the alias name and pointers to tell dBASE where fields not in the current work area can be found. As an example, try this command:

```
SET FIELDS TO ABCSTAFF->LASTNAME, ABCSTAFF->FIRSTNAME,
SOCIALSEC, HOURS, ASSIGNMENT, WEEKENDING
```

When the command is entered, you will have the six named fields available for further use without the need of any names or pointers. Enter the command

```
EDIT
```

and you will see the fields from both files, and only those fields specified with the SET FIELDS command.

NOTE You should avoid making changes with BROWSE or EDIT to multiple files related with SET RELATION. If you change the field used to link the files, a link between records may be broken. It is better to make changes to one file at a time.

Press ESC to get back to the dot prompt, and then try this command:

```
LIST LASTNAME, FIRSTNAME, HOURS, WEEKENDING
```

The results show that you do not now need the alias and pointer to retrieve the LASTNAME and FIRSTNAME data from the related file:

Record#	LASTNAME	FIRSTNAME	HOURS	WEEKENDING
1	Jones	Judi	35.0	01/16/88
2	Westman	Andrea	30.0	01/16/88
3	Robinson	Shirley	27.0	01/16/88
4	Morse	Marcia	32.0	01/16/88
5	Robinson	Wanda	35.0	01/16/88

6	Jackson	Cheryl	28.0	01/16/88
7	Jackson	David	30.0	01/16/88
8	Hart	Edward	30.0	01/16/88
9	Mitchell	Mary Jo	28.0	01/23/88
10	Hart	Edward	35.0	01/23/88
11	Jackson	David	30.0	01/23/88
12	Jackson	Cheryl	32.0	01/23/88
13	Robinson	Wanda	32.0	01/23/88
14	Westman	Andrea	35.0	01/23/88
15	Jones	Judi	33.0	01/23/88

HINT If you need to establish the same relationship often, save the relationship to a view file with CREATE VIEW *filename* FROM ENVIRONMENT. Then use SET VIEW TO to restore the view file as needed.

The use of SET FIELDS is also valuable with reports, because unless you either design a view or use SET FIELDS, the report generator won't know where to find those fields in a related file (unless you add them to the report as calculated fields). All of the fields you specify in a SET FIELDS command are available within a quick report or from the pick list that appears in the report generator.

To see how this works, enter

```
CREATE REPORT TEST1
```

When the Report Design screen appears, open the Layout menu with ALT-L. Choose Quick Layouts, and then select Form Layout from the next menu. Notice that the fields that appear are the fields you specified with the SET FIELDS command. Save this report with CTRL-END, and run the report from the dot prompt by entering this to see the results:

```
REPORT FORM TEST1
```

Prior to using this report, you would have to establish the relations with the SET RELATION command, and you would need to set up the pool of available fields with the SET FIELDS command. To verify this, enter the following commands at the dot prompt:

```
CLOSE DATABASES
SELECT 1
USE HOURS
USE ABCSTAFF IN 2 ORDER SOCIALSEC
SET RELATION TO SOCIALSEC INTO ABCSTAFF
LIST ABCSTAFF->LASTNAME, HOURS, WEEKENDING
```

The listing that results shows that you've established the needed relationship to get the data from both files. Now try running the report you just created with the command

```
REPORT FORM TEST1
```

The error message that appears, "Variable not found", means the report form cannot find a field named LASTNAME, because you haven't established the pool of fields. Choose Cancel and press ESC to get back to the dot prompt. Then enter the command

```
SET FIELDS TO ABCSTAFF->LASTNAME, ABCSTAFF->FIRSTNAME,
SOCIALSEC, HOURS, ASSIGNMENT, WEEKENDING
```

Try running the report again with the command

```
REPORT FORM TEST1
```

This time, the report runs normally.

A Warning

When you are working with related files from the dot prompt, it is completely up to you to make sure the indexes that allow the use of the SET RELATION command are kept updated. If you or another user opens a database without using an accompanying .NDX index file and adds or edits records, the resulting incomplete index files can cause incorrect results when you are trying to establish relationships or generate relational reports. If in doubt, use REINDEX to rebuild any indexes you are using. (This is only a problem with .NDX index files, since production .MDX files are opened and updated automatically.)

You can minimize this sort of potential problem by making effective use of catalogs and keeping all your needed indexes in the catalog. As long as you start work by opening the catalog, your databases and index files will be in use until you remove the index or the database from the catalog.

Analyzing Types of Relationships

Before you delve deeply into working with relationships between multiple files, you may find it necessary to do some analysis on paper, and determine the relationships that need to be drawn between the fields. The different types of possible relationships mean you can establish your links in different ways.

When one field in one record of a database relates in a unique manner to a field in another record in a different database, you have a *one-to-one* relationship. An example is a personnel system that contains medical and benefit information in one file and salary information in another file. Each database contains one record per employee, meaning that for every record in the medical file, there is a corresponding record for that same employee in the salary file. The relationship between the files is a one-to-one relationship. Figure 12-15 shows two such databases and the relationship between them. In this case, things are relatively simple; you use the SET RELATION command to link on the common field used between the two files (in this example, a unique employee ID number).

When relating files, it is often advantageous to have a field that will always contain unique data for each record, as in this example; unless an incorrect entry is made, no two employees ever have the same employee ID number. Customer numbers, social security numbers, and stock numbers are other types of data commonly used for the same purpose of unique identification.

In some cases, a single field with unique data may not be available; for example, you may have a list of customers, but your company may not assign customer numbers as a practice. If you can't convince management to change the way it tracks customers, you have the alternative of creating a link based on more than one field. In the case of customers, you could index on a combination of LASTNAME + FIRSTNAME + ADDRESS, and establish the relation on the expression with a command like

```
SET RELATION TO (LASTNAME+FIRSTNAME+ADDRESS) INTO MYFILE
```

This would work, assuming you never have two customers with the same name living at the same address.

By comparison, if one field of one record in the first file relates to a field in one or more records in the second file, you have a *one-to-many* relationship. An example is the relationship between the ABC Temporaries ABCSTAFF and HOURS database files. For every employee in the ABCSTAFF file, there are a

Figure 12-15.

EMPLOYEEID	LASTNAME	FIRSTNAME	SALARY	GRADE	HIRED
X288	Anderson	Terence	750.55	8	03/17/69
X289	Smith	Linda	890.00	10	06/25/75
G343	Robinson	James	790.40	6	08/19/86

EMPLOYEEID	HEALTHNAME	HEALTHCOST	DENTALNAME	DENTALCOST
G343	Blue Cross	95.50	Prudential	33.00
X288	Kaiser	62.00	Kaiser	27.00
X289	Prudential	55.00	Kaiser	27.00

One-to-one relationship

number of records in the HOURS file corresponding to a different weekly entry of hours worked by that employee. Again, SET RELATION is used to establish the link, as was demonstrated earlier in this chapter.

One-to-many relationships are more complex, however, because you must keep track of which file is active when performing data retrieval operations. In this example, the ABCSTAFF file is the "one" file, and the HOURS file is the "many" file. When a listing of all hours worked by the employees was needed, the HOURS file had to be the active file, and the relation had to be set out of that file, because it contained the "many" data. If the ABCSTAFF file had been the active file and a relation had been set out of ABCSTAFF into HOURS, only the first matching record in the "many" file (HOURS) would appear in any listing, and you would have to use SET SKIP to allow all the matching records in the "many" database to be properly listed. The point is to keep in mind the nature of the one-to-many relationship, and plan your relationships accordingly.

Finally, a type of relationship that is not as common as the first two but that occasionally arises is the *many-to-many* relationship. This relationship exists when a field in several records in one database relates to a field in several records in another database. A classic example of this is that of student tracking at a high school or college, where many students are assigned to many different classes. To set up this or any many-to-many relationship under dBASE IV, you will need at least three database files. The first two files contain the "many" data, and the third file serves as an intermediate or "linking" file between them. In this example, the three files needed are a student file with the names of each student and a unique student ID number; a classes file, containing a unique class ID number for each class, the class name, room number, and teacher name; and finally, a schedule file, containing a record for each student's enrollment in a class. Figure 12-16 shows the databases and illustrates the relationships between the files. You can duplicate the files and the data shown if you care to try the following examples. Call the file of student names STUDENTS, the file of scheduled classes SCHEDULE, and the file of class names CLASSES.

Once the databases are created, you can use the SET RELATION command to link the SCHEDULE file to both the STUDENTS file and the CLASSES file. Depending on the data you need, you could use various LIST commands or design different reports to produce the desired results. If you duplicated the sample files, you could try these commands:

```
SELECT 1
USE STUDENTS
INDEX ON SOCIAL TAG STUDENTS
SELECT 2
USE SCHEDULE
SELECT 3
USE CLASSES
INDEX ON CLASSID TAG CLASSES
SELECT 2
SET RELATION TO SOCIAL INTO STUDENTS, CLASSID INTO CLASSES
```

Figure 12-16.

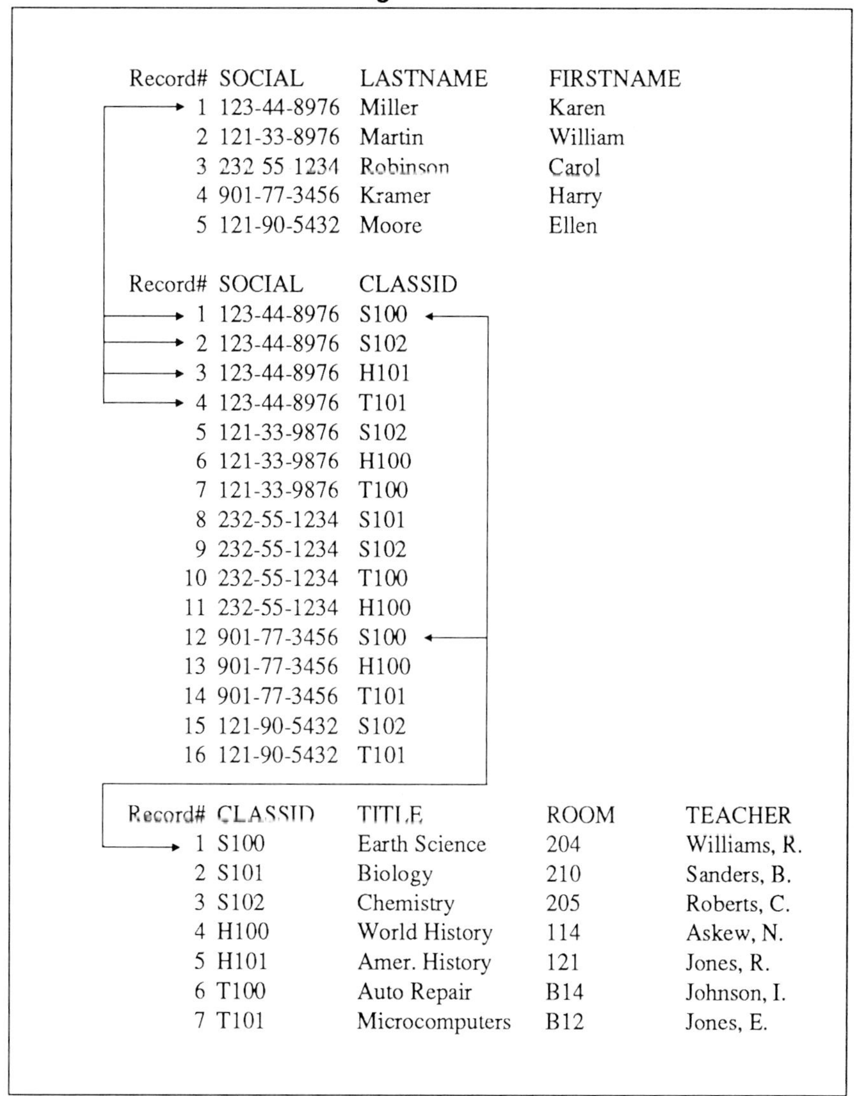

Record#	SOCIAL	LASTNAME	FIRSTNAME
1	123-44-8976	Miller	Karen
2	121-33-8976	Martin	William
3	232-55-1234	Robinson	Carol
4	901-77-3456	Kramer	Harry
5	121-90-5432	Moore	Ellen

Record#	SOCIAL	CLASSID
1	123-44-8976	S100
2	123-44-8976	S102
3	123-44-8976	H101
4	123-44-8976	T101
5	121-33-9876	S102
6	121-33-9876	H100
7	121-33-9876	T100
8	232-55-1234	S101
9	232-55-1234	S102
10	232-55-1234	T100
11	232-55-1234	H100
12	901-77-3456	S100
13	901-77-3456	H100
14	901-77-3456	T101
15	121-90-5432	S102
16	121-90-5432	T101

Record#	CLASSID	TITLE	ROOM	TEACHER
1	S100	Earth Science	204	Williams, R.
2	S101	Biology	210	Sanders, B.
3	S102	Chemistry	205	Roberts, C.
4	H100	World History	114	Askew, N.
5	H101	Amer. History	121	Jones, R.
6	T100	Auto Repair	B14	Johnson, I.
7	T101	Microcomputers	B12	Jones, E.

Many-to-many relationship

If you wanted to use this relationship at a later date, you could save it with a command like CREATE VIEW SCHOOL FROM ENVIRONMENT. You could then proceed to retrieve the needed data. As an example, a cross-list of student names and instructor names could be produced with a command like

```
LIST CLASSES->TEACHER, STUDENTS->LASTNAME,
STUDENTS->FIRSTNAME
```

The results would resemble the following:

Record#	CLASSES->TEACHER	STUDENTS->LASTNAME	STUDENTS->FIRSTNAME
1	Williams, R.	Miller	Karen
2	Roberts, C.	Miller	Karen
3	Jones, R.	Miller	Karen
4	Jones, E.	Miller	Karen
5	Roberts, C.	Martin	William
6	Askew, N.	Martin	William
7	Johnson, I.	Martin	William
8	Sanders, B.	Robinson	Carol
9	Roberts, C.	Robinson	Carol
10	Johnson, I.	Robinson	Carol
11	Askew, N.	Robinson	Carol
12	Williams, R	Kramer	Harry
13	Askew, N.	Kramer	Harry
14	Jones, E.	Kramer	Harry
15	Roberts, C.	Moore	Ellen
16	Jones, E.	Moore	Ellen

If you needed a course list for all students, you could use a command like

```
LIST STUDENTS->LASTNAME, STUDENTS->FIRSTNAME, CLASSID,
CLASSES->TITLE
```

and the results would resemble this:

Record#	STUDENTS->LASTNAME	STUDENTS->FIRSTNAME	CLASSID	CLASSES->TITLE
1	Miller	Karen	S100	Earth Science
2	Miller	Karen	S102	Chemistry
3	Miller	Karen	H101	Amer. History

4	Miller	Karen	T101	Microcomputers
5	Martin	William	S102	Chemistry
6	Martin	William	H100	World History
7	Martin	William	T100	Auto Repair
8	Robinson	Carol	S101	Biology
9	Robinson	Carol	S102	Chemistry
10	Robinson	Carol	T100	Auto Repair
11	Robinson	Carol	H100	World History
12	Kramer	Harry	S100	Earth Science
13	Kramer	Harry	H100	World History
14	Kramer	Harry	T101	Microcomputers
15	Moore	Ellen	S102	Chemistry
16	Moore	Ellen	T101	Microcomputers

If you wanted a list of classes for a single student, you could include a FOR clause, as in

```
LIST STUDENTS->LASTNAME, STUDENTS->FIRSTNAME, CLASSID,
CLASSES->TITLE FOR STUDENTS->LASTNAME = "Kramer"
```

The results include only those classes for the student named, as shown here:

Record#	STUDENTS->LASTNAME	STUDENTS->FIRSTNAME	CLASSID	CLASSES->TITLE
12	Kramer	Harry	S100	Earth Science
13	Kramer	Harry	H100	World History
14	Kramer	Harry	T101	Microcomputers

You could use similar techniques to obtain listings of all students for a given teacher, as shown in the following example:

```
LIST STUDENTS->LASTNAME, STUDENTS->FIRSTNAME, CLASSID,
CLASSES->TITLE FOR CLASSES->TEACHER = "Roberts, C."
```

The results will appear as follows:

Record#	STUDENTS->LASTNAME	STUDENTS->FIRSTNAME	CLASSID	CLASSES->TITLE
2	Miller	Karen	S102	Chemistry
5	Martin	Williams	S102	Chemistry
9	Robinson	Carol	S102	Chemistry
15	Moore	Ellen	S102	Chemistry

While the management of a many-to-many application like this one gets fairly complex, it also demonstrates the power and usefulness of a well-planned relational database system. To manage this data in a single database file would call for an enormous amount of redundant data entry; student names and teacher names would be repeated needlessly dozens or hundreds of times in such a file. In spite of this, database users create single files to manage tasks like this all too often (either to avoid learning the relational commands necessary, or because student data-entry labor is cheap). If you take the time now to learn the techniques of relating files in dBASE IV, your database applications will be much more efficient, saving you time and hassle in the future.

Quick Reference

To establish a relationship between multiple files Design a query, and use the Add File To Query option of the Layout menu to add multiple files to the query. Place the same sample variable in the common field of the file skeletons used to provide the link. Or, from the dot prompt, use the SET RELATION command to establish a link between database files.

To use AND selection criteria in a query with multiple files Place multiple criteria, as desired, in different fields of the file skeletons. The multiple criteria need not be in the same file; you can have one condition in a field of one file skeleton, and another condition in a field of another file skeleton.

To use OR selection criteria in a query with multiple files Place multiple criteria on multiple lines of each file skeleton. Use the DOWN ARROW key to add new lines to either file skeleton. Again, the conditions (or criteria) need not be in the same file.

To generate relational reports First design and save a relational query. Place the query in use, and then design the desired report with the Create option of the Reports panel (or the CREATE REPORT command from the dot prompt). Before using the report, be sure to place the relational query in use.

CHAPTER

13

Introduction To dBASE IV Programming

While you may not have purchased dBASE IV with the intent of becoming a computer programmer, you'll find that programming with dBASE IV is not as difficult as you might expect. As you will see in this chapter, you program in dBASE through the use of *command files*. Using programs that automate the way dBASE IV works for you is well worth the effort spent in designing and writing command files.

Any computer program is simply a series of instructions to a computer. These instructions are commands that cause the computer to perform specific tasks. The commands are written in a file contained on a disk, and they are performed each time the file is retrieved from the disk. A dBASE IV command file is made up of dBASE IV commands. Each time you use a command file, dBASE IV will execute the list of commands in sequential order unless you request it to do otherwise.

HINT If you repeat the same commands over and over in your work, command files will save you considerable effort.

Let's look at an example that uses the ABC Temporaries database. If an ABC Temporaries manager wanted a printed listing of employees' last names, salary amounts, cities, and states, that manager could enter commands like those you have already learned to use to produce the listing. This may not seem like a complex task; in fact, it could be done with the following two commands:

```
USE ABCSTAFF
LIST LASTNAME, FIRSTNAME, SALARY, CITY, STATE
```

If, however, the manager needed to reprint this list frequently, typing the same commands over and over would be a waste of time. Instead, these commands could be placed inside of a command file, and then the manager would only type one command to execute all of the commands in the file.

Two characteristics of command files make them a powerful feature of dBASE IV:

- Any series of dBASE IV commands entered from the dot prompt can be stored in a command file. When the command file is run, the dBASE IV commands present in the file will be executed just as if they had been entered from the keyboard.

- One command file can call and execute another command file, and information can be transferred between command files. This means that complex systems can be designed efficiently by creating a series of smaller command files for individual tasks.

Using command files, you can create a system that relies on menus appearing on the screen. An example of a menu screen is shown in Figure 13-1. Rather than entering individual commands, the user simply makes choices from the menu to retrieve and manipulate information in the database. Such a menu-driven system can easily be learned and used by people unfamiliar with dBASE IV commands.

Figure 13-1.

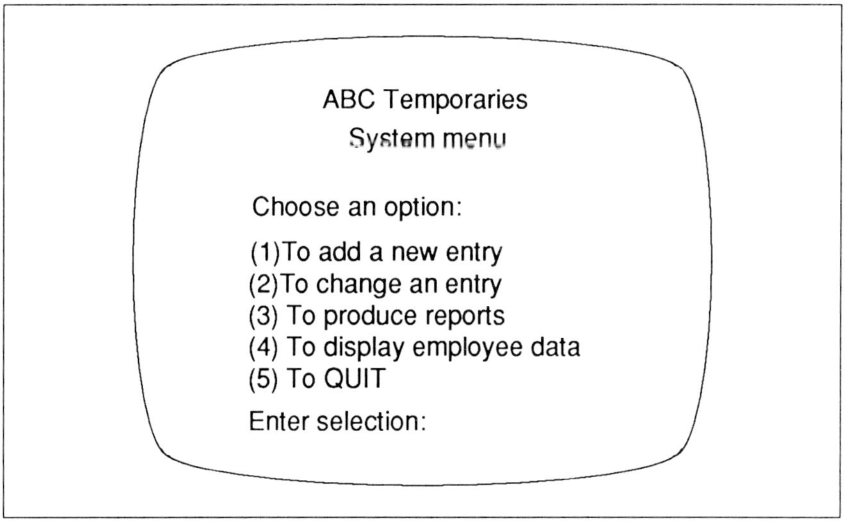

```
ABC Temporaries
  System menu

Choose an option:

(1)To add a new entry
(2)To change an entry
(3) To produce reports
(4) To display employee data
(5) To QUIT

Enter selection:
```

Sample menu for ABC Temporaries

Creating Command Files

You can create command files with the MODIFY COMMAND command. From the dot prompt, its format is

MODIFY COMMAND *filename*

Entering **MODIFY COMMAND** along with a filename brings up the dBASE IV editor. You then use the editor (which is dBASE IV's built-in word processor) to type commands that will be stored as a command file.

When you use MODIFY COMMAND, the file you create will

Table 13-1.

Key	Function
↑ or CTRL-E	Moves cursor up one line
↓ or CTRL-X	Moves cursor down one line
→ or CTRL-D	Moves cursor one character forward
← or CTRL-S	Moves cursor back one character
CTRL-N	Inserts a blank line
CTRL-T	Deletes word beginning at the cursor to the next word
CTRL-Y	Deletes line
INS or CTRL-V	Turns Insert mode on or off
DEL	Deletes character at the cursor position
BACKSPACE	Deletes character to the left of the cursor
PGUP or CTRL-R	Scrolls screen upward
PGDN or CTRL-C	Scrolls screen downward
CTRL-END	Saves file on disk
ESC	Exits the word processor without saving

Editing Keys in the dBASE IV Editor

have an extension of .PRG (for "program") unless you enter a different extension. If the filename you enter already exists on the disk, it will be recalled to the screen. If the filename does not exist, a blank screen within the editor is displayed.

You can also create command files from the Control Center. To do so, you choose the Create option of the Applications panel and choose dBASE Program from the next menu to appear.

Let's create a command file now. Get to the dot prompt if you are not already there, and enter

```
MODIFY COMMAND TEST
```

The dBASE IV editor appears. At this point, the screen is like a blank sheet of paper. You type the commands that you wish to place in your command file, pressing ENTER as you complete each line. If you make any mistakes, you can correct them with the arrow keys and the BACKSPACE or DEL key. The editing keys available in the editor are listed in Table 13-1. When you are using the dBASE IV editor, any characters you type will overwrite any existing characters in the same position unless you are in Insert mode, which you can get in and out of by pressing INS. When you are in Insert mode, "Ins" appears at the right side of the status bar, and any characters to the right of the cursor will be pushed to the right as you type new characters.

Type the following series of commands now, pressing ENTER after you complete each line; only one command should appear on each line. (If you don't have a printer attached to your system, omit SET PRINT ON, SET PRINT OFF, and EJECT.)

```
USE ABCSTAFF
SET PRINT ON
LIST LASTNAME, FIRSTNAME, CITY, SALARY FOR STATE = "MD"
LIST LASTNAME, FIRSTNAME, CITY, SALARY FOR STATE = "VA"
LIST LASTNAME, FIRSTNAME, CITY, SALARY FOR STATE = "DC"
SET PRINT OFF
EJECT
```

Whenever you finish editing with the dBASE IV editor, choose Save Changes and Exit from the Exit menu (or press CTRL-END) to save the command file. (If you want to leave the editor without saving the file, you can choose Abandon Changes and Exit from the Exit menu to get back to the dot prompt.)

HINT You can also run programs from the Control Center by choosing the program from the Applications panel and selecting Run Application from the next menu.

The simple command file that you have created will print a listing of employees grouped by state, including employee names, city names, and salary amounts. Make sure that your printer is turned on; then, to see the results of your work, enter

```
DO TEST
```

The commands in the file will be carried out in sequential order, just as if you had entered them individually. Figure 13-2 shows the result.

You can also create a command file by using other word processing programs. Although the dBASE IV editor is convenient and relatively powerful, you may prefer to use your favorite word processing program. Any word processor that can save files as ASCII text (text without any control codes) can be used to create a dBASE IV command file. This includes WordPerfect, MultiMate, WordStar, and Microsoft Word. In WordPerfect, save the file with the CTRL-F5 and **1** key combination. In WordStar, save the file in nondocument mode. In Microsoft Word, save the file as unformatted. The important points to remember are to save the file as an ASCII file and to use the .PRG extension when naming the file; otherwise, dBASE IV won't recognize the file as a command file unless you include the extension when calling the program with the DO command.

Figure 13-2.

Record#	LASTNAME	FIRSTNAME	CITY	SALARY
1	Morse	Marcia	Chevy Chase	9.00
2	Westman	Andrea	Silver Spring	16.50
5	Robinson	Shirley	Takoma Park	8.00

Record#	LASTNAME	FIRSTNAME	CITY	SALARY
3	Jackson	David	Falls Church	8.00
4	Mitchell	Mary Jo	Arlington	8.00
6	Jackson	Cheryl	Falls Church	12.00
8	Hart	Edward	Fairfax	8.50
9	Jones	Judi	Reston	12.50

Record#	LASTNAME	FIRSTNAME	CITY	SALARY
7	Robinson	Wanda	Washington	8.00

Results of command file

Also note that dBASE creates programs whenever you save a report, label, or query. When you save a report, a file with the report's name and the .FRG extension contains a program that will generate the report. The same is true of labels, except that the filename's extension will be .LBG. Queries are stored as a single file with a .QBE extension, but the file will contain a series of program statements along with some other control codes. This is worth knowing, because you can use the TYPE command (either at the dot prompt or from DOS outside of dBASE) to examine the contents of these files. For example, if you get to the dot prompt and enter the command

```
TYPE ABCMAIL.LBG
```

you will see the contents of a program created by dBASE when you saved the label you designed in Chapter 11.

REMEMBER If you use other word processors to create command files, be sure to save the files as ASCII text. Also, be sure to read the next section, "A Note About Compiling."

Examining programs that dBASE creates in this manner can be helpful in learning how to design your own programs. Also, you can often save time by incorporating the programs dBASE creates into your own programs.

A Note About Compiling

dBASE IV uses a compiler to run programs on a compiled basis, rather than an interpreted basis. Interpreters convert each line of a program into machine language each time the program runs; compilers translate the entire program once into what is known as object code, and then each time the program runs it uses that object code. The use of a compiler offers a significant speed advantage over an interpreter. (Earlier versions of Ashton-Tate's dBASE, including dBASE II, dBASE III, and dBASE III PLUS, were interpreter-based.)

When you run a dBASE IV program by entering **DO *filename*,** dBASE IV looks for a compiled object code file with an .OBJ extension. If dBASE IV finds the file, it runs the program using the already-compiled object code. If dBASE IV can't find the file, it looks for a "source" file, which is an ASCII text file of commands with a .PRG extension. dBASE IV compiles this file, creating an object code file of the same filename, and then runs the program. Thus, if you enter **DO *filename*** and you see the message "Compiling" on the screen, dBASE IV is compiling the program. Compiling takes place only the first time you run a new or modified program.

It is important to know this if you use your own editor to modify existing programs. When you change an existing program using the dBASE IV editor, dBASE IV recompiles to a new object file when you run the program. If you use your own editor to change a program and the existing object code file is not erased, entering **DO *filename*** will cause the old version of the program to be run. When making changes with your editor, you must erase the old object code (.OBJ file) version of the program, or you must use the SET DEVELOPMENT ON command when you start your dBASE IV session. Entering **SET DEVELOPMENT ON** will tell dBASE IV to compare creation dates and times between source (.PRG) and object (.OBJ) files; if they differ, dBASE IV will recompile the program before running it.

Programming Concepts

There are various concepts and terms associated with programming that you should know about before you delve into the topic of dBASE IV command files. These are constants, variables, expressions, operators, and functions.

Constants

A constant is fixed data, or data that does not change. Unlike fields (whose values change, depending on the position of the record pointer), a constant's value is dependent on nothing; once established, the constant remains the same. There are numeric, character, date, or logical constants. For example, 5.05 might be a numeric constant, while "a" might be a character constant. All character constants must be surrounded by quotes.

Memory Variables

A memory variable (or just "variable" for short) is a memory location within the computer that is used to store data. A variable name must not have more than 10 characters. It must consist of letters, numbers, and underscores only, and it must start with a letter. You cannot use the names of commands; it is also advised that you not use field names.

Because the contents of a memory variable are stored apart from the contents of a database, memory variables are useful for the temporary processing of values and data within a dBASE program. Data can be stored in the form of memory variables and can then be recalled for use by the program at a later time.

! ***HINT*** Think of a memory variable as a temporary place to put a piece of information that will be needed later in the program.

The STORE command is commonly used to assign data to a variable. Its format is

STORE *expression* TO *variable-name*

An alternate way of assigning data to a variable is to use the *variable* = *X* format, as shown here:

variable-name = *expression*

dBASE IV allows four types of variables: character, numeric, date, and logical. Character variables store strings of characters, which can be letters, numbers, or a combination of both. Numbers in a character variable are treated as characters. Numeric variables contain whole or decimal numbers. Date variables contain dates written in date format (for example, 12/16/84). Logical variables contain a logical value of T (true) or F (false), or Y (yes) or N (no).

You do not have to designate the type when you create a variable—just assign the value you will be using. Use a descriptive name to help you remember what is stored in the variable. For example, the following STORE command assigns a numeric value of 18 to the variable LEGALAGE:

```
STORE 18 TO LEGALAGE
```

If you prefer the alternate format, you could accomplish the same result with the statement

```
LEGALAGE = 18
```

You can change the value by using the STORE command again:

```
STORE 21 TO LEGALAGE
```

The contents of a field can be stored to a memory variable. As an example, the command

```
STORE LASTNAME TO ROSTER
```

would store the contents of the LASTNAME field to a memory variable named ROSTER. When a list of characters is stored in a variable, the list of characters, known as *character string,* must be surrounded by single or double quotation marks. For example, the command

```
STORE "BILL ROBERTS" TO NAME
```

would store the character string BILL ROBERTS in the variable NAME.

Surround the logical variable T, F, Y, or N with periods to distinguish it from a regular character: while .T. has a logical value of true, "T" is simply the letter T. Logical values can also be stored in variables with the STORE command. The following command would assign a logical value of false to the variable CHOICE:

```
STORE .F. TO CHOICE
```

To initialize a date variable, surround the date with curly braces. As an example,

```
STORE {11/01/88} TO MYDAY
```

would store the date, 11/01/88, to a date variable named MYDAY.

In addition to STORE, other commands assign values to variables. These commands will be discussed in later chapters. To display a list of the variables you have used and their values, type **DISPLAY MEMORY**.

You can use memory variables in direct commands and in command files. However, all memory variables that you use are only temporary; as soon as you turn off the computer, they vanish. You can make a memory variable permanent by storing the variable to a memory file on disk. As you might expect, when the values are stored on disk, they can be recalled by a dBASE IV program. Each memory variable must be assigned a unique name.

Try entering the following:

```
STORE 25 TO QUANTITY
STORE "Jefferson" TO NAMES
STORE TIME() TO CLOCK
```

```
? QUANTITY, NAMES, CLOCK
```

The previous example displayed the values stored in memory with the STORE command. However, you can use the DISPLAY MEMORY command to take a look at all variables that have been defined in memory. Enter

```
DISPLAY MEMORY
```

to display a listing of variables, a letter designating the type of variable, and what each variable contains. The letter C indicates a character variable, N a numeric variable, D a date variable, and L a logical variable. The designation "Pub" beside each variable indicates that these are "public" variables, available to all parts of dBASE IV. Variables can be public or private (see the PUBLIC command in Appendix A for details). For now, you needn't be concerned about this designation. Along with the memory variables you have created, you will also see information on print system memory variables that dBASE IV uses; you can ignore these.

You should keep two guidelines in mind when using memory variables. First, it's a good idea to not name variables after a field. If a program encounters a name that can be either a variable or a field, the field name will take precedence over the memory variable. If you must give a variable the same name as a field, use the M-> prefix ahead of the variable name so that dBASE IV knows when you are referring to the variable. For example, if ABCSTAFF were in use, LASTNAME would refer to the LASTNAME field, while M->LASTNAME would refer to a variable called LASTNAME.

Second, note that dBASE IV requires that store some type of value, even if it is a worthless one, to a memory variable before you can begin using the variable. If you attempt to use variables in a program before defining them with the STORE command, dBASE IV will respond with a "variable not found" error message.

The exceptions to this are the ACCEPT, INPUT, and WAIT commands, which can create memory variables as they are used.

To save variables on disk, use the SAVE TO command. The format of this command is

SAVE TO *filename*

where *filename* is the name of the file that you want the variables saved under. The .MEM extension will automatically be added to the filename.

Right now, you have at least four memory variables defined from the previous examples—WORDS, QUANTITY, NAMES, and CLOCK. (You may also have other variables, created from prior examples.) To save the variables currently in memory, enter the following:

```
SAVE TO FASTFILE
```

Once the variables have been stored, you can clear the memory of variables with the RELEASE ALL command. Enter the following:

```
RELEASE ALL
DISPLAY MEMORY
```

You'll see that the memory variables no longer exist in memory. To get the memory variables back from FASTFILE, use the RESTORE FROM *filename* command. This command will restore variables from *filename* to memory. You do not have to include the .MEM file extension. Enter

```
RESTORE FROM FASTFILE
DISPLAY MEMORY
```

The variables are again in the system, ready for further use. When you use the RESTORE FROM *filename* command, all variables currently in memory will be removed to accommodate variables from the file. If you want to keep existing variables in memory while loading additional variables that were saved to a disk file, use the RESTORE FROM *filename* ADDITIVE variation of the command.

With the RELEASE command, you can also select specific variables to remove from memory by including either the EXCEPT or the LIKE option. (You will need to use the word ALL before the words EXCEPT or LIKE.) RELEASE with EXCEPT eliminates all variables except those that you list after EXCEPT. RELEASE with LIKE, on the other hand, removes the variables that you list after LIKE. As an example, the command

```
RELEASE ALL LIKE N*
```

would cause all memory variables starting with the letter N to be erased from memory.

You can use LIKE to erase some memory variables and leave other variables untouched. For example, try the following:

```
RESTORE FROM FASTFILE
RELEASE ALL LIKE Q*
DISPLAY MEMORY
```

This causes all memory variables beginning with the letter Q, including the memory variable QUANTITY, to be erased from memory, while leaving the others untouched. Note that you can use the same LIKE and ALL options in a similar manner with the SAVE command. For example, you could enter the command

```
SAVE ALL LIKE Q* TO QFILE
```

in order to save all of the memory variables starting with the letter Q.

Expressions

An expression can be a combination of one or more fields, functions, operators, memory variables, or constants. As an example, Figure 13-3 shows a statement combining a field, a memory variable, and a constant to form a single expression. This statement calculates total rent over a period of months, deducting 5% for estimated utilities (water, garbage, and so on).

Each part of an expression, whether that part is a constant, a field, or a memory variable, is considered an element of the expression. All elements of an expression must be of the same type. You cannot, for example, mix character and date fields within the same expression unless you use functions to convert the dates to characters. If you try to mix different types of fields

Figure 13-3.

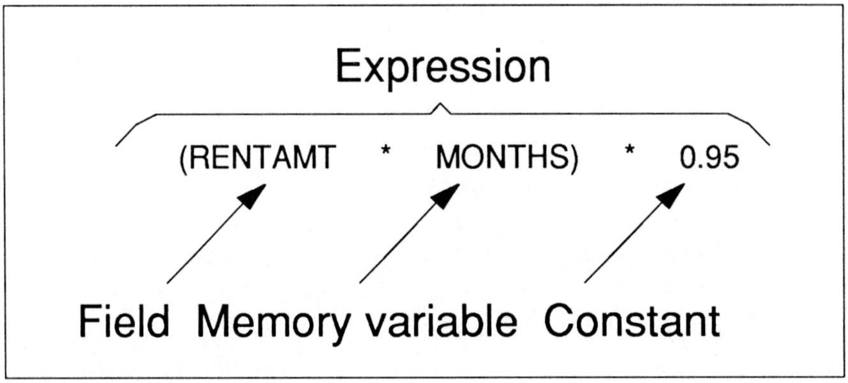

An example of an expression

within an expression, dBASE IV will display a "Data type mismatch" error message.

The most common type of expression found in dBASE programs is the math expression. Math expressions contain the elements of an expression (constants, fields, memory variables, or functions) linked by one or more math operators (+, -, *, /). Examples of math expressions include the following:

```
SALARY * 12

HOURLYRATE - SALARY

SALARY + (SALARY * .05)

SALARY * 40

637.5/HOURLYRATE

82
```

Character expressions are also quite common in dBASE IV programs. They are used to manipulate character strings or groups of characters. Examples of character expressions include the following:

```
"Bob Smith"

"Mr." + FIRSTNAME + " " + LASTNAME + " is behind in payments."
```

Operators

Operators, which are represented by symbols, work on related values to produce a single value. Operators that work on two values are called *binary* operators; operators that work on one value are called *unary* operators. Most of dBASE IV's operators are binary operators, but there are a couple of unary operators. dBASE IV has four kinds of operators: mathematical, relational, logical, and string operators.

Mathematical Operators Mathematical operators are used to produce numeric results. Besides addition, subtraction, multiplication, and division, dBASE IV has operators for exponentiation and unary minus (assigning a negative value to a number). The symbols for math operators are as follows:

Operation	Symbol
Unary minus	-
Exponentiation	** or ^
Division	/
Multiplication	*
Subtraction	-
Addition	+

If an expression contains more than one math operator, dBASE IV executes the operations in a prescribed order. Unary minus is performed first, followed by exponentiation; then multiplication or division is calculated, and then addition or subtraction. In the case of operators with equal precedence—division and multiplication, subtraction and addition—calculation will be from left to right. You can alter the order of operations by grouping them with matched pairs of parentheses. For example, the parentheses in (3 + 6) * 5 force dBASE IV to add 3 + 6 first and then multiply the sum by 5. You can also group operations within operations with *nested* parentheses. dBASE IV begins with the innermost group and calculates outward, as in the case of ((3 + 5) * 6) ^ 3, where 3 + 5 is added first, multiplied by 6, and then raised to the power of 3.

Relational Operators Relational operators are used to compare character strings with character strings, date values with date values, and numbers with numbers. The values you compare can be constants or variables. The relational operators are as follows:

Operation	Operator
Less than	<
Greater than	>
Equal to	=
Not equal to	< > or #
Less than or equal to	<=
Greater than or equal to	>=

Any comparison of values results in a logical value of true or false. The simple comparison 6 < 7 would result in .T.. The result of 6 < NUMBER depends on the value of NUMBER. You can also compare such character strings as "canine" < "feline" because dBASE IV orders letters and words as in a dictionary. However, uppercase letters come before lowercase letters, so "Z" < "a" is a true comparison even though the letter a comes before Z in the alphabet.

Logical Operators Logical operators compare values of the same type to produce a logical true, false, yes, or no. The logical operators are as follows:

.AND.
.OR.
.NOT.

Table 13-2 lists all possible values produced by the three logical operators. .AND. and .OR. are binary operators, while .NOT. is a unary operator.

Table 13-2.

First Value	Operator	Second Value	Result
.T.	.AND.	.T.	.T.
.T.	.AND.	.F.	.F.
.F.	.AND.	.T.	.F.
.F.	.AND.	.F.	.F.
.T.	.OR.	.T.	.T.
.T.	.OR.	.F.	.T.
.F.	.OR.	.T.	.T.
.F.	.OR.	.F.	.F.
.T.	.NOT.	N.A.	.F.
.F.	.NOT.	N.A.	.T.

Truth Table for Logical Operators .AND., .OR., and .NOT.

String Operators The string operator you will commonly use in dBASE IV is the plus sign (+), which is used to combine two or more character strings. This is known as *concatenation*. For example, "Orange" + "Fox" would be combined as "OrangeFox" (remember, a blank is a character).

Strings inside variables can also be concatenated; for example, if ANIMAL = "Fox" and COLOR = "Orange", then COLOR+ANIMAL would result in "OrangeFox".

Functions

Functions are used in dBASE IV to perform special operations that supplement the normal dBASE IV commands. dBASE IV has 70 different functions that range from calculating the square root of a number to finding the time. To discuss all of dBASE IV's functions would require a detailed explanation of programming, which is not the purpose of this book. However, you should know about some functions that are commonly used in command files. These are discussed in the following sections.

EOF

The EOF function indicates when the dBASE IV record pointer has reached the end of a database file. The normal format of the function is simply EOF( ). To see how EOF is set to true when the pointer is past the last record, enter

```
GO BOTTOM
```

This moves the pointer to the last record. Now enter

```
DISPLAY
```

and you will see that you are at record 9, the final record in the database. Next, enter

```
? EOF( )
```

to display the value of the EOF function. dBASE IV returns .F. (false), meaning that the value of the EOF function is false because you are not yet at the end of the file. The SKIP command, discussed shortly, can be used to move the dBASE IV record pointer. Enter

```
SKIP
```

to move the pointer past the last record. Next, enter

```
? EOF( )
```

The .T. (true) value shows that the pointer is now at the end of the file.

BOF

The BOF function is the opposite of the EOF function. The value of BOF is set to true when the beginning of a database file is reached. The format is simply BOF( ). To see how BOF operates, enter

```
GO TOP
```

The pointer moves to the first record. Now enter

```
DISPLAY
```

and the first record in the database is displayed. Next, enter

```
? BOF( )
```

to display the value of the BOF function, which is .F. (false) because the pointer is at the first record and not at the beginning of the file. Enter

```
SKIP -1
```

to move the pointer above record 1, and then enter

```
? BOF( )
```

The .T. (true) value shows that the pointer is at the beginning of the file.

DATE and TIME

The DATE and TIME functions are used to provide the current date and time, respectively. dBASE IV provides the date and time by means of the clock built into your computer. For this reason, if the date and time are set incorrectly in your computer, the DATE and TIME functions of dBASE IV will also be incorrect. The format for DATE is DATE( ), and it provides the current date in the form MM/DD/YY. Dates follow the American date format—month, day, year—unless you use the PICTURE option (see Chapter 15) or the SET DATE command to tell dBASE IV otherwise. The format for TIME for is TIME( ), and it provides the current time in HH:MM:SS format. From the dot prompt, you could display the current date and time by entering

```
? DATE( )
? TIME( )
```

The output of the DATE and TIME functions can be stored as a variable for use within a program, as in the example shown here:

```
? "Today's date is: "
?? DATE( )
STORE TIME( ) TO BEGIN
?
LIST LASTNAME, FIRSTNAME, TAPELIMIT, EXPIREDATE
?
? "Starting time was: "
?? BEGIN
? "Ending time is: "
?? TIME( )
```

HINT Use ? DATE( ) or ? TIME( ) in your programs to display the date or time on the screen or print them in reports (if SET PRINT is on).

UPPER

The UPPER function converts lowercase letters to uppercase letters. UPPER can thus be used to display text and variables in a uniform format if consistency is desired. You can use it with a character field, a character string, a constant, or a memory variable that contains a character string. For example try entering the following:

```
? UPPER ("This is not really uppercase")
THIS IS NOT REALLY UPPERCASE

STORE "not uppercase" TO WORDS
? UPPER(WORDS)
NOT UPPERCASE

? WORDS
not uppercase
```

As you can see the UPPER function displays characters in uppercase, but does not actually alter the data. This function is especially useful to search for data when you are not sure whether the data was entered as all uppercase or with initial capital letters only. For example, a command like

```
LIST FOR UPPER(LASTNAME) = "SMITH"
```

would find a record whether the last name was entered as "Smith" or "SMITH."

LOWER

The LOWER function is the opposite of UPPER: it converts uppercase characters to lowercase characters. As with the UPPER function, the LOWER function does not convert the actual data; it only changes the appearance of the data. Here is an example:

```
STORE "NOT CAPS" TO WORDS
? LOWER(WORDS)
not caps
```

CTOD and DTOC

CTOD and DTOC are the character-to-date and date-to-character functions, respectively. CTOD converts a string of characters to a value that is recognized as a date by dBASE IV. DTOC performs the opposite function, converting a date into a string of characters. Acceptable characters that can be converted to dates range from "01/01/0100" to "12/31/9999." The full century is optional. Usually, you only specify the last two digits of the year, unless the date falls in a century other than the current one. Any character strings that have values that fall outside this range of values will produce an error message if the CTOD function is used. As an example of the CTOD function, the following command might be used within a program to convert a string of characters to a value that could then be stored within a date field:

```
MYEAR = STR(YEAR(DATE( )))
STORE CTOD("01/01/" + MYEAR) TO JAN1
```

As an example of the DTOC function, the following command would convert a date to a text string and combine it with another:

```
? "The expiration date is: " + DTOC(EXPIREDATE)
```

DTOS

The DTOS function converts a date to a character string that follows the YYYYMMDD format. For example, the DTOS function would convert a date of 12/03/1986 to the character string "19861203". This function is very useful when building indexes based on dates, so that any dates spanning multiple years will appear in the correct chronological order. (If you were to use the DTOC function to build the index instead, dates would only appear in true chronological order if they all occurred within a single year.) As an example, the command

```
INDEX ON DTOS(EXPIREDATE) TAG BYDAYS
```

would create an index in chronological order, with records arranged by order of the expiration date.

SPACE

The SPACE function creates a string of blank spaces, up to a maximum length of 254 spaces. As an example, the following commands make use of a variable called BLANKS, which contains 10 spaces (the variable was created with the SPACE function).

```
STORE SPACE(10) TO BLANKS
LIST LASTNAME + BLANKS + CITY + BLANKS + STATE
```

TRIM

The TRIM function removes trailing blanks or (spaces that follow characters) from a character string. You have already seen this function used in expressions on reports and labels. The expression TRIM(CITY) + ", " + STATE + " " + ZIPCODE, for example, was used to print the contents of the CITY and STATE fields separated by one space. The TRIM function also is useful as part of an expression when displaying information with LIST or DISPLAY to close large gaps of space that often occur between fields. For example, the commands

```
USE ABCSTAFF
GO 2
SET PRINT ON
? FIRSTNAME, LASTNAME, ADDRESS
```

result in an unattractive printout that looks like this:

```
Andrea          Westman            4807 East Avenue
```

Using the TRIM function, the large gaps between the fields can be eliminated, as shown in the following example:

```
USE MEMBERS
GO 2
SET PRINT ON
? TRIM(FIRSTNAME), TRIM(LASTNAME), ADDRESS
```

The printout now looks like this:

Andrea Westman 4807 East Avenue

Note that you should not use the TRIM function as part of an indexing expression, such as INDEX ON TRIM(LASTNAME) + FIRSTNAME TO NAMES. Such an index would result in variable-length index keys, which can cause problems in searching for data.

LTRIM

The LTRIM function performs an operation similar to that of the TRIM function, but it trims leading spaces (spaces that occur at the start of the expression), rather than trailing spaces. The following example shows the effect of the LTRIM function:

```
STORE "          ten leading spaces here." TO TEXT
? TEXT
```

```
        ten leading spaces
? LTRIM(TEXT)
ten leading spaces
```

STR

The STR function is used to convert a numeric value into a character string. This type of conversion lets you mix numeric values with characters within displays and reports. As an example of the STR function, the command

```
? "Name is " + LASTNAME + " and the salary is " + SALARY
```

will produce an operator/operand type mismatch error, because SALARY is a numeric field and the rest of the expression contains character values. You can use the STR function to convert the numeric value into a character value, as follows:

```
? "Name is " + LASTNAME + " and limit is " + STR(SALARY)
```

Some Commonly Used Commands

Some dBASE IV commands are often used within command files but are rarely used elsewhere. Since you will be using command files with increasing regularity in the rest of this book, these commands deserve a closer look. At the end of this chapter, you will begin using the commands to design a program.

SET TALK

SET TALK ON displays on-screen execution of the commands within a command file. When SET TALK OFF is executed within a command file, visual responses to the dBASE IV commands will halt until a SET TALK ON command is encountered. You can use SET TALK OFF to stop the display of such messages as the "% of file indexed" message during indexing or the record number displayed after a GO TO command. When you begin a session with dBASE IV, SET TALK is on.

SKIP

The SKIP command moves the record pointer forward or backward. The format of the command is

SKIP [+/-*integer*]

The integer specified with SKIP will move the pointer forward or backward by that number of records. For example, entering **SKIP 4** moves the record pointer forward by four records. Entering **SKIP -2** moves the record pointer backward by two records. Entering **SKIP** without an expression moves the pointer one record forward.

The values can be stored in a memory variable, which can then be used as part of SKIP. For example, entering **STORE 4 TO JUMP** assigns 4 to JUMP; then entering **SKIP JUMP** moves the record pointer forward by four records. If you attempt to move the record pointer beyond the end of the file or above the beginning of the file, an error message will result.

RETURN

The RETURN command is used to halt the execution of a command file. When a RETURN command is encountered, dBASE IV will return to the dot prompt. If the RETURN command is encountered from within a command file that has been called by another command file, dBASE IV will return to the command file that called the file containing the RETURN command.

ACCEPT and INPUT

Two dBASE IV commands display a string of characters and wait for the user to enter a response that is then stored in a variable. These commands are ACCEPT and INPUT. The ACCEPT command stores characters; the INPUT command stores values. The format for ACCEPT is

ACCEPT "*prompt*" TO *variable-name*

For INPUT, the format is

INPUT "*prompt*" TO *variable-name*

The order of the commands is the same whether you are dealing with characters or numbers. You enter the command, followed by the question or message that is to appear on the screen (which must be enclosed in single or double quotes), followed by TO, followed by the memory variable in which you want to store the response.

HINT ACCEPT works well when you want to ask for a character response, like a name. INPUT works well when you want to ask for a numeric response.

Let's use this format with the ACCEPT statement to store a name in a memory variable. Enter the following:

```
ACCEPT "What is your last name?" TO LNAME
```

When you press ENTER, you'll see the message "What is your last name?" appear on the screen. dBASE IV is waiting for your response, so enter your last name. When the prompt reappears, enter the following:

```
? LNAME
```

(The ? command, as you may recall from earlier use, displays the contents of the expression following the question mark.) You'll see that dBASE IV has indeed stored your last name as a character string within the memory variable LNAME.

The same operation is used for numbers, but you use the INPUT statement instead. For example, enter

```
INPUT "How old are you?" TO AGE
```

In response to the prompt, enter your age. Next, enter

```
? AGE
```

You'll see that the memory variable AGE now contains your response.

COUNT

The COUNT command is used to count a number of occurrences of a condition within a database. One condition might be to count the number of occurrences of the name "Robinson" in a file, another to find out how many employees live in Washington. The general format of COUNT is

COUNT FOR *fieldname = condition* TO *variable-name*

Fieldname is the field that COUNT will search for the occurrence of *condition*; thus, *condition* should match the field type of *fieldname* (if *condition* is a character string, it should be enclosed in quotes). The number of occurrences of *condition* will be stored in *variable-name*. The variable can then be used in another part of the program for calculations or for printing.

As an example, the command

```
COUNT FOR LASTNAME = "Robinson" TO NAMECOUNT
```

would count the occurrences of the last name Robinson in the LASTNAME field of ABCSTAFF. That count would then be stored as a memory variable, NAMECOUNT. The FOR clause, used in this example, is optional. You could accomplish the same type of selective counting by setting a filter with the SET FILTER command and then using the COUNT command.

SUM

The SUM command provides the total for any numeric field. The basic format of the command is

SUM [*scope*] [*field-list*] [FOR *fieldname* = *condition*] [WHILE *fieldname* = *condition*] TO [*variable-list*]

SUM can be used with or without conditions in a number of ways. The *scope* parameter identifies the magnitude of the summation. If *scope* is absent, all records will be checked; if *scope* is NEXT followed by an integer, then only the specified number of records from the current record will be summed. If scope is ALL, all records are summed, which is the same as when no scope is specified. The record pointer is considered to be at the beginning of the current record, so a command like SUM NEXT 5 sums the current record plus the next four records. If *scope* is REST, all records from the current record will be summed. If the word "RECORD" is used instead of a scope, only the current record will be summed (which is rather ridiculous, since there is nothing to add).

The *field-list* parameter is a list of the numeric fields to be summed by the SUM command. Entering **SUM** without a field list will cause dBASE IV to add and display the totals of all the numeric fields within the database.

The *variable-list* parameter assigns the memory variables the values produced by SUM will be stored in. For example, the command

```
SUM SALARY TO TOTAL
```

will store the total of the SALARY field in a memory variable called TOTAL.

```
SUM SALARY, HOURLYRATE TO C,D
```

will store the total of the SALARY field in variable C and the total of the HOURLYRATE field in variable D.

```
SUM SALARY FOR LASTNAME = "Robinson" TO E
```

would store salary amounts for the name Robinson in variable E.

The WHILE clause, which is optional, is used with indexed files to sum the records while (or as long as) a particular condition is in effect. For example, in a file indexed by last names, you could find the first occurrence of the name "Smith" and then use a command like

```
SUM WHILE LASTNAME = "Smith"
```

to obtain the sum of any numeric fields for all the persons named Smith. You can use the FOR clause to accomplish the same task, but in a large database, using WHILE is considerably faster.

AVERAGE

The AVERAGE command calculates the average value of a numeric field. Its basic format is

AVERAGE [FOR *fieldname, ...*] [WHILE *fieldname=condition*] [TO *variable, ...*]

The *fieldname* parameter must be a numeric field (there can be more than one *fieldname*). The average of each *fieldname* will be stored in *variable*.

The command AVERAGE SALARY TO F would store the average value of the SALARY field in variable F.

@, ?, ??, and TEXT

Four commands are commonly used to display or print text: @, ?, ??, and TEXT. The ? and ?? commands will display a single line of text at a time. If ? is used, a linefeed and carriage return occur before the display. A ?? command does not include the linefeed and carriage return operation before the display.

If the ? or ?? command is preceded by a SET PRINT ON command, output is also routed to the printer. An example is shown in the following command file:

```
SET PRINT ON
? "The last name is: "
?? LASTNAME
?
? "The salary per 40-hour week is: "
?? SALARY * 40
SET PRINT OFF
```

You can also add the optional AT clause and a column position to the ? or ?? commands to control where on the line the data appears. For example, the command

```
? "Lastname:" AT 26
```

would print "Lastname:" starting at column 26 on the current line.

For more selective printing or display, the @ command moves the cursor to a specific location on the screen, and when combined with SAY displays the information there. dBASE IV divides the screen into 24 rows and 80 columns. The top-left coordinate is 0,0, and the bottom-right coordinate is 23,79. The general format of the @ command is as follows:

@ *row,column* [SAY *character-string*]

To try this, enter

```
CLEAR

@ 12, 20 SAY "This is a display"
```

Using the @ command with the SAY option, you can generate report headings or statements at any required location. Screen formatting with the @ command will be covered in greater detail in Chapter 15.

The TEXT command is useful for displaying large amounts of text. TEXT is commonly used to display operator warnings, menu displays, and notes that appear during various operations of the program. TEXT is followed by the text to be displayed, and then ended with ENDTEXT. The text need not be surrounded by quotes. Everything between TEXT and ENDTEXT is displayed.

The following example will erase the screen with CLEAR and then display a copyright message:

```
CLEAR
TEXT
****************************************************************
        dBASE IV Copyright (C) 1988 Ashton-Tate
Personnel Director Copyright (C) 1987 J Systems, Inc.
For technical support, phone our offices at 555-5555
****************************************************************
ENDTEXT
```

The TEXT command must be used from within a command file. Any attempt to use TEXT as a direct command will result in an error message.

Overview of a Program Design

Programming involves more than entering commands and statements into the computer correctly—in fact, that's the simplest part. Programming requires careful planning of the code and rigorous testing afterward. How do you start to write a program, and after it is operational, how do you determine whether the program is efficient? Unfortunately, there is no one correct way to write a program or determine when it is efficient or good.

However, most programmers have a natural tendency to follow five steps in the design of a program:

1. Defining the problem
2. Designing the program
3. Writing the program
4. Verifying the program
5. Documenting the program

As these steps imply, the process of good programming is more than just writing a series of commands to be used in a particular command file. If you are programming, you are probably building *applications* (which are a group of programs that perform a general task). Designing an application is somewhat similar to the process of designing a database (outlined in Chapter 2), but because you are designing an application and not a database, you must think about how the application will use information in the source database, how the application will produce reports, and how the application can be designed so that it is easy to use. Once these design steps have been clearly defined, you can proceed to design and create the programs that will make up the application.

Designing and Writing a Program

Since most applications begin with a menu of choices, the menu module is normally written first. Each selection within the menu should then lead to the part of the program that performs the appropriate function. For example, selecting a Run Report option from a menu could result in a REPORT FORM command being issued to print a report. An Add New Entries option could activate an APPEND command that adds data to the database.

When you design your own systems, you'll find it helpful to design the menu first and then use it as a starting point for the other modules in the program. In this example, however, you will design the menu module of the program in the next chapter, because it will use various commands that will be explained there.

It often helps, particularly if you are new to designing programs, to use *pseudocode*. Pseudocode is the English equivalent to the dBASE IV language. You write the program in pseudocode and then convert it into actual code. For instance, the process that would allow users to display a list of names and edit a particular name would look like this in pseudocode:

1. Clear screen

2. List all names in the database

3. Ask user for number of record to be edited, and store that number as a variable

4. Edit specified record

5. Return to main menu

When you know what steps are needed to perform the task, you store the corresponding commands in a command file. As an example, enter

```
MODIFY COMMAND CHANGES
```

to create a new command file called CHANGES.PRG. When the dBASE editor appears, enter the following commands, and then choose Save Changes and Exit from the Exit menu to save the command file:

```
CLEAR
LIST LASTNAME, FIRSTNAME
INPUT "Edit what record?" TO RECNO
EDIT RECNO
RETURN
```

Verifying the Program

Any errors in the program are corrected during this step. The program is also examined to see if the needs of all users have indeed been met; if not, you may need to make changes or additions to some modules. In addition, you should now make any improvements that can speed up the system or minimize user confusion.

The best way to find errors in a program is to use the program, so verify the program's operation by entering

```
DO CHANGES
```

The program will display a list of all employee names. The corresponding record numbers will be shown to the left of the names:

```
Record#     LASTNAME     FIRSTNAME
      1     Morse        Marcia
      2     Westman      Andrea
```

```
3       Jackson      David
4       Mitchell     Mary Jo
5       Robinson     Shirley
6       Jackson      Cheryl
7       Robinson     Wanda
8       Hart         Edward
9       Jones        Judi

Edit what record?
```

The last line of the program now asks for the number of the record that you wish to edit. In response to the prompt, enter **8** (for record 8). If the program works as designed, the Edit screen for record 8 should appear. Change the salary for Edward Hart to 10.50, and save the change by pressing CTRL-END. (Later, as a convenience for users unfamiliar with dBASE IV, you may want to display a message explaining how to save changes.)

You should return to the dBASE IV prompt, and for now, that is all that is expected of the program. In later chapters, you'll add commands that will use more attractive designs, like the data entry screen you created in Chapter 5, to view and edit data.

Documenting the Program

The *documentation* of a program takes one of two forms: written directions (like a manual) explaining how the program operates, and comments within the program itself about how the program is designed. The use of clear and simple menus and instructions within the program can help minimize the need for written documentation. A few sentences on how to start dBASE IV and run the command file that displays the menu may be sufficient. For directions and remarks within the program, dBASE IV lets you put comments, in the form of text, at any location in a command file. Comments are preceded by an asterisk (*) or by the

NOTE command. When dBASE IV sees a line beginning with an asterisk or the word "NOTE," no action is taken by the program.

Comments are simply an aid to you or any other person who modifies your command files. For example, this short command file documents the program with NOTE and the asterisk (*):

```
CLEAR
NOTE Display the employees' names
LIST LASTNAME, FIRSTNAME
NOTE Ask for a record number and store it.
INPUT "Edit what record?" TO RECNO
*Edit the record.
EDIT RECNO
RETURN
```

This file may seem to have an overabundance of comments because it does not need elaboration. If a command file consists of dozens of commands, however, comments become more necessary. Not only do they make the program easier to understand, but if any other person must make changes to your dBASE IV program, the task will be much easier.

Quick Reference

To create a dBASE IV program At the dot prompt, enter **MODIFY COMMAND *filename***, where *filename* is the name to be assigned to the program file. From the Control Center, select the Create option of the Applications panel, and from the next menu to appear, choose dBASE Program.

When the dBASE editor appears, enter the desired statements, one on each line. You can enter a long statement on two lines by placing a semicolon (;) at the end of the first line. When done, press CTRL-END (or choose Save Changes and Exit from the Exit menu) to save the program.

To run a program At the dot prompt, enter **DO *filename***, where *filename* is the name of the program file. From the Control Center, select the program from the Applications panel, then select Run Application from the next menu to appear. (Note that programs created at the dot prompt will not appear in the Applications panel, unless you use the Add File to Catalog option of the Catalog menu to add them to a catalog.)

To design a program First define the problem the program is to solve, and then design the overall layout of the program in modular parts. You can then proceed to write the program based on the design.

CHAPTER

Decision Making Within a dBASE IV Program

The ability of command files to automate the storing and retrieval of records provides even more flexibility when you use decision-making conditions from within a command file. A program can prompt the user for a response, and the user's response will determine what the program does next.

To program a condition, you will need a way to evaluate user responses and, based on those responses, cause dBASE IV to perform certain actions. In this chapter you'll use the IF, ELSE,

ENDIF, DO WHILE, and ENDDO commands to perform these operations within a program.

Going in Circles

There will be many times when your program will need to perform the same task repeatedly. dBASE IV has two commands, DO WHILE and ENDDO, that are used as a matched pair to repeat a series of commands for as long as necessary. The commands that you wish to repeat are enclosed between the DO WHILE and the ENDDO commands.

The DO WHILE command always begins the loop, and the ENDDO command normally ends the loop. The series of commands contained within the DO WHILE loop will continue to execute until the condition specified immediately next to the DO WHILE command is no longer true. You determine when the loop should stop by specifying the condition; otherwise, the loop could go on indefinitely. The format of the command is

DO WHILE *condition*
        [*commands...*]
ENDDO

As long as the condition within the DO WHILE loop is true, the commands between the DO WHILE and the ENDDO commands are executed. Whenever ENDDO is reached, dBASE IV evaluates the condition to see if it is still true. If it is true, dBASE IV executes the commands within the loop again; if the condition is not true, dBASE IV jumps to the command following the ENDDO command. If the condition is false when the DO WHILE command is first encountered, none of the commands in the loop are executed, and the program proceeds to the first command that follows the ENDDO command.

REMEMBER ENDDO is a matching statement for DO WHILE. For every DO WHILE there must be an ENDDO or you will encounter errors in your program.

You could use the DO WHILE and ENDDO commands in a command file that will print the names and addresses in the ABC Temporaries database with triple line spacing between them. Get to the dot prompt, and then open a command file and call it TRIPLE by entering

```
MODIFY COMMAND TRIPLE
```

When the dBASE IV editor comes up, enter the following command file:

```
SET TALK OFF
USE ABCSTAFF
SET PRINT ON
DO WHILE .NOT. EOF()
        ? FIRSTNAME + LASTNAME
        ? ADDRESS
        ? CITY + STATE + " " + ZIPCODE
        ?
        ?
        ?
        SKIP
ENDDO
? "Triple report completed."
SET PRINT OFF
EJECT
```

HINT After indenting lines, you can get back to the left margin with SHIFT-TAB.

Before you save this command file, take a brief look at its design. After such preliminaries as activating the ABCSTAFF file and routing the output to the printer, the program begins the DO WHILE loop. The condition for the DO WHILE is .NOT. EOF( ), which simply means, "As long as the end of the file is not reached, continue the DO WHILE loop." The first three statements in the loop print the name and address from the current record. The next three question marks print the three blank lines between each name and address. SKIP moves the pointer down a record each time the body of the DO WHILE loop is executed. If this command were absent, the pointer would never reach the end of the file, the condition would never be false, and the program would never leave the loop. The ENDDO command is then reached, so dBASE IV returns to the DO WHILE statement to evaluate the condition. If the pointer hasn't reached the end of the file, the loop is repeated. Once the end of the file has been reached, dBASE IV proceeds past the ENDDO command. The final three commands in the program are executed, and you are returned to the dot prompt.

Indenting the commands between DO WHILE and ENDDO will help you identify the body of the loop. This is especially helpful if you have nested DO WHILE loops—a DO WHILE loop within a DO WHILE loop.

After you enter the commands in the file, press CTRL-END to save the command file to disk; then make sure your printer is on, and enter **DO TRIPLE**. The command file will print the names and addresses on your printer using triple line spacing between each name.

SCAN and ENDSCAN

Another set of commands that you may encounter as you work with dBASE programs is SCAN and ENDSCAN. These commands, like DO WHILE and ENDDO, are a matched pair, and like DO WHILE and ENDDO, they let you create a repetitive loop in which operations are performed for a group of records in a database. The syntax for these commands is

SCAN [*scope*] [FOR *condition*] [WHILE *condition*]
    [*commands...*]
ENDSCAN

SCAN and ENDSCAN are simpler alternatives to the DO WHILE and ENDDO commands. If you simply wish to use DO WHILE and ENDDO to perform repetitive processing, you can often use SCAN and ENDSCAN instead and use slightly fewer lines of programming code. As an example, perhaps you wanted to write a program that would use a DO WHILE loop to print the name and salary for every person in the database who earns more than $9.00 per hour. You could accomplish the task with a program like this:

```
USE ABCSTAFF
SET PRINT ON
DO WHILE .NOT. EOF( )
        IF SALARY > 9
```

```
        ? LASTNAME, FIRSTNAME
        ?? SALARY
    ENDIF
    SKIP
ENDDO
```

By comparison, you could use the SCAN and ENDSCAN commands to accomplish the same task. An example of the program code if you use SCAN and ENDSCAN is shown here:

```
USE ABCSTAFF
SET PRINT ON
SCAN FOR SALARY > 9
    ? LASTNAME, FIRSTNAME
    ?? SALARY
ENDSCAN
```

Because you combine FOR or WHILE clauses with the SCAN command to specify the condition (a salary greater than $9.00), the IF and ENDIF conditionals are not needed; hence, less lines of program code accomplish the same task.

IF, ELSE, and ENDIF

In many command files, dBASE IV will need to perform different operations depending on the user's response to a condition from a previous calculation or operation, or depending on different values encountered in a database. For example, if the user has a choice of editing or printing a record in a main menu, the program must be able to perform the chosen operation. dBASE IV lets you use the IF, ELSE, and ENDIF commands to branch to the part of the program where the chosen operation is performed.

Like the DO WHILE and ENDDO commands, the IF and ENDIF commands are used as a matched pair enclosing a number of commands. The ELSE command is optional and is used within the body of IF-ENDIF as another decision step. The IF command along with the ENDIF command can be used to decide between actions in a program. The format of the command is

```
IF condition
        [command...]
ELSE
        [command...]
ENDIF
```

This decision-making command must always start with IF and end with ENDIF. The commands that you place between the IF and ENDIF commands determine exactly what will occur if *condition* is true, unless an ELSE is encountered.

A good way to write IF, ELSE, and ENDIF commands is to write them in pseudocode first and then compare them:

Pseudocode	**dBASE IV**
If last name is Cooke, then display last name.	IF LASTNAME = "Cooke" ? LASTNAME ENDIF
If monthly rent is less than $300, then display "Reasonably priced."	IF RENTMONTH < 300 ? "Reasonably priced" ENDIF

Using IF and ENDIF alone will work fine for making a single decision, but if you wish to add an alternative choice, you'll need the ELSE statement:

Pseudocode	**dBASE IV**

If last name is Cooke, then print last name; or else print "There is no one by that name in this database."	IF LASTNAME = "Cooke"
	? LASTNAME
	ELSE
	? "There is no one by that name in this database."
	ENDIF

dBASE IV will evaluate the condition following the IF command to see if any action should be taken. If no action is necessary, dBASE IV will simply move on to the next command after the ENDIF command. In the example

```
IF SALARY = 10
     STORE SALARY TO MATCH
ENDIF
```

if SALARY is not 10, the STORE command will not be executed and dBASE IV will proceed to the command following ENDIF. You can also use multiple IF-ENDIF commands if you need to have the program make more than one decision. Consider this example:

```
? "Enter 1 to print mailing labels or 2 to edit."
INPUT "What is your choice?" TO CHOICE
IF CHOICE = 1
     DO TRIPLE
ENDIF
IF CHOICE = 2
     DO CHANGES
ENDIF
```

The answer that the user types will be stored in a variable called CHOICE. One of two things can happen then, depending on whether the user types 1 or 2 in response to the question. If CHOICE equals 1, the TRIPLE program will be run from disk. If CHOICE equals 2, the CHANGES program will be run. If CHOICE does not equal 1 or 2, the program will proceed to the next command after the ENDIF command. Again, indenting the commands within the body of IF-ENDIF will make the flow of thc program easier to follow.

Nesting IF-ENDIF Statements

You can use nested IF-ENDIF statements, which are IF-ENDIF statements placed inside of other IF-ENDIF statements. For the innermost IF-ENDIF statement to be processed, the condition tested by the outermost IF-ENDIF statement must be true. The following is an example of a nested IF-ENDIF statement:

```
INPUT "Display report on (S)creen or (P)rinter?" TO ANS
IF UPPER(ANS) = "P"
   INPUT "Ready printer, press Enter, or type C then;
   press ENTER to cancel report." TO ANS2
   IF UPPER(ANS2) = "C"
      *user cancelled print run.
      RETURN
   ENDIF
   REPORT FORM MEMBERS TO PRINT
   EJECT
ENDIF
```

In this example, whether the innermost IF-ENDIF is ever processed is determined by the response supplied to the outermost IF-ENDIF statement. If the user does not input "P" for printer, dBASE skips ahead to the outermost ENDIF statement. If the user does respond with "P" for printer, dBASE displays the "Ready printer" message, and the innermost IF-ENDIF tests for a response, and takes appropriate action.

HINT If you are going to nest IF-ENDIF statements, indenting helps keep track of whether you have a matching statement (an ENDIF for each IF).

The Immediate IF Function

Within programs, you may want to make use of the Immediate IF( ) function. The syntax for the function is

IIF(*condition, expression1, expression2*)

If the condition specified is true, dBASE IV returns the first expression; if the condition is false, dBASE IV returns the second expression. Note that *expression1* and *expression2* must be of the same data type. As an example, the statement

```
CREDITOK = IIF(INCOME=15000, "yes", "no")
```

would, when processed in a program, store a character expression of "yes" to the CREDITOK variable if the amount in INCOME was equal to or greater than 15,000. In effect, this statement performs the same task as the following commands:

```
IF INCOME = 15000
   CREDITOK = "yes"
ELSE
   CREDITOK = "no"
ENDIF
```

The advantage of the Immediate IF function is that it takes less lines of code to accomplish the same task, and it is executed slightly faster.

You can use IF and ENDIF commands in a command file to search for and display the data regarding a specific entry in the database. If you want to find an employee named Mitchell, you can use the ACCEPT and IF-ENDIF commands to search for the record. (This operation can be done faster with SEEK, but for demonstration purposes IF and DO WHILE will be used here.) First use pseudocode to outline what needs to be done:

USE ABCSTAFF database
ACCEPT the last name
BEGIN the DO-WHILE loop
IF the last name field = the ACCEPT variable
PRINT (on the screen) name, address, salary, hourly rate, and date of hire
END the IF test
SKIP forward one record
END the DO-WHILE loop
RETURN to the dBASE IV dot prompt

Now create a command file by entering

```
MODIFY COMMAND SHOW
```

When the dBASE IV editor appears, enter the following command file:

```
*This command file finds and displays data in a record.
USE ABCSTAFF
SET TALK OFF
CLEAR
*Begin loop that contains commands to display record.
ACCEPT "Search for what last name? " TO SNAME
DO WHILE .NOT. EOF( )
```

```
        IF LASTNAME = SNAME
        ? "Last name is: "
        ?? LASTNAME
        ? "First name is: "
        ?? FIRSTNAME
        ? "Address is: "
        ?? ADDRESS
        ? CITY + STATE + " " + ZIPCODE
        ?
        ? "Salary is: "
        ?? SALARY
        ? "Billing rate is: "
        ?? HOURLYRATE
        ? "Date of hire is: "
        ?? DATEHIRED
        ?
        ENDIF
        SKIP
ENDDO
WAIT
RETURN
```

When the prompt reappears, try the program by entering **DO SHOW**. In response to the last-name prompt that appears on the screen, enter **Mitchell**, and dBASE IV will search the database for the record containing "Mitchell."

In this search you used the ACCEPT, IF, and ENDIF commands. The ACCEPT command stored the name that you entered into the memory variable SNAME. The IF loop began a decision-making process that stated the condition, "If the memory variable SNAME contains the same name as the LASTNAME field, then execute the commands that follow the IF command."

There is no limit to the number of commands that you can place between IF and ENDIF in the loop. You can also link multiple IF-ENDIF and ELSE commands if multiple choices are needed within a program.

The CASE Statement

Your program may need to make more than two or three decisions from a single response. A series of IF-ENDIF statements could do the job, but using more than three IF-ENDIFs to test one procedure is unwieldy. There is an easier way: the CASE statement. With the CASE statement, the IF-ENDIF tests are made into cases, and dBASE IV then chooses the first case, the second case, or another case.

The CASE statement is a matched pair of DO CASE and ENDCASE. All choices are declared between DO CASE and ENDCASE. OTHERWISE is treated exactly like the ELSE in an IF-ENDIF statement. The general format is

```
DO CASE
        CASE condition
        [commands...]
        [CASE condition...]
        [commands...]
        [OTHERWISE]
        [commands...]
ENDCASE
```

Whenever dBASE IV encounters a DO CASE command, it will examine each case until it finds a condition that is true; then it will execute the commands below the CASE until it encounters the next CASE statement or ENDCASE, whichever comes first.

If you want to create a menu that offers to display a record, print labels, edit a record, or add a record, you could create a command file like this one:

```
? "1. Display a record"
?
? "2. Print the database"
?
? "3. Change a record"
?
INPUT "Choose a selection" TO SELECT
DO CASE
        CASE SELECT = 1
                DO SHOW
        CASE SELECT = 2
                DO TRIPLE
        CASE SELECT = 3
                DO CHANGES
ENDCASE
```

In this example, dBASE IV will query the user for a selection with the INPUT statement (the CHANGES file for the third selection was created in the last chapter). When the user enters the choice, it will be stored in the variable SELECT. Then, in the DO CASE series, dBASE IV will examine the SELECT variable for each CASE until it finds one that matches the value of SELECT. Once a match has been found, no other CASE statement will be evaluated. If no match is found, dBASE IV will proceed to the next statement after the ENDCASE command. Like IF-ENDIF, the DO CASE-ENDCASE commands are used in pairs; you must always end a CASE series with an ENDCASE command.

You should use DO CASE if you have more than three choices. For example, if you wanted to offer the same three selections from the last program by using IF-ENDIF and ELSE, the command file might look like this:

```
? "1. Display a record"
?
? "2. Print the database"
?
? "3. Change a record"
?
INPUT "Choose a selection" TO SELECT
```

```
IF SELECT = 1
      DO SHOW
ENDIF
IF SELECT = 2
      DO TRIPLE
ENDIF
IF SELECT = 3
      DO CHANGES
ENDIF
```

Using IF-ENDIF is more complex than using DO CASE as the number of choices increases.

Let's use a CASE statement to create a main menu for the users of the ABC Temporaries database. Enter **MODIFY COMMAND MENU**, and when the dBASE IV editor appears, enter the following command file:

```
USE ABCSTAFF
SET TALK OFF
STORE 0 TO CHOICE
DO WHILE CHOICE < 5
        CLEAR
        * Display the menu.
        ? "ABC Temporaries Database System Menu"
        ?
        ? " 1. Add a new entry to the database."
        ? " 2. Change an existing entry."
        ? " 3. Produce the personnel report."
        ? " 4. Display data regarding a particular employee."
        ? " 5. Exit this program."
INPUT "Enter selection: " TO CHOICE
DO CASE
           CASE CHOICE=1
           APPEND
           CASE CHOICE=2
           DO CHANGES
           CASE CHOICE=3
           REPORT FORM RFORM1
           CASE CHOICE=4
           DO SHOW
           CASE CHOICE=5
```

```
        CLOSE DATABASES
        SET TALK ON
        RETURN
ENDCASE
ENDDO
```

There are five choices, and the INPUT command stores the response in the corresponding CHOICE variable. When dBASE IV finds a matching choice, it executes the command that follows that choice.

Save this command file by pressing CTRL-END. When the prompt reappears, enter **DO MENU**. Try some of the menu choices on your own to see how the system operates.

EXIT

The EXIT command is used when you are within a DO WHILE-ENDDO programming loop. EXIT lets dBASE IV exit from a DO WHILE-ENDDO loop to the first command below ENDDO. An EXIT command arbitrarily placed within a DO WHILE-ENDDO loop will prevent dBASE IV from ever reaching the commands below EXIT to ENDDO; thus, EXIT only makes sense if it is executed conditionally. For this reason, you will frequently find EXIT commands with IF-ENDIF and CASE statements.

Consider the following example, in which a program lists a name based on a desired address. The same task could be done with a LOCATE command, but for purposes of demonstrating the EXIT command, this program uses a DO WHILE-ENDDO loop.

```
USE ABCSTAFF
SET TALK OFF
GO TOP
```

```
ACCEPT "What is the address- " TO CHOICE
DO WHILE .NOT. EOF()
   IF ADDRESS = CHOICE
      ? LASTNAME, FIRSTNAME
      EXIT
   ENDIF
   SKIP
ENDDO
```

If the contents of ADDRESS, a field, match CHOICE, a variable, the EXIT command will cause the DO WHILE loop to terminate. If no match is found, the commands below the IF will be executed and finally will drop from the loop when the last record is accessed.

Use EXITs conservatively: a program that is always jumping out of loops, and around the program for that matter, is difficult to follow and debug, contrary to good program design. Most DO WHILE loops that have EXITs can be redesigned without them.

CANCEL

The CANCEL command will exit a dBASE IV command file and return you to the dot prompt. It can be useful when you are testing various commands and program files; however, using CANCEL in a completed dBASE IV program may be unwise. CANCEL will drop the user at the dot prompt, and the inexperienced user may not know how to exit dBASE IV to DOS or return to the program. QUIT is used more often to exit programs and return to the DOS prompt. You can add a selection at the main menu that executes a QUIT command to let the user get out of dBASE IV and back to the computer's operating system when the work is completed.

WAIT

The WAIT command halts execution of a dBASE IV program until a key is pressed. WAIT can optionally display a message or prompt and store the value of the key pressed as a character variable. The format of the command is

WAIT *prompt* [TO *memory variable name*]

Both the prompt and the memory variable name are options. If a prompt is not specified, dBASE IV supplies the message "Press any key to continue..." as a default prompt. For example, to display a message, halt execution of a program until a key is pressed, and store that key as a variable named ANSWER, the following command might be used:

```
WAIT "Enter Y to begin processing transactions, any other key to continue:" TO
ANSWER
```

You could then use an IF-ELSE-ENDIF structure to test the value of ANSWER, and take different actions depending on the result.

ZAP

The ZAP command is a one-step command for erasing all records from a database while leaving the structure of the database intact. Using ZAP is functionally equivalent to entering DELETE ALL and then entering PACK, but ZAP operates considerably faster. If you include ZAP in a program, you may want to include a SET SAFETY OFF command near the start of the program; this tells dBASE IV not to ask for confirmation before erasing all records from the file.

Using Programming Macros

dBASE IV has a handy macro-substitution function. (It is used specifically within programs, and is not to be confused with the types of macros covered in Chapter 9.) Macro substitution works by placing an ampersand (&) in front of a memory variable name. This combination of ampersand and variable name becomes the dBASE IV macro. Then, whenever dBASE IV sees that macro, it will replace it with the contents of the memory variable. If, for example, you had a memory variable called NAME, you could store names of people in variables at different times during a program. When you prefix NAME with an ampersand, it become a macro. Each time dBASE IV encounters &NAME, it references the value of &NAME instead of the name of the variable. Try a macro operation in interactive mode by entering the following commands from the dot prompt:

```
USE MEMBERS
INDEX ON LASTNAME TO NAME
STORE "Zachman" TO TEST
FIND &TEST
DISPLAY
```

Commands that require literal values can also use macros to convert a variable to a literal when the program runs. One such command is FIND. With the FIND command, you normally would be required to enter the literal value or the actual name of the item to be found. But with the macro function, you can substitute a variable for the actual name. In this example, you could have easily specified the contents of the variable instead of creating the variable to use as a macro. Using macros saves time in programming since the variable probably exists in your program. You can use macro substitution in response to a user's query to search a database selectively for information. Once you have found the item, you can edit or delete it. An example of these techniques will be used in a routine for editing records in the next chapter.

Quick Reference

Use DO WHILE and ENDDO To repeat a series of statements a specified number of times. All statements between a DO WHILE command and the corresponding ENDDO command will be repeated for as long as the condition specified by the DO WHILE statement is true.

Use SCAN and ENDSCAN As simpler alternatives to DO WHILE and ENDDO when you are testing all records in a file for a given condition. SCAN and ENDSCAN start at the beginning of a database, and process records until the end of the database is reached. For each record, if the condition named in the SCAN statement is true, the statements between SCAN and ENDSCAN are carried out.

Use IF and ENDIF To make conditional decisions, such as "IF age is greater than 21, DISPLAY this record." When the condition specified by the IF statement is true, all statements between the IF statement and ENDIF statement (or an optional ELSE statement) are carried out. Use the optional ELSE statement between IF and ENDIF to specify statements between the ELSE and the ENDIF that should be carried out when the condition specified by IF is not true.

Use DO CASE, CASE, and ENDCASE To make one selection out of a group of possible selections.

Use CANCEL To cancel the execution of a program and return to the dot prompt or the Control Center (if the program was started from the Control Center).

Use WAIT To temporarily halt program execution and wait for the user to press a key.

CHAPTER

15

Programming for Data Entry and Editing

dBASE IV can help you design screen displays that will not confuse the people who use your database management system. The appearance of screen displays may at first seem like a minor point of importance. However, if you were a new dBASE IV system user, which of the two screen displays in Figure 15-1 would be easier to use: the top screen (*a*) or the bottom screen (*b*)?

Obviously, the bottom screen will make more sense to the novice user of dBASE IV; it is clearer and less cluttered than the top screen. As you will see in this chapter, you can easily create well-designed screens by storing various screen-display com-

Figure 15-1.

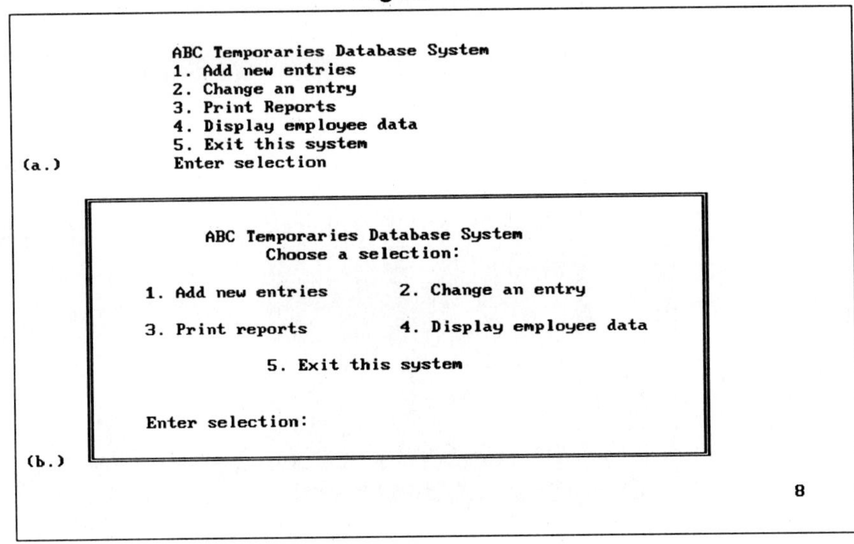

Badly designed (a) and well-designed (b) screen displays

mands within a dBASE IV command file. You'll use the @, SAY, and GET commands to place prompts and information at selected locations on the screen, and the READ command to allow responses to the prompts displayed by the system. You'll also examine how the Form Design screen can provide most of the commands you need to format screens.

Putting Information on the Screen

The @ command (commonly referred to as the "at" command) tells dBASE IV where to place the cursor on the screen. The dBASE IV screen is divided into 25 lines and 80 columns, as shown in Figure 15-2. Rows are numbered from 0 to 24, and columns are

Figure 15-2.

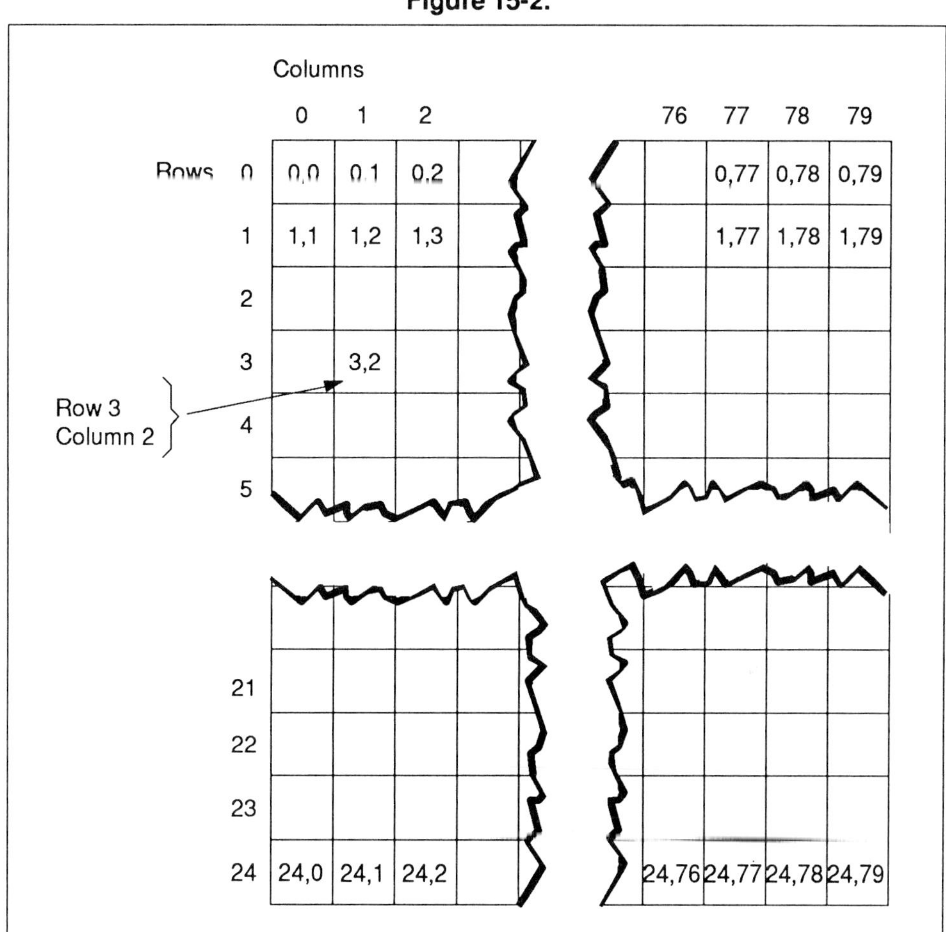

Screen coordinates

numbered from 0 to 79. Row 0, column 0 is in the upper-left corner of the screen. Row 24, column 79 is in the lower-right corner. The cursor can be placed in any screen position.

Once the cursor has been placed in the proper position with the @ command, you can print a message with the SAY option. It causes the text or the contents of a string variable that follows the command to appear on the screen. The SAY option can be used, along with the @ command, in one of two possible formats:

@ *row,column* SAY "*message*"

or

@ *row,column* SAY *varname*

In the first format, SAY is followed by one or more characters, which must be enclosed by double or single quotes. (You should use double quotes whenever there is an apostrophe in the message itself.) The characters will be displayed on the screen exactly as they appear between the quotes. In the second format, *varname* is a variable name. Any value that your program stores in that variable will be displayed.

To try the first format, let's display a message beginning at row 12, column 40 on the screen. Get to the dot prompt, and then enter

```
CLEAR
@ 12,40 SAY "Enter name."
```

This displays the prompt "Enter name." beginning at row 12, column 40 on the screen.

Now let's try the second format. Enter this:

```
STORE 1200.57 TO AMOUNT
@ 6,30 SAY AMOUNT
```

This stores 1200.57 in the variable AMOUNT and then displays the value at row 6, column 30.

! ***HINT*** When calculating screen locations, figure the possible length of an expression to be sure it will fit. For example, you would not want to display a 30-character field at row 5, column 55, because it would wrap onto the next line.

Keep in mind that when you use the @ command and SAY option to design screen displays, the coordinates for the edges of the screen may or may not actually be displayed at your screen's edges. Some monitors cut off the edges, so to be safe you may want to stay away from the outer edges of the screen. Because dBASE IV puts system and error messages on lines 22, 23, and 24 on the screen, it is a good idea to avoid these lines altogether.

You can erase any part of the screen with the @ command and CLEAR option. The format for this is

@ *row,column* CLEAR

The screen beginning at *row,column* will be erased to the lower-right corner. You use the @ command and CLEAR option in a manner similar to the @ command and SAY option, but don't enter any prompts or variables after the word "CLEAR." As an example, the command

```
@ 9,7 CLEAR
```

would erase the screen from row 9, column 7 to the lower-right corner.

Using GET and READ with @ and SAY

Now that you know how to display information at selected places on the screen, you need a way to store responses to screen prompts. This is done with two new options, GET and READ.

Used together, they display existing variables or field names and the field length of the record being referenced by the pointer, as well as storing the typed replies to screen messages and prompts. There are two formats:

@ *row,column* SAY "*prompt*" GET *varname*... READ

and

@ *row,column* SAY "*prompt*" GET *fieldname*... READ

The GET option tells dBASE IV to get ready to accept information. The information displayed with GET can be either an existing memory variable or any field in the database in use. The READ command then tells dBASE IV to enter full-screen Edit mode, which allows the user to move the cursor around the screen; to accept responses from the keyboard for any of the preceding GET options; and to store the responses in memory. In addition, the READ option lets you edit the displayed information. A READ command applies to all GET statements between the READ command and any previous use of the READ command, or the start of the program, whichever is closest.

A GET option does not have to be immediately followed by a READ option; it can be the last command in a series of GETs. If you use a GET without READ, however, you cannot enter any responses from the keyboard. READ options are only used following GET options. You could, for example, create a command file like this one:

```
@ 5,10 SAY "Enter name." GET LASTNAME
@ 7,10 SAY "Enter address." GET ADDRESS
@ 9,10 SAY "Enter city." GET CITY
@ 11,10 SAY "Enter state." GET STATE
READ
```

If you were to use the database containing the field names and run this command file, dBASE IV would provide a screen display that would prompt you for the desired information. The prompts would appear at the screen locations identified by the @ command and SAY option. Once the READ option was encountered, the full-screen Edit mode would be entered, and the cursor would be placed at the start of the first area identified by a GET option. As data was entered, dBASE IV would store all of the entries in memory under the field names or variable names used. The name would be stored in LASTNAME, the address in ADDRESS, the city in CITY, and so on. Once a READ occurred, data entered under the field names would be written to the database file itself.

You could also use the INPUT command along with a prompt to place information on the screen and store a response. With INPUT, however, it is not easy to specify where on the screen the information appears. The example that follows will show how the use of the @ command and the SAY, GET, and READ options can result in a clear, well-designed menu screen.

Designing a Menu With @, SAY, and GET

You now have a main menu system for the ABC Temporaries database, but it uses ? and INPUT commands that do not provide much flexibility when it comes to placing the information on the screen. To change this, you must get into the dBASE IV editor and edit the command file used to display the menu. Enter this:

```
MODIFY COMMAND MENU
```

When the dBASE IV editor appears, the menu command file you developed in Chapter 14 will appear along with it. Change the file so it looks like this one:

```
USE ABCSTAFF
SET TALK OFF
STORE 0 TO CHOICE
DO WHILE CHOICE < 5
    CLEAR
    *Display main menu.
    @ 5,15 SAY "ABC Temporaries Database System Menu"
    @ 7,18 SAY "Choose a selection shown below:"
    @ 10, 5 SAY "1 Add new entries."
    @ 10,34 SAY "3 Produce Reports"
    @ 12, 5 SAY "2 Change existing entries."
    @ 12,34 SAY "4 Display employee data"
    @ 15,21 SAY "5 Exit this program."
    @ 4, 3 TO 20,60 DOUBLE
    * above line draws double line box around menu.*
    @ 19,7 SAY "Enter selection: " GET CHOICE
    READ
    DO CASE
        CASE CHOICE = 1
            APPEND
        CASE CHOICE = 2
            DO CHANGES
        CASE CHOICE = 3
            REPORT FORM RFORM1
        CASE CHOICE = 4
            DO SHOW
        CASE CHOICE = 5
            RETURN
    ENDCASE
ENDDO
```

When you have finished entering the command file, choose Save Changes and Exit from the Exit menu to save it. You then might want to try using the system; start it by entering **DO MENU**. Choose the menu choice for adding a record, and while you are watching the system's operation, you might want to think about ways to improve further on the system design. Perhaps you can modify the command files used by your system, so that other choices from the menu will provide screen displays that are easy to understand. When you are finished using the system, the CTRL-END key combination will get you out of Edit or Append mode and back to the system menu.

Customizing a Data Entry Screen

One area of the system that could stand improvement is in the adding of data. Currently, the system relies on the APPEND command. With the @ command and the SAY, GET, and READ options, you can display the prompts more neatly than you could with the APPEND command and you can store the data in the fields of the database. Let's create a new command file, called ADDER, that will be used whenever you want to add a record to the database. Enter **MODIFY COMMAND ADDER**, and enter the following as the command file:

```
USE ABCSTAFF
CLEAR
APPEND BLANK
@ 1,0 SAY "Social Sec.:" GET SOCIALSEC
@ 2,0 SAY "Lastname:" GET LASTNAME
@ 3,0 SAY "Firstname:" GET FIRSTNAME
@ 4,0 SAY "Address:" GET ADDRESS
@ 5,0 SAY "City:" GET CITY
@ 6,0 SAY "State:" GET STATE
@ 7,0 SAY "ZIP Code:" GET ZIPCODE
@ 8,0 SAY "Telephone:" GET PHONE
@ 9,0 SAY "Birth date:" GET BIRTHDAY
@ 10,0 SAY "Hire Date:" GET DATEHIRED
@ 11,0 SAY "Dependents:" GET DEPENDENTS
@ 12,0 SAY "Salary:" GET SALARY
@ 13,0 SAY "Assignment:" GET ASSIGNMENT
@ 14,0 SAY "Hourly Rate:" GET HOURLYRATE
```

```
@ 15,0 SAY "Evaluate:" GET EVALUATE
READ
RETURN
```

You should examine this command file before you save it. After opening the file with USE and clearing the screen, you then use the BLANK option of the APPEND command. Whenever dBASE IV sees APPEND BLANK as a command, it adds a blank record to the end of the database, and the record pointer is positioned at the last record. Each @ command and SAY option prints a query, such as "Birth Date:". The GET option not only displays the contents of each field listed, but it displays them in reverse video in the dimensions of the field width. Since the record pointer is referencing the last record, which is empty, only the reverse video will be displayed.

The READ command toward the bottom of the file activates the full-screen entry and editing specified by the GET options. When data entry or editing has been completed for the last field, you then return to the main menu section of the program.

Choose Save Changes and Exit from the Exit menu to save the command file. Now you'll need to make one change in the main menu's command file to integrate the new ADDER command file into the system. Enter **MODIFY COMMAND MENU**, and change the word "APPEND" in the command file to "DO ADDER"; then press CTRL-END to save the file.

Try out the new command file by entering **DO MENU**. Choose menu 1, and try entering a new employee of your own choosing.

Using PICTURE

The PICTURE option is used with the @ command to format data. With PICTURE, you can display dollar amounts with both commas and decimal places, or you can display dates in American or

European date formats. PICTURE restricts the way data can be entered into the system. You can accept numbers only (for dollar amounts) or a date only, rejecting any other characters.

The PICTURE option is divided into function and template symbols (see Table 15-1). The format is

@ *row,column* SAY *expression* PICTURE "*clause*"

You use the PICTURE option by adding the word "PICTURE" and then the letters or symbols that specify the function or template. The functions or templates in the clause are surrounded by quotes. An @ symbol must appear as the first character in a function.

Two examples of the PICTURE option are shown here:

```
@ 12,40 SAY "Enter effective date-" GET MYDAY PICTURE "@E"
@ 14,20 SAY "Customer name is: "LASTNAME PICTURE"!!!!!!!!!!!!!!!"
```

In the first example, the @ symbol after the word "PICTURE" defines the clause as a function. The letter E defines the function as European date format. A template is used in the second example. The exclamation points in the template will result in a display of uppercase letters, regardless of how the letters are stored in the database.

Some of the functions used with PICTURE apply only to certain kinds of data. The C, X, B, (, and Z functions apply only to numeric data. The @ and ! functions apply to character data only, but the D and E functions apply to date, character, and numeric data. You can combine function symbols for multiple functions. For example, the function symbols BZ align numeric data at the left side of the field and display any zero values as blanks.

You can get a better idea of how the PICTURE option is used if you try a few examples. First try the X and C functions. The X function will display "DB" for debit after a negative number, and

Table 15-1.

Symbol	Meaning
FUNCTIONS	
A	Displays alphabetic characters only
B	Left-justifies numeric data
C	Displays "CR" for credit, after a positive number
D	Displays American date format
E	Displays European date format
X	Displays "DB" for debit, after a negative number
Z	Displays any zeros as blanks
!	Displays capital letters only
(	Surrounds negative numbers with parentheses
TEMPLATES	
9	Allows only digits for character data, or digits and signs for numeric data
#	Allows only digits, blanks, and signs
A	Allows only letters
L	Allows only logical data (.T. or .F.; .Y. or .N.)
N	Allows only letters and digits
X	Allows any characters
!	Converts letters to uppercase
$	Displays dollar signs in place of leading zeros
*	Displays asterisks in place of leading zeros
.	Specifies a decimal position
,	Displays a comma if there are any numbers to the left of the comma

Functions and Templates Used with PICTURE

the C function will display "CR" for credit after a positive number. Try the following commands to illustrate these functions:

```
CLEAR
STORE -1650.32 TO A
STORE 795 TO B
@5,0 SAY A PICTURE "@X"
@10,0 SAY B PICTURE "@C"
```

These commmands have the following results:

```
1650.32 DB

795 CR
```

This is useful in accounting.

The ! template is useful when you want character displays to appear in all uppercase letters. Try this:

```
CLEAR
STORE "small words" TO WORDS
@10,10 SAY WORDS PICTURE "!!!!!!!!!!!"
```

The # template reserves space for digits, blanks, or signs, and the comma template specifies where the comma should appear in numeric data. Try these templates with the following example:

```
STORE 1234.56 TO A
@16,0 SAY A PICTURE "#,###.##"

1,234.56
```

When you are using templates, you must use a symbol for each character that is to be displayed with SAY or GET. To display a character field that is ten characters wide in uppercase, for example, you would need ten exclamation points in the template. The template would look like this:

```
@20,10 SAY "Name is--" NAME PICTURE "!!!!!!!!!!"
```

Let's try a PICTURE option in the command file for adding a record. Enter **MODIFY COMMAND ADDER**. Change the line of the program that reads

```
@ 1,0 SAY "Social Sec.: " GET SOCIALSEC
```

so that it contains the following command:

```
@ 1,0 SAY "Social Sec.: " GET SOCIALSEC PICTURE "999-99-9999"
```

Save the program with CTRL-END, and then run the system with the DO MENU command. Choose the Add New Entries option and enter another record. You'll see the new format caused by the PICTURE specification as you enter the social security number; the hyphens will be added automatically. You can get out of the system without making changes to the database by pressing the ESC key and then typing **5** to return to the dot prompt.

Note that when you use functions and templates along with a GET command as you did in this example, the data is stored in the specified format, not just displayed that way (as with the SAY command). Functions and templates along with GET commands can be very useful for forcing data entries into uppercase.

Using Format Files

Let's say that you wanted to enter only last names, first names, and salary amounts without being required to step through all of the other fields that normally appear on the screen—addresses, phone numbers, birth dates, hire dates, and so on. You can limit the amount of information shown on a screen in either Append or Edit mode by using a *format file*. A format file is a special file with the extension .FMT that contains an @ command and SAY and GET options that will display messages and prompts according to your arrangements. Once you have created the format file, you can implement it with the SET FORMAT TO command.

REMEMBER The PICTURE and FUNCTION templates discussed earlier can be used in format files.

For an example, create a format file with the dBASE editor by entering

```
MODIFY COMMAND QUICKIE.FMT
```

This will create a file called QUICKIE with the format extension of .FMT. Now enter the following commands:

```
@ 10,10 SAY "The last name is: " GET LASTNAME
@ 12,10 SAY "The first name is: " GET FIRSTNAME
@ 14,10 SAY "The salary amount will be: " GET SALARY
```

Choose Save Changes and Exit from the Exit menu to save the format file. When the prompt reappears, enter **GO TOP**, and then enter **EDIT** (be sure that ABCSTAFF is the active file). Notice that what you see is the normal editing screen with all of its fields. Press ESC to get back to the dot prompt.

To use the format file, you must use the SET FORMAT TO *filename* command (you don't have to supply the .FMT extension). Enter

```
SET FORMAT TO QUICKIE
```

Now enter **APPEND**. With the new format file in effect, only the specified fields are shown. Press ESC to leave Append mode without making changes.

Now enter **GOTO 5**. This will move the pointer to record 5. Enter **EDIT**. Instead of the normal editing screen, you will see just those fields specified in the format file that apply to record 5. Press ESC to get out of Edit mode without making any changes. To disable a format file when you finish using it, simply enter

CLOSE FORMAT without specifying a filename (because only one format file may be opened at a time).

Format files can come in handy when you want to use the same screen format many times in different parts of a program. You can include a SET FORMAT TO *filename* command anywhere in a dBASE IV command file, and that format file will take effect for any appending or editing until you use CLOSE FORMAT.

An Easier Way

Now that you've learned how to write @-SAY-GET commands to place information on the screen and prompt the user for a response, let's consider why you shouldn't bother to write such files—at least in some cases, such as for common data entry screens. The Form Design screen, discussed in Chapter 5, automatically creates format files with all of the @-SAY-GET commands you may ever need.

To summarize what you learned in Chapter 5, the Form Design screen is a menu-driven feature of dBASE IV that creates data entry screens, complete with descriptive titles and borders, when desired. The information used within the Form Design screen to design a particular screen is stored in a screen file that is assigned the .SCR extension. The Form Design screen also creates a format file with an .FMT extension. This file contains the @-SAY-GET commands that would be required if you were to write a command file that would display the same information in the same format as the Form Design screen.

HINT Study the contents of format files to get a better idea of how to use the PICTURE and FUNCTION templates.

The Form Design Screen And Format Files

If you use the Form Design screen to create forms, any modification of the form (with MODIFY SCREEN from the dot prompt or with the Create option of the Screen panel) will update both the screen (.SCR) file and the format (.FMT) file. If you use the format files along with your programs and you make any changes manually to the format file by using the dBASE editor, you should rename the file with a name that is different from the corresponding screen file. This will prevent the format file from being accidentally overwritten if you later use the Form Design screen to make changes to the screen.

If you do use the dBASE editor to make changes manually to a format file, remember that the corresponding screen file is not updated. To update the screen file, you must make your changes within the Form Design screen.

Using Windows

One significant asset of dBASE IV, that you should be aware of when designing programs is its ability to display information within windows. From the prior use of commands like BROWSE, it is obvious that dBASE IV lets you add and edit data within windows. What may not be obvious is that you can use certain window-related commands within programs to display or edit data inside of windows. There are three often-used commands that relate to window management within dBASE IV. These are

- DEFINE WINDOW *window name*, which is used to define the screen coordinates (or location) and the display attributes for a window.
- ACTIVATE WINDOW *window name* [ALL], which is used to activate a window that has been defined. Once activated, all screen output appears in the window until another window is activated, or until the current window is deactivated. The ALL option, when used, activates all previously-defined windows, and current screen output appears in the last window to be defined.
- DEACTIVATE WINDOW *window name* [ALL], which is used to deactivate, or turn off, an active window. The ALL option, when used, deactivates all active windows.

To use windows in your program, you first use the DEFINE WINDOW command to define as many windows as will be needed (one DEFINE WINDOW command is used for each window). Window names can be up to ten characters in length. Then, as you need to display data in a window, use the ACTIVATE WINDOW command to make the window active. When done with the window, use the DEACTIVATE WINDOW command to deactivate the window.

Defining the Window

You can use a number of options with the DEFINE WINDOW command to control the appearance and colors of the window. All the options are covered in detail in Appendix A; for now, here is a brief description of some of them. The options take the format shown in the following commands:

DEFINE WINDOW *window name* FROM *row1, col1* TO *row2, col2*[DOUBLE/PANEL/NONE][COLOR *standard / enhanced* [*,border*]]

The *row1, col1* coordinates indicate the row and column number for the upper-left corner of the window. The *row2, col2* coordinates indicate the row and column number of the lower-right corner of the window.

The DOUBLE, PANEL, or NONE options can be used to define a different border for the window. The default border, if no option is specified, is a single line box. DOUBLE gives the window a double-line box. PANEL gives the window a panel border. NONE specifies no border.

The COLOR option lets you define color attributes for the window using the appropriate letters separated by a slash, to indicate standard and enhanced colors (separate the standard color pair from the enhanced color pair with a comma). The first letter in the pair is the foreground color, and the second letter is the background color. The color codes are as follows:

Black - N	Yellow - GR+
Cyan - BG	Blue - B
White - W	Magenta - RB
Blank - X	Brown - GR
Green - G	Red - R

As an example, you could define the window as having standard colors of black on a white background, and enhanced colors of blue on a red background, by adding the option

```
COLOR N/W, B/R
```

to the DEFINE WINDOW command.

As an example of a window definition, the command

```
DEFINE WINDOW Staff1 FROM 8,8 TO 22,75 PANEL COLOR B/W
```

would define a window with a panel border, and place its upper-left corner at row 8, column 8 of the screen and it's lower-right corner at row 22, column 75 of the screen. The window colors would be blue characters on a white background.

Activating and Using The Window

Once you have defined the window with the DEFINE WINDOW command, use the ACTIVATE WINDOW *window name* command to activate, or turn on, the window. Once you activate a window, all screen output appears inside of that window. When using @SAY commands to place data inside a window, it is important to realize that the coordinates are now *relative to the window*. This means that row 0, column 0 is no longer the upper left corner of the screen; it is now the upper-left corner of the window. It will remain this way until you stop using the window with a DEACTIVATE WINDOW command. You need to understand this to avoid errors in your program. If, for example, you activate a window that is only 5 rows deep in size, and you then try to display data at row 15, your program will halt with a "position is off the screen" error message, because the window you are using has no row 15.

You can use LIST or DISPLAY commands to display data without worrying about screen locations, and the data will appear completely contained within the window. If the data wraps around lines in an unattractive fashion, you can either change the size of the window to fit more data, or include less fields in the LIST or DISPLAY command. You can also activate a window and then use a BROWSE, CHANGE, or EDIT command to allow changes inside the window. You might find such a technique useful if, for some reason, you wanted a Browse or Edit window of a specific size to appear at a specific screen location.

Deactivating the Window

Once you are done with the window, use the DEACTIVATE WINDOW *window name* command to turn it off. Screen output is then restored to the normal screen. If you have activated a number of windows, you can use the ALL clause in place of *window name* to deactivate all the windows.

An Example of the Use of Windows

From the dot prompt, you can define and activate a window, and you will see that all successive screen output takes place in the window. For example, try the following command now at the dot prompt:

```
CLEAR
DEFINE WINDOW SHOWME FROM 5,5 TO 15,70 DOUBLE
ACTIVATE WINDOW SHOWME
```

As soon as you activate the window, the dot prompt and cursor appear inside the window. Enter the commands

```
USE HOURS
LIST
BROWSE
```

and you will see the results of the LIST and BROWSE commands appear within the window. Press ESC to exit the Browse mode, and enter

```
DEACTIVATE WINDOW SHOWME
```

to restore output to the full screen.

Assuming you've created the ABCSTAFF and HOURS files in earlier chapters, you can try the following program to see how multiple windows can be used to visually enhance your application. Perhaps ABC Temporaries would like a program that asks for an employee name, and then displays all hours worked by that employee. The following program presents the information inside multiple windows.

```
*windows.prg shows off window use.*
STORE SPACE(15) TO MLAST
DEFINE WINDOW Staff1 FROM 5,5 TO 9,50 DOUBLE
DEFINE WINDOW Hours1 FROM 8,8 TO 22,75 PANEL COLOR N/W, B/R, G
DEFINE WINDOW askthem FROM 3,15 TO 6,45 DOUBLE
USE ABCSTAFF
SET ORDER TO NAME
ACTIVATE WINDOW askthem
@ 1,1 SAY "Last name? " GET MLAST
READ
SEEK MLAST
IF .NOT. FOUND( )
   @ 1,1 SAY "NAME NOT FOUND IN DATABASE!"
   WAIT
   DEACTIVATE WINDOW askthem
   CLOSE DATABASES
   RETURN
ENDIF
```

```
STORE SOCIALSEC TO FINDER
ACTIVATE WINDOW Staff1
@ 1,2 SAY "Name: " + TRIM(FIRSTNAME) + " " + LASTNAME
WAIT "Press a key to see hours worked..."
SET ESCAPE OFF
ACTIVATE WINDOW Hours1
SELECT 2
USE HOURS
DISPLAY ALL OFF FOR SOCIALSEC = FINDER
WAIT "Press a key when done viewing..."
DEACTIVATE WINDOW ALL
CLOSE DATABASES
SET ESCAPE ON
RETURN
```

At the beginning of the program, three DEFINE WINDOW commands are used to define three different windows for later use. After opening a database file and using SET ORDER to activate the desired index, the program activates the window called "askthem" and displays a prompt for a last name within that window.

Once the user responds with a last name, a SEEK command finds the name in the index, and the window called "Staff1" is activated. The employee's full name is displayed in this window, and the user is asked to press a key to see the hours worked. Once the user presses a key, the window called "Hours1" is activated, and all hours worked by that employee are shown in this window. At the end of the program, all the windows are deactivated, and the files are closed.

You may notice the addition of the SET ESCAPE OFF command just before the final window is opened. This is used to prevent a user from halting the program in midstream by pressing the ESC key. You may want to use the SET ESCAPE OFF command early on in most of your programs, so users cannot interrupt a program by pressing ESC.

A Note for Users of Version 1.1

If you are going to be using windows in programs often, you should be aware of the SAVE SCREEN and RESTORE SCREEN commands added to version 1.1 of dBASE IV. These commands let you save the current screen image to a memory variable, and later restore that screen image. Use SAVE SCREEN TO *varname*, where *varname* is the memory variable name of your choice, to save the screen image. You can then open and use various windows, or create other displays with appropriate @SAY commands. When you later want to restore the original screen display, use RESTORE SCREEN FROM *varname*, where *varname* is the memory variable name that you saved the screen under.

This is an important addition, because dBASE leaves a blank portion of a screen underneath any window that is deactivated. You can use RESTORE SCREEN to easily restore the screen image that was underneath a window before that window was activated.

Another advantage is that with visually complex screen designs, SAVE SCREEN and RESTORE SCREEN can be much faster than repainting an entire screen with @SAY commands. Note that each screen you save requires about 4K of free memory.

Using Programs to Display And Edit Records

You know that you can edit records with the EDIT command or by @-SAY-GET and READ commands, but you must first display the record before you can change it. Let's use macro substitution for the displaying and editing functions of the ABC Temporaries database system. Remember that CHANGES.PRG, the editor program, displays all records in the database. The system then asks you for the record number to be edited, and the EDIT command is used to edit that record. But if the database has grown beyond a screenful of members, you won't be able to see all of the records on the screen at once. Obviously, a better method of editing is needed.

The employees of ABC Temporaries have agreed that it would be best if they could enter the last name of the member to have dBASE IV search for the record. When you first think about what must be done, you might draw up this list:

1. Ask for the last name of the member whose record is to be edited.

2. Store the name to a variable.

3. Using the macro function, find the name in the database.

4. Edit the record whose number corresponds to that name.

Let's change the editor command file so that it does this task. Enter **MODIFY COMMAND CHANGES**, and change the program so that it looks like this:

```
CLEAR
STORE SPACE(15) TO TEST
USE ABCSTAFF
SET ORDER TO NAME
@ 5,10 SAY "Editing a record."
@ 7,10 SAY "Enter the last name of the employee."
@ 10,10 SAY "Last name: " GET TEST
READ
IF TEST = " "
   RETURN
ENDIF
```

```
FIND &TEST
IF .NOT. FOUND( )
    CLEAR
    @5,10 SAY "There is no such name in the database."
    WAIT
    *wait command causes a pause.
    RETURN
ENDIF
EDIT
RETURN
```

Choose Save Changes and Exit from the Exit menu to save the file. Try the system again by entering **DO MENU**, and choose the Change an Existing Entry selection. Try entering the name **Hart**.

If all went well, the selected record will appear on the screen. This is made possible by the FIND &TEST macro function. Whatever name is entered with the @-SAY-GET command will be substituted for the macro when the FIND command is executed. Observant readers may be aware that the SEEK command, which accepts a memory variable directly, could be used in place of FIND and a macro. In this example, FIND was used instead to demonstrate the use of the macro (&) function.

One obvious flaw in the above design is that the search routine is based on last name only. If two persons have the same last name, such a design may or may not find the name you want. However, you can apply the same logic to combinations of fields if you use an index built on that same combination of fields to perform the search. You could, for example, build the NAME index tag on a combination of LASTNAME and FIRSTNAME with the commands

```
USE MEMBERS
INDEX ON LASTNAME + FIRSTNAME TAG NAME
```

The search routine just shown could then be rewritten to prompt for both the last and the first names. The responses could be combined using the plus symbol, which combines ("concatenates") text strings, and the combined expression could then be used as the search term. As an example, the following search routine would work if the index was built on a combination of last and first names:

```
CLEAR
STORE SPACE(15) TO TESTLAST
STORE SPACE(15) TO TESTFIRST
USE ABCSTAFF
SET ORDER TO NAME
@ 5,10 SAY "Editing a record."
@ 7,10 SAY "Enter the last name of the employee."
@ 8,10 SAY "Last name: " GET TESTLAST
@ 10,10 SAY "Enter the first name of the employee."
@ 11,10 SAY "First name: " GET TESTFIRST
READ
STORE TESTLAST + TESTFIRST TO TEST
IF TEST = " "
   RETURN
ENDIF
FIND &TEST
IF .NOT. FOUND( )
   CLEAR
   @ 5,10 SAY "There is no such name in the database."
   WAIT
   RETURN
ENDIF
EDIT
RETURN
```

Using Programs to Delete Records

If you're going to be writing your own applications, you should add a routine similar to those for editing to delete unwanted records. This is too often left out of a system's initial design, as if users want to add but never want to delete records from a database. The logic for a delete program is very similar to that of a search-and-edit program, because in the case of both editing and deleting, you have to find the record first. To delete a record, the design of your program may look like this:

```
open database, index files
prompt user for variables to search by
FIND variable in index file
IF NOT FOUND
   show error message, exit routine
ELSE
   show record to user with @SAY commands
   ask user for confirmation to delete record
   IF confirmation is given
      DELETE the record
   ELSE
      move to next record to see if it is same name
      ask user for confirmation to delete record
   ENDIF
ENDIF
```

The fastest way to build such a routine is probably to copy your edit routine, remove the lines of code that allow for changing the fields, and add lines of code that ask for confirmation and proceed to delete the record. The following example uses a modified version of the program created earlier for editing records based on a last and first name:

```
CLEAR
STORE SPACE(15) TO TESTLAST
STORE SPACE(15) TO TESTFIRST
USE ABCSTAFF
SET ORDER TO NAME
*Name tag is indexed on lastname + firstname.*
@ 5,10 SAY "DELETING a record."
@ 7,10 SAY "Enter the last name of the member."
@ 8,10 SAY "Last name: " GET TESTLAST
@ 10,10 SAY "Enter the first name of the member."
```

```
@ 11,10 SAY "First name: " GET TESTFIRST
READ
STORE TESTLAST + TESTFIRST TO TEST
SEEK TEST
IF .NOT. FOUND( )
    CLEAR
    @5,10 SAY "There is no such name in the database."
    WAIT
    *wait command causes a pause.
    RETURN
ENDIF
DO WHILE .NOT. EOF( )
    STORE "N" TO DOIT
    @ 5, 5 SAY " Lastname:"
    @ 5,15 SAY LASTNAME
    @ 6, 5 SAY "Firstname:"
    @ 6,15 SAY FIRSTNAME
    @ 7, 5 SAY "  Address:"
    @ 7,15 SAY ADDRESS
    @ 8,15 SAY TRIM(CITY) + " " + STATE + " " + ZIPCODE
    @ 12, 20 SAY "DELETE THIS MEMBER? Y/N or C to CANCEL: "
    @ 12, 62 GET DOIT
    READ
    DO CASE
      CASE UPPER(DOIT) = "Y"
      DELETE
      RETURN
      CASE UPPER(DOIT) = "N"
      SKIP
      CASE UPPER(DOIT) = "C"
      RETURN
    ENDCASE
ENDDO
RETURN
```

The advantage of placing the portion of the program that displays the member and asks for confirmation in a DOWHILE loop is that if two members have the same last and first names, the user can press N for No and automatically view the next member. Once the user views the desired member to delete and presses Y for Yes, the record is deleted.

Note also that this routine does not perform a PACK, because packing a database can be time-consuming (particularly with larger databases). Most systems provide the user with an option to pack the file at some point in time. It probably isn't wise to do this all too often, nor is it necessary, since you can place a SET DELETED ON statement near the start of the program to hide the deleted records. Given that a PACK is going to be time-consuming with all but the smallest of databases, it should be an option that is performed at the user's discretion. Many systems provide a pack option in the form of a question that the user sees just before exiting the system. This can be done with a program like that shown in this example:

```
CLEAR
ACCEPT "  ==PACK database now? Y/N: " TO PACKANS
IF UPPER(PACKANS) = "Y"
   CLEAR
   @ 5,5 SAY "Please wait... do NOT interrupt!"
   SET TALK ON
   USE ABCSTAFF
   PACK
   SET TALK OFF
ENDIF
QUIT
```

This gives the user of your application, who may not want to spend the time at that particular instant, the option of performing or not performing the pack.

Helpful Hints on Screen Design

Think about these aspects of screen design when you are designing a dBASE IV system:

- Use menus as often as necessary. They should clearly say what choices are available to the person using the system.
- Avoid overly cluttered menus or data entry screens. It may be better to break the entry screen in half, input half of the information, clear the screen with CLEAR, and then input the other half of the information, rather than trying to fit a large number of fields on one data entry screen. You can apply the same tactic to a menu by grouping a number of choices in a second menu—a reports menu, for example—that can be reached by a single choice on the main menu.
- Give users a way out; that is, give them a way to change their minds after making a choice from a menu or selecting a particular entry screen. Many applications designers handle this need by making the last option in any menu serve as an exit back to the previous menu with a RETURN statement.
- Finally, never leave the screen blank for any noticeable period of time. Few things are as unnerving to a computer user as a blank screen. A simple message that states that the computer is doing something (sorting, indexing, or whatever) is reassuring to the user.

Quick Reference

To place information at a specific location on the screen Use the @SAY command, with either of the following formats:

@ row,column SAY "message"
@ row, column SAY *memory variable name*

To accept information from the user Use the @-SAY-GET command, and include the name of a memory variable after the GET option. Then use the READ command after one or more @-SAY-GET commands to activate the series of GETs. The responses typed by the user will be stored in the memory variables named by the GET options.

To quickly set up a screen design for adding or editing records in a program Design and save a screen form, using the techniques covered in Chapter 5. Then use the statement SET FORMAT TO *filename*, where *filename* is the name of the screen form you created, followed by an appropriate APPEND or EDIT command.

To use windows within a program Define the window with the DEFINE WINDOW command. When the window is needed, activate it with the ACTIVATE WINDOW command. All further screen operations will take place inside the window until you deactivate it with the DEACTIVATE WINDOW command.

CHAPTER

16

Programming for Data Retrieval

This chapter covers ways to retrieve data in the form of reports from within your programs. The chapter assumes that you are already familiar with the ways to design reports, as detailed in Chapters 8 and 11. The stored reports created by the report generator can be called from within a program to produce a variety of reports. You can also write programs that produce reports, although the flexibility of the report generator makes this task necessary only on the rarest of occasions.

Generating Reports with Stored Report Forms

If you have designed your reports with the report generator, all that is needed to generate a report is to place the REPORT FORM command (detailed in Chapter 8) at the appropriate place in your program. You may also want to build selective indexes or set some sort of filter before generating the report, and it is a good idea to give users a way to cancel the report before it starts generating. A simple report-producing program, called from one of the options in the main menu, might resemble the following:

```
*REPORTER.PRG produces the membership report.*
CLEAR
TEXT
*****************************************************
This menu option prints the employee report.
Make sure that the printer is turned on, and that
paper is loaded.
Press C to CANCEL, any other key to start printing.
*****************************************************
ENDTEXT
WAIT TO DOIT
IF UPPER(DOIT) < > "C"
     REPORT FORM RSIMPLE TO PRINT
ENDIF
RETURN
```

Using stored reports like the one used by this program is by far the easiest way to generate reports within a program. You can limit the records that are printed by including an INDEX ON-FOR command (version 1.1 and above only) or a SET FILTER command within the program. With SET FILTER, for example, you could offer various menu options that select different filter conditions, then print the same stored report. As an example, one user might want to see the employees in the staff database restricted by a specific ZIP code, while another user might want to see all employees who lived in a specific state. You could provide menu options in a simple reporting program like the one shown here to handle this task:

```
*REPORTER.PRG produces the membership report.*
CLEAR
@ 5, 5 SAY "1. All employees    "
@ 6, 5 SAY "2. By State         "
@ 7, 5 SAY "3. By ZIP code range"
@ 4, 4 TO 8, 25 DOUBLE
STORE 1 TO CHOICE
@ 10,5 SAY "Your selection?" GET CHOICE PICTURE '9'
READ
CLEAR
DO CASE
    CASE CHOICE = 2
       STORE SPACE(2) TO MSTATE
       @ 12,10 SAY "For which state? " GET MSTATE
       READ
       SET FILTER TO UPPER(STATE) = UPPER(MSTATE)
       GO TOP
    CASE CHOICE = 3
       STORE SPACE(10) TO STARTZIPS
       STORE SPACE(10) TO ENDZIPS
       @ 12,10 SAY "Starting ZIP code? " GET STARTZIPS
       @ 13,10 SAY "  Ending ZIP code? " GET ENDZIPS
       @ 15,10 SAY "(enter same ZIP code for a single ZIP.)"
       READ
       SET FILTER TO ZIPCODE = STARTZIPS .AND. ZIPCODE <=ENDZIPS
       GO TOP
    OTHERWISE
       WAIT "All employees chosen. Press a key."
ENDCASE
CLEAR
TEXT
*****************************************************

Ready to print the staff report. Make sure that
the printer is turned on, and that paper is loaded.
Press C to CANCEL, any other key to start printing.
*****************************************************
```

```
ENDTEXT
WAIT TO DOIT
IF UPPER(DOIT) <> "C"
     REPORT FORM RSIMPLE TO PRINT
ENDIF
SET FILTER TO
*above line needed to clear effects of filter.*
RETURN
```

In this example, depending on the menu choice selected, one of two filters may be set to limit the records printed. Note the inclusion of the SET FILTER TO statement near the end of the program to clear any existing filter. If a filter is set and not cleared after the report is done, it could cause havoc in other parts of your program when records suddenly appear to be "missing" from the database.

You can also place stored queries into effect before printing reports with the SET VIEW TO *filename* command, where *filename* is the name that you saved the query under. This can be particularly useful for providing options to print relational reports within a program.

Providing the Option to Report to The Screen, the Printer, or a Disk File

Often a report is needed for both screen and printer. A program may need to display a report on the screen or optionally send the output to the printer. Anyone who has designed a single report to try to meet the two different needs of screen and printer has discovered that the two tasks are similar but not identical. The screen limitation of 24 lines puts a severe constraint on the amount of information you can display at once; the program must prompt for each display, or the data scrolls by so fast as to be useless. When sending output to a printer, there is no need to stop every 24 lines; however, page ejects must be taken into consideration. One way to handle such a situation is to use a program like this:

```
PRINANS = "S"
@ 5, 5 SAY 'Screen (S) or Printer (P)?" GET PRINANS
READ
IF UPPER(PRINANS) = "P"
     REPORT FORM RSIMPLE TO PRINT
ELSE
     GO TOP
     WAIT "Press C to CANCEL, any other key to view employees."
     CLEAR
     DO WHILE .NOT. EOF()
          REPORT FORM RSIMPLE NEXT 20
          WAIT TO KEEPGOING
          IF UPPER(KEEPGOING) = "C"
               EXIT
          ENDIF
     ENDDO
ENDIF
RETURN
```

As long as the report fits within 80 columns, this lets the same stored report form work for both screen and printer. If the user answers the prompt with "S" for screen, the DO WHILE loop causes the REPORT FORM RSIMPLE NEXT 20 statement to repeat over and over, until the end of the file is reached. The scope of NEXT 20 limits the report to 20 records—the total that fit on the screen in this example—and the WAIT command pauses the screen for the user to view the records. In your application, you could change the NEXT 20 option of the REPORT FORM command to whatever number of records will fit on your screen at one time.

Keep in mind that users will often desire an option to print a report to a disk file; you can add options to your menu choices accordingly. For printing to a disk file, you can use the TO FILE options of the REPORT FORM command if you are using stored reports. If you write your reports with program code, you can instead use the SET ALTERNATE command to store all output that appears on the screen to a disk file in ASCII format. Use the statement SET ALTERNATE TO *filename*, where *filename* is the name to be assigned to the ASCII text file. Then, use the statement SET ALTERNATE ON when you want to begin storing all text displayed on the screen to the disk file. When you are done with the report, use a CLOSE ALTERNATE statement to close the text file. Note that SET ALTERNATE captures all screen display except that produced with @-SAY commands. If your reports are designed with @-SAY commands, you will need to use the SET DEVICE TO FILE command in place of the SET ALTERNATE command. The SET DEVICE TO FILE *filename* command redirects all screen output resulting from @-SAY commands to the named disk file.

Writing Reports with Program Code

Before proceeding with this topic, you should know that producing stored reports with the report generator is far easier than the following methods of writing reports manually with program code. The methods are described here primarily because you may run into dBASE IV applications written by other programmers who chose to use these methods, because of the limitations of earlier versions of dBASE. The report generators in dBASE III and dBASE III PLUS did not let you create form-oriented reports with ease, so many programmers resorted to writing report programs to accomplish the task. It may help to be familiar with these methods of programming in case you ever want to modify another programmer's work. But if at all possible, you should avoid these techniques and instead write your reporting programs with stored reports created by the report generator.

There are about as many ways to design a reporting program as there are ways to build data entry screens. About the only thing such programs have in common are one or more repetitive (DO WHILE) loops that print selected contents of a record for each record within a group of records. Beyond this, the commands you will need vary with the complexity of the reports, the levels of grouping, whether or not the report is relational, and numerous other factors. Many reports written with program code do follow a common methodology, which is something like the following:

```
OPEN Database and Index tags
FIND first record in desired group, or SET FILTER and go
top
Initialize any memory variables for page and line counters
Route output to the printer
Print report headings
DO WHILE not at the end of the file or the desired data
group
        Print the desired fields or expressions for one record
        Update counter for page position
        IF form feed counter exceeds max lines per page
                Print footers, if any
                EJECT the paper
                Print headers, if any
        ENDIF
        SKIP to the next record in logical sequence
ENDDO
```

There are two ways to route the data to the printer: by using SET PRINT ON and a series of ? statements, or by using SET DEVICE TO PRINT followed by a series of @-SAY statements. The following program demonstrates the use of the first approach, within the design framework just described.

```
*MEMLIST.PRG prints membership roster.*
CLEAR
STORE 4 TO LINES
STORE 1 TO PAGES
USE MEMBERS INDEX NAMES
SET PRINT ON
? "****************************************************"
? "    Membership Address and Phone Roster"
? "****************************************************"
DO WHILE .NOT. EOF( )
      ? "Name: " + TRIM(FIRSTNAME) + " " + LASTNAME
      ? "Phone: " + PHONE
      ?? "Expiration Date: " + DTOC(EXPIREDATE)
      ? "Home address: " + ADDRESS
      ? SPACE(15) + TRIM(CITY) + " " + STATE + " " + ZIPCODE
      ? "********************************"
      STORE LINES+ 5 TO LINES
      IF LINES > 55
            ?
            ? SPACE(40) + "Page " + LTRIM(STR(PAGES))
            EJECT
            STORE 1 + PAGES TO PAGES
            STORE 4 TO LINES
            ? "******************************************************"
            ? "    Membership Address and Phone Roster"
            ? "******************************************************"
      ENDIF
      SKIP
ENDDO
IF LINES > 1
      EJECT
ENDIF
SET PRINT OFF
RETURN
```

Using SET PRINT ON and the ? statements get the job done, but it doesn't offer precise control over where the data appears in the report. For more precision, you can use the other method of printing in a program, which is to use SET DEVICE TO PRINT to reroute screen output to the printer, combined with @-SAY commands to position the data on the printed page. The following example of a printing program uses this approach to create a simple tabular report with custom headers and footers:

```
CLEAR
STORE 5 TO LINES
STORE 1 TO PAGES
USE MEMBERS INDEX NAMES
SET DEVICE TO PRINT
@ 2, 15 SAY "MEMBERSHIP EXPIRATION DATES REPORT"
@ 3, 10 SAY "**********************************************"
@ 4, 10 SAY "Name                City"
@ 4, 50 SAY "Tape Limit    Exp.Date"
DO WHILE .NOT. EOF( )
      @ LINES, 5 SAY TRIM(FIRSTNAME) + " " + LASTNAME
      @ LINES, 32 SAY CITY
      @ LINES, 50 SAY TAPELIMIT
      @ LINES, 64 SAY EXPIREDATE
      STORE LINES + 1 TO LINES
      IF LINES > 50
            @ LINES + 2, 40 SAY "PAGE " + TRIM(STR(PAGES))
            STORE PAGES + 1 TO PAGES
            STORE 5 TO LINES
            @ 2, 15 SAY "MEMBERSHIP EXPIRATION DATES REPORT"
            @ 3, 10 SAY "**********************************************"
            @ 4, 10 SAY "Name                City"
            @ 4, 50 SAY "Tape Limit   Exp.Date"
      ENDIF
      SKIP
ENDDO
IF LINES > 5
      EJECT
ENDIF
SET DEVICE TO SCREEN
RETURN
```

You can use whichever approach best suits you and modify it to handle any complex reporting need. Multiple file reporting, for example, is simple to implement by selecting appropriate work areas and including filenames and pointers, as discussed in Chapter 12, to find the related data. In one-to-many relationships where one record in the controlling database may have dozens or hundreds of records in a related file, you can add program code to monitor the page count and line count, and eject pages and print new headings when appropriate.

While on the subject of page numbers and line counts, note that both examples of report code just shown use memory variables incremented by the program to keep track of page numbers and line counts. This approach was also common in dBASE III PLUS and other earlier dBASE compatible languages. In dBASE IV, however, there are system memory variables (discussed shortly under "Controlling Your Printer") that can be used to keep track of page numbers and line positions. These system memory variables work with the stored reports, and you may want to consider using them if you need reports that begin with a specific page number other than 1.

Creating Columnar Listings With LABEL FORM

Sometimes what you need is a report with data in a two-across or three-across fashion. You can spend an inordinate amount of time writing a program to handle this need, or you can use the LABEL FORM command as a part of your report. This works well when the data needed follows a format like this one:

```
                                        Page 1
                                        10/06/89
              Employee Address Roster
                  ABC Company
Marcia Morse          Carol Levy          David Jackson
4260 Park Avenue      1207 5th Street     4102 Valley Lane
Chevy Chase, MD       Washington, DC      Falls Church, VA
```

The trick to using the LABEL FORM command is similar to earlier described uses of the REPORT FORM command within a program. Create a label form with the CREATE LABEL command, and choose 3-across or 2-across as desired from the Label menu. Decide how many records you wish to have appear on each page, and use the command

LABEL FORM *filename* NEXT *no. of recs per page* TO PRINT

within your program. The following program shows how this can be handled:

```
SET TALK OFF
USE ABCSTAFF
SET ORDER TO NAMES
STORE 1 TO PAGES
SET DEVICE TO PRINT
DO WHILE .NOT. EOF( )
      @ 3, 50 SAY "Page: " + LTRIM(STR(PAGES))
      @ 4, 50 SAY DATE( )
      @ 5, 20 SAY "ABC Temporaries Employee Address Roster"
      @ 7, 0
      LABEL FORM ABCMAIL NEXT 20 TO PRINT
      STORE PAGES + 1 TO PAGES
      EJECT
```

```
ENDDO
SET DEVICE TO SCREEN
EJECT
```

This will give you a report in the format of the example just shown, with a minimum amount of programming. You will need to decide how many records can appear on each page based on the size of the paper and the position of your headers and footers, and adjust the number that you use with the NEXT scope in the LABEL FORM command accordingly.

Controlling Your Printer

By changing the printer memory variables, you can control various print settings used when stored report forms are generated with the REPORT FORM command. The printer memory variables are special memory variables that dBASE IV uses to control the output produced when a REPORT FORM command is directed to the printer. The printer memory variables will affect settings like page length, page offset from the left margin, the number of pages printed within a report, and line spacing. You can change the values of these memory variables by storing different values to the variables before running the report with the REPORT FORM command. If you perform a LIST MEMORY command, you can see the printer memory variables, which will be similar to the following example. Names of the printer memory variables start with _P.

```
LIST MEMORY
     0 variables defined,        0 bytes used
   256 variables available,      6000 bytes available
Print System Memory Variables
```

```
_ALIGNMENT     Pub   C  "LEFT"
_BOX           Pub   L  .T.
_INDENT        Pub   N            0   (    0.00000000)
_LMARGIN       Pub   N            0   (    0.00000000)
_PADVANCE      Pub   C  "FORMFEED"
_PAGENO        Pub   N            1   (    1.00000000)
_PBPAGE        Pub   N            1   (    1.00000000)
_PCOLNO        Pub   N           55   (   55.00000000)
_PCOPIES       Pub   N            1   (    1.00000000)
_PDRIVER       Pub   C  ""
_PECODE        Pub   C  ""
_PEJECT        Pub   C  "BEFORE"
_PEPAGE        Pub   N            1   (    1.00000000)
_PFORM         Pub   C  ""
_PLENGTH       Pub   N           66   (   66.00000000)
_PLINENO       Pub   N           52   (   52.00000000)
_PLOFFSET      Pub   N            0   (    0.00000000)
_PPITCH        Pub   C  "DEFAULT"
_PQUALITY      Pub   L  .F.
_PSCODE        Pub   C  ""
_PSPACING      Pub   N            1   (    1.00000000)
_PWAIT         Pub   L  .F.
_RMARGIN       Pub   N           80   (   80.00000000)
_TABS          Pub   C  ""
_WRAP          Pub   L  .F.
```

Here is a brief description of each of the printer memory variables:

- _PADVANCE: Contains a character expression of either "LINEFEED" or "FORMFEED." Depending on the value of the expression, new pages are generated either with multiple line feeds, or with form feeds.
- _PAGENO: Indicates the page number to use on the first page of a report. The default is 1, but you can enter any value from 1 to 32,767.
- _PBPAGE: Indicates the beginning page of a report when you don't want to print the entire report.

- _PCOLNO: Indicates a new starting column position. This repositions the printer at the specified cursor location before the report begins.
- _PCOPIES: Indicates the number of copies of a report desired; the default is 1.
- _PDRIVER: Contains a character expression that is the name of the printer driver in use, such as "EPSONFX" (for Epson FX series) or "HPLAS1" (for Hewlett-Packard LaserJet 1). If no printer has been chosen with the Printer Setup option, the default will be a null string ("").
- _PECODE: Contains any ending escape codes you want to send to the printer after the report is completed.
- _PEJECT: Indicates when to eject a page, with the character expression "NONE," "BEFORE," "AFTER," or "BOTH." NONE indicates no formfeed is needed (other than those that naturally occur inside the report); BEFORE indicates a formfeed should occur at the start of printing; AFTER indicates a formfeed should occur at the end of printing; and BOTH indicates a formfeed is needed both before and after printing.
- _PEPAGE: Indicates the ending page of a report when you don't want to print the entire report.
- _PFORM: Contains a character expression that evaluates to the name of a stored report form file.
- _PLENGTH: Indicates the page length for the printed page. The default of 66 matches standard 11-inch (US) paper; you can store 84 to this value if you are using 14-inch (US legal size) paper.
- _PLINENO: Indicates a new starting line number. This repositions the printer at the specified row location before the report begins.

- _PLOFFSET: Indicates the left offset (the distance from the left edge of the page) where printing will begin. Enter a desired numeric value, such as 15 for a left offset of 15 spaces.

- _PPITCH: Contains a character expression that selects the printing typestyle. Valid choices are "PICA," "ELITE," "COMPRESSED," or "DEFAULT." Note that a printer driver must be installed and your printer must support the option for the desired typestyle to be used successfully.

- _PQUALITY: Indicates whether quality printing mode will be used. A logical false stored to this variable turns off quality printing, and a logical true turns on quality printing. Note that a printer driver must be installed, and your printer must support quality printing, for this variable to have an effect.

- _PSCODE: Contains any starting escape codes you want to send to the printer before the report begins printing.

- _PSSPACING: Contains a numeric value of 1, 2, or 3, indicating the line spacing to be used within a report. The default value is 1.

- _PWAIT: Indicates whether the printer should pause between each page. A logical value of false indicates no pause, while a logical value of true indicates a pause.

Most of these parameters can be controlled in other ways, such as through various menu selections when designing or printing a report, or by entering other commands, such as SET MARGIN TO (the command equivalent of the left offset variable). These variables, however, can be quite useful if you want to offer your users multiple options for report printing while under program control. Depending on the user's response to various menu options, you could store certain values to different printer variables, then print the report with the REPORT FORM command. As an example, a user could print from one to three copies of a report from within a program if the following statements were used in the program:

```
CLEAR
INPUT "Number of copies to print (3 maximum):" TO ANS
IF ANS > 3
      STORE 3 TO ANS
      ? "Sorry. I'll only print three."
ENDIF
IF ANS < 1
      RETURN
ENDIF
*assign number of copies to print system memvar.*
STORE ANS TO _PCOPIES
REPORT FORM ABCSTAFF TO PRINT
```

Sending Escape Codes To the Printer

In its default mode, dBASE IV treats the printer as a simple device capable of receiving ASCII, and sends that information. This saves you the worry of trying to get a particular printer to match the output of dBASE IV, but it also means that dBASE IV will not by default use any special effects that your printer has to offer.

If you are using stored report forms, you can take advantage of special effects with the Style options of the Words menu, as detailed in Chapter 8. Within programs, you can take advantage of printer special effects by sending escape codes to your printer with the CHR( ) function.

As an example, the code for compressed print from Epson-compatible printers is the ASCII value of 27, followed by the ASCII value of 15. You can therefore switch an Epson-compatible printer into compressed mode with commands like

```
SET PRINT ON
??? CHR(27) + CHR(15)
SET PRINT OFF
```

and the printer will remain in this mode until you send another escape code that clears the prior one or selects a different font, or until you manually reset the printer. (Note the use of the ??? command, which is ideal for sending data to the printer. Unlike the ? commands, the use of ??? does not affect the printer row or column position.) Consult your printer manual for a listing of your escape codes; the popular escape codes for Epson-compatible printers are listed as follows:

CHR(27) + CHR(52)	Italics On
CHR(27) + CHR(53)	Italics Off
CHR(15)	Compressed On
CHR(18)	Compressed Off
CHR(27) + CHR(69)	Emphasized On
CHR(27) + CHR(70)	Emphasized Off
CHR(27) + CHR(71)	Bold On
CHR(27) + CHR(72)	Bold Off

If you use the escape codes to select different print styles often, consider storing them as memory variables, and saving those variables as a part of a configuration file. By having the escape codes stored as variables, you can use them where appropriate in your various printer routines, by using a SET PRINT ON statement followed by ??? *memvar*, where *memvar* is the memory variable that contains the escape code. As an example, you can store an escape code to a variable with a command like this:

```
BOLD = CHR(27) + CHR(71)
```

Within your printer routines, you can start printing with commands like

```
WAIT "Press a key to begin printing report..."
SET PRINT ON
??? BOLD
...more commands to print report...
```

If you are using the Hewlett-Packard LaserJet printer, or another laser printer compatible with the HP description language, you can use similar escape codes to select fonts, assuming they are available with your particular printer. The following simple menu program stores the escape codes for the HP LaserJet to a series of memory variables and then, depending on the chosen selection, routes the escape codes to the printer to select the desired fonts.

```
*Fonts.PRG for HP Laserjet and compatibles.*
STORE CHR(27)+"(0U"+CHR(27)+"(s 1p 10v 0s 0b 5T" to TmsRoman
STORE CHR(27)+"(0U"+CHR(27)+"(s 1p 10v 0s 3b 5T" to TmsRomanB
STORE CHR(27)+"(0U"+CHR(27)+"(s 1p 10v 0s 0b 5T" to TmsRomanC
STORE CHR(27)+"(0U"+CHR(27)+"(s 1p 10v 1s 0b 5T" to TmsRomanI
STORE CHR(27)+"(8U"+CHR(27)+"(s 0p 10h 12v 1s 0b 3T" to CourierI
STORE CHR(27)+"(8U"+CHR(27)+"(s 0p 10h 12v 0s 3b 3T" to CourierB
STORE CHR(27)+"(0U"+CHR(27)+"(s 1p 10h 14.4v 0s 3b 4T" to HelvBold
CLEAR
@ 3, 25 SAY      [SELECT A PRINTER FONT    ]
@ 5, 15 SAY      [ 1. Times Roman          ]
@ 7, 15 SAY      [ 2. Times Roman Italic   ]
@ 9, 15 SAY      [ 3. Times Roman Bold     ]
@ 11, 15 SAY     [ 4. Times Roman Compressed ]
@ 13, 15 SAY     [ 5. Courier Italic       ]
@ 14, 15 SAY     [ 5. Courier Bold         ]
@ 15, 15 SAY     [ 6. Helvetica Bold       ]
@ 17, 28 SAY     [       0. EXIT           ]
STORE 0 TO SELECTNUM
@ 19, 10 SAY " YOUR CHOICE?" GET SELECTNUM PICTURE '9'
READ
SET PRINT ON
DO CASE
      CASE SELECTNUM = 1
      ??? TmsRoman
```

```
        CASE SELECTNUM = 2
        ??? TmsRomanI
        CASE SELECTNUM = 3
        ??? TmsRomanB
        CASE SELECTNUM = 4
        ??? TmsRomanC
        CASE SELECTNUM = 5
        ??? CourierI
        CASE SELECTNUM = 6
        ??? CourierB
        CASE SELECTNUM = 7
        ??? HelvBold
ENDCASE
SET PRINT OFF
RETURN
```

If you are using an HP-compatible laser printer, you may want to experiment with the various fonts before using them in an application. Because dBASE IV assumes a standard character width for each printed character, the proportionally-spaced fonts generated by a laser printer may or may not appear where you would like to see them. Figure 16-1 shows the results of a LIST command using the Courier Italic font of the HP LaserJet, while Figure 16-2 shows the results of the same LIST command with the HP LaserJet set to the Helvetica Bold font. Without the ability to incrementally space characters on the printed page, it is impossible to maintain proper character spacing with the laser's

Figure 16-1.

```
J.E. Jones Associates             Reston      VA   22094
The Software Bar, Inc.            Herndon     VA   22070
Computers R Us                    Pasadena    CA   90556
Chapel Hill Life & Casualty       Carrboro    NC   27805
Sun City Transit Corporation      El Paso     TX   78809
Osborne-McGraw Hill               Berkeley    CA   94710
```

Results of LIST with Courier Italic font

Figure 16-2.

```
J.E. Jones Associates Reston VA 22094
The Software Bar, Inc. Herndon VA 22070
Computers R Us  Pasadena CA 90556
Chapel Hill Life & Company Carrboro NC 27805
Sun City Transit Corporation El Paso TX 78809
Osborne-McGraw Hill Berkeley CA 94710
```

Results of LIST with Helvetica Bold font

proportional fonts. This limits the use of the proportional fonts to items like headings and cover pages.

Quick Reference

To include reporting options in your programs Use the REPORT FORM comand along with the TO PRINT option at appropriate locations in your programs. Be sure to provide users with a way to cancel the report choice before starting to print the report.

To provide selective reports in your programs Use the SET FILTER, SET VIEW, or INDEX ON-FOR (version 1.1 only) command before you use the REPORT FORM command to limit the records that will be made available to the report.

When writing reports using program code Use SET PRINT ON, followed by ? or ?? statements, to route output to the printer.

Or use SET DEVICE TO PRINT followed by @-SAY statements, to route output to the printer. You will need to include statements that will count lines and pages processed to handle your own page breaks.

To control a printer when using stored reports in a program Store desired values to the printer system memory variables before calling the report with the REPORT FORM...TO PRINT command.

To control a printer when using reports written from program code Send the desired escape codes to the printer, using the ??? command. (See your printer documentation for appropriate escape codes.)

To print a report to a disk file When using stored reports, add the TO FILE *filename* clause to the end of the usual REPORT FORM command. When using reports produced from program code, use SET ALTERNATE statements if your reports do not use @-SAY commands, or use SET DEVICE TO *filename* statements if your reports use @-SAY commands.

CHAPTER

17

Using The Applications Generator

If you've closely followed this text, you should now know how you can put dBASE IV to work in your application. You have created different database files, used the menu choices for getting information from those database files, designed custom reports, and used macros to automate your work. If you've covered the last four chapters, you've also been introduced to programming with the dBASE language. But what may for many be the most advanced feature of dBASE IV has been saved for this chapter.

The dBASE IV applications generator is an applications development tool that you can use to create complete applications, with custom menus and help screens, for users of your database files, reports, and forms. You do not need to learn to program to create these applications; you can create them by choosing from a series of menu selections.

HINT Applications allow users who are unfamiliar with dBASE IV to manage you databases and generate reports with little training.

An Application, Defined

Why are applications so important to database users? In a nutshell, an application makes things easier on the average user because it combines a series of "building blocks," like database files, forms, reports, and labels, into a complete system. An application is what makes an accounts receivable system different from a database containing accounts receivable information. Both deal with the same kinds of information—dollar amounts and bills addressed to recipients that contain breakdowns of those amounts. But the accounts receivable database can only store the data, while the accounts receivable system has the database and all the other files (indexes, forms, reports, and programs) needed to solve a particular business problem.

In addition to helping you meet the needs of a specific task, an application binds together the building blocks of a database system. If you consider the parts of a database system—one or more database files, the indexes, the forms, labels, and the reports—to be building blocks of a sort, the application can be thought of as a kind of mortar that binds these building blocks into a complete, operating unit.

Applications are nothing new in the computer world, and there is a good chance that you have already used some types of specialized applications based on some sort of a database. The programs that handle mailing lists, inventory, sales tracking, and accounting are all specialized applications that make use of databases. To use these types of applications, however, you had to buy a software package designed for the application (or pay a programmer to write it), and then you were often stuck with something that did most, but not all, of what you wanted. The major difference with the dBASE IV applications generator is that you can build custom applications designed to do precisely what you want, while greatly reducing the time you need to write programs.

Much of what you need to know in order to use the dBASE IV applications generator is already familiar to you if you have been through the rest of this book. The dBASE IV applications generator uses the same kind of menus as are used throughout dBASE IV. A series of thorough help screens are accessible by pressing F1 anytime you are using the applications generator.

The Design of a Typical Application

To further illustrate how an application can make things easier, consider the work you've done in the examples throughout this book to create a usable system for ABC Temporaries. You have database files for tracking both employees and the time worked for clients, and you have custom forms and custom reports. With your familiarity with dBASE IV, if you want to add or edit data or to generate reports, you can load dBASE IV and use the various menu options to accomplish the desired results. When you want to show someone *else* in the office how to add or edit data or how to produce reports, however, you find quite a task ahead of you. That person must go through the same kind of learning process, getting sufficiently familiar with the dBASE IV menus until she or he can accomplish the same kind of results that you can manage. If your office has the usual moderate-to-high staff turnover common in today's business world, you could be faced with having to show others how to use dBASE IV for the same application, year in and year out.

The answer to this sort of dilemma, as proven by thousands of human programmers year after year, is to build custom applications containing menu choices that casual users will need no specialized training to understand. The applications generator lets you design the application to communicate in terms that people in your office will understand. As an example, the employees of ABC Temporaries commonly need to perform the following tasks:

- Add employees to the ABCSTAFF database file
- Edit employees in the ABCSTAFF database file
- Add client time to the HOURS database file
- Edit client time in the HOURS database file
- Add clients to the CLIENTS database file
- Edit clients in the CLIENTS database file
- Print a list of employees
- Print a list of client time records
- Print a list of clients

- Print a relational report containing names, "week ending" dates, client names, and city locations

You can automate these tasks by using the applications generator to create an application that provides a menu choice for each of the options just shown.

If you were to try to sketch out the design of such an application on paper, it might resemble the sketch in Figure 17-1. This example design makes use of multiple menus, one main menu leading to other secondary or submenus. As you design your own applications, you may find the use of secondary menus for specific areas, such as working with a particular database file or generating reports, to be a wise idea. If you try to place too many menu choices on a single menu, the application can become visually confusing.

Figure 17-1.

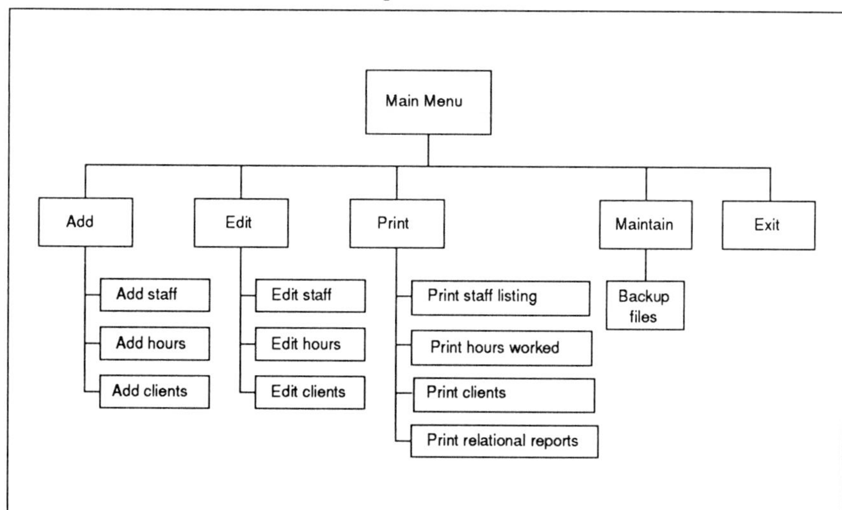

Design of application for ABC Temporaries

Figure 17-2.

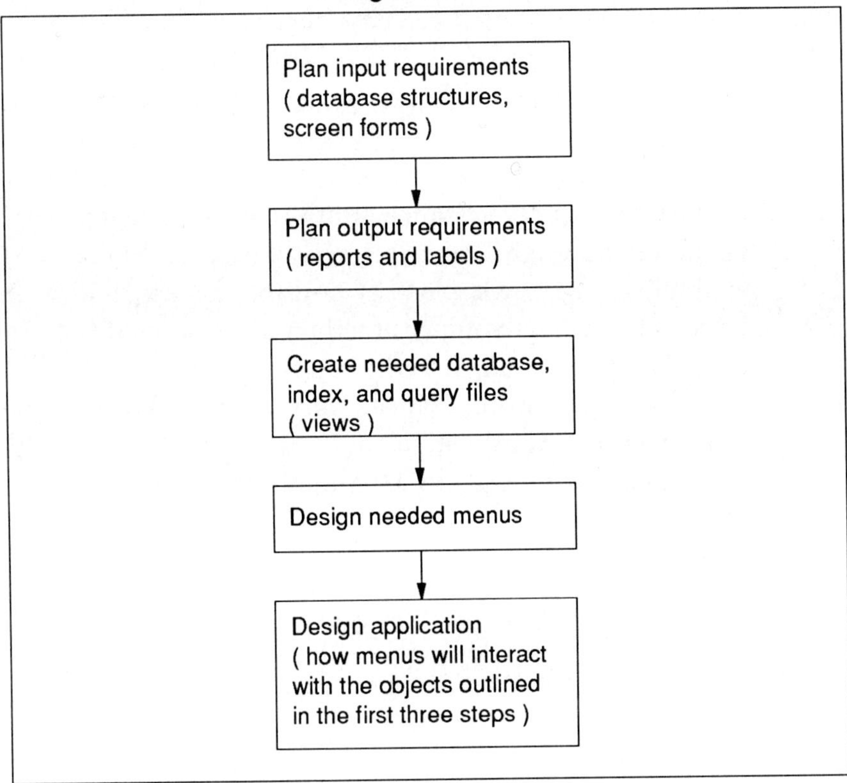

Planning an application

When designing any application, it is usually helpful to sketch out a preliminary design like this on paper before you start to use the applications generator. Figure 17-2 shows a logical sequence of steps you can follow when designing an application. Having the design outlined in this manner can give you a reference point to work from when you are actually building the application with the applications generator.

Because the applications generator is quite flexible, you can create applications that range from the very simple to the very complex. This chapter will provide you with examples of two applications, both based on the ABC Temporaries database files, forms, and reports. The first example demonstrates the Quick Application option, whereby you can create a simple application for managing a single database file within a matter of minutes. The second example is patterned after the illustration in Figure 17-1. This example will demonstrate the use of the applications generator to build a more complex, customized application with different database files, different forms, and different reports.

HINT Although you can build an application and design queries, forms, reports and labels at the same time, it's generally easier to design the needed queries, forms, reports, and labels first, and then build the application.

Using the Applications Generator

To start the applications generator, you can enter the CREATE APPLICATION *filename* command from the dot prompt, or from the Control Center you can select the Create option within the Applications panel. Get to the Control Center now, and select the Create option in the Applications panel. The next menu will ask if you want to create a dBASE program or use the applications generator. (The dBASE Program option simply puts you in the editor, where you can proceed to write dBASE programs manually.) In this case, choose Applications Generator from the menu. In a moment a new menu will appear, along with a dialog box, as shown in Figure 17-3.

In the dialog box you will enter information that defines the application, such as a filename for the application, the type of menu used as the main menu, and the database file and index

Figure 17-3.

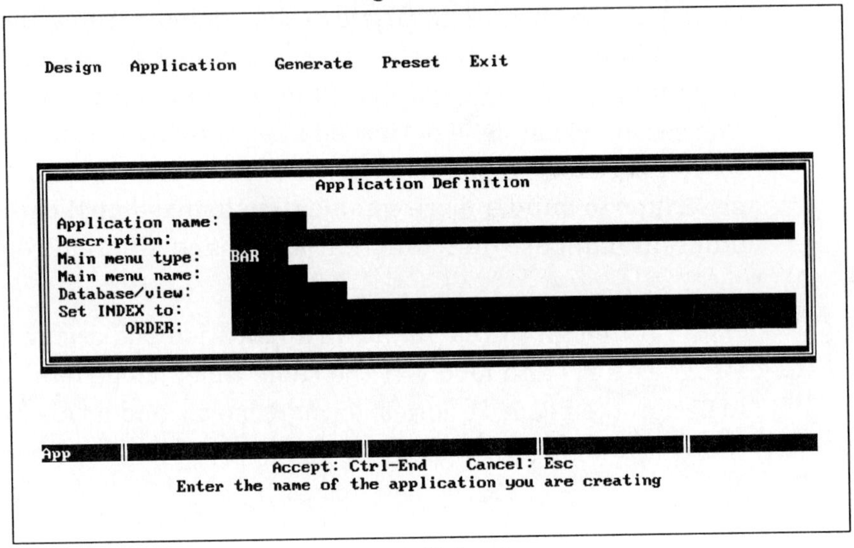

```
Design   Application   Generate   Preset   Exit

                 Application Definition
Application name:
Description:
Main menu type:  BAR
Main menu name:
Database/view:
Set INDEX to:
       ORDER:

App
              Accept: Ctrl-End     Cancel: Esc
        Enter the name of the application you are creating
```

Applications Generator menu and dialog box

used with the application. At the top of the screen are five menu options: Design, Application, Generate, Preset, and Exit. These menus (which cannot be chosen currently) will be used shortly to control the building of the application; before using any of them, however, you must fill in the information for the application's definition in the dialog box.

The cursor is currently in the Application Name box. In this box, you must enter a valid DOS name, up to eight characters long, for the application. For this example, enter **ABCQUICK**. Once you press ENTER, the cursor will move to the Description area, which can contain an optional description of the application. Enter the following:

```
Quick application for use with ABCSTAFF database.
```

After the description has been entered, the cursor moves to the Main Menu Type entry, and the default, Bar, currently appears in the entry. There are three choices offered by the applications generator for this entry: Bar, Pop-Up, and Batch. Bar menus appear in a bar at the top of the screen, like the dBASE menus themselves. Pop-up menus appear in a box that "pops up" at a specified location on the screen. "Batch" actually does not refer to a type of menu; rather it refers to a process (or sequence of dBASE commands) called a *batch process,* which can perform several operations, one of which might include opening a menu. To keep things simple, this chapter will use the bar and pop-up types for this choice.

Press the spacebar until "Pop-Up" appears in the entry. Then press ENTER to accept this type of menu and move to the next entry, Main Menu Name. In this area, you must enter a DOS name (1 to 8 characters, no spaces) that will be used for a program file that will contain the instructions used for the main menu. In this example, enter **ABCMAIN**.

In the Database/View area, enter **ABCSTAFF.DBF**. Note that you are allowed to enter the name of either a database file or a view here. When designing your own applications of a relational nature, it may be helpful to remember that you can use view names in this field as an option.

In the next area, Set Index To, enter **ABCSTAFF.MDX**. This will tell the applications generator to use the production index as the index for the application. In the last area, for the index order, enter **NAME**. This will cause the NAME tag of the production index (based on last names) to be used as the controlling index.

After entering the last item, press CTRL-END to save your entries. The dialog box will be replaced with an application object (Figure 17-4). The screen that you now see is the applications generator *desktop*. The menus will now be available, and the center of the screen contains the application object.

Figure 17-4.

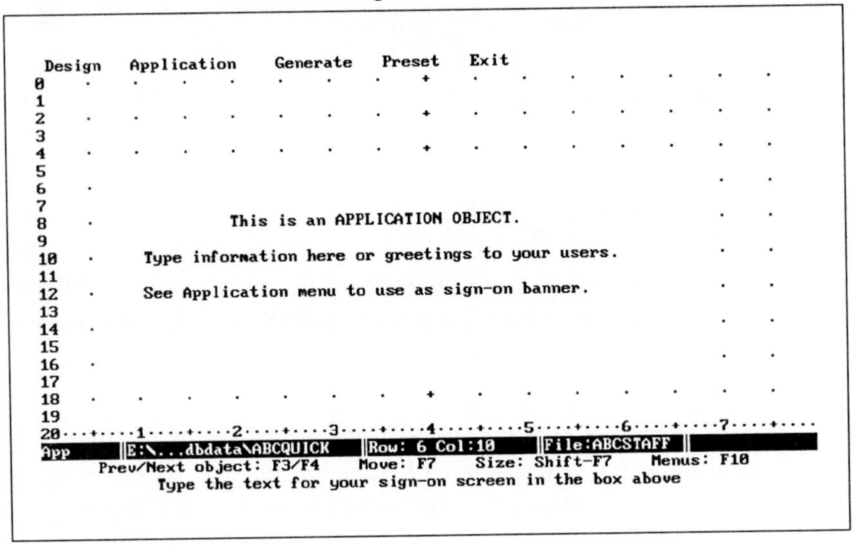

```
 Design   Application    Generate   Preset   Exit
0
1
2
3
4
5
6
7
8                This is an APPLICATION OBJECT.
9
10        Type information here or greetings to your users.
11
12        See Application menu to use as sign-on banner.
13
14
15
16
17
18
19
20····+····1····+····2····+····3····+····4····+····5····+····6····+····7····+····
App     E:\...dbdata\ABCQUICK    Row: 6 Col:10    File:ABCSTAFF
     Prev/Next object: F3/F4    Move: F7    Size: Shift-F7    Menus: F10
          Type the text for your sign-on screen in the box above
```

Application object

An application object will always appear on the desktop, although you can change its size, if desired, to reveal more of the desktop work surface. You can also work with additional objects as you design the application, so you may put away one object as it is replaced with another. You can also use the application object as a *sign-on banner,* which is an introductory screen seen by users when they start the application.

Press F10 now, and the Design menu will open (Figure 17-5). It lets you choose additional objects (such as menus) that you will create or modify while building the application.

Press the right arrow key once to see the Application menu (Figure 17-6). The various choices in this menu will apply to objects on the desktop that you are working with. As an example, you will shortly apply the Display Sign-On Banner option to the application object currently on the screen. If you were working with an object that would be used as a main menu, you could use the Assign Main Menu option with that object.

Figure 17-5.

```
Design  Application    Generate   Preset   Exit
 Horizontal bar menu
 Pop-up menu
 Files list
 Structure list
 Values list

 Batch process
                      s an APPLICATION OBJECT.
9
10  ·     Type information here or greetings to your users.
11
12  ·     See Application menu to use as sign-on banner.
13
14  ·
15
16  ·
17
18  ·
19
20···+····1····+····2····+····3····+····4····+····5····+····6····+····7····+····
App      ||E:\...dbdata\ABCQUICK  ||               ||File:ABCSTAFF ||
    Prev/Next object:F3/F4   Change menu:↔   Select:◄┘   Work surface:Esc
                   Create or modify a horizontal bar menu
```

Design menu

Figure 17-6.

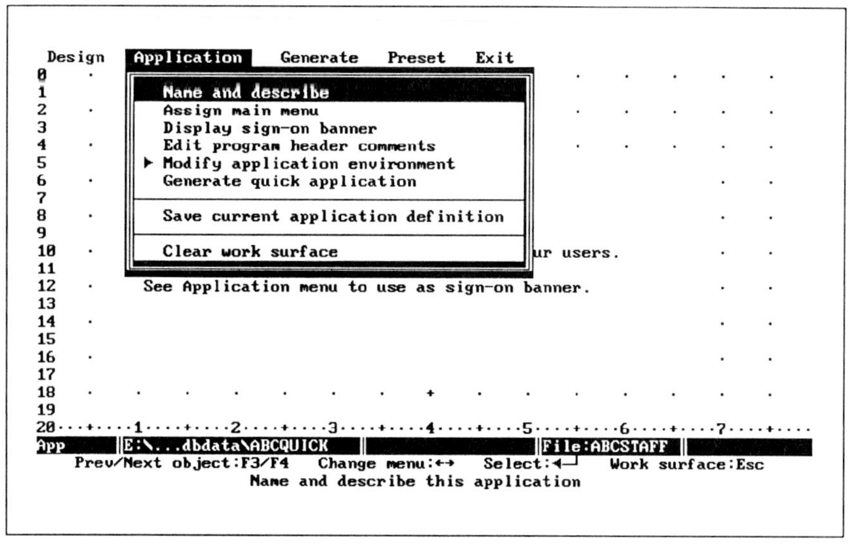

Application menu

☞ ***REMEMBER*** You can also use the ALT key plus the first letter of a menu to open a menu.

Press the right arrow key once, and the Generate menu will open (Figure 17-7). Using the options within this menu, you can generate the dBASE programs that will make up your application. You can also generate descriptions for the application objects that you create.

Press the right arrow key once, and the Preset menu will open (Figure 17-8). This menu lets you set the defaults for various options in the applications generator, such as the default text in a sign-on banner, display options for the application, environmental settings, and the disk drive and path normally used.

Finally, the Exit menu is the same as other Exit menus throughout dBASE IV, with two choices: Save Changes and Exit, or Abandon Changes and Exit.

Press ESC now to close any open menu and get back to the application object. This first application object will be used as a sign-on screen for our application, so press CTRL-Y repeatedly until all the existing lines of text have been deleted. Place the cursor at row 8, column 20 (you can determine the row and column positions from the status bar), and enter this:

```
ABC Temporaries Staff File Manager
```

Then move the cursor to row 10, column 20, and enter the following text:

```
Press any key to begin...
```

Open the Application menu with ALT-A. You'll need to tell dBASE that the application object currently on the screen will be used as a sign-on banner. Choose Display Sign-On Banner from the menu, and then select Yes from the confirmation menu that next appears.

Figure 17-7.

```
 Design    Application    Generate   Preset    Exit
0                        Begin generating
1                        Select template
2                        Display during generation
3
4
5
6
7
8              This is an APPLICATION OBJECT.
9
10      Type information here or greetings to your users.
11
12      See Application menu to use as sign-on banner.
13
14
15
16
17
18
19
20····+····1····+····2····+····3····+····4····+····5····+····6····+····7····+····
App   E:\...dbdata\ABCQUICK                    File:ABCSTAFF
    Prev/Next object:F3/F4   Change menu:←→   Select:◄┘   Work surface:Esc
        Generate dBASE program or doc using currently selected template
```

Generate menu

Figure 17-8.

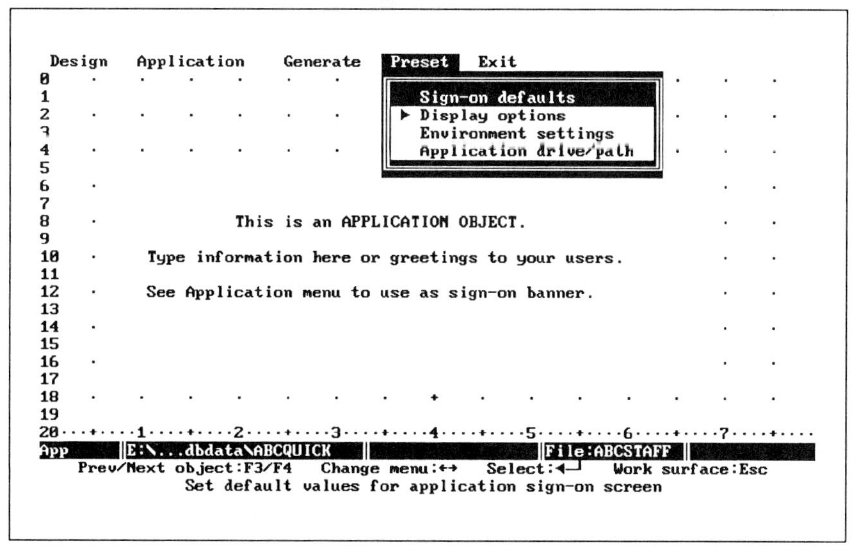

Preset menu

If you were creating a complex application, you could now proceed to use the various options of the Design menu to create custom menus, and link those menus with actions that dBASE should perform when the application is run. However, the applications generator offers a Generate Quick Application option to create a simple application for adding and editing records and for producing reports or labels, without requiring any detailed menu design on your part. From the Application menu (which should still be open), choose Generate Quick Application now. Another dialog box will open, as shown in Figure 17-9.

In this dialog box you can enter a name for the database, report format, screen format, label format, and indexes used by the quick application. From viewing this screen, you may realize a limitation of the "quick application"—you can only use one report and one label. If you want to give your users a choice of more than one

Figure 17-9.

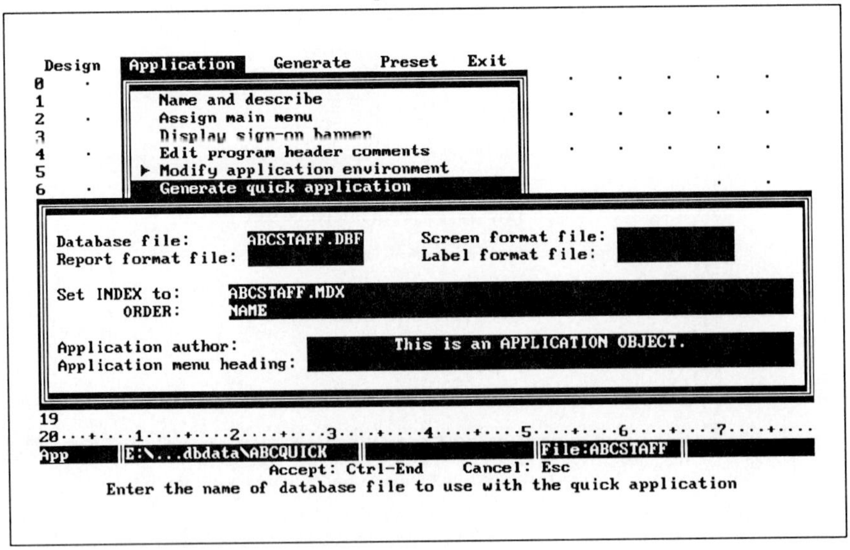

```
Design   Application   Generate   Preset   Exit
0
1            Name and describe
2            Assign main menu
3            Display sign-on banner
4            Edit program header comments
5          ▸ Modify application environment
6            Generate quick application

  Database file:         ABCSTAFF.DBF        Screen format file:
  Report format file:                        Label format file:

  Set INDEX to:        ABCSTAFF.MDX
          ORDER:       NAME

  Application author:              This is an APPLICATION OBJECT.
  Application menu heading:

19
20···+····1····+····2····+····3····+····4····+····5····+····6····+····7····+····
App      E:\...dbdata\ABCQUICK                       File:ABCSTAFF
                      Accept: Ctrl-End     Cancel: Esc
          Enter the name of database file to use with the quick application
```

Dialog box for Generate Quick Application

report, you would need to design the more detailed type of application and skip the Generate Quick Application option. You'll build the more detailed type of application later in this chapter.

HINT Generate Quick Application is an excellent choice when you need an application to manage a single database file.

Since you selected the database name and the index earlier, these already appear in the Database File, Set Index To, and Order areas. Press ENTER to move to the file entry for Screen Format. While you can enter this name manually, you can also choose the file from a list of available screen format files. Press SHIFT-F1 now to display the list, and select ABCFORM from the list.

The cursor now moves to the Report Format file entry. Again, press SHIFT-F1, and choose RFORM1 from the list of reports. In the Label Format file entry, press SHIFT-F1, and choose ABCMAIL from the list.

Finally, press ENTER until the cursor moves down to the last entry, Application Menu Heading. Enter the following:

```
ABC Temporaries Staff Management System
```

With the final entry made, press CTRL-END. Another menu box will appear, displaying the prompt

```
Select YES to generate the quick application; select NO to cancel.
```

Choose Yes from the menu box to begin generating the quick application. When the process has been completed, you will see the message

```
Generation is complete--press any key to continue
```

at the bottom of the screen. Press a key, and you will be returned to the desktop.

Open the Exit menu with ALT-E, and choose Save All Changes and Exit. You will be returned to the Control Center, and the application, called ABCQUICK, will now appear in the Applications panel.

Running the Application

To run an application, you can enter the DO *filename* command from the dot prompt, or you can select the application within the Applications panel and choose Run Application from the next menu to appear. Choose ABCQUICK from the Applications panel now, and select Run Application from the next menu. Finally, confirm the choice by choosing Yes from the next menu to appear.

After the application has been loaded, the sign-on banner will appear. You can either press a key or wait a few moments, in which case the sign-on banner will eventually vanish. When the sign-on banner disappears, the menu for the quick application appears (see Figure 17-10).

All applications created with the Generate Quick Application option of the applications generator will resemble this one, with choices for adding information, changing information, using Browse mode, deleting marked records, and printing reports or mailing labels. If you do not specify a mailing-label format file during the design of the application, the menu choice for labels is omitted from the resulting application; the same is true for reports. You might want to spend some time trying the various options of the application to see how they work. When you are done experimenting with your new application, choose the Exit from Abcquick option of the menu to get back to the Control Center.

Figure 17-10.

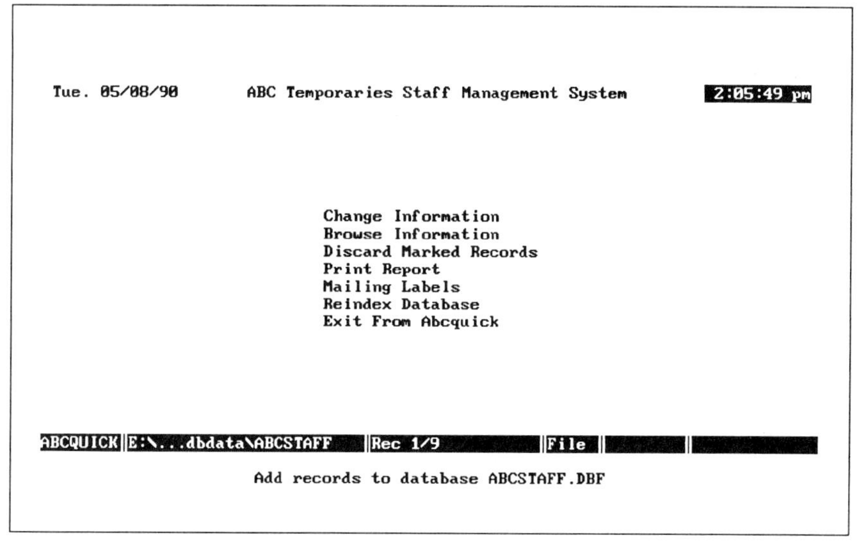

Menu for quick application

Creating a Complex Application

As mentioned earlier, you may want to offer your users more options in an application, such as the ability to work with different database files and use different reports. You may also want to design complex menu structures in your application. You can do all of this with the options provided by the applications generator. The next example will use database files, forms, and reports you created in earlier chapters to form a more complex application.

Highlight the Create option of the Applications panel, and press ENTER; then choose Applications Generator from the next menu to appear. The dialog box for the application definition will again appear on the screen. Enter **ABCFULL** for the application name. For a description, enter

```
ABC Temporaries Complex Application
```

For the Main Menu type, press ENTER to accept Bar as the default menu type. For the Main Menu Name, enter **ABCTEMPS**. For the Database/View name, enter **ABCSTAFF.DBF**. For the Set Index To entry, enter **ABCSTAFF.MDX**. For the Order entry, enter **NAME**. Finally, press CTRL-END to store the entries. The application object will appear on the desktop.

Press CTRL-Y repeatedly until the text in the application object is deleted, and then enter the following at row 10, column 12:

```
ABC Temporaries Staff Management System. Press a key.
```

Open the Application menu with ALT-A, and choose Display Sign-On Banner. Then select Yes from the confirmation prompt that appears.

The next logical step in designing the application is to create the main menu, since it is used as a focal point for all operations within the system. The Design menu is used to design objects (including menus), so open it now with ALT-D.

Choose the Horizontal Bar Menu option from the Design menu. Another list box appears, containing the Create option; select it now. The next dialog box to appear asks for a name, description, and message-line prompt for the menu you are designing. For the name, enter **ABCTEMPS**. For the description, enter

```
ABC Temporaries System Main Menu
```

For the message-line prompt, enter

```
Use the left, right arrow keys to highlight a selection.
```

Then press CTRL-END to save the entries. When you do this, an empty bar menu appears at the top of the screen.

When designing a horizontal bar menu, you use the F5 (Field) key to mark the beginning and end of the options you place within the menu. This particular menu is to have five options: Add, Edit, Print, Maintain, and Exit. Move the cursor to column 3, and press F5 (Field) to begin entering the option name. Type **Add**, and then press F5 again. Next, move the cursor to column 18. Press F5, type **Edit**, and press F5 again. Move the cursor to column 33. Press F5, type **Print**, and press F5 again. Move the cursor to column 52. Press F5, type **Maintain**, and press F5 again. Finally, move the cursor to column 70, press F5, and type **Exit**. Press F5 again.

Next, you'll need to define a series of secondary menus that will appear when the menu choices in the main menu are selected. The first main menu choice, Add, needs to specify whether data will be added to the ABCSTAFF file, to the HOURS file, or to the CLIENTS file. Open the Design menu with ALT-D and choose Pop-Up Menu. Choose Create from the next option list. When the dialog box asks you for the name, description, and message-line prompt for the new menu, enter the following:

(Name:) ADD

(Description:) Add new records to file

(Message-line prompt:) Choose a database to add records to.

Press CTRL-END to store the changes, and a new empty pop-up menu will appear in the center of the screen.

With pop-up menus, you don't need to use the F5 key as you did with the horizontal bar menus; you just enter the desired menu option on each line of the pop-up menu. Enter the following on the first three lines of the menu:

Add to staff file
Add to hours file
Add to clients file

Then press SHIFT-F7 (Size), and press the up arrow key three times to shrink the size of the menu. Press ENTER to accept the new size. Press F7, and choose Entire Frame from the next menu to move the entire frame. Using the cursor keys, move the frame to row 1, column 1, and press ENTER to place the menu in its new location.

Highlight the Add to Staff File menu choice, and open the Item menu with ALT-I. The Item menu lets you control what your items on the desktop do, so you'll use this menu to assign desired actions to an item (in this case, a menu choice). Choose Change Action from the Item menu. Select the Edit Form option from the next menu to appear. A dialog box with various options now appears, as shown in Figure 17-11.

You could enter various choices to limit or control what the user is allowed to do when adding records. In this case, nearly all of the default options will be accepted. One option that would

Figure 17-11.

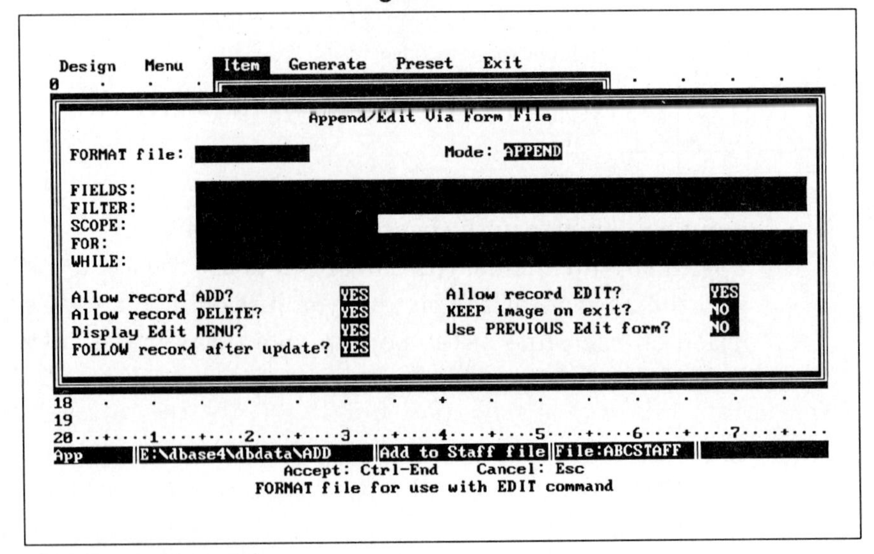

Edit Form dialog box

improve the look of things would be to use the screen format file for adding records. With the cursor in the Format File entry, press SHIFT- F1, and choose ABCFORM from the list that appears. Finally, press CTRL-END to store the entries.

Press ESC to close the Item menu, and press the down arrow key once to highlight the Add to Hours File choice. Open the Item menu with ALT-I, and choose Override Assigned Database or View. You use this option to tell dBASE that the menu choice you are now defining should make use of a different database file than the default, which was entered when you started defining the application. When the dialog box appears, press the spacebar once to change the highlighted entry from Above to Entered Below. Doing this will tell dBASE to use the filename and index name you are about to enter along with this menu choice.

Press ENTER, and the cursor will move to the Database/View entry at the bottom of the screen. Press SHIFT-F1 to display the list of available files, and choose HOURS.DBF. In the Set Index To area, enter **HOURS.MDX**. In the Order area, enter **SO-CIALSEC**. Press CTRL-END to store the entries.

Choose Change Action from the Item menu to tell dBASE what action this menu choice should perform. From the next menu, choose Browse. (For the sake of experience, this application will use Browse mode for adding records, since there are few fields in the HOURS database.) When the dialog box appears, press ENTER until the cursor moves to the Fields to Lock Onscreen entry. Enter **1** as the value. The remaining Browse mode options will do fine for this example, so accept the options by pressing CTRL-END.

Press ESC to close the Item menu, and press the down arrow key once to highlight the Add to Clients File choice. Open the Item menu with ALT-I, and choose Override Assigned Database or View. When the dialog box appears, press the spacebar once to change the highlighted entry from Above to Entered Below. Press ENTER, and the cursor will move to the Database/View entry at the bottom of the screen. Press SHIFT-F1 to display the list of available files, and choose CLIENTS.DBF. In the Set Index To area, enter **CLIENTS.MDX**. In the Order area, enter **CLIENT**. Press CTRL-END to store the entries.

Choose Change Action from the Item menu. From the next menu, choose Browse. Press ENTER until the cursor moves to the Fields to Lock Onscreen entry. Enter **1** as the value. Press CTRL-END to accept the remaining default options for Browse mode.

Open the Menu menu with ALT-M, and choose Put Away Current Menu. Another menu appears, asking if you want to save your changes. Choose Save Changes from this menu. Open the Design menu with ALT-D, and choose Pop-Up menu. Choose Create from the next option list. When the dialog box asks for the name, description, and message-line prompt, enter the following:

(Name:) EDIT

(Description:) Edit records in a file

(Message-line prompt:) Choose a database to edit

Press CTRL-END to store the changes, and a new, empty pop-up menu will appear. Enter the following on the first three lines of the menu:

```
Edit staff file
Edit hours file
Edit clients file
```

Then press SHIFT-F7 (Size), and press the up arrow key three times to shrink the size of the menu. Press ENTER to accept the new size. Then press F7, and choose Entire Frame from the next menu. Move the frame to row 1, column 18, and press ENTER to place the menu in its new location.

Highlight the Edit Staff File menu choice, and open the Item menu with ALT-I. Choose Change Action from the Item menu. Select the Edit Form option from the next menu to appear. Again, nearly all the default options will be acceptable in this case. With the cursor in the Format File entry, press SHIFT-F1, and choose ABCFORM as the screen format.

Once you make the selection, the cursor will move down to the Mode entry. Press the spacebar once to change this entry from Append to Edit. Next, press ENTER until the cursor moves to the Allow Record ADD? entry. Press the spacebar to change this option to No. Finally, press CTRL-END to store the entries.

Press ESC to close the Item menu, and press the down arrow key once to highlight the Edit Hours File choice. Open the Item menu with ALT-I, and choose Override Assigned Database or View. When the dialog box appears, press the spacebar once to change the highlighted entry from Above to Entered Below. Press ENTER, and the cursor will move to the Database/View entry at the bottom of the screen. Press SHIFT-F1 to display the list of available files, and choose HOURS.DBF. In the Set Index To area, enter **HOURS.MDX**. In the Order area, enter **SOCIALSEC**. Press CTRL-END to store the entries.

Choose Change Action from the Item menu. From the next menu, choose Browse. When the dialog box appears, press ENTER until the cursor moves to the Fields to Lock Onscreen entry. Enter **1** as the value. Press ENTER until the cursor moves to the Allow Record ADD? entry. Press the spacebar to change this option to No. The remaining Browse mode options will again serve for this example, so accept them by pressing CTRL-END.

Press ESC to close the Item menu, and press the down arrow key once to highlight the Edit Clients File choice. Open the Item menu with ALT-I, and choose Override Assigned Database or View. When the dialog box appears, press the spacebar once to change the highlighted entry from Above to Entered Below. Press ENTER, and the cursor will move to the Database/View entry at the bottom of the screen. Press SHIFT-F1 to display the list of available files, and choose CLIENTS.DBF. In the Set Index To area, enter **CLIENTS.MDX**. In the Order area, enter **CLIENT**. Press CTRL-END to store the entries.

Choose Change Action from the Item menu. From the next menu, choose Browse. Press ENTER until the cursor moves to the Allow Record ADD? entry, and press the spacebar to change this option to No. Press CTRL-END to accept the default options for Browse mode. Open the Menu menu with ALT-M, and choose Put Away Current menu. Choose Save Changes from the menu box that appears next.

You have now defined the pop-up menus that will be used for adding and editing records. The menus for reports, file maintenance, and exiting the application remain to be created, but first you must create two new reports that will be used in the application. You can use the default quick report design to do this.

Open the Exit menu with ALT-E, and choose Save All Changes and Exit from the menu. In a moment you will be returned to the Control Center. Highlight the HOURS file in the Data panel, and open the file by pressing ENTER twice. Then choose the Create option of the Reports panel to create a new report. When the Report Design screen appears, choose Quick Layout, and then choose Column Layout. A default report design will appear in the design screen. Open the Exit menu with ALT-E, and choose Save Changes and Exit. For a filename, enter **HOURSREP**.

When the report has been saved and the Control Center reappears, highlight the CLIENTS file in the Data panel, and open the file by pressing ENTER twice. Then choose the Create option of the Reports Panel to create another report. When the Report Design screen appears, choose Quick Layout and then choose Column Layout. A default report design will appear in the design screen. Open the Exit menu with ALT-E, and choose Save Changes and Exit. For a filename, enter **CLIENTRP**.

When the Control Center reappears, select ABCFULL at the Applications panel, and choose Modify Application to continue the process of application design. Open the Design menu with ALT-D, and choose Pop-Up menu. Choose Create from the next option list. When the dialog box asks for the name, description, and message-line prompt, enter the following:

(Name:) PRINT

(Description:) Print Reports

(Message-line prompt:) Choose the desired report.

Press CTRL-END to store the changes, and a new, empty pop-up menu will appear. Enter the following on the first four lines of the menu:

Print Staff Listing
Print Hours Worked
Print Clients
Relational Report

Then press SHIFT-F7 (Size), and press the up arrow key three times to shrink the size of the menu. Press ENTER to accept the new size.

Press F7, and choose Entire Frame from the next menu. Move the frame to row 1, column 30, and press ENTER to place the menu in its new location. Highlight the Print Staff Listing choice within the new menu, and open the Item menu with ALT-I. Choose Change Action from the Item menu. At the next menu, choose Display or Print, and then select Report Form.

A dialog box for entering information about the report will now appear (Figure 17-12). Note that you can choose report formats, heading formats, and where the output of the report should be directed. You can also enter filter conditions, a scope, and FOR or WHILE conditions to further limit the records that are displayed or printed in response to a menu selection.

With the cursor in the Form Name entry, press SHIFT-F1 to display the list of available reports. Choose RFORM1 from the list. (If you don't want to waste paper, you may also prefer to change the Before Printing option to Do Not Eject. This will tell dBASE not to eject a sheet of paper before starting the report.) Press CTRL-END to accept the remaining default options.

Figure 17-12.

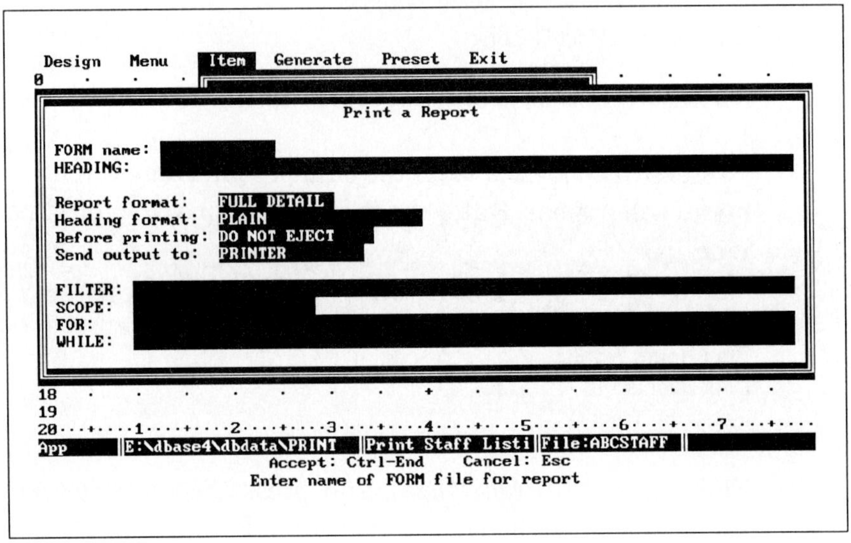

```
Design   Menu   Item   Generate   Preset   Exit
0
                         Print a Report

FORM name:
HEADING:

Report format:    FULL DETAIL
Heading format:   PLAIN
Before printing:  DO NOT EJECT
Send output to:   PRINTER

FILTER:
SCOPE:
FOR:
WHILE:

18
19
20···+····1····+····2····+····3····+····4····+····5····+····6····+····7····+····
App     E:\dbase4\dbdata\PRINT   Print Staff Listi  File:ABCSTAFF
                Accept: Ctrl-End      Cancel: Esc
              Enter name of FORM file for report
```

Dialog box for reports

Press ESC to close the Item menu, and highlight the Print Hours Worked option of the menu. Open the Item menu with ALT-I, and choose Override Assigned Database or View. When the dialog box appears, press the spacebar once to change the highlighted entry from Above to Entered Below. Press ENTER, and the cursor will move to the Database/View entry at the bottom of the screen. Press SHIFT-F1 to display the list of available files, and choose HOURS.DBF. In the Set Index To area, enter **HOURS.MDX**. In the Order area, enter **SOCIALSEC**. Press CTRL-END to store the entries.

Choose Change Action from the Item menu. From the next menu, choose Display or Print, and then choose Report Form. With the cursor in the Form Name entry, press SHIFT-F1, and choose HOURSREP as the report name. Then press CTRL-END to accept the remaining options.

Press ESC to close the Item menu, and highlight the Print Clients option of the menu. Open the Item menu with ALT-I, and choose Override Assigned Database or View. When the dialog box appears, press the spacebar once to change the highlighted entry from Above to Entered Below. Press ENTER, and the cursor will move to the Database/View entry at the bottom of the screen. Press SHIFT-F1 to display the list of available files, and choose CLIENTS.DBF. In the Set Index To area, enter **CLIENTS.MDX**. In the Order area, enter **CLIENT**. Press CTRL-END to store the entries.

Choose Change Action from the Item menu. From the next menu, choose Display or Print, and then choose Report Form. With the cursor in the Form Name entry, press SHIFT-F1, and choose CLIENTRP as the report name. Then press CTRL-END to accept the remaining options.

Press ESC to close the Item menu, and highlight the Relational Report option of the menu. Open the Item menu with ALT-I, and choose Override Assigned Database or View. When the dialog box appears, press the spacebar once to change the highlighted entry from Above to Entered Below. Press ENTER, and the cursor will move to the Database/View entry at the bottom of the screen. Press SHIFT-F1 to display the list of available files, and choose RELATE3.QBE. This time, you may ignore the index and order entries. Press CTRL-END to store the entries.

☞ ***REMEMBER*** Whenever you enter the name of a view query in the Database/View entry of the applications generator, the data made available to that portion of the application will be dependent on the view query you designed earlier.

Choose Change Action from the Item menu. From the next menu, choose Display or Print, and then choose Display/List. Press CTRL-END to accept the remaining options. For simplicity's sake, this selection will tell dBASE to use the LIST command to display the available fields in the relational query you created in Chapter 12.

Open the Menu menu with ALT-M, and choose Put Away Current menu. Choose Save Changes from the next menu to appear. The next menu, Maintain, will have only one choice for backing up the files. Open the Design menu with ALT-D, choose Pop-Up menu, and choose Create. When the dialog box asks for a name, description, and message prompt, enter the following:

(Name:) MAINTAIN

(Description:) Maintenance menu

(Message-line prompt:) Perform file maintenance.

Press CTRL-END to save the entries and display the new menu. Next, enter the following on the first line of the menu:

Backup file

Then press SHIFT-F7 (Size), and press the up arrow key five times. Press ENTER to accept the new menu size. Press F7 and choose Entire Frame from the next menu. Move the menu frame to row 1, column 52, and press ENTER to place the menu in its new location.

Highlight the Backup File option of the new menu, and open the Item menu with ALT-I. Choose Change Action from the menu. At the next menu that appears, choose Perform File Operation. A menu of various file operations will appear (Figure 17-13). Select File Copy from this menu. A new dialog box containing areas for "COPY file" (the source) and "TO file" (the destination) will appear. Enter **ABCSTAFF.DBF** in the COPY file area. Enter **ABCSTAFF.DBK** in the TO file area. Press CTRL-END to accept the entry.

To keep things simple, our menu option will create a backup file only for the ABCSTAFF database. In actual design you would

Figure 17-13.

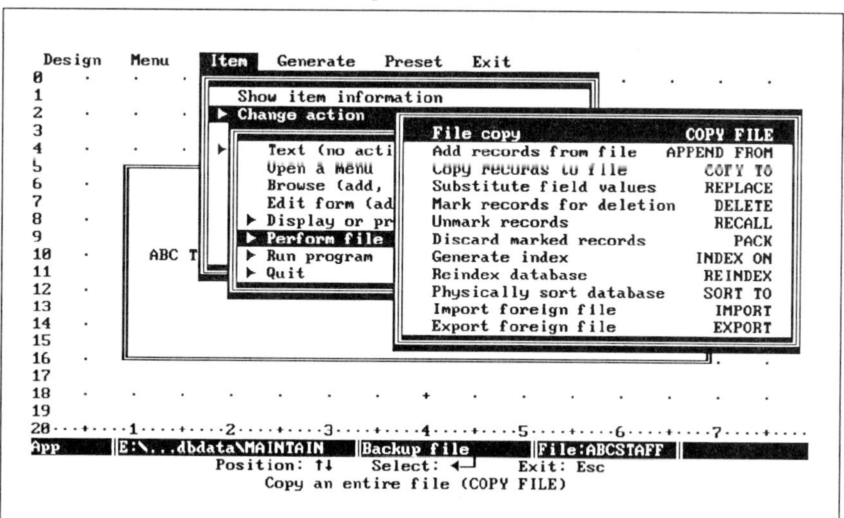

File operations

want to be more thorough and provide menu options to back up the memo field file (ABCSTAFF.DBT), the index files, and other databases as well.

Open the Menu menu by using ALT-M, and choose Put Away Current menu. Choose Save Changes from the next menu that appears.

The final menu, Exit, will also have just one choice, for exiting the application. Open the Design menu with ALT-D, choose Pop-Up menu, and choose Create. When the dialog box asks for a name, description, and message prompt, enter the following:

(Name:) EXIT

(Description:) Exit application

(Message-line prompt:) Choose this option to leave the system.

Press CTRL-END to save the entries and display the new menu. Next, enter the following on the first line of the menu:

```
Exit System
```

Then press SHIFT-F7 (Size), and press the up arrow key five times. Press ENTER to accept the new menu size. Press F7 and choose Entire Frame from the next menu. Move the menu frame to row 1, column 58, and press ENTER to place the menu in its new location.

Highlight the Exit System option of the new menu, and open the Item menu with ALT-I. Choose Change Action from the menu. At the next menu to appear, choose Quit. Then choose Return from the next menu displayed, and confirm your choice by selecting OK from the prompt box. Open the Menu menu with ALT-M, and choose Put Away Current menu. Choose Save Changes from the next menu to appear.

As a final step, you must tell dBASE what actions the main menu items should take; you need to link the main menu choices with the pop-up menus you have created. Open the Design menu with ALT-D, choose Horizontal Bar menu, and select ABCTEMPS from the list to bring the bar menu you designed earlier back onto the screen. Next, move the cursor within the bar menu to the word "Add" so it is highlighted, and open the Item menu with ALT-I. Choose Change Action, and then select Open a Menu. Press the spacebar until "Pop-Up" appears, and then press ENTER. Enter **ADD** in the menu name field, and then press CTRL-END. This action links the bar menu choice, Add, to the Add pop-up menu.

Press ESC to close the Item menu, and then move the cursor to the Edit option within the bar menu. Open the Item menu with ALT-I. Choose Change Action, and then select Open a Menu. Press the spacebar until "Pop-Up" appears, and then press ENTER. Enter **EDIT** in the menu name field, and then press CTRL-END.

This action links the bar menu choice, Edit, to the Edit pop-up menu. The next three steps will perform the same task for the remaining pop-up menus.

Press ESC to close the Item menu, and then move the cursor to the Print option within the bar menu. Open the Item menu with ALT-I. Choose Change Action, and then select Open a Menu. Press the spacebar until "Pop-Up" appears; then press ENTER. Enter **PRINT** in the menu name field, and then press CTRL-END.

Press ESC to close the Item menu, and then move the cursor to the Maintain option within the bar menu. Open the Item menu with ALT-I. Choose Change Action, and then select Open a Menu. Press the spacebar until "Pop-Up" appears, and then press ENTER. Enter **MAINTAIN** in the menu name field, and then press CTRL-END.

Press ESC to close the Item menu, and then move the cursor to the Exit option within the bar menu. Open the Item menu with ALT-I. Choose Change Action, and then select Open a Menu. Press the spacebar until "Pop-Up" appears; then press ENTER. Enter **EXIT** in the menu name field, and press CTRL-END.

Open the Menu menu with ALT-M, and choose Put Away Current menu. Choose Save Changes from the next menu. Note that it is important to put away the menu before you choose the Begin Generating option to generate the application. If a menu or another object (other than the application object) is still in use when you tell dBASE to begin generating an application, the applications generator will generate the necessary code for that object and not for the entire application.

You have designed all the menus and provided dBASE with the information it needs to know to build the application. Open the Generate menu with ALT-G. Choose Display During Generation, and then confirm this choice by selecting Yes from the prompt box. (This choice is by no means mandatory; although it slows the process slightly, it is entertaining to see the results as dBASE proceeds to write the programs needed for the application.)

Finally, choose Begin Generating from the Generate menu. The applications generator will proceed to generate the application. As it does so, program code will scroll rapidly up the screen. When the process is finished, you will see the message

```
Generation is complete--press any key to continue
```

at the bottom of the screen. Press a key, and you will be returned to the application generator desktop. Open the Exit menu with ALT-E, and choose Save All Changes and Exit to get back to the Control Center.

Running the Complex Application

To run the application, choose ABCFULL from the Applications panel now, and select Run Application from the next menu. Finally, confirm the choice by choosing Yes from the next menu to appear.

After the application loads, the sign-on banner will appear. You can either press a key or wait a few moments for the sign-on banner to vanish. When the sign-on banner disappears, the menu for the application appears (Figure 17-14). Unlike the quick application, this application is tailored to perform the specific design you outlined with the various choices of the applications generator.

You might want to spend some time trying the various options of the application to see how they work. When you are done experimenting with your new application, choose the Exit option of the menu to get back to the Control Center.

Figure 17-14.

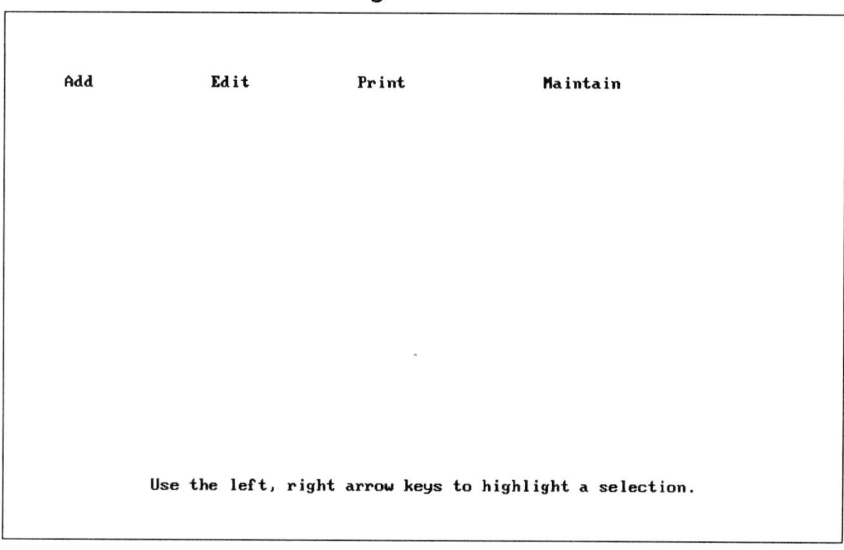

Menu for complex application

REMEMBER From the dot prompt, enter DO *appname* (where *appname* is the name you saved an application under) to run an application.

Just the Beginning

This chapter has given you an idea of the power and ease of use that a professional application, written with the help of the applications generator, can provide. Chapter 20, "Sample Applications," provides additional examples of how the applications generator can be used to aid in the design and implementation of complete applications.

If your job can be made easier through the presence of applications, take the time to explore all of the features of the applications generator. The resulting applications will be well worth the time you spend.

Quick Reference

To start the applications generator From the Control Center, select the Create option in the Applications Panel. From the next menu to appear, choose Applications Generator. Or from the dot prompt enter **CREATE APPLICATION *filename***, where *filename* is the name for the application.

To design menus used in an application Open the Design menu and select the type of menu desired (horizontal or pop-up). When the new menu appears, assign the desired selections to the menu choices. Repeat these steps for all menus needed in the application.

To specify an action for a menu item Highlight the menu item,open the Item menu with ALT-I, and choose Change Action. At the next screen, select the type of action needed. Repeat these steps for each item in the menu.

To generate the application Make sure the application object is highlighted, and open the Generate menu with ALT-G. Choose Begin Generating to generate the application.

To save all design changes to the application Open the Exit menu with ALT-E, and choose Save Changes and Exit.

CHAPTER

18

Using dBASE IV With Other Programs

The ability to exchange information with other programs enhances the power of dBASE IV. dBASE IV allows you to transfer files between it and nearly all popular software available for the PC. There is just one condition to dBASE IV's ability to receive transferred information: the other programs must be able to transfer information in a format acceptable to dBASE IV.

File Formats

You can transfer information between dBASE IV and another program in various formats. These include ASCII format, delimited format, system data format (SDF), document interchange format (DIF), symbolic link format (SYLK), PFS:FILE format, RapidFile format (RPD), Framework-II format, and Lotus worksheet format (WKS and WK1). Delimited and SDF files are composed of ASCII text in a special format.

ASCII Format

The term *ASCII format* refers to files that are composed of characters and spaces not necessarily arranged in any particular order. ASCII stands for the American Standard Code for Information Interchange, an international method of representing information in computers. Text files created by word processors are stored as ASCII text. You'll use ASCII files if you need to merge the contents of a database with a document created by a word processor. If, for example, your database contains a list of names, you can save those names to a text file in ASCII format. You can then use your word processor to call up the text file and use it as part of a document.

Delimited Format

Delimited format ASCII files are composed of records in which the fields are delimited, or separated, by a specific character or a space. If the records are separated by a certain character (such as a quotation mark), the format is called *character delimited.* If the fields are separated by a single space, the format is called *blank delimited.*

While you can use any character as the delimiter in character-delimited files, the most commonly used format is to surround the data in each field with quotation marks and to separate each field from other fields by commas. Each record occupies a separate line, so each record is followed by a carriage return. The following example shows a character-delimited file in this common format:

```
"Morse","Marcia","4260 Park Avenue","Chevy Chase","MD","20815-0988"
"Westman","Andrea","4807 East Avenue","Silver Spring","MD","20910-0124"
"Jackson","David","4102 Valley Lane","Falls Church","VA","22044"
"Mitchell","Mary Jo","617 North Oakland Street","Arlington","VA","22203"
"Robinson","Shirley","270 Browning Ave #2A","Takoma Park","MD","20912-1234"
"Jackson","Cheryl","1617 Arlington Blvd","Falls Church","VA","22044"
"Robinson","Wanda","1607 21st Street, NW","Washington","DC","20009-0101"
"Hart","Edward","6200 Germantown Road","Fairfax","VA","22025"
"Jones","Judi","5203 North Shore Drive","Reston","VA","22090"
```

As an example, WordStar's MailMerge option uses this format for storing information.

SDF Format

Like delimited files, SDF files store each record as an individual line, so the records are separated from each other by carriage returns. However, the records in an SDF file maintain a preset width for the individual fields. SDF format is also referred to as *fixed-length fields.*

dBASE IV has the ability to store files in SDF format for use by other programs. Many spreadsheets can store data on a disk in SDF. dBASE IV can then read those files, using an SDF option of the APPEND command (which will be discussed shortly). The following example shows a file in SDF format created by dBASE IV using the LASTNAME, CITY, and SALARY fields of the ABC Temporaries database:

```
Morse      Chevy Chase       9.00
Westman    Silver Spring    16.50
Jackson    Falls Church      8.00
Mitchell   Arlington         8.00
Robinson   Takoma Park       8.00
Jackson    Falls Church     12.00
Robinson   Washington        8.00
Hart       Fairfax          10.50
Jones      Reston           12.50
```

The SDF format uses a fixed number of spaces for each field, regardless of the actual size of the information in the field. Information that is too long to fit in an SDF file will be truncated.

SYLK, DIF, and WKS/WK1 Formats

In addition to using ASCII text, many programs can transfer data in one of three common file formats: SYLK, DIF, and WKS/WK1. The SYLK format (an abbreviation for Symbolic Link), developed by Microsoft Corporation, is commonly used by Microsoft products as a means of exchanging files. Microsoft's Chart (graphics), Multiplan (spreadsheet), and File (database manager) can all work with files written in SYLK format.

The DIF format (an abbreviation for Document Interchange Format) can be used by a wide assortment of programs, including VisiCalc (spreadsheet), R:base, and PC-File III (database managers). Internally, the DIF format bears a resemblance to character-delimited format files.

Finally, the WKS and WK1 file formats are used by Lotus 1-2-3 and by most other products that can directly read and write Lotus 1-2-3 files. The WKS files that are created by dBASE IV can be used by both versions of Lotus 1-2-3 (version 1.A and the newer Release 2) and by Symphony. Files with a .WR1 extension created by Symphony and files with a .WK1 extension created by Lotus 1-2-3 Release 2 can be read by dBASE IV, although dBASE IV cannot write files in this format.

Which Format to Use

When you transfer data out of dBASE IV, you must decide what format you wish to use. A list of some of the better-known programs and the types of data they can exchange is shown in Table 18-1.

As a general rule, most word processors will transfer ASCII, delimited, or SDF. (The abbreviation SDF is used by Ashton-Tate; many other vendors call the same type of files flat files, fixed-length files, or DOS text files.) Many spreadsheets will transfer data in WKS, DIF, or SDF format, and most database managers will transfer data in DIF or delimited format. Lotus 1-2-3 and Symphony can use the WKS file format. If it isn't obvious which format your software package uses, check your owner's manual.

HINT Some lesser-known software packages may use a more commonly-known file format, such as WKS (Lotus), to transfer files. If dBASE IV cannot read or write files in the format of the package you are using, you may be able to use a common format, such as the Lotus format, to transfer data between dBASE IV and the other software.

Table 18-1.

Brand	Type of Package	File Type
WordPerfect	Word processor	ASCII, delimited, or SDF
WordStar	Word processor	ASCII, delimited, or SDF
MailMerge	Option of WordStar	Delimited
Microsoft Word	Word processor	ASCII, delimited, or SDF
MultiMate	Word processor	ASCII, delimited, or SDF*
Lotus 1-2-3	Spreadsheet	WKS or WK1**
PC-File III	Database manager	Delimited
R:base	Database manager	DIF or delimited
Microsoft Multiplan	Spreadsheet	SYLK
Microsoft Chart	Graphics	SYLK

* Newer versions of MultiMate can read .DBF files directly.
** WK1 and WKS can be read by 1-2-3 Release 2.0; WKS can be read by 1-2-3 version 1.A.

Software Interchange Formats

Data Sharing with APPEND And COPY

Many exchanges of data between dBASE IV and other programs can be accomplished with the aid of certain TYPE options within the COPY and APPEND commands. Using COPY, you can copy data from dBASE IV to another program; using APPEND, you can append (transfer) data from another program into a dBASE IV database. The normal format for these commands, when used with a TYPE option, is shown here:

COPY TO *filename* [*Scope*] [FIELDS *field-list*] TYPE [*type*]

APPEND FROM *filename* [*Scope*] [FIELDS *field-list*] TYPE [*type*]

In this case, *filename* is the name of the file to be transferred between dBASE IV and the other program, and *type* is one of the acceptable types. With COPY, the acceptable types are DELIMITED [WITH], SDF, DBASEII, RPD, FW2, SYLK, DIF, DBMEMO3, and WKS. With the APPEND command, the acceptable types are DELIMITED [WITH], DIF, FW2, RPD, SDF, SYLK, WKS, and WK1. The WITH parameter of the DELIMITED option lets you specify a character to use as the field delimiter in place of the default question marks.

As a brief example, to copy the ABC Temporaries database into a Lotus-compatible file, you might use this command:

```
COPY TO 123FILE TYPE WKS
```

You might use the following command to transfer a file from Microsoft's Multiplan to dBASE IV:

```
APPEND FROM MPFILE TYPE SYLK
```

You can add other options, such as a scope (ALL, NEXT, or a record number) or a list of fields to the COPY and APPEND commands when you use these commands to tranfer data to other programs. You can also use the FOR condition to specify records that will be transferred.

While most exercises in this chapter use dot-prompt commands, you can also use the Control Center menus to transfer data if you prefer. Use the Import and Export options of the Tools menu to transfer data to other file formats. When you select either option, another menu appears, displaying the various available file formats. Choose the desired file format, and enter the filenames when prompted.

Examples of Transferring Files

This section provides working examples of transferring files. Since you may not be using the software packages described, you may not be able to follow along with the examples. If you have a software package mentioned here or a similar software package with the ability to use the file formats acceptable to dBASE IV, try using the examples with your software.

From dBASE IV to WordStar And Other Word Processors

Most word processors work with ASCII format, so let's try it first. Suppose you needed to pull names and salary amounts from the database in order to give the company president a memo containing all employees' salary amounts. You can use the TO FILE option of the LIST command to help you perform this task. When you enter the LIST command (along with any preferred fields) followed by TO FILE and a filename, the data displayed with LIST is also stored as ASCII text in the file you named within the command.

Try using the TO FILE option of the LIST command by entering the following:

```
USE ABCSTAFF
LIST LASTNAME, FIRSTNAME, SALARY TO FILE PEOPLE.TXT
```

Now exit dBASE IV and load your word processor. Enter the command normally used by your word processor to read an ASCII file. When your word processor asks you for the name of the file to load, enter the drive and path of your dBASE data directory, followed by the filename PEOPLE.TXT. The file should then appear on your screen. For WordStar the screen should resemble Figure 18-1.

Note that you can also store the output of a report in a file by adding the TO FILE option at the end of a REPORT FORM command. As an example, the command

```
REPORT FORM RSIMPLE TO FILE REPS.TXT
```

would create a file named REPS.TXT containing the data in the report format generated by the stored report, RSIMPLE.

WARNING Depending on what word processor you are using, at the bottom of the file that was transferred with dBASE IV there may be a left-pointing arrow or a similar graphics character. If

Figure 18-1.

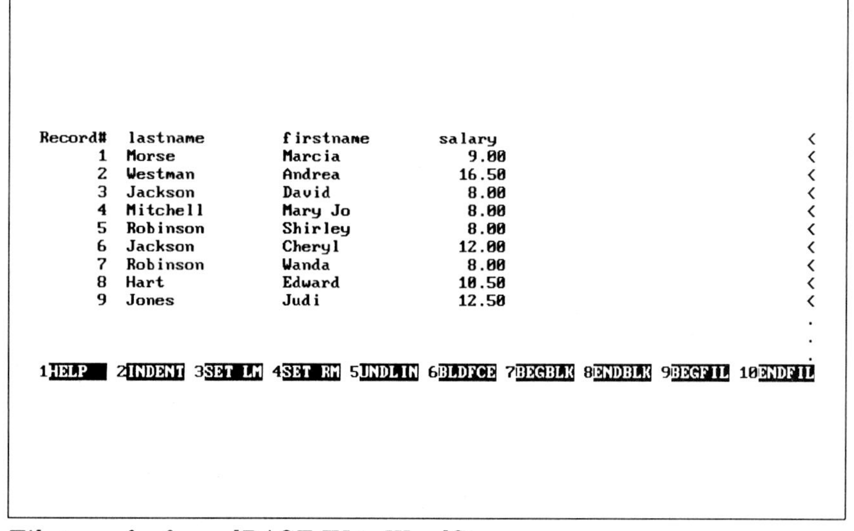

File transfer from dBASE IV to WordStar

you are using WordStar, you may see one or more ^@ symbols at the end of the file. This represents an end-of-file marker that dBASE IV produced when it was finished writing to the file. You can use the BACKSPACE key or a DELETE command to erase this unwanted character. Different word processors interpret the end-of-file marker in different ways, so you may see a character other than ^@.

Get out of your word processor in the usual manner, and reload dBASE IV now.

From dBASE IV to MailMerge And Other Database Managers

If you need data in delimited format, you'll use the DELIMITED option of the COPY command. Delimited formats are used by WordStar's MailMerge option and by many other database managers.

First copy the fields from the active database to a separate file used by the other program. The format of the COPY command with the DELIMITED option is

COPY TO *filename* [*scope*] [FIELDS *field-list*,] [DELIMITED]

Here, *filename* is the name of the file that will contain the fields. You can limit the records to be copied by including [*scope*], specified by ALL, NEXT, or RECORD. Fields can be limited by FIELD and the *field-list* option. When you specify the DELIMITED option, the .TXT extension is automatically appended to *filename*.

As an example, let's say that you need to transfer a list of the names, addresses, and cities from ABCSTAFF to a file named DATAFILE that will be used by another database manager. Enter the following commands:

```
USE ABCSTAFF
COPY TO DATAFILE FIELDS LASTNAME, FIRSTNAME, ADDRESS, CITY
TYPE DELIMITED
```

The DATAFILE.TXT file created by COPY TO will contain one line for each record that was copied from ABCSTAFF. Each record includes the employee's last name, first name, address, and city. Each field is enclosed by quotation marks, and each field is separated by a comma. dBASE automatically adds the .TXT extension unless you specify otherwise.

The TYPE command can be used to list on the screen the contents of any disk file. Let's examine DATAFILE with the TYPE command to see the delimited file format. With TYPE you are required to supply the file extension (in this case, .TXT). From the dot prompt, enter

```
TYPE DATAFILE.TXT
```

and your display will resemble the following:

```
10/8/88                    DATAFILE.TXT

"Morse","Marcia","4260 Park Avenue","Chevy Chase"
"Westman","Andrea","4807 East Avenue","Silver Spring"
"Jackson","David","4102 Valley Lane","Falls Church"
"Mitchell","Mary Jo","617 North Oakland Street","Arlington"
"Robinson","Shirley","270 Browning Ave #2A","Takoma Park"
"Jackson","Cheryl","1617 Arlington Blvd","Falls Church"
"Robinson","Wanda","1607 21st Street, NW","Washington"
"Hart","Edward","6200 Germantown Road","Fairfax"
"Jones","Judi","5203 North Shore Drive","Reston"
```

This file can be used by almost all other database managers, including PC-File III and R:base, or it can be used by WordStar's MailMerge option to create a form letter. In such cases, you must use the appropriate commands of the particular database manager or MailMerge to import a file in delimited format. MailMerge works very well with delimited files, and with a few MailMerge commands inserted within a WordStar file, you can create form letters that gather information from a delimited file.

An example of a template for a form letter, written with WordStar for use with MailMerge, is shown in Figure 18-2. The template letter uses a number of WordStar and MailMerge com-

Figure 18-2.

```
.op
.df datafile.txt
.rv lastname,firstname,address,city

                    January 1, 1989

&firstname& &lastname&
&address&
&city&

Dear Mr./Ms. &lastname&

    Our records indicate that your assignment will be ending within the
next 60 days.  If you prefer an extension of your present assignment,
please contact our personnel office as soon as possible.

Sincerely,


O.J. Springs, Manager
ABC Temporaries, Inc.
```

WordStar form letter for use with MailMerge and dBASE IV

Figure 18-3.

January 1, 1989

David Jackson
4102 Valley Lane
Falls Church

Dear Mr./Ms. Jackson

Our records indicate that your assignment will be ending within the next 60 days. If you prefer an extension of your present assignment, please contact our personnel office as soon as possible.

Sincerely,

O.J. Springs, Manager
ABC Temporaries, Inc.

Letter produced by using the form in Figure 18-2 and MailMerge

mands. The .op command tells WordStar not to use page numbers when printing the form letter. The .df command identifies the delimited file that will be used by MailMerge. The .rv command identifies the names and order of the fields in the delimited file. The ampersands surrounding the field names in the form letter will be replaced by the data contained in the appropriate fields of the delimited file. When the MailMerge option of WordStar is used, it generates a form letter similar to the one that is shown in Figure 18-3.

For database managers and other programs that accept data in DIF format, use the DIF option with the COPY and APPEND commands, as demonstrated in the following examples:

```
COPY TO B:STOCKS.VC1 FIELDS LASTNAME, FIRSTNAME, CITY, STATE
TYPE DIF

APPEND FROM C:MAILER TYPE DIF
```

The first example will copy the contents of the named fields within a database in use to a file named STOCKS.VC1 on drive B. The file will be stored in DIF format. In the second example, records will be copied from a DIF file called MAILER into the database in use. Remember that when you are importing data into dBASE IV with the APPEND command, the database structure must match the structure of the records within the file that contain the data. In other words, the fields must be in the same order, and the fields in the dBASE database should be wide enough to accommodate the incoming data.

From dBASE IV to Microsoft Word

With Microsoft Word, the process is very similar to that used with WordStar. Again, you can create a delimited file with the default delimiters. Microsoft Word, however, does not expect to see the names of the fields defined within the form letter; instead, it expects the names of the fields to appear as the very first line of text in the foreign file, with the fields separated by commas. Using the prior example again, the foreign file that Microsoft Word would need to use would resemble this:

```
last,first,address,city,state,zip
"Miller","Karen","4260 Park Avenue","Chevy Chase","MD","20815-0988"
"Martin","William","4807 East Avenue","Silver Spring","MD","20910-0124"
"Robinson","Carol","4102 Valley Lane","Falls Church","VA","22043-1234"
"Kramer","Harry","617 North Oakland Street","Arlington","VA","22203"
"Moore","Ellen","270 Browning Ave #2A","Takoma Park","MD","20912"
```

A quick and painless way to do this is to build a file that contains the heading, and then use the DOS COPY command to combine the heading file with the foreign file to produce a file ready for use by Microsoft Word. This could be done entirely within dBASE IV with commands like these:

```
SET TALK OFF
SET ALTERNATE TO HEADS
SET ALTERNATE ON
? "Last,First,Address,City,State,Zip"
?
CLOSE ALTERNATE
COPY TO WFILE FIELDS LAST, FIRST, ADDRESS,;
CITY, STATE, ZIPCODE TYPE DELIMITED
RUN COPY HEADS.TXT + WFILE.TXT WORDFILE.TXT
```

The resultant file, called WORDFILE.TXT in this case, would resemble the foreign file just shown, with the header containing the field names for use by Microsoft Word appearing as the first line in the foreign file.

When designing the form letter within Microsoft Word, press CTRL-[(left bracket) to mark the start of each field, and CTRL-] (right bracket) to mark the end of each field. The CTRL-[key combination produces a symbol that resembles a double less-than sign, and the CTRL-] key combination produces a symbol that resembles a double greater-than sign. Using these characters, you can create a form letter like this:

<<data wordfile.txt>>

Johnson, Johnson
Fennerson & Smith
303 Broadway South
Norfolk, VA 56008

<<first> ><<last>>

<<address>>
<<city>>, <<state>> <<zip>>

Dear <<first>> <<last>>:

In response to your letter received, we are pleased to enclose a catalog of our latest products. If we can answer any questions, please do not hesitate to call.

Sincerely,

Mike Rowe
Sales Manager

You can then generate the form letters with the Print Merge command from within Microsoft Word. (See your Microsoft Word documentation for details.)

An Export Program for WordPerfect

If you wish to use the MailMerge feature of WordPerfect, you must operate a little differently than with most other software. WordPerfect expects to see data on individual lines, all flush left, with the ends of fields marked by a Control-R followed by a carriage return. The end of a record is indicated by a Control-E followed by a carriage return. A data file when loaded within WordPerfect would resemble the following:

Jerry^R
Sampson^R
1412 Wyldewood Way^R
Pheonix^R
AZ^R
78009^R
^E

```
Paris^R
Williamson^R
P.O. Box 1834^R
Herndon^R
VA^R
22070^R
^E
Mary^R
Smith^R
37 Mill Way^R
Great Neck^R
NY^R
12134^R
```

Unfortunately, you cannot create a file like this with something as simple as a COPY command. You can, however, write a short program to accomplish this task. To generate such a file, simply write each desired field out to a line of a file, and end that line with a Control-R (ASCII 18). After the last field of the record, write a line containing only Control-E (ASCII 5).

You can use the SET ALTERNATE TO and SET ALTERNATE ON commands to turn on the output to a foreign text file, and write each desired line until done; then, close the foreign file with the CLOSE ALTERNATE command. As an example, the following program would perform such a task. You could enter **MODIFY COMMAND *filename*,** where *filename* is the name you want to give the program, and enter the program as shown, saving it with CTRL-END. Substitute your field names and database filename for the ones used in the example.

```
*CREATES Word Perfect MAIL MERGE FILES.*
USE ABCSTAFF
SET TALK OFF
STORE CHR(18) TO ENDFIELD
STORE CHR(5) TO ENDREC
SET ALTERNATE TO PERFECT
SET ALTERNATE ON
GO TOP
DO WHILE .NOT. EOF( )
```

```
    ? TRIM(FIRSTNAME) + ENDFIELD
    ? TRIM(LASTNAME) + ENDFIELD
    ? TRIM(ADDRESS) + ENDFIELD
    ? TRIM(CITY) + ENDFIELD
    ? STATE + ENDFIELD
    ? ZIPCODE + ENDFIELD
    ? ENDREC
    SKIP
ENDDO
CLOSE ALTERNATE
RETURN
```

When you run the program with the DO command, the result will be a foreign file similar to this one, with each field on a separate line, terminated by the ASCII character Control-R, with Control-E on lines between the records.

To use the files in a WordPerfect form letter document, first make note of the order of the fields as output by your program (the first field after an end-of-record indicator is field 1, the next is field 2, and so on). In WordPerfect, when creating the form letter, use the ALT-F9 key combination to define the field numbers desired. For example, when you press ALT-F9, enter **F** followed by **3** (to indicate the third field), and then press the ENTER key, WordPerfect will enter the symbol (^F3^), which indicates that the contents of the third field in the sequence will appear in that position when the form letters are generated. Your WordPerfect form letter might resemble the following:

```
                Johnson, Johnson
                Fennerson & Smith
                303 Broadway South
                Norfolk, VA 56008


^F1^ ^F2^
^F3^
^F4^, ^F5^ ^F6^
```

Dear ^F1^ ^F2^:

In response to your letter received, we are pleased to enclose a catalog of our latest products. If we can answer any questions, please do not hesitate to call.

Sincerely,

Mike Rowe
Sales Manager

Save the letter by using the usual save commands for WordPerfect. To generate the form letters in WordPerfect, first use CTRL-F5 to import the dBASE IV file, and then select 2 (Retrieve) and enter the name of the file you created in dBASE with the SET ALTERNATE command. Eliminate any blank lines at the top of the document, and save the file with F10 under a new name. Use F7 to exit the document and get to a blank screen. Then press CTRL-F9, choose Merge, enter the name of the form letter, and then enter the name of the file containing the data. WordPerfect will proceed to create the letters, which can then be printed in the usual manner.

Two programs that this section did not deal with are IBM's DisplayWrite and Ashton-Tate's MultiMate. IBM's DisplayWrite uses a complex data transfer language called DCA (Document Content Architecture). This format does not transfer easily between any of the available dBASE IV formats, so if you are faced with trying to do a mailmerge of sorts and DisplayWrite is your word processor of choice, consider creating the form letter completely in dBASE IV using the report generator (see Chapter 11). MultiMate users who are using later versions of the software should refer to the MultiMate documentation; recent versions of MultiMate can directly read dBASE files, so you can use the dBASE IV database directly, or use the DBMEMO3 type option if memo fields are in the file.

Between dBASE IV and PFS:FILE

Databases from PFS:FILE can be converted to dBASE IV format, and dBASE IV databases can be converted to PFS:FILE format. PFS:FILE is a special case and does not require the COPY and APPEND commands used with other software packages. Instead, dBASE IV provides two commands, IMPORT and EXPORT, to perform the task of sharing files with PFS:FILE. You can use the IMPORT and EXPORT commands at the dot prompt, or you can choose PFS FILE from the Import and Export options of the Tools menu. (IMPORT and EXPORT can also be used with RapidFile and Framework as described later in this chapter.)

The IMPORT command, when used with PFS as the type, reads a PFS:FILE database and creates a dBASE IV database with a matching database structure. The command also creates a screen format file that matches the screen format of the PFS:FILE database. In addition, a view file is created; when used, it will link the database and screen format files together.

The format of the IMPORT command from the dot prompt is

IMPORT FROM *D:filename* TYPE PFS

where *filename* is the name of the PFS:FILE database and *D:* is the designator of the disk drive containing the database. As an example, to import a PFS:FILE database named PATIENTS, you could use a command like this one:

```
IMPORT FROM B:PATIENTS TYPE PFS
```

To use IMPORT from the Control Center, open the Tools menu and select Import. Then choose PFS:FILE from the menu of file types that appears. You will be prompted for the disk, directory, and desired database to import (Figure 18-4). Select the database

Figure 18-4.

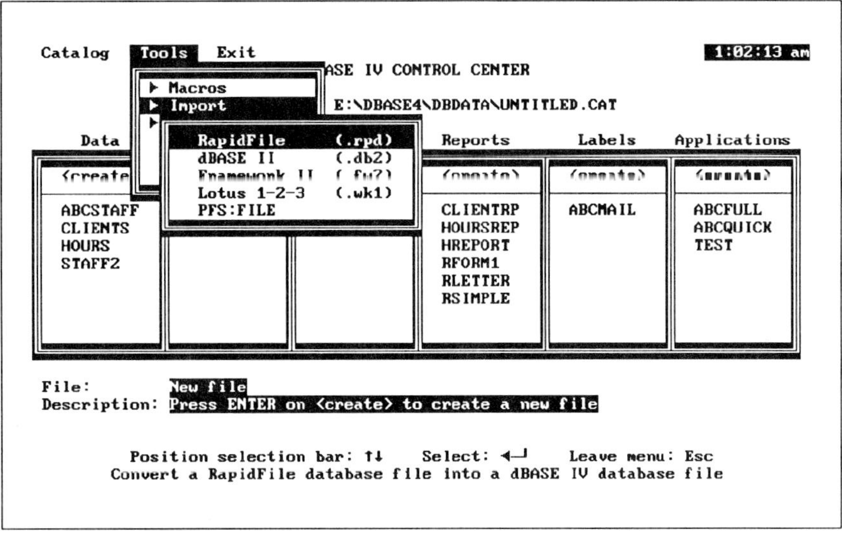

Import choice of Tools menu

from the list that appears, and the conversion process will take place.

You can use the converted database separately or with the view file or screen format file created along with the database by the IMPORT command. All field types contained in the converted database will be character fields, because PFS:FILE treats all fields as character fields.

The EXPORT command used with the PFS type converts a dBASE IV database to a PFS:FILE database. The format of this command is

EXPORT TO *D:filename* TYPE PFS

where *filename* is the name of the PFS:FILE database, and *D:* is the drive designator of the disk drive containing the database.

For example, to export to a database named CLIENTS as a PFS:FILE database, you could use a command like this one:

```
EXPORT TO B:CLIENTS TYPE PFS
```

To use EXPORT from the Control Center, open the Tools menu and select Export. Then choose PFS from the menu of file types that appears. You will be prompted for the desired database to export (Figure 18-5). Select the database that is to be converted from the list, and the conversion process will take place. All fields in the database are converted to character fields in the PFS:FILE database. If a screen format file is in use when the conversion takes place, that form will be used as a screen design within the PFS:FILE database. If no screen format is used, the file structure

Figure 18-5.

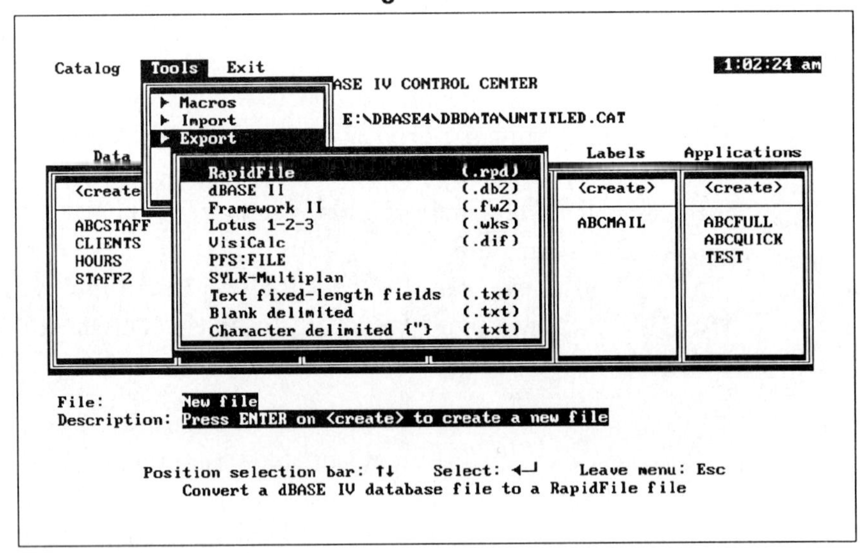

Export choice of Tools menu

of the dBASE database will be used as the screen design within PFS:FILE.

Between dBASE IV and Lotus 1-2-3 or Symphony

Exchanging data between Lotus 1-2-3 or Symphony and dBASE IV is a simple matter. dBASE IV has the ability to directly read and write files in Lotus 1-2-3 format. dBASE IV can exchange data between 1-2-3 version 1.A and between the newer 1-2-3 Release 2 and Symphony. (If you are using Release 3.0 of Lotus 1-2-3, you should use the Translate option within 1-2-3 to convert spreadsheets to 1-2-3 Release 2.0 format before exporting them to dBASE.)

To transfer data to and from Lotus 1-2-3 or Symphony, you use the APPEND and COPY commands with the worksheet file type, as shown in this example:

```
APPEND FROM LOTUSFIL TYPE WKS        (for version 1.A)

APPEND FROM LOTUSFIL TYPE WK1        (for Release 2)

COPY TO LOTUSFIL TYPE WKS            (for all Lotus products)
```

When the APPEND command is used in this manner, it reads the contents of an existing 1-2-3 or Symphony spreadsheet and adds those contents to a database that is in use. (If no database to store the data exists, you must first create a database with a structure that matches the column layout of the spreadsheet.) The COPY command copies the contents of an existing database to a file that can be read by Lotus 1-2-3 or by Symphony. The file will have the .WKS extension.

If you have Lotus 1-2-3, try the following commands to create a WKS file for a 1-2-3 spreadsheet:

```
USE HOURS
COPY TO 123FILE TYPE WKS
```

The 123FILE.WKS file created by these commands will contain a 1-2-3 spreadsheet with one record in each row. The individual columns of the spreadsheet represent the fields of the database. Enter **QUIT** to leave dBASE IV and return to the DOS prompt. If your copy of 1-2-3 is in a different subdirectory of your hard disk, then use the DOS COPY command to copy the file called 123FILE.WKS to that directory.

Load Lotus 1-2-3 in your usual manner. When the opening 1-2-3 screen appears, press any key to get a blank spreadsheet on the screen. The FILE LOAD command of Lotus 1-2-3 can be used to load the file. Once you are in the spreadsheet, type a slash (/) to bring the 1-2-3 commands to the top of the screen. Then type **F** (for File), which will display the 1-2-3 file transfer menu, and type **R** (for Retrieve File). 1-2-3 will respond by displaying the names of any spreadsheets in your default directory.

Highlight the correct filename (123FILE.WKS) and press ENTER. The spreadsheet will be loaded and will appear on the screen. In our example, the Set Column-Width command in Lotus 1-2-3 was used to widen the columns, allowing for the full display of the SOCIALSEC, WEEKENDING, and HOURS fields as shown in Figure 18-6.

To read Lotus 1-2-3 files into dBASE IV, no special preparation in 1-2-3 is needed (unless you are using Release 3.0, in which case you should save the worksheets in Release 2.0 formats). Simply store a 1-2-3 file in the usual manner, and use the APPEND command of dBASE IV to add the contents of the file to a dBASE IV database. To import a 1-2-3 spreadsheet named FINANCE,

Figure 18-6.

```
                                   < Ready !>
A1 [W20]: 'ASSIGNMENT

   1 ASSIGNMENT           SOCIALSEC    WEEKENDING  HOURS
     National Oil Co.     909-88-7654  16-Jan-88      35.0
     National Oil Co.     121 33 9076  16 Jan 88      30.0
     National Oil Co.     121-90-5432  16-Jan-88      27.0
     National Oil Co.     123-44-8976  16-Jan-88      32.0
     City Revenue Dept.   343-55-9821  16-Jan-88      35.0
     City Revenue Dept.   495-00-3456  16-Jan-88      28.0
     City Revenue Dept.   232-55-1234  16-Jan-88      30.0
     Smith Builders       876-54-3210  23-Jan-88      30.0
     Smith Builders       901-77-3456  23-Jan-88      28.0
     Smith Builders       876-54-3210  23-Jan-88      35.0
     City Revenue Dept.   232-55-1234  23-Jan-88      30.0
     City Revenue Dept.   495-00-3456  23-Jan-88      32.0
     City Revenue Dept.   343-55-9821  23-Jan-88      32.0
     National Oil Co.     121-33-9876  23-Jan-88      35.0
     National Oil Co.     909-88-7654  23-Jan-88      33.0
```

Lotus 1-2-3 spreadsheet

created by 1-2-3 version 1.A, you would use the following command from the dot prompt:

```
APPEND FROM FINANCE TYPE WKS
```

To import a spreadsheet named FINANCE, created by Lotus 1-2-3 Release 2, you would use this command:

```
APPEND FROM FINANCE TYPE WK1
```

And to import a Symphony worksheet named FINANCE, you would use the following command:

```
APPEND FROM FINANCE.WR1 TYPE WK1
```

The only difference between these commands is the use of the WK1 type in the second example, and the inclusion of the .WR1 extension to the filename in the third example; .WR1 is the extension used by Symphony.

REMEMBER You'll need to include the extension with the filename when reading Symphony files into dBASE IV.

Spreadsheet users should keep in mind that nearly all spreadsheets are limited in size by the available memory of the computer, while dBASE files are limited in practice by available disk space. It is possible to export a file so large that it cannot be loaded into your spreadsheet. When you are creating files for spreadsheets from large databases, you may find it necessary to export small portions of the file. You can use the FOR conditional with the commands, or you can set a filter with the SET FILTER command before exporting the data to the spreadsheet file.

From dBASE IV to Non-Lotus-Compatible Spreadsheets

Users of Microsoft's Multiplan can transfer a dBASE IV database to a Multiplan spreadsheet by using the SYLK option of the COPY command. The SYLK file format is used for the transfer of data to Multiplan and other Microsoft products. The normal format for the COPY command, when used with this option, is

COPY TO *filename* [*Scope*] [FIELDS *field-list*] TYPE SYLK

As an example, the following commands could be used to create a spreadsheet that could be read by Microsoft's Multiplan:

```
USE ABCSTAFF
COPY TO MPFILE FIELDS LASTNAME, CITY, STATE, SALARY TYPE SYLK
```

The spreadsheet would contain columns for each of the fields named. Multiplan users should note that when the file is loaded into Multiplan, the Transfer Options choice should be selected from the main Multiplan menu, and Symbolic should then be chosen from the menu that appears. This will tell Multiplan to load symbolic-link type (SYLK) files.

If you need to save a file in SDF format, you should use the SDF option of the COPY command. The SDF format is used for transferring data from dBASE IV to spreadsheets that cannot read SYLK or WKS format files. (This format is also useful for exchanging data with mainframe computers.) Try this variation of the COPY command to create an SDF file:

```
COPY TO CALCFILE FIELDS LASTNAME, CITY, SALARY TYPE SDF
```

The CALCFILE file created by this command will contain one line for each record, with each record containing LASTNAME, CITY, and SALARY fields. Instead of being surrounded by quotes and separated by commas, each field is allotted space according to its width. To see the file in SDF format, enter

```
TYPE CALCFILE.TXT
```

The following will be displayed on your screen:

```
Morse       Chevy Chase     9.00
Westman     Silver Spring  16.50
Jackson     Falls Church    8.00
Mitchell    Arlington       8.00
Robinson    Takoma Park     8.00
Jackson     Falls Church   12.00
```

Robinson	Washington	8.00
Hart	Fairfax	10.50
Jones	Reston	12.50

How you will load the file into your spreadsheet will depend on what spreadsheet you are using. It would be impossible to present the file-loading command for each spreadsheet, but in every case you will need to perform two steps to import the dBASE IV file into your spreadsheet. First, you must set your spreadsheet's load command so that the spreadsheet is ready to receive files in the SDF format. Second, you must use your spreadsheet's external load or import command to load the SDF file.

From Other Spreadsheets to dBASE IV

An increasing number of spreadsheets (including Microsoft Excel, Twin, and VP-Planner) can work with the popular Lotus 1-2-3 (WKS) format. Check your spreadsheet manual to see if your spreadsheet can save files in Lotus 1-2-3 file format. Quattro users should note that Quattro can read and write dBASE files directly, except that memo fields will not be transferred. See your Quattro manual for details.

Most spreadsheets that cannot write 1-2-3-compatible files do provide an option for printing a file onto disk. The resulting disk file matches the SDF format. Different spreadsheets use different commands to create such files, so check your spreadsheet manual for instructions. In most cases, the way to get a spreadsheet into SDF format is to use the "print to disk" option of the particular spreadsheet. Table 18-2 gives methods for creating dBASE-compatible files with some of the more popular spreadsheets.

Table 18-2.

Lotus 1-2-3 Users

1. Press the slash key (/) to display Lotus 1-2-3 commands.
2. Type **F** (for File).
3. Type **S** (for Save).
4. Specify a name for the file you will create.
5. Press the slash key.
6. Type **Q** (for Quit).

Multiplan Users

1. Press ESC to highlight Multiplan commands.
2. Type **T** (for Transfer).
3. Type **O** (for Options).
4. Type **S** (for Symbolic) and press ENTER.
5. Type **T** (for Transfer).
6. Type **S** (for Save).
7. Specify a name for the file you will create.

Note: Use the SYLK option of the APPEND command to read a Multiplan file into a dBASE IV database.

SuperCalc 2 and 3 Users

1. Press the slash key (/) to display SuperCalc commands.
2. Type **O** (for Output).
3. Type **D** (for Display Option).
4. Specify a range of the spreadsheet to be transferred to the file.
5. Type **D** (for Disk).
6. Specify a name for the SDF file.

Note: SuperCalc saves all non-SuperCalc files with an extension of .PRN. You must include this extension when naming the file in the dBASE IV APPEND command. Users of SuperCalc 4 and above can save the files in Lotus (WKS) format; see the SuperCalc manual for details.

Steps for Creating dBASE-Compatible Files with Popular Spreadsheets

Before transferring an SDF file into a database, be sure that the database field types and field widths match the SDF format precisely. You can use the APPEND command with the SDF option to transfer the data into dBASE IV. The format of this command is

APPEND FROM *filename* TYPE SDF

Note that you cannot use a condition with APPEND when appending from non-dBASE files. APPEND FROM with TYPE SDF operates exactly like APPEND FROM with TYPE DELIMITED; *filename* is the name of the file that will be transferred and appended to the active database file. The fields in the database must be as wide as or wider than the fields in the SDF file. If the database fields are narrower, the incoming data will be truncated to fit the field.

An alternate method for transferring data from a spreadsheet is to convert the SDF file to a delimited file. This is done by using your word processor to edit the file, removing extra spaces between fields, and adding commas and quotation marks to separate the fields. You can then transfer the data with the DELIMITED option of the APPEND command, but this time you need not be concerned that the field widths precisely match the width of the SDF files.

From WordStar and Other Word Processors to dBASE IV

Transferring data from other programs into a dBASE IV database may take just a little more work than the process of sending dBASE IV data to other programs (particularly to word processors). This is because files brought into a dBASE IV database must follow a precise format, such as an SDF or delimited format. Thus, when you send data from your word processor to a dBASE IV database, you must edit the file from your word processor until it matches the format of a delimited or an SDF file.

WordPerfect users should note that it is possible to create a delimited file in WordPerfect that can then be read easily into dBASE IV. To do this, you must merge a secondary file (a file containing data) with a primary file (a merge document containing only quotes, commas, and field markers). Consult your WordPerfect manual for additional details.

After your word processor creates a file in delimited or SDF format, you can use dBASE IV's APPEND command to load the file. At first glance, it may seem easier to use SDF format instead of delimited format, because you don't have to type all of the quotes and commas. If you choose SDF format, however, you must keep track of the size of each field. Each field must have the same width as the database field in which you will be transferring data, and the fields must be in the same order as those in the database. For this reason, it is sometimes easier to use delimited format.

When you transfer files created by your word processor (or any other program) to dBASE IV, you must also create or use a dBASE IV database with a structure that matches the design of the files you wish to transfer. For purposes of simplicity, the following examples assume that the files created by other software match the structure of the ABC Temporaries database. Let's try a transfer using a delimited file. Suppose you have created a mailing list with a word processor; you now want to use that mailing list with dBASE IV. If you have a word processor that can create files in ASCII text, follow along.

Use your word processor to create the following delimited file, and give it the name MAIL2.TXT. (If you are using WordStar, type **N** from the No-File or Opening menu to create a document that does not contain WordStar formatting codes. If you are using Microsoft Word, WordPerfect, or IBM DisplayWrite, save the file as ASCII text.)

```
"123-80-7654","Johnson","Larry","4209 Vienna Way","Asheville","NC","27995"
"191-23-5566","Mills","Jeanette","13 Shannon Manor","Pheonix","AZ","87506"
"909-88-7654","Simpson","Charles","421 Park Avenue","New York","NY","10023"
```

Save the file as ASCII text with your word processor's save commands. Now load dBASE IV. You'll use the DELIMITED option of APPEND to append the file to ABCSTAFF. The format of the APPEND command when used to import a delimited file (without conditions, which is discussed in Chapter 4) is

APPEND FROM *filename* DELIMITED

To transfer MAIL2.TXT to dBASE IV, enter the following from the dBASE IV dot prompt:

```
USE ABCSTAFF
APPEND FROM MAIL2.TXT DELIMITED
```

dBASE IV will respond with the message "3 records added." To examine the database, enter **GO TOP** and then **LIST**, and at the bottom of the database you will see that the names and addresses from the mailing list have been added to the database.

In this example, fields are in order of last name, first name, address, city, state, and ZIP code. Fortunately, this is the same order as the fields in ABCSTAFF. In real life, however, things may not be so simple. If, for example, the list of employees were in order by first name and then last name, you would have to transpose the names before transferring the file to dBASE IV. When the fields in the database used by the other program do not match the database used by dBASE IV, you will need to perform whatever work is necessary to make them match. You can do this in one of two ways: either change the order of the data in the other file or design a new database in dBASE IV that matches the order of the data in the other file.

In most cases, it is easier to first create a matching file structure in dBASE and then append the data from the other file. After the data has been appended to dBASE, you can either modify the structure of the file or copy the data into a second file that has the fields in the desired order (in which case, dBASE will match fields by the field names.)

Transferring Databases Between dBASE IV and Ashton-Tate Products

Users of Ashton-Tate's RapidFile database manager and Framework II integrated software will find that databases can be exchanged easily between dBASE IV and Framework or RapidFile. (This is not surprising, considering that the same company is behind these packages.) You can use the COPY and APPEND commands with the TYPE RPD and TYPE FW2 options. The RPD option reads and writes RapidFile database files. The FW2 option reads and writes Framework II files. (Framework III can directly read and write dBASE files, so no conversion is needed.)

REMEMBER RapidFile will not read dBASE IV memo fields. Framework will transfer the memo fields, but only the first 255 characters of each memo will appear in the Framework database.

As an example, to copy the ABCSTAFF database into a database compatible with RapidFile, you could use the command

```
COPY TO ABCSTAFF TYPE RPD
```

This would create a new file, ABCSTAFF.RPD, which could be used within RapidFile. To read an existing database called CLIENTS.RPD saved in RapidFile, you could use the command

```
APPEND FROM CLIENTS.RPD TYPE RPD
```

Use similar commands to import and export files from Framework II. The following examples could be used to read a Framework II database, STUDENTS, and write the ABCSTAFF file out to a database that can be used within Framework II:

```
APPEND FROM STUDENTS.FW2 TYPE FW2

USE ABCSTAFF
COPY TO ABCSTAFF.FW2 TYPE FW2
```

One warning for users of Framework II: the maximum size of a Framework database is limited by the amount of memory in your PC. dBASE IV, on the other hand, is in practice limited only by disk space. If a dBASE IV database is too large to fit within a Framework II database, Framework II will import as much of the file as it can handle and then display a warning message indicating the number of records that are present in the Framework database.

If this becomes a problem, you can break the dBASE database into smaller pieces with the optional *scope* parameter of the COPY command. As an example, you could copy the contents of a 550-record dBASE database into three separate files with the following commands:

```
USE MAILDATA
COPY NEXT 200 TO FWONE
COPY NEXT 200 TO FWTWO
COPY NEXT 150 TO FWTHREE
```

These commands would create three files, each containing specific records in the dBASE database. The files could then be exported to Framework II files and used on an individual basis.

dBASE IV and Other Versions Of dBASE

Files from dBASE III and dBASE III PLUS can be used in dBASE IV without any changes. You can also use dBASE IV database files within dBASE III and dBASE III PLUS. If the dBASE IV file contains memo fields, use the COPY TO command with the DBMEMO3 type option to create a dBASE III or dBASE III PLUS compatible file.

To transfer dBASE IV files to dBASE II, you must convert them by using the DBASEII type option of the COPY command. As an example, a command like

```
USE ABCSTAFF
COPY TO A:ABCSTAFF.DBF TYPE DBASEII
```

would create a dBASE II-compatible database file on the disk in drive A under the name specified (ABCSTAFF.DBF). Note that because dBASE II is rather limited in its field types, some fields will not be converted and some will be converted as different types. For example, there are no memo fields in dBASE II, so any data in the memo fields will not get converted. Logical fields are also unsupported in dBASE II, so these come across as a character field containing the letter T or the letter F.

Finally, if you are sharing data with dBASE Mac, no preparation needs to be done on the dBASE IV side. dBASE Mac can read a dBASE IV database file directly (once it has been stored in a Macintosh-compatible disk format). Because dBASE Mac has no equivalent field type for memo fields, memo-field data will not be read by dBASE Mac.

Before you try to export a dBASE Mac file to dBASE IV, you must save the file in dBASE III format while you are still in dBASE Mac. Once the file is saved in dBASE III format, use your preferred means to copy the file to an IBM-compatible disk format, and load it in dBASE IV in the usual manner.

Quick Reference

To transfer data from dBASE IV to another program From the Control Center, select the Export option of the Tools menu. From the next menu to appear, select the desired file format, then enter the filenames when prompted. From the dot prompt, use the COPY TO command with an appropriate TYPE clause.

To transfer data from another program to dBASE IV From the Control Center, select the Import option of the Tools menu. From the next menu to appear, select the desired file format, then enter the filenames when prompted. From the dot prompt, use the APPEND FROM command with an appropriate TYPE clause.

To produce dBASE files compatible with dBASE III PLUS Use the COPY TO command with the TYPE DBMEMO3 clause added to the end of the command. Any memo fields in the resultant file will be compatible with dBASE III PLUS and with most other products that can directly read dBASE III PLUS data files.

CHAPTER

19

Using dBASE IV On a Local Area Network

This chapter provides information that you will need if you intend to use the network version of dBASE IV. The first half of the chapter provides an overview of local area networks, requirements for using dBASE IV on a network, hints for installing and using dBASE IV on a network, and general hints for effective network use. The second half of the chapter explains the use of the Protect menu options that provide security to a dBASE system, along with considerations for programmers who write applications that will be used on a network.

Because of the complexity of local area networks, the material presented in this chapter assumes a higher level of knowledge than most other chapters in this book. It is assumed that the reader is already familiar with the use of dBASE IV, basic DOS commands and DOS subdirectories, and network commands for the particular network on which dBASE IV will be installed. The appropriate manuals for network operation should be referred to for any questions regarding the use of the network operating system commands.

dBASE and Networks

A local area network, or LAN, is a system of computer communications that links together a number of personal computers, usually within a single building, for the transfer of information and the sharing of peripherals between users of the computers. In its minimal configuration, a local area network consists of two PCs connected by some type of wire that allows information transfer and resource sharing between the two machines.

A local area network allows the sharing of resources—printers, modems, hard disks, and other devices—that may be attached to computers on the network. Files (such as databases) and commonly used software can also be shared among the users of a local area network. Figure 19-1 shows how computers can be linked together by means of a local area network.

There are different designs for local area networks, but all LANs are made up of the same basic components: servers, workstations, and the physical cable linking the components together. Servers are computers that provide the devices that can be used

Figure 19-1.

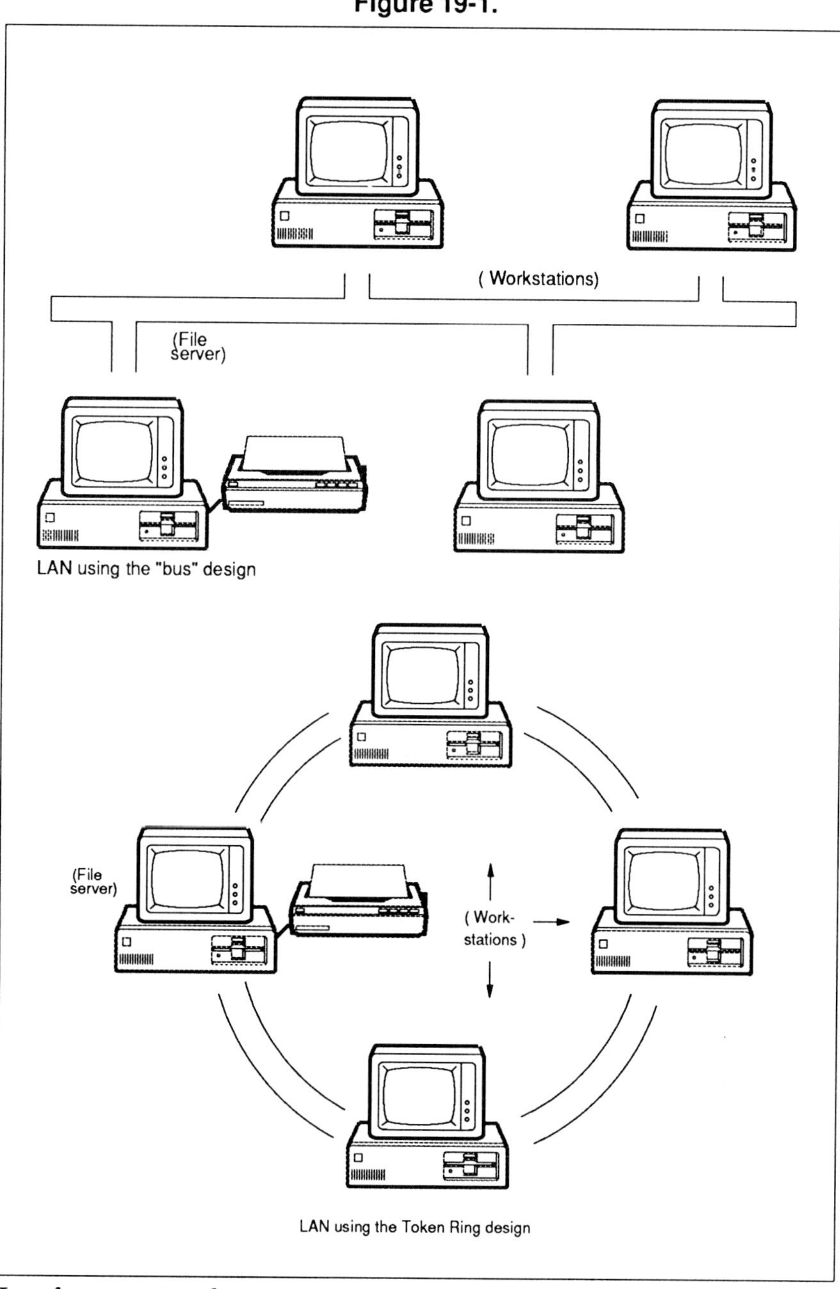

Local area network

by all users of the network. Most servers are one of three types: file servers, which provide shared hard disks; print servers, which provide shared printers; and communications servers, which provide shared modems. Servers can provide more than one of these functions simultaneously; a single server, for example, may have a hard disk and a printer attached, making that server both a file server and a print server.

Workstations are computers that are attached to the network but do not normally provide shared resources for other users. They are used by the individual users of the network to run software that may be present on a workstation or on the file server. Some types of networks allow the simultaneous use of the same computer for a file server and a workstation, although this practice is not recommended; network performance suffers as a result.

dBASE IV and Compatible Networks

At the time of this writing, a number of local area networks are compatible with dBASE IV. The IBM PC Token Ring Network, the 3Com 3Plus network, the Ungermann-Bass Net /One network, and the Novell S/Net Network can be operated with dBASE IV installed on any of the file servers. You can also use dBASE IV on networks that are 100% NETBIOS compatible with these networks. The network must use DOS version 3.1 or above, or OS/2 version 1.0 or above.

dBASE IV, when used on a local area network, contains the necessary operational and programming features to provide file and record locking. dBASE IV also recognizes any security limitations outlined through the use of the Protect option. dBASE IV can be installed on one or more file servers throughout a network.

The dBASE Access Control program is a program used at a server to enable additional users to access dBASE IV. The standard version of dBASE IV permits one user at a time to access the program on a network. (The Developer's Release edition of dBASE IV permits three users at a time.) To allow additional users to gain access to dBASE IV, you must use the Access Control program, which is installed on the desired server. See the installation guides provided with dBASE IV or with the dBASE Lan Pack for more details on adding users.

Protect is a menu option that lets you control access to dBASE IV and to databases residing on the file server. The Protect option lets you specify the authorized users and passwords, whether databases will be encrypted, and whether users can make changes to databases or only view (read) those databases. Protect is an optional feature of dBASE IV; you do not have to use Protect on your network. If security is an issue, however, the use of Protect is recommended.

Database Integrity

Users of database software on any local area network face the consideration of database integrity. Database integrity—the completeness of the database—is threatened whenever two users attempt to modify the same database record at the same time. If the software is not designed to operate on a network, serious problems can occur. One user may write over another user's changes, or in more extreme cases, the network operating software may crash and bring the entire network down. In network lingo, such a potential disaster is known as a *collision*. Another common problem, known as a *deadly embrace,* can occur when programs execute endless loops, trying to provide exclusive use of the same file to more than one user on the network.

To prevent such problems, dBASE IV offers two features: file locking and record locking. File locking causes a database file that is in use by one user to be made unavailable to any other users on the network. Record locking performs the same type of safeguard, but does so for an individual record within a file. dBASE IV will automatically perform file and record locking as needed to maintain data integrity for any database that you use. Commands that change data, such as EDIT, APPEND, and INDEX ON will cause dBASE IV to lock the file or record automatically. In addition to the file and record locking that is automatic, you can use specific programming commands to turn file and record locking off or on.

Requirements for Network Use

To use dBASE IV on a local area network, you will need workstations with a minimum of 640K of memory (on Novell networks) or with 640K base memory plus 360K extended memory or 64K additional DOS-contiguous memory (on non-Novell networks). The server or one workstation on the network must have one 5 1/4-inch 360K or 1.2Mb floppy, or one 3 1/2-inch, 720K floppy. The server must have a hard-disk drive. The network operating system can be any of the following:

- Novell SFT Netware/286 TTS version 2.10 or above
- IBM Token Ring Network with IBM PC Local Area Network Program version 1.2 or above

- 3Com 3Plus share version 1.3.1 or above
- Ungermann-Bass Net /One PC version 16.0 or above
- Any other network configuration that is 100% NETBIOS compatible with DOS 3.1 or above and with the networks just listed.

If more than three workstations are to make regular use of the network, an IBM PC AT, AT-compatible, or 80386-based system is recommended instead of a PC-compatible or an XT-compatible (8088-based systems). Serious speed degradation usually occurs when a large number of workstations use a server that is a PC or XT compatible.

A Note on Installation

Because the specific steps for installation of dBASE IV on a network vary widely and may change with each revision of dBASE IV, this text will not attempt to detail the specific steps. For instructions on the installation of dBASE IV on your particular network, consult the Network Installation supplement provided with your dBASE IV documentation. The remainder of this chapter assumes that your network administrator (the person who manages the network) has already installed dBASE IV on your network for your use.

If you are faced with the task of installing dBASE IV on a network, you should thoroughly study the "Introduction" and "Network Planning" sections of the Network Installation supplement, and then proceed to the section on dBASE IV installation.

Starting dBASE on a Network

To use dBASE on the network, you must first ensure that the file server and workstations to be used are turned on and started in the usual manner. See your network operator's manual, if necessary, for instructions on starting workstations and file servers on the network.

Once the file server and workstation are up and running, log on to the network at the workstation. If necessary, change to the subdirectory containing dBASE, and enter **DBASE** to start the program. One of two things should happen: you will see the normal copyright message followed by the Control Center or the dot prompt, or you will see a message box asking you for a user name, group name, and password. The message box appears if a security system has been set up with the Protect option by your network administrator. Contact your network administrator for information about the names and passwords you should be using.

Using dBASE IV on a network is in most respects identical to using it in a single-user environment. Users should remember to use proper disk-drive designators, since most network workstations have a large number of available disk drives. As an example, a workstation may have available drives A and B (dual floppies in the workstation), drive C (a hard disk attached to the workstation), and drives D, E, F, and G (four hard disks at the file server). Many networks also map drive letters to shared drives (often drives Z, Y, W, or X). The SET DEFAULT command should be used, when appropriate, to select the desired drive for storage of files and programs on a network.

Network Commands

There are some additional commands available to network users of dBASE IV; these commands provide information and control certain functions within dBASE IV. The DISPLAY STATUS, LIST STATUS, and SET PRINTER commands, while available with single-user dBASE, provide additional information or options when you are using a network. The DISPLAY USERS command is specific to the network use of dBASE. This list is by no means all-inclusive, but many other commands are for advanced programming uses and are therefore beyond the scope of this text.

DISPLAY STATUS/LIST STATUS

The DISPLAY STATUS and LIST STATUS commands provide the same information in network dBASE IV as they do in the single-user versions of dBASE IV: the name of the database in use, status of most SET commands, and the status of the programmable function keys. In addition to this information, the DISPLAY STATUS and LIST STATUS commands also indicate whether database files are locked and whether individual records within a file are locked. An example of the display resulting from the DISPLAY STATUS or LIST STATUS command is shown in Figure 19-2.

Figure 19-2.

```
Currently Selected Database:
Select area: 1, Database in Use: C:\DBASE4\DBDATA\ABCSTAFF.DBF Alias:
ABCSTAFF
Production  MDX file:  C:\DBASE4\DBDATA\ABCSTAFF.MDX
            Index TAG:    SOCIALEC  Key: SOCIALSEC
            Memo file:  C:\DBASE4\DBDATA\ABCSTAFF.DBT
            Lock list:     2,    3,    7,   8  locked


File search path:
Default disk drive: C:
Print destination:  PRN:
Margin =     0
Refresh count =    0
Reprocess count =    0
Number of files open =    9
Current work area =    1

ALTERNATE- ON   DELIMITERS  - OFF    FULLPATH - OFF    SAFETY    - ON
AUTOSAVE - OFF  DESIGN      - ON     HEADING  - ON   SCOREBOARD- ON
BELL      - ON  DEVELOP     - ON     HELP     - OFF    SPACE     - ON
CARRY     - OFF DEVICE      - SCRN   HISTORY  - ON     SQL       - OFF
CATALOG   - OFF ECHO        - OFF    INSTRUCT - ON     STATUS    - ON
CENTURY   - OFF ENCRYPTION  - ON     INTENSITY- ON     STEP      - OFF
CONFIRM   - OFF ESCAPE      - ON     LOCK     - ON     TALK      - OFF
CONSOLE   - ON  EXACT       - OFF    NEAR     - OFF    TITLE     - ON
DEBUG     - OFF EXCLUSIVE   - OFF    PAUSE    - OFF    TRAP      - OFF
DELETED   - OFF FIELDS      - OFF    PRINT    - OFF    UNIQUE    - OFF

Programmable function keys:
F2          - assist;
F3          - list;
F4          - dir;
F5          - display structure;
F6          - display status;
F7          - display memory;
F8          - display;
F9          - append;
F10         - edit;
CTRL-F1     - Hello.
CTRL-F2  -
```

Example of display resulting from DISPLAY STATUS or LIST STATUS command

Figure 19-2. *(continued)*

```
CTRL-F3  -
CTRL-F4  -
CTRL-F5  -
CTRL-F6  -
CTRL-F7  -
CTRL-F8  -
CTRL-F9  -
CTRL-F10 -
SHIFT-F1 -
SHIFT-F2 -
SHIFT-F3 -
SHIFT-F4 -
SHIFT-F5 -
SHIFT-F6 -
SHIFT-F7 -
SHIFT-F8 -
SHIFT-F9 -
```

Example of display resulting from DISPLAY STATUS or LIST STATUS command

Both commands operate in an identical manner, except that LIST STATUS displays the information without pausing and DISPLAY STATUS pauses every 24 lines. The TO PRINT option can be added to either command if you want the status to be printed on your printer.

DISPLAY USERS/LIST USERS

The DISPLAY USERS and LIST USERS commands show all users currently sharing dBASE IV on the file server. The names shown by the commands are the names assigned through the use of the network's operating-system software. An example of the

DISPLAY USERS command is shown here. The greater-than sign indicates the user who is currently logged on the network and using dBASE IV.

```
DISPLAY USERS

Server Phoenix
--------------

>STA-ALLEN
STA-JUDIE
>STA-BILL
STA-LARRY
STA-CATHY
```

Both commands operate in an identical manner, except that LIST USERS displays the names of all users without pausing and DISPLAY USERS pauses every 24 lines. The TO PRINT option can be added to either command if you want the list of users to be printed on your printer.

SET PRINTER

The SET PRINTER command is used to specify whether print output should be sent to a "local" printer (one attached to a workstation) or to a printer attached to a server. The normal syntax of the SET PRINTER command is

SET PRINTER TO *computer-name**printer-name* = *destination*

where *computer-name* is the name of the workstation as assigned by the network operating software; *printer-name* is the network name assigned to the desired printer; and *destination* is the DOS device that identifies the printer (LPT1, LPT2, and so on). If no destination is specified, the default destination will be the first parallel port (LPT1).

As an example, to redirect printer output to parallel printer port 1 (LPT1) connected to a workstation named Chicago, where an attached laser printer has been named LASER by the network operating system software, you would use the following command:

```
SET PRINTER TO \\CHICAGO\LASER = LPT1
```

To redirect output to a printer attached to a file server that has been named PUBLIC by the network software, you would use the command

```
SET PRINTER TO \\PUBLIC
```

To redirect output to a printer attached to your workstation and choose LPT1 for the printer port, you would enter

```
SET PRINTER TO LPT1
```

General Network Hints

There are several points you should keep in mind to make the most effective use of dBASE IV on a network:

- In any multiuser environment, large numbers of files tend to clutter the working space on the file server. To hold such clutter to a minimum, heavy users should be provided with individual subdirectories on the file server. The dBASE SET PATH command can be used to cause all dBASE commands that read files to search private subdirectories. (See Appendix A for information on the SET PATH command.)

- If users are going to create smaller files that will not be used by other users of the network, encourage those users to store such files at their workstations, rather than on the file server.
- Back up all databases regularly to floppy disks or a tape backup.
- Create new applications and databases at a workstation, in a single-user mode, and thoroughly test those applications before placing the files in shared space on the file server. A multiuser environment is not the best place to get all of the "bugs" out of a system's design.

Introducing Protect

The next section of this chapter describes the use of Protect, a menu-driven option that builds a security system around dBASE IV and the databases present on the file server. Protect should be used by your network administrator to assign security procedures and levels of file access to users of the network. Protect controls access only to dBASE IV and dBASE databases; to establish security for other files on a network, you should continue to use the security features available within your version of network operating-system software. Three kinds of security are provided by Protect: log-in security, file and field access levels, and database encryption.

About Log-In Security

Log-in security requires users to enter names and passwords before the system can be used. The names and passwords for each user are stored in a file that is read by dBASE IV when a user attempts to use the system. Log-in security will require three items from the users: a group name, a user name, and a password. Each item is entered on a separate line of a log-in screen presented by dBASE IV. If valid names and passwords are provided by the user, access to dBASE IV is granted.

File and Field Access

File and field access levels are used to assign privilege access levels to each user, restricting changes that can be made to a database in varying degrees. (Privilege access levels are also referred to as the *file privilege scheme.*) Such privilege access levels are optional; a network administrator can choose to allow all users unrestricted access to all fields in all databases.

Access to databases and the fields present in the databases are controlled by the matching of file and field access levels with user access levels. User access levels are varying levels granted to users, on a sliding scale of 1 (the least restrictive) to 8 (the most restrictive). The network administrator controls what privileges are available at the different user access levels.

At the database file level, privileges can control the ability to read (read privilege), edit (update privilege), append (extend privilege), and delete (delete privilege) records within a database. At the field level, privileges can control whether users have full access (FULL), read-only access (R/O), or no access (NONE) to particular fields within a database.

When you are creating a file privilege scheme, you must keep in mind how Protect works. First, the file access controls that you specify within Protect cannot override any read-only limitations set by the network operating-system software. In general, limitations set by network operating-system security commands will take priority over limitations set by the Protect option. Second, you can specify the most restrictive access level for each type of privilege (read, extend, update, and delete). When you do this, all levels that are less restrictive than the specified level will be given the privilege, while all levels that are more restrictive than the specified level will be denied the privilege. As an example, if you choose level 5 as a level to grant delete privileges, then all users with access levels of 1 through 5 will have the ability to delete records, while users with access levels of 6 through 8 will not be able to delete records.

Database Encryption

Database encryption causes each database identified by Protect to be encrypted. Encrypted databases cannot be read unless proper user names, group names, and passwords are supplied. Protect automatically creates encrypted versions of database files. Whenever you specify privileges while using the Protect option, the database file will be encrypted, which means it will be encoded to protect it from unauthorized access. Once a database has been encrypted, it cannot be used without proper entry of the user name, group name, and password when dBASE is initially started.

REMEMBER Encrypting databases is useless unless you remember to delete the unencrypted originals after you finish encrypting your files.

The Protect option creates a copy of the original database file; the copy is encrypted, while the original file remains in its original condition. Encrypted database files have an extension of .CRP. For maximum security following the use of Protect, you should delete the database file with the .DBF extension and rename the database file with the .CRP extension to a .DBF extension.

User Groups

Each user is assigned a security profile when you add a user to the file of user names and passwords with the Protect option. In addition to user name and password, the security profile will also contain the name of a group to which the user is assigned. Various users should be assigned to various groups in a logical order (a TAX group, a LEGAL group, a PERSONNL group, and so on). Each group will be associated with a set of database files.

Once the files have been encrypted by Protect, a user must belong to a qualified group to access a database. You give groups the ability to access various database files through a menu selection within the Protect option. Users can belong to more than one group. However, to gain access to a database that belongs to a different group, a user must log out with the LOGOUT command and log back in as a member of the other group.

The DBSYSTEM.DB File

The Protect option stores the security profile information in a special file named DBSYSTEM.DB. The file is a special form of database that contains a record for each user, with the user's name, group name, password, and assigned access level. The file is encrypted, so you cannot use dBASE IV to directly read the DBSYSTEM.DB file.

User names, group names, passwords, and access levels should be written down and stored in a safe place so that if the DBSYSTEM.DB file is accidentally erased, the network administrator will have a copy of the information. It is also a good idea to copy the DBSYSTEM.DB file created by Protect to a backup disk for safekeeping.

When a user tries to access dBASE IV, the program will first attempt to read a file called DBSYSTEM.DB. If no such file is present, no log-in sequence will be required by dBASE IV. However, the database encryption codes are stored within the database files, so if the DBSYSTEM.DB file is missing, the users will not be able to open encrypted databases until the missing file has been restored by the network administrator.

Using Protect

To use Protect, enter **PROTECT** from the dot prompt or choose the Protect Data option of the Tools menu. In a moment, the screen will be replaced by the log-in screen (Figure 19-3).

NOTE Before entering a password, you should write down the password in a safe place. Once you have defined a password, you must know that password to use the Protect option. There is no way to retrieve the password from the system; therefore, do not lose the password!

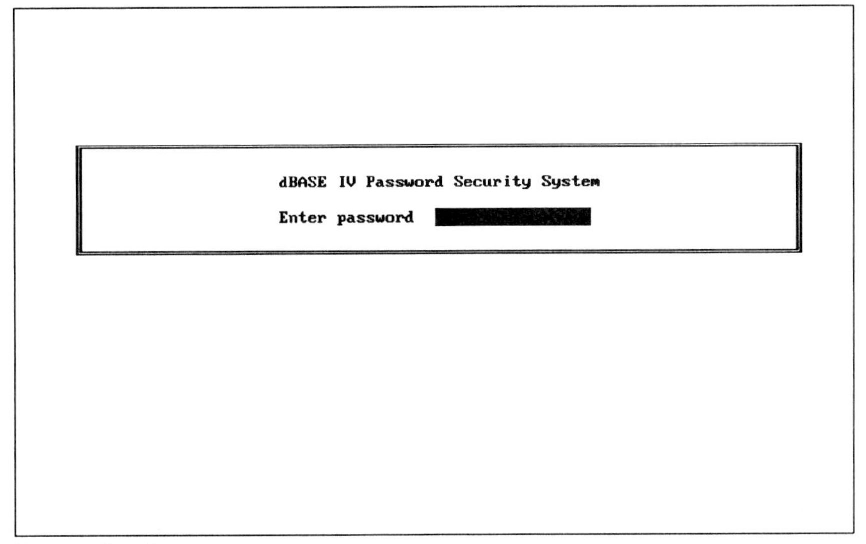

Protect log-in screen

You must enter a password of eight characters or less in the Login screen. The first time that you use Protect, it will ask for the password just once when you start the program. An incorrect password entry will result in the user being returned to the dot prompt or the Control Center.

Once the password has been entered correctly, the Protect menu appears (Figure 19-4).

The Protect menu is similar in design to other menus used throughout dBASE IV. The menu bar offers four choices: Users, Files, Reports, and Exit. The Users menu is used to specify the user names, passwords, group names, full names, and access levels for network users. You can also delete existing users from a group of dBASE IV users through the Users menu.

Figure 19-4.

```
Users  Files  Reports  Exit                                    10:25:55 am

 Login name
 Password
 Group name

 Full Name
 Access level          1

 Store user profile

 Delete user from group

Protect
        Position selection bar: ↑↓   Select: ◄┘   Cancel: Esc
                 Enter the login name for this user
```

Protect menu

The Files menu lets you identify file and field access privileges for a specific database file. Varying levels of privileges let you identify whether groups of users can read, edit (update), append to (extend), or delete records in the specified database.

The Reports menu lets you display on the screen or print security information about the users or the protected files. The Exit menu lets you save the changes you made while you are in the User or Files menus. You can also abandon any changes without saving them.

Adding Users

The first step in creating a security system with Protect is to add authorized users. To do this, you normally perform the following steps:

1. Open the Users menu.
2. Enter a user's log-in name of eight characters or less.
3. Enter a user password of eight characters or less.
4. Enter a group name of eight characters or less.
5. Enter a full name. (This is an option; you use full names to give further definition to the user names.)
6. Select a user access level from 1 (least restrictive) to 8 (most restrictive). This access level will be matched to privileges that you specify when you use the Files menu.
7. Select Store User Profile to store the data for the user.
8. Repeat steps 1 through 7 for each additional user.

Figure 19-5 shows a filled-in Users menu for a sample user on a network. If you decide that you do not wish to save the information entered during any of the steps, you can cancel the changes by selecting the Abandon option of the Exit menu.

Figure 19-5.

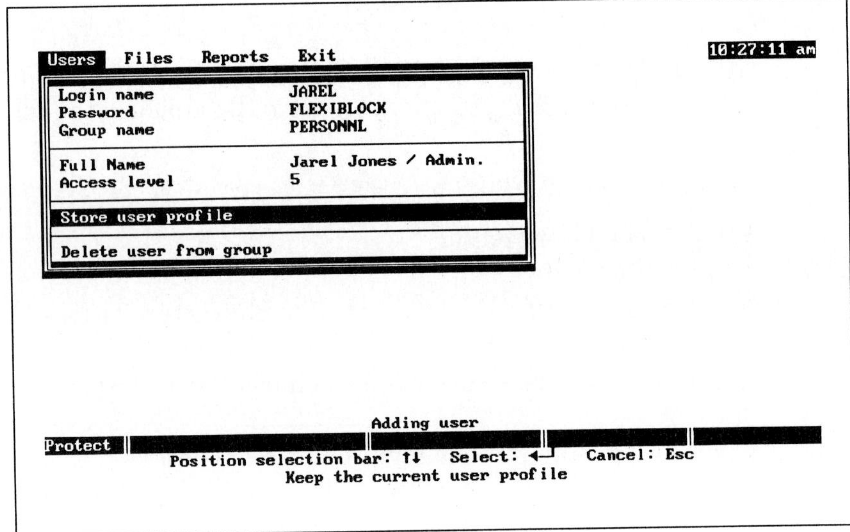

Filled-in Users menu

Changing and Deleting Users

To change the user information for an existing user, simply enter the log-in name, password, and group name already established for that user. The remaining fields within the Users menu will be filled in with the existing data for that user. You can then make any desired changes and save the updated user information with the Save option of the Exit menu.

To delete a user from a specified group of users, select the Delete User from Group option of the Users menu. Then save the selection with the Save option of the Exit Menu.

Creating File Privileges

The Files menu (Figure 19-6) is used to assign file and field access privileges to a database file. You can assign any combination of read, update (edit), extend (append to), and delete privileges to a specific group of users. Up to eight access levels can be specified, and you control precisely what privileges are available at each of these access levels. You may choose to use one, two, or all of the available access levels. If you do not use the Files menu to specify privileges, all users of the network can read and write to all database files.

By using the Field Access Privileges section of the Files menu, you can specify access to individual fields. Such access to a particular field can be FULL (read/write), R/O (read-only), or NONE (no access). The default value is FULL access, so if you do not specify field privileges, all users of the network can access all database fields.

To identify file privileges with the Files menu, perform the following steps:

1. Open the Files menu.

2. Choose the New File option. A menu of files will appear, as shown in Figure 19-7.

3. Highlight the desired database and press ENTER.

4. Select Group Name, and enter the name of a group that will have access to the file.

5. Using a number of your choice from 1 (least restrictive) to 8 (most restrictive), specify the access level for the read, update, extend, and delete privilege levels.

Figure 19-6.

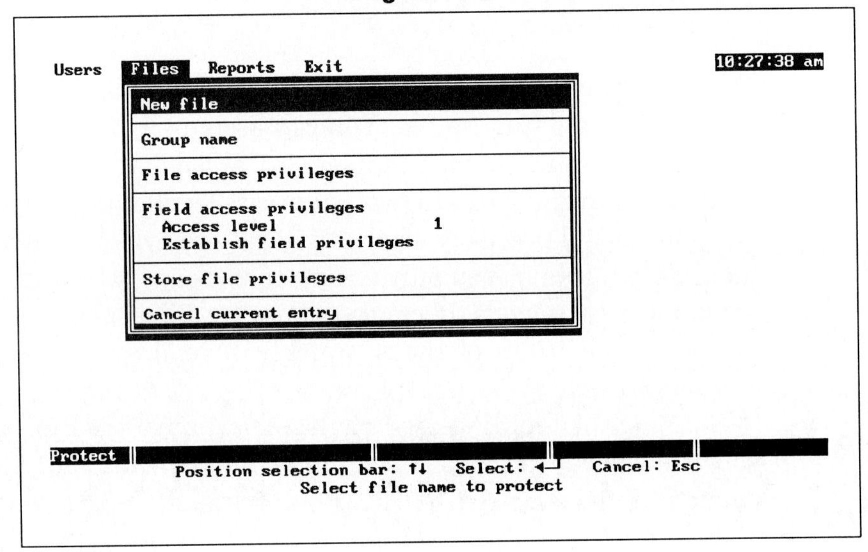

Files menu

Figure 19-7.

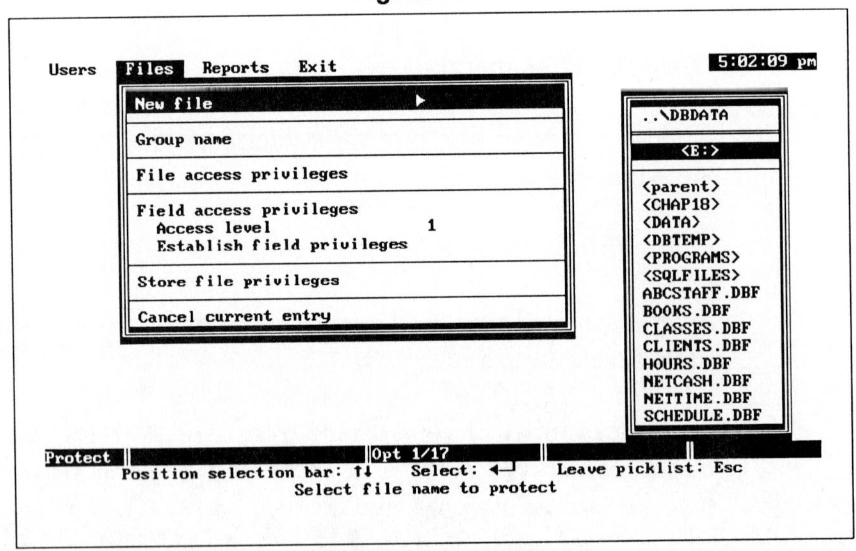

Files menu with available database files

6. If field privileges are also desired, select an access level, and enter the desired field privileges for that access level. When you enter a number (from 1 to 8) for the access level and then select the Establish Field Privileges option, a list of fields will appear, as shown in Figure 19-8. Choose the desired field privilege for each field by highlighting the field and pressing ENTER to display the available options. As you press ENTER, the field privilege will switch between FULL (full access), R/O (read-only), and NONE (no access to the field). When the desired option appears, use the up or down arrow key to move to the next field. After all desired privileges have been set, press ESC to leave the list of fields and return to the Files menu.

You can repeat step 6 for each access level desired. Doing so lets you set individual field privileges for all access levels that you have specified for groups of users. Note that when you specify field privileges as any choice other than the default value (FULL), all field privileges for more restrictive user

Figure 19-8.

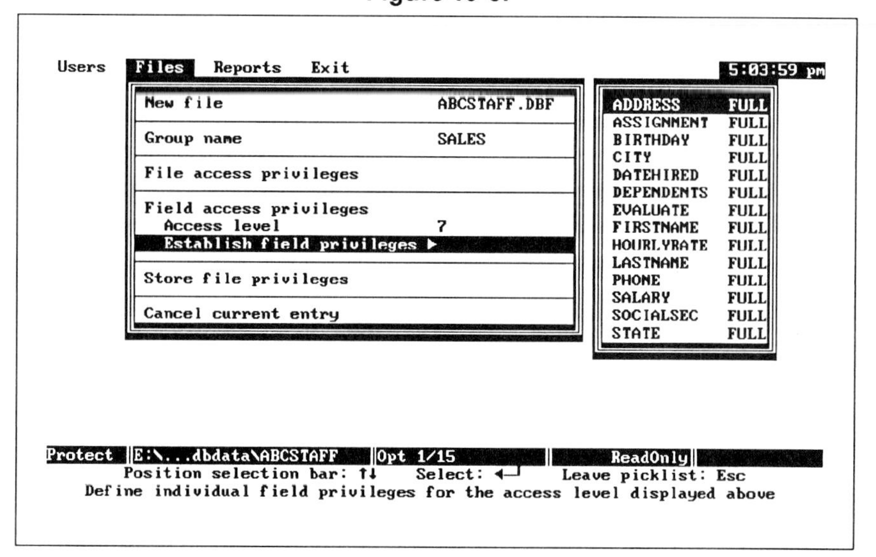

List of fields

access levels are changed to NONE unless you specify otherwise.

7. Select the Store File Privileges option from the Files menu. The privileges will be stored in memory, and the New File option will be highlighted at the top of the menu.

8. Repeat steps 1 through 7 for each additional database for which you wish to assign privileges. You can also choose to assign different privileges for the same database to different groups. To do so, simply specify a different group name while giving the same filename when in the Files menu. Note that you can only enter privileges for up to ten databases at a time. You must save all changes with the Save option of the Exit menu if you wish to select privileges for more than ten database files.

Figure 19-9 shows a filled-in Files menu for a sample database on a network. If you decide that you do not wish to save the information entered during any of the steps, you can cancel the operation by selecting the Cancel Current Entry option of the Files menu.

To change the file and field privileges for an existing group, simply open the Files menu and enter the name of the database file and the name of the group. The rest of the information previously entered will then be accessible through the menu selections. Make the required changes, and choose the Store File Privileges option to save any changes.

Figure 19-9.

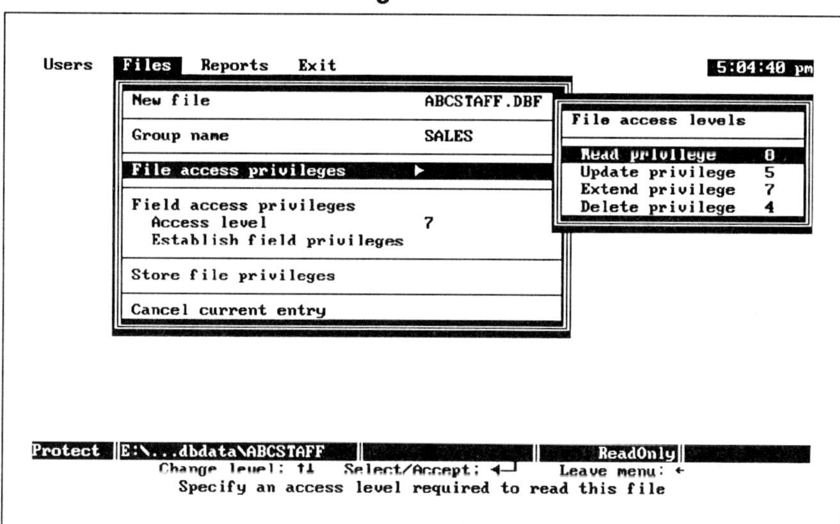

Filled-in Files menu

Using the Reports Menu

When you choose Reports from the menu bar, the choices shown in Figure 19-10 appear. The choices are User Information and File Information. If you select the User Information option, you are asked if the report should be directed to the printer. If you select the Files Information option, you are asked to pick a file from the list of files; then you are asked if the report should be directed to the printer. Enter **Y** to send the report to the default printer, or enter **N** to display the report on the screen.

Figure 19-10.

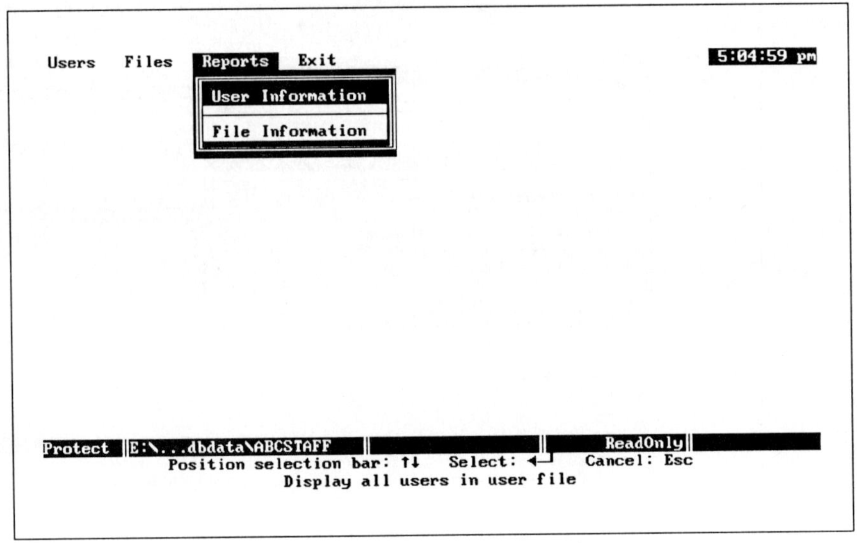

Reports menu

The User Information report lists the names of all authorized users, passwords, group names, full names, and security levels. The File Information report lists the names of your dBASE files, the groups that own those files, file privileges, the names of each field in the files, and the field privileges. Note that if you have just created a new database and you have not yet closed that file, you cannot list information on that file.

Exiting from the Protect Option

The Exit menu (Figure 19-11) contains choices for saving changes, abandoning any changes, and exiting the Protect option. To save any entries while you are within Protect and to continue using

Figure 19-11.

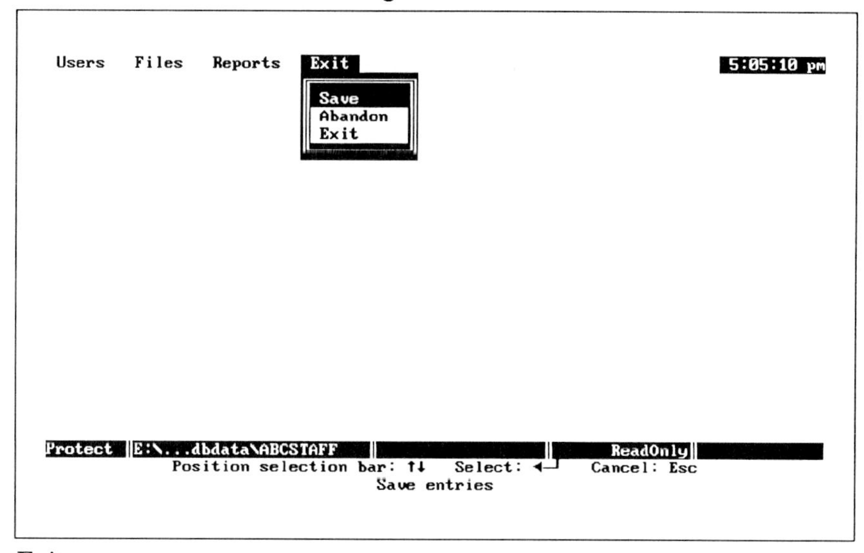

Exit menu

the Protect option, choose the Save option. To cancel any entries and continue using Protect, choose the Abandon option. To save your entries and exit the Protect option, choose the Exit option. Once you select Exit, the appropriate databases will be encrypted, and user, password, and access level information will be stored in the DBSYSTEM.DB file. With large databases, the encryption process may take a few moments. When the process is complete, the Control Center or the dot prompt will reappear.

Once dBASE IV has been protected with the Protect option, any attempt to load dBASE will result in the Log-in screen being presented to the workstation user (Figure 19-12). The user must enter a valid user name, group name, and password before dBASE IV will display a dot prompt or run a program. The user name and group name are displayed during the entry process, but the password remains hidden as it is entered. If the entries match valid entries specified during the use of Protect, the user will be allowed access to the system. If the entries are invalid, the user

Figure 19-12.

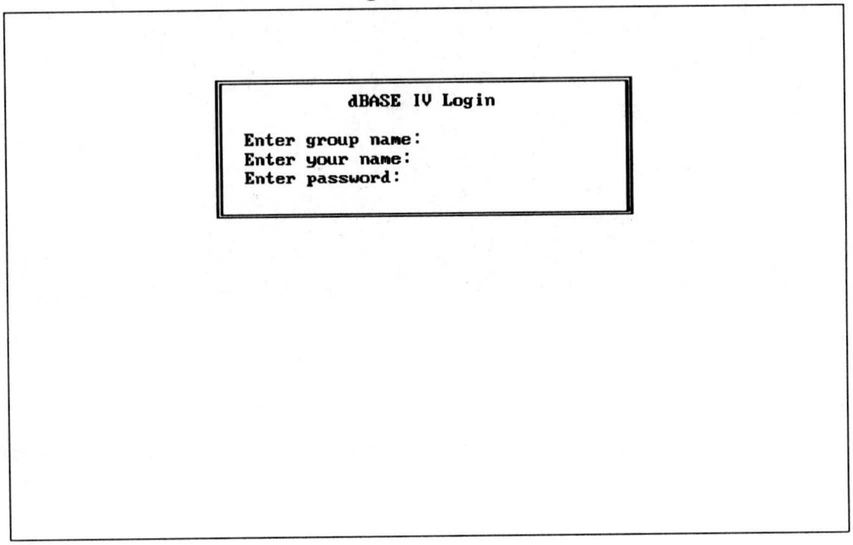

```
dBASE IV Login

Enter group name:
Enter your name:
Enter password:
```

Log-in screen

will be given a maximum of three chances to enter valid information. If valid information is not entered, the message

```
Unauthorized Login
***dBASE IV initialization error
```

will appear, and the user will be returned to the DOS prompt.

General Security Hints

Network administrators should keep some general hints in mind when implementing security for dBASE IV on a network.

- A record of user names and passwords should be kept in a safe place.

- Users should be encouraged to memorize passwords and to avoid using passwords that are easy to decipher (like the name of a spouse).
- Only the network administrator and a responsible backup administrator should have access to the Protect option password.
- If encryption of databases is important in your application, remember to delete the unencrypted (.DBF) database files once the encrypted versions have been created, and rename the encrypted (.CRP) files to files with .DBF extensions.

Any security system is only as strong as its weakest link. In most large organizations, the network administrator (this probably means *you*) is usually held responsible for any breach of security due to carelessness. The network version of dBASE IV has effective tools to increase security on a network, but it is up to you to put those tools to proper use.

Programming Considerations

Additional programming tools available with dBASE IV are designed to maintain database integrity and security in a network environment. Effective use of these tools calls for an in-depth discussion of programming for networks, which is beyond the scope of this book. This section of the chapter will make the reader aware of the existence of these tools and will suggest additional resources that can provide more information for a network programmer.

The additional programming tools, which consist of various commands and functions, are needed to prevent potential problems when users share files. Collisions between users, caused when users try to use the same file at the same time, can cause additional problems for the network programmer, because the program must be provided with enough "intelligence" to sense such problems and find a solution. Certain commands and functions can be used to provide a program with routines that test for activity on the network. Included in these programming tools are the SET EXCLUSIVE and the UNLOCK commands, and the LOCK, FLOCK, and RLOCK functions. These are not all of the available programming commands and functions that can be used for control of dBASE programs on a network, but they do provide important features, and they serve as an introduction to programming for network use.

Using SET EXCLUSIVE

The SET EXCLUSIVE command controls whether files are available on a shared basis, or are available only for the exclusive use of the first user to access the file. The format for this command is

```
SET EXCLUSIVE ON/OFF
```

As an alternative, you can also add the word "EXCLUSIVE" after the USE command when a file is opened to open that file for exclusive use only.

If SET EXCLUSIVE is on, only one user can access a database file at a time. Until the file is closed, no other user can gain access. If SET EXCLUSIVE is off, a database file can be accessed simultaneously by multiple users. Once a program opens a file with SET EXCLUSIVE turned off, it is the responsibility of the program to guard against potential collisions by checking the status of files and records with the locking functions (FLOCK, RLOCK, and LOCK).

Using Locking Functions

In dBASE IV, locking functions can be used to prevent collisions and occurrences of deadly embrace. Locking functions let a program know if a file or a record is locked by another user on the network. Locking functions operate in a slightly different manner than other functions. Where other dBASE functions usually return a value (such as true or false), the locking functions can perform an action (the locking of a file or a record) as well as returning a value.

There are three locking functions within dBASE IV: FLOCK, RLOCK, and LOCK. The RLOCK and LOCK functions perform identical tasks: both are used to check the status of a record and to lock that record (if it is presently unlocked). The FLOCK function checks the status of a file and locks the file if it is not already locked. Like all functions, the locking functions can be used in an interactive mode (from the dot prompt) or from within a command file.

Let's look at an example. The commands

```
USE ABCSTAFF
? FLOCK( )
```

will cause dBASE IV to respond with true (.T.), assuming no other users are using the ABCSTAFF file. The FLOCK function causes the ABCSTAFF file to be locked and reports the file-lock status as true. If another user then logs on to the system and enters the same commands, dBASE IV will respond with false (.F.), which indicates that the ABCSTAFF file is already locked.

Within a program, you can combine IF expressions with various locking functions and pass program control to appropriate parts of a program, depending on the status reported by the locking functions. As an example of a simple method of protection against collisions, a program might include a SET EXCLUSIVE command and the FLOCK function, as shown here:

```
ON ERROR DO ERRFIND
SET SAFETY OFF
SET TALK OFF
SET EXCLUSIVE OFF
USE ABCSTAFF
*test for file lock.
IF .NOT. FLOCK( )
            *file not locked, so exit program.
            CLEAR
            ? "Another user is using the ABC staff database."
            ? "try your choice again later."
            RETURN
ENDIF
*file lock successful, so continue.
DO MAINMENU
(rest of program...)
```

The UNLOCK Command

Once your program has completed operations with a record or a file, the UNLOCK command can be used to clear all locks. The format of the command is simply UNLOCK.

As an alternate method of clearing a lock, you can lock a different record or file, or close the database with a CLEAR ALL, USE, or QUIT command. Any of these operations will release a previous lock on a record or file.

The SET REPROCESS Command

The SET REPROCESS command, which is valid in programs or when stored in the CONFIG.DB file as REPROCESS = *n*, sets the number of times dBASE attempts to open a previously locked file or record before it displays an error message. The default is 0, which means that if dBASE tries to open a locked file or record, it immediately displays an error message. You can use the command

```
SET REPROCESS TO n
```

where *n* is a number from 1 to 32,000 and dBASE will then retry the operation the specified number of times before the error condition is reported.

The Deadly Embrace

Many programs written for a single-user environment must be rewritten to contend adequately with the demands of a network environment. A very common fault of single-user dBASE programs running on a network is an inability to guard against the deadly embrace that results when programs executed by two or more users contend for the same files and become locked in an endless loop. Even with the simple type of file locking used in the program example you saw with locking functions, a deadly embrace can occur.

Consider the example shown in Figure 19-13, where two users are running the same program and one of them happens to start the program an instant before the other user. In the deadly

Figure 19-13.

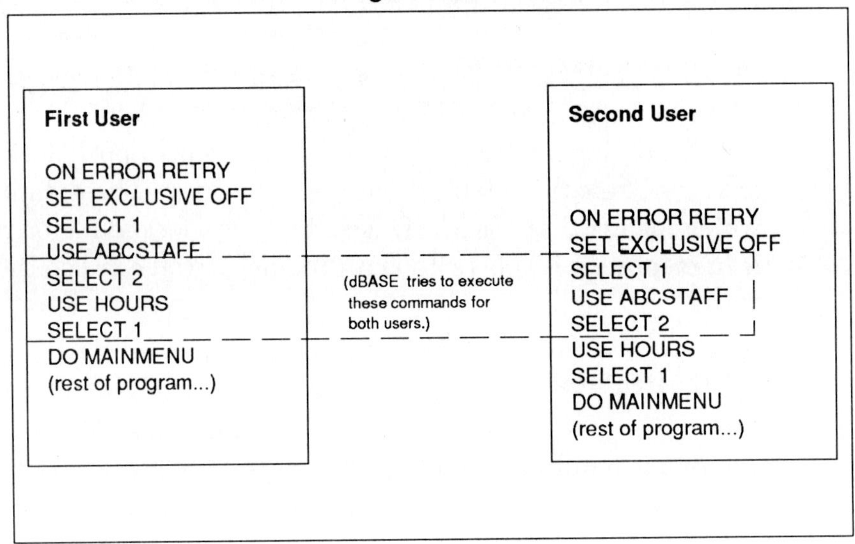

Deadly embrace

embrace illustrated by this example, the following chain of events takes place. The first user's program opens ABCSTAFF in work area 1. Then the HOURS file is opened in work area 2. At the same instant in time, the second user's program opens ABC-STAFF. The first user's program now tries to open ABCSTAFF with the SELECT 1 command but is unsuccessful because ABC-STAFF is now locked by the second user's program. The second user's program is trying to open HOURS but is unsuccessful because HOURS is locked by the first user's program. Normally, both users would get "File in use" error messages at this point, but because the programs contain an ON ERROR RETRY statement, dBASE IV gets caught in an infinite loop, trying to give both users exclusive access to the same files.

This example demonstrates the planning that is necessary when you are programming applications that will be used on a network. In this case, a better use of the ON ERROR command would be to transfer control to a part of the program that would use the locking functions to test the status of the desired files. Depending on the results, the program could then take appropriate action.

Where Do I Go from Here?

As stated earlier, the programming of applications for a network environment requires additional considerations not covered in this brief introduction to such a complicated topic. Programmers who plan to develop serious applications on a network should take advantage of all available resources, including the network operator's manual for the particular network in use, the "Network Programming Concepts" section of the dBASE documentation, and various programmers' reference guides for dBASE IV, such as *Advanced dBASE IV Programming and Techniques* by Miriam Liskin (Osborne/McGraw-Hill, Berkeley, 1988).

Quick Reference

Additional commands useful on a network include DISPLAY STATUS and LIST STATUS, which show the locking status of database files and records; DISPLAY USERS and LIST USERS, which show network names of all users logged onto dBASE IV on the file server; and SET PRINTER, which lets you redirect printer output to a different printer on the network.

Commands and functions that are useful when writing programs for use on a network SET EXCLSIVE, to determine whether files are opened for exclusive use; UNLOCK, to clear locks on a record or file; SET REPROCESS, to change the number of attempts dBASE makes on a locked file or record; and FLOCK(), LOCK(), and RLOCK(), to lock records or files.

To start the Protect Utility From the Control Center, choose the Protect option of the Tools menu. From the dot prompt, enter **PROTECT**.

CHAPTER

20

Sample Applications

This chapter describes how you can build two sample applications: a mailing list and a payroll system. Rather than present you with the daunting task of typing in hundreds of lines of program code, this chapter tells you which options to use to build the applications with the applications generator. It is assumed that you are already familiar with the applications generator and with the other dBASE IV features and concepts presented throughout this text. When new options of the applications generator are used in this chapter, they are explained, but for the most part only the steps you need will be provided here. For a detailed explanation of how to use the applications generator, see Chapter 17.

If you prefer to save the time involved in building these applications, they are available on disk, along with other sample dBASE IV applications and programs. See the form at the front of this book for details.

Before building each application, you may want to create a new catalog so that the various files will not clutter your current catalog.

HINT You can also create new directories to store you applications while in dBASE. Open the Tools menu, choose DOS Utilities, open the DOS menu, and choose Perform DOS Command. Enter the appropriate MD\ command to create a directory. (See your DOS manual for details on the MD\ command.

Membership Roster and Mailing List

The Mailer application maintains a membership roster and mailing list. It lets you add new names to the list, edit existing names, print a membership roster, or print mailing labels. The Print options of this application let you print the membership roster alphabetically or by expiration dates, and the mailing labels may be printed by expiration date or by ZIP code.

Before designing the application, you should create a database that will contain the membership records. The database should be assigned the name MAILERS.DBF. Specify the fields and their characteristics as shown here:

MAILERS.DBF

Field#	Field Name	Type	Width	Dec	Index
1	LASTNAME	Character	20		N
2	FIRSTNAME	Character	20		N
3	COMPANY	Character	20		N
4	ADDRESS	Character	25		N
5	CITY	Character	20		N
6	STATE	Character	2		N
7	ZIP	Character	10		N
8	PHONE	Character	12		N
9	CONTRIBUTE	Numeric	7	2	N
10	EXPIRATION	Date	8		N

To allow for printing in order of expiration date, ZIP code, or alphabetically, three index tags are needed. After you create the database, go to the dot prompt and enter the following commands to create the desired indexes:

```
USE MAILERS
INDEX ON LASTNAME + FIRSTNAME TAG NAMES
INDEX ON ZIP TAG ZIPS
INDEX ON EXPIRATION TAG DATES
```

Then enter **ASSIST** to get back to the Control Center.

Select the Create option of the Forms panel to build a new form for data entry and editing. When the Form Design screen appears, choose Quick Layouts. Make any cosmetic changes you desire to the form. When you are finished, save the form with CTRL-END. For a form name, enter **MAILERS**.

Next, select the Create option of the Reports panel to create the report that will be used for the membership roster. When the Report Design screen appears, choose Quick Layouts, and then select Form Layout. Make any cosmetic changes you wish to the design of the report. (You might want to add a blank line after the final field in the Detail band, so that records printed within the report will be separated by sufficient space.) When you are done, save the report with CTRL-END. Enter **MAILERS** when you are prompted for a report name.

Choose the Create option of the Labels panel to create mailing labels. When the design screen for the mailing label appears, open the Dimensions menu. With the Predefined Size option highlighted, press ENTER to display the list of available sizes. Select the label size you prefer from the list, and press ENTER until the menus have closed.

Open the Fields menu, choose Add Field, select FIRSTNAME from the list, and then press CTRL-END. Depending on the label size you selected, you may or may not have sufficient room to fit the LASTNAME field on the same line. If you do have room, press the spacebar once and then proceed to the next paragraph. If you don't have room, move the cursor to the beginning of the next line.

Open the Fields menu, choose Add Field, select LASTNAME from the list, and then press CTRL-END to accept the display options. Press ENTER to move to the start of the next line.

Open the Fields Menu and choose Add Field again. Select ADDRESS from the list, and press CTRL-END to accept the display options. Press ENTER to move to the start of the next line. Open the Fields Menu and choose Add Field again. Select CITY from the list, and press CTRL-END to accept the display options. Type a comma, and then press the spacebar once.

Open the Fields menu and choose Add Field. Select STATE from the list, and press CTRL-END to accept the display options. Press the spacebar twice to add two spaces between the state and the ZIP code. Open the Fields menu and choose Add Field. Select ZIP from the list. Then press CTRL-END to accept the display options.

Make any cosmetic changes desired to the label, and save the label with CTRL-END. When you are prompted for a name for the label, enter **MAILERS**.

Now that the necessary objects are complete, the application can be constructed. Select the Create option of the Applications panel. Select Applications Generator from the next menu to appear. When the Application Definition screen appears, enter **MAILER** as the application name. Add a description of your choosing in the Description entry. When in the Main Menu Type entry, press the spacebar until "Pop-Up" appears as the menu choice.

Press ENTER to move the cursor to the Main Menu Name entry. For a main menu name, enter **MAILMENU**. For the Database-/View entry, enter **MAILERS.DBF**. For the Set Index To entry, enter **MAILERS.MDX**. For the Order entry, enter **NAMES**. Then press CTRL-END to save these options. The application object will now appear on the desktop. If you wish, you can replace the message within the application object with one of your own choosing, and select Display Sign-On Banner from the Application menu to tell dBASE that you will use the object as a sign-on banner.

Open the Design menu and choose Pop-Up Menu. From the list of menus that appears, choose the Create option. When prompted for a name, enter **MAILMENU**. (The next line, Description, is optional and can be filled in if you wish.) For the Message-line prompt, enter **Choose a desired option**. Press CTRL-END to save the options, and a new pop-up menu will appear. Enter the following choices on the first five lines of the menu:

```
Add New Members

Edit/Delete Members

Print Reports/Labels

Export To Framework

Quit System
```

Press SHIFT-F7 (Size), press the up arrow key twice to reduce the size of the menu, and press ENTER. Next, press F7 (Move) and choose Entire Frame from the next menu to appear. Press the up arrow key three times, and then press ENTER to place the menu in the new location.

Open the Design menu and choose Pop-Up Menu. From the list box that appears, choose the Create option. For a name, enter **PRINTER**. (Add any description in the Description entry if desired.) At the Message Line Prompt entry, enter **Choose report or labels desired**. Then press CTRL-END to accept these options. The new pop-up menu will appear in the center of the screen.

Press SHIFT-F7 (Size). Press the right arrow key ten times to widen the menu for additional text. Then press the up arrow key three times to reduce the depth of the menu. Press ENTER to set the menu to its new size. Next, press F7 (Move), choose Entire Frame from the next menu, and press the right arrow key eight times. Press ENTER to set the menu in its new location.

Enter the following choices on the first five lines of the menu:

```
Print Members Alphabetically

Print Members By Exp. Date

Print Labels By Exp. Date

Print Labels By ZIP Code

Return To Main Menu
```

Press F4 (Next) until the first menu you created is the highlighted object. Highlight the first option, Add New Members, and open the Item menu.

Choose Change Action from the Item menu, and then select Edit Form from the next menu to appear. In the Format File entry, enter **MAILERS**. Press CTRL-END to accept the remaining options.

Press the PGDN key once. (This selects the next menu option, Edit /Delete Members, without your having to close and open the Item menu. You can verify this by looking at the center of the status bar.) Choose Change Action from the Item menu, and then choose Edit Form.

For the Format File entry, enter **MAILERS**. In the Mode entry, press the spacebar until "EDIT" appears. Press ENTER repeatedly until the cursor moves down to the Allow Record Add entry, and then press the spacebar to change the entry from Yes to No. Press CTRL-END to save the options.

To allow a particular record to be selected for editing, a short program will now be added by means of the Embed Code option of the Item menu. The program will prompt the user for the last and first name of the desired individual. A SEEK operation will then be performed to find the desired record.

Choose Embed Code from the Item menu. The next menu to appear provides two choices, Before and After. These options let you choose whether your program will be executed before the action assigned to the menu is performed or after. Select Before from the menu. When the full-screen editing window appears, enter the following program:

```
STORE SPACE(20) TO LAST, FIRST
CLEAR
@ 5, 5 SAY "Last name?" GET LAST
@ 7, 5 SAY "First name?" GET FIRST
READ
FINDIT = LAST + TRIM(FIRST)
SEEK FINDIT
IF .NOT. FOUND( )
        CLEAR
        @ 5, 5 SAY "No such record in database!"
        WAIT
        CLEAR
        RETURN
ENDIF
CLEAR
```

When you have finished, press CTRL-END twice, once to close the full-screen window and once to close the Before/After menu box.

Press PGDN once to move to the Print Reports/Labels menu choice. Choose Change Action from the Item menu and then choose Open a Menu. In the Menu Type entry, press the spacebar until "Pop-Up" appears. For the menu name, enter **PRINTER**. Press CTRL-END to store the options.

Press ESC to close the Item menu. Press F4 (Next) until the Printer menu is the highlighted object. Highlight the first choice of the menu, Print Members Alphabetically, and open the Item menu with ALT-I. Choose Change Action, and then select Display or Print.

From the next menu, select Report Form. For a form name, enter **MAILERS**. If desired, change the Before Printing option to Do Not Eject.

Press ENTER until the cursor moves to the Send Output To entry. Press the spacebar until "Ask at Run Time" appears in the entry. This will cause the application to display a menu when the user requests a report. The menu will provide options for selecting one of two printer ports, a serial port, a disk file, or the screen as the output device for the report.

Press CTRL-END to store the options. Next, press PGDN to select the next menu item, Print Members by Expiration Date. Choose Change Action from the Item menu. Select Display/Print from the next menu, and then choose Report Form. For a form name, enter **MAILERS**. If desired, change the Before Printing option to Do Not Eject. Press ENTER until the cursor moves to the Send Output To entry. Press the spacebar until "Ask at Run Time" appears in the entry, and then save the options with CTRL-END.

Since this report is to be printed in the order of expiration date, a new index tag must be selected. Choose Reassign Index Order from the Item menu. When the Set Order To entry appears, enter **DATES** as the new order.

To allow a group of records to be selected for printing, a short program will be added by means of the Embed Code option of the Item menu. The program will prompt the user for a range of dates and then set a filter based on the response. Similar programs will be used for the remaining menu options for printing labels.

Choose Embed Code from the Item menu, and then select Before from the next menu. A full-screen window for editing text will appear. Enter the following program:

```
STARTDAY = {01/01/01}
ENDDAY = {12/31/99}
CLEAR
@ 5, 5 SAY "Starting expiration date?" GET STARTDAY
@ 7, 5 SAY "Ending expiration date?" GET ENDDAY
@ 9, 5 SAY "Leave both fields as-is to print ALL records."
READ
IF STARTDAY <> {01/01/01} .OR. ENDDAY <> {12/31/99}
        SET FILTER TO EXPIRATION >= STARTDAY .AND. EXPIRATION;
        <= ENDDAY
        GO TOP
ENDIF
CLEAR
```

When you have completed entering the code and checked it for errors, press CTRL-END. The full-screen window containing the program will vanish, and the menu with the Before and After options will still be visible.

Choose After from the menu. When the full-screen window again appears, enter the following statement:

```
SET FILTER TO
```

Press CTRL-END twice, once to close the full-screen editing window and once to close the Before/After menu. This one-line program will be executed after the report runs, so that any filter that was set previously will be cleared.

Press PGDN once to select the Print Labels by Expiration Date option of the menu. Choose Reassign Index Order from the Item menu. When the Set Order entry appears, enter **DATES** as the new order.

Choose Change Action from the Item menu. Select Display/Print from the next menu, and then choose Labels. For a label name, enter **MAILERS**, and then save the options with CTRL-END.

Choose Embed Code from the Item menu. The next menu to appear provides the Before and After choices. Select Before from the menu. The full-screen window for editing text will appear. Enter the following program:

```
STARTDAY = {01/01/01}
ENDDAY = {12/31/99}
CLEAR
@ 5, 5 SAY "Starting expiration date?" GET STARTDAY
@ 7, 5 SAY "Ending expiration date?" GET ENDDAY
@ 9, 5 SAY "Leave both fields as-is to print ALL records."
READ
IF STARTDAY < > {01/01/01} .OR. ENDDAY < > {12/31/99}
        SET FILTER TO EXPIRATION >= STARTDAY .AND. EXPIRATION;
        <= ENDDAY
        GO TOP
ENDIF
CLEAR
```

When you have finished entering the code and checked it for errors, press CTRL-END. The full-screen window containing the program will vanish, and the menu with the Before and After options will still be visible.

Choose After from the menu. When the full-screen window again appears, enter the following statement:

```
SET FILTER TO
```

Press CTRL-END twice, once to close the full-screen editing window and once to close the Before/After menu.

Press PGDN once to select the Print Labels by ZIP Codes option of the menu. Choose Reassign Index Order from the Item menu. When the Set Order entry appears, enter **ZIPS** as the new order.

Choose Change Action from the Item menu. Select Display/Print from the next menu, and then choose Labels. For a label name, enter **MAILERS**, and then save the options with CTRL-END.

Choose Embed Code from the Item menu, and then select Before from the next menu to appear. The full-screen window for editing text will appear. Enter the following program:

```
STORE SPACE(10) TO STARTZIP
STORE SPACE(10) TO ENDZIP
CLEAR
@ 5, 5 SAY "Starting ZIP code?" GET STARTZIP
@ 7, 5 SAY "Ending ZIP code?" GET ENDZIP
@ 9, 5 SAY "Leave both fields BLANK to print ALL records."
READ
IF STARTZIP <> " " .OR. ENDZIP <> " "
          SET FILTER TO ZIP >= STARTZIP .AND. ZIP <= ENDZIP
          GO TOP
ENDIF
CLEAR
```

When you have completed entering the code and checked it for errors, press CTRL-END. The full-screen window containing the program will vanish, and the menu with the Before and After options will still be visible.

Choose After from the menu. When the full-screen window again appears, enter the following statement:

```
SET FILTER TO
```

Press CTRL-END twice, once to close the full-screen editing window and once to close the Before/After menu. Press PGDN once to select the Return to Main Menu option in the Printer menu. From the Item menu, choose Reassign Index Order. In response to the Set Order To prompt, enter **NAMES**.

Next, choose Change Action from the Item menu, and then select Quit. From the next menu to appear, choose Return, and confirm the choice by selecting OK from the confirmation box. Open the Menu menu with ALT-M, and choose Put Away Current Menu. From the next prompt to appear, choose Save Changes.

Press F4 (Next) until Main menu is the highlighted object. Highlight the Export to Framework menu option. Open the Item menu, and choose Change Action. At the next menu, select Perform File Operation. From the menu that appears next, select Export Foreign File.

In the To File entry area that appears, enter **FWMAIL**. When the entry moves into the Type field, press the spacebar until "FW2" appears as the export type. If you use RapidFile or dBASE II, you might want to select one of those types instead (and relabel the menu option accordingly). For exporting any other file types, you could select the Copy Records to File option from the Perform File operation menu, and then specify the appropriate Type option (see Chapter 18 for details).

Press CTRL-END to store the options, and then press PGDN to select the Quit System option of the menu. Choose Change Action from the Item menu, and select Quit. From the next menu to appear, choose either Return or Quit according to your preference. Choosing Return will cause the application to exit back to dBASE when finished; choosing Quit will cause the application to exit to DOS. Confirm your choice by selecting OK from the next menu to appear.

Open the Menu menu with ALT-M, and choose Put Away Current Menu. From the next menu to appear, choose Save Changes. Finally, open the Generate menu, and choose Begin Generating to generate the code for the application.

When the applications generator completes the application, choose Save Changes and Exit from the Exit menu to save the application and return to the Control Center. Try your application by selecting it by name from the Applications panel.

A Payroll System

Meeting the payroll has always been a major task at businesses for obvious reasons. Making sure everyone gets paid the proper amount on time is of prime importance in the minds of the staff. The application described in this section manages a payroll and contains a reporting function that prints checks.

The application requires two databases. The first, STAFF.DBF, contains a record of each employee with vital information such as name, social security number, and hourly salary rate. The second, CHECKS.DBF, contains a record for each work week completed by the employee. In this file are recorded the number of hours worked, withholding amounts for taxes and other deductions, and the resulting net pay. The social security number is used as a link for relations between the files; the SOCIALSEC fields are indexed in both database files. The database structures are shown here; create these databases before building the application.

STAFF.DBF

Field	Field Name	Type	Width	Dec	Index
1	SOCIALSEC	Character	11		Y
2	LASTNAME	Character	15		N
3	FIRSTNAME	Character	15		N
4	MIDDLEINIT	Character	1		N
5	DEPARTMENT	Character	15		N
6	HOURLYSAL	Numeric	5	2	N
7	SICKDAYS	Numeric	2		N
8	VACDAYS	Numeric	2		N
9	EXEMPTIONS	Numeric	2		N
10	MEDICAL	Logical	1		N
11	DENTAL	Logical	1		N
12	LIFE	Logical	1		N

CHECKS.DBF

Field	Field Name	Type	Width	Dec	Index
1	SOCIALSEC	Character	11		Y
2	WEEKENDING	Date	8		N
3	HOURS	Numeric	4	1	N
4	GROSSPAY	Numeric	7	2	N
5	FEDTAX	Numeric	6	2	N
6	FICA	Numeric	6	2	N
7	STATETAX	Numeric	6	2	N
8	OTHERDEDUC	Numeric	6	2	N
9	NETPAY	Numeric	7	2	N

Select Staff from the Data panel and then choose Use File to open the STAFF.DBF database file. Next, select Create at the Forms panel to create a data entry screen. When the Layout menu appears, choose Quick Layouts. Make any cosmetic changes you desire to the form. (You might want to change the abbreviations used as the field names to more descriptive terms.) When you have finished any changes, save the form with CTRL-END. For a form name, enter **STAFF**.

Select Checks from the Data panel and then choose Use File to open the CHECKS.DBF database file. Select Create at the Forms panel to create a data entry screen. When the Layout menu appears, choose Quick Layouts. Make any cosmetic changes you desire to the form. (You might want to change the abbreviations used as the field names to more descriptive terms.) When you have finished any changes, save the form with CTRL-END. For a form name, enter **CHECKS**.

You'll also need a relational query to link the checks file to the proper name in the staff file when checks are printed. Choose the Create option of the Queries panel. When the file skeleton for the CHECKS.DBF file appears in the Query Design screen, press TAB once to move to the SOCIALSEC field. Enter the following:

```
FINDMATCH
```

Then open the Layout menu with ALT-L and choose Add File to Query. Select STAFF.DBF from the list of files that appears.

When the file skeleton for STAFF.DBF appears, press TAB once to move to the SOCIALSEC field and again enter

```
FINDMATCH
```

Press TAB to move to the LASTNAME field, and press F5 to add the field to the view. Press TAB once more to move to the FIRSTNAME field, and again press F5 to add this field to the view. Using the same technique, proceed to add the MIDDLEINIT, DEPARTMENT, and HOURLYSAL fields to the view. Press CTRL-END to save the view. For a filename, enter **RELATED**.

Next, you'll need a salary report, a report for listing the staff names and addresses, and a report that will be used for printing checks. Select the Create option of the Reports panel. When the Report Design screen appears with the Layout menu open, press ESC to close the Layout menu. Move the cursor into the Detail band, and with Insert mode on, press ENTER once to add a line.

Move the cursor to column 55, open the Fields menu, choose Add Field, and select Date from the Predefined panel. Press CTRL-END to accept the default values. Press ENTER twice. Move to line 3, column 10, and open the Fields menu. Choose Add Field, and select FIRSTNAME from the list; then accept the default values with CTRL-END.

! ***HINT*** When the list of fields appears, you can quickly move the cursor to the desired field by typing the first letters of the field name.

Press the spacebar once to add a space, and open the Fields menu. Choose Add Field, and select MIDDLEINIT from the list; then accept the default values with CTRL-END. Press the spacebar once to add a space, and open the Fields menu. Choose Add Field, and select LASTNAME from the list; then accept the default values by pressing CTRL-END.

Move the cursor to column 60 of the same line. Open the Fields menu, choose Add Field, and select NETPAY from the list. Accept the default options with CTRL-END. Press ENTER twice, and then move to column 10 of line 5. Open the Fields menu, choose Add Field, and select the Create option of the Calculated panel. For the name of the field, enter **DOLLARS**. In the Expression entry area for the field, enter the following:

```
TRANSFORM(NETPAY,"@$ # , # # # . # #")
```

Press ENTER, and move down to the Template option. Press Enter again to select that option. Add five more X's to the end of the template, and press ENTER. Then press CTRL-END to accept the options.

This report will be used for printing the checks. If you plan to make use of automated check printing with preprinted checks for computer printers, you will probably need to experiment with the exact locations of these fields before the names and amounts appear in the proper locations on your checks.

Press CTRL-END to save the report. For a report name, enter **PRINTCHK**.

When the Control Center appears, choose Create from the Reports panel to begin another report. When the Report Design screen appears, press ESC to close the Layout menu. Move the cursor into the Report Intro band. At column 30, enter the heading

```
Salary Report
```

and press ENTER twice to add two blank lines below the heading. Move the cursor into the Detail band, and press ENTER once. Open the Fields menu, choose Add Field, and select LASTNAME from the fields list. Accept the default display options with CTRL-END.

Press ENTER once to move to the next line, open the Fields menu, and choose Add Field. Select FIRSTNAME from the list of fields, and then press CTRL-END to accept the default options. Press the spacebar once, open the Fields menu, and choose Add Field. Select MIDDLEINIT from the list of fields, and press CTRL-END to accept the default options.

Move the cursor up one line and over to column 22. Open the Fields menu, choose Add Field, and select HOURS from the list of fields. Accept the default options with CTRL-END. Move the cursor over to column 30. Open the Fields menu, choose Add Field, and select FEDTAX from the list of fields. Accept the default options with CTRL-END.

Move the cursor over to column 40. Open the Fields menu, choose Add Field, and select FICA from the list of fields. Accept the default options with CTRL-END. Move the cursor over to column 50. Open the Fields menu, choose Add Field, and select STATETAX from the list of fields. Accept the default options with CTRL-END.

Move the cursor over to column 60. Open the Fields menu, choose Add Field, and select OTHERDEDUC from the list of fields. Accept the default options with CTRL-END. Move the cursor over to column 70. Open the Fields menu, choose Add Field, and select NETPAY from the list of fields. Accept the default options with CTRL-END.

Move the cursor down one line, and press ENTER to add a new line directly below the field masks for the first name and middle initial. Type

```
For week ending:
```

and add a space after the colon. Open the Fields menu, choose Add Field, and select WEEKENDING from the list of fields. Accept the default options with CTRL-END.

Press ENTER once more to add a blank line at the bottom of the Detail band. Then move the cursor up into the Report Intro band, onto the blank line just above the start of the Detail band. Add the following headings above the respective field masks:

At column 22, enter **Hours**

At column 30, enter **Fed. Tax**

At column 40, enter **FICA**

At column 50, enter **State Tax**

At column 60, enter **Other**

At column 70, enter **Net Pay**

Move the cursor down into the Summary band of the report, to column 68. Open the Fields menu and choose Add Field. Select Sum from the Summary panel. For the field name, enter **TOTALPAY**. For the Field to Summarize On entry, choose NETPAY. Press CTRL-END to accept the options.

Move the cursor to column 43 of the same line, and enter the following text:

```
Total for all salaries:
```

Then press CTRL-END to save the report. For a report name, enter **SALARYRP**.

Once you are back at the Control Center, open the STAFF file by choosing STAFF from the Data panel and selecting Use File from the next menu to appear. Then choose Create from the Reports panel. When the Report Design screen appears, choose Quick Layouts and then Form Layout. Make any desired cosmetic changes you may prefer to the headings of the report that appears. You may want to add a blank line after the last field, so that records are separated by a sufficient amount of blank space when printed. If you would prefer that each employee's record be printed on a separate page, move the cursor into the Detail band and choose Begin Band on New Page from the Bands menu. When you are done with any desired changes, press CTRL-END to save the report. For a filename, enter **STAFF**.

With all of the needed objects completed, you can proceed to build the application. Choose the Create option of the Applications panel and select Applications Generator from the next menu to appear. For an application name, enter **PAYROLL**. Enter a description of your choice, if desired. For the Main Menu Type, choose Pop-Up by pressing the spacebar until "Pop-Up" appears in the Main Menu entry.

For the Main Menu Name, enter **PAYCHECK**. For the Database/View entry, enter **CHECKS.DBF**. For the Set Index To entry, enter **CHECKS.MDX**. For the Order entry, enter **SOCIALSEC**. Then press CTRL-END to accept the options. In a moment, the desktop containing the application object will appear.

Open the Design menu with ALT-D and choose Pop-Up Menu. Select Create from the list box that appears. For a name, enter **PAYCHECK**. As a description, enter **Payroll System**. As a message-line prompt, enter

```
Use arrow keys, and press ENTER to select option
```

Press CTRL- END, and the new menu will appear in the center of the screen.

Enter these headings in the first seven lines of the menu:

```
Enter Weekly Salary

Edit Weekly Salary

Add New Employee

Edit/Delete Employee
```

Print Staff Report

Print Paychecks

Exit System

Highlight the Enter Weekly Salary option, and open the Item menu. Choose Change Action. From the next menu, choose Edit. In the Format File box, enter **CHECKS**. Press CTRL-END to accept the remaining options.

Press the PGDN key once. (This will select the next menu item, Edit Weekly Salary, without your having to close and reopen the Item menu. You can tell which item is selected by looking at the status bar.) Again choose Change Action from the Item menu. From the next menu, choose Edit. In the Format File box, enter **CHECKS**. In the Mode box, press the spacebar until "Edit" appears. Press ENTER until the cursor is in the Allow Record Add box, and press the spacebar to change this option to No. Press CTRL-END to accept the remaining options.

Press the PGDN key once to select the next menu item, Add New Employee, without having to close and reopen the Item menu. Select Override Assigned Database or View from the Item menu. Press the spacebar once to change Values from Above to Entered Below. Press ENTER to move down to the Database/View entry, and enter **STAFF.DBF**. In the Set Index To entry, enter **STAFF.MDX**. (The Order entry may remain blank.) Accept these values by pressing CTRL-END.

Choose Change Action from the Item menu. From the next menu, choose Edit. In the Format File box, enter **STAFF**. Press CTRL-END to accept the remaining options.

Press the PGDN key once to select the next menu item, Edit/Delete Employee. Select Override Assigned Database or View from the Item menu. Press the spacebar once to change Values from Above to Entered Below. Press ENTER to move down to the Database/View entry, and enter **STAFF.DBF**. In the Set Index

To entry, enter **STAFF.MDX**. In the Order entry, enter **SOCIALSEC**. Accept these values by pressing CTRL-END.

Choose Change Action from the Item menu. From the next menu, choose Edit. In the Format File box, enter **STAFF**. In the Mode box, press the spacebar until "Edit" appears. Press ENTER until the cursor is in the Allow Record Add box, and press the spacebar to change this option to No. Press CTRL-END to accept the remaining options.

Press PGDN once to select the Print Staff Report menu choice. With the Item menu still open, choose Override Assigned Database or View. Press the spacebar once to change Values from Above to Entered Below. Press ENTER to move down to the Database/View entry, and enter **STAFF.DBF**. In the Set Index To entry, enter **STAFF.MDX**. In the Order entry, enter **SOCIALSEC**. Accept these values by pressing CTRL-END.

Choose Change Action from the Item menu. From the next menu, choose Display or Print, and then choose Report Form. For a report form name, enter **STAFF**. Change any of the other defaults to options you may prefer, and then save the options with CTRL-END.

Press PGDN once to select the Print Paychecks menu option. Choose Override Assigned Database or View from the Item menu. Press the spacebar once to change the Values entry to Entered Below. Press ENTER to move down to the Database/View entry, and enter **RELATED.QBE** as the view name. Then press CTRL-END to save the options.

Choose Position Record Pointer from the Item menu. When the next screen appears, press the spacebar once to change the Display positioning at Run-Time entry from No to Yes. Then press CTRL-END to save the option. This action will cause the application to display a record-positioning menu when the option for printing checks is selected; with the menu, the user will be able to select a FOR condition (usually all checks for a given "week ending" date).

Next, choose Change Action from the Item menu, and then choose Display or Print. From the next menu to appear, choose Report Form. In the Form Name entry, enter **PRINTCHK**. Press CTRL-END to save the options.

Press PGDN once to choose the Exit System option of the menu. Select Change Action from the Item menu, and choose Quit from the next menu to appear. From the next menu, choose Quit to DOS or choose Return to Calling Program according to your preference.

Open the Menu menu with ALT-M, and choose Put Away Current Menu. Choose Save Changes from the next menu that appears. Finally, choose Begin Generating from the Generate menu to generate the application.

When the applications generator completes the application, choose Save Changes and Exit from the Exit menu to save the application and return to the Control Center. Try your application by selecting it by name from the Applications panel.

Possible Improvements

With this example payroll system, the task of entering the weekly salary records is more tedious than it could be, because you must manually enter the federal tax, state tax, and social security (FICA) deductions. You could ease this task with a program that would calculate those amounts, based on the number of exemptions. Once such a program were written, you could provide access to that program from within the application by adding a menu choice that calls the program with the Embed Code option of the Item menu.

APPENDIX

Glossary of dBASE IV Commands

This appendix contains a listing of dBASE IV commands. Each command name is followed by the syntax of the command and a description of how the command works. You will recognize most commands from the tutorial section; others will be introduced here.

Glossary Symbols and Conventions

1. All commands are printed in UPPERCASE, although you can enter them in either upper- or lowercase letters.

2. All parameters of the command are listed in *italics*.

3. Any part of a command or parameter that is surrounded by [and] (left and right brackets) is optional.

4. When a slash separates two choices in a command, as in ON/OFF, you specify one choice, not both.

5. Ellipses (...) following a parameter or command mean that the parameter or command can be repeated "infinitely"— that is, until you exhaust the memory of the computer, or reach the limit of 1,024 characters on a single line.

6. The parameter *scope,* which is always an option, can have three different meanings, depending upon the command: ALL, for all records; NEXT *n,* for *n* number of records beginning at the current position of the record pointer; and RECORD, for only one record beginning at the current position of the record pointer.

? or ?? or ???

Syntax

? / ?? [*expression* [PICTURE "*clause*"]
[FUNCTION "*function-list*"] [AT *expN*]
[STYLE *font-character*]]

or

??? expC

The ? command displays the value of a dBASE IV expression. If a single question mark (?) is used, the cursor executes a carriage return and linefeed, and then the value of the expression is displayed. If the double question mark (??) is used, the cursor is not moved before the value of the expression is displayed. The PICTURE, FUNCTION, and STYLE options may be used to customize the appearance of the displayed information. The AT option may be used to place the expression at a specific column location. The STYLE option uses one or more letters indicating a font style. Use B for bold, I for italic, U for underline, R for raised (superscript), and L for lowered (subscript).

The ??? command sends characters to the printer without changing the current row and column positions. Use this command to send control codes and other escape sequences to the printer. To specify control codes, enclose the ASCII code in curly braces.

Syntax

@ row,col [SAY expression] [GET *variable*]
[PICTURE expression] [FUNCTION *list*] [RANGE *low, high*]
[VALID *condition*] [ERROR *expC*] [COLOR *std./enhanced*]
[CLEAR][DOUBLE]

The @ command places the cursor at a specific screen location identified by *row,col.* The @ command can be used with one or more of the named options. The SAY option displays the expression following the word "SAY." The GET option allows full-screen editing of *variable.* The PICTURE option allows the use of templates, which specify the way data will be displayed or accepted in response to the GET option. The RANGE option is used with the GET option to specify a range of acceptable entries. The VALID option specifies acceptable entries for GET. ERROR displays a custom message if VALID is not met. COLOR defines new color settings for the @...SAY...GET command.

When used with the DOUBLE option, the @ command draws single or double lines or borders (or a combination of these) on the screen. The first value represents the upper-left screen coordinate, and the second value represents the lower-right screen coordinate. If both coordinates share a horizontal or vertical coordinate, a line is drawn; otherwise, a rectangular border is drawn. The CLEAR option can be used to clear the screen to the right and below the specified location.

@...FILL

Syntax

@row 1, col1
FILL TO *row2,col2* [COLOR
std./enhanced]

The @...FILL command changes the color of the screen within the defined area. The *std. / enhanced* parameter is *X / Y,* where *X* is the code for the standard color and *Y* is the code for the enhanced color. If the COLOR option is omitted, the screen is cleared within the defined area.

ACCEPT

Syntax

ACCEPT [*prompt*] TO *memvar*

The ACCEPT command stores a character string to the memory variable *memvar*. ACCEPT can be followed by an optional character string. If this string is included, it will appear on the screen when the ACCEPT command is executed.

ACTIVATE MENU

Syntax

ACTIVATE MENU *menu-name* [PAD *pad-name*]

The ACTIVATE MENU command activates a predefined menu and displays that menu on the screen. If the PAD option is specified, the highlight bar appears at the named pad; otherwise, the first pad in the menu is highlighted. To implement a bar menu, first define the menu with the DEFINE MENU and DEFINE PAD commands. Then use the ACTIVATE MENU command to activate the menu.

ACTIVATE POPUP

Syntax

ACTIVATE POPUP *popup-name*

The ACTIVATE POPUP command activates a predefined pop-up menu and displays it on the screen. Pop-up menus are vertical menus, with each successive choice under the prior choice. To implement a pop-up menu, first define the menu with the DEFINE POPUP and DEFINE BAR commands. Then use the

ACTIVATE POPUP command to activate the menu. You can deactivate a menu by pressing ESC, or by using the DEACTIVATE MENU command.

ACTIVATE SCREEN

Syntax

ACTIVATE SCREEN

The ACTIVATE SCREEN command switches screen display from an active window to the full screen. The active window remains on the screen, and you can later use the ACTIVATE WINDOW command to redirect screen output to the window. Keep in mind that when you use ACTIVATE SCREEN, you are returning from virtual screen coordinates to physical screen coordinates. In other words, the *row,col* positioning used with @...SAY commands was relative to the upper-left corner of the window; once you restore full-screen display with ACTIVATE SCREEN, the *row,col* positioning is now relative to the upper-left corner of the screen. This may call for different values for your cursor positioning within programs.

ACTIVATE WINDOW

Syntax

ACTIVATE WINDOW *window-name-list* / ALL

The ACTIVATE WINDOW command activates a predefined window from memory. After the ACTIVATE WINDOW command is used, all screen output is directed to that window. If the ALL option is used, all defined windows in memory are displayed in the order in which they were defined.

APPEND

Syntax

APPEND [BLANK]

The APPEND command appends records to a database. When the APPEND command is executed, a blank record is displayed, and dBASE IV enters full-screen Edit mode. If the BLANK option is used, a blank record is added to the end of the database and full-screen Edit mode is not entered.

APPEND FROM/APPEND FROM ARRAY

Syntax

APPEND FROM *filename* [FOR/WHILE *condition*] [TYPE *file-type*]
APPEND FROM ARRAY *array-name FOR condition*

APPEND FROM copies records from *filename* and appends them to the active database. The FOR/WHILE option specifies a condition that must be met before any records will be copied. If the filename containing the data to be copied is not a dBASE IV database, an acceptable type option must be used. Valid types are DBASEII, DELIMITED, DELIMITED WITH BLANK, DELIMITED WITH "*specified-character*", DIF, FW2, RPD, SDF, SYLK, WKS, and WK1.

The APPEND FROM ARRAY command appends records to a database file from a named array. The contents of each row in the array are transferred to a new record in the database file. The first column in the array becomes the first field, the second column in the array becomes the second field, and so on. If there are more columns in the array than fields in the database, the extra columns are ignored. If there are more fields in the database than there are columns in the array, the extra fields remain empty. The FOR clause, which is optional, lets you define a condition that must be met before data in the array will be added to a new record. An array must exist (be defined with DECLARE, and data stored to the array with STORE) before you can successfully use the APPEND FROM ARRAY command.

APPEND MEMO

Syntax

APPEND MEMO *memo-field-name* FROM *filename* [OVERWRITE]

The APPEND MEMO command imports a file into a memo field. The contents of the file are normally added to the end of any existing text in the memo field.

If the OVERWRITE option is used, the contents of the file will overwrite any existing text in the memo field. dBASE assumes that the file has an extension of .TXT. If this is not the case, the extension must be specified along with the filename.

ASSIST

Syntax

ASSIST

The ASSIST command lets you operate dBASE IV from the Control Center. The Control Center provides access to various dBASE IV commands through a series of menus.

AVERAGE

Syntax

AVERAGE *field-list* [*scope*][FOR/WHILE *condition*]
[TO *memvar-list*] [TO ARRAY *array-name*]

The AVERAGE command computes an average of a specified numeric field listed in *field-list.* If the TO option is not used, the average is displayed on the screen. If TO is used, the average of the first field is assigned to the first memory variable, the average of the second field to the second memory variable, and so on down the list; the average is stored as the memory variable specified. If the *scope* option is not used, the quantifier of ALL is assumed, meaning all records in *field-list* will be averaged. The FOR/ WHILE option can be used to specify a condition that must be met for the fields to be averaged.

BEGIN TRANSACTION

Syntax

BEGIN TRANSACTION

The BEGIN TRANSACTION and END TRANSACTION commands start and end the recording of a transaction file, a procedure that tracks all changes made to a database file. Use BEGIN TRANSACTION to start the recording of all database file changes in a transaction log; then perform the desired operations for adding and changing records. When the operations are complete, use END TRANSACTION to stop the transaction recording and erase the transaction log. If an abnormal occurrence (power failure, hardware malfunction) halts the process before the END TRANSACTION command is used, the ROLLBACK command can be used to safely restore the database files to the status they had before the BEGIN TRANSACTION command was used. (*See* ROLLBACK.)

BROWSE

Syntax

BROWSE FIELDS [*field-list*] [NOINIT] [NOFOLLOW]
[NOAPPEND] [NODELETE] [NOCLEAR] [COMPRESS]
[NOEDIT] [FORMAT] [LOCK *expN*] [WIDTH *expN*]
[WINDOW *window-name*]

The BROWSE command displays a database on the screen. If the database is too large for the screen, BROWSE displays only the fields that will fit on the screen. More fields can be viewed by scrolling to the left or right (holding the CTRL key down and pressing the left or right arrow key). The contents of any field can be edited while in Browse mode. To save changes made during BROWSE, press CTRL-END; to exit BROWSE, press ESC. The FIELDS option will display only the fields listed in *field-list*. The NOINIT option tells BROWSE to use the settings used in the prior use of BROWSE. The NOAPPEND, NOEDIT, and NODELETE options restrict the use of appending, editing, or deleting when in Browse mode. The LOCK and WIDTH options let you lock specified fields at the left margin or adjust the width of columns. The WINDOW option causes the Browse display to appear in a previously defined window. The COMPRESS option reduces the normal-size Browse display slightly to allow for viewing of two additional records.

CALCULATE

Syntax

CALCULATE [*scope*] *options* [FOR *condition*]
[WHILE *condition*][TO *memvar-list*/TO ARRAY *array-name*]

The CALCULATE command calculates amounts, using standard financial and statistical functions. The functions are defined as part of the options list shown here. All records are processed until the scope is completed or the condition is no longer true. The following financial and statistical functions can be used within the options list:

AVG(*expN*) Calculates the numerical average of value *expN*.

CNT( ) Counts the records in a database file. If a condition has been specified with the FOR clause, the condition must be met before the record will be counted.

MAX(*exp*) Determines the maximum value in a field. *exp* is usually a field name or an expression that translates to a field name.

MIN(*exp*) Determines the minimum value in a field. *exp* is usually a field name or an expression that translates to a field name.

NPV(*rate,flows,initial*) Calculates the net present value where *rate* is the discount rate, *flows* is a series of signed periodic cash flow values, and *initial* is the initial investment.

STD(*exp*) Determines the standard deviation of values stored in a database field. *exp* is usually a field name or an expression that translates to a field name.

SUM(*exp*) Determines the sum of the values in a database field. *exp* is usually a field name or an expression that translates to a field name.

VAR(*exp*) Determines the variance of the values in a database field. *exp* is usually a field name or an expression that translates to a field name. The value supplied by VAR(*exp*) is a floating-point number.

CALL

Syntax

CALL *module-name* [WITH *expression*]

The CALL command executes a binary (assembly-language) program that was previously loaded into memory with the LOAD command (*see* LOAD). The WITH option is used to pass the value of the expression to the binary program. The CALL command should only be used with external programs designed as binary modules. Normal executable programs should be accessed with the RUN/! command.

CANCEL

Syntax

CANCEL

The CANCEL command halts execution of a command file and returns dBASE IV to the dot prompt.

CHANGE

Syntax

CHANGE [*scope*][FIELDS *field-list*][FOR/WHILE *condition*]

The CHANGE command permits full-screen editing of the fields listed in *field-list.* If the *scope* option is absent, the quantifier ALL is assumed. The FOR/WHILE option allows editing only to records satisfying the condition.

CLEAR

Syntax

CLEAR

The CLEAR command erases the screen and returns the cursor to location 0,0 (the upper-left corner). CLEAR can also be used as an option of the @ command, clearing the screen below and to the right of the location specified by the @ command.

CLEAR [ALL/FIELDS/GETS/MEMORY/POPUPS /TYPEAHEAD/WINDOWS]

Syntax

CLEAR ALL or CLEAR FIELDS or CLEAR GETS or CLEAR MEMORY or CLEAR POPUPS or CLEAR TYPEAHEAD or CLEAR WINDOWS

The CLEAR ALL command closes all open database, memo, index, and format files. The current work area is set to 1.

The CLEAR FIELDS command clears the list of fields specified by the SET FIELDS command. The CLEAR FIELDS command has no effect if the SET FIELDS command was not previously used to specify fields. (*See* SET FIELDS.)

The CLEAR GETS command clears values from variables provided by the GET statements that were accessed with a READ command.

The CLEAR MEMORY command erases all current memory variables.

The CLEAR POPUPS command clears all pop-up menus and erases them from memory.

The CLEAR TYPEAHEAD command clears the contents of the typeahead buffer. (*See* SET TYPEAHEAD.)

The CLEAR WINDOWS command clears all active windows and erases all windows from memory. (*See* DEFINE WINDOW.)

CLOSE

Syntax

CLOSE *file-type*

The CLOSE command closes all file types listed in *file-type*. The *file-type* parameter can be: ALTERNATE, DATABASES, FORMAT, INDEX, or PROCEDURE.

COMPILE

Syntax

COMPILE *filename*

The COMPILE command reads a dBASE program (or command) file and creates an object (.DBO) file, which is an execute-only dBASE program file.

CONTINUE

Syntax

CONTINUE

The CONTINUE command resumes a search started by LOCATE. After LOCATE finds the record that matches the criteria specified in the command, you can find additional records that meet the same criteria by entering CONTINUE. (*See* LOCATE.)

CONVERT

Syntax

CONVERT [TO *expN*]

The CONVERT command prepares a database used in single-user mode for use on a network. The command adds a field to the active database file. The field is used to store locking information used by other dBASE operations when on a network.

The new field added to the database is named _dbaselock. It contains a default value of 16, unless a numeric expression (*expN*) has been added along with the TO option of the command. If used, the numeric expression can range from 8 (which will restrict the size of the network user name stored with each locked record or file to 0) to 24 (which will allow a network user name of up to 16 characters to be stored with each locked record or file).

COPY

Syntax

COPY TO *filename* [*scope*] [FIELDS *field-list*]
[FOR/WHILE *condition*] [TYPE WKS/RPD/DBASEII/FW2/SDF/SYLK/DIF
/DBMEMO3/DELIMITED [WITH *delimiter*]]

The COPY command copies all or part of the active database to *filename*. If *scope* is not listed, ALL is assumed. The FIELDS option is used to pinpoint the fields to be copied. The FOR/WHILE option copies only those records meeting the condition. Specifying SDF will copy the file in system data format; specifying DELIMITED will copy the file in delimited format. WKS type is Lotus 1-2-3, RPD is RapidFile, and FW2 is Framework II. DIF is data interchange format (used by VisiCalc), and SYLK is Microsoft symbolic link format.

COPY FILE

Syntax

COPY FILE *source-file* TO *destination-file*

The COPY FILE command creates an identical copy of a file. You must supply the extension in both *source-file* and *destination-file*.

COPY INDEXES

Syntax

COPY INDEXES *.ndx-files-list* [TO *.mdx- filename*]

The COPY INDEXES command converts dBASE III/III PLUS style (.NDX) index files into multiple index (.MDX) files. If the TO clause is omitted, the .NDX index files are added as tags to the production .MDX file. If the TO clause is included, the .NDX files are added as tags to the .MDX filename specified in the option.

COPY MEMO

Syntax

COPY MEMO *memo-field-name* TO *filename* [ADDITIVE]

The COPY MEMO command is used to copy the contents of a memo field to a text file. A drive name and path can be included as a part of the filename. If the ADDITIVE option is used, the text of the memo field will be added to the end of an existing filename; if the ADDITIVE option is omitted, any existing file with the same name will be overwritten.

COPY STRUCTURE /COPY STRUCTURE EXTENDED

Syntax

COPY STRUCTURE *TO filename* [FIELDS *field-list*]
COPY TO *filename* STRUCTURE EXTENDED

The COPY STRUCTURE command copies the structure of an active database to *filename*. Specifying FIELDS with *field- list* will copy only those fields to the structure.

The COPY STRUCTURE EXTENDED command creates a new database with records that contain field information about the fields of the old database. The new database contains fields called FIELD_NAME, FIELD_TYPE, FIELD_LEN, FIELD_DEC, and FIELD_IDX. One record in the new database is added for each field in the old database.

COPY TAG

Syntax

COPY TAG *tag-name* [OF *.mdx-filename*] TO *.ndx-filename*

The COPY TAG command converts a multiple index (.MDX) file's tag information into a dBASE III style (.NDX) index file. If the TO clause is omitted, the .NDX file has the same name as the .MDX file that is in use.

COPY TO ARRAY

Syntax

COPY TO ARRAY *array-name* [FIELDS *fields-list*]
[*scope*] [FOR *condition*] [WHILE *condition*]

The COPY TO ARRAY command copies data from the fields of a database into an array. For each record in the database, the first field is stored in the first column of the array, the second field in the second column, and so on. (You must first declare the array with the DECLARE command.) If the database has more fields than the array has columns, the contents of extra fields are not stored to the array. If the array has more columns than the database has fields, the extra columns in the array are not changed. Note that memo fields are not copied into the array.

COUNT

Syntax

COUNT [*scope*] [FOR/WHILE *condition*] [TO *memvar*]

The COUNT command counts the number of records in the active database that meet a specific condition. The *scope* option quantifies the records to be counted. The FOR/WHILE option can be used to specify a condition that must be met before a record will be counted. The TO option can be used to store the count to the memory variable *memvar*.

CREATE

Syntax

CREATE *filename*

The CREATE command creates a new database file and defines its structure. If CREATE is entered without a filename, dBASE IV will prompt you for one. If CREATE is followed by a filename, a database with that filename will be created. The filename extension .DBF is added automatically to the filename unless you specify otherwise.

CREATE APPLICATION

Syntax

CREATE APPLICATION *filename*

The CREATE APPLICATION command starts the applications generator. A filename with the extension .APP is created when the application is saved. If an application by that name already exists, the existing application is loaded into the applications generator.

CREATE LABEL

Syntax

CREATE LABEL *filename*

The CREATE LABEL command creates a label form file. This file can be used with the LABEL FORM command to produce mailing labels.

CREATE QUERY/VIEW

Syntax

CREATE QUERY *filename*
CREATE VIEW *filename*

The CREATE QUERY creates or modifies a query (.QBE) file by providing access to the Query Design screen. Using this you can create queries that will select specific records and/or establish relational links between database files. The CREATE VIEW alternative is provided for compatibility with dBASE III PLUS. If a catalog is active when CREATE QUERY is used, the query file and its contents will be added to the catalog.

CREATE REPORT

Syntax

CREATE REPORT

The CREATE REPORT (or as an alternative, MODIFY REPORT) command creates (or allows the user to modify) a report form file for producing reports. Once the report has been outlined with the CREATE REPORT command, the report can be displayed or printed with the REPORT FORM command.

CREATE SCREEN

Syntax

CREATE SCREEN *filename*

This command creates or modifies a custom screen form that is used for the display and editing of records. Three files are created by the CREATE SCREEN command. Upon entry of the command, the Form Design screen appears. Options within the Form Design screen allow the design of the custom screen. If a catalog is active when CREATE SCREEN is used, the resulting screen files will be added to the catalog.

DEACTIVATE MENU/DEACTIVATE POPUP

Syntax

DEACTIVATE MENU

or

DEACTIVATE POPUP

The DEACTIVATE MENU command deactivates the active bar menu and clears the menu from the screen. The menu remains in memory and can be recalled with the ACTIVATE MENU command.

The DEACTIVATE POPUP command deactivates the active pop-up menu and erases it from the screen. The pop-up menu remains in memory and can be recalled to the screen with the ACTIVATE POPUP command.

DEACTIVATE WINDOW

Syntax

DEACTIVATE WINDOW *window-name*/ALL

The DEACTIVATE WINDOW command deactivates the window or windows named in the command and erases them from the screen. The windows remain in memory and can be restored to the screen with the ACTIVATE WINDOW command. If the ALL option is not used, the most recently activated window is deactivated. If a window is underlying the most recent window, it becomes the active window. If the ALL option is included, all active windows are deactivated.

DEBUG

Syntax

DEBUG *program-name/procedure-name* [WITH *parameter-list*]

The DEBUG command provides access to the dBASE IV full-screen debugger.

DECLARE

Syntax

DECLARE *array-name 1* [*no.-of-rows,no.-of-columns*]
[*array-name2*][*no.-of-rows,no.-of-columns*]

The DECLARE command creates an array. In the definition list, you enter the array name and the dimensions of the array. Array names may be up to 10 characters in length. Array dimensions consist of the row and column numbers. If a column number is omitted, dBASE creates a one-dimensional array. If row and column numbers are used, they must be separated by a comma, and dBASE creates a two-dimensional array. Arrays declared within programs are private unless declared public with the PUBLIC command.

DEFINE BAR

Syntax

DEFINE BAR *line-number* OF *popup-name* PROMPT *expC*

[MESSAGE *expC*] [SKIP [FOR *condition*] [NOSPACE]]

The DEFINE BAR command defines one bar option within a pop-up menu. The *popup-name* parameter must have been previously defined with the DEFINE POPUP command. The *line-number* parameter specifies the line number within the pop-up menu; line 1 appears on the first line of the pop-up, line 2 on the second line of the pop-up, and so on. The text specified with PROMPT appears as text in the bar of the menu. The MESSAGE option can be used to specify text that will appear at the bottom of the screen when the specified menu bar is highlighted. The SKIP option causes the bar to appear, but not be selectable within the menu.

DEFINE BOX

Syntax

DEFINE BOX FROM *print-column* TO *print-column* HEIGHT *exp*
[AT LINE *print-line*] [SINGLE/DOUBLE/*border-definition-string*]

The DEFINE BOX command lets you define a box that will appear around text in a report. Use the specified options in the command to define the starting column on the left, the ending column on the right, the starting line for the top of the box, and the height of the box. The *border-definition-string* option lets you specify a character that will be used as the box border; the default, if this option is omitted, is a single line.

DEFINE MENU

Syntax

DEFINE MENU *menu-name* [MESSAGE *expC*]

The DEFINE MENU command defines a bar menu. If the MESSAGE option is added, the text of the message appears at the bottom of the screen when the menu is displayed. (*See* ACTIVATE MENU.)

DEFINE PAD

Syntax

DEFINE PAD *pad-name* OF *menu-name* PROMPT *expC* [AT *row,col*]
[MESSAGE *expC*]

The DEFINE PAD command defines one pad of a bar menu. Use a separate statement containing this command for each desired pad within the menu. The text specified with PROMPT appears inside the menu pad. If the AT *row,col* option is omitted, the first pad appears at the far left, and each successive pad appears one space to the right of the previous pad. Any text that accompanies the MESSAGE option appears at the bottom of the screen when that pad is highlighted within the menu.

DEFINE POPUP

Syntax

DEFINE POPUP *popup-name* FROM *row1,col1* [TO *row2,col2*]
[PROMPT FIELD *field-name*/PROMPT FILES [LIKE *skeleton*]/PROMPT STRUCTURE]
[MESSAGE *expC*]

Use the DEFINE POPUP command to define a pop-up menu. The FROM and TO row and column coordinates define the upper-left and lower-right corners of the pop-up. If the TO coordinate is omitted, dBASE will make the menu as large as needed to contain the prompts within the menu. The PROMPT FIELD, PROMPT FILE, and PROMPT STRUCTURE clauses are optional. These allow you to display selection lists of field contents, filenames, or field names from a database structure.

DEFINE WINDOW

Syntax

DEFINE WINDOW *window-name* FROM *row1,col1* TO *row2,col2*
[DOUBLE/PANEL/NONE/*border-definition-string*]
[COLOR [*standard*][,*enhanced*][,*frame*]]

The DEFINE WINDOW command defines display attributes and screen coordinates for a window. The FROM and TO coordinates define the upper-left and lower-right corners of the window. The default border is a single-line box; you can use the DOUBLE, PANEL, NONE, or *border-definition-string* option to specify a different border for the window. (Use ASCII codes for the border definition option.)

DELETE

Syntax

DELETE *record-number* [*scope*] [FOR/WHILE *condition*]

The DELETE command marks specific records for deletion. If DELETE is used without a record number, the current record is marked for deletion. The *scope* option is used to identify the records to be deleted. The FOR/WHILE option can be used to specify a condition that must be met before a record will be deleted. DELETE marks a file for deletion; the PACK command actually removes the record.

DELETE TAG

Syntax

DELETE TAG *tag-name1* [OF *.mdx-filename*]/*.ndx- filename1*
[,*tag-name2* [OF *.mdx-filename*]/*.ndx-filename2*]

The DELETE TAG command removes the named tag from a multiple index file if it is the named file, or the command closes an .NDX index file if it is the named file.

DIR

Syntax

DIR [*drive:*][*filename*]

The DIR command displays the directory of all database files or files of a specific type if a file extension is specified. The *drive:* parameter is the drive designator (A:, B:, or C: for hard-disk users), and *filename* is the name of a file with or without an extension. Wildcards, which are asterisks or question marks, can be used as part of or as a replacement for *filename*. For database files, the display produced by DIR includes the number of records contained in the database, the date of the last update, and the size of the file (in bytes).

DISPLAY

Syntax

DISPLAY [*scope*] [*field-list*] [FOR/WHILE *condition*] [OFF]

The DISPLAY command displays a record from the active database. You can display more records by including the *scope* option. The FOR/WHILE option limits the display of records to those satisfying *condition*. Only the fields listed in *field- list* will be displayed; if *field-list* is absent, all fields will be displayed. The OFF option will prevent the record number from being displayed.

DISPLAY HISTORY

Syntax

DISPLAY HISTORY [LAST *number*] [TO PRINT]

DISPLAY HISTORY displays all commands stored in HISTORY, unless the LAST option, where *number* equals the number of commands to display, is used to specify a certain number of commands. The TO PRINT option will cause the displayed commands to be printed on the printer.

DISPLAY MEMORY

Syntax

DISPLAY MEMORY [TO PRINT]

The DISPLAY MEMORY command displays all active memory variables, their sizes, and their contents. From a total of 500 variables the numbers of active variables and available variables are listed, along with the numbers of bytes consumed and bytes available. These statistics will be displayed on the printer as well as on the screen if TO PRINT is included.

DISPLAY STATUS/DISPLAY STRUCTURE/ DISPLAY USERS

Syntax

DISPLAY STATUS

or

DISPLAY STRUCTURE

or

DISPLAY USERS

The DISPLAY STATUS command displays the names and aliases of all currently active work areas and active files. Any key fields used in index files, the current drive designator, function-key settings, and settings of SET commands are also displayed.

The DISPLAY STRUCTURE command displays the structure of the active database. The complete filename, along with the current drive designator, number of records, date of last update, and names of fields, including their statistics (type, length, and decimal places), are listed.

The DISPLAY USERS command displays the users currently using dBASE IV on a local area network.

DO

Syntax

DO *filename* [WITH *parameter-list*]

The DO command starts the execution of a dBASE IV command file. The filename extension of .PRG or .DBO is assumed unless otherwise specified. If the WITH option is specified and followed by a list of parameters in *parameter-list,* those parameters are transferred to the command file.

DO CASE

Syntax

```
DO CASE
        CASE condition
        commands...
        [CASE condition]
        [commands...]
        [OTHERWISE]
        [commands...]
ENDCASE
```

The DO CASE command selects one course of action from a number of choices. The conditions following the CASE statements are evaluated until one of the conditions is found to be true. When a condition is true, the commands between the CASE statement and another CASE, or OTHERWISE and ENDCASE, will be executed. If none of the conditions in the CASE statements are found to be true, any commands following the optional OTHERWISE statement will be executed. If the OTHERWISE statement is not used and no conditions are found to be true, dBASE IV proceeds to the command following the ENDCASE statement.

DO WHILE

Syntax

DO WHILE *condition*
    commands...
ENDDO

The DO WHILE command repeatedly executes commands between DO WHILE and ENDDO as long as *condition* is true. When dBASE IV encounters a DO WHILE command, the condition following the command is evaluated. If it is false, dBASE IV proceeds to the command following the ENDDO command, but if it is true, dBASE IV executes the commands following the DO WHILE command until the ENDDO command is reached. When the ENDDO command is reached, the condition following the DO WHILE command is again evaluated. If it is still true, the commands between DO WHILE and ENDDO are again executed. If the condition is false, dBASE IV proceeds to the command below the ENDDO command.

EDIT

Syntax

EDIT [RECORD *n*] [NOINIT] [NO FOLLOW] [NOAPPEND]
[NOMENU] [NOEDIT] [NODELETE] [FIELDS *field-list*]
[FOR *condition*] [WHILE *condition*]

The EDIT command allows full-screen editing of a record in the database. If no record number is specified by RECORD (*n* being the record number), the current record, which is identified by the current position of the record pointer, will be edited.

The FIELDS option will display only the fields listed in *field-list*. The NOINIT option tells EDIT to use settings used with the prior use of EDIT. The NOAPPEND, NOEDIT, and NODELETE options restrict the use of appending, editing, or deleting in Edit mode. The FOR and WHILE options let you specify conditions that must be met before a record will appear in the Edit screen.

EJECT

Syntax

EJECT

The EJECT command causes the printer to perform a form feed.

EJECT PAGE

Syntax

EJECT PAGE

The EJECT PAGE command causes the printer to perform a form feed. The output of the EJECT PAGE command is directed to all destinations that are available to the ? command.

END TRANSACTION

Syntax

END TRANSACTION

The END TRANSACTION command ends the recording of a transaction file, which tracks all changes made to a database file. (*See also* BEGIN TRANSAC-

TION, ROLLBACK.) When the operations are complete, use END TRANSACTION to stop the transaction recording, and erase the transaction log.

ERASE

Syntax

ERASE *filename.ext*

The ERASE command erases the named file from the directory. The name must include the file extension. You can also use the command DELETE FILE *filename.ext* to erase a file. If the file is on a disk that is not in the default drive, you must include the drive designator.

EXIT

Syntax

EXIT

The EXIT command exits a DO WHILE loop and proceeds to the first command below the ENDDO command.

EXPORT

Syntax

EXPORT TO *filename* [TYPE] PFS/DBASEII/FW2/RPD
[FIELDS *field-list*] [*scope*] [FOR *condition*]
[WHILE *condition*]

This command exports a file to the file type named with the TYPE option. Valid types are PFS (PFS:File), DBASEII (dBASE II), FW2 (Framework II), or RPD (RapidFile).

FIND

Syntax

FIND "*character-string*"

The FIND command positions the record pointer at the first record containing an index key that matches *character-string*. If there are leading blanks in *character-string*, it must be surrounded by single or double quotes; otherwise, no quotes are necessary. If the specific character string cannot be found, the EOF value is set to true, and a "No Find" message is displayed on the screen (if dBASE IV is not executing a command file). An index file must be open before you use the FIND command.

FUNCTION

Syntax

FUNCTION *procedure-name*

The FUNCTION command identifies a procedure that serves as a user-defined function.

GO or GOTO

Syntax

GO or GOTO BOTTOM/TOP/*expression*

The GO and GOTO command positions the record pointer at a record. GO TOP will move the pointer to the beginning of a database, and GO BOTTOM will move it to the end of a database.

HELP

Syntax

HELP *command-name*

The HELP command provides instructions on using dBASE IV commands and functions, as well as other information. If you enter **HELP** without specifying a command or function, a menu-driven system of help screens allows you to request information on various subjects. If HELP is followed by a command or function, information about it will be displayed.

IF

Syntax

```
IF condition
        commands...
[ELSE]
        commands...
ENDIF
```

IF is a decision-making command that will execute commands when certain conditions are true. If the condition for the IF statement is true, the commands between the IF and ENDIF will be executed. Should the condition be false and there is an ELSE, the commands will be executed between ELSE and ENDIF. On the other hand, if the condition for IF is not true and there is no ELSE, dBASE IV will drop to the ENDIF statement without executing any commands.

IMPORT

Syntax

IMPORT FROM *filename* [TYPE] PFS/DBASEII/FW2/RPD/WKS
[FIELDS *field-list*] [*scope*] [FOR *condition*]
[WHILE *condition*]

This command imports a file of the file type named with the TYPE option. Valid types are PFS (PFS:File), DBASEII (dBASE II), FW2 (Framework II), WKS (Lotus 1-2-3), and RPD (RapidFile).

INDEX

Syntax

INDEX ON *field-list* TAG *filename* [UNIQUE] [DESCENDING]
INDEX ON *field-list* TO *filename* [UNIQUE] [DESCENDING]

The INDEX command creates an index file based on a field from the active database. Depending on the field, the index file will be indexed alphabetically, numerically, or chronologically. If the index based on the first field has duplicate entries, the duplicates are indexed according to the second field in *field-list,* provided a second field has been listed. The TAG variation of the INDEX command adds the index as a tag in the .MDX index file. The TO variation of the command creates an .NDX index file, compatible with dBASE III and III PLUS. When the UNIQUE option is used, duplicate entries are omitted from the index. The indexing occurs in ascending order unless you add the DESCENDING option.

In dBASE IV version 1.1, the FOR expression can be used to build a selective index. The index will contain only those records that meet the condition specified by the FOR clause. For example, the following command can be used in dBASE IV version 1.1:

```
INDEX ON LASTNAME + FIRSTNAME FOR SALARY > 20
```

INPUT

Syntax

INPUT [*prompt*] [TO *memvar*]

The INPUT command stores a numeric entry assigned to a memory variable by the user. An optional prompt can display a message to the user during keyboard entry. The prompt can be a memory variable of a character string.

INSERT

Syntax

INSERT [BLANK][BEFORE]

The INSERT command adds a new record below the record pointer's position and renumbers the records below the insertion. Specifying BEFORE causes the record to be inserted at the record pointer; thus, if the pointer is at record 3, the new record will be 3 and the records below it renumbered. If the BLANK option is omitted, dBASE IV allows full-screen editing of the new record; otherwise, the record will be blank.

JOIN

Syntax

JOIN WITH *alias* TO *filename* [FIELDS
field-list] [FOR *condition*]

The JOIN command creates a new database by combining specific records and fields from the active database and the database listed as *alias*. The combined database is stored in *filename*. You can limit the choice of records from the active database by specifying a FOR condition. All fields from both files will be copied if you do not include a field list; but if you do, only those fields specified in the field list will be copied. Specify fields from the nonactive database by supplying *filename → field-name*.

KEYBOARD

Syntax

KEYBOARD *ExpC*

The KEYBOARD command (available only in dBASE IV version 1.1 and above) stuffs the keyboard buffer with a character string. The data will remain in the keyboard buffer until the program seeks input from the keyboard. The KEY-

BOARD command can be very useful for creating self-executing demonstrations that showcase your programs.

LABEL FORM

Syntax

LABEL FORM *label-filename* [*scope*] [SAMPLE]
[FOR/WHILE *condition*] [TO PRINT] [TO FILE *filename*]

The LABEL FORM command is used to print mailing labels from a label form file (extension .LBL). The SAMPLE option allows a sample label to be printed. The FOR/WHILE option can be used to specify a condition that must be met before a label for a record will be printed. The TO PRINT option sends output to the printer, while the TO FILE option sends output to a named disk file.

LIST

Syntax

LIST [OFF][*scope*][*field-list*][FOR/WHILE
condition][TO PRINT][TO FILE *filename*]

The LIST command provides a list of database contents. The *scope* option is used to quantify the records to be listed. If *scope* is absent, ALL is assumed. The FOR/WHILE option specifies a condition that must be met before a record will be listed. The OFF option will prevent the record number from being listed. If the TO PRINT option is used, the listing will be printed on the printer.

LIST MEMORY/LIST STATUS

Syntax

LIST MEMORY [TO PRINT] [TO FILE *filename*]
LIST STATUS [TO PRINT] [TO FILE *filename*]

The LIST MEMORY command lists the names, sizes, and types of memory variables. If the TO PRINT option is used, the listing will be printed on the printer. If the TO FILE option is used, the listing will be directed to the named disk file.

The LIST STATUS command lists information on currently open work areas, the active file, and system settings. All open files and open index filenames are displayed, along with work area numbers, any key fields used in index files, the default disk drive, function-key settings, and settings of the SET commands. If the TO PRINT option is used, the listing will be printed on the printer. LIST STATUS does not pause during the listing, which is the only difference between LIST STATUS and DISPLAY STATUS.

LIST STRUCTURE

Syntax

LIST STRUCTURE [TO PRINT] [TO FILE *filename*]
[IN ALIAS *alias-name*]

The LIST STRUCTURE command lists the structure of the database in use, including the name, number of records, all names of fields, and the date of the last update. If the TO PRINT option is used, the listing will be printed on the printer. The TO FILE option may be specified to redirect the output to a file. LIST STRUCTURE does not pause during the listing, which is the only difference between LIST STRUCTURE and DISPLAY STRUCTURE. The IN ALIAS option may be used to list the structure of a file in another work area.

LOAD

Syntax

LOAD *binary-filename*

The LOAD command is used to load binary (assembly language) programs into memory for future use. An extension is optional; if omitted, it is assumed to be .BIN.

LOCATE

Syntax

LOCATE [*scope*] [FOR *condition*] [WHILE *condition*]

The LOCATE command finds the first record that matches *condition*. The *scope* option can be used to limit the number of records that will be searched, but if *scope* is omitted, ALL is assumed. The LOCATE command ends when a record matching *condition* is found, after which dBASE IV prints the location of the record but not the record itself.

LOGOUT

Syntax

LOGOUT

The LOGOUT command logs a user out of dBASE IV when running in a multiuser mode on a network.

LOOP

Syntax

LOOP

The LOOP command causes a jump back to the start of a DO WHILE loop. The LOOP command is normally executed conditionally with the IF statement.

MODIFY APPLICATION

Syntax

MODIFY APPLICATION *application-name*

The MODIFY APPLICATION command starts the applications generator. This command is functionally equivalent to the CREATE APPLICATION command. (*See* CREATE APPLICATION.)

MODIFY COMMAND/MODIFY LABELS/ MODIFY QUERY/MODIFY VIEW

Syntax

MODIFY COMMAND *filename* or MODIFY LABELS *filename* or MODIFY QUERY *filename* or MODIFY VIEW *filename*

MODIFY COMMAND starts the dBASE IV editor, which can be used for editing command files or any ASCII text files. The filename will be given the extension .PRG unless a different extension is named.

The MODIFY LABELS command creates or allows the editing of a label form file. This file can be used with the LABEL FORM command to produce mailing labels. The filename will be given the extension .LBL.

The MODIFY QUERY and MODIFY VIEW commands create or modify a query (.QBE) file by providing access to the Query Design screen. Using the Query Design screen, you can design queries that will select specific records and/or establish relational links between database files. The MODIFY VIEW alternative is provided for compatibility with dBASE III PLUS. If a catalog is active when MODIFY QUERY is used, the query file and its contents will be added to the catalog.

MODIFY REPORT/MODIFY SCREEN/ MODIFY STRUCTURE

Syntax

MODIFY REPORT *filename* or MODIFY SCREEN *filename* or MODIFY STRUCTURE *filename*

The MODIFY REPORT command allows you to use the Report Design screen to create or modify a report form file for producing reports. The filenames produced will be given the extensions .FRM and .FRG.

MODIFY SCREEN modifies an existing custom screen form. (This command is identical in operation to the CREATE SCREEN command.) Upon entry of the command, the Form Design screen appears. Options within the Form Design screen allow modifications to the design of the custom screen form. If a catalog is active when MODIFY SCREEN is used, the modified files will be added to the catalog.

The MODIFY STRUCTURE command allows you to alter the structure of a database. The filename extension .DBF is given to *filename* unless specified otherwise. A backup copy is created to store the data from *filename.* The data is later returned to the modified file; the backup file remains on disk with the same filename but with an extension of .BAK.

MOVE WINDOW

Syntax

MOVE WINDOW *window-name* TO *row,col*
/BY *delta-row,delta-column*

The MOVE WINDOW command moves a predefined window to a new location on the screen.

NOTE or *

Syntax

NOTE or *

The NOTE or * command is used to insert comments in a command file. Text after the * or the word "NOTE" in a command file will be ignored by dBASE IV.

ON

Syntax

ON ERROR *command*
ON ESCAPE *command*
ON KEY *command*

This command causes a branch within a command file, specified by *command*, to be carried out when the condition identified by ON (an error, pressing the ESC key, or pressing any key) is met. If more than one ON condition is specified, the order of precedence is ON ERROR, ON ESCAPE, and then ON KEY. All ON conditions remain in effect until another ON condition is specified to clear the previous condition. To clear an ON condition without specifying another condition, enter **ON ERROR**, **ON ESCAPE**, or **ON KEY** without adding a command.

Use of the ON KEY syntax of the command will result in the key that is pressed being stored in the keyboard buffer. The routine that is called by the ON KEY command should use a READ command or INKEY function to clear the buffer.

ON PAD

Syntax

ON PAD *pad-name* OF *menu-name*
[ACTIVATE POPUP *popup-name*]

The ON PAD command ties a given pad within a bar menu to a specific pop-up menu. When the named pad is selected from the menu, the associated pop-up menu appears.

ON PAGE

Syntax

ON PAGE [AT LINE *expN command*]

The ON PAGE command executes the command named after the ON PAGE command whenever the end of a page is reached. The page length is defined by the system print variables when PRINTJOB is active. (*See* PRINTJOB.)

ON READERROR

Syntax

ON READERROR [*command*]

The ON READERROR command runs a program or executes a named command or procedure after testing for an error condition. The ON READERROR command is called in response to invalid dates, improper responses to a VALID clause, or improper entries when a RANGE clause is in effect.

ON SELECTION PAD

Syntax

ON SELECTION PAD *pad-name* OF *menu-name* [*command*]

The ON SELECTION PAD command links a program, procedure, or a command to a specific pad of a bar menu. When the named pad is chosen from the menu, the command, procedure, or program named within the ON SELECTION statement will be executed.

ON SELECTION POPUP

Syntax

ON SELECTION POPUP *popup-name* /ALL [*command*]

The ON SELECTION POPUP command names a program, procedure, or command that executes when a selection is made from a pop-up menu. If no command or procedure is named, the active pop-up is deactivated. If the ALL option is used, the command or procedure applies to all pop-ups.

PACK

Syntax

PACK

The PACK command removes records that have been marked for deletion by the DELETE command.

PARAMETERS

Syntax

PARAMETERS *parameter-list*

The PARAMETERS command is used within a command file to assign variable names to data items that are received from another command file with the DO command. The PARAMETERS command must be the first command in a command file; the parameter list is identical to the list of parameters included with the WITH option of the DO command that called the command file.

PLAY MACRO

Syntax

PLAY MACRO *macro-name*

The PLAY MACRO command plays a previously stored macro.

PRINTJOB/ENDPRINTJOB

Syntax

PRINTJOB/*commands*/ENDPRINTJOB

The PRINTJOB command places stored print-related settings into effect for the duration of a printing job. The command also activates the ON PAGE command if it was used earlier. Desired values must be stored to the memory variables used by PRINTJOB before the command is encountered. When PRINTJOB is executed, starting codes stored to _pscodes are sent to the printer; a form feed is sent if _peject contains "BEFORE" or "BOTH"; _pcolno is initialized to 0; and _plineno and ON PAGE are activated. When the printing process is complete and the ENDPRINTJOB command is encountered, any ending print codes stored to _pecodes are sent to the printer; a form feed is sent if _peject contains "AFTER" or "BOTH"; dBASE returns to the PRINTJOB command if the _pcopies variable contains more than 1 (set to more than one copy of the report); and _plineno and ON PAGE are deactivated.

PRIVATE

Syntax

PRIVATE [ALL [LIKE/EXCEPT*skeleton*]]
[*memvar-list*] [ARRAY *array-definition-list*]

This command sets named variables to private, hiding the values of those variables from all higher-level parts of a program. Skeletons are the acceptable asterisk (*) and question mark (?) DOS wildcards. Memory variables are private by default.

PROCEDURE

Syntax

PROCEDURE

The PROCEDURE command identifies the start of each separate procedure within a procedure file.

PROTECT

Syntax

PROTECT

The PROTECT command starts the menu-driven Protect utility, which lets you control data security within the dBASE environment.

PUBLIC

Syntax

PUBLIC [memvar-list]/ [ARRAY
array-definition-list]

This command sets named variables to public, making the values of those variables available to all levels of a program.

QUIT

Syntax

QUIT

The QUIT command closes all open files, leaves dBASE IV, and returns you to the DOS prompt.

READ

Syntax

READ [SAVE]

The READ command allows full-screen data entry from an @ command with GET option. Normally, a READ command clears all GETs when all data entry or editing is completed. The SAVE option is used to avoid clearing all GETs after completion of data entry or editing.

RECALL

Syntax

RECALL [*scope*] [FOR/WHILE *condition*]

The RECALL command unmarks records that have been marked for deletion. If *scope* is not listed, ALL is assumed. The FOR/WHILE option can be used to specify a condition that must be met before a record will be recalled.

REINDEX

Syntax

REINDEX

The REINDEX command rebuilds all open index files in the current work area, including multiple index (.MDX) files. If any changes have been made to the database while its index file was closed, you can update the index file with REINDEX.

RELEASE

Syntax

RELEASE [*memvar-list*] [ALL [LIKE/EXCEPT *wildcards*]]
[RELEASE MODULE *module-name*]
[RELEASE MENUS *menu-name-list*]
[RELEASE POPUP *popup-name-list*]
[RELEASE WINDOW *window-name-list*]

The RELEASE command removes all or specified memory variables from memory. Wildcards (asterisks or question marks) are used with the LIKE and EXCEPT options. The asterisk can be used to represent one or more characters, the question mark to represent one character. The variations RELEASE MODULE, RELEASE MENUS, RELEASE POPUP, and RELEASE WINDOW of the command release the named objects from active memory.

RENAME

Syntax

RENAME *filename.ext* TO *new-filename.ext*

The RENAME command changes the name of a file. The name must include the file extension. If the file is on a disk that is not in the default drive, the drive designator must also be included.

REPLACE

Syntax

REPLACE [*scope*] [*field* WITH *expression* ...*field2*
WITH *expression2*] [FOR/WHILE *condition*] [ADDITIVE]

The REPLACE command replaces the contents of a specified field with new values. You can replace values in more than one field by listing more than one *field* WITH *expression;* be sure to separate each field replacement with a comma. The FOR/WHILE option can be used to specify a condition that must be met before a field in a record will be replaced. If *scope* or the FOR/WHILE options are not used, the current record (at the current record-pointer location) will be the only record replaced. The ADDITIVE option can be used to build a memo field with the contents of character strings.

REPLACE FROM ARRAY

Syntax

REPLACE FROM ARRAY *array name* [*scope*] [FIELDS *field-list*]
[FOR *condition*] [WHILE *condition*]

The REPLACE FROM ARRAY command (available only in dBASE IV versions 1.1 and above) updates the fields of a database record with data that is contained in the elements of an array. For each record in the database, the first array element is stored in the first database field, the second array element in the second database field, and so on. If the database has more fields than the array has elements, the contents of extra fields remain unchanged. If the array has more elements than the database has fields, the extra elements in the array are ignored. Note that memo fields are not copied from an array. In operation, the REPLACE FROM ARRAY command is the opposite of the COPY TO ARRAY command.

REPORT FORM

Syntax

REPORT FORM *filename* [*scope*] [FOR *condition*]
[WHILE *condition*] [PLAIN] [HEADING *character-string*]
[SUMMARY] [NOEJECT] [TO PRINT] [TO FILE *filename*]

The REPORT FORM command uses a report form file (previously created with the CREATE REPORT command) to produce a report. A filename with the extension .FRM is assumed unless otherwise specified. The FOR or WHILE *condition* option can be used to specify a condition to be met before a record will be printed. If *scope* is not included, ALL is assumed. The PLAIN option omits page numbers and the system date. The HEADING option (followed by a character string) provides a header in addition to any header that was specified when the report was created with CREATE REPORT. The NOEJECT option cancels the initial form feed. The SUMMARY option causes a summary report to be printed. TO PRINT directs output to the screen and the printer, while TO FILE directs output to a disk file.

RESET

Syntax

RESET [IN *alias-name*]

The RESET command removes the integrity flag from a file. This flag is normally removed by the END TRANSACTION command, or when a successful ROLLBACK operation has occurred. If a successful ROLLBACK is not possible, use the RESET command to remove the integrity flag.

RESTORE

Syntax

RESTORE FROM *filename* [ADDITIVE]

The RESTORE command reads memory variables into memory from a memory variable file. RESTORE FROM assumes that *filename* ends with .MEM; if it does not, you should include the extension. If the ADDITIVE option is used, current memory variables will not be deleted.

RESTORE MACROS

Syntax

RESTORE MACROS FROM *macro-filename*

The RESTORE MACROS command restores to memory any macros that were saved in a macro file. Macros in memory that are assigned to the same keys when you use this command will be overwritten.

RESTORE SCREEN

Syntax

RESTORE SCREEN [FROM *memvar*]

The RESTORE SCREEN command (available in only dBASE IV versions 1.1 and above) restores a screen from the buffer or from the named memory variable. (The corresponding command, SAVE SCREEN, is used to store the screen in the memory buffer or to a memory variable.) RESTORE SCREEN and SAVE SCREEN can be useful when you want to display messages over screen displays, and you want to avoid having to redraw the screen display after the message is removed. Use SAVE SCREEN [TO *memvar*] to save the screen image to a variable and then display the message. When the message has been viewed, clear the message, and use RESTORE SCREEN [FROM *memvar*] to redisplay the original screen.

RESTORE WINDOW

Syntax

RESTORE WINDOW *window-name-list*/ALL FROM *filename*

The RESTORE WINDOW command restores window definitions that were saved in a file with the SAVE WINDOW command.

RESUME

Syntax

RESUME

This command is a companion to the SUSPEND command. RESUME causes program execution to continue at the line that follows the line containing the SUSPEND command. (*See* SUSPEND.)

RETRY

Syntax

RETRY

The RETRY command returns control to a calling program and executes the same line that called the program containing the RETRY command. The function of RETRY is similar to the function of the RETURN command; however, whereas RETURN executes the following line of the calling program, RETRY executes the same line of the calling program. RETRY can be useful in error-recovery situations, where an action can be taken to clear the cause of an error and the command repeated.

RETURN

Syntax

RETURN [TO MASTER] [*expression*]

The RETURN command ends execution of a command file or procedure. If the command file was called by another command file, program control returns to the other command file. If the command file was not called by another command file, control returns to the dot prompt. If the TO MASTER option is used, control returns to the highest-level command file. The *expression* option is used to return the value in a user-defined function to another procedure or command file.

ROLLBACK

Syntax

ROLLBACK [*database-name*]

The ROLLBACK command restores a database and associated index files back to the original status they had before the BEGIN TRANSACTION command was encountered. (*See* BEGIN TRANSACTION, END TRANSACTION.)

RUN

Syntax

RUN *filename*

The RUN command executes a non-dBASE IV program from within the dBASE IV environment. The program must have an extension of .COM or .EXE. When the program completes its execution, control is passed back to dBASE IV. You can also execute DOS commands with RUN, provided there is enough available memory.

SAVE

Syntax

SAVE TO *filename* [ALL LIKE/ EXCEPT *wildcard*]

The SAVE command copies memory variables to a disk file. Wildcards, which are asterisks or question marks, are used with the LIKE and EXCEPT options. The asterisk can be used to represent one or more characters, the question mark to represent one character.

SAVE MACROS

Syntax

SAVE MACROS TO *macro-filename*

The SAVE MACROS command saves macros currently in memory to a macro file.

SAVE SCREEN

Syntax

SAVE SCREEN [TO *memvar*]

The SAVE SCREEN command (available only in dBASE IV versions 1.1 and above) saves a screen to the buffer or to the named memory variable. (The corresponding command, RESTORE SCREEN, is used to restore the screen currently in the memory buffer or from a memory variable.) SAVE SCREEN and RESTORE SCREEN can be useful when you want to display messages over screen displays, and you want to avoid having to redraw the screen display after the message is removed. Use SAVE SCREEN TO *memvar* to save the screen image to a variable and then display the message. When the message has been viewed, clear the message, and use RESTORE SCREEN FROM *memvar* to redisplay the original screen. This presents less programming work than re-drawing the original screen, and with complex screens it is considerably faster.

SAVE WINDOW

Syntax

SAVE WINDOW *window-name-list*/ALL TO *window-filename*

The SAVE WINDOW command saves the windows named in the list to a disk file. If the ALL option is used, all windows in memory are saved to a file. The windows can be restored to memory by using RESTORE WINDOW.

SCAN

Syntax

```
SCAN [scope] [FOR condition] [WHILE condition]
      [commands...]
```

```
        [LOOP]
        [commands]
        [EXIT]
ENDSCAN
```

The SCAN and ENDSCAN commands are simplified alternatives to the DO WHILE and ENDDO commands. The SCAN and ENDSCAN commands cause the file in use to be scanned, processing all records that meet the specified conditions.

SEEK

Syntax

SEEK *expression*

The SEEK command searches for the first record in an indexed file whose field matches a specific expression. If *expression* is a character string, it must be surrounded by single or double quotes. If *expression* cannot be found and dBASE IV is not executing a command file, the EOF value is set to true and a "No Find" message is displayed on the screen. An index file must be open before you can use the SEEK command.

SELECT

Syntax

SELECT *n* or SELECT *alias*

The SELECT command chooses from among ten possible work areas for database files. When dBASE IV is first loaded into the computer, it defaults to work area 1. To use multiple files at once, you must select other work areas with the SELECT command; other files can then be opened in those areas. Acceptable work areas are from 1 through 10.

SET

Syntax

SET

SET causes the Set menu to be displayed. The Set menu can then be used to select most available SET parameters within dBASE IV.

SET ALTERNATE

Syntax

SET ALTERNATE ON/OFF

and

SET ALTERNATE TO *filename* [ADDITIVE]

The SET ALTERNATE TO command creates a text file with extension .TXT, and when actuated by SET ALTERNATE ON, stores all keyboard entries and screen displays to the file. The SET ALTERNATE OFF command halts the process, after which CLOSE ALTERNATE is used to close the file. If the ADDITIVE option is used, the SET ALTERNATE command appends to the end of any existing file.

SET AUTOSAVE

Syntax

SET AUTOSAVE ON/OFF

The SET AUTOSAVE command, when turned on, causes dBASE to save changes to disk after each I/O operation. This procedure reduces the chances of data loss due to power or hardware failure. The default for the SET AUTOSAVE command is OFF.

SET BELL

Syntax

SET BELL ON/OFF SET BELL TO *frequency/duration*

The SET BELL command controls whether audible warnings will be issued during certain operations, and it controls the frequency and duration of the bell. The frequency is the desired tone in hertz, and each unit of duration is approximately .0549 seconds. Available frequency is from 18 to 10,001, and available duration is from 2 to 20.

SET BLOCKSIZE

Syntax

SET BLOCKSIZE TO *expN*

The SET BLOCKSIZE command changes the block size used to store data in memo fields. The default, which is the only size compatible with dBASE III PLUS and dBASE III, is 1. With large amounts of text, larger blocks often increase performance. The value multiplied by 512 represents the actual size of the blocks in bytes.

SET BORDER

Syntax

SET BORDER TO [SINGLE/DOUBLE/PANEL/NONE/
border-definition-string]

The SET BORDER command redefines the default border, which is a single-line box. The SINGLE option defines a single line; the DOUBLE option defines a double line; the PANEL option defines a panel built with the ASCII 219 character; and NONE defines no border. The *border-definition-string* option may contain eight ASCII values separated by commas. Value 1 defines the top of the border; value 2 the bottom; values 3 and 4 the left and right edges; and values 5, 6, 7, and 8 the upper-left, upper-right, lower-left, and lower-right corners, respectively.

SET CARRY

Syntax

SET CARRY ON/OFF

The SET CARRY command controls whether data will be copied from the prior record into a new record when APPEND or INSERT is used.

SET CATALOG

Syntax

SET CATALOG ON/OFF
SET CATALOG TO

The SET CATALOR ON/OFF command causes or does not cause files that are opened to be added to an open catalog. The SET CATALOG TO command opens a catalog, or if the named catalog does not exist, creates a new catalog. Any catalog previously opened will be closed when the SET CATALOG TO command is used.

SET CENTURY

Syntax

SET CENTURY ON/OFF

This command causes or does not cause the century to be visible in the display of dates. For example, a date that appears as 12/30/86 will appear as 12/30/1986 after the SET CENTURY ON command is used.

SET CLOCK

Syntax

SET CLOCK ON/OFF
SET CLOCK TO *row,col*

The SET CLOCK command defines the location of the system clock and whether the clock will appear. The default location, if one is not defined, is row 1, column 68. SET CLOCK ON displays the clock, while SET CLOCK OFF hides the clock.

SET COLOR

Syntax

SET COLOR TO *standard*
[,*enhanced*][,*perimeter*][,*background*]

The SET COLOR command is used to select screen colors and display attributes.

SET CONFIRM

Syntax

SET CONFIRM ON/OFF

The SET CONFIRM command controls the behavior of the cursor during full-screen editing. When SET CONFIRM is ON, the ENTER key must be pressed to move from one field to another in full-screen editing.

SET CONSOLE

Syntax

SET CONSOLE ON/OFF

The SET CONSOLE command turns output to the screen on or off. SET CONSOLE does not control output to the printer.

SET CURRENCY TO/SET CURRENCY LEFT/RIGHT

Syntax

SET CURRENCY TO [*expC*]
SET CURRENCY LEFT/RIGHT

The SET CURRENCY command changes the symbol used for currency. A character expression containing up to nine characters may be used as the currency symbol.

The SET CURRENCY LEFT/RIGHT command changes the currency symbol, allowing the symbol to appear to the left or the right of the value.

SET CURSOR

Syntax

SET CURSOR ON/OFF

The SET CURSOR command (available only in dBASE IV version 1.1) enables or disables the cursor. Use SET CURSOR OFF to hide the cursor, use SET CURSOR ON to redisplay the cursor. The setting of SET CURSOR does not affect other operations taking place within your program. SET CURSOR OFF is useful in programs when you do not want the cursor to be displayed during processing operations. In a program, the cursor must be visible only when a user is editing some type of field or entry.

SET DATE

Syntax

SET DATE AMERICAN/ANSI/BRITISH/ITALIAN/FRENCH/GERMAN /JAPAN/USA/MDY/DMY/YMD

This command sets the display format for the appearance of dates. American displays as MM/DD/YY; ANSI displays as YY.MM.DD; British displays as DD/MM/YY; Italian displays as DD-MM-YY; French displays as DD/MM/YY; German displays as DD.MM.YY; Japan displays as YY/MM/DD; USA displays as MM-DD-YY; MDY displays as MM/DD/YY; DMY displays as DD/MM/YY; and YMD displays as YY/MM/DD. The default value is American.

SET DEBUG

Syntax

SET DEBUG ON/OFF

The SET DEBUG command routes the output of the SET ECHO command to the printer instead of to the screen.

SET DECIMALS

Syntax

SET DECIMALS TO *expN*

The SET DECIMALS command changes the minimum number of decimal places that are normally displayed during calculations.

SET DEFAULT

Syntax

SET DEFAULT TO *drive:*

This command changes the default drive used in file operations. Usually *drive:* is A or B; it is usually C for hard-disk drives.

SET DELETED

Syntax

SET DELETED ON/OFF

With SET DELETED ON, all records marked for deletion will be displayed when commands such as LIST are used. With SET DELETED OFF, delete markers are turned off, even though they are still present.

SET DELIMITERS

Syntax

SET DELIMITERS TO [*character-string*] [DEFAULT]
SET DELIMITERS ON/OFF

The SET DELIMITERS command assigns characters other than the default colon (:) to be used to mark the field area. Once assigned, SET DELIMITERS ON activates the delimiters, and SET DELIMITERS OFF deactivates the delimiters. DEFAULT restores the colon as the delimiter.

SET DESIGN

Syntax

SET DESIGN ON/OFF

The SET DESIGN command prevents access to the design screens with SHIFT-F2. Use this command within applications to keep end users from redesigning your objects. SET DESIGN OFF prevents design access with SHIFT-F2; SET DESIGN ON restores access to the design screens.

SET DEVELOPMENT

Syntax

SET DEVELOPMENT ON/OFF

The SET DEVELOPMENT command, when ON, tells dBASE IV to compare creation dates of .PRG files and compiled (.DBO) files so that when a program is run, an outdated .DBO file will not be used. The dBASE editor automatically deletes old .DBO files as programs are updated, so the SET DEVELOPMENT command is not needed if you use the dBASE editor. If you use another editor to create and modify program files, add a SET DEVELOPMENT ON statement at the start of your programs.

SET DEVICE

Syntax

SET DEVICE TO PRINTER/SCREEN/FILE *filename*

The SET DEVICE command controls whether @ commands are sent to the screen or printer. SET DEVICE is normally set to SCREEN, but if PRINTER is specified, output will be directed to the printer. The FILE option directs output to the named disk file.

SET DIRECTORY

Syntax

SET DIRECTORY TO [*drive*][*path*]

The SET DIRECTORY command (available only in dBASE IV version 1.1) sets the default directory for both dBASE IV and for the operating system (usually DOS or OS/2). Use SET DIRECTORY to change both the dBASE default drive and the operating system drive and directory in a single step.

SET DISPLAY TO

Syntax

SET DISPLAY TO MONO/COLOR/EGA25/EGA43/MONO43

The SET DISPLAY command chooses a monitor type and sets the number of lines displayed. For the number of lines option to have effect, the graphics hardware must support the type chosen within the SET DISPLAY command.

SET ECHO

Syntax

SET ECHO ON/OFF

The SET ECHO command determines whether instructions from command files will be displayed or printed during program execution. It is mostly used with SET DEBUG. The default for SET ECHO is OFF.

SET ENCRYPTION

Syntax

SET ENCRYPTION ON/OFF

The SET ENCRYPTION command, when ON, causes all databases created by copying existing files to be encrypted. The encryption affects database files created with commands like SORT and COPY TO. Existing database files and new files created with the CREATE command are not directly encrypted by the use of SET ENCRYPTION; such files can be protected with the PROTECT utility, accessible by entering the PROTECT command. Note that SET ENCRYPTION must be OFF before you can write foreign files with the TYPE options of the COPY TO command or with the EXPORT command.

SET ESCAPE

Syntax

SET ESCAPE ON/OFF

The SET ESCAPE command determines whether the ESC key will interrupt a program during execution. The default for the SET ESCAPE command is ON.

SET EXACT

Syntax

SET EXACT ON/OFF

The SET EXACT command determines how precisely two character strings will be compared. With SET EXACT deactivated, which is the default case, comparison is not strict: a string on the left of the test is equal to its substring on the right if the substring acts as a prefix of the larger string. Thus, "turnbull" = "turn" is true even though it is clearly not. SET EXACT ON corrects for this lack of precision.

SET FIELDS

Syntax

SET FIELDS ON/OFF

This command respects or overrides a list of fields specified by the SET FIELDS TO command.

SET FIELDS TO

Syntax

SET FIELDS TO [*list-of-fields* [ALL [LIKE/EXCEPT *skeleton*]]]
[ADDITIVE]

This command sets a specified list of fields that will be available for use. The ALL option causes all fields present in the active database to be made available. The LIKE/EXCEPT *skeleton* options select fields that match (or do not match) the skeleton. The ADDITIVE option adds the fields to a prior list of fields.

SET FILTER

Syntax

SET FILTER TO [*condition*][FILE][*query-filename*]

The SET FILTER command displays only those records in a database that meet a specific condition. The FILE option retrieves the condition from a query file that was saved earlier.

SET FIXED

Syntax

SET FIXED ON/OFF

The SET FIXED command has no effect in dBASE IV. It is provided to maintain compatibility with dBASE III and III PLUS command files.

SET FORMAT

Syntax

SET FORMAT TO *filename*

The SET FORMAT command lets you select *filename* for the format of screen displays. If *filename* has the extension .FRM, you need not supply the extension.

SET FUNCTION

Syntax

SET FUNCTION *expN* TO *character-string*

The SET FUNCTION command resets a function key to a command of your choice (75 characters maximum). You can view the current settings with the DISPLAY STATUS command.

SET HEADING

Syntax

SET HEADING ON/OFF

The SET HEADING command determines whether column headings appear when the LIST, DISPLAY, AVERAGE, or SUM command is used.

SET HELP

Syntax

SET HELP ON/OFF

If SET HELP is ON, the help message prompt appears if dBASE cannot understand the command you entered.

SET HISTORY

Syntax

SET HISTORY TO *numeric-expression*

SET HISTORY identifies the maximum number of commands that will be stored within HISTORY. The default value provided if the command is not used is 20.

SET HOURS

Syntax

SET HOURS TO [12/24]

The SET HOURS command changes the time display to the desired format (12 or 24 hours).

SET INDEX

Syntax

SET INDEX TO *filename*

The SET INDEX command opens the index file *filename*. If your file has the extension .NDX or .MDX, you do not need to include it in the command. If you do not specify an extension, SET INDEX will first look for an .MDX file by that name and then an .NDX file by that name.

SET INSTRUCT

Syntax

SET INSTRUCT ON/OFF

The SET INSTRUCT command activates or deactivates the display of information boxes that normally appear when you are in full-screen operations like Browse or Edit mode. SET INSTRUCT OFF turns off the information boxes; SET INSTRUCT ON restores the boxes.

SET INTENSITY

Syntax

SET INTENSITY ON/OFF

The SET INTENSITY command determines whether reverse video is on or off during full-screen operations. SET INTENSITY is ON when you begin a session with dBASE IV.

SET LOCK

Syntax

SET LOCK ON/OFF

The SET LOCK command enables or disables the automatic file- and record-locking facilities of dBASE IV when used on a local-area network. Use SET LOCK OFF to disable automatic locking. The default for SET LOCK is ON.

SET MARGIN

Syntax

SET MARGIN TO *expN*

The SET MARGIN command resets the left printer margin from the default value of 0.

SET MARK

Syntax

SET MARK TO *expC*

The SET MARK command specifies the delimiter used to separate the month, day, and year of a date. The character expression must be a single character surrounded by quotes.

SET MEMOWIDTH

Syntax

SET MEMOWIDTH TO *numeric-expression*

This command controls the width of columns containing the display or printed listings of contents of memo fields. The default value provided if this command is not used is 50.

SET MENU

Syntax

SET MENU ON/OFF

The SET MENU command has no effect in dBASE IV; it is retained as a valid (but nonoperational) command only to maintain compatibility with programs written for dBASE III PLUS.

SET MESSAGE

Syntax

SET MESSAGE TO *character-string*

The SET MESSAGE command allows a user-definable message to appear on the message line at the bottom of the screen. SET MESSAGE must be ON for the message to appear.

SET NEAR

Syntax

SET NEAR ON/OFF

The SET NEAR command positions the record pointer at the nearest record when a FIND or a SEEK is unsuccessful. If SET NEAR is ON, the record pointer will be placed at the next record after the expression that could not be located. If SET NEAR is OFF, the record pointer is placed at the end of the file when the expression is not found.

SET ODOMETER

Syntax

SET ODOMETER TO [*expN*]

The SET ODOMETER command tells dBASE how often commands that display a record count should update the screen display. The default value is 1, and the maximum value is 200.

SET ORDER

Syntax

SET ORDER TO *index-filename*

SET ORDER makes the named index tag or file the active index without changing the open or closed status of other index files.

SET PATH

Syntax

SET PATH TO *pathname*

The PATH command identifies a DOS path that will be searched for files if a file is not found in the current directory. For more information on path names, read your DOS manual (version 2.1 or later).

SET POINT

Syntax

SET POINT TO *expC*

The SET POINT command changes the character used as the decimal point. The specified expression can be any single character surrounded by quotes.

SET PRECISION

Syntax

SET PRECISION TO *expN*

The SET PRECISION command specifies the number of digits that dBASE IV should use for internal precision in math operations that use type N (fixed) numbers. The default value is 16. Acceptable values are from 10 to 20.

SET PRINT

Syntax

SET PRINT ON/OFF
SET PRINTER ON/OFF

The SET PRINT command directs output to the printer as well as the screen. The default for SET PRINT is OFF. (The SET PRINTER ON/OFF command is identical to this command.)

SET PRINTER TO

Syntax

SET PRINTER TO LPT1, COM1, COM2,...*other-DOS-device*
SET PRINTER TO *computer**printer-name* =
destination/ \\SPOOLER\\CAPTURE
SET PRINTER TO FILE *filename*

This command reroutes printer output to the specified device, network device, or disk file.

SET PROCEDURE

Syntax

SET PROCEDURE TO *procedure-filename*

The SET PROCEDURE command opens the named procedure file. SET PROCEDURE is placed in the command file that will reference the procedures in a procedure file.

SET REFRESH

Syntax

SET REFRESH TO *expN*

The SET REFRESH command specifies the amount of time, in seconds, between screen refreshes when full-screen operations on a network are used. The minimum value is 0, and the maximum value is 3600 (or one hour). The default is 0.

SET RELATION

Syntax

SET RELATION [TO *key-expression*/*numeric-expression*]
INTO *alias*

The SET RELATION command links the active database to an open database in another area. If the *key-expression* option is used, the active file must contain that key, and the other file must be indexed on that key.

SET REPROCESS

Syntax

SET REPROCESS TO *expN*

The SET REPROCESS command sets the number of times that dBASE will retry an operation against a locked file or record before displaying an error message. The minimum value is 1, and the maximum value is 32,000. Any negative value may be entered, in which case dBASE retries the operation on an infinite basis.

SET SAFETY

Syntax

SET SAFETY ON/OFF

The SET SAFETY command determines whether a confirmation message will be provided before existing files are overwritten. SET SAFETY is normally set to ON.

SET SCOREBOARD

Syntax

SET SCOREBOARD ON/OFF

When SET SCOREBOARD is ON and SET STATUS is OFF, dBASE displays the scoreboard (keyboard) indicators on line 1 of the screen. When SET STATUS is ON, the keyboard indicators are displayed on the status bar, and SET SCOREBOARD has no effect.

SET SEPARATOR

Syntax

SET SEPARATOR TO *expC*

The SET SEPARATOR command specifies the symbol that should be used to separate hundreds in numeric amounts. The default is the comma, which is standard in U.S. currency. The expression may be any single character surrounded by quotes.

SET SKIP

Syntax

SET SKIP TO [*alias-name1*][,*alias-name2*...]

The SET SKIP command, which is used along with SET RELATION, lets you access all records within the linked file that match a particular index-key value.

SET SPACE

Syntax

SET SPACE ON/OFF

The SET SPACE command, when ON, tells dBASE to add a space between expressions printed with the ? and ?? commands. The default for SET SPACE is ON.

SET SQL

Syntax

SET SQL ON/OFF

The SET SQL command enables or disables the SQL (structured query language) mode of dBASE IV.

SET STATUS

Syntax

SET STATUS ON/OFF

SET STATUS turns on or off the display of the dBASE IV status line.

SET STEP

Syntax

SET STEP ON/OFF

SET STEP is a debugging command that determines whether processing will stop each time a command in a command file is executed. The default of SET STEP is OFF.

SET TALK

Syntax

SET TALK ON/OFF

The SET TALK command determines whether responses from dBASE IV commands are displayed on the screen. The default for SET TALK is ON.

SET TITLE

Syntax

SET TITLE ON/OFF

The SET TITLE command enables or disables the prompt for the catalog title that appears when a new file is saved and SET CATALOG is ON.

SET TRAP

Syntax

SET TRAP ON/OFF

The SET TRAP command, when ON, automatically starts the program debugger when a program error occurs. If SET TRAP is OFF, the debugger will not start automatically if a program error occurs.

SET TYPEAHEAD

Syntax

SET TYPEAHEAD TO *numeric-expression*

This command sets the size, in number of keystrokes, of the typeahead buffer. The default value provided if this command is not used is 20. The size of the typeahead buffer can be increased to prevent fast typists from outrunning the keyboard. Acceptable values are any number between 0 and 32,000.

SET UNIQUE

Syntax

SET UNIQUE ON/OFF

This command is used with the INDEX command to create lists of items with no duplicates. The list may not be indexed adequately if there are duplicates. The default setting for SET UNIQUE is OFF.

SET VIEW

Syntax

SET VIEW TO *query-filename* / *view-filename* / [?]

The SET VIEW command selects the query (.QBE) or view (.VUE) file specified by *filename.* If the question-mark option is used in place of a valid filename, a menu of all available query or view files will appear. dBASE IV first looks for a .QBE file with the given name, and if none is found, it then looks for a .VUE (dBASE III PLUS style) view file with that name.

SET WINDOW

Syntax

SET WINDOW OF MEMO TO *window-name*

The SET WINDOW command sets a window for use in editing the contents of memo fields. The window listed as *window-name* must have been previously defined with the DEFINE WINDOW command.

SHOW MENU

Syntax

SHOW MENU *menu-name* [PAD *pad-name*]

The SHOW MENU command displays a menu without activating the menu. The command is used primarily in the program design process to check the visual appearance of a menu.

SHOW POPUP

Syntax

SHOW POPUP *popup-name*

The SHOW POPUP command displays a pop-up menu without activating the menu. The command is primarily used in the program design process to check the visual appearance of a menu.

SKIP

Syntax

SKIP *expression* [IN *alias-name*]

The SKIP command moves the record pointe. SKIP moves one record forward if no value is specified. Values can be expressed as memory variables or as constants. The IN *alias-name* option can be used to move the record pointer within a file in another work area.

SORT

Syntax

SORT TO *filename* ON *field1* [/A][/C][/D]
[,*field2* [/A][/C][/D]...] [ASCENDING/DESCENDING]
[*scope*] [FOR *condition*] [WHILE *condition*]

The SORT command creates a rearranged copy of a database. The order of the new copy depends on the fields and options specified. The /C option creates a sorted file in dictionary order, where there is no differentiation between upper- and lowercase. Use /A for ascending order on a specific field and /D for descending order on a specific field. Use the ASCENDING or DESCENDING options to specify ascending or descending order for all fields. (The /A or /D option can be used with any field to override the effects of the ASCENDING or DESCENDING options.) Up to ten fields can be combined in a single sort; you cannot sort on memo fields or on logical fields.

STORE

Syntax

STORE *expression* TO *memvar-list* / *array-element-list*

The STORE command creates a memory variable and stores a value to that variable or to the named array.

SUM

Syntax

SUM [*scope*] [*field-list*] [TO *memvar-list*]

This command provides a sum total of *field-list* involving numeric fields. If the TO option is not used, the sum is displayed. If the TO option is used, the sum is stored as the memory variable specified. If the *scope* option is not used, ALL is assumed by dBASE IV. The FOR/WHILE option can be used to specify a condition that must be met before an entry in a field can be summed. The TO ARRAY option stores the values summed to the elements of the named array.

SUSPEND

Syntax

SUSPEND

This command suspends execution of a command file or procedure and returns program control to the dot prompt, leaving current memory variables intact. Execution of the command file or procedure can be restarted where it was interrupted with the RESUME command.

TEXT

Syntax

TEXT
    text to be displayed
ENDTEXT

This command displays blocks of text from a command file.

TOTAL

Syntax

TOTAL TO *filename* ON *key* [*scope*] [FIELDS *field-list*]
[FOR/WHILE *condition*]

This command adds the numeric fields in a database and creates a new database containing the results.

TYPE

Syntax

TYPE *filename.ext* [NUMBER] [TO PRINT] [TO FILE *filename*]

The TYPE command displays the contents of a disk file on the screen. If the TO PRINT option is used, the file will be printed. The TO FILE option directs the output of the TYPE command to a named disk file. The NUMBER option causes line numbers to be included.

UNLOCK

Syntax

UNLOCK [ALL]

The UNLOCK command releases the last lock placed on a record or a file in the current work area. If UNLOCK is used, any lock that applies to the active file is released. If the ALL option is included, all locks in all work areas are released.

UPDATE

Syntax

UPDATE [RANDOM] ON *key-field* FROM *alias* REPLACE
field WITH *expression* [,*field2* WITH *expression2...*]

The UPDATE command uses data from a specified database, *alias,* to make changes to the database in use. Both files must be sorted or indexed on the key field unless RANDOM is included, in which case only *alias* need be indexed.

USE

Syntax

USE [*database-file* /?] [IN *work-area-number*]
[INDEX *.mdx-or-.ndx-file-list*]
[ORDER *.ndx-filename* /*.mdx-file-tag* [OF *.mdx-name*]]
[ALIAS *alias-name*] [EXCLUSIVE]

The USE command opens a database file and related index files in a work area. If the ? is used in place of the database filename, a list of available files appears. Use the INDEX and ORDER options to specify index tags or files that will be open or active. Use the ALIAS option to open the file in a different work area. Use the EXCLUSIVE option to open the file for exclusive use on a local-area network. Entering the USE command without specifying a filename will close the file that is currently open.

WAIT

Syntax

WAIT [*prompt*] [TO *memvar*]

The WAIT command halts operation of a command file until a key is pressed. If a prompt is included, it will be displayed on the screen. If the TO option is used, the key pressed will be stored as a memory variable.

ZAP

Syntax

ZAP

The ZAP command removes all records from the active database file. It is equivalent to a DELETE ALL command followed by a PACK command.

APPENDIX

B

Glossary of Functions

This appendix summarizes the dBASE IV functions. Following the name of each function is the function's syntax, and a description of its purpose. (For a similar summary of dBASE IV commands, see Appendix A.)

Glossary Symbols and Conventions

1. All functions are printed in UPPERCASE, although you can enter them in either upper- or lowercase letters.

2. The term *ExpC* indicates a character expression, *ExpN* indicates a numeric expression, *ExpD* indicates a date expression, and *ExpL* indicates a logical expression. Where data type does not matter, the term *expression* is used.

3. Whenever a function calls for or permits an *alias* argument, you can use the alias name (in quotes), or you can use the work area number or letter.

4. Any part of a parameter that is surrounded by [ ] (left and right brackets) is optional.

5. Ellipses (...) following a parameter means that the parameter can be repeated "infinitely;" that is, until you exhaust the memory of the computer or reach the limit of 1024 characters on a single program line.

ABS( )

Syntax

ABS(*ExpN*)

The ABS( ) function returns the absolute (or unsigned) value of the specified numeric expression.

ACCESS( )

Syntax

ACCESS( )

The ACCESS( ) function returns the access level of the user when dBASE IV is running on a local area network.

ACOS( )

Syntax

ACOS(*ExpN*)

The ACOS( ) function returns the arc cosine of *ExpN*, as measured in radians between zero and +pi (3.14159). Allowable values for *ExpN* are from +1 to -1.

ALIAS( )

Syntax

ALIAS([*ExpN*])

The ALIAS( ) function returns the alias of the database open in the work area specified by *ExpN*. If *ExpN* is omitted, ALIAS( ) returns the alias of the current work area.

ASC( )

Syntax

ASC(*ExpC*)

The ASC( ) function returns the decimal ASCII code for the leftmost character in *ExpC*.

ASIN( )

Syntax

ASIN(*ExpN*)

The ASIN( ) function returns the arcsine of *ExpN*, as measured in radians between -pi/2 and +pi/2 (-1.57079 to 1.57079). Acceptable values for *ExpN* are from +1 to -1.

AT( )

Syntax

AT(*ExpC1*, *ExpC2*)

The AT( ) function finds *ExpC1* in *ExpC2*. (Note that *ExpC2* may be a memo field.) The function returns (as an integer) the starting position of *ExpC1*. If *ExpC1* is not found, the function returns a zero.

ATAN( )

Syntax

ATAN(*ExpN*)

The ATAN( ) function returns the arctangent of *ExpN*, as measured in radians between -pi/2 and +pi/2 (-1.57079 to 1.57079). *ExpN* can be any value.

ATN2( )

Syntax

ATN2(*ExpN1*, *ExpN2*)

The ATN2( ) function returns the arctangent angle (as measured in radians) for all four quadrants. You specify the X and Y coordinates (or sine and cosine of the angle) instead of specifying the tangent value, as with the ATAN( ) function. *ExpN1* is the X coordinate or sine of the angle, while *ExpN2* is the Y coordinate, or cosine of the angle.

BAR( )

Syntax

BAR( )

The BAR( ) function returns the number of the menu item most recently selected from the active pop-up menu. Use the DEFINE BAR command to assign each menu item a number. If no pop-up menu is active, the BAR( ) function returns a zero.

BOF( )

Syntax

BOF([*alias*])

The BOF( ) function returns a logical true (.T.) if the record pointer is at the beginning-of-file (above the first record in the database file.) Use the optional *alias* to test for beginning-of-file in a different work area.

CALL( )

Syntax

CALL(*ExpC,ExpC/memvar name*)

The CALL( ) function executes a binary program previously loaded with the LOAD command, and passes a value to the binary program. *ExpC* is the name of the binary program (a .BIN extension is assumed). *Memvar name* is the name of the variable containing the value to be passed to the binary routine. The value returned by the function can be used in an expression or stored to a variable.

CDOW( )

Syntax

CDOW(*ExpD*)

The CDOW( ) function returns the name of the day of the week for the given date expression.

CEILING( )

Syntax

CEILING(*ExpN*)

The CEILING( ) function returns the nearest integer greater than or equal to *ExpN*. Positive numbers with decimals are rounded up to the next highest number, and negative numbers with decimals are rounded up to the number next closest to zero.

CERROR( )

Syntax

CERROR( )

The CERROR( ) function (available in dBASE IV versions 1.1 and above) returns the error code number of the last error reported by the dBASE IV compiler. If a compiler error has not been reported, CERROR( ) returns a value of zero.

CHANGE( )

Syntax

CHANGE( )

The CHANGE( ) function returns a logical value indicating whether the current record has been changed since it was opened. CHANGE( ) can be used in network applications to determine whether a record should be updated on the screen due to changes by another user on the network. If CHANGE( ) returns a logical true, the record has been changed since it was opened. If CHANGE( ) returns a logical false, the record is unchanged. Note that CHANGE( ) operates correctly only if the records in the database have been converted for network use with the CONVERT command.

CHR( )

Syntax

CHR(*ExpN*)

The CHR( ) function returns the character whose decimal ASCII code is equivalent to *ExpN*.

CMONTH( )

Syntax

CMONTH(*ExpD*)

The CMONTH( ) function returns the name of the month that corresponds to the date expression.

COL( )

Syntax

COL( )

The COL( ) function returns the current column location of the cursor.

COMPLETED( )

Syntax

COMPLETED( )

The COMPLETED( ) function returns a logical value indicating whether a transaction opened with BEGIN TRANSACTION has completed. If the transaction is complete, COMPLETED( ) returns a logical true. If the transaction is not complete, COMPLETED( ) returns a logical false.

COS( )

Syntax

COS(*ExpN*)

The COS( ) function returns the cosine of *ExpN*, as measured in radians. To convert an angle from degrees to radians, use the DTOR( ) function.

CTOD( )

Syntax

CTOD(*ExpC*)

The CTOD( ) function returns the date value that corresponds to *ExpC*, in the default date format (usually mm/dd/yy). Use the SET DATE and SET CENTURY commands to change the default format.

DATE( )

Syntax

DATE( )

The DATE( ) function returns the current system date.

DAY( )

Syntax

DAY(*ExpD*)

The DAY( ) function returns the numeric day of the month that corresponds to the date expression.

DBF( )

Syntax

DBF([*alias*])

The DBF( ) function returns the database filename for the file open in the specified work area. If no alias is specified, the DBF( ) function returns the filename for the currently selected work area. If no file is open in the work area, the function returns a null string.

DELETED( )

Syntax

DELETED([*alias*])

The DELETED( ) function returns a logical true (.T.) if the current record is marked for deletion; otherwise, it returns a logical false (.F.). Use the optional *alias* to test for deleted records in an unselected work area.

DIFFERENCE( )

Syntax

DIFFERENCE(*ExpC1, ExpC2*)

The DIFFERENCE( ) function returns a numeric value between 0 and 4 representing the phonetic difference between two character strings *ExpC1* and *ExpC2*. The DIFFERENCE( ) function can be useful for searching databases when the precise spelling of an entry is not known. A value of 4 represents the closest match between *ExpC1* and *ExpC2*.

DISKSPACE( )

Syntax

DISKSPACE( )

The DISKSPACE( ) function returns the number of bytes available on the default drive.

DMY( )

Syntax

DMY(*ExpD*)

The DMY( ) function returns a date expression in European (DD-Month-YY) format for the given date expression.

DOW( )

Syntax

DOW(*ExpD*)

The DOW( ) function returns the numeric day of the week corresponding to the date expression. The value returned ranges from 1 (for Sunday) to 7 (for Saturday).

DTOC( )

Syntax

DTOC(*ExpD*)

The DTOC( ) function returns a character string containing the date that corresponds to the date expression. Use the SET DATE and the SET CENTURY commands to change the format of the string.

DTOR( )

Syntax

DTOR(*ExpN*)

The DTOR( ) function converts the angle specified by *ExpN* from degrees to radians.

DTOS( )

Syntax

DTOS(*ExpD*)

The DTOS( ) function returns a character string in the format YYYYMMDD for the given date expression. This function is useful when indexing on a date field.

EOF( )

Syntax

EOF([*alias*])

The EOF( ) function returns a logical true (.T.) if the end-of- file is reached (the record pointer passes the last record in the database, or a FIND, LOCATE, or SEEK command was unsuccessful). Use the optional *alias* to test for end-of-file in a different work area. Note that if you establish a relation with SET RELATION and the related file does not contain a record with the key matching the current record, the record pointer will be at the end-of-file in the related file.

ERROR( )

Syntax

ERROR( )

The ERROR( ) function returns the number of the error causing the ON ERROR condition. An ON ERROR routine must be in effect for the ERROR( ) function to return a value other than zero.

EXP( )

Syntax

EXP(*ExpN*)

The EXP( ) function returns the value of e raised to *N*th power. *ExpN* is the exponent *N* in the equation e^*N*. The value of e is roughly 2.71828 (the base of natural logarithms).

FIELD( )

Syntax

FIELD(*ExpN1*[, *alias*])

The FIELD( ) function returns the name of the field in the active database that corresponds to the numeric position specified in the expression. If there is no corresponding field in the active database, FIELD( ) returns a null string. Use the optional *alias* to return a field name from a database that is open in an unselected work area.

FILE( )

Syntax

FILE(*ExpC*)

The FILE( ) function returns a logical true (.T.) if the character expression matches the name for an existing file in the default directory. If no such file can be found, the FILE( ) function returns a logical false (.F.).

FIXED( )

Syntax

FIXED(*ExpN*)

The FIXED( ) function converts floating point numbers (data type F in dBASE IV) to binary coded decimal numbers (data type N in dBASE IV). *ExpN* denotes the floating point number that is to be converted to the numeric type. The value returned by the function is the number in type N format.

FKLABEL( )

Syntax

FKLABEL(*ExpN*)

The FKLABEL( ) function returns the name of the function key that corresponds to *ExpN*.

FKMAX( )

Syntax

FKMAX( )

The FKMAX( ) function returns the number of programmable function keys available on your keyboard.

FLOAT( )

Syntax

FLOAT(*ExpN*)

The FLOAT( ) function converts a numeric value (data type N in dBASE IV) to a floating-point value (data type F in dBASE IV). *ExpN* specifies the number that is to be converted to a floating-point number. The value returned by the function is the floating-point equivalent.

FLOCK( )

Syntax

FLOCK([*alias*])

The FLOCK( ) function attempts to lock a file on a network, and returns a logical true if the attempt is successful. The file remains locked until you close the file, or use the UNLOCK command or the RLOCK( ) function. Use the optional *alias* to lock a file in another work area. If a relationship has been established with SET RELATION, the related files are also locked.

FLOOR( )

Syntax

FLOOR(*ExpN*)

The FLOOR( ) function returns the nearest integer value less than or equal to the numeric expression. All positive numbers with a decimal will be rounded down to the next lowest number, and all negative numbers with a decimal will be rounded down to the next number farther from zero.

FOUND( )

Syntax

FOUND([*alias*])

The FOUND( ) function returns a logical true (.T.) if the last CONTINUE, FIND, LOCATE, or SEEK command was successful. A logical false (.F.) is returned if the search command was unsuccessful. Note that if you have established a relation with SET RELATION, and you specify the related file with *alias*, the function returns a logical true if the pointer is on a record with a key value matching that of the current record in the active database.

FV( )

Syntax

FV(*ExpN1, ExpN2, ExpN3*)

The FV( ) function returns the future value of an investment. FV( ) calculates the future value of a series of equal payments earning a fixed interest rate. The future value is the total of all payments, plus the interest. *ExpN1* is the payment amount, *ExpN2* is the interest rate, and *ExpN3* is the number of periods. If the payments are compounded monthly and the interest rate is compounded yearly, divide the interest rate by 12 to get the proper results.

GETENV( )

Syntax

GETENV(*ExpC*)

The GETENV( ) function returns a character string that contains the contents of the DOS environmental variable named as the character expression.

IIF( )

Syntax

IIF(*ExpL, expression1, expression2*)

The IIF( ) function (immediate IF) returns the value of *expression1* if the logical expression is true, and returns the value of *expression2* if the logical expression is false. *Expression1* and *expression2* must be of the same data type.

INKEY( )

Syntax

INKEY([*ExpN*])

The INKEY( ) function returns an integer value, between 0 and 255, corresponding to the decimal ASCII code for the key that was pressed. A zero is returned if the keyboard buffer is empty and no key has been pressed.

INT( )

Syntax

INT(*ExpN*)

The INT( ) function returns the integer portion of *ExpN*. No rounding occurs; any decimal values are simply dropped.

ISALPHA( )

Syntax

ISALPHA(*ExpC*)

The ISALPHA( ) function returns a logical true (.T.) if the first character of *ExpC* is a through z or A through Z. A logical false (.F.) is returned if *ExpC* begins with a nonalphabetic or a numeric character.

ISCOLOR( )

Syntax

ISCOLOR( )

The ISCOLOR( ) function returns a logical true (.T.) if the system has color capability (whether or not a color monitor is being used) and returns a logical false (.F.) if the system has noncolor (monochrome) capability.

ISLOWER( )

Syntax

ISLOWER(*ExpC*)

The ISLOWER( ) function returns a logical true (.T.) if the first character in *ExpC* is a lowercase alphabetical character, or a logical false (.F.) if the first character is anything other than a lowercase alphabetical character.

ISMARKED

Syntax

ISMARKED([*alias*])

The ISMARKED( ) function returns a logical true if a database is in a state of change, as defined by a BEGIN TRANSACTION command. The optional *alias* denotes the alias for the database; if omitted, ISMARKED checks the status of the database in the current work area. If BEGIN TRANSACTION has not been used, ISMARKED( ) returns a logical false. If BEGIN TRANSACTION has been used and END TRANSACTION or ROLLBACK has not yet been used, ISMARKED( ) returns a logical true.

ISUPPER( )

Syntax

ISUPPER(*ExpC*)

The ISUPPER( ) function returns a logical true (.T.) if the first character in *ExpC* is an uppercase alphabetical character, or a logical false (.F.) if the first character is anything other than an uppercase alphabetical character.

KEY( )

Syntax

KEY([*.MDX filename*,] *ExpN* [, *alias*])

The KEY( ) function returns the index expression of the specified index file. If an .MDX file is named, the numeric expression refers to the tag in that .MDX file. If an .MDX file is not named, the numeric expression identifies the index file, where 1 is the first index file opened, 2 is the second index file opened, and so on. Use the *alias* option to return the key expression for an index file that is open in an unselected work area.

LASTKEY( )

Syntax

LASTKEY( )

The LASTKEY( ) function returns the decimal ASCII value for the last key pressed. (The LASTKEY( ) function returns the same ASCII values as the INKEY( ) function.)

LEFT( )

Syntax

LEFT(*ExpC, ExpN*)

The LEFT( ) function returns the leftmost number of characters specified in *ExpN* from the character expression *ExpC*, starting with the first or leftmost character. Note that *ExpC* can be the name of a memo field.

LEN( )

Syntax

LEN(*ExpC*)

The LEN( ) function returns the length of a character string expression specified in *ExpC*. *ExpC* can be a memo field name, in which case the length of the text stored within the memo field is returned. Note that in the case of character fields, LEN( ) returns the length of the field, not the length of the text within the field; you must add a TRIM( ) function to get the length of the text stored in the field.

LIKE( )

Syntax

LIKE(*ExpC1*, *ExpC2*)

The LIKE( ) function compares two character expressions and returns a logical true (.T.) if the character string in *ExpC2* contains the characters in *ExpC1*. The pattern can include the wildcard characters * (representing any sequence of characters) and ? (representing any single character). Note that the LIKE( ) function is case sensitive.

LINENO( )

Syntax

LINENO( )

The LINENO( ) function returns the line number of the next statement in the program that is currently running.

LKSYS( )

Syntax

LKSYS(*ExpN*)

The LKSYS( ) function returns information regarding a locked record on a network. *ExpN* determines what information is returned by LKSYS( ). If *ExpN* is 0, LKSYS( ) returns the time that the lock was placed. If *ExpN* is 1, LKSYS( ) returns the date that the lock was placed. If *ExpN* is 2, LKSYS( ) returns the log-in name of the user who placed the lock, as determined by the network operating system. Note that the CONVERT command must have been used to convert the database for network use; otherwise, LKSYS( ) will return a null string ("").

LOG( )

Syntax

LOG(*ExpN*)

The LOG( ) function returns the natural logarithm of a number specified by *ExpN*. *ExpN* must be greater than zero. Use the SET DECIMALS command to specify the number of decimal places returned.

LOG10( )

Syntax

LOG10(*ExpN*)

The LOG10( ) function returns the common (base 10) logarithm of a number specified by *ExpN*. *ExpN* must be greater than zero. Use the SET DECIMALS command to specify the number of decimal places returned.

LOOKUP( )

Syntax

LOOKUP(*return field,look-for exp,look-in field*)

The LOOKUP( ) function searches a database for a record and returns a value from a specified field when the record is found. *Look-in field* specifies the field name you want to search, *look-for exp* is the expression used as the basis for the search, and and *return field* is the name of the field that returns data once a search is completed. The LOOKUP( ) function assumes the use of a database in the current work area, unless you specify a file in another work area by including alias names and pointers along with the field names. LOOKUP( )

performs a sequential search, unless an index based on the same expression as the search is available. If such an index is open, LOOKUP( ) will use the index to speed the search.

LOWER( )

Syntax

LOWER(*ExpC*)

The LOWER( ) function converts all uppercase letters in *ExpC* to lowercase. The function will not affect non-alphabetic characters. The LOWER( ) function does not change the way the data is stored, unless you use the function as part of a STORE or REPLACE command. The function is generally used to find or compare data when you do not know what case data was originally entered as.

LTRIM( )

Syntax

LTRIM(*ExpC*)

The LTRIM( ) function trims all leading blanks from the character expression defined as *ExpC*.

LUPDATE( )

Syntax

LUPDATE(*alias*)

The LUPDATE( ) function returns the last update of the active database. Use the optional *alias* to return the last update for a file open in an unselected work area.

MAX( )

Syntax

MAX(*expression1, expression2*)

The MAX( ) function returns the maximum value of two possible values. The values denoted by the expressions can be numeric or date types, but both expressions must be of the same type.

MDX( )

Syntax

MDX (*ExpN* [,*alias*])

The MDX( ) function returns a character expression representing the filename for the .MDX file specified by *ExpN*. *ExpN* is a numeric expression that denotes the position of the .MDX file in the list specified with the SET INDEX TO command. MDX( ) also assumes the use of the database in the current work area; you can use the optional *alias* to specify a database file open in a different work area. If no .MDX file matches the number you denote with *ExpN*, MDX( ) returns a null string (" ").

MDY( )

Syntax

MDY(*ExpD*)

The MDY( ) function returns a Month DD, YY (or Month DD, YYYY) character string for a given date expression. The Month is always spelled out, and the day always takes the DD format. If SET CENTURY is OFF, the year takes the YY format; otherwise, it takes the YYYY format.

MEMLINES( )

Syntax

MEMLINES(*memo_field*)

The MEMLINES( ) function returns the number of lines in the named memo field for the current record. Note that the number of lines in the memo field will be affected by the current value of SET MEMOWIDTH (see SET MEMOWIDTH in Appendix A).

MEMORY( )

Syntax

MEMORY( )

The MEMORY( ) function returns the amount of free conventional memory as a numeric value in kilobytes.

MENU( )

Syntax

MENU( )

The MENU( ) function returns the name of the currently active menu. If a menu is not active, MENU( ) returns a null string.

MESSAGE( )

Syntax

MESSAGE( )

The MESSAGE( ) function returns the current error message, useful in situations in which dBASE IV detects an error within a program. The MESSAGE( ) function can be used along with the ON ERROR command for error-trapping and recovery purposes.

MIN( )

Syntax

MIN(*expression1, expression2*)

The MIN( ) function returns the minimum value expression from two possible expressions. The expressions can be numeric or date types, but they both must be of the same type.

MLINE( )

Syntax

MLINE(*memo_field, ExpN*)

The MLINE( ) function returns the specified line *ExpN* from the named memo field in the current record. Note that the value of SET MEMOWIDTH will affect the number of lines in a memo field (see SET MEMOWIDTH in Appendix A).

MOD( )

Syntax

MOD(*ExpN1, ExpN2*)

The MOD( ) function returns the remainder when *ExpN1* is divided by *ExpN2*. A positive number is returned if *ExpN2* is positive and a negative number is returned if *ExpN2* is negative. If there is no remainder, a zero is returned.

MONTH( )

Syntax

MONTH(*ExpD*)

The MONTH( ) function returns the numeric month (1 to 12) that corresponds to the date expression. The numbers 1 through 12 correspond to January through December.

NDX( )

Syntax

NDX(*ExpN* [, *alias*])

The NDX( ) function returns the name of an open index file in the current work area. The numeric expression specifies the order of the index file, 1 being the first index file opened, 2 the second index file opened, and so on. Use the optional *alias* to return the name of an open index file in an unselected work area.

NETWORK( )

Syntax

NETWORK( )

The NETWORK( ) function returns a logical value that indicates whether dBASE IV is running on a local area network. NETWORK( ) returns a logical true if dBASE IV is running on a network. On a single-user system, the-NETWORK( ) function returns a logical false.

ORDER( )

Syntax

ORDER([*alias*])

ORDER( ) returns the name of the master (or active) index file in the current work area. Use the optional *alias* to return the name of the active index in an unselected work area.

OS( )

Syntax

OS( )

The OS( ) function returns the name and version of the operating system.

PAD( )

Syntax

PAD( )

The PAD( ) function returns the name of the pad last chosen from the active menu bar. The function returns a null string if no menu is active.

PAYMENT( )

Syntax

PAYMENT(*ExpN1, ExpN2, ExpN3*)

The PAYMENT( ) function returns the amount of a loan payment. ThePAYMENT( ) function assumes a constant interest rate and that payments are made at the end of each period. *ExpN1* is the principal amount, *ExpN2* is the interest rate, and *ExpN3* is the number of payments. If the payments are compounded monthly and the interest rate is compounded yearly, divide the interest rate by 12 to get the proper results.

PCOL( )

Syntax

PCOL( )

The PCOL( ) function returns the current column position of the printer.

PI( )

Syntax

PI( )

The PI( ) function returns the numeric constant pi (approximately 3.14159).

POPUP( )

Syntax

POPUP( )

The POPUP( ) function returns the name of the active pop-up menu.

PRINTSTATUS( )

Syntax

PRINTSTATUS( )

The PRINTSTATUS( ) function returns a logical true (.T.) if the printer is ready, or a logical false (.F.) if it is not.

PROGRAM( )

Syntax

PROGRAM( )

The PROGRAM( ) function returns the name of the program currently running, or the program that was running when an error occurred.

PROMPT( )

Syntax

PROMPT( )

The PROMPT( ) function returns the prompt for the last option chosen from the active menu pad or pop-up menu. The function returns a null string if no pop-up menu is active.

PROW( )

Syntax

PROW( )

The PROW( ) function returns the current row position of the printer. Note that when an EJECT command is issued, PROW( ) is reset to zero.

PV( )

Syntax

PV(*ExpN1, ExpN2, ExpN3*)

The PV( ) function returns the present value of an investment, or the amount which must be invested to earn a known future value. *ExpN1*is the payment made each period, *ExpN2* is the interest rate, and *ExpN3* is the number of periods. If the payments are compounded monthly and the interest rate is yearly, divide the interest rate by 12 to get the proper results.

RAND( )

Syntax

RAND([*ExpN*])

The RAND( ) function returns a random number between 0 and 1. The optional numeric expression can be used to provide a seed different than the default for generating the random number. A given seed will always produce the same sequence of random numbers; you can vary the sequence of random numbers by varying the seed. If *ExpN* is negative, the seed is taken from the system clock. To obtain a random number in a particular range, multiply the result of the RAND( ) function by a chosen value. For example, you could get a random number between 50 and 100 by using (RAND( )*50)+50.

READKEY( )

Syntax

READKEY( )

The READKEY( ) function returns an integer value that indicates the key pressed when exiting from the editing commands APPEND, BROWSE, CHANGE, CREATE, EDIT, INSERT, MODIFY, and READ. The READKEY function provides a value between 0 and 36 if no changes were made to the data, or a value between 256 and 292 if changes were made to the data.

RECCOUNT( )

Syntax

RECCOUNT([*alias*])

The RECCOUNT( ) function returns the number of records in the database open in the current work area. If no database is open, RECCOUNT( ) returns a zero. Use the optional *alias* to return the number of records in a database open in an unselected work area.

RECNO( )

Syntax

RECNO([*alias*])

The RECNO( ) function returns the current record number. Use the optional *alias* to return the current record number in a database open in an unselected work area.

RECSIZE( )

Syntax

RECSIZE([*alias*])

The RECSIZE( ) function returns the size of the database record in the current work area. Use the optional *alias* to return the size of the database record for a database open in an unselected work area. If no database is open, RECSIZE( ) returns a zero.

REPLICATE( )

Syntax

REPLICATE(*ExpC, ExpN*)

The REPLICATE( ) function returns a character string consisting of *ExpC* repeated *ExpN* times.

RIGHT( )

Syntax

RIGHT(*ExpC / memvar, ExpN*)

The RIGHT( ) function returns the rightmost part of the character string *ExpC* or memory variable *memvar*. Use the numeric expression *ExpN* to specify the number of characters that will be returned.

RLOCK( )

Syntax

RLOCK([*ExpC list,alias*] / [*alias*])

The RLOCK( ) function attempts to lock a record and returns a logical true if the attempted lock succeeds. The record remains locked until you close the file or use the UNLOCK command. Note that LOCK( ) can be used as a synonym for RLOCK( ). *ExpC list*, which is optional, is a list of record numbers to lock. Use the optional *alias* to specify records to lock in another work area.

ROLLBACK( )

Syntax

ROLLBACK( )

The ROLLBACK( ) function returns a logical value indicating whether the last ROLLBACK command completed successfully. If ROLLBACK( ) returns a logical true, the last ROLLBACK command was successful. If ROLLBACK( ) returns a logical false, the last ROLLBACK command was unsuccessful, or a ROLLBACK was never attempted.

ROUND( )

Syntax

ROUND(*ExpN1*, *ExpN2*)

The ROUND( ) function rounds off the number supplied in *ExpN1*. Use *ExpN2* to specify the number of decimal places to round off to. If *ExpN2* is negative, the rounded number returned is a whole number.

ROW( )

Syntax

ROW( )

The ROW( ) function returns the current row location of the cursor.

RTOD( )

Syntax

RTOD(*ExpN*)

The RTOD( ) function converts radians to degrees. The numeric expression is the value in radians, and the value returned by the function is the equivalent value in degrees.

RTRIM( )

Syntax

RTRIM(*ExpC*)

The RTRIM( ) function strips the trailing spaces from the named character string. The RTRIM( ) function is identical to the TRIM( ) function.

SEEK( )

Syntax

SEEK(*expression*[, *alias*])

The SEEK( ) function returns a logical true (.T.) if the search expression can be found in the active index. A successful result positions the record pointer at the found record. If the search expression is not found, the function returns a logical false (.F.), and the record pointer is placed at the end of the file. Use the optional *alias* to search an open index in an unselected work area.

SELECT( )

Syntax

SELECT( )

The SELECT( ) function returns the number of the highest unused work area.

SET( )

Syntax

SET(*ExpC*)

The SET( ) function returns the status of the various SET commands. The character expression contains the name of the desired SET command. Note that you need to use quotes around *ExpC* if it is a character string rather than a memory variable.

SIGN( )

Syntax

SIGN(*ExpN*)

SIGN( ) returns a numeric value that represents the sign of the numeric expression. If *ExpN* is positive, SIGN( ) returns a value of 1. If *ExpN* is negative, SIGN( ) returns a value of -1. If *ExpN* is zero, SIGN( ) returns a 0.

SIN( )

Syntax

SIN(*ExpN*)

The SIN( ) function returns the sine of *ExpN*, where *ExpN* is an angle measured in radians. To convert degrees to radians, use the DTOR( ) function.

SOUNDEX( )

Syntax

SOUNDEX(*ExpC*)

The SOUNDEX( ) function returns a four-character string that represents the phonetic "Soundex" code for the character expression *ExpC*. The four-character code returned by the SOUNDEX( ) function can be useful for finding similar-sounding names, or for building an index to perform lookups based on the sound of a word.

SPACE( )

Syntax

SPACE(*ExpN*)

The SPACE( ) function returns a character string containing the specified number of blank spaces. The maximum number of spaces that can be specified by *ExpN* is 254.

SQRT( )

Syntax

SQRT(*ExpN*)

The SQRT( ) function returns the square root of the numeric expression *ExpN*. The numeric expression must be a positive number.

STR( )

Syntax

STR(*ExpN1* [, *ExpN2* [, *ExpN3*]])

The STR( ) function converts a numeric expression to a character expression, where *ExpN1* is the numeric expression to be converted to a character string. Use the optional *ExpN2* to specify a length (including the decimal point and decimal places), and use the optional *ExpN3* to specify the number of decimal places.

STUFF( )

Syntax

STUFF(*ExpC1*, *ExpN1*, *ExpN2*, *ExpC2*)

The STUFF( ) function inserts or removes characters from any part of a character string. *ExpC1* is the existing character string, *ExpN1* is the starting position in the string, *ExpN2* is the number of characters to remove from the right of *ExpC1*, and *ExpC2* is the character string to insert. Note that the STUFF( ) function cannot be used with memo fields.

SUBSTR( )

Syntax

SUBSTR(*ExpC*, *ExpN1* [, *ExpN2*])

The SUBSTR( ) function extracts a portion of a string from a character expression. *ExpC* is the character expression to extract the string from, *ExpN1* is the starting position in the expression, and *ExpN2* is the number of characters to extract from the expression. Note that *ExpC* can be a memo field.

TAG( )

Syntax

TAG([.*MDX name*,]*ExpN* [,*alias*])

The TAG( ) function returns a character expression that is the name of the index tag identified by *ExpN*, in the file named by *.MDX name*. *ExpN* represents the position of the tag in the .MDX file; for example, a value of 3 would denote the third tag in the .MDX file. *.MDX name* is a character expression representing the name of the multiple index file. The optional *alias* can be used to return the name of an index tag in an .MDX file open in a different work area.

TAN( )

Syntax

TAN(*ExpN*)

The TAN( ) function returns the tangent of *ExpN*, where *ExpN* is measured in radians. To convert degrees to radians, use the DTOR( ) function.

TIME( )

Syntax

TIME( )

The TIME( ) function returns the current system time in the format of HH:MM:SS (if SET HOURS is set to 24), or in the format of HH:MM:SS am/pm (if SET HOURS is set to 12).

TRANSFORM( )

Syntax

TRANSFORM(*expression, ExpC*)

The TRANSFRM( ) function formats character strings or numbers with PICTURE options, without using the @SAY command. *Expression* is the variable or field to format, and *ExpC* is a character expression that contains the PICTURE clause.

TRIM( )

Syntax

TRIM(*ExpC*)

The TRIM( ) function trims trailing spaces from a character string. If the character string is composed entirely of spaces, TRIM( ) returns a null string. The TRIM( ) function is identical to the RTRIM( ) function.

TYPE( )

Syntax

TYPE(*ExpC*)

The TYPE( ) function returns a single character indicating the data type of the expression named in *ExpC*. The letter C denotes character type, L denotes logical type, N denotes numeric type, F denotes floating numeric type, D denotes date type, M denotes memo type, and U denotes an undefined type.

UPPER( )

Syntax

UPPER(*ExpC*)

The UPPER( ) function converts all alphabetic characters in *ExpC* to uppercase letters. The UPPER( ) function does not change the way the data is stored, unless you use the function as part of a STORE or REPLACE command. The function is generally used for finding or comparing data when you do not know what case the data was originally entered as.

USER( )

Syntax

USER( )

The USER( ) function returns a character string that is the log-in name of the current user, as defined by the PROTECT utility in dBASE IV. If PROTECT has not been used to establish user names and passwords, USER( ) returns a null string (" ").

VAL( )

Syntax

VAL(*ExpC*)

The VAL( ) function converts a character expression containing numbers into a numeric value. Starting at the leftmost character and ignoring leading blanks, VAL( ) processes digits until a non-numeric character is encountered. If the first character of *ExpC* is not a number, VAL( ) returns a value of 0.

VARREAD( )

Syntax

VARREAD( )

The VARREAD( ) function returns the name of the field or variable currently being edited. The function can be useful when designing context-sensitive help systems, so that different help messages can appear for different fields.

VERSION( )

Syntax

VERSION( )

The VERSION( ) function returns a character string indicating the version number of dBASE IV.

YEAR( )

Syntax

YEAR(*ExpD*)

The YEAR( ) function returns the numeric year corresponding to the date expression.

Index

D

E

Index

G

H

M

N

O

P

S

T

X

Y

Z